BREAKING NEW GROUND

BREAKING NEW GROUND

Mining, Minerals, and Sustainable Development

The Report of the MMSD Project

from Routledge

First published by Earthscan in the UK and USA in 2002

Earthscan
2 Park Square, Milton Park, Abingdon, Oxon OX14 4RN
711 Third Avenue, New York, NY 10017

Earthscan is an imprint of the Taylor & Francis Group, an informa business

ISBN 13: 978-1-85383-942-9 (hbk)

Design and layout by Spencer Landor and Asset Graphics
Cover photographs © MMSD and Rio Tinto plc

Photo credits: Adrian Arbib/Still Pictures: p. 291; Anglo American: pp. 123, 136, 185, 212, and 217; Alan Baker: p. 265; Anne-Marie Fleury: p. 197; Adrian Phillips: p. 165; Ben Sandbrook: pp. 3, 9, 13, 27, 33, 57, 85, 111, 141, 203, 269, 271, and 361; Frank McShane: p. 113; Gabriela Flores: p. 176; Klein/Hubert/Still Pictures: p. xiii; Luke Danielson: pp. 3, 147, 231, 233, 287, 313, 335, and 357; Meredith Sassoon: pp. 151, 160, 227, and 308; Peter Frischmuth/Still Pictures: p. 108; Richard Sandbrook: pp. 171 and 375; Rio Tinto plc: pp. 73, 255, and 295; Ron Giling/Still Pictures: p. 345; Silvia Kyeyune: p. 3; Tricia Caswell: pp. 3, 12, 31, and 369.

A catalogue record for this book is available from the British Library

Executive Summaries are also available in French, Spanish, and Portuguese from http://www.earthprint.com.

Mining, Minerals and Sustainable Development was a project of the International Institute for Environment and Development (IIED) in London, UK. The project was made possible by the support of the World Business Council for Sustainable Development. IIED is a company limited by guarantee and incorporated in England. Reg. No. 2188452. VAT Reg. No. GB 440 4948 50. Registered Charity No. 800066

FOREWORD

This report represents the end of the second productive partnership between IIED and WBCSD.

Our first joint project was a major study of the paper industry and how it could better contribute to sustainable development. That was five years ago. Many acknowledge it was a turning point for the sector. Now, and on a more ambitious scale, we are proud to present *Breaking New Ground*, the first in-depth review of the mining and minerals sector from the perspective of sustainable development, undertaken with the support and engagement of mining companies, mining communities, labour, the research community, and a broad range of other stakeholders.

The project has not been without controversy for the report challenges all sides in the debate. The stakeholders in the chain of production and use of minerals extends in some sense to almost everyone. The project has had considerable success in engaging with stakeholders in some parts of the globe, but has fallen short of a deep involvement with every interest group. Indeed it has been explicitly rejected by some special interest groups, sometimes before there was anything concrete to judge by.

We need a more informed understanding of the industry's actual and potential contribution to sustainable development. It is no longer enough to argue that because society needs its products, it must tolerate whatever occurs in their production. Nor is it enough to play to a public audience conditioned to expect the worst from mining or the other minerals industries. We need to get past scoring points by addressing the obvious: a large part of the world's public has a negative view of the industry and feels it is not meeting legitimate needs and expectations of others.

But if we cannot do without the industry – and we clearly can't – we need to define what higher performance amounts to, and create sanctions and incentives to achieve it.

This report stands up to rigorous scrutiny. It has been executed with integrity by the IIED project team under the supervision of a distinguished, balanced, 25-member global Assurance Group. Now, with it in hand (and a wealth of background material available on the CD-ROM and, in some cases, in forthcoming publications), there is a real opportunity for big and small companies, governments and inter-governmental organizations, labour, non-governmental organizations and civil society to raise the game to higher and more accountable standards of performance.

Finally, while full acknowledgements are elsewhere, we should pay tribute to Luke Danielson, Project Director, and Richard Sandbrook, Project Coordinator, without whose leadership, integrity, and vision this report, and its associated research and publications, would not have been possible.

Nigel Cross
Executive Director, International Institute for Environment and Development

Björn Stigson
President, World Business Council for Sustainable Development

STATEMENT BY THE MMSD ASSURANCE GROUP

The Assurance Group's key responsibilities were to seek to ensure the highest quality, balance, and integrity of the work of the Mining, Minerals and Sustainable Development (MMSD) project.

Consistent with its role, the Assurance Group held seven meetings during the process of consultation, preparation, and review of the effort that has led to the project report. In these meetings, members of the Assurance Group, in their individual capacities, gave feedback to the project Work Group on both process and substantive issues. In particular, members assisted in identifying priority issues, and commented on the scope of the project, the stakeholder processes being undertaken, and draft versions of the report.

The issues with which the report deals are highly complex and often extremely controversial. Because the Assurance Group is composed of individuals with diverse expertise, backgrounds, and perspectives, we did not attempt to reach consensus on the conclusions and recommendations contained in this report. We believe, however, that the Work Group have conducted themselves in accordance with their Charter, have maintained the independence of their perspective, have sought consultation broadly, have worked openly, and have produced a project report that is respectful of differing views.

We also recognize the enormous effort made by the Work Group in bringing the report to its final state. The MMSD project has been a substantial and innovative effort that has thoughtfully considered important issues that must be addressed. The Assurance Group challenges companies, governments, unions, communities, non-governmental organizations, and other stakeholders to take the report's recommendations forward.

Duma Nkosi, *Chair*

Glenn Miller, *Vice-Chair*

Jacqueline Aloisi de Larderel
Richard Baldes
Patricia Caswell
Anna Cederstav
Mick Dodson
Cholpon Dyikanova
Colin Filer
Douglas Fraser
Reg Green
Gerard Holden
Namakau Kaingu
Antonio La Viña
Kathryn McPhail
Daniel Meilán
Maria Ligia Noronha
Manuel Pulgar-Vidal
Leon Rajaobelina
Charles Secrett
John Stewart
Osvaldo Sunkel
Helmut Weidner
Doug Yearley
Senzeni Zokwana

Detailed information on the MMSD Assurance Group may be found in Appendix 1.

STATEMENT BY THE MMSD SPONSORS GROUP

The following organizations abided by the MMSD Sponsors Group Charter, which entrusted them with the mandate of supporting and financing the project as well as ensuring its independence. They held regular meetings related to contractual and budgetary matters and participated in the MMSD process as stakeholders – that is, they attended workshops, contributed papers and presentations, submitted comments on drafts, and provided contacts from their particular stakeholder groups. Their sponsors' status did not afford them any special access to the process, nor was their participation considered any differently to that of other stakeholders.

Accordingly, the sponsors of the MMSD project:

• had no authority over the contents or production of any final material by MMSD;
• do not necessarily endorse the findings and conclusions of MMSD;
• accept no responsibility for the accuracy, lawfulness, or completeness of any material produced by MMSD; and
• are not bound by the conclusions of MMSD.

Alcan Inc
Alcoa Inc
Anglo American plc
Anglovaal Mining Ltd
BHP Billiton
Caterpillar Inc
Codelco Chile – Corporación Nacional del Cobre
Colorado School of Mines
Comisión Chilena del Cobre
Conservation International
CRU International Ltd
Department for International Development, Government of the United Kingdom
Environment Australia, Government of Australia
Freeport-McMoRan Copper and Gold Inc
Gold Fields Ltd
HATCH Associates Ltd
International Federation of Chemical, Energy, Mine and General Workers' Unions (ICEM)
IUCN – The World Conservation Union
KPMG
Lonmin plc
Mackay School of Mines, University of Nevada, Reno
M.I.M. Holdings Ltd
Mitsubishi Materials Corporation / Mitsubishi Corporation
Mitsui Mining and Smelting Co., Ltd
Natural Resources Canada, Government of Canada
Newmont Mining Corporation
Nippon Mining & Metals Co., Ltd
Noranda Inc
Norsk Hydro ASA
Pasminco Ltd
Phelps Dodge Corporation
Placer Dome Inc
PricewaterhouseCoopers
Rio Tinto plc
Sibirsky Aluminium Group (Sibal)
Somincor
Sumitomo Metal Mining
Teck Cominco Ltd
United Nations Environment Programme
WMC Resources Ltd
The World Bank Group

Support from the Rockefeller Foundation is gratefully acknowledged. Thanks also to the Global Reporting Initiative for its collaboration with MMSD.

A copy of the MMSD Sponsors Group Charter is available on the CD-ROM.

CONTENTS

EXECUTIVE SUMMARY

Mineral products are essential to contemporary societies and economies. Many basic needs cannot be met without them. But simply meeting market demand for mineral commodities falls far short of meeting society's expectations of industry. The process of producing, using, and recycling minerals could help society reach many other goals – providing jobs directly and indirectly, aiding in the development of national economies, and helping to reach energy and resource efficiency targets, among many others. Where industry is falling far short of meeting these objectives, it is seen as failing in its obligations and is increasingly unwelcome.

The mining and minerals industry faces some of the most difficult challenges of any industrial sector – and is currently distrusted by many of the people it deals with day to day. It has been failing to convince some of its constituents and stakeholders that it has the 'social licence to operate' in many parts of the world, based on the many expectations of its potential contributions:

- Countries expect that minerals development will be an engine of sustained economic growth.
- Local communities expect that the industry will provide employment, infrastructure, and other benefits that counter the risks and impacts they experience and will leave them better off than when the project started.
- The industry's employees expect safer and healthier working conditions, a better community life, and consideration when their employment ends.
- Local citizens and human rights campaigners expect companies to respect and support basic rights, even when they are operating where government does not.
- Environmental organizations expect a much higher standard of performance and that the industry will avoid ecologically and culturally sensitive areas.
- Investors expect higher returns and have shown considerable concern about the industry's financial results.
- Consumers expect safe products produced in a manner that meets acceptable environmental and social standards.

Companies must do much more, sometimes with fewer resources. There are boundaries to the responsibilities companies can take on in society: most people would be uncomfortable in a world where companies were the main sources of education and

health care, the principal agencies protecting individual rights, or surrogate governments. Other actors have important roles to play – governments above all. Government must provide an enabling environment, define the standards expected of industry, assure those standards are being met, and have meaningful incentives and sanctions to encourage compliance. It must be a better service provider and a better protector of minority rights.

Success will require improved capacity and performance by all in the minerals sector – industry at all stages from exploration to processing, government, international organizations, non-governmental organizations (NGOs), academia, civil society, communities, labour, lenders, insurers, and consumers. All will need to learn to pursue their own objectives in ways that move society as a whole forward.

Against this background, and with the World Summit for Sustainable Development planned for 2002 in mind, nine of the world's largest mining companies decided to initiate a project to examine the role of the minerals sector in contributing to sustainable development, and how that contribution could be increased. Through the World Business Council for Sustainable Development, they contracted with the International Institute for Environment and Development to undertake a two-year independent process of research and consultation – the Mining, Minerals and Sustainable Development Project (MMSD). The project ultimately attracted support from more than 40 commercial and non-commercial sponsors. From April 2000, project teams in London and four key regions worked to meet four broad objectives:
- to assess the global mining and minerals sector in terms of the transition to sustainable development,
- to identify how the services provided through the minerals supply chain can be delivered in ways that support sustainable development,
- to propose key elements for improving the minerals system, and
- to build platforms of analysis and engagement for ongoing communication and networking among all stakeholders in the sector.

The project was supervised by an independent Assurance Group of 25 experienced individuals from different perspectives and regions who served as individuals rather than representatives of any organizations. The group met eight times to review progress and advise on future direction. The project management maintained independence throughout the process. The main components of the project are set out in Box ES–1.

Breaking New Ground presents an analysis of a large and heterogeneous sector through the many stages of minerals and metals exploration, production, use, re-use, recycling, and final disposal. The project assumed from the start that sustainable development could provide a useful framework to guide the minerals sector. It also believed that by setting out the challenges – from all perspectives, in a balanced way – new ways forward would emerge. This Executive Summary provides a basic guide to the priority issues facing the sector, which MMSD identified in its consultations

with different stakeholders, and outlines some of the most important policy recommendations that came out of the process of consultation and analysis.

A process of this nature has not been attempted on this scale before in any major industrial sector. It has not been an easy task, given the low levels of trust in the sector on the one hand and the complexity of the issues on the other. Though it is premature to attempt an assessment of all the lessons from MMSD, Box ES–2 provides some preliminary observations from the process.

Much of the substance of *Breaking New Ground* is based on research and consultation undertaken through the regional processes in Australia, North America, South America, and Southern Africa. Mirroring the global process, the regional reports are based on extensive dialogue with key stakeholders through workshops, regional forums, and regionally convened advisory groups and on research commissioned on priority topics. The regional partners generated a picture of the sector's contribution to sustainable development and the key priorities in their respective regions. Most important, they identified regionally

Box ES–1. The MMSD Process

Regional Partnerships. The project included four regional partnerships, each with its own governance structure, research priorities, and process of consultation: Southern Africa, South America, Australia, and North America.

National Projects. Through the regional partnerships, or in some cases directly from the project centre, MMSD organized national efforts in approximately 20 countries. In some cases these were simply reconnaissance research reports; in others they included more ambitious research and consultation processes.

Global Workshops. Some 700 people from diverse backgrounds attended the 23 global workshops or expert meetings that dealt with issues from the handling of large-volume wastes and biodiversity to indigenous concerns, human rights, and corruption.

Commissioned Research. Approximately 175 individual pieces of research were commissioned globally and by the regional partners in the course of the project. Much of this was discussed or debated at the workshops or consultation meetings.

Presentations, Communications, and Bulletins. The MMSD staff presented emerging ideas to a wide variety of audiences and asked for comment. The project posted key documents on its website and received substantial communication in response. Over the course of the project, 21 Project Bulletins were sent to a list of more than 5000 people, updating them on project activities and asking for ideas and feedback and comment on the draft report.

Box ES–2. Multistakeholder Processes: Some Observations from the MMSD Project

- A broad-based, inclusive process of initiation is fundamental to the success of the effort.
- The time frame must take into account the differing capacities of participants as well as the need for a timely outcome.
- No one group should own access to the process or its follow-up.
- A group that is trusted for its diversity and its insights must be given primary responsibility for steering the process on behalf of all others.
- No process should override the importance of local endowments (cultural, environmental, and economic); thus decentralization should be the guiding rule.
- The initial scope must be agreed to by all, and be subject to revision as the dialogue unfolds.
- The process cannot succeed if any one stakeholder attempts prematurely to claim the high ground in public, or works in private to circumvent due process.
- The rules of evidence are crucial – everyone needs to work to the same standards of rigour, honesty, and transparency.
- Any financial resources applied should not affect the relationship; at the same time, appropriate responsibilities for follow-up have to be recognized.

specific actions for the way forward. The regional analyses and outcomes are available as separate reports.

Sustainable Development

One of the greatest challenges facing the world today is integrating economic activity with environmental integrity, social concerns, and effective governance systems. The goal of that integration can be seen as 'sustainable development'. In the context of the minerals sector, the goal should be to maximize the contribution to the well-being of the current generation in a way that ensures an equitable distribution of its costs and benefits, without reducing the potential for future generations to meet their own needs. The approach taken to achieve this has to be both comprehensive – including the whole minerals chain – and forward-looking, setting out long-term as well as short-term objectives. It requires:

- a robust framework for sustainable development based on an agreed set of broad principles;
- an understanding of the key challenges and constraints facing the sector at different levels and in different regions and the actions needed to meet or overcome them, along with the respective roles and responsibilities of actors in the sector;
- a process for responding to these challenges that respects the rights and interests of all involved, is able to set priorities, and ensures that action is taken at the appropriate level;
- an integrated set of institutions and policy instruments to ensure minimum standards of compliance as well as responsible voluntary actions; and
- verifiable measures to evaluate progress and foster consistent improvement.

Box ES–3 provides a framework based on a set of guiding principles for each of the four dimensions or 'pillars' of sustainable development. These should be seen as high-level aspirations and be interpreted in a way that recognizes diversity, limitations in knowledge and capacity, and society's need for minerals. Although laid out here in different spheres for ease of interpretation, these principles should be applied in an integrated manner in decision-making. Thus, for example, the role of mineral wealth in maximizing human well-being should be acknowledged, but it must be managed in a way that protects the environment and other social and cultural values.

Similarly, the decision of whether or not to mine in a certain area should be undertaken through a democratic decision-making process and be based on an integrated assessment of ecological, environmental, economic, and social impacts.

Box ES–3. Sustainable Development Principles

Economic Sphere
- Maximize human well-being.
- Ensure efficient use of all resources, natural and otherwise, by maximizing rents.
- Seek to identify and internalize environmental and social costs.
- Maintain and enhance the conditions for viable enterprise.

Social Sphere
- Ensure a fair distribution of the costs and benefits of development for all those alive today.
- Respect and reinforce the fundamental rights of human beings, including civil and political liberties, cultural autonomy, social and economic freedoms, and personal security.
- Seek to sustain improvements over time; ensure that depletion of natural resources will not deprive future generations through replacement with other forms of capital.

Environmental Sphere
- Promote responsible stewardship of natural resources and the environment, including remediation of past damage.
- Minimize waste and environmental damage along the whole of the supply chain.
- Exercise prudence where impacts are unknown or uncertain.
- Operate within ecological limits and protect critical natural capital.

Governance Sphere
- Support representative democracy, including participatory decision-making.
- Encourage free enterprise within a system of clear and fair rules and incentives.
- Avoid excessive concentration of power through appropriate checks and balances.
- Ensure transparency through providing all stakeholders with access to relevant and accurate information.
- Ensure accountability for decisions and actions, which are based on comprehensive and reliable analysis.
- Encourage cooperation in order to build trust and shared goals and values.
- Ensure that decisions are made at the appropriate level, adhering to the principle of subsidiarity where possible.

Decision-making processes are as vital as the end results and usually entail making choices and trade-offs between competing interests. There may be conflicts among different groups of stakeholders and between global and local priorities. Various groups, acting in concert, need to evaluate the acceptability of, for example, sustaining minor environmental damage in exchange for major social and economic gain, or of sacrificing economic and social goals for a significant environmental benefit. In each case, the principle of subsidiarity should be adhered to, which recognizes that decisions should be taken as close as possible to and with the people and communities most directly affected.

Implementation of sustainable development principles in the minerals sector requires the development of integrated tools capable of bringing these diverse principles and objectives into focus in a manageable decision-making structure. A wide range of instruments is available, including regulatory, fiscal, educational, and institutional tools. Instruments need to be effective; administratively feasible; cost-efficient, with incentives for innovation and improvement; transparent; acceptable and credible to stakeholders; reliable and reproducible across different groups and regions; and equitable in the distribution of costs and benefits.

Any suggested actions have to be:
- consistent with the sustainable development framework;
- based on clearly defined objectives and incentives to change towards better practice;
- SMART (specific, monitorable, achievable, realistic, and time-bound);
- moving towards higher levels of trust and cooperation; and
- where possible, built on existing structures and institutions.

Challenges Faced by the Minerals Sector

MMSD focused stakeholders' concerns into nine key challenges facing the sector, as laid out in Box ES–4. These represent the most pressing issues identified through the various consultative mechanisms used by MMSD through its almost two-year life.

Box ES–4. Nine Key Challenges

Viability of the Minerals Industry. The minerals industry cannot contribute to sustainable development if companies cannot survive and succeed. This requires a safe, healthy, educated, and committed work force; access to capital; a social licence to operate; the ability to attract and maintain good managerial talent; and the opportunity for a return on investment.

The Control, Use, and Management of Land. Mineral development is one of a number of often competing land uses. There is frequently a lack of planning or other frameworks to balance and manage possible uses. As a result, there are often problems and disagreement around issues such as compensation, resettlement, land claims of indigenous peoples, and protected areas.

Minerals and Economic Development. Minerals have the potential to contribute to poverty alleviation and broader economic development at the national level. Countries have realized this with mixed success. For this to be achieved, appropriate frameworks for the creation and management of mineral wealth must be in place. Additional challenges include corruption and determining the balance between local and national benefits.

Local Communities and Mines. Minerals development can also bring benefits at the local level. Recent trends towards, for example, smaller work forces and outsourcing affect communities adversely, however. The social upheaval and inequitable distribution of benefits and costs within communities can also create social tension. Ensuring that improved health and education or economic activity will endure after mines close requires a level of planning that has too often not been achieved.

Mining, Minerals, and the Environment. Minerals activities have a significant environmental impact. Managing these impacts more effectively requires dealing with unresolved issues of handling immense quantities of waste, developing ways of internalizing the costs of acid drainage, improving both impact assessment and environmental management systems, and doing effective planning for mine closure.

An Integrated Approach to Using Minerals. The use of minerals is essential for modern living. Yet current patterns of use face a growing number of challenges, ranging from concerns about efficiency and waste minimization to the risks associated with the use of certain minerals. Companies at different stages in the minerals chain can benefit from learning to work together exploring further recycling, re-use, and re-manufacture of products and developing integrated programmes of product stewardship and supply chain assurance.

Access to Information. Access to information is key to building greater trust and cooperation. The quality of information and its use, production, flow, accessibility, and credibility affect the interaction of all actors in the sector. Effective public participation in decision-making requires information to be publicly available in an accessible form.

Artisanal and Small-Scale Mining. Many millions of people make their living through artisanal and small-scale mining (ASM). It often provides an important, and sometimes the only, source of income. This part of the sector is characterized by low incomes, unsafe working conditions, serious environmental impacts, exposure to hazardous materials such as mercury vapours, and conflict with larger companies and governments.

Sector Governance: Roles, Responsibilities, and Instruments for Change. Sustainable development requires new integrated systems of governance. Most countries still lack the framework for turning minerals investment into sustainable development: these need to be developed. Voluntary codes and guidelines, stakeholder processes, and other systems for promoting better practice in areas where government is unable to exercise an effective role as regulator are gaining favour as an expedient to address these problems. Lenders and other financial institutions can play a pivotal role in driving better practice.

Viability of the Minerals Industry

The greatest challenge to embedding sustainable development in minerals companies is the difficulty of linking the concept to financial success. Most companies are struggling to establish a clear business case for pursuing this path. There is indeed a business case for addressing sustainable development concerns: lower labour and health costs, improved access to lenders and insurers, lower post-closure costs, and often reputational and market advantage.

Some companies are undertaking specific measures to integrate the principles of sustainable development into corporate practice, but most are far from developing a detailed vision. Several tools are commonly used, including corporate strategy and policy, change management programmes, formal risk management procedures, implementation and auditing of internal objectives and targets, project appraisals, and core staff training programmes.

Many of the large international publicly quoted mining and mineral companies state that they are committed to shareholder value. A properly implemented switch from the cost culture to the value culture can potentially ensure that sustainable development issues are factored into business decision-making on a more disciplined and systematic basis.

Minerals companies as a group have a poor record of safe and healthy working conditions. There has been significant progress in recent years, but more needs to be done to ensure that employees can work without injury or illness. Effective safety management on a day-to-day basis requires partnership among management, workers, and unions. Companies need to demonstrate that they are meeting the minimal standards required under the International Labour Organization core conventions, including the right of workers to choose to form trade unions and the observation of minimum standards for health, safety, and hours of work.

The Control, Use, and Management of Land

Exploration and mining pose some significant challenges in terms of land access and management. The most appropriate use of land is best decided within an integrated land planning framework that seeks to balance competing interests between national and local levels, for example, or between mining and conservation. There are trade-offs that may be made in order to generate benefits in one domain, but decisions on these can only be achieved through inclusion of and negotiation with all of those likely to be directly affected by the results. The planning process will be more effective in the presence of equitable and inclusive rules of tenure, compensation schemes for those affected, and strong governance, including mechanisms for arbitration where necessary.

Land, Mining, and Indigenous Peoples

Indigenous lands have been and, many would say, are still under threat from all sorts of exploitative uses, including mining. Land is often used without the consent of indigenous peoples. Companies should act as if consent to gain access to land were required even when the law does not demand this. Decision-making processes appropriate to the cultural circumstances of indigenous peoples must be respected.

Resettlement

Resettlement has often been accompanied by

landlessness, unemployment, homelessness, and loss of access to common resources, among other problems. Companies today would not support the practices of the past, and there is a more equitable approach to resettlement issues around contemporary projects. Where resettlement takes place, companies need to ensure that living standards are not diminished, that community and social ties are preserved, and that they provide fair compensation for loss of assets and economic opportunity among others. Roles and responsibilities for ensuring the long-term well-being of resettled communities need to be defined and monitored.

Protected Areas

Protected areas are essential to the conservation of key ecological, social, and cultural values. There should be broader discussion of protected areas management and trade-offs. Both the local stake in the success of protected areas and the resources available to manage them need to be increased. Minerals development could in principle help fill these gaps, but there is profound suspicion of any proposal to mine in or near protected areas. A lack of successful examples where this principle has been concretely demonstrated is a major obstacle to progress. Environmental, mining, and other interests should be considered in conjunction with those of the often poor and politically marginalized peoples who commonly live in these areas.

Minerals and Economic Development

Minerals development is hard to justify if it does not bring economic benefits, particularly to countries and regions that lack alternative sources of development and are otherwise unattractive to foreign investors. In addition to gaining hard currency from taxes and royalties, benefits from mineral development should include employment, infrastructure such as roads and hospitals, linkages upstream to industries that supply goods and services or downstream to industries that process mineral outputs, and technology transfer. In some countries, however, mineral activities have not brought sustained economic development. Sudden wealth may have detrimental effects on social and political life, leading to or supporting corruption, authoritarian government, human rights abuse, or armed conflict.

Tariff and non-tariff barriers have also inhibited developing economies from capturing more value added in the minerals chain. A lack of economic resources, institutional capacity, and political will are often the source of inequities and underdevelopment. Where governance and national-local linkages are weak, communities may see little of the mineral revenues. The solution is to find better ways to capture and manage mineral wealth and to ensure that it is invested for lasting benefits in support of national, regional, and local development.

Corruption

Corruption is a major obstacle to the equitable distribution of minerals revenues. Many operations take place in countries where corruption is prevalent. Some companies in the minerals sector may have colluded in a variety of illicit activities – bribery to obtain licences and permits; to get preferential access to prospects, assets, or credit; or to sway judicial decisions. The minerals sector also has characteristics that heighten the risk of corruption, such as the large capital expenditures involved, the extensive regulation required, and the fixed locations.

Human Rights

Some mining companies have been accused of human rights abuses, for actions taken either independently or in collusion with governments. Some of the worst cases have occurred when companies have relied on national security forces to gain control over land or defend established premises. Miners' rights are also threatened by difficult and dangerous working conditions, with a long history of labour-management conflict, particularly in authoritarian states. Some advocates argue that multinationals should take responsibility not just for respecting but for promoting human rights.

Conflict

In politically unstable areas of the world, mining has provided a source of funds to sustain outbreaks of violence – where combatants sell minerals through illegal channels to fund military campaigns. Large-scale in-migration at mine sites can cause resentment among those already living there. When mining revenues are not equitably shared, armed conflict may be provoked. Similar disruption can occur at mine closure.

Local Communities and Mines

Few areas present a greater challenge than the relationship between mining companies and local communities. The legacy of abuse and mistrust is clear. Widespread community demands for relevant, direct, and sustained benefits from mineral wealth are a relatively recent phenomenon, so frequently neither government institutions nor companies or communities themselves have been properly equipped to respond to them. In areas of weak governance, communities often turn to the operating companies, which have found themselves providing development services to obtain or to maintain their social licence to operate.

A new relationship is beginning to emerge, based on recognition of the rights of communities and the need for community participation in decision-making. Moreover, new initiatives seek to avoid the company assuming the role and responsibilities of government, but rather focus on improving the capacity of local government and other local institutions to deliver mine-derived benefits over the long term. It is increasingly recognized that NGOs and other civil society groups can also act as independent mediators, facilitating the flow of information to and from communities and implementing actions in partnership with companies and government.

Ideally, the share of revenue received by the community should be determined through a democratic process and incorporated into initial agreements between governments and mining companies. The design of policy, regulations, and agreements must reflect the capacity to implement them. In the short term, where there is insufficient capacity, the best option is to take a collaborative approach. Of course, the most appropriate path will vary on a case-by-case basis, depending on the community's relationship with government and the availability of economic activities, services, and savings opportunities to which funds and revenues can be directed.

It is important to ensure that the benefits from minerals development are sustained beyond the life span of the projects for the communities. Support for local businesses, preferential procurement policies towards local suppliers and distributors, employment of locals, and skills training are important means of benefiting local communities and building human and financial resources. There are also initiatives that are geared towards the concerns of workers who lose their jobs. Such efforts will be of limited success if initiated only when retrenchment is a reality.

Health services provided by companies to employees and communities have generally reflected an inadequate understanding of local needs, as well as a lack of consideration for the inability to sustain such services after the operation closes. Beyond work-related diseases, few endeavours attempt to prevent diseases that affect the wider community or to consider the community's broader well-being. Some companies are now taking on a broader role in community health programmes by working in partnership with other stakeholders.

Multistakeholder forums run by independent parties can provide an effective means of facilitating community awareness, capacity-building, and involvement, as well as reducing the power differential between the community and company.

Mining, Minerals, and the Environment

The best modern mining operations represent a great improvement over past practice, and most major mining companies are committed to continuous progress on environmental performance. But past practice was sometimes bad, and in some cases this continues. Even the best modern operations may have some undesirable environmental impacts, and good practice has far to go before it spreads to all parts of the industry. The objective of improved performance is to ensure that critical natural capital is maintained, that ecosystems are enhanced where possible, and that minerals wealth contributes to net environmental continuity. The challenge is to define where, in the short and medium term, resources can be targeted to ensure the best chance of meeting these objectives in the future.

Large-Volume Waste

Mining produces very large volumes of waste, so decisions about where and how to dispose of it are often virtually irreversible. Facilities designed to contain this waste are among the largest structures ever built. The long-term impacts of the options for waste disposal are among the most important in the minerals cycle.

Mine Closure Planning

Because decisions about waste handling and other aspects of operations are often so difficult and expensive to reverse, they need to be right in the first place. The best way is to ensure that development of a closure plan at the outset of operations. This can guide individual decisions taken during the mine life to ensure they are oriented towards this objective. Most mine closure planning now focuses only on environmental aspects of closure. Integrating social and economic aspects is a necessary step to transform mining investment into sustainable development.

Environmental Legacy

The environmental issues of current and prospective mining operations are daunting enough. But in many ways far more troubling are some of the continuing effects of past mining and smelting. These sites have proved that some impacts can be long term and that society is still paying the price for natural capital stocks that have been drawn down by past generations.

Environmental Management Systems

Environmental impact assessment (EIA) is perhaps the most widely used tool of environmental management in the minerals sector and elsewhere. EIAs are now mandatory for most large-scale development projects. However, their implementation is often abysmal. Recently, social and economic factors have tended to creep into this environmental exercise; this should be deliberately promoted as part of a move towards integrated impact assessments.

EIA, as part of an environmental management system (EMS), should integrate environmental responsibilities into everyday management practices through changes to organizational structure, responsibilities, procedures, processes, and resources. An EMS provides a structured method for company management and the regulating authority to have awareness and control of the performance of a project that can be applied at all stages of the life cycle.

Biodiversity

A loss of biodiversity is a loss of natural capital. It is irreversible. Some companies have formulated biodiversity policies and introduced innovative design and operating management. Such remedial actions are encouraging, but still largely restricted to the major players. Governments have found it difficult to create the incentives to encourage conservation. The Convention on Biological Diversity provides the minerals sector with a politically sound basis for engaging in constructive dialogue and partnerships with the biodiversity community. It is a

key instrument of the global programme for sustainable development.

An Integrated Approach to Using Minerals

The use and downstream supply of mineral products has implications for sustainable development and must be considered along with mining and processing of minerals. Current patterns of minerals use raise concerns about efficiency and the need for more equitable access to resources world-wide. Much of the concern, policy, and regulation regarding the use of minerals has focused on environmental issues, health risks associated with use, and the long-run availability of these resources. A number of conceptual tools aimed at increasing efficiency and calculating optimal levels for recycling have been developed to this end. The social and economic dimensions of use and of potential future changes are generally not given equal consideration.

Environmentalists and others have called for a reduction in the material throughputs that support many national economies, particularly in industrial countries. Such calls challenge those who directly influence the ways in which minerals are used in products and challenge users to reduce their levels and patterns of use and disposal. Resource efficiency can be increased in numerous ways, including recycling, product re-manufacture and re-use, substitution, and in some cases avoidance of use.

The environmental and health impacts of different mineral products in use need to be carefully managed. Where the risks associated with use are deemed unacceptable or are not known, the costs associated with using certain minerals may outweigh the benefits. It is primarily a government responsibility to balance these uncertainties using the precautionary approach. Industry can generate much of the information required to ensure that such judgements are science-based.

Recycling is associated with many of the same trade-offs between environmental and social factors as the extraction of minerals and ores. If recycling is to be encouraged, broader integration and consistency in environmental policy-making, including difficult trade-offs between different environmental goals, are needed. Technological advances are also key, as is information on the material available for recycling.

Access to Information

Sustainable development requires increased openness and greater transparency in information production and dissemination throughout the minerals life cycle. Access to information is also linked to the ability of individuals to obtain and defend fundamental rights to resources. The processes by which information is generated and communicated play a key role in improving all participants' ability to negotiate effectively and with legitimacy. Information should be a 'leveling tool' so that all stakeholders might participate in decision-making on equal ground.

Authoritative, independent sources are critical for ensuring that information is regarded as legitimate and respecting the right of stakeholders to have access to accurate and relevant data. Systems of accountability and verification are essential to monitoring the performance of companies, governments, and civil society. The digital divide also presents imbalance. International and multilateral bodies, governments, NGOs, and industry all have an important role in making new information resources available. The processes for establishing the norms and standards of information generation and transfer, the regulatory system to ensure conformity to these standards, the opportunities for reaction in the public domain, and the freedom to participate without fear of reprisal are largely the responsibility of state governments, with the cooperation of other actors.

Open information regimes are critical to more efficient economic decisions by all and effective public participation in decision-making. They will not work without access to justice.

Artisanal and Small-Scale Mining

In many parts of the world minerals are extracted by artisanal and small-scale miners – people working with simple tools and equipment, usually in the informal sector, outside the legal and regulatory framework. There are also many artisanal mineral processors, such as diamond polishers. The vast majority are very poor, exploiting marginal deposits in harsh and often dangerous conditions – and with considerable impact on the environment. Small-scale mining is thought to involve 13 million people directly and affect the livelihoods of a further 80–100 million. A broad range of minerals is extracted by artisanal and small-scale miners, including gold, gems, precious stones, and metals.

ASM is an important aspect of rural livelihoods. It often represents the most promising, if not the only, income opportunity available. But it can also be very disruptive – particularly when it takes the form of a sudden 'rush' causing local people to desert their farms or resulting in in-migration. When the rush is over, most of the profits are likely to have disappeared – while the social and environmental damages persist.

The environmental impacts of ASM are of greatest concern to many observers: mercury pollution, direct dumping of tailings and effluents into rivers, threats from improperly constructed tailings dams, river damage in alluvial areas, river siltation, erosion damage and deforestation, and landscape destruction. A lack of awareness combined with a lack of information about affordable methods to reduce impacts and a lack of obvious incentives to change all contribute to these problems. To many people these are unacceptable and a sufficient reason to ban many forms of ASM.

Sector Governance: Roles, Responsibilities, and Instruments for Change

Achieving effective governance is a major challenge facing the sector and is a key to dealing with many of the issues discussed in *Breaking New Ground*. Many of these relate to poor governance, which results from numerous factors, including a lack of resources and capacity, power imbalances, a lack of political will, a lack of coordination and integration, or a lack of representation of stakeholders in decision-making. In some cases, existing governance structures fail to resolve issues and enforce legislation due to bureaucracy, authoritarian systems, lack of accountability and transparency, or corruption. At the extreme, poor governance can go hand in hand with abuses of human rights and conflict between different actors. Prevailing governance structures continue to reflect imbalances in power among different actors and in the priorities given to their interests at the national and international level. Minerals development has in the past decades been the province of the investor, who was often foreign.

Sustainable development requires understanding and defining the roles, rights, and responsibilities of all actors – and introducing new instruments for change. It is important to focus on capacity building throughout the sector. Government has a central and unavoidable role to play in improving governance for sustainable development through a national policy framework, regulation, and enforcement. But not all governments have the capacity to make the changes. Therefore it is especially important to focus on strengthening the capacity of national and local governments to design and enforce regulations.

Capacity can also be strengthened through voluntary collaboration among different actors. Agreed standards and benchmarks will need to be established, together with agreed mechanisms to deal with the legacy of past mining operations and any future effects of today's activities. Efforts are needed to avoid the proliferation of competing schemes – norms, standards, guidelines, and criteria for the minerals sectors. To achieve this, effective and trusted systems of stakeholder engagement are required. These need to ensure that those with most at stake, especially the most vulnerable groups, are able to participate in appropriate and effective ways.

An Agenda for Change

Given the heterogeneous nature of the minerals sector, few generalizations can or should be made. With that disclaimer in mind, here are some general conclusions of the MMSD Project:

Need – Society's need for mineral commodities is clear, as they provide the substrate for numerous products upon which modern society depends. Even in the case of non-recyclable mineral commodities such as coal, it will take years to phase out use, given current dependencies. It is not currently possible to meet the world's legitimate basic needs without more of at least some kinds of mineral commodities in circulation.

Structure of the Sector – Though there is a great deal of interdependence among companies along the value chain, the lack of vertical integration in some of the minerals industry can be an obstacle to effective product stewardship. Improving this situation will require much more collaboration in the industry than has occurred in the past. If the industry is to move towards providing mineral 'services' as opposed to material supply, restructuring and alliances will need to be established.

Stakeholders – The sector includes stakeholders from the local to the global – with a wide variety of interests. There is a difference between those with a direct and often involuntary interest and those who are concerned indirectly because they choose to be. The term 'stakeholder' therefore requires further clarification. Talking of multistakeholder processes without some clarity around the different kinds of 'stakes' is too simplistic.

Subsidiarity – Local issues should be solved locally, as local endowments and priorities differ from place to place. While international action and solidarity remain crucial, decentralizing decision-making to the point as close to the impact as possible should be the norm. Local actors often resent interventions from national or international quarters 'on their behalf', particularly if this involves the assumption of a mandate.

Best Practice – Similarly, the concept of 'best practice' requires local solutions. A frequent response to questions about what constitutes 'best practice' is that 'it all depends'. Best practice should be defined by decentralized and iterative processes, not by a fixed set of parameters that can be read out of a manual.

Incentives – Win–win solutions are not always possible; voluntary approaches alone are insufficient where there is a compelling priority but little or no business case to justify the additional expenditures needed to meet it. There are then two options: collective action on a voluntary basis that is enforced internally by a group, or governmental intervention or regulation to achieve the same result. Unless the law is clear and enforced, some enterprises will resist change. In addition, if civil society groups put pressure only on a large few companies and fail to recognize progress, the rest will ride free. Market-based incentives on sustainable development criteria are difficult, though probably not impossible, to design. At present, the discussion is couched in terms of the management of risk, increasing shareholder value, and the occasional marketing advantage. Devising a system of customer-driven certification is also problematic due to the heterogeneity of the industry.

Capacities – There is a critical need to build the capacity of all the actors. Sustainable development for the sector calls for a new and different mix of skills.

Managing Mineral Wealth – The potential contribution of minerals to national economies is mostly far from realized. In all too many instances, incentives for foreign investment reduce the wealth available to the host nation. The ability of mineral-rich countries to add value to their wealth by way of beneficiation and processing is often denied by lack of capacity, tariffs, and other trade barriers. In some cases, subsidies make the position worse for others. The mismanagement of wealth through inefficiency and corruption does not help. Those who have mineral wealth now should be determined to use it to produce diverse and stable economies for tomorrow – and they need help to do so.

Legacies – The negative social and environmental legacy of the sector is a major obstacle to building trust and moving forward. Abandoned sites and communities, persistent waste and pollution issues, aggrieved peoples: the list is long. Historically, consumers – mostly in the industrial world – have not paid the full costs of using mineral commodities; the failure to internalize many of these costs has only been recognized recently. The obstacles to progress in dealing with legacies include establishing priorities on the worst sites, identifying who will pay, and deciding on the source of the funding.

Collective Efforts – Corporate performance in the minerals sector, measured against any indicator, is variable. Some good companies are improving, but the bad are inexcusable, and the past record is even worse. Action by companies, individually and collectively, is clearly required. In an open trading and competitive world, a 'rush to the bottom' caused by 'free riders' is a real danger. In many areas, small companies are crucial to the standards of large ones. If, for example, projects near closure are simply sold by multinationals to private, less visible entities, other routes are opened to avoid obligations. Collective action must include companies of all sizes in order to produce positive results.

Use of Existing Institutions – Existing organizations should be encouraged to continue facilitating collective action. Institutions such as national and international chambers of mining and regional governmental organizations currently offer the best opportunity for collective action to move forward. Mutual recognition of their respective roles and collaboration is needed. All need to engage more openly with other constituencies.

Dilemmas remain on a range of issues, including how to:

- raise the capacity of all to act to the best of standards,
- define the boundaries of responsibility among different actors when governance is weak,
- balance the role of regulation with that of voluntary initiatives,
- apply the precautionary principle so as to have a proportional response,
- remove subsidies and trade barriers that favour the better-off,
- achieve better balances between risks and opportunities,
- act when there is a democratic and governance deficit,
- stop the free riders yet maintain competition in an open trading world, and
- ensure that the price of a product reflects its total costs.

A Vision of the Minerals Sector

The MMSD process sought to create a picture of what the minerals sector would look like if it were to maximize its contribution to sustainable development. In this vision of the future, the minerals industry is integrated throughout the value chain and providing mineral services rather than primary products. To raise the performance of all, a leading group of companies – both large and small – provides a model and supports the efforts of others.

Legal and regulatory frameworks will be complemented by voluntary initiatives, such as mine-site or company-wide verification. These measures will be developed through transparent and inclusive processes, defining concrete performance standards at the global, national, and local levels. Governments will have sufficient capability and willingness to impose sanctions on those who will not meet these standards. There will be fair and accepted mechanisms to facilitate access to information, public participation in decision-making processes, and access to justice to resolve disputes.

All actors will have sufficient capacity to meet higher standards, to define and enforce constructive interventions, and to monitor performance and facilitate sustainable development objectives. Costs will be much better internalized, and there will

be a concerted effort to address the legacies of
abandoned mines.

There will be clear incentives for all actors. Companies
that perform well will retain their social licence to
operate – including lower operating costs, favourable
borrowing terms, and lower insurance rates.
Governments will benefit from harmonious social,
economic, and political relations. Labour will enjoy
better working conditions and better health. NGOs
will play a positive role in meeting society's needs.
Consumers will be assured that their use of mineral
products is supporting sustainable livelihoods.
And communities overall will have better standards
of living and greater involvement in decision-making
processes.

Supporting Sustainable Development in the Minerals Sector

Broad steps that can be taken to integrate many of the
individual suggestions in *Breaking New Ground* can be
grouped into four major categories of actions to
support sustainable development in the minerals sector:

• Increase understanding of sustainable development.
• Create organizational-level policies and management
  systems for implementing the principles of
  sustainable development.
• Collaborate with others with common interests to
  take joint steps towards sustainable development.
• Increase the ability to work towards sustainable
  development at the local, national, and global levels.

The proposals are directed principally to those with a
high level of interest and involvement in the sector.
Many of the proposals are more applicable to some
actors than to others.

Step One – Understanding Sustainable Development
A commitment to education and research is required,
including a focus on the development of practical tools
for making decisions and taking actions. This should
include incorporating sustainable development into the
curricula for mineral professionals, and increasing
understanding among employees of minerals
companies, relevant government agencies, labour and
civil society organizations, and others with important
roles in the sector.

Research will face increasing demands to ensure
relevance to the concerns of stakeholders in the sector,
and there is a need to find mechanisms to ensure this
broadening of focus occurs. Any organization funding
significant research in this area should have clearly
stated policies ensuring the rigour of the research it is
supporting, including publication of data, citation to
publicly available sources, and peer review. More
funding could be committed to research that aims to
integrate disparate sets of knowledge or expertise
within a sustainable development framework.

Specialists of different disciplines and technical fields at
all stages of the minerals cycle – from geology to
accounting – will need to evaluate how to apply the
principles of sustainable development to their current
activities. This task may be aided by collaboration with
others in the same fields, through, for example, the
work of professional associations.

Step Two – Creating Organizational Policies and Management Systems
Most organizations do not have sustainable
development policies and should consider developing
them. This is important for all actors, including
large consumers of mineral products, lenders, and
institutional investors. As a first step in developing
such a policy, an organization should review its
overall objectives and functions from a sustainable
development perspective. Those that already have
sustainable development policies should review the
extent to which these have penetrated the organization
and its decision-making processes, and should
consider more effective ways of integrating them into
practices and deriving organizational value from
them.

Companies should develop a sustainable development
policy, which incorporates other relevant company
policies such as those on environmental issues, worker
health and safety, employee integrity, community
relations, human rights, reporting, and so on. This
should enable the integration of these policies within a
coherent, more efficient and effective, and less costly
management system. The whole company should be
engaged.

Companies can develop management systems for key
issues, even where such policies have not been
established. For minerals companies, an example of this
is establishing a management system to review end-of-

life plans at existing operations, to take necessary action to strengthen them, and to continue to monitor them throughout the project life. The review should focus on whether existing plans fully address the end-of-life environmental, social, and economic conditions for affected communities; care and opportunities for displaced workers; and the implications for government and other actors at all levels. This process can be useful in surfacing potential future liabilities and allowing them to be managed.

Labour organizations could develop sustainable development policies as a way of bringing members together in a shared understanding of priorities and objectives for themselves and for the organization as a whole.

Government sustainable development policy for the minerals sector would provide a useful tool to integrate, coordinate, and harmonize the missions of different departments in pursuit of common objectives. The departments involved in developing and adopting the policy should at a minimum include those dealing with minerals exploration and development, the environment, trade and industry, labour, and economic development. A country with significant mineral endowments should consider undertaking a comprehensive review of the impact of its legal and policy framework for the minerals sector.

NGOs could develop policies to clarify the link between organizational purposes and broader sustainable development goals, to provide guidance to employees in making decisions, and to make the organization's position clear to other actors. NGOs can also enhance their effectiveness and credibility, and reduce risks by developing clear and public policies and management systems of investigation and assurance that they apply to data they use.

Step Three – Achieving Cooperation Among Those With Similar Interests

Groups of actors with common roles, responsibilities, and interests can benefit from collaboration in a number of ways. For example, they can form associations or networks to share understanding and lessons of good practice, and to enable more effective communication with other groups to pool resources, and to minimize transaction costs. Collaboration may occur from the local to international level and may

take a number of different forms – everything from informal information-sharing networks to formal associations requiring membership and adherence to a set of structures and certain norms.

Existing Associations and Networks

These should review current practices with a view to developing sustainable development policies, where they do not already exist. Networks such as the World Mines Ministries Forum, regional associations such as the Mines Ministries of the Americas (CAMMA) and ministries in Asia Pacific Economic Cooperation (APEC), and NGO initiatives such as the Global Mining Campaign should consider adopting sustainable development policies.

Forming Associations or Networks

Where appropriate, stakeholder groups in the minerals sector should be encouraged to form associations. The impetus must come from within the groups themselves, but others can help create opportunities for engagement.

A key goal is to develop the ability of small-scale and artisanal miners to articulate their views, through their own associations, in policy and other processes that affect their interests. The Communities and Small-Scale Mining initiative is critical in providing a forum to facilitate communication and coordination between miners, donors, and other stakeholders.

Communities affected by mineral activities could benefit from the development of stronger networks for sharing experience and bringing their views to attention at the national and global level. Conferences of local governments and other community organizations, supported by donors and organized on an inclusive basis, might be a first step towards building these stronger networks.

An international indigenous peoples organization could be established to share experience and strategically advise, direct, and monitor industry performance in the arena of indigenous relations.

Protocols and Statements of Principle

Within associations of actors, standards can be improved collectively through the development of and agreement on norms and principles.

• *A Global Declaration and Establishment of a Protocol*
The minerals industry should consider adopting a
Declaration on Sustainable Development and
establishing a Protocol to support its commitment.
This would simplify the current multiple codes of
conduct and sources of guidance by providing a way to
bring these together over time into one management
system. It would start by building on the recently
adopted Sustainable Development Charter of ICMM.

Phase I – ICMM and other appropriate organizations
could develop the Declaration unilaterally in
consultation with stakeholders. (See Box ES–5 for
suggested basic elements and Box ES–6 for candidates
for inclusion.) Companies would be encouraged to
adopt and sign on to it. The Declaration might be
most effective if it includes a commitment to develop
specific, measurable criteria as a set of protocols, along
with a system of verification of performance.
It suggests how that system of protocols could be
extended more broadly to all parts of the industry.

Phase II –The goal of Phase II would be to create the
basis for an accepted Protocol for individual minerals

> **Box ES–5. Basic Elements of the Declaration on Mining, Minerals, and Sustainable Development**
>
> Companies could agree to:
>
> • Participate in review of their association charters and policies in light of the conclusions of this report.
> • Work with other companies, within a defined time, to establish a Protocol dealing with key issues of sustainable development and corporate performance, in a process acceptable to key external stakeholders.
> • Work with other companies to develop an accepted system of verification to accompany the Protocol.
> • Devise a set of immediate commitments embodied in the Declaration; one approach would be the adoption of the basic principles outlined in a manageable number of existing agreements and guidelines.
> • Develop internal management procedures to familiarize employees with the meaning of these commitments, their importance as company policy, and their alignment with business success.
> • Develop reporting procedures that address the principles in the Declaration.
> • Conduct, over a defined period, an independent audit by a reputable outside organization of the state of company compliance with the requirements of the Declaration.

> **Box ES–6. Candidates for Inclusion in Initial Declaration**
>
> • Rio Declaration.
> • The United Nations Global Compact.
> • Environmental, social, and economic guidelines on corporate reporting that have been developed within the Global Reporting Initiative.
> • OECD Guidelines for Multinational Enterprises.
> • World Bank Group's Operational Guidelines, including, but not limited to, those on Environmental Assessment, Involuntary Resettlement, Indigenous Peoples, and Projects in Disputed Areas.
> • OECD Convention on Combating Bribery of Foreign Officials.
> • ILO Convention 98 on the Right to Organize and Collective Bargaining; ILO Convention 169 Concerning Indigenous and Tribal Peoples in Independent Countries; ILO Convention 176 on Safety and Health in Mines and ILO Recommendation 183, which accompanies it.
> • Voluntary Principles on Security and Human Rights.

facilities or projects. Protocols for individual sets
of issues could be adopted as they were agreed. The
Protocol should be accompanied by a clear system of
rigorous third-party verification. Representatives of key
stakeholder groups should be involved in development
of the Protocol and the verification process.

Phase III – This phase is envisioned to be an expanded
Protocol for company-wide application. Participation
by external stakeholders in management of the process
would be deepened. It may lead to a system of
company-wide certification or verification. Phase III
could ultimately consider product certification for
certain mineral commodities.

While ICMM must have the key role in reviewing its
own Charter, and should take leadership in developing
the language of the Declaration and the subsequent
adoption of the Protocol, companies choosing not to
join ICMM should be able to participate in this
system. It should be open to all levels of the industry,
and therefore should be a subject of early discussion
with national associations and such bodies as the
Prospectors and Developers Association of Canada
(PDAC) or Eurométaux. Any or all of these bodies
could eventually – as the Australian Minerals Council
has – decide that adhering to the Protocol is a
requirement of membership. But the Protocol should
not require membership in ICMM.

The Declaration could call for an immediate set of commitments that could be adopted by individual companies, together with a commitment to a longer-term process of multistakeholder engagement to develop the more comprehensive and specific protocols for the industry. It should also provide for a company commitment to adopt and comply with national or regional industry codes of conduct where they exist. For example, companies operating in Australia should initially comply with the Australian Minerals Industry Code for Environmental Management, and those in Canada should adhere to the Mining Association of Canada's environmental policy and sustainable development principles as they are developed.

• *National and Regional Industry Codes of Conduct*
Many issues can be dealt with more effectively at the national or regional level. A number of national industry associations have adopted sustainable development policies. There may be benefits in developing these further into codes of conduct, on the model of the environmental codes already in place in some associations.

• *Regional Statements of Principle by Governments*
Regional government organizations such as SADC, APEC, or CAMMA may want to consider adopting sustainable development policies for the minerals sector that can help governments seek greater convergence and harmonization.

• *Statements of Principles by Nongovernmental Organizations*
A collective statement of principles by NGOs that focuses on mineral-related issues might strengthen their influence and increase the contribution they are able to make.

Developing the Capacity to Prevent and Respond to Emergencies

Preventing accidents is a high priority. An international facility, supported principally by industry and with appropriate involvement of other stakeholders, could play an important role. It could mobilize world-class experts to supplement government capacity to assess, respond, and control accidents and emergencies, or to reduce the chance of them happening. This approach could assure the public that the best possible advice is available to responsible officials. This facility would rely on experts from consulting firms, universities, governments, companies, NGOs, or other institutions on an 'as needed' basis.

Step Four – Building Capacity for Effective Actions at All Levels

Community Level
Where a local community is affected by minerals development, a shared vision of the development path for the community is required.

• *Community Engagement*
For most mining operations, engagement with local communities must begin at the exploration stage. Companies should develop plans for continuous engagement during the operation's life – from exploration through to closure. This plan should be discussed with the community to ensure that the mechanisms proposed are considered appropriate. Companies must ensure that those in charge have the right skills and proper authority and that there is continuity of involvement. They must also be willing to invest time in the community.

• *Integrated Impact Assessment*
Environmental and social assessment tools should be combined to enable a transition to integrated impact assessment. This should be universal for new projects and include an early phase of consultation with the community to identify local concerns, and to ensure those are addressed. It could become the basis for the development of a Community Sustainable Development Plan (CSDP). The Seven Questions framework developed by MMSD NORTH AMERICA provides a useful example of an integrated assessment framework that goes beyond 'impacts'.

• *Community Sustainable Development Plans*
The CSDP should be based on the community's concept of how the mine can best contribute to achieving its social, environmental, and economic goals. The plan should provide the fundamental framework for relationships among the company, the community, and the government (and any other parties) through the project life and into post-closure. It should identify the specific actions needed and the respective roles and responsibilities to achieve the agreed-upon vision. It could also create some obligations, on all sides, for taking those steps. Independent mechanisms for monitoring and evaluation, including clear and agreed indicators of performance, need to be included. The plan will need to evolve and be amended over the life of the project to reflect changing priorities and capacities.

Key Actions at the Community Level	
Actions	**Responsibilities**
• Community Engagement • Integrated Impact Assessment • Community Sustainable Development Plans • Integrated Planning for Closure • Labour-management agreement for sustainable development • Disputes and conflict resolution mechanisms • Cooperation between large companies and artisanal and small-scale miners	• Companies, communities, local institutions • Companies, communities, local government, consultants • Companies, labour unions, local government, communities, civil society organizations • Companies, labour unions, local government, communities, civil society organizations • Labour organizations, companies • Companies, communities, labour unions, local government, civil society organizations

While a company may facilitate and promote the process, the leadership role belongs to local government to the extent it has the capacity and willingness. Otherwise an NGO or development organization could step into this role. The World Bank could evaluate the usefulness of requiring or encouraging contractual CSDPs, where they will be useful, in projects funded by the International Finance Corporation (IFC) or insured by the Multilateral Investment Guarantee Agency. Commercial banks could review whether adopting a parallel requirement would be a way to reduce their exposure to the results of proceeding without such plans.

• *Integrated Planning for Closure*
Since many mineral projects depend on specific deposits that have a finite life span, there is a need to focus on where the community wants to be when the project closes. This requires defining desired end-of-life environmental, social, and economic conditions; identifying the resources required to achieve them; and clearly allocating roles and responsibilities of each of the actors. There needs to be a focus on sustaining benefits in areas such as housing, community health, and education.

• *Dispute Resolution Mechanisms*
Where there is restricted access to justice, especially at the community level, or when existing mechanisms are inadequate or not trusted, it may be necessary to design dispute resolution mechanisms at the community level.

• *Large Companies and Artisanal and Small-Scale Mining*
Large companies could engage directly with small-scale miners and their communities, helping them to work in a more sustainable fashion and where

necessary to find alternative economic activities.

National Level
Effective policy, coordination, and action at the national level will help to maximize the benefits of minerals activities and minimize the negative impacts. Governments with mineral activities may consider comprehensive reviews of their legal and policy frameworks for the minerals sector to ensure that they are consistent with the vision of sustainable development.

• *Access to Information*
All levels of governments should have legal and regulatory provisions for citizens to access information in government possession for which there is not a valid and publicly stated reason for non-disclosure. Mechanisms to support this may include contact points for regular exchange of information with civil society. Governments and civil society organizations should also establish clear and agreed procedures for requesting, receiving, and disseminating information.

• *Public Participation*
Governments should continue the process of regulatory reform to facilitate public participation. Access to information and public participation cannot be established and maintained unless there is a right to access to the legal means to enforce them.

• *Clarifying Land Regimes*
National frameworks should provide clear rules for access to and use of land, including elements such as extensive consultation with local communities; clearly defined rights for those with established occupancy and use of land or communal land holdings, even where they hold no legal title; compensation for loss

of rights; and effective access to systems of justice. Governments should also ensure that when bilateral negotiations do take place around land issues, the rules are understood and followed by all actors.

• *Traditional Indigenous Territories*
Governments and companies could make considerable progress by maintaining respect for the principle of prior informed consent freely given. The extent of indigenous territories needs to be clearly defined for the security of traditional peoples, and open dialogue needs to be maintained on this issues. Other actors such as the NGO community can assist.

• *Frameworks to Maximize and Sustain the Benefits of Minerals Development*
Governments should consider developing long-term strategic plans for the creation and management of mineral wealth that include appropriate methods of capturing the rent from minerals and distributing the revenues; the creation of human, physical, and other forms of capital; and planning for the effects of mine closure at both the local and the national level. In addition, governments could develop measures, such as commodity loans and fiscal restraint, to prevent undue stress on public financing resulting from minerals price volatility.

• *Frameworks for Artisanal and Small-Scale Mining*
Governments need to develop a policy and regulatory framework that focuses on both the facilitation and management of artisanal and small-scale mining, and creates sufficient financial and regulatory incentives for small-scale miners to formalize their activities.

• *Frameworks for Community Development*
Governments should consider incorporating integrated impact assessment, CSDPs, and integrated closure planning and its existing frameworks and assigning responsibilities among agencies – in consultation with relevant stakeholder groups.

• *Mining-Induced Displacement and Resettlement*
Governments must put in place regulations that ensure free and willing negotiation on any resettlement proposal; mechanisms for monitoring and arbitration are a natural accompaniment to such regulations. Although it is premature to institute insurance on involuntary displacement and resettlement, a contingency clause could be proposed as an interim solution.

• *Anti-Corruption Initiatives*
Concerted effort is needed to combat corruption – governments should adopt national legislation to put the anti-corruption convention of the Organisation for Economic Co-operation and Development into effect. Companies could work with organizations such as Transparency International at the national level to establish industry-wide guidance. Industry

Key Actions at the National Level	
Actions	**Responsibilities**
Review and Development of Legal and Policy Frameworks • Access to information • Public participation • Land rights regimes and compensation systems • Traditional indigenous territories • Maximizing the benefits of mineral development • Artisanal and small-scale mining • Community development • Mining-induced displacement and resettlement	• Governments and relevant stakeholders
Other Actions • An international register of payments to combat corruption • Audits, guidelines, and standards for environmental management • Capacity building • Labour-company agreements • National multistakeholder processes	• Companies, industry associations, NGOs, governments, international organizations • Government, affected communities, companies • Governments, international organizations such as the World Bank, the UN, NGOs, donors • National unions, companies • All relevant actors

organizations should consider taking the initiative, possibly in partnership with an international organization such as the World Bank, to establish an international and public register of all payments by mining companies to governments at all levels.

• *Audits, Guidelines, and Standards for Environment Management*
Governments and funding agencies should require regular independent audits of all tailings storage facilities and find ways to act on the results. Equally, governments should set up clear guidelines for evaluating different disposal methods for mining waste on a case-by-case basis, with a clear value in the short term of the need to avoid riverine disposal.

Government agencies charged with managing impact assessment processes should develop standards for baseline data and analysis for special issues, such as acid drainage assessment, closure planning, and water quality. A high priority in many countries should be communicating the results of these assessments more effectively to interested parties, and integrating these concerns into decision-making from the permitting stage through closure.

• *Capacity Building*
The World Bank and the United Nations, working with member governments, could develop a clearer picture of the kind of capacities needed and those that are already in place at the national level.

• *National Multistakeholder Processes*
Governments could be an effective convenor of multistakeholder processes at the national level for policy discussions and change.

Global Level
There are a number of initiatives that are best taken at the global level by different groups of actors working together. Some are already under way in some form and need to be supported. Others have yet to be initiated. It should be noted that calling for action at the international level does not preclude these initiatives being undertaken at other levels.

• *A Complaints and Dispute Resolution Mechanism*
All parties in the sector should be committed to establishing fair, reasonable ways to resolve grievances and disputes. A dispute resolution mechanism should bring parties together, in a neutral forum, to work out

a mutually acceptable facilitated settlement. The elements of the mechanism are envisioned as similar to the methods and procedures of an ombudsman, such as the IFC's Advisor/Ombudsman or the Mining Ombudsman Project operated by Community Aid Abroad in Australia. Clearly, where possible, complaints would be better handled by an independent organization operating at a regional or national level.

The overall programme could be overseen by a balanced multistakeholder Board. Commercial lenders could support this proposal by requiring a demonstration that an effective dispute resolution mechanism is available as a condition of loans.

• *A Product Stewardship Initiative*
A Product Stewardship Initiative could promote greater exchange of information and integration of views with the industry's principal customers and intermediary processors, recyclers, and others. This initiative could build on the work already undertaken by the Non-Ferrous Metals Consultative Forum on Sustainable Development.

As part of this process, national governments need to continue to identify incentives and disincentives for recycling, extended product life, and innovative design in metals use and to develop policies on them. These should include measurable targets, collection networks, infrastructure, and investment in recycling technologies.

A Product Stewardship Initiative would lead to improved understanding of: energy, water, land use, recycling, and re-use issues; life-cycle analysis as a management tool for sustainable development; appropriate recycling technology transfers to developing countries; and possible product certification schemes.

• *A Sustainable Development Support Facility*
A Sustainable Development Support Facility could be developed to serve as a central clearinghouse for information on who is doing what in the sector and to suggest ways to coordinate and target the efforts of donors and others. It could serve:
• as an independent source of capacity building or advice to government on issues such as emergency planning or implementation of local emergency preparedness plans;
• as a supplement to government departments charged with technical tasks such as safety inspection of tailings dams;

- to help develop the technical standards necessary for effective impact assessment in the minerals sector;
- to assess potential for acid drainage and strategies for dealing with it; and
- to assist in the development of CSDPs and to strengthen the capacity needed for effective planning for closure.

The Facility could be supported by donor agencies, and could be administered by the World Bank Group as a trust fund. An important role in its management could also be played by the World Conservation Union–IUCN.

Applications for assistance could be made by any government, NGO, UN body, trade union, or other appropriate organization that was committed to cooperative approaches to sustainable development challenges in the minerals sector.

- *Reporting Guidelines*
A harmonized system of reporting guidelines is needed to ensure that key aspects of company practice are publicly reported to a standard that informs internal and external stakeholders about the sustainable development performance of corporations and major projects. A multilateral organization such as the World Bank could convene an experts group to draft a broad set of principles and operational guidelines for reporting. In defining guidelines, the sector should work with organizations such as the Global Reporting Initiative and the International Organization for Standardization to achieve comparability between sectors and to ensure the transfer of existing knowledge.

Research into the identification and development of key indicators for public reporting needs to continue. Through organizations such as the Minerals and Energy Research Network (MERN), the eventual aim is to construct a set of 'must have' generic, yet sector-specific indicators at the project and corporate level, supported by a secondary set of indicators that could be applicable at particular sites.

- *Protected Areas and Mining Initiative*
Increased collaboration is required at the international level among key actors including IUCN and other conservation organizations, governments, and NGOs to resolve issues related to protected areas management. Possible actions could include:

- Establish a multistakeholder forum that aims to achieve consensus on 'no-go' zones for mining, on a case-by-case basis, with a priority for World Heritage Sites.
- Develop a package of published 'better-practice' guidance on mining and protected areas.
- Establish clear criteria that can be used to decide if mining is possible near protected areas, which should then be applied to its control and to the assessment of existing mines in protected areas.
- Work towards improving the transparency of decision-making around the assignment of protected areas categories.
- Undertake 'high resolution' mapping through key institutions that will identify the scale and extent of threats to and opportunities for protected areas posed by mining and other sectoral activities.

- *Mineral Legacies Initiative*
Improving conditions at abandoned sites can yield immense social and environmental benefits for a relatively small investment. The focus at least initially should be on true 'orphan' sites, where no former owner or operator can be identified. Priority should be given to sites where remedial action will offer a clear payoff in improved public health and safety, more usable water supplies, or other demonstrable benefits, such as protection of biodiversity. Another priority is sites in low-income countries with significant abandoned mine legacy problems and those with particularly pressing social legacies of mining communities.

Governments with many abandoned mines but few resources could be given grants to determine priorities for the cases most urgently needing attention and to develop project proposals that could then be funded.

Most observers agree on the need for such action, but not on its financing or administration. Yet there are good if not perfect models for the administration – the Global Environment Facility is one; a trust fund established by donors and administered by the World Bank or regional development banks would be another. The World Bank has financed work at abandoned mines or other mineral facilities in the past. At a minimum it could coordinate its future support for such activities with a trust or other entity managing this work. One possibility would be for a group of companies to take the initiative by pledging an initial contribution to the trust fund on the condition that it be matched by government and other donors.

At the World Summit on Sustainable Development in August–September 2002, world leaders could use the opportunity of meeting in one of the world's most important mining centres – and one that shares with others a legacy of problems from that activity – to call for a full-scale feasibility study of a Mineral Legacies Initiative. Establishing this fund would require a number of nations to commit together to a programme to make it viable for at least several years. Protection of public goods such as water supply and public health and safety would have to be the primary goals, but the programme could also be useful in building skills and generating employment.

• *Financial Surety*
Governments recognize that some industries (such as power plants, chemical facilities, and mines) have the potential to leave behind large social costs. To make sure they do not inherit these costs, some insist that companies provide a bond or financial guarantee to ensure that they will comply with closure plans and not leave behind such costs. Developing countries have often not adopted financial surety. Some way must be found to capture its benefits. Progress on this issue is important. The World Bank recognizes this as a priority concern.

The best way forward seems to be for the World Bank and the world's mines ministers together to convene a dialogue, starting with a high-level conference, to find ways of reconciling the clear benefits to be achieved by appropriate guarantee systems, national policies for minerals investment, and the growing desire of many commercial and non-commercial lenders to ensure that the projects they finance do not wind up adding to the world's inventory of sites abandoned without proper precaution.

• *A Global Labour-Management Agreement*
There could be a global-level agreement between labour federations representing workers in the minerals sector, such as the International Federation of Chemical, Energy, Mine and General Workers' Unions (ICEM), and international organizations representing companies for broad cooperation in support of sustainable development. Organized labour could take the lead to suggest elements of the agreement. These may include traditional areas of interest such as the training, health, and safety of workers, but could also include broader community concerns. The agreement could be linked to counterpart agreements at the national and local levels.

• *Forum on Mining, Minerals, and Sustainable Development*
A Forum on Mining, Minerals, and Sustainable Development could be established as a process, or processes, that can stay in effective communication with all principal stakeholders, and is not controlled by any of them individually but 'belongs' to all of them as a group. In the forest products industry, a similar need led to the creation of a Forest Stewardship Council.

Key Actions at the Global Level

Actions	Responsibilities
• Complaints and Dispute Resolution Mechanism	• Companies, representatives of affected stakeholder groups, commercial lenders
• Product Stewardship Initiative	• Non-Ferrous Metals Consultative Forum on Sustainable Development, industry associations, NGOs, governments, labour
• Sustainable Development Support Facility	• Governments, international organizations, NGOs such as IUCN, stakeholders
• Reporting Guidelines	• ICMM–industry associations, NGOs and stakeholders, Global Reporting Initiative, companies, international organizations
• Protected Areas and Mining	• Conservation NGOs such as IUCN, governments, companies, associations such as ICMM, communities
• Dialogue on Mineral Legacies	• Mining industry, world leaders
• Dialogue on Financial Surety	• World Bank, mine ministers
• Global Labour-Management Agreement	• International labour unions such as ICEM and international industry associations such as ICMM
• Forum on Mining, Minerals, and Sustainable Development	• All actors

In the dam building sector, it led to the World Commission on Dams. The Responsible Care initiative in the chemicals industry has a multistakeholder stewardship council. In the minerals sector, this model has been pursued, with variations, for things such as the recent cyanide code, the White Horse Mining Initiative, and the MMSD Project itself. Processes of this type can create results that cannot be created in any other way.

The Forum would not have to be a permanent bureaucracy. It could, for example, resemble the Global Mining Initiative Conference in May 2002, but in a more advanced version at some determined intervals in the future. The Forum could perhaps achieve these goals:

- Establishing priorities for a wide range of actors in the sector, so that each could focus on a manageable number of tasks in the near term.
- Setting guidelines for processes directed at individual issues, to give all concerned a greater confidence in their legitimacy and reduce the transaction costs in setting them up.
- Endorsing processes if they met those guidelines, adding to their legitimacy and increasing peoples' confidence in participating in them.
- Endorsing the results of these processes, giving them broader acceptance and ensuring that their principles are more quickly incorporated into company policy, industry protocols, best practice guidelines, lending policies of banks, and laws and regulations.

The MMSD project has identified a number of issues ripe for progress in a Forum – management of tailings and other large-volume wastes, action against corruption, integrated planning for closure, community health and mining, and biodiversity and protected areas, to name just a few. But progress on any of them will require engagement of a variety of stakeholders. Effective engagement that produces results will require attention to process, which requires investment. There is no effective alternative. A way to proceed, and one that could yield better long-term results, would be to make the investment once, instead of every time an issue came up.

There is an informal proposal for such a forum from the UN family. Others suggest that the Forum could develop out of existing mechanisms such as the International Study Group's Non-Ferrous Metals Consultative Forum on Sustainable Development.

Whatever the future of the Forum proposal, at a minimum there should be a recognition that establishing communication and discussion among interested parties on a national, regional, or global basis requires a committed effort and a significant investment of time and money. Processes are expensive at least in part because of the investment needed to establish these links. Finding a home in an institution capable of maintaining the databases that projects – including MMSD – have established and of circulating periodic bulletins, perhaps containing a registry of current research activities, is an important investment in the future of dialogue. MERN, the UNCTAD/UNEP Mineral Resources Forum, or a new Union for Minerals and Sustainable Development are all possible homes for such a body.

A Final Thought...

The MMSD Project did not try to resolve the many economic, environmental, social, and governance issues facing the mining and minerals sector – no single effort could. But the project did try to turn a spotlight on the range of challenges raised by society's need for and production of minerals. Judging by the input and reactions during the two years of the Project, that goal was achieved. The many people who made contributions to the process – through papers, workshop participation, comments on successive drafts, emails with news from all corners of the world – confirmed that the minerals sector involves much more than digging ore out of the ground.

Although *Breaking New Ground* is the final report of the MMSD Project, it is not, of course, the final word on this complex subject. But we hope that for the minerals sector it is a helpful step along a road towards sustainable development that includes all those affected: policymakers, business leaders, public interest campaigners, people working in mines, local communities, and – very important – consumers. All these people must join the discussion and take action if the world is to find a better way to meet society's needs.

BREAKING NEW GROUND

INTRODUCTION

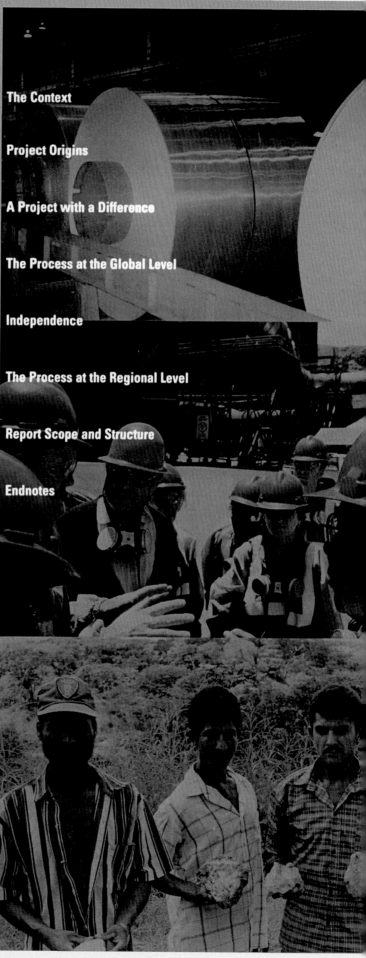

This report is the result of nearly two years of research, analysis, and consultation by the Mining, Minerals and Sustainable Development (MMSD) Project at the International Institute for Environment and Development (IIED). This Introduction describes what the project set out to do and the process that evolved to accomplish those goals.

The Context

In the past decade, the mining and minerals industry has come under tremendous pressure to improve its social, developmental, and environmental performance. Like other parts of the corporate world, companies are more routinely expected to perform to ever higher standards of behaviour, going well beyond achieving the best rate of return for shareholders. They are also increasingly being asked to be more transparent and subject to third-party audit or review. In response, a number of companies, either independently or with other actors, are establishing 'voluntary standards' that often go beyond any law. But even so, some observers remain suspicious that many businesses are merely engaging in public relations exercises and doubt their sincerity. In particular, the industry has been failing to convince some of its constituencies and stakeholders that it necessarily has the 'social licence to operate' in many areas of the world.

Despite the industry's undoubted importance in meeting the need for minerals and its significant contributions to economic and social development, concerns about aspects of its performance prevail. Mining, refining, and the use and disposal of minerals have in some instances led to significant local environmental and social damage. It is not always clear that mining brings economic and social benefits to the host countries, as the minerals sector sometimes operates where there is poor governance, including corruption, and is thus associated with it. In some cases, communities and indigenous groups near or around mines allege human rights abuses. The litany of concerns is long.

Project Origins

Against this background, and with the tenth anniversary of the Rio Earth Summit in mind, in late 1998 nine of the largest mining companies decided to embark on a new initiative intended to achieve a serious change in the way industry approached today's problems. They called this the Global Mining Initiative. It included a programme of internal reform, a review of the various associations they belonged to, and a rigorous study of the societal issues they had to face. Through the World Business Council for Sustainable Development (WBCSD), they commissioned IIED to undertake a scoping study in May 1999 to set out the global challenge of sustainable development facing the mining sector and to propose the scope of a two-year process of participatory analysis to explore the role of the sector in the transition to sustainable development.[1]

A team of IIED researchers reviewed existing initiatives and materials, and consulted over 150 separate individuals and organizations to understand their views of how the minerals sector's contribution to sustainable development could be improved and to develop a more detailed framework for the process. The Mining and Energy Research Network (MERN) held an experts meeting to review the findings. There were few precedents to go by. The nearest was a project on the paper sector, conducted by IIED in partnership with the WBCSD in the mid-1990s.[2] There was also the comprehensive study of large dams, but it was conducted by a World Commission and at the time was just getting under way.[3] While various 'multistakeholder' processes had been attempted, most were not convened on such a scale.[4]

IIED published its results in October 1999, making recommendations for the design and scope of the process that became known as the MMSD Project.[5] It proposed four objectives of the new project. (See Box 1.)

- To assess the global mining and minerals sector in terms of the transition to sustainable development. This would cover the current contribution – both positive and negative – to economic prosperity, human well-being, ecosystem health, and accountable decision-making, as well as the track record of past practice.
- To identify how the services provided by the minerals system can be delivered in accordance with sustainable development in the future.
- To propose key elements for improving the minerals system.
- Crucial for long-term impact, to build platforms of analysis and engagement for ongoing cooperation and networking among all stakeholders.

It was clear the MMSD Project had to be independent and collaborative if the results were to lead to trusted and accepted outcomes. In short, the project needed to build on past achievements and involve the sector as a whole. (Throughout this report, the term sector is used to describe all the key stakeholders associated with the minerals sector: industry from explorationists through to processors, government, international organizations, non-governmental organizations (NGOs), academia, civil society, communities, and labour.) It also needed to decentralize – to confer much of the responsibility for undertaking the work to regional institutions in the principal centres of mineral production and consumption. Finally, from the outset it needed to integrate the element of planning for implementation in order to ensure that its efforts resulted in more than just a documentation of ideas.

Moreover, since mining is driven by society's use of, and need for, the products of the mining industry, the project needed to be inclusive in its scope and seek to examine the whole life cycle of minerals in the context of sustainable development. There would be little point in having perfect standards at a coal mine, for example, if society considered the use of coal too undesirable in terms of its potential climate effects.

Following the publication of the scoping report, WBCSD appointed IIED to undertake the MMSD Project. One key criterion for the selection of the study's host institution was that it would have no long-term institutional interest in the findings and outcomes of the report, nor would it seek to be the centre of mining expertise. It was on this basis, and on the

strength of its experience, that IIED was asked to house the project.

IIED then held a series of discussions with the main industry sponsors to clarify the MMSD Project design and objectives. Some important limits on the project emerged:

- The project would not be about building consensus on how to proceed in any area – there was insufficient time or capacity to do so (although should a consensus emerge, so much the better). Instead, MMSD hoped to set out key issues related to the minerals sector in ways that would fairly reflect different perspectives and suggest ways of moving forward.
- Consistent with this, MMSD would not be the same as a 'commission' of enquiry – the sector was too heterogeneous and divided for such a process to be contemplated. Rather, MMSD would be more in the nature of a feasibility study of what might lead to better outcomes.
- Limits to MMSD's geographical and 'stakeholder' reach were assumed from the outset. The project would not be expected to reach or understand the plight and problem of the last affected group or person in the world. The report would therefore not be 'speaking on behalf of any stakeholders' unless the project had been asked to do so.
- The project – it was hoped – would lay the basis for an ongoing process by many actors. It was not intended to be an end-point that would stop in 2002. It was intended to lay the ground for a strategic approach to solving problems based on analysis and consultation in which the boundaries of rights and responsibilities of all the relevant actors were clearer.

A Project with a Difference

Conducting the MMSD Project turned out to be a major challenge. The objectives were ambitious. Several realities shaped the way it was designed and then proceeded, and these too are reflected in the results. It was recognized from the start that a project on mining and minerals was bound to be more controversial and complex than earlier projects, such as the one based on the paper cycle. For example, the paper industry is based on a single 'renewable resource', instead of a multiplicity of very different non-renewable resources.

MMSD Managing Mineral Wealth Workshop, London, August 2001

One issue at the core of controversy concerning mining and minerals is the idea that the use of 'non-renewable resources' is inherently undesirable. Some groups oppose all mining on this basis. This idea is, of course, not new. Many environmentalists from the 1970s onwards have campaigned against the extraction and use of non-renewable resources, either because these will ultimately run out or because of the adverse impacts of extraction and use.

Many stakeholders, however, are supportive of the minerals sector and of mining – not least, governments and some communities in developing countries seeking employment and sources of revenue. The MMSD Project convened several workshops where valuable exchanges of ideas occurred on such issues. But the low level of trust and high level of animosity between the minerals industry and many of its critics was problematic for the project from the start. This was a critical issue, especially if some sense of convergence were to be achieved for the future.

The critics of this industry include a diverse range of constituencies, such as communities in and around the mines and public advocacy groups concerned with the environment, human rights, indigenous peoples, poverty alleviation, and economic development. Labour, too, is in some instances in dispute with management. In order to tackle the public policy issues facing the minerals sector, the MMSD Project needed to have enough breadth to comprehend many of these concerns and their interconnections and implications. But most important, it had to try to create opportunities for the different constituencies to express themselves in confidence and, should confidence be

built, engage in dialogue to seek solutions. This objective was not entirely achieved. While participants from many diverse interest groups took part in the MMSD process, a distinct group of NGOs chose not to. Indeed, persuading others not to take part became a campaign for these groups in its own right.

The project design of MMSD recognized that campaigning by environmental and political groups has played an important role in catalysing major changes in the standards pursued by minerals industry in the past, and that these groups would continue to be major drivers of change. But these changes have taken place in a patchy fashion. For example, stringent environmental requirements in Europe and many parts of North America have made it more difficult for companies to operate mines in these regions. This is one reason why little mining is done within the European Union today, save in the building materials sector. The parts of the minerals cycle that have been retained are those where the business of adding value is less controversial (and more profitable). In contrast, governments of developing countries are perceived by some to be lowering social and environmental standards, fuelling a 'race to the bottom' as countries use lower standards to attract investment. Given the complexity and interconnections of all these issues, MMSD needed to examine the sector from regional and global perspectives. Understanding the practical politics of these intricate issues was a major challenge too.

MMSD also had to address a clear paradox. While consumers in the industrial world enjoy mined products – cars or planes, jewellery, mobile phones, computers, and even the fabric of buildings – they are less fond of the 'holes in the ground' needed for their supply. This disconnect between source and product is even reflected in the structure of parts of the minerals industry, which is quite stratified. The supply chains of minerals are different from those of timber, food, or even oil and gas. At its simplest, miners sell to refiners, who sell onto commodity exchanges used by fabricators, who sell to wholesalers, who sell to retailers and, eventually, to the consuming public. Some companies in the metals industry in Europe are keen to deny their connection to mining on the basis that much of their material comes from secondary sources. Such an approach mirrors the attitudes of many governments in Europe, which seem disinterested in the problems of metal and mineral supply even though much of the minerals sector's investment and the demand for its products come from industrial countries and all economies are dependent on such products. As a result, it was difficult at times to get the cooperation of key actors along the commodities chain.

There is great variation in the scale of enterprise. Some mineral commodities are largely produced by some of the world's millions of small-scale and artisanal miners, or processed by individuals or village artisans. Others are produced almost entirely by a small number of large multinational corporations.

The crisis of confidence that the minerals industry has been undergoing in some quarters has given rise to many defensive and divided attitudes. This industry is also diverse and heterogeneous, and the responses of different companies to a growing array of regulations and criticisms vary considerably. Many might like to dismiss criticisms as unreasonable, not least because some critics do not take into account the positive contributions the industry can make to development or acknowledge that society has a need for minerals. Leaders of the industry might argue that 'best practice' today is far ahead of the standard a decade ago, that the industry has been judged on the basis of the worst offenders, and that nothing has been done to recognize the failures of other players involved in the sector as a whole, such as governments or the users and consumers of minerals and metals. Others argue that the best practice of today is still not good enough. This is merely an example of the many perspectives that MMSD had to accommodate as best it could.

The Process at the Global Level

The MMSD Project began in April 2000. Before work could commence in full, it was necessary to recruit a new team into IIED to work alongside existing staff. The team, which reached a peak of 17, was drawn internationally and included people with a range of expertise on one or another aspect of the sector.

The project quickly set out to work with as many groups and individuals as it could in the process, and thereby include as many perspectives as possible. Four main functions to be fulfilled by MMSD were identified: research and analysis, stakeholder

engagement, information and communications, and planning for outcomes. These interconnected roles constituted the 'MMSD approach' and aimed to ensure the relevance of the research topics selected and the action plans derived from stakeholder input and the project's analysis, as well as the effectiveness with which they could be implemented.

In May 2000, soon after the project began, a two-day Strategic Planning Workshop for some 50 people known to be engaged in the issues was held. As with subsequent workshops, participants were drawn from a diverse range of backgrounds and experiences including industry and its trade associations, labour, governments, academia, indigenous peoples, UN and international organizations, and NGOs concerned with environment and social issues. Participants attended meetings as individuals rather than as representatives of organizations.

At the Strategic Planning Workshop, participants advised on the scope of issues and on the process that was envisaged. One result was a list of topics that different groups felt to be important, together with the work that had already been done on them. It became apparent at this early stage that a key feature of the process had to be a concentration on 'strategic issues', for there was not going to be time to enter into every last detail on specifics. The workshop also provided guidance on the process of stakeholder engagement, the project's governance structure, and decentralization of project activities.[6]

By the end of 2000 the project's scope at the global level had been condensed to a series of challenges. These were still wide subject areas, but they seemed to constitute the major issues that had to be faced. From August 2000 to February 2002, MMSD commissioned research and held a series of workshops organized around these challenges. Thematic research, workshops, and stakeholder engagement exercises were also conducted through the MMSD regional processes around regionally defined topics.

At the global level, workshops were organized around themes such as the management of mineral wealth; human rights, conflict, and corruption; the role of financial institutions; public participation; environmental issues, including land use, biodiversity, waste, and mine closure issues; life-cycle assessment; the reporting and verification of information; indigenous peoples' issues; and artisanal and small-scale mining. (See Appendix 1 for a full list of meetings.)

Throughout the project there were many bilateral meetings and presentations to UN organizations, the World Bank, the Organisation for Economic Co-operation and Development, the European Union, governments, and other significant groups and players. In addition, the process had numerous informal routes by which input and opinion were gathered. A project website was regularly updated and contained all documents generated by the project. A monthly news bulletin – in English and Spanish – was disseminated through the project's database to at least 5500 contacts.

Clear rules were observed throughout the MMSD process. These included a set of principles of stakeholder engagement that were developed early in the project and disseminated through its Bulletin and website. Among the key principles observed were:

- First, by attending or in some way taking part in the process, no one was represented as endorsing the process, much less the report itself.[7]
- Second, no person or group or entity was mentioned by name in workshop proceedings without a published reference or their agreement.
- Third, the Work Group – including all those in the regions – attempted to maintain a sense of fairness, balance, transparency, and openness to critics throughout.

Independence

This report hopes to reflect all these different perspectives in a balanced fashion. One of the project's aims was to create a structure that would guarantee the project's independence and the quality of the analysis and outcomes. The safeguards put in place centred on three issues: diversification of funding, quality control, and editorial control.

MMSD's funding comes from what is known as the Sponsors Group. To ensure a diversity of funding, the Sponsors Group was expanded to include companies other than the original 9 who initiated the Scoping Study (the 9 grew to 25), four consulting groups, the public sector (several donor governments), international organizations (including the UN

Environment Programme and the World Bank), one foundation, and six non-governmental sponsors. A target ratio of funding sources was set at 60% commercial to 40% non-commercial. Although in the end this was not achieved in cash terms, many of the non-commercial sponsors provided significant 'in kind' contributions.

An Assurance Group made up of recognized individuals with experience from different constituencies of the minerals sector – the so-called stakeholders – was established to ensure the quality, independence, and balance of the process and report. (See Appendix 1 for a list of the Assurance Group.) Members served as individuals rather than as representatives of any organizations. Initial members were appointed by the Project Coordinator in consultation with the Project Director. Subsequent members were selected and approved by the group itself through its Nominations Committee, which assessed under-represented stakeholder clusters, held independent consultation to identify candidates, and selected individuals. The Assurance Group met eight times through the life of the Project to review progress and advise on future direction. To ensure editorial freedom, IIED retained the right to publish the final report independently if in its judgement this was necessary.

The Sponsors Group, the Assurance Group, and the Work Group were governed by a set of charters that were agreed to by one and all who were directly involved (but not by some constituencies that were interested). A Project Coordinator worked on behalf of the WBCSD and facilitated communication and coordination among the three groups.

The Process at the Regional Level

One of MMSD's most important elements was the regional partnerships established in four of the world's principal mineral-producing and -consuming regions: MMSD AUSTRALIA, MMSD NORTH AMERICA, MMSD SOUTH AMERICA, and MMSD SOUTHERN AFRICA. In each case, the partner organization was asked to establish a broad-reaching process of consultation and research. MMSD's regional partners designed the regional research work, through a consultation process, to reflect the issues and the locally derived options for change suggested by regional stakeholders. As regional workshops, meetings, and other events took place, all documentation and meeting records were posted on the partners' websites. All publications – including draft and final regional reports – were made available for public review. The work in each case was overseen, guided, and reviewed by a regional advisory group or steering committee. The research issues, methods of consultation, and structure of the project were never exactly the same, reflecting the diversity of the regions. Yet there were often strikingly similar ways forward suggested as outcomes of the regional MMSD processes.

MMSD Australia

The Australian Minerals and Energy Environment Foundation (Ameef) managed the MMSD process in Australia. Ameef is an independent not-for-profit organization established in 1991 to promote sustainable development in the resources sector.

Priority areas for research were agreed to at a multistakeholder workshop in Melbourne in December 2000, video-linked to Brisbane and Perth. MMSD AUSTRALIA commissioned seven studies, including a baseline assessment of the Australian minerals sector and research into the management of industry impacts on biodiversity, the management of mineral wealth, and the operation of voluntary initiatives in support of sustainable development. The project also commissioned work on the development of new approaches to stakeholder engagement, case studies of formal consultation processes in Victoria, and research into mining company agreements with indigenous communities.

MMSD AUSTRALIA facilitated extensive multistakeholder engagement and dialogue. Research proposals and findings were presented to multistakeholder workshops at the initiation, mid-point, and conclusion of research. The draft report of the MMSD AUSTRALIA project was presented to a series of workshops in February 2002. In all, nine workshops brought together key representatives of industry, federal and state governments, NGOs, labour unions, universities, community, and indigenous representative groups. They provided a neutral forum in which stakeholders could express their views, explore common ground, and begin to address commonly recognized problems. This established a basis for longer-term dialogue, communication, and trust-building in the Australian sector.

MMSD meeting with a local village NGO, Kyrgyzstan, June 2001

MMSD North America

The North American regional process began in late 2000 with a scan of issues and interests. This led to the development of an initial Working Draft Action Plan that was vetted at workshops in Canada and the United States. As a result of these workshops, a five-task workplan for MMSD NORTH AMERICA was established that consisted of a profile of the North American mining and minerals industry, scenarios for the future, developing a guideline for assessing an operation's contribution to sustainability, an action plan for change, and a final report.

The general approach used by MMSD NORTH AMERICA was to convene work groups of approximately 25 individuals focused on specific tasks. To as great an extent as possible, participants were drawn from a range of interests, including companies (small, intermediate, large, and service), mining-affected communities, First Nations/Native Americans, NGOs, government, organized labour, and universities (teachers, researchers, and students). While participants were asked to share their knowledge and expertise, they were not asked to 'represent' any organization. Further, although a great effort was made to incorporate everyone's perspective and reach consensus on issues, neither participants nor their affiliated organizations (where they existed) were asked to endorse the results. Thus the end result is a reflection of a multiparty deliberation, though the final treatment of the various topics may not be fully supported by all participants. Rather, the output of MMSD NORTH AMERICA is seen as a contribution to a continuing and evolving discussion about how mining and minerals can best contribute to the broader societal shift to sustainable development.

MMSD South America

MMSD SOUTH AMERICA was led by the Centro de Investigación y Planificación del Medio Ambiente (CIPMA) in Santiago, Chile, and the Mining Policy Research Initiative (MPRI) in Montevideo, Uruguay. The South American process had two components: research (coordinated by CIPMA) and participation (coordinated by MPRI). Both components were carried out in close coordination to produce a final regional report that addressed a research agenda supported by the participatory process. The Partners relied on an Advisory Group drawn from different countries and constituencies for guidance and orientation.

The process was carried out in a decentralized manner with national teams conducting research and participatory activities – in Bolivia (Servicios Ambientales S.A. MEDMIN), Brazil (Centro de Tecnologia Mineral), Chile (Centro de Investigación y Planificación del Medio Ambiente), Ecuador (Fundación Ambiente y Sociedad/Fundación Futuro Latinoamericano), and Peru (Grupo de Análisis para el Desarrollo). These national-level processes worked in close cooperation with one another and with the regional coordinators.

Stakeholder profiles were developed for each country, which was an important first step for the planning of the engagement process. A survey was designed, applied, and completed by 345 individuals from 15 Latin American countries. The results helped establish priorities on the main issues of concern for different groups in the various countries and refined the regional research and participatory agenda.

MMSD Indigenous Peoples Workshop, Quito, September 2001

Some 50 workshops, attended by more than 700 participants, were conducted at the national level. Three regional meetings of the Advisory Group, Regional Coordinators, National Coordinators, and interested observers were held to review findings and receive feedback and advice. Five national reports were produced, which were synthesized by the regional coordinators into the MMSD SOUTH AMERICA's regional report.

MMSD Southern Africa

The University of the Witwatersrand in Johannesburg, South Africa, and the Council for Scientific and Industrial Research in Stellenbosch, South Africa, were responsible for MMSD activities in Southern Africa. For the purposes of this process, Southern Africa was defined as consisting of countries within the Southern African Development Community (SADC), and consisted of Angola, Botswana, Democratic Republic of Congo, Lesotho, Malawi, Mozambique, Namibia, South Africa, Swaziland, Tanzania, Zambia, and Zimbabwe. A regional Steering Committee, with members from South Africa, Tanzania, Zambia, Zimbabwe, and the SADC Mining Coordinating Unit, was established early in the process to appoint and oversee the regional Working Group. The Steering Committee members also represented stakeholder groups in the region.

The first major outcome of the stakeholder engagement process was the identification of the issues in the region that stakeholders believed should be the topics of the research component of the process. This was initially done by questionnaire, followed by a multistakeholder meeting in November 2000. The areas identified for research were small-scale mining, HIV/AIDS, mining and society, the biophysical environment, and managing mineral wealth. Researchers and reviewers were chosen on the basis of sound knowledge of and wide experience in the region and to ensure good regional and demographic representation.

Focus group meetings were held in Botswana, Mozambique, Namibia, South Africa, Tanzania, and Zimbabwe. Stakeholders had the opportunity to gain clarity about the MMSD process and to articulate the priority issues in their countries. In addition to national focus groups, meetings were also held with specific stakeholder groups. The first results of the process were presented to about 100 participants, drawn from eight SADC countries, at a multistakeholder workshop in September 2001. The process has resulted in an inclusive regional MMSD report.

Other Regions

From the outset it was difficult to establish a broad-based process in Europe, for several reasons. First, the metals industry perceived the project to be about mining and thus irrelevant to their major concerns around metals in use and market access. Most European environmental NGOs either had little interest in mining or were more concerned about mining issues overseas. The key governmental institutions concerned with trade, environment, and development were already engaged in initiatives with the relevant major trade and commodity associations. Despite many efforts, it was impossible to establish any process comparable with other regions.

In other areas of the world, MMSD worked at the national rather than the regional level because of difficulties either establishing broad regional entities within the project time frame and resources or defining a cohesive regional unit for the purposes of the project. In Indonesia, the Philippines, and Papua New Guinea, MMSD worked with local organizations or individuals to produce baseline studies on the diversity of local issues, but did not attempt to go into the depth of consultation achieved through other regional partnerships.

Similar arrangements were made in the former Soviet Union through baseline studies done in Russia, Kyrgyzstan, and the Republic of Khakassia. In the last two cases, the work was reviewed by a multistakeholder committee. A baseline study was also commissioned for India. Some areas of the world were beyond the scope and resources of the project, notably China and Japan. This is not an indication of the importance of these countries in terms of their mining and processing activity, but a reflection on the MMSD Project's capacity and resources.

Report Scope and Structure

Some final points on the scope of the MMSD report and lessons learnt from the process (See Box 2).

Box 2. Multistakeholder Processes: Some Observations from the MMSD Project

- A broad-based, inclusive process of initiation is fundamental to the success of the effort.
- The time frame must take into account the differing capacities of participants as well as the need for a timely outcome.
- No one group should own access to the process or its follow-up.
- A group that is trusted for its diversity and its insights must be given primary responsibility for steering the process on behalf of all others.
- No process should override the importance of local endowments (cultural, environmental, and economic); thus decentralization should be the guiding rule.
- The initial scope must be agreed to by all, and be subject to revision as the dialogue unfolds.
- The process cannot succeed if any one stakeholder attempts prematurely to claim the high ground in public or works in private to circumvent due process.
- The rules of evidence are crucial – everyone needs to work to the same standards of rigour, honesty, and transparency.
- Any financial resources applied should not affect the relationship; at the same time, appropriate responsibilities for follow-up have to be recognized.

The project excluded all considerations around the consumption part of the coal chain, as it did not wish to enter into the energy and climate debates associated with this commodity since they are well covered elsewhere. Similarly, the downstream part of the uranium cycle was excluded because the issues of weapons proliferation, security, and waste disposal are so complex and controversial that adequate attention to them all was beyond the available resources of time, personnel, and funding. The project focused heavily on the minerals that are traded in global markets, such as metals, and less on those traded primarily in local markets, such as aggregates, sand, and gravel. And it did not deal with cement (the topic of a separate WBCSD-sponsored exercise).[8]

Much of this report is derivative. The project sought to consolidate the existing knowledge base from key actors such as the United Nations, the industry's trade associations, MERN, and the many specialist university departments around the world. It commissioned reviews, synthesis, and reports of existing knowledge. But it also held events to engage those who might be

MMSD Assurance Group visit to El Teniente smelter, Chile, January 2001

interested in critiquing its results as they developed.

Thus the MMSD Project was a considerable challenge from many points of view, particularly given the very tight timeline. The sponsors were asked to invest in a process they could not control (as a condition of their contract). For IIED, a Work Group had to be recruited, the regional processes had to be organized, and the funding had to be diversified – and then the analysis and consultation with all the stakeholders done across a subject area capable of supporting a thousand PhDs. Readers need to bear these limitations in mind. This report is principally a consolidation and synthesis of what has been done and is known by others – and a beginning for those who now want to move forward.

The Work Group retained both editorial and project management independence throughout the project. The industry players honoured their original 'hands off' pledge in full. None of the sponsors interfered in the selection of the Work Group or the Assurance Group but were consulted on the same basis as other interested parties. In addition to the companies, many other constituents, such as civil society groups, labour unions, academics, politicians, and civil servants, took part in the MMSD process and meetings. The engagement was tremendous. Of course, as indicated, the involvement of these individuals and groups in no way constitutes their endorsement of the final report, for which MMSD takes full responsibility.

To some extent this effort has brought the issues just past the starting line. This project was the first attempt, and an ambitious one, to tackle the issues of both supply and demand of minerals throughout the world

by whatever means and affecting anyone. The players live in different worlds, work to different ethics, have different values, want different things. Many of these people, institutions, and cultures had rarely if ever exchanged ideas on these important issues before.

It does appear that at a high level, they share certain views: a realization that the status quo is good for very few of them; a desire to have a better, more functional sector that delivers better results for everyone; and a frustration that there seems to be such difficulty in getting good ideas advanced on all sides brought forward to action. This is a basis on which a way forward can be built.

Above all, MMSD hopes that it has succeeded in condensing a large mass of information and ideas into a few key questions of strategic importance – a long process to reduce hundreds of concerns to a manageable number of issues to be taken forward. These form the basis of the nine chapters in Part III of this report, after Parts I and II provide a sustainable development framework and a review of current trends and actors. Part IV suggests responses and recommendations by reviewing regional perspectives and presenting an overall Agenda for Change.

Endnotes

[1] The original nine companies are now eight.

[2] IIED (1996).

[3] World Commission on Dams (2000).

[4] Hemmati (2002).

[5] IIED (1999).

[6] The minutes of this meeting are on the CD-ROM accompanying this report.

[7] The MMSD 'Principles of Engagement' developed early in the project can be found in Appendix 1.

[8] WBCSD (2002).

PART I

A FRAMEWORK FOR CHANGE

CHAPTER 1

THE MINERALS SECTOR AND SUSTAINABLE DEVELOPMENT

One of the greatest challenges facing the world today is integrating economic activity with environmental integrity and social concerns. The goal of that integration can be seen as 'sustainable development'.

This chapter lays out a proposed sustainable development framework for the minerals sector and considers how it applies to nine areas of concern faced by all actors in the sector – government, industry, labour, and civil society.[1] These concerns are the main focus of Part III of *Breaking New Ground*. The process for moving forward within this framework is discussed in detail in the Agenda for Change in Part IV.

Sustainable Development: Why Now?

The sustainable development concept has grown out of concern about several trends. One is the growing imbalance in development between different countries, often simplified into the categories North and South. Poverty reduction is an enormous global challenge. Almost half of the world's population – 2.8 billion people – subsists on less than US$2 per day. Although aggregate development trends have been positive, since 1965 average annual economic growth has been almost twice as fast in low-income countries as in high-income ones – 5.9% a year compared with 3.0%. Average gains in human development in low- and middle-income countries have been higher than gains in incomes: for example, life expectancy increased by 59% between 1950 and 1998 and illiteracy was reduced from 39% in 1970 to 25% in 1998. Yet performance across regions has varied widely: there has been remarkable progress in Asia but no discernible reduction in poverty in Latin America and Africa. In the last decade, poverty rates increased dramatically in the transition economies of Eastern Europe and the former Soviet Union. In parallel, inequality between and within countries has also risen – the ratio of the average income of the richest to the poorest country in the world increased from 9 to 1 at the end of the nineteenth century to about 30 to 1 in 1960 to more than 60 to 1 today.[2]

Another concern is the high and increasing consumption of scarce resources and resulting pollution, particularly in the most industrialized countries. This concern is compounded by population growth. It has also become clear that economic development that disregards environmental and social

impacts can bring unintended and undesirable consequences, as evidenced by the threat of climate change and loss of ecosystem integrity and biological diversity. Cultures, too, have changed irreversibly – in some cases, nearly disappearing. Indeed, there are countless examples from different sectors and circumstances of the immediate or long-term environmental and social costs of development that have to be weighed alongside the gains. Increased understanding of these concerns has been accompanied by a growing realization that existing institutions are not able to manage these problems effectively unless their roles and responsibilities are clearly defined, appropriate integrated policy frameworks are in place, and there is sufficient capacity to implement change.

In the last decade, these concerns have been brought to a head by a range of trends loosely grouped under the term 'globalization'. The processes of economic globalization – trade and investment liberalization and the spread of market-oriented development approaches – have created a deeper and broader connection among the world's nations than ever before. Many have benefited from the process, but to many observers it is the shareholders of large multinational companies of the world who are the principal winners.

The ability of large companies, which operate in many countries and are sometimes hard for individual governments to manage, to influence people's lives is also feared by many. People often feel disenfranchised because economic activity is increasingly subject to international rather than local forces. The world trading system is seen to be failing to deal with all aspects of market access: industrial countries have in many cases failed to remove perverse subsidies that protect their own interests, and many environmental standards are seen as protectionist. Meanwhile, the capacity of public institutions has, it seems, failed to keep up with the pace of change. The resulting mismatch has contributed to a deep and widespread mistrust of the institutions of governance, both public and private. These are the perceptions of the situation today – right or wrong – and they do matter.

At the same time, international competition, another aspect of globalization, is changing the face of enterprise. Improvements in technology and the efficiency of production challenge those who do not keep pace. These have also reduced the requirement for labour per unit of output in many activities. At a global level, reductions in employment in some sectors, such as manufacturing and other industrial activities, have been offset by increases in the demand for labour in others, such as the service and information sectors. But in some industries and at the local level, reductions in employment cause significant hardship, particularly in poor countries without social safety nets.

Despite these real concerns, globalization also provides an unprecedented opportunity for change for the better. Although not evenly spread across the globe, it has brought access to new technologies that give people the potential to learn, communicate, and participate in decision-making as never before. The pace of technological and scientific innovation has brought with it new uncertainties and half-understood risks, but also hope for a better world. To capitalize on the opportunities brought by globalization, the wealth and power of the private sector need to be harnessed and steered in a direction that respects social needs and environmental limits and thus contributes to sustainable development.

The minerals sector is part of this web of issues. Many countries and communities depend on minerals production as a source of income and a means of development. And with growing trade liberalization and privatization, much of the investment in minerals exploration and production has turned to developing and transition countries. Mining is important in 51 developing countries – accounting for 15-50% of exports in 30 countries and 5-15% of exports in a further 18 countries, and being important domestically in 3 other countries. About 3.5 billion people live in these countries, with about 1.5 billion living on less than US$2 per day.[3]

Minerals development can create many opportunities, including jobs, a transfer of skills and technology, and the development of local infrastructure and services. However, there is sometimes a lack of capacity, knowledge, and incentives to turn investment into development. The industry has generated wealth in direct and indirect ways but, it is alleged, there is a mismatch of opportunities and problems – the wealth often being enjoyed far from the communities and environments that feel the adverse impacts. The operational life of a mine is finite. Unless there is effective planning, the economic and social benefits brought by minerals development may last only as long as the mine, while the environmental damage may

remain indefinitely. The challenge of ensuring that local communities benefit from minerals production becomes more difficult with increasing mechanization and declining employment levels.

There is also concern about disparities in the use of mineral products between rich and poor and, mainly in the North, about ever-increasing demand. These concerns are heightened by the non-renewable nature of mineral resources and fears of eventual depletion. Moreover, the process of extraction may incur social and environmental costs that are considered by some to be unacceptable. The energy used to mine and process minerals is a growing concern in a world preoccupied by climate change.

The mining industry, at least at the level of multinationals, is becoming increasingly concentrated in fewer hands, exacerbating the perceived or real imbalance of decision-making power between them and other stakeholders.

Perhaps the greatest challenge of all is the fact that past practices and social and environmental legacies, combined with continuing examples of poor performance and inadequate accountability, have undermined trust among companies, governments, and some in civil society. The public's perception of what industry is doing is often very different from what company managers think they are doing. As far as some observers outside the industry are concerned, companies have been resisting or at best offering only token improvements: they are seen as failing to meet rising standards of accountability, transparency, and participation.

People in the industry often feel differently. They dispute many of the assertions made about them. They wonder how society can want the products of their industry so much and yet hold some companies in such low esteem. They ask how – in a world of internationally traded mined commodities and one where prices do not reflect all costs – they are going to meet the implicit costs of sustainable development. They also wonder how to achieve a framework of enforced law to control 'free riders' and internalize such costs over time.

Despite these differing perspectives, however, there is a high degree of consensus on some of the fundamental issues. There is recognition of the magnitude of the challenges and opportunities that exist and of the unacceptable or less-than-desirable distribution of them. There is also a strong desire to improve the quality of life, particularly for the poor. This consensus points to possible ways forward, and sustainable development provides a useful framework for advancing this change.

What Is Sustainable Development?

Sustainable development is one of a range of ideas about how humans should best interact with each other and the biosphere. (See Box 1–1 for a description of the evolution of this concept.) It involves integrating and meeting economic, social, and environmental goals. The more that unsustainable activities pose unacceptable risks to communities, nations, and humanity as a whole, the stronger the argument for change. Sustainable development has become the logical framework for change and for identifying best practice. As British environmentalist Jonathon Porritt puts it:

> Sustainable development is the only intellectually coherent, sufficiently inclusive, potentially mind-changing concept that gets even half-way close to capturing the true nature and urgency of the challenge that now confronts the world. There really is no alternative.[4]

The concept has gained widespread currency since becoming the cornerstone of the United Nations Conference on Environment and Development (the Rio Earth Summit) in 1992. It is integral to *Agenda 21* (the blueprint for change adopted in Rio), and to many other international declarations of intent. It will be central to the World Summit on Sustainable Development in Johannesburg in August 2002.

Institutions at different levels have taken on elements of the sustainable development challenge. Governments have increasingly integrated the concept into national planning, and companies are beginning to integrate it into corporate strategies and practice. UN Secretary-General Kofi Annan speaks often of the need for sustainable development to end poverty and environmental degradation. The preamble to the Marrakesh Agreement establishing the World Trade Organization refers to the importance of working towards sustainable development.[5] In Europe, the Treaty of Rome, which established the European Community, was effectively amended in 1992 by the

---

Box 1–1. Sustainable Development Roots and Prospects

Particularly over the last century, national governments have been taken to be the prime movers in ensuring domestic prosperity. After World War II, the idea of governments' responsibility for 'development' started to take root internationally, including the notion that richer countries had followed a path to development that poorer countries could also tread, with the help of foreign aid. The motives behind post-war foreign aid were complex. Thinking about development assistance was dominated by both the reconstruction experience in Europe and cold war politics. Aid donors had often conflicting objectives of promoting long-term growth in developing countries and furthering their own short-term interests by helping political allies.

Since the end of World War II, many governments of developing countries saw their lack of physical and human capital as the main obstacle to progress, though even then they worried that the international trading and financial systems were biased against them. The solution was assumed to be government action financed by development assistance. A great deal of aid money went to infrastructure projects and technology, with a corresponding focus on higher education and training. There were some positive results in some countries, but there were also unmitigated failures.

In most countries the record was mixed: projects with poor economic returns as a result of poor planning or management or because funds leaked away through corruption or tied aid, and apparently successful projects that triggered problems such as social displacement, marginalization, and environmental damage. Developing-country debts racked up. The distorted pattern of development heightened inequality in many countries. An economic elite reaped the rewards while the burden of the social and environmental damage was borne largely by the poor and underprivileged. Even in the best cases, uneven development created tensions and sharpened existing cultural, ethnic, or racial divides.

The reaction to these disappointments took many forms. Some activists concentrated on supporting local communities undermined or by-passed by the formal development processes. Other groups argued that development was inherently destructive, and either opposed it completely or fought against mega-projects that threatened pristine areas. And some people worked to improve the theory and practice of development.

The 1972 Stockholm Conference and Its Aftermath
Alongside this development debate was the environmental story.
It had begun in the West with a concern over pollution. By the
early 1970s the environmental costs of development were
recognized. Among the first widely read books on this was *Only
One Earth*, by Barbara Ward and Rene Dubos, which explained
for a popular audience the concerns that had led to the 1972 UN
Conference on the Human Environment in Stockholm.[a] The book
considered, for example, what would be needed 'to maintain the
earth as a place suitable for human life not only now but for
future generations.' Also in 1972 the Club of Rome, a group of
scientists that had been established in 1968, published its first
major report – *Limits to Growth*. Although this overstated the
speed with which the world was exhausting many natural
resources, particularly minerals, it was an important precursor
of modern debates.

Following Stockholm, environmental concerns moved up the
political agenda in industrial countries. Many argued that
focusing solely on rapid economic growth would cause so much
environmental damage that it would restrict future growth.
Others pointed out the link between environmental damage and
poverty – poor people displaced to the most marginal land could
be driven to overexploit it, cutting trees for firewood, for
example, and exacerbating soil erosion. The natural environment
could suffer from both overdevelopment and underdevelopment.

These debates on environmental degradation continued through
the 1970s. One significant reflection was a joint effort by the UN
Environment Programme, the World Wildlife Fund, and the
International Union for Conservation of Nature and Natural
Resources. In 1980 they jointly presented the *World
Conservation Strategy*, arguing that local groups needed rights
over their own environment and benefits from development: 'For
development to be sustainable, it must take account of social and
ecological factors, as well as economic ones; of the living and
non-living resource base; and of the long-term as well as the
short-term advantages and disadvantages of alternative actions.'[b]

The notion that environment and development were not so much
in conflict as interdependent signalled a radical shift for the
early environment movement and established the importance of
'sustainable development'. Development advocates, including
those in the South, began to focus more on the spectacular
failures of some development projects, sometimes due to
unforeseen alterations of the environment.

Still, demand for economic growth remained stronger than calls
for environmental protection. Economic imperatives grew even
stronger during the early 1980s. Internationally, a new tone was set

by the Reagan and Thatcher administrations, with the World Bank
and the International Monetary Fund (IMF) prescribing similar
ideas to developing countries that needed finances: deregulation,
economic liberalization, and export-led economic growth.

An important counter to these ideas appeared in 1987, when the
World Commission on Environment and Development presented
its report. *Our Common Future* (known as the Brundtland Report)
returned sustainable development to the international agenda.
The Commission's members were not only conservationists but
also important figures in international development who insisted
that 'progress' should be judged by more than naked economic
growth as conventionally defined.

The 1992 Rio Conference
The Brundtland Report also fed into an emerging political and
economic commitment to environmental concerns, culminating
in the 1992 UN Conference on Environment and Development
held in Rio de Janeiro. The Rio conference accelerated agreements
on climate and biodiversity as well as setting out a new style of
development as laid out in Agenda 21. But it did little to convert
the principles of sustainable development into action and paid
too little attention to social development. Suggestions that
developing countries that adopted more environmentally friendly
agendas would get more aid came to nothing.

In retrospect, Rio was the last time the international community
believed that collective government decisions could save the
world. After 1992, the role of states became to establish
enabling frameworks for markets and civil society. Their task
was to juggle the goals of economic efficiency, social equity,
and environmental quality. The balance of resource flows to
developing countries also shifted. In the early 1990s, around half
the investment funds going to developing countries arrived as
official aid; by 2000, it was just 13%, with most of the rest from
private sources.

But Rio did establish the 'three pillars' of sustainable
development: economic, environmental, and social. The first
pillar uses the market to signal the relative scarcity of goods and
services and create a robust economy that can serve as the
foundation for social and environmental progress. Rio also
validated the environmental pillar, probably its greatest
achievement: the development process, if it was to yield lasting
results, had to safeguard life-support systems, use renewable
resources within their regenerative limits, and respect the
capacity of ecosystems to absorb and break down wastes. It
also recognized the value of the diversity of nature. While these
disciplines place some limits on economic activity, they also
allow more opportunities for human creativity, and will ultimately

give a better result. But the 'social' pillar of sustainable development was not developed much further in Rio, perhaps because its advocates were not as well organized as their economic and environmental counterparts. Exploring social issues went little beyond rhetorical statements about tackling poverty and lessening the impact of western consumption. Rio coincided with the beginning of a recession in western industrial countries, reining back the prospects for reducing poverty through economic growth. It also marked the beginning of a massive expansion of participatory democracy.[c] After the collapse of the Soviet Union, many developing and transition economies were radically changing their political and economic frameworks. The spread of democracy was opening up greater space for all kinds of activism, including environmental campaigns. Though uneven and far from universal, the process provided openings for stronger voices from communities, non-governmental groups, and individuals in Asia, Africa, and Latin America.

The Washington Consensus

Despite Rio's best efforts, in other respects the options for environmental protection were narrowing. Economic liberalization continued to sweep across the world. The IMF and the World Bank urged developing countries to reform their economies along the lines of the 'Washington Consensus' – a view of what a poor country should do to become more prosperous.[d] The core argument was that liberalizing markets and dismantling barriers to trade and investment would cause rapid economic growth. This radical medicine might worsen social dislocation, harm cultural identity, or strain environmental resources, but it was assumed that economic growth would create enough wealth to repair the damage.

The five years after Rio seemed to confirm the validity of this approach. After the early 1990s recession there was unprecedented growth, especially in richer countries. The more advanced developing countries that had opened their economies – such as Argentina, Brazil, China, Hungary, India, Malaysia, Mexico, the Philippines, and Thailand – became major recipients of foreign direct investment. As a result, their economies were growing by 5% per year. For the first time in history, world-wide poverty numbers actually dropped, even if the sheer number of people living on less than US$1 per day was still a daunting 1.2 billion. Meanwhile the 'non-globalizers' lagged further and further behind, with average annual growth rates of only 1.4%.

There had certainly been formal progress on the environmental front too. Many countries developed environmental policies, laws, and institutions. Most major multilateral development banks and bilateral development agencies incorporated environmental requirements into their policies. The social dimension of development continued to lag, however, even though *Human Development Reports* from the UN Development Programme had established the importance of looking beyond a narrow fixation on economic growth as a measure of human achievement – and that all too many trends were still in the wrong direction. Unfortunately, the opportunities for promoting human development through governments were limited by rising populations, shrinking domestic budgets, and declines in international aid. Development assistance peaked in 1992 and then went into decline – by 1998 reaching levels lower in real terms than since the 1960s.[e]

With this 'retreat' of the state from direct economic or production activity, it was feared that much of the economic power has been transferred to the 60,000 or more transnational corporations.

While these companies had greater opportunities to grow, they did not appear to assume more responsibility. In reaction, a rainbow alliance of interest groups sprang up concerned with social justice, the environment, human rights, and poverty eradication.

From Rio onwards there has been a distinct change in atmosphere and a shift from confrontation to cooperation in the intergovernmental world. UN agencies started to encourage partnerships with business. Some corporations have become more proactive and now work more closely with their critics. Initiatives include codes of conduct for self-regulation and 'green' business networks (the largest of which is the World Business Council for Sustainable Development).[f]

But a groundswell of popular opinion now asserts that neither governments nor corporations can be trusted to promote sustainable development. Such distrust is also directed at international organizations, which surfaced most visibly as the protests against globalization at the 1999 World Trade Organization meeting in Seattle.

Returning to Sustainable Development

Despite this gloomy prognosis, there is better news. Parallel to the protests has come a significant wave of policy experimentation. This can be seen as a 'second coming' of sustainable development – more subtle and potentially more powerful. It relies on practical ways to harness the power of capital and markets. Examples are the Fair Trade movement, the rise of eco-labelling and green certification, and the growth in 'ethical' investment funds. Many corporations have also tried to become more responsible, forming partnerships with civil society organizations.

Among the most serious obstacles to these changes is the lack of good government. Many economists argue that trade liberalization will only lead to solid economic growth if the right institutions of governance are in place, including an independent judiciary, well-functioning banks, and a non-corrupt bureaucracy.[g]

The search is on for a new direction.[h] Some see this to be human development administered by the state, while others put their faith more in 'rights-based' development that empowers individuals and groups to demand not just political but also economic and social rights and to assume responsibilities to match them.

What confronts the World Summit on Sustainable Development, to be held in Johannesburg in August–September 2002, is the very question of whether 'sustainable development' can solve the problems posed by globalization. Who should be involved in global discussions and decision-making? What is the future role of the UN and how can it operate most effectively? What are the barriers to sustainable development at local and national levels, and how can global attention help to deal with them? The summit is also a chance to move beyond vague commitments to sustainable development and demonstrate that its principles can be at the heart of international collaboration.

[a] Ward and Dubos (1972).

[b] UNEP/WWF/IUCNNR (1980).

[c] Fisher (1993).

[d] The Washington Consensus was the name that economist John Williamson gave in 1989 to a list of ten policy recommendations for countries willing to reform their economies. His prescriptions were fiscal discipline, redirect public expenditure, tax reform, financial liberalization, a single and competitive exchange rate, trade liberalization, eliminate barriers to foreign direct investment, privatize state-owned enterprises, deregulate market entry and competition, and secure property rights. See Williamson (1990).

[e] German and Rande (1998).

[f] UNRISD (2000) p.76.

[g] Amartya Sen sets out the fundamental conditions for development investments to yield the desired results. See Sen (1999). David Dollar and Lant Pritchett have come to similar conclusions for development aid. See Dollar and Pritchett (1998).

See UNDP (1997).

Maastricht Treaty, which included specific references to sustainable development. In the minerals sector, the International Council on Mining & Metals has recently adopted a Sustainable Development Charter.[6]

The overall framework of what sustainable development means and how to put it into practice still has some murky areas but is becoming increasingly coherent. The most widely accepted definition of sustainable development is the one used in 1987 by the World Commission on Environment and Development (known as the Brundtland Commission):

> Sustainable development is development that meets the needs of the present without compromising the ability of future generations to meet their own needs.[7]

This definition has received broad support, not least because it is a deceptively simple formulation. But it has multiple layers of meaning and some profound implications. It allows flexibility within defined boundaries, and can be applied to the development of many activities. There is no single goal or path for getting there; sustainable development presents more a framework for change than a list of prescriptions to achieve it. In this sense, it is as hard to define as other ideas that guide society – such as democracy, or justice, or freedom of speech.

The original Brundtland definition can be broken down into four conditions for sustainable development:[8]
- material and other needs for a better quality of life have to be fulfilled for people of this generation
- as equitably as possible
- while respecting ecosystem limits and
- building the basis on which future generations can meet their own needs.

A core principle of sustainable development is to improve human well-being and to sustain those improvements over time. The goal is for children to have as good a life as their parents did, or better. This requires passing the means of survival on to future generations unimpaired and building, or at least not diminishing, the total stock of capital. It also requires the integration of social, economic, environmental, and governance goals in decision-making.

Sustainable development has also brought to the fore the notion of equity in access to opportunities and in the distribution of costs and benefits. It focuses attention on righting the enormous imbalances in political and economic power – between rich and poor people; among corporations, states, and communities; between rich and poor countries.

The idea of 'capital' lies at the heart of sustainable development. This goes well beyond the common idea of financial capital and has five main forms:
- *natural capital*, which provides a continuing income of ecosystem benefits, such as biological diversity, mineral resources, and clean air and water;

- *manufactured capital*, such as machinery, buildings, and infrastructure;
- *human capital*, in the form of knowledge, skills, health, and cultural endowment;
- *social capital*, the institutions and structures that allow individuals and groups to develop collaboratively; and
- *financial capital*, the value of which is simply representative of the other forms of capital.

Some theorists of sustainable development see all these forms of capital as completely substitutable – it does not matter what form the stock of capital takes so long as the total, in some agreed unit of account, does not decline. This is the 'soft' view of sustainable development. While this view is consistent with all views of sustainable development in demanding that equivalent or increased amounts of capital are passed to future generations, it allows the form of this capital to change. This opens the door to passing on to the next generation less of one kind of capital so long as there is more of another to balance it. To a proponent of 'soft' sustainable development, natural resources do not occupy a privileged position, and the environment is merely one form of capital among others.

Others, however, argue that the different types of capital are not substitutable, since the loss of some forms of 'critical' natural capital – such as the ozone layer or biological diversity – could threaten the very survival of the human race. Moreover, while most manufactured and human capital can be replaced (with a few exceptions like cultural diversity), the destruction of natural capital is often irreversible within generational time frames. This approach narrows the range of options by forbidding certain trade-offs. It is the 'hard' view of sustainable development.

This discussion of 'soft' versus 'hard' sustainable development is not just a theoretical concern. It goes right to the heart, for example, of why some people think there should be no mining in protected areas. Some people believe that certain areas of the planet should be beyond reach for any human activity that will disturb them, including mining, because they contain irreplaceable critical natural or human capital.

There is an emerging consensus that there are in fact some 'non-negotiable' or non-tradable types of capital. While many agree they exist, the difficulty comes in

agreeing what they are. A fundamental problem is that denying the possibility of substitution may imply that certain forms of capital have an 'absolute' value, greater than any other objective or consideration. Are human rights any more negotiable than biological diversity? Where should the line be drawn? It is often difficult to reconcile this 'hard' concept of sustainable development with a people-centred approach.[9]

The on-going theoretical debates about sustainable development should not obscure its usefulness as a decision-making tool. Perhaps one way of understanding how to use the idea of 'capital' is to divide decisions into three groups:

- *'Win–win–win' decisions* – Some decisions advance all the goals identified by sustainable development simultaneously: they improve material well-being for this generation, spread that well-being more equitably, enhance the environment, strengthen our ability to manage problems, and pass on enhanced stocks of capital to future generations. These are obvious 'wins' and should be acted upon.
- *'Trade-off' decisions* – Other decisions will result in both gains and losses. If the gains are great enough and the losers can be compensated, the decision should be to proceed. This is the zone of trade-offs and requires an agreed mechanism for reaching a decision.
- *'No-go' decisions* – A final group of decisions may go past some widely accepted limit, such as destroying critical natural capital or transgressing fundamental human rights. If these conditions hold, the decision should be to not proceed.

Many of the complicated decisions that need to be made on the path towards sustainable development will involve compromises or trade-offs: between different objectives and dimensions, between different groups of stakeholders, between different generations. There may be conflicts between global and local priorities. Long-term needs will have to be balanced against short-term imperatives. The various constituencies, acting in concert, will have to evaluate the acceptability of, for example, sustaining minor environmental damage in exchange for major social and economic gain, or of sacrificing economic and social goals for a significant environmental benefit.

Different disciplines have used different language or concepts to describe the challenges spoken of earlier.

An economist has a quite different perspective than an anthropologist or a natural scientist. Recent thinking includes work using terms such as rights-based approaches to development, sustainable livelihoods, impact analysis and life-cycle thinking, and various resource efficiency concepts. None of these alone can provide all the answers, just as no one of the sciences can do so. Each is designed for particular purposes. Although views and priorities will always differ between stakeholder groups and regions, sustainable development provides a common vocabulary for discussion and agreement on some first principles. In applying these principles, the chance of maximizing win–win–wins and minimizing trade-offs among social, environmental, economic, and governance objectives is improved through the integration of otherwise conflicting goals.

The Importance of Governance

A sustainable development framework should be defined only in part in terms of social, environmental, and economic principles. It should also be defined by the decision-making processes it promotes: the mechanisms for reaching decisions and where necessary making the trade-offs it identifies in ways that are widely regarded as fair. New principles for governance are required – these can be seen as the fourth dimension of sustainable development. Where existing institutions are not capable of applying those principles and making the trade-offs in acceptable ways, there may even be need for some new institutions.

Actors should strive to have consensus on a long-term vision, which distinguishes between long-term and short-term priorities. Effective participation by all constituents in shaping the vision is crucial to ensure acceptability and legitimacy. The adoption of strategic approaches is required to identify means of achieving this vision. This will mean adopting approaches that are based on credible evidence, set priorities, and lay out the main tactics for achieving them. It will also require defining and redefining the roles and responsibilities of different actors and the overlapping boundaries of responsibilities.[10] This will have important institutional, capacity, and budget implications, making cooperation between different actors key.

Over time, many stakeholders will need to make big changes, and will naturally need to see some benefit

from doing so. If there is to be rapid progress towards sustainable development, a mix of strong, overlapping, and mutually reinforcing incentives is required. A meaningful system of independent evaluation, backed up by the ability to encourage good behaviour and discourage inadequate performance, is needed. Many, although not all, of these incentives will be market-based. Appropriate education, regulation, and policy will also be key.

Different challenges have to be addressed at different levels. Fundamental questions should be asked about the appropriate level (local to international) and value systems for decisions. Some challenges to sustainable development should be addressed at the global level (climate change), and others should be addressed at the national (regulatory changes) or local level (resource use). In each case, the principle of subsidiarity should be adhered to, which recognizes that decisions should be taken as close as possible to and with the people and communities most directly affected.

There are also financial costs associated with moving towards sustainable development. In some cases, these costs may outweigh the benefits of improvements. Though this report talks of minimizing impacts, in economic terms the aim is to reduce the impacts to the point where the additional costs of reducing these impacts would outweigh the additional benefits. Moreover, the costs of reaching the goals of sustainable development have to be apportioned in a way that ensures that economies remain sufficiently viable to meet the needs of humankind for development and for various products and services – which in turn implies that the prices paid for products must reflect the true costs of providing them. Some change will be achieved by win–win efficiency gains (such as a reduction in energy use), but much more will involve internalizing costs that have been outside the market system thus far.

Last but not least, sustainable development also requires democratic processes to ensure that people can participate in the decisions that affect their lives, as well as legal and political structures to guarantee their civil and political rights. Transparent and democratic governance confers legitimacy on development and holds organizations and corporations to account for their actions.

A Sustainable Development Framework for the Minerals Sector

Applying the concept of sustainable development to the minerals sector does not mean making one mine after another 'sustainable' – whatever that means. The challenge of the sustainable development framework is to see that the minerals sector as a whole contributes to human welfare and well-being today without reducing the potential for future generations to do the same. Thus the approach has to be both comprehensive – taking into account the whole minerals system – and forward-looking, setting out long-term as well as short-term objectives. Moving from the concept of sustainable development to action requires:

- a robust framework based on an agreed set of broad principles;
- an understanding of the key challenges and constraints facing the sector at different levels and in different regions and the actions needed to meet or overcome them, along with the respective roles and responsibilities of actors in the sector;
- a process for responding to these challenges that respects the rights and interests of all those involved, is able to set priorities, and ensures that action is taken at the appropriate level;
- an integrated set of institutions and policy instruments to ensure minimum standards of compliance as well as responsible voluntary actions; and
- verifiable measures to evaluate progress and foster consistent improvement.

If the minerals sector is to contribute positively to sustainable development, it needs to demonstrate continuous improvement of its social, economic, and environmental contribution, with new and evolving governance systems. The sector needs a framework within which it should judge and pursue any development.

Table 1–1 provides a set of guiding principles for each of the four dimensions of sustainable development. These principles should be seen as high-level aspirations that could equally be applied to other parts of the economy. They should be interpreted in a way that recognizes diversity, the limits of existing levels of knowledge and capacity, and society's continuing need for minerals. Under the guiding framework of these principles, goals and priorities should be agreed at the appropriate level (from local to global), as should the strategic approaches for achieving them.

Table 1–1. Sustainable Development Principles

Economic Sphere
- Maximize human well-being.
- Ensure efficient use of all resources, natural and otherwise, by maximizing rents.
- Seek to identify and internalize environmental and social costs.
- Maintain and enhance the conditions for viable enterprise.

Social Sphere
- Ensure a fair distribution of the costs and benefits of development for all those alive today.
- Respect and reinforce the fundamental rights of human beings, including civil and political liberties, cultural autonomy, social and economic freedoms, and personal security.
- Seek to sustain improvements over time; ensure that depletion of natural resources will not deprive future generations through replacement with other forms of capital.

Environmental Sphere
- Promote responsible stewardship of natural resources and the environment, including remediation for past damage.
- Minimize waste and environmental damage along the whole of the supply chain.
- Exercise prudence where impacts are unknown or uncertain.
- Operate within ecological limits and protect critical natural capital.

Governance Sphere
- Support representative democracy, including participatory decision-making.
- Encourage free enterprise within a system of clear and fair rules and incentives.
- Avoid excessive concentration of power through appropriate checks and balances.
- Ensure transparency through providing all stakeholders with access to relevant and accurate information.
- Ensure accountability for decisions and actions, which are based on comprehensive and reliable analysis.
- Encourage cooperation in order to build trust and shared goals and values.
- Ensure that decisions are made at the appropriate level, adhering to the principle of subsidiarity where possible.

Although laid out here in different spheres for ease of interpretation, these principles should be applied in an integrated manner in decision-making. Thus, for example, the role of mineral wealth in maximizing human well-being should be encouraged, but it must be undertaken in a way that protects the environment and other social and cultural values. Similarly, the decision of whether or not to mine in a certain area should be undertaken through a democratic decision-making process and be based on an integrated assessment of ecological, environmental, economic, and social impacts.

Key Areas of Action and Challenges

Some progress has already been made by various actors in the minerals sector towards the goals of sustainable development, but a great deal remains to be done. Through a consultative process (see Introduction), the MMSD Project focused stakeholders' concerns into nine key challenges facing the sector:
- the viability of the industry;
- control, use, and management of land;
- national economic and social development;
- community development;
- environmental management;
- the use of minerals;
- information flow;
- artisanal and small-scale mining; and
- roles and responsibilities.

These nine challenges are put forward to reflect the most pressing issues facing the industry, which MMSD identified in its consultations with different stakeholders. They are not definitions of what sustainable development means in the minerals sector. This report represents an attempt to apply the overarching sustainable development principles outlined in Table 1–1 to these challenges in order to demonstrate how the sector can best contribute to sustainable development.

This section examines how the goals and principles of sustainable development apply in each challenge area. The points made here have emerged from the MMSD process but should not be taken as a consensus list. It is intended as a draft 'wish list' rather than as something that can be achieved immediately.

Viability of the Minerals Industry
The minerals industry has a key role to play in assisting the sector to make a substantial positive contribution to sustainable development. Important changes will take place, and the ultimate shape of the industry cannot be known with any certainty. But two challenges are clear:

- The global market for minerals must develop in a way that enables rather than constrains the transition to sustainable development, notably in terms of internalizing costs over time, while maintaining viable enterprises and rewarding good practice. Creating incentives for industry through market-based solutions must go hand in hand with enforcing standards and guidelines.
- The fundamentals of sustainable development must become embedded in the culture of mining companies. If this can be done successfully, it will have significant and cumulative effects on a whole range of aspects of company life – from the health and safety of workers and the communities they operate in to long-term skills training.

The Control, Use, and Management of Land
The development of minerals unavoidably competes with other land uses. Uncertainty over the ability to obtain access to land for mineral exploration and development imposes serious constraints on industry. At the same time, many other actors – including local communities and indigenous peoples – have vital interests in how land is used and who makes decisions regarding land use.

- Land use decisions should be arrived at through a process that respects the principle of prior informed consent arrived at through democratic decision-making processes that account for the rights and interests of communities and other stakeholders, while still allowing for the negotiated use of renewable and non-renewable resources. This should equally apply to negotiations for access to land used by people whose rights to that land are not formally recognized by the state or who do not have the capacity to defend those rights.
- The decision of whether or not to explore and mine in a certain area must be based on an integrated assessment of ecological, environmental, economic, and social impacts and thus be governed by a land use strategy that incorporates the principles of sustainable development.
- Decision-making processes must be open to the decision not to mine in circumstances where cultural, environmental, or other factors override access to minerals or where mining would impose unacceptable loss in the view of those it is being imposed on.
- There must be compensation for any harm that occurs as a result of land use decisions.

National Economic and Social Development

The potential for mining to bring economic and social development, particularly to developing countries, should be harnessed. Mining should bring benefits that can be sustained at the national level even after mining ceases. Potential benefits are by no means automatic, however. Any country that wishes to translate mineral wealth in the ground into human development for its people faces stiff challenges.

- Creating and sustaining mineral wealth can play an important role in maximizing human well-being, but it must be undertaken in a way that protects environmental quality and other social and cultural values while recognizing the sovereign rights of governments to act in the best interest of the nation.
- Economic efficiency of mineral production should be achieved such that the marginal benefits and costs to society are equalized.
- A portion of the rents derived from minerals and other non-renewable resources needs to be set aside and re-invested, in order to ensure a sustainable income when the resource is used up. This may include investing in financial assets or physical and human resources.
- Revenues should be shared equitably between the public and private sectors and among central, regional, and local levels. Decisions on how the surpluses are distributed should be arrived at through democratic decision-making processes.
- Revenue management – which pertains to how these rents are used by the public sector to support development at national and, increasingly, at regional and local levels – will require a sound macro-economic framework of pro-poor policies and transparent public expenditure management, as well as adequate capacity on the part of government to manage project-generated revenues.

Community Development

Best use should also be made of the potential for mining to contribute to sustainable development at the local level. The challenge at the community level, as elsewhere, is to maximize the benefits and to avoid or mitigate any negative impacts of mining.

- Priorities and ultimately choices regarding trade-offs relating to different social, environmental, and economic goals need to be determined through participatory processes, involving all relevant actors,

including members of the affected community, and in accord with the local context. This requires appropriate processes for participation and dialogue, as well as adequate capacity and access to information for all involved. Potentially disadvantaged groups, such as women, indigenous peoples, and minorities, should be included.

- The relationship between the mining company and other actors needs to be one of collaboration, trust, and respect.
- The goal should be that no one be made worse off, although it is inevitable that there will be losers in both the absolute and the relative sense.
- Priority should be given to ensuring that the rights of marginalized individuals and groups in communities are protected and that they receive a fair share of the benefits.
- The economic benefits brought by mining should be shared equitably within communities.
- To ensure that benefits are sustained, a proportion of the rents should be invested in other forms of capital, such as trust funds, skills training, or social infrastructure.
- Mining should not leave unacceptable environmental or other negative legacies.
- Where it does not already exist, sufficient capacity should be developed at the local level to manage revenues for legitimate development needs. Public–private partnerships should be encouraged.

Environmental Management

There is a considerable degree of environmental impact associated with most exploration, mining, and mineral processing, and negative impacts can be spread over large areas. Though ideally the minerals sector should not operate at the expense of the environment, in practice there is a balance to be struck if the decision to proceed with an operation is made. The challenge becomes how to optimize the trade-off between environmental damage and the potential development benefits to local and national economies.

- The negative effects of minerals and metal products on the environment and human health should be minimized through all phases of the minerals life cycle.
- Long-term damage should be avoided. No permit should be sought on the basis of a trade-off today against long-term and irreparable legacies that may harm future generations. Prudence should be exercised where the environmental impacts or

damage are not known.

- Best-practice appropriate technologies and modern management techniques should be adopted, and research and technological innovation accelerated, to produce the smallest possible environmental footprint while not entailing excessive cost. This can be achieved through improved resource and energy efficiency as well as cleaner technologies.
- Minerals and metals themselves can play a crucial role in minimizing negative environmental impacts, as they are important components of pollution prevention and cleaner production technologies.
- Consistent with the need to internalize costs, polluters should pay for clean-up, remediation, and prevention. Where no owner can be located, mechanisms to set priorities and deal with the legacy of liabilities must be developed.
- Mine closure and, more important, post-closure should be planned for. This should ensure that the land and structures can be restored for alternative uses after the mine closes.
- By paying much closer attention to the potential to restore and replenish natural ecosystems, the minerals sector can play a part in maintaining the diversity of plant and animal species on which the survival of the planet depends.

An Integrated Approach to Minerals Use

The use of minerals is essential for modern living – for meeting basic requirements and the aspirations for improved welfare for current and future generations. Yet current patterns of use face a growing number of challenges, ranging from concerns about efficiency and waste minimization to the risks associated with the use of certain minerals. Added to this is the call for more equitable shares in mineral use world-wide.

- The basic needs of individuals and communities for mineral products should be met. Clearly, this requires sufficient income and the availability of minerals.
- Effort should be made to attain a more equitable distribution of use between industrial and developing countries.
- While recognizing the essential need for minerals, efficient use should be encouraged to reduce waste, depletion, and pollution. Re-manufacture, re-use, and recycling should be encouraged. The social and economic impacts associated with these changes must be assessed and responded to.

- Life-cycle thinking should be used as a decision-making tool to assess production processes, mineral uses, and the impacts and alternative materials choice. Where the risks associated with certain end-uses are unknown, prudence should be exercised.
- Responsible stewardship of minerals should be promoted throughout the life cycle.
- Minerals and metals consumers, many of whom are large equipment manufacturers and contractors, must increasingly be prepared to give preference and potentially pay more to minerals producers who behave in a responsible manner. Ultimately, end-use consumers must be prepared to pay the full internalized costs of metals and minerals production.
- Best use of mineral products and metals should be made in facilitating development through their input to physical infrastructure and other applications.
- In its use of non-renewable resources, the present generation needs to consider the needs of future societies.

The Flow of Information

Sustainable development requires increased openness and greater transparency in information production and dissemination throughout the minerals life cycle. The processes by which information is generated and communicated play a key role in building or undermining trust and in improving all players' ability to negotiate effectively.

- Authoritative, independent sources are critical to ensure that information is trusted and to respect the right of stakeholders to have access to accurate and relevant data.

Metal products may be re-used many times over

- Access to information is linked to the ability of individuals to secure and defend fundamental rights to resources. Information must be collected and distributed in an equitable manner to ensure this.
- Systems of accountability and verification are essential to monitor the performance of companies, governments, and civil society.
- Knowledge needs to be shared and gaps progressively filled.

Artisanal and Small-scale Mining

Artisanal and small-scale mining (ASM) activities can play a crucial role in providing sources of income in poor areas. The sector is better known, however, for its high environmental costs and poor health and safety record. Irrespective of whether it is a net contributor to sustainable development, the fact remains that ASM activities will persist for at least as long as poverty continues to make them attractive.

- ASM's contribution to poverty alleviation and local economic development must be optimized by investing a proportion of the revenue generated in other forms of capital, such as education and alternative income-producing opportunities, and through ensuring that ASM activities are incorporated into broader local development planning.
- The negative environmental and social impacts of small-scale mining as well as adverse impacts on human health should be avoided or reduced.
- Where applicable or feasible, alternative economic activities more appropriate for working towards sustainable development should be sought.
- The collective capacity of artisanal and small-scale miners should be developed to enable them to better contribute to sustainable development.
- The development of 'fair trade' markets for artisanal and small-scale mining products should be encouraged to ensure that producers get a fair return and that they adhere to the practices of sustainable development.

Roles, Responsibilities, and Instruments for Change

Accompanying the rights of different groups are corresponding responsibilities to safeguard the interests of others. The boundaries of responsibility and what is considered good behaviour have to be agreed upon and respected if progress is to be made. These will be

led by the best practice of the day, but may well change as knowledge improves.

- Participatory and democratic decision-making structures should be adhered to.
- Decisions should be decentralized and taken as close as possible to the stakeholders most directly affected.
- No one component of the minerals sector alone can drive the evolution in thinking and practice that is required; coordinated action is necessary. This also requires the development of trust.
- All actors need to develop the institutional culture, resources, and skills required for the transition to sustainable development.
- Decision-making and dispute resolution need to take place in ways that treat people with equal concern and respect and that recognize their unequal power relationships and vulnerabilities.
- Alliances will need to be constructed between the private sector, the public sector, civil society, and external development assistance partners to manage many of the dimensions of sustainable development. In turn, this will require agreement on mutually agreed objectives, shared responsibilities for outcomes, distinct accountabilities, and reciprocal obligations.

The Challenge of Implementation

One of the key challenges for the minerals sector is implementation. In this it is not alone – as the ten years since Rio have demonstrated, achieving the goals and objectives of sustainable development presents tremendous challenges for all parts of society.

Various instruments are available to facilitate putting sustainable development into practice. Some of these are well known; others are in experimental stages. (See Box 1–2.) These are discussed further in Chapter 14. Policy-makers will need to select a mixture of these, based on the principles outlined in the sustainable development framework described earlier.

For the minerals sector, implementation requires the development and refining of integrated tools from the international to the local level and at all stages. Some of these are already available and in use, such as impact assessments of mining operations (whether social, environmental, or conflict impacts), life-cycle thinking and analysis, and planning for mine closure, but they

Box 1–2. Instruments of Change

Legislative, regulatory, and juridical instruments include constitutional guarantees on sustainable development and its elements, as well as laws, by-laws, and regulations that set standards governing ownership, production, consumption, trade, environmental liability, associations, and contracts. Numerous national and international agreements govern social, environmental, and economic behaviour. Legal instruments can set absolute limits and provide clear sanctions, especially in areas with clear consensus. However, they can quickly become outdated in relation to society's rapidly changing aspirations, scientific discovery, technology, and economic conditions. The 'mandate, regulate, and litigate' approach can also be costly to implement in several ways – in direct financial terms, in its blindness to differences in the cost of compliance, in the hostilities it produces, in locking in outmoded or irrelevant technologies, and in the innovation that it may stifle. In addition, regulation can be 'captured' to serve the interests of powerful or narrow interest groups. Finally, public-sector capacity to enforce legal instruments may be weak.

Financial and market instruments include:
* *property rights-based approaches,* including tradable pollution permits or other licences, concessions, and liability claims for environmental damages;
* *price-based approaches,* including pollution or disposal taxes, payments for environmental amenities, auctions of publicly owned resources, user fees, tax credits for socially responsible investment funds, and performance bonds;
* *reform of perverse subsidies* to encourage more efficient use of resources; and
* *market-enabling measures,* including information disclosure requirements, product certification and labelling, and procurement policies.

These various instruments work by influencing behaviour through price signals. Their advantages centre on their ability to benefit from competition and efficiency in the market. They can produce a desired outcome at much lower cost than regulation by encouraging innovation and continuous improvement, by finding solutions suitable for the local situation, and by reducing enforcement and administration costs. However, considerable capacity is needed to develop and implement these instruments and they should not be introduced without careful preparation and negotiation, as they may lead to severe economic dislocation. In addition, imposing charges for previously 'free' use of natural resources may not be politically feasible or even desirable for poor groups that are significantly affected.

In the category of *educational and informational instruments* are accessible information on resources, stakeholders and their performances, sustainable development challenges, and opportunities to improve performance; research and pilot projects, especially where stakeholders are themselves involved; and demonstration projects. Also included in this category are public awareness campaigns. The advantage of educational instruments is the ability to raise awareness, encourage self-regulation, and bring about positive peer pressure. They can also reinforce other instruments by improving understanding of the latter's rationale and benefits.

Voluntary instruments tend to rely on self-interest and the innovation that can be found in multistakeholder approaches. There are real limits to what can be achieved through voluntary approaches, partly because real change in behaviour may be less evident than rhetoric implies (especially in the absence of 'sticks and carrots'). In addition, these efforts can actually be so successful that government is left behind, producing a climate of neglect by the state in which weaker groups may become more vulnerable. Included in this category are fora and facilities for dialogue; partnerships (public-private) and associations (corporate or mixed); environmental management systems; full privatization of resources, rights, and services to companies or communities; decentralization of rights and responsibilities; codes of conduct by individual corporations and associations; citizens' actions; contracts and agreements on access, management, and service provision; and common property management regimes.

Source: Dalal-Clayton and Bass (2001) pp.22–24

may need to be improved. Tools that need to be developed include reliable and accessible measures of sustainable development plus methods for assessing trade–offs and balancing conflicting interests. These and other tools are discussed throughout Part III.

Putting sustainable development into practice also requires actors in the minerals sector to be publicly committed to explicit and well–understood goals and objectives. Leadership from the top is a must, as is the need to ensure that all employees understand what sustainable development entails. This is necessary not only for companies but also for government ministries and departments at all levels, as well as labour, civil society organizations, and communities. Capacity building is also key to moving forward.

Conclusion

The concept of sustainable development is not new –
it brings together ideas from a long history of human
development into one common framework. This is
becoming an increasingly important guide and judge
for many actors – whether from government, industry,
or civil society. There is little disagreement about the
broad principles contained in the framework, although
different groups and individuals accord different
priorities to the various spheres – economic,
environmental, social, and governance – depending on
their interests and their level of understanding and
implementation. These priorities will determine the
paths of action for implementation of the principles.
The differences do not detract from the high-level vision
of sustainable development, which allows for different
iterative and ever-improving approaches.

Because there is no one way – no magic bullet – all
that this report can do is to propose a set of sustainable
development principles and to test and test again all
the activities along the minerals supply chain to see
how they stand up to the principles and ideas in the
sustainable development lexicon. Equally important is
understanding how these activities should change for
the better, and how such change can be implemented.
Chapter 16, the Agenda for Change, reflects four
criteria that have to be applied. Any suggested actions
have to be:

- consistent with the sustainable development
  framework;
- based on clearly defined objectives and incentives to
  change towards better practice;
- SMART – specific, monitorable, achievable, realistic,
  and time-bound;
- moving towards higher levels of trust and
  cooperation; and,
- where possible, built on existing structures and
  institutions.

In many ways the picture today is already more
positive than it was a decade ago. Concerns about the
social and environmental effects of minerals
development and disparities in the distribution of costs
and benefits are still very real. There remains much to
be done in improving the sector's contribution to all
aspects of sustainable development. But the largest
companies and their newest operations at least are now
being held to higher standards. Indeed, the best mining

operations are now in the sustainable development
vanguard – not merely ahead of what local regulations
demand, but achieving higher social and environmental
standards than many other industrial enterprises.
Similarly, many governmental and other players are
continually raising the bar. This report is designed to
see that these trends continue, that the best performers
continue to improve, and that the standards of poor
performers are raised.

Endnotes

[1] Throughout this report, the term minerals sector is used to
describe all the key stakeholders associated with the sector:
government, industry, international organizations, non-
governmental organizations, civil society, communities, and labour.

[2] World Bank (2000b).

[3] World Bank – International Finance Corporation (2002).

[4] Cited in Dalal-Clayton and Bass (2001) Chapter 7, p.4.

[5] Agreement signed in April 1994. See http://wto.org.

[6] ICMM SD Charter can be found at http://www.icmm.com/
html/charter_intro.php.

[7] World Commission on Environment and Development (1987)
p.43.

[8] See Secrett (1995) for an example of sustainable development
broken down into concrete ideas, p.7.

[9] Dalal-Clayton and Bass (2001) Chapter 8, p.14.

[10] Ibid., Chapter 2, p.21.

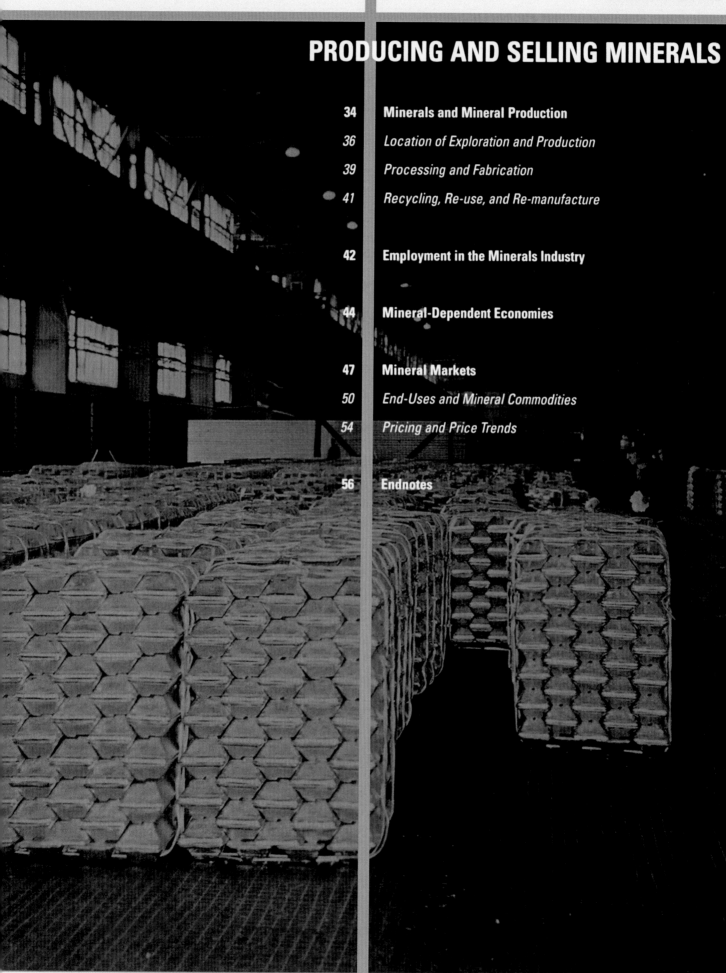

CHAPTER 2

PRODUCING AND SELLING MINERALS

The minerals industry is enormously diverse, which means that no easy generalizations can be made about mineral production or use.[1] Any policy proposal or idea for change or regulation must be based on, and take into account, the distinctive characteristics of different parts of the industry.

This chapter provides a summary overview of the minerals cycle (see Figure 2–1) from the location of minerals and exploration to the different types of end-uses of mineral commodities. It also considers employment levels, economic dependency on mineral production, and trends in mineral prices.

Minerals and Mineral Production

Approximately 99% of the mass of Earth's crust is made up of eight elements: oxygen (47%), silicon (29%), aluminium (8%), and iron (4%), followed by calcium, sodium, magnesium, and potassium.[2] The remaining 1% contains about 90 elements of natural origin. Some minerals are geographically abundant in economic terms, such as coal, iron, quartz, silica, and limestone, and can be found in most countries. Others are concentrated in relatively few places, like some minor metals (tantalum and vanadium) and industrial minerals (borates and phosphate rock). The varying patterns of occurrence of minerals depend largely on the processes that form them, whether they be geological, fluvial, or biological.

Geological sciences are used to estimate the size and grade of ore bodies and to define ore reserves. Different classifications are used to define ore resources and reserves in different parts of the world. The most commonly used definition is that a mineral resource is an *in-situ* concentration or occurrence of a material of

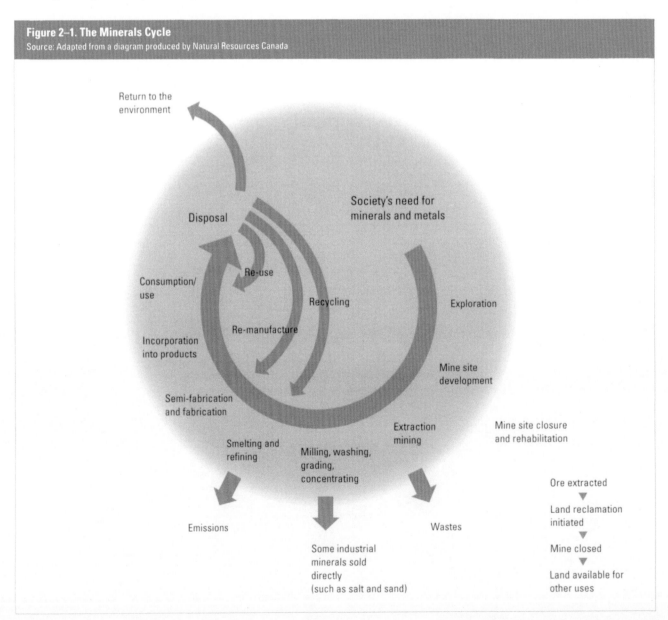

Figure 2–1. The Minerals Cycle
Source: Adapted from a diagram produced by Natural Resources Canada

Return to the environment

Disposal

Society's need for minerals and metals

Re-use

Consumption/ use

Recycling

Exploration

Re-manufacture

Incorporation into products

Mine site development

Semi-fabrication and fabrication

Extraction mining

Mine site closure and rehabilitation

Smelting and refining

Milling, washing, grading, concentrating

Emissions

Wastes

Some industrial minerals sold directly (such as salt and sand)

Ore extracted
▼
Land reclamation initiated
▼
Mine closed
▼
Land available for other uses

economic interest in or on Earth's crust that has reasonable prospects for extraction. The resource is subdivided, in order of increasing geological confidence, into inferred, indicated, and measured categories.[3] After appropriate assessments have been carried out to justify extraction under realistically assumed technical and economic conditions, the mineable part of the measured or the indicated resource is known as the mineral reserve. Mineral reserves are sub-divided, in order of increasing geological, technical, and economic confidence, into probable and proven reserves.

Definitions of minerals range from strictly geological – 'a structurally homogenous solid of definite chemical composition formed by the inorganic processes of nature' – to commodity-oriented. According to the US Geological Survey, for example, there are at least 80 mineral commodities. The majority are metals but there are also important non-metals, a few of which are known as metalloids (such as silicon, arsenic, selenium, and tellurium) because they have some metallic properties.[4] Some metals have been used for many thousands of years. Copper, for instance, can be traced as far back as 7000 B.C. In contrast, metals such as titanium, tantalum, niobium, molybdenum, and zirconium have been used commercially for only 50 years.

The principal classes of mineral commodities are:
• metalliferous minerals (including base metals, ferrous metals, precious metals, and minor metals);
• energy minerals;
• industrial and construction minerals; and
• diamonds and precious gems.

Mineral commodities can also be categorized according to the way they are traded. There are three broad groups:

• Some mineral commodities have a high enough value that they are sold in the global market. These include, among others, gold, diamonds, copper, and aluminium.
• Some mineral commodities have a high enough value per unit weight that they can be marketed in broad regions (as with many grades of coal, limestone, and steel) even if they cannot be marketed truly globally.

• Some mineral commodities have a very low value per unit of weight, such as sand, gravel, and stone, and are therefore marketed mainly locally.

Traditionally, minerals were most commonly produced in deposits in or near the regions where they were used. Today, relatively cheap transport allows the globalization of much production except for ores and minerals that have a low value relative to the transport cost. Where they have ample deposits of high-grade ores, countries such as Australia and Canada are still competitive in mineral production.

But there has been a gradual migration of minerals production to many developing countries, largely because low-cost mineral deposits in these countries have in many cases been mined out. The difficulties and longer lead times in getting environmental permits and the higher labour costs for projects in the most industrialized countries have also contributed to this change. The extent of the migration varies widely with different minerals. It has gone further for many metals than for industrial minerals and construction materials.

However, the fact that some minerals are sold in global markets does not mean they are not also sold regionally or domestically. Domestic output to satisfy domestic demand accounts for a substantial share of global mining (for example in China, India, Brazil, and the US). This is true for metallic minerals as well as construction materials and industrial minerals.

This report focuses largely on globally traded mineral commodities. It is worth noting, however, that locally and regionally traded mine products often dominate in volume terms within regions.

Mineral commodities are supplied in different quantities, reflecting their scarcity and their value in use. Common mineral commodities can be produced cheaply, as they can be extracted from large deposits with economies of scale. Rare mineral commodities are expensive to produce because they tend to occur as trace elements in only a few deposits. They are also supplied in different forms. Common metals are chiefly produced from ores where the principal recoverable metal constitutes a high proportion of the weight of the ore. Iron ore, for example, can contain as much as 67% iron. For rare and precious metals, in contrast, the volume of the recoverable metal may be so small that it is measured in grams per tonne.

Table 2–1. Production and Prices of Some Major Mineral Commodities, 2000

Mineral commodity	2000 Production (thousand tonnes)	Price (US$/tonne)	Annual value (US$ million)
Finished steel	762,612	300	228,784
Coal	3,400,000	40	136,000
Primary aluminium	24,461	1,458	35,664
Refined copper	14,676	1,813	26,608
Gold	2.574	8,677,877	22,337
Refined zinc	8,922	1,155	10,305
Primary nickel	1,107	8,642	9,566
Phosphate rock	141,589	40	5,664
Molybdenum	543	5,732	3,114
Platinum	0.162	16,920,304	2,734
Primary lead	3,038	454	1,379
Titanium minerals	6,580	222	1,461
Fluorspar	4,520	125	565

Source: CRU International (2001)

There is enormous diversity in volumes and dollar values of minerals mined and processed. (See Table 2–1.) In sheer volume terms, aggregates or construction minerals (such as sand and gravel) constitute by far the largest material volumes mined, with world production estimated to exceed 15 billion tonnes per year.[5] Of the metalliferous ores, iron – used mainly in the form of steel – is the largest in volume. In 2000, finished steel production was 763 million tonnes, dwarfing the 24 million tonnes of aluminium, which is the largest non-ferrous metal in terms of volume. At the other end of the scale, 162 tonnes of platinum and smaller tonnages of other rare metals were produced.

The prices of minerals and metals also vary wildly. Platinum prices averaged nearly US$17 million per tonne in 2000, while coal and phosphate rock averaged around US$40 per tonne.[6] Finished steel is the largest mineral commodity traded in sales value, followed by coal. These are the only minerals or metals for which the value of sales exceeded US$100 billion in 2000. Copper, aluminium, zinc, and gold were all in the US$10–100 billion range, while fluorspar, at the low end, was well below US$1 billion in value.

Location of Exploration and Production
In 2001, an estimated US$2.2 billion was spent on mining exploration looking for new deposits. This was

15% less than in 2000 and about 58% below peak exploration spending of US$5.2 billion in 1997.[7] A number of factors may account for this decline, including the Asian financial crisis, recent mergers among the major companies, lower expenditures on exploration by the large multinationals, reduced access to finance for smaller companies, and a downswing in commodity prices. Exploration spending has been more severely affected in the US due to tough environmental laws and in the Pacific and Southeast Asia due to civil unrest, some of which is directly related to anti-mining activities. Metal prices also affect exploration spending by means of their influence on the free cash flow of mining companies and the expected profitability of any discoveries. Today, Canadian companies spend the most on exploration, followed by those based in Australia. Canadian companies have a stronger focus on overseas opportunities. (See Figure 2–2.)

As in other industries, the pattern of mining in terms of products and location of mineral development has changed over time, and these dynamics have significant implications for the sector's contribution to sustainable development. To mention just a few trends, the last two decades witnessed the decline in coal mining in Europe, a rapid increase in copper production in Latin America, and the emergence of China as a formidable player in the supply of many mineral commodities, such as coal.

PRODUCING AND SELLING MINERALS **CHAPTER 2**

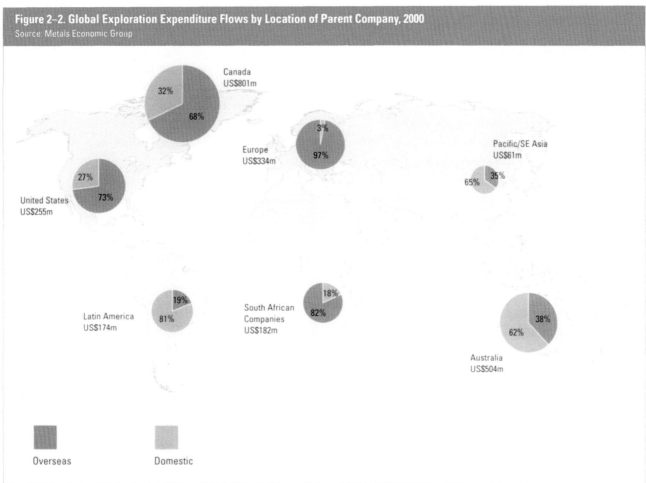

Figure 2–2. Global Exploration Expenditure Flows by Location of Parent Company, 2000
Source: Metals Economic Group

Canada
US$801m
32%
68%

Europe
US$334m
3%
97%

Pacific/SE Asia
US$61m
65% 35%

United States
US$255m
27%
73%

Latin America
US$174m
19%
81%

South African
Companies
US$182m
18%
82%

Australia
US$504m
38%
62%

Overseas

Domestic

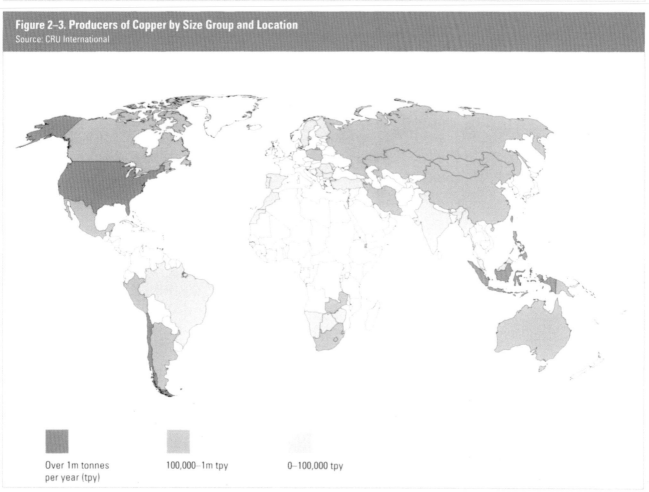

Figure 2–3. Producers of Copper by Size Group and Location
Source: CRU International

Over 1m tonnes
per year (tpy)

100,000–1m tpy

0–100,000 tpy

MMSD THE MINING, MINERALS AND SUSTAINABLE DEVELOPMENT PROJECT

Each mineral resource currently exploited has a unique pattern of geographical occurrence, as indicated by brief descriptions of copper, aluminium, and iron ore and steel production.

Copper

Chile is the biggest producer of copper minerals, followed by the US and Indonesia. (See Figure 2–3.) Copper can be found in many other parts of the world, though less in Europe and much of Africa. Most copper oxide ores are refined where they are found, but there is significant international trade in copper concentrates from sulphide ores. Important countries with refining but no mining are Germany, Italy, and South Korea.

The four chief producers of refined copper are Chile, the US, China, and Japan. Chile is the world's prime producer of copper ore, while China and Japan are big importers of copper concentrates. (China imports 70% of its concentrates; Japan has no domestic production.) Elsewhere, major smelting and refining facilities are divided among countries that are major producers of copper raw materials (for example, Peru, Zambia, and Indonesia), countries that are major users (such as

Germany) and countries that are both (the US).

Aluminium

Bauxite, the main raw material for aluminium, is produced in large countries such as Brazil and Australia and in smaller countries such as Jamaica and Guinea. (See Figure 2–4.) There is little production, by contrast, in North America, Europe, or Africa (apart from Guinea).

Alumina is an intermediate product between bauxite and aluminium. Australia, which has many bauxite mines and some major aluminium smelters, is the largest producer of alumina in the world. Alumina is often produced near the mines, such as the high volumes found in Australia, Jamaica, Guyana, and Guinea, before it is shipped to smelters. Elsewhere bauxite is shipped to regions with aluminium smelting capacity, such as Europe and North America, though not necessarily to final destinations. There is no automatic correlation between the location of bauxite mines and aluminium smelters. Aluminium smelters tend to be located in countries where electric power is plentiful and cheap or in industrial countries where utilities grant special power rates to aluminium

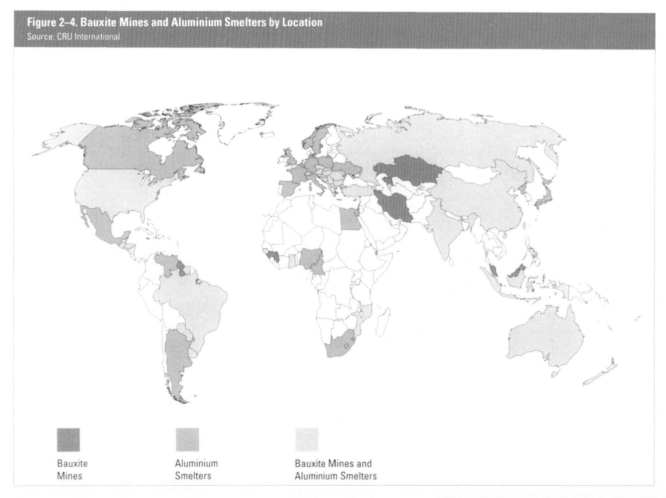

Figure 2–4. Bauxite Mines and Aluminium Smelters by Location
Source: CRU International

Bauxite Mines

Aluminium Smelters

Bauxite Mines and Aluminium Smelters

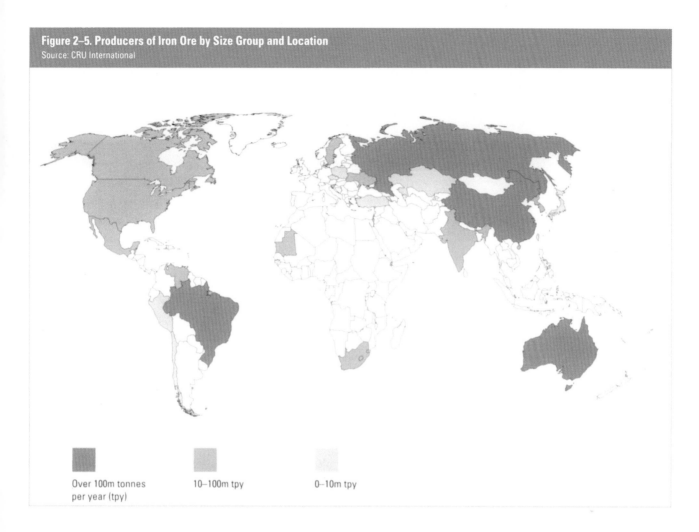

Figure 2–5. Producers of Iron Ore by Size Group and Location
Source: CRU International

Over 100m tonnes per year (tpy)   10–100m tpy   0–10m tpy

producers. Aluminium smelting can be an attractive means of exploiting power resources (which may be based on hydro, gas, or coal) in countries with few alternative markets for their power. Examples include Norway and Iceland.

Iron Ore and Steel
The big producers of iron ore are Australia, Brazil, China, and Russia. (See Figure 2–5.) Australia and Brazil are big exporters, while China and Russia produce mainly for domestic use. Production in Africa is generally confined to Mauritania and South Africa, while there is little production in South Asia apart from India. Sweden is the biggest producer in Europe. Significant production takes place in North America; in South America, production occurs in Brazil, Chile, Peru, and Venezuela.

Most iron ore-producing countries also smelt iron ore (in blast furnaces or in direct reduction plants) and produce steel. Iron ore production and use are seldom in balance within any single country. Many countries that use iron ore do not produce it – that is, most of Europe, all of South and East Asia (except China and

India), and several countries in South America and Africa.

China and Japan are the largest users of iron ore globally but they compete with the US to be the largest steel producers. The US obtains a greater proportion of the iron used in steel making from scrap, hence its need for iron ore is smaller. The number of countries that produce crude steel is much larger than the number that use iron ore. Many smaller countries produce steel by the electric arc furnace method, using scrap as a feed.

Processing and Fabrication
Most metallic minerals go through many processing steps in the transformation to a saleable metal or metallic-based product. The steps from the material in the ground to the processing plants also varies widely. In a classical 'concentrator', ore is crushed, ground down to very fine particles (which is quite energy-intensive), and then put through a range of processes to optimize the separation of valuable minerals from waste (or gangue). These processes include gravity separation, flotation, magnetic separation, electrostatic

separation, and a range of other pre-treatments, involving an array of chemical processes or reagents.

In the aluminium sector, there is one generic process to commercial aluminium. Bauxite is mined and digested (or dissolved) in caustic soda at high temperature and pressure. From this liquor, pure hydrated alumina is precipitated. It is shipped globally as pure alumina powder. At smelter sites, the alumina and fluxes are fed to a 'pot line', where electricity is applied to reduce the alumina to aluminium metal. The metal is removed from the pots as a liquid and cast directly as ingots for shipping or future alloying, reheating, rolling, and shaping. Auxiliary plants for power, anode production, gas cleaning, and utilities mean that aluminium smelters are complex facilities.

Base metals occur normally as either sulphide or oxide minerals. The major processing routes are dictated by the specific valuable minerals, by the mix of minerals, and by the minor commercially interesting elements such as silver, gold, or platinum group metals that can be present. The minor components that present significant environmental or occupational health and safety risks, such as arsenic, bismuth, selenium, cadmium, and so on, may also dictate the processing route.

Base metal extraction plants are generally all different, but fall in two major process groupings: pyrometallurgical, working with very-high-temperature molten materials, and hydrometallurgical, working with normally aqueous solutions. Pyrometallurgical plants will typically contain separate or combined steps for melting, crude metal production, primary refining, casting, re-refining, alloying, and product casting. There will be additional steps for minor and by-product treatment and production. For hydrometallurgical processing, there is a primary ore dissolution step. This can be in acid or alkali at high or low temperature and pressure, or can be bacterially assisted (bioleach), depending on the ore and economically desirable products. The solution is then typically purified by selective precipitation of products, by-products, or impurities. Depending on the metal and the desired product, electrodeposition of product from solution is often used (electrowon copper, electrolytic nickel or cobalt, and commercial zinc).

In the iron and steel sector there are three main routes to production of finished steel. Integrated steel mills use iron ore as a feed. Iron ore is mined and may be upgraded prior to shipping to the steel works by a range of techniques. A major percentage of iron ore is shipped as hardened pellets, which involves crushing and grinding the ore, upgrading, forming into pellets, and heating to give the pellets strength for shipping and for proper operation of the blast furnaces where they are used. The heart of an integrated mill is the blast furnace where iron ore (typically as a pellet) is mixed with coke in a high-temperature reduction process to produce liquid iron. The coke is produced by heating coal in an oxygen-free atmosphere. Fuel gas is simultaneously produced and used in other parts of the steel works. The liquid iron is then typically 'blown' to steel by injecting oxygen, again producing a usable fuel gas. The steel is then refined and cast into slabs or shapes for downstream rolling to commercial product for shipping.

In electric arc steel making, scrap steel is remelted, refined, and cast into intermediate shapes. These shapes typically, with reheating, are passed through a variety of rolling mills that reduce the size and finalize the shape to specific commercial tolerances. Historically, scrap-based steel was used in low-value products. In the last decade technology has allowed casting of sheet and plate of commercial quality to challenge 'integrated' mills. Over the last 20 years a substantial portion of electric arc furnaces feed has switched to Direct Reduced Iron in place of scrap. In this, high-quality iron ore pellets are typically reduced to iron with natural gas products or other carbon-reducing agents. The Direct Reduced Iron is substituted for scrap (up to 100%) and typically results in higher quality steels. There is a wide range of emerging processes.

By far the largest tonnage of materials mined are coal, sand, and gravel. All of these have basic processing steps involving sizing, screening, washing and other waste separation steps prior to shipping.

For most metals, the refined product is sold on for further processing or fabricating, whether rolling, extruding, machining, or forming into semi-fabricated products that will be used in original equipment manufacture. The number of processing stages and the amount of further working depends on the individual mineral and the end-use application. The process of adding value to minerals is often known as 'minerals beneficiation'. (See Figure 2–6.)

Recycling, Re-use, and Re-manufacture

Mineral commodities vary in the extent to which they can be re-used, re-manufactured, or recycled. Some commodities, once produced, can be used only once, such as coal. Others may stay in use almost indefinitely; supposedly Cleopatra's gold is still in circulation. Many industrial metals also stay in use for long periods. For instance, perhaps 85% of all the copper ever mined is still in use.

Thus recycling activity depends on the nature of the mineral commodity. The key determinant is that the commodity retains its chemical form in use. Steel is always steel and can therefore be recycled, even if it requires remelting and refining to become usable once more. Lead, copper, and aluminium also keep their basic properties. Some metals are principally recycled in the form of alloys. Nickel, for example, is largely used in stainless steel and other non-ferrous alloys but the stainless steel and the alloys are themselves largely recycled.

If a metal is converted into a new chemical form, as in the production of chemicals, recycling is usually impossible. It is also often impossible to recover metals that are widely dispersed in use. By definition, fertilizer and energy minerals cannot be recycled. Energy minerals are burnt and lost, while the final products of fertilizer minerals disappear into the soil.

There are basically three different kinds of scrap: home or revert scrap is generated at the metal refining or processing stage and is usually reintroduced into the melting furnaces; new or prompt industrial scrap is produced by manufacturing processes, such as car production, and can be collected and recycled relatively quickly; and old or obsolete scrap is recovered post-use, which may be many tens of years in the case of much infrastructure and other capital goods. It is important to understand the differences among these three types in order to discuss the recyclability of various metals.

Many metals are not available for recycling as they are applied in structural uses that have long lives, such as railways, bridges, pipelines, and electricity distribution systems. Continuing construction means that increasingly more metal will be stored as structures in use (although this should still be counted as part of the world's reserves of metal).

Recycling reduces the demand for primary metals and requires considerably less energy than producing primary metal would. For example, scrap aluminium requires about 5% and scrap steel about 25% of the energy required to produce the primary metals.

In the iron and steel industry, over one-third of production currently comes from scrap, from different sources. Producers generate and recycle their own scrap in steelworks. Foundries and steel fabricators collect scrap and supply it to traders who send it back to the steel producers. A significant volume of scrap also comes back to the industry after use. Steel food

Figure 2–6. Minerals Benefication Process
Source: Chamber of Mines of South Africa

Stage	Mineral benefication process category	Process flow-chart		Labour intensity	Capital intensity
1	Mining and producing an ore or concentrate (primary product)	Run-of-mine ores →	Washed and sized concentrates	High	High
2	Converting a concentrate into a bulk tonnage intermediate product (such as metal or alloy)	Mattes/slags/ bulk chemicals →	Ferro alloys/ pure metals	Low	High
3	Converting the intermediate goods into a refined product suitable for purchase by both small and sophisticated industries (semis)	Steel/alloys →	Worked shapes and forms	Low	High
4	Manufacturing a final product for sale	Worked shapes and forms →	Worked shapes and forms	Medium to high	Medium to high

and beverage cans are often returned relatively soon after use. Other steel products have a longer life and some are eventually collected and returned. Most old motor vehicles are eventually shredded, and the scrap returns to the steel industry. Demolition scrap, including obsolete building elements, plant and equipment, rails, and so forth, is heavily recycled. In recent years, more than 50% of total steel use has been derived from recycled material.

Primary aluminium production totalled 24.4 million tonnes in 2000, while 15.6 million tonnes were recycled. The sources of the scrap are diverse, but over half was generated in the production of semi-finished aluminium products. Over one-quarter was post-consumer scrap, and the rest came from aluminium fabricators and secondary foundries. Beverage cans are a major source of post-consumer scrap. Old post-consumer scrap is also recovered from buildings, other construction, and motor vehicles.

Estimates of the residence time for metals in use by society depend principally on assumptions regarding the life span of metal-containing products.[8] For example, it has been estimated that 40 years is the average lifetime for copper in use in the US.[9] This masks considerable variation between applications. In Sweden, 80–90% of the copper that has been produced and used since the Middle Ages is still either in use or in long-lived products that are no longer in use but have not been discarded into known landfills.[10] This compares with an estimate that 75% of the annual use of refined copper (excepting inputs from recycled scrap) in the US is accumulated in use, the remainder being subject to dissipative uses.[11] (See Figure 2–7.)

Scrap recovery depends on the number of end-use applications and the ease and cost of collection. For example, the recovery of lead from batteries is now about 90% in the US, but recovery from other uses such as radiation shielding, sound proofing, weights, and ammunition is much lower. Overall recovery of lead is about 55% of use.[12] A high proportion of spent lead–acid batteries is collected and reprocessed, despite the low intrinsic value of a spent battery (typically about US$2). In industrial countries, the recycling rate for lead–acid batteries is over 90%. Secondary lead now accounts for 66% of total lead use in the US (59% if only old scrap is considered). The majority of any future growth in secondary lead production will

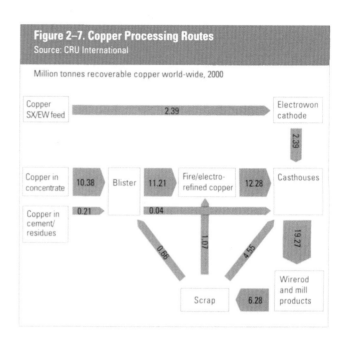

Figure 2–7. Copper Processing Routes
Source: CRU International

Million tonnes recoverable copper world-wide, 2000

come from greater use of batteries and better recycling rates in these transition countries. This trend is largely driven by the predominance of use in one application – lead-acid batteries – and the existence of an easy system for collection at replacement battery centres.

On the other hand, the great majority of zinc is used either as an alloying material or as a coating to steel. At the end of the life of products containing zinc, the metal cannot readily be separated and recycled as pure zinc. The recycling of zinc therefore takes many forms and is not done by one dedicated industry, in contrast to lead. As the recycling routes are diverse, the statistics on the volume of zinc recycled are by no means complete. About 1.7 million tonnes of zinc were recycled in 1999, but many countries lack data on this, so the true total is certainly larger.

It is important to remember that while recycling will be an ever-important component in the supply of metals, new virgin metal will be required in order to meet the demands of the world's growing population.

Employment in the Minerals Industry

No one knows how many jobs the minerals industry provides world-wide. The uncertainty becomes greater further down the minerals value chain. For instance, is someone who works in a recycling yard that handles both metals and other materials working in the minerals industry? Is a bricklayer, working all day with bricks and mortar – both made wholly from minerals – working in the minerals sector? What about a jeweller? Even if answers to such questions were available, statistical agencies often do not gather employment data in ways that provide this type of information.

Explorationists, miners, and smelter workers clearly belong to the minerals industry. Even for them, however, the available information is less than clear and does not allow cross-national comparisons.[13] The most comprehensive source of employment statistics is the International Labour Organization (ILO), which reports data for the extractive industries from 73 countries extending back at least 10 years.[14] Since country-specific data include employment for both mining and oil and gas exploration, however, in countries where both are important – such as Russia, Mexico, and Indonesia – there remains great uncertainty.

In addition to the country-specific data, the ILO provides a global estimate of 30 million people involved in mining itself (excluding oil and gas), 10 million of whom produce coal.[15] This represents 1% of the world's work force but it excludes at least 13 million small-scale miners. Taking into account dependants, the ILO estimates that the number of people relying on mining, both large- and small-scale, for a living is likely to be about 300 million.[16]

Recycling is an important employer in the minerals sector, particularly for metals. For example, the Bureau of International Recycling estimated that there were 1 million workers employed in ferrous and non-ferrous recycling industries in 1996.[17] Employment numbers vary considerably among regions. The ILO data also indicate that the largest concentration of mining employment (60%) is in Asia.[18] This is concentrated in China, which has about half the world's mining employees.

Employment statistics for the minerals industry in a selection of the most important mineral-producing countries are given in Figure 2–8.[19] Many of these data relate to mining, while others include smelting and refining. The regional distribution of employment is not proportional to production. Of the estimated 400,000 people employed directly in mining, smelting, and refining of copper, nearly 60% of them are in China and the former Soviet Union.[20] This is despite the fact that these regions produce just over 10% of the world's output.[21] In contrast, South America

employs 10% of the labour force to mine over 40% of global copper supply.

The relative importance of the minerals industry as a source of employment can be demonstrated by comparison with the total work force. In both Australia and Chile, employment in the mining industry for the period 1999-2000 represented almost 0.9% of the total work force.[22] In South Africa, the mining industry represented 2.7% of the economically active population or some 9% of workers in the non-agricultural formal sectors of the economy in 1999.[23]

The number of people employed in mining and minerals processing has been in decline. In some countries, such as the UK and Germany, employment has fallen as mines have closed or production has fallen and the sector became less important. More generally, most of the industry has become more capital-intensive due to technological change. In some parts of the world, such as Eastern Europe and the former Soviet Union, a decrease in employment is due to the changing structures of mining enterprises. The general trend for a decrease in employment is most clearly illustrated by the case of South Africa, where 360,000 mineworkers, or 46% of the industry's 1990 work force, lost their jobs between 1990 and 2000.[24]

In many countries, employment is concentrated in certain parts of the industry. In Australia, the black coal industry is the largest minerals sector employer, accounting for approximately 25% of the work force in the minerals sector in 1999.[25] In India, the coal industry is estimated to have accounted for 70% of the 700,000 formally employed in mining in 1999.[26] In Chile, the copper industry accounts for over 30% of the mine labour force.[27]

Changes in employment levels have varied within countries, depending on the mineral being produced. For instance, in Chile between 1995 and 1999, employment in the copper sector dropped by 21%, compared with 60% in the gold/silver sector.[28] However, the non-metal mining industry in the same period increased employment by 61%.[29] Although employment in the US mining industry decreased by 31% between 1985 and 2000, within this sector the coal industry is the biggest employer and showed the largest decrease – almost 60%.[30] In Canada, employment in the minerals industry experienced a modest increase of about 3% in the 1990s.[31] Despite

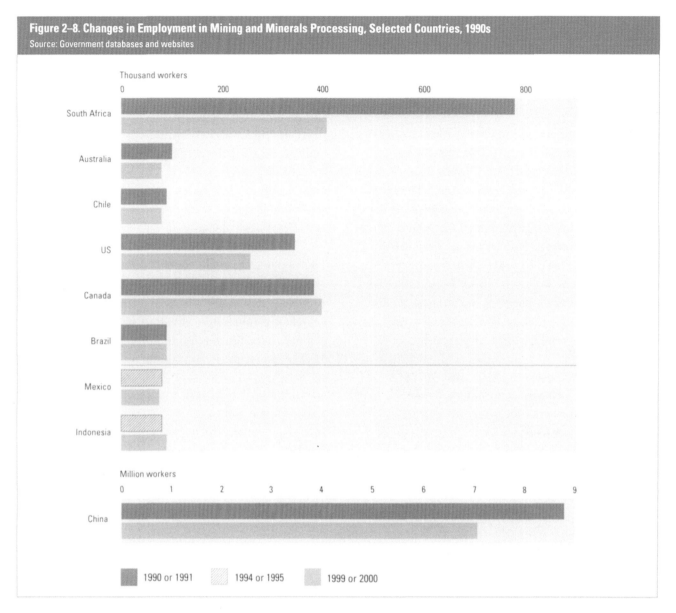

Figure 2–8. Changes in Employment in Mining and Minerals Processing, Selected Countries, 1990s
Source: Government databases and websites

this, the chain of production that includes metal, non-metal, quarrying, and coal mining registered a decrease of 26%, while the structural materials sector showed an important recovery, with the number of employees increasing by about 60%.[32]

The impact on employment of the introduction of more capital-intensive technologies is demonstrated by the steel industry. Global steel production has risen by approximately 30% in the past 25 years.[33] Over the same period, estimated employment in the major steel-producing countries (excluding China) has fallen from around 2.5 million to fewer than 900,000 people. (See Table 2–2.) This enormous reduction – more than 60% – has been the result of major capital investments by steel companies in steel-making processes and technologies.[34]

Employment figures are greater if downstream

activities are included. The greatest employment in the minerals industry is often not at the mining stage. For example, the zinc industry is estimated to provide direct employment to about 210,000 people worldwide.[35] Zinc mining, excluding that occurring in China, employs about 55,400 people, or 26% of the total.[36] Zinc refining and smelting employs an estimated 65,000 people and the zinc oxide industry a further 6000 people.[37] Most of the employment in the zinc industry is in galvanizing (where zinc is coated on iron and steel for corrosion resistance); the total for this activity is about 85,000 people.[38]

Mineral-Dependent Economies

Mineral production and processing are important economic activities in many parts of the world. Classifying mineral dependence is difficult because of

Table 2–2. Steel Industry Employment in Selected Countries, 1974 and 2000

Country	1974	2000	Decline
	(thousand)		(per cent)
European Union	996	278	72
UK	197	51	85
France	158	37	77
Yugoslavia	42	15	64
US	521	151	71
Brazil	118	63	47
South Africa	100	47	53
Japan	459	197	57
Australia	42	21	50

Source: International Iron and Steel Institute website http://www.worldsteel.org

the number of ways in which this can be measured. Common measures record mineral output as a percentage of gross domestic product (GDP) or the value of minerals in relation to exports. In 34 countries, mainly developing ones and those in transition, mineral exports represent at least 25% of total merchandise exports. (See Table 2–3.) These countries, often known as 'mineral-dependent economies', differ not only in terms of their reliance on fuel or non-fuel minerals (see Figure 2–9), and geographical location, but also in terms of their broader development performance. (See Chapters 8 and 9 for discussion of the impact of mineral development on national and local economic development.)

The importance of mineral production to regional and national economies is demonstrated by the findings of MMSD's regional processes. Australia relies substantially on mineral commodities for export income – 45% of its merchandise export income, accounting for 9% of GDP, comes from basic mineral commodities.[39]

In the Southern African Development Community region, mining output constitutes about 8% of GDP. In South Africa, which is responsible for more than 70% of the region's mining output, the figure is 6.5%.[40] The range within Southern Africa is considerable – from 34% of GDP in Botswana to less than 1% in Mozambique.[41] Mining contributed 43% to the region's exports, with Botswana, Democratic Republic of the Congo, Namibia, and Zambia deriving over 50% of their export earnings from mining.[42]

In Latin America the contribution is also important. Bolivia gests 3.6% of its GDP and 32% of the value of its national exports from mining.[43] In Brazil, mining activities (including oil and gas extraction) account for 8.5% of the GDP and 32% of national exports.[44] Chile obtains 10.3% of its GDP and 44% of the value of its nationals exports from mining.[45] And mining in Peru contributes almost 50% of the exports and 5.5% of the GDP.[46]

The US has the largest minerals sector in the world by volume, although less than 0.5% of its GDP comes from direct mineral extraction (20% of which

Figure 2–9. Countries Dependent on Ore and Metal Exports, 1999

Source: Based on data arranged by Eggert (2001). Data source: World Bank (2001b) and (for data on ore and metal exports in DR Congo, Mauritania, Mongolia, Tajikistan, and Zambia) UNCTAD (2001).

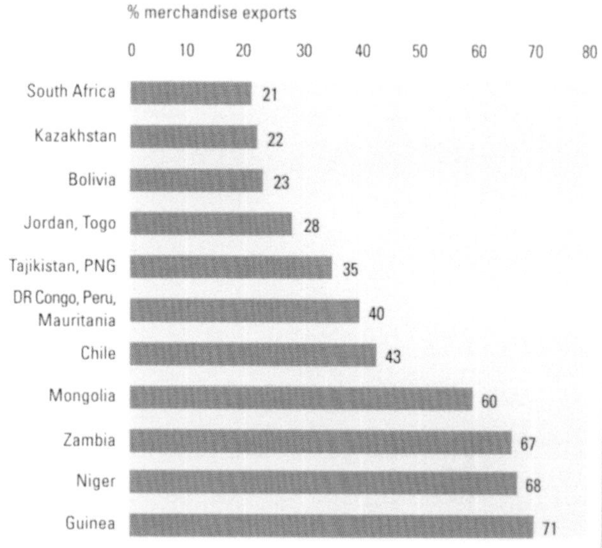

% merchandise exports

South Africa	21
Kazakhstan	22
Bolivia	23
Jordan, Togo	28
Tajikistan, PNG	35
DR Congo, Peru, Mauritania	40
Chile	43
Mongolia	60
Zambia	67
Niger	68
Guinea	71

Table 2–3. Mineral Dependence in the Structure of Exports, 1999

Country	Ores and Metals	Fuels	Total
	(per cent of merchandise exports)		
Nigeria	0	99	99
Algeria	0	96	96
Libya	0	95	95
Yemen	0	93	93
Saudi Arabia	1	85	86
Venezuela	4	81	85
Kuwait	0	79	79
Oman	1	77	78
Guinea	71	0	71
Azerbaijan	1	69	70
Syrian Arab Republic	1	68	69
Niger	67	0	67
Zambia	66[a]	0	66
Kazakhstan	22	42	64
Mongolia	60[a]	0	60
Norway	7	50	57
Trinidad and Tobago	0	54	54
Russian Federation	11	41	52
Peru	40	5	45
Chile	43	0	43
Colombia	1	40	41
Egypt	4	37	41
Congo, Dem. Rep.	40[a]	0	40
Mauritania	40[a]	0	40
Australia	17	19	36
Papua New Guinea	35	0	35
Tajikistan	35[a]	0	35
Ecuador	0	33	33
South Africa	21	10	31
Bolivia	23	6	29
Indonesia	5	23	28
Jordan	27	0	27
Senegal	10	17	27
Togo	27	0	27

[a] Includes SITC 522.66 in addition to SITC Section 3.
Source: Eggert (2001), based on World Bank and UNCTAD data

is from the metals sector).[47] In Canada, the mining industry contributes 3.7% of GDP and about 14% of exports.[48] Construction and industrial minerals form a significant percentage of total mineral production in the US and Canada. (See Figures 2–10 to 2–13.)

Europe has significant mineral production, mostly of natural aggregates (sand and gravel), crushed rock aggregates, and other construction minerals. Countries in the European Union represent around 20% of world production of industrial and construction minerals.[49] Some of these are among the world's largest producers of natural stone, feldspar, and kaolin.

Mineral Markets

The quantity and type of mineral commodities used varies considerably between countries. Historically, Europe, Japan, and the US have been the largest mineral-using regions. But this is changing as markets mature,

especially as use increases in Brazil, China (see Box 2–1), and other Asian countries, such as Malaysia and Thailand.

Europe and Asia are the two principal regions using most of nine metals and minerals: aluminium, lead, zinc, copper, nickel, steel, gold, coal, and phosphate rock. (See Table 2–4.) The European Union mainly depends on imports for its raw materials supply, with a negative minerals trade balance in 1998 of about 8 billion euros (US$7 billion).[50] North America is also important, especially for aluminium, lead, and coal. Coal is perhaps the most anomalous of these commodities. Regional consumption as a share of the world total is much higher for coal than for other commodities in the former Soviet Union and Australasia. Phosphate rock use depends on the proximity of phosphoric acid and phosphate plants as well as on the location of final use; North America and Asia are the largest regions if use in this case. Africa is also an important user, largely because Morocco is the largest producer in the world. It should be noted that

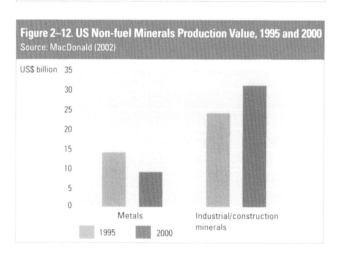

Figure 2–10. Value of Non-fuel Mineral Products in Canada, by Type, 1999
Source: MacDonald (2002)

Non-metals 24%
Structural materials 19%
Metals 57%

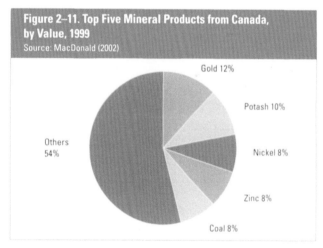

Figure 2–11. Top Five Mineral Products from Canada, by Value, 1999
Source: MacDonald (2002)

Gold 12%
Potash 10%
Others 54%
Nickel 8%
Zinc 8%
Coal 8%

Figure 2–12. US Non-fuel Minerals Production Value, 1995 and 2000
Source: MacDonald (2002)

US$ billion

Metals
Industrial/construction minerals

1995   2000

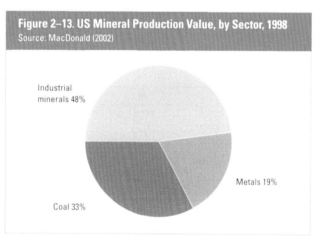

Figure 2–13. US Mineral Production Value, by Sector, 1998
Source: MacDonald (2002)

Industrial minerals 48%
Metals 19%
Coal 33%

Box 2–1. Focus on China

One of the most important developments in the global mining industry in the last decade has been the rapid development of China in the world market. From a small but significant exporter of minor mineral commodities such as tungsten and magnesite, China has become a significant influence in virtually all the major mineral markets by virtue of the sheer volumes it is now using, importing, and exporting during its rapid industrialization. Annual use grew at double-digit percentage rates through the 1990s. Chinese use accounted for one-third of the entire world growth in copper use between 1990 and 2000 and 40% of world growth in aluminium use. More than 60% of this copper must be imported, and it is increasingly being imported as concentrates rather than metal or semi-fabricated products.

China is the world's largest steel producer and user. The growth in production has moved China's share of the sea-borne market for iron ore from 4% in 1990 to 16% in 2000, accounting for 60% of all growth in this market. China is expected to import more than 80 million tonnes in 2001. In the last two years, China has also become a significant exporter of coal, doubling its share of the traded coal market from 6% to 12%, and it is expected to export in excess of 75 million tonnes.

Source: Humphreys (2001b).

data on use only record the countries of first use. There is considerable trade in semi-manufactured and mineral-containing products.

On a per capita basis, it is clear that the industrialized regions of Europe and North America use the lion's share of metals and minerals. Just taking one example, only 0.7 kilograms of aluminium is used a year in Africa per capita compared with 22.3 kilograms in the US. Americans use about 600 kilograms of metals per person a year.[51] During an average 70-year lifetime, West Europeans on average use about 460 tonnes of sand and gravel, about 39 tonnes of steel, 100 tonnes of limestone, and more than 360 tonnes of fuel to heat houses, produce electricity, or keep cars running.[52] Several studies have proposed that intensity of use of a mineral (the use of a mineral commodity divided by GDP) depends on the level of economic development, as measured by GDP per capita, and that the pattern of intensity of use follows an inverted U-shape as economies develop.[53] (See Figures 2–14 and 2–15.) As development takes place, countries focus on building infrastructure (such as rails, roads, and bridges, and water supply and electricity transmission) and people buy more durable goods, which rapidly increases the demand for mineral commodities. As economies mature, all other things being equal, they move to a less materials-intensive phase, spending more on education and other services, which reduces the intensity of mineral use. Other factors that affect intensity of use include government policies, shifts in demographics, materials substitution, and new technologies.

The available empirical evidence suggests that the intensity of use of many important mineral commodities is falling over the long run.[54] But it remains difficult to forecast future demand given all the factors that can affect intensity, some of which,

Table 2–4. Consumption of Selected Metals and Minerals, 2000

	North America	South America	Europe	Former Soviet Union	Asia	Africa	Other
	(thousand tonnes)						
Aluminium	7,291	823	6,632	612	8,819	294	421
Lead	1,924	212	1,854	179	1,866	118	47
Zinc	1,714	352	2,572	280	3,563	162	240
Copper	3,649	534	4,551	270	5,868	116	176
Nickel	165	24	416	25	449	31	2
Steel (million tonnes)	170	33	206	25	377	18	9
Gold (tonnes)	306	83	906	42	2,423	179	7
Coal (million tonnes oil equivalent)	613	37	241	197	767	123	158
Phosphate rock	44,580	6,298	11,008	8,965	43,210	23,087	2,718

Source: CRU International (2001)

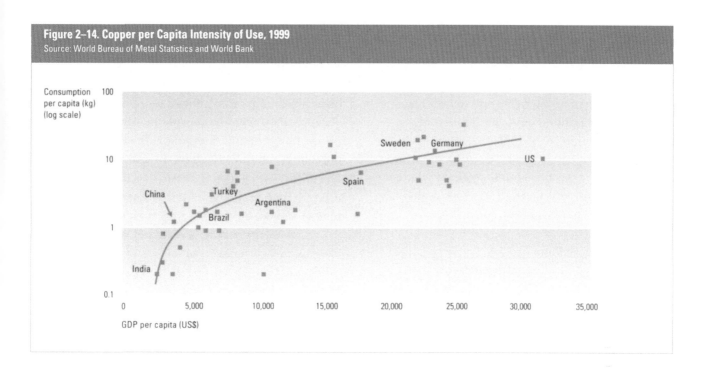

Figure 2–14. Copper per Capita Intensity of Use, 1999
Source: World Bureau of Metal Statistics and World Bank

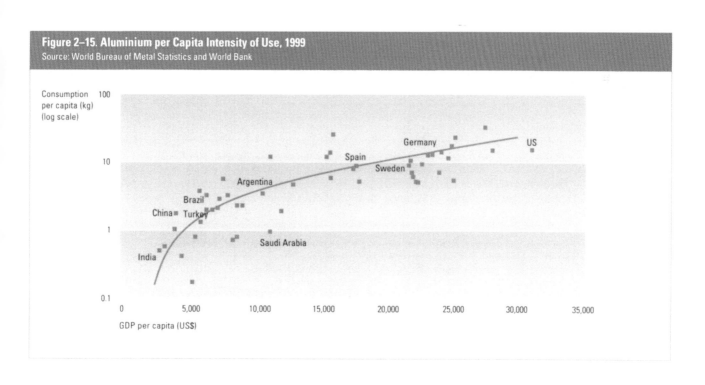

Figure 2–15. Aluminium per Capita Intensity of Use, 1999
Source: World Bureau of Metal Statistics and World Bank

such as new technology, are impossible to predict.

End-Uses and Mineral Commodities

The list of applications for metals and minerals is endless – aerospace, automotive, electronics, energy generation and transmission, high-rise construction, wide-span bridges, railway tracks, weapons of war, and so on. (See Table 2–5.) In addition, most manufacturing processes for most products in the world use metal equipment as an integral part of the process.

There are 31 metals in the standard personal computer.[55] A modern jet engine is composed of 41%

titanium, 34% nickel, 11% chromium, 7% cobalt, and lesser amounts of aluminium, niobium, and tantalum.[56] Nickel-based super alloys are used in jet engines because of high temperature stability and strength. These super alloys may contain more than 15 elements, including iron, vanadium, tungsten, cobalt, carbon, molybdenum, aluminium, titanium, and niobium. A car contains about 10 different types of steel alloys that constitute about 70% of all the materials used in it.[57] Mineral commodities have a large number of non-mechanical uses, such as kaolin in paper, zinc in agriculture, and copper sulphate as a chemical raw material.

By end-use, metals are found in all sectors of

Table 2–5. Common Uses of Mined Products

Aggregates	Concrete, building construction, roads, bridges, sewer and water systems
Aluminium	Aircraft parts, automotive parts (truck and automobile engine blocks and cylinder heads, heat exchangers, transmission housings, engine parts and automobile wheels), railroad cars, seagoing vessels, packaging (foil, cans, cookware), building construction (siding, windows, skylights, weather-proofing, doors, screens, gutters, down spouts, hardware, canopies, and shingles), electrical applications (overhead power lines, wires and cables), pharmaceutical uses (antacid, antiperspirants), water treatment
Antimony	Alloys, flame-proofing compounds, batteries, plastics, ceramics, glass, infrared detectors and diodes, cable sheathing, small arms, paints, medicine
Arsenic	Glass production, semi-conductors, wood preservation, pesticides, bronzing, pyrotechnics, laser material
Asbestos	Cement building materials (roofing, cladding, pipes), heat and acoustic insulation, fire proofing
Beryllium	Structural material for high performance aircraft, missiles, spacecraft and communication satellites, automotive parts, computer and laser technology, X-ray windows, ceramics, nuclear industry
Bismuth	Malleable irons, thermocouple material, carrier for uranium fuel in nuclear reactors, low-melting fire detection and extinguishing systems, acrylic fibres, medicine, cosmetics
Borates	Fertilizers, disinfectant, detergent, water softener, corrosion inhibitor for antifreeze, flux in brazing, ceramics, paint, coated paper, enamels, heat-resistant glass (Pyrex), pharmaceuticals, food preservative
Cadmium	Electroplating, nuclear reactor parts, television phosphors, batteries
Chromium	Metal plating, alloys, pigments, corrosion resistance, glass and ceramics, catalyst, oxidizing agents, anodizing aluminium, tanning leather, refractory products
Clays	Bricks, ceramics, nutritional additives, concrete, mortar
Coal	Electricity generation; steel making; chemical manufacture; production of liquid fuels, plastics and polymers
Cobalt	Super alloy (used in jet engines and gas turbine engines), magnets, stainless steel, electroplating, batteries, cemented carbides (hard metals) and diamond tools, catalysts, pigments, radiotherapeutic agent
Copper	Building construction (wire, cable, plumbing and gas tubing, roofing and climate control systems), aircraft parts (undercarriage components, aeroengine bearings, display unit components, and helicopter motor spindles), automotive parts (wire, starter motor, bearings, gears, valve guides), industrial applications and machinery (tools, gears, bearings, turbine blades), furniture, coins, crafts, clothing, jewellery, artwork, musical instruments, cookware

Table 2–5. Common Uses of Mined Products (continued)

Dolomite	Building stone, nutritional additives
Feldspar	Glass, ceramics, enamel, tile glazes, source of alkalies and alumina in glazes, paint, plastics, mild abrasives, welding electrodes
Fluorspar	Steel making, aluminium, fluorocarbons (used in refrigerants, blowing agents, solvents, aerosols, sterilants, fire extinguishers)
Gallium	Compound semiconductors in mobile phones, glass and mirror coatings, transistors
Germanium	Semiconductors, infrared imaging and detector systems, optical fibres, phosphor in fluorescent lamps, catalyst, radiation detectors, lasers and light detectors, medical and biological uses
Gold	Ornamental, electronics, dentistry, decorative plating of costume jewellery, watchcases, pens and pencils, spectacle frames and bathroom fittings, decoration of china and glass, store of value
Graphite	High-temperature lubricants, brushes for electrical motors, brake and friction linings, battery and fuel cells, pencil fillings, seals and gaskets, conducting linings on cables, antistatic plastics and rubbers, heat exchanger, electrodes, apparatuses and linings for the chemical industry
Gypsum	Building construction (plasterboard, plaster and cement), agriculture, glass, chemicals
Iron	Steel making, alloy
Kaolin	Filler for paper, rubber, plastic, paint and adhesives, refractories, ceramics, fibreglass, cement, catalyst for petroleum refining
Lead	Batteries, cable sheathing, lead crystal, solder and radiation protection, anti-knock compound in petrol, plumbing, ammunition
Limestone	Aggregate, cement, fertilizer, soil conditioner, iron flux, paints, plastics, livestock feed
Lithium	Lubricants, glass and ceramics, lithium carbonate (used for aluminium reduction, batteries, pharmaceuticals), high-performance alloys for aircraft, carbon dioxide absorber in spacecrafts, nuclear applications
Manganese	Steel making, alloys, batteries, colourants and pigments, ferrites, welding fluxes, agriculture, water treatment, hydrometallurgy, fuel additives, oxidizing agents, odour control, catalysts, sealants, metal coating, circuit boards
Magnesite	Agricultural fertilizer, refractory bricks, filler in plastics and paints, nuclear reactors and rocket engine nozzles, manufacture of Epsom salts, magnesia, cosmetics, insulating material and disinfectant, fire retardant
Magnesium	Alloys used for aircraft, car engine casings, and missile construction; refractory material; agriculture (feed and fertilizer); filler in paper, paints, and plastics; automobile and machinery; ceramics; fire retardant; pyrotechnics and flares; reducing agent for the production of uranium and other metals from their salts
Mercury	Thermometers, barometers, diffusion pumps, electrical apparatus, electrode, batteries, chlorine and sodium hydroxide manufacture, plant treatments, lighting, pesticides, dentistry
Molybdenum	Alloys, catalyst in petroleum refining, heating elements, lubricants, nuclear energy applications, missile and aircraft parts, electrical applications
Nickel	Stainless steel, corrosion-resistant alloys, gas turbines, rocket engines, plating, coins, catalysts, burglar-proof vaults, batteries
Niobium	Alloys, stainless steels, advanced engineering systems (space programs), nuclear industry, electrical products, jewellery
Palladium	Jewellery, watches, surgical instruments, catalysts, dentistry (crown), electrical contacts, hydrogen gas purification
Phosphate rock	Fertilizers, detergents, flame retardants, food and beverages, animal feeds, metal treatment, water treatment, pulp and paper, glass and ceramics, textiles and synthetic fibres, plastics, rubber, pharmaceuticals, cosmetics, petroleum production and products, construction, pesticides, toothpaste, mining, leather, paints, fuel cells

Table 2–5. Common Uses of Mined Products (continued)

Phosphorus	Safety matches, pyrotechnics, incendiary shells, smoke bombs, tracer bullets, glass, calcium phosphate (used to produce fine chinaware), steel making, cleaning agent, water softener, pesticides
Platinum	Jewellery, coins, autocatalysts, electronics, glass, dentistry, chemical and electrochemical, catalysts, petroleum, laboratory equipment, antipollution devices in cars, investment, anti-cancer drugs, implants (pacemakers, replacement valves)
Plutonium	Nuclear fuel and weapons, pacemakers
Potash	Fertilizer, soap and detergents, glass and ceramics, chemical dyes and drugs, food and beverages
Pumice	Construction, stonewashing in textile industries, glass and metal polishing, dental supplies and paste, agriculture, sport and leisure facilities, cosmetics
Rhodium	Alloys (used for furnace windings, thermocouple elements, bushings for glass fibre production, electrodes for aircraft spark plugs, laboratory crucibles), electrical contact material, optical instruments, jewellery, industrial catalysts, car catalytic converter
Sand and gravel	Concrete, bricks, roads, building materials
Selenium	Photoreceptors (used in the manufacture of plain paper photocopiers and laser printers), electronic applications, glass, pigments, alloys, biological applications, rubber, lubricants, catalysts
Silica	Glass (bottles and jars)
Silver	Photography (X-ray film for medical, dental, industrial uses), jewellery, electrical applications, batteries, solder and brazing alloys, tableware, mirrors and glass, coins
Soda ash	Glass, detergents, chemicals, water treatment, flue gas desulphurization, pulp and paper
Sulphur	Sulphuric acid, ammunition, fungicide, vulcanization of natural rubber
Talc	Paper, plastics, paints, ceramics, refractories, roofing, rubber, cosmetics, pharmaceuticals, agrochemical, animal feed, cement, glass fibre
Tantalum	Electrolytic capacitors, alloys (use in aircraft and missile manufacture), lining for chemical and nuclear reactors, wires, surgery (used in sutures and as cranial repair plates), cameras
Tin	Tinplates, alloys, solder, pewter, chemicals, panel lighting, frost-free windshields
Titanium	Production of lightweight alloys, aircraft components (jet engines, aircraft frames), automotive components, joint replacement (hip ball and sockets), paints, watches, chemical processing equipment, marine equipment (rigging and other parts exposed to sea water), pulp and paper processing equipment, pipes, jewellery
Tungsten	Alloys (used in filaments for electric lamps, electron and television tube, metal evaporation work), ammunition, chemical and tanning industry, paints, X-ray targets
Uranium	Nuclear fuel, nuclear weapons, X-ray targets, photographic toner
Vanadium	Alloys (especially in steel), catalysts, pigments for ceramics and glass, batteries, medical, pharmaceutical, electronics
Zinc	Galvanizing, alloys, brass, batteries, roofing, water purification, coins, zinc oxide (used in manufacture of paints, rubber products, cosmetics, pharmaceuticals, floor coverings, plastics, printing inks, soap, textiles, electrical equipment, ointments), zinc sulphide (used in making luminous dials, X-ray and TV screens, paints, fluorescent lights)
Zirconium	Ceramics, refractories, foundry sands, glass, chemical piping in corrosive environments, nuclear power reactors, hardening agent in alloys, heat exchangers, photographic flashbulbs, surgical instruments

Source: ICMM, MERN, CRU International (2001), industry association websites

manufacturing, although some are particularly large-volume users, such as transportation and appliances. Construction is also important. Some high-value metals are used in very small volumes in specialized uses. Non-metallic mineral commodities are also used in manufacturing, but some mineral commodities have other distinct uses, including agriculture (phosphates and borates, for example) and power generation (coal).

The future demand for metals is not, however, determined solely by the development of new applications for these materials or changes in existing ones. Metals may be substituted for alternative materials and vice versa, and this may occur at various levels, although the availability of the substitute materials must also be considered.

At the level of national and regional economies, the relative contribution of different materials towards economic output may change. These 'compositional shifts in economic activity' are most commonly measured by intensity of use.[58] Steel and copper use in the US, for example, was relatively stable between 1960 and 1985, while that of aluminium and plastics increased significantly. Similar trends may be identified in the construction materials sector.[59] Substitution may also occur with strategic uses of metals, which do not involve incorporation into products. In recent years, there has been a trend among central banks to exchange gold reserves for currency reserves. (See Chapter 5.)

Substitution also occurs within individual product applications. (See Box 2–2.) For instance, copper is now used in brake linings (together with plastics) instead of asbestos. Several important factors must be considered when choosing materials in product design. The market for fuel-efficient vehicles has been fundamental to materials choice in the motor industry, for example. A key limiting factor in the substitution of metals for other materials is not just the technology to produce the materials but also the infrastructure to incorporate them into finished products.[60] Some metals have unique physical characteristics that, based on current knowledge, make them essentially non-substitutable. An example is copper, which is fundamental in many electrical applications. While aluminium is a good electrical conductor and has considerable application in high-voltage transmission lines, it is not an economic alternative to copper for the distribution of electricity in most manufactured

---

Box 2–2. Choosing Between Metals and Other Materials

The motor industry is a key metal user. Vehicle manufacturers in the US account for approximately 20% of aluminium, 14% of steel, and 10% of the copper used in the economy. The composition of cars world-wide has, however, changed considerably. For instance, 5% of the mass of Japanese cars in 1973 was composed of plastics, whereas in 1997 this increased to 7.5%. Plastics and composites have been used instead of steel in instrument panels, bumpers, and outer body panels. Cast aluminium has increasingly replaced cast iron in engine blocks. The bodies of several models of mass-produced cars have been made from fibre-reinforced polymers. Even though these are a small percentage of the market, it is still suggested that plastic may be the material choice for car bodies of the future. A key factor in this is the desire of manufacturers to reduce the weight of cars in order to achieve fuel efficiency.

In food and beverage packaging, there is intense competition between aluminium, steel, plastics, and glass as materials choices. The rivalry between suppliers of these materials has been a driver of significant technological advances that have, in turn, led to a reduction in the amount of material used per unit of product. The weight of a steel food can fell by 60% between 1960 and 1990. Simple materials choice decisions are also influenced by market distortions (including bans) and inertia (preferences based on familiarity).

There are significant regional variations in choices between materials. Soft drinks in North America come in aluminium cans, whereas glass dominates in South America. Where metals are used, consumer lifestyle and pressures have had an overwhelming influence on the demand. In the case of long-term food packaging, metals remain the dominant material in use because of the need for strength during vacuum processing. Free market competition between materials has often been strongly influenced by regulation. In Denmark, aluminium cans were banned on the basis of a government analysis of the environmental impacts of this and other forms of packaging. Biodegradable plastics may be an increasingly competitive form of packaging in the future.

Source: Metal use by vehicle manufacturers in US from Rocky Mountain Institute http://www.rmi.org/sitepages/pid422.php; metal use in Japanese cars from Samel (2001); general trends in materials use in cars from Eggert (1990); weight of steel can from Nappi (1990).

---

products and local electricity networks.

Consideration of the social, economic, and environmental impacts of different mineral commodities is also key. For example, copper is 30% more efficient at transmitting electricity. Replacing copper with aluminium in electricity transmission would therefore lead to an increase in any global warming effects associated with the provision of electricity. Life-cycle assessment provides a useful tool for the comparative analysis of the various impacts. (See Chapter 11.)

Pricing and Price Trends

The London Metal Exchange (LME) is a market in which copper, aluminium, nickel, lead, zinc, tin, and silver may be brought and sold, for delivery either immediately or at fixed dates in the future. LME prices refer to refined metals and are used as the basis price for transactions in these metals (apart from silver) world-wide. LME prices are also used as the basis for products upstream from refined metals (such as ores and concentrates) and for downstream products, such as some semi-fabricated products. They are even used as the basis for scrap prices.

Only an estimated 5% of the metals produced annually are physically traded through the LME. Companies with physical metal to sell will normally deal directly with their customers or through merchants. The vast majority of LME contracts are hedging transactions where the buyer or seller of the metal can enter into forward contracts on the LME to secure a fixed price, even though the counterparty will quote a price based on the unknown future price of the metal.

Understanding variations in the price of mineral commodities is critical to evaluating the future of the mining and minerals industry. This is principally because prices simultaneously reflect and affect both demand and supply. They are also influenced by artificial price-setting interventions by industry and governments. With a proper understanding of price setting, prices can be an important tool in analysing long-term trends in the minerals sector. For example, they can signal changes in the availability of minerals for extraction, as well as technological and organizational changes in mining and minerals processing.

Long-term descriptions of price depend on the methods used to account for inflation, all of which have relative merits.[61] Attempts have been made to use labour costs, the price of goods that do not result from resource extraction, and general national price indexes. Potter and Christy made one of the first attempts at a systematic description of price trends for mineral commodities, using the US Producer Price Index as a means of adjusting for inflation.[62] They showed that when the prices of all the mineral commodities were amalgamated, prices had declined by 40% between 1870 and 1957. This illustrates the potential for misinterpretation of data, for when the first ten years of the data they used are excluded, the long-term trend is quite stable. Potter and Christy's work has been updated several times – most recently by Howie, who reported on real prices for selected commodities between 1870 and 1997.[63] (See Figure 2–16.)

Howie's analysis illustrates several points. First, the long-term trend for mineral commodities depends entirely on the product in question. Prices shift according to technology. Aluminium is perhaps the example of greatest price reduction associated with technological change. There have been major reductions in both the cost of energy and the amount of energy required to convert bauxite to alumina and then to aluminium ingot. Other mineral commodities such as copper have remained relatively stable, which may reflect the balance between technological change, physical availability, and demand.

Second, there is considerable volatility. The appearance of this can be even more exaggerated if price fluctuations are quoted for frequencies less than a year. Some of the year-by-year price changes can be attributed to global events such as economic crises and wars. Price volatility is a key issue in mineral commodity markets. This can significantly affect the revenues of mining and minerals processing companies and host governments as well as the costs to consumers, such as the fabricators of metal products.

The value of long-term historic price trends in predicting future patterns is debatable. Although numerous models for price are available, the complexity of issues relating to the availability of minerals and technology to extract them means that the past is no sure guide to the future.

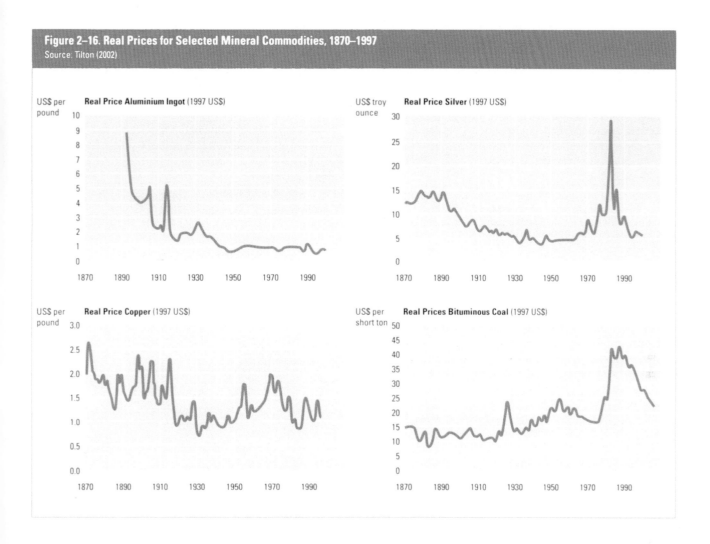

Figure 2–16. Real Prices for Selected Mineral Commodities, 1870–1997
Source: Tilton (2002)

Endnotes

[1] Unless otherwise indicated, statistical information in this chapter is from CRU International (2001b).

[2] Wedepohl (1995).

[3] For more detail on these definitions, see Canadian Institute of Mining, Metallurgy and Petroleum (1998).

[4] US Geological Survey, at http://minerals.usgs.gov/minerals/pubs/mcs

[5] Regueiro et al. (2000).

[6] The prices of the major non-ferrous and precious metals are evaluated by their average value on commodity exchanges. There is no terminal market for low-volume, and often heterogeneous, metals and mineral commodities. Moreover, because transport costs are high relative to costs of production, the price of the commodities may vary significantly from one region to the next. The prices for finished steel, coal, phosphate rock, titanium minerals, and fluorspar are all notional prices that are quoted merely to show the approximate position of each product in the value hierarchy. Actual prices may have been significantly higher or lower for each of these commodities in 2000, depending on the specification of the product and the location where it was used.

[7] Metals Economics Group, Canada quoted in *Financial Times*, 1 November 2001.

[8] Ayres et al. (2001).

[9] US EPA (1983).

[10] Ayres et al. (2001).

[11] Jolly (2000).

[12] Henstock (1996).

[13] The diverse statistical sources that are available include international organizations, regional associations, national governments, labour unions, and industry information. The most important problem in reporting employment data is the lack of a common methodology, which would allow reliable comparisons between nations. This problem of aggregation occurs because different proportional shares of direct and indirect employment and different stages of the chain of production are included (some figures include mining only, while others do not discriminate between extraction, smelting, refining, and fabrication workers). Finally, both reliability and quality of the data vary between countries.

[14] ILO (2001b). The data referred to from the ILO are the total number of people employed by economic activity according to the International Standard Classification of all Economic Activities; these statistics cover mining, quarrying, and extraction of oil and natural gas activities.

[15] http://www.ilo.org/public/english/dialogue/sector/sectors/mining.htm.

[16] Ibid.

[17] Bureau of International Recycling, at http://www.bir.org/biruk/index.asp.

[18] ILO (2001b).

[19] *South Africa:* Government of South Africa, Department of Minerals & Energy (2001) p.9. *Australia:* Data exclude metal ore extraction, smelting, refining, and basic metal fabrication. Source: Hancock (2001). *Chile:* Includes both direct employment and contractors. Includes coal but excludes oil. Source: Chilean Copper Commission (2001). US: Includes all mining, processing, independent shops and yards, and office workers. Source: Mine Safety and Health Administration, US Department of Labor. *Canada:* Includes all mining, smelting, refining, and fabrication. Source: Mining Association of Canada (2001). *Brazil:* Mining, smelting, and refining. Source: Brazilian Bureau of Mines (2001). Mexico: Earliest available data are for 1994–95. Source: Secretaria de Trabajo y Prevision Social (2001) http://www.stps.gob.mx. *Indonesia:* Earliest available data are for 1994–95. Excluding mining

services. Source: Wiriosudarmo (2001). *China:* Source: Chinese Statistical Information Network (2000).

[20] CRU International (2001b).

[21] Of the 60%, 160,000 are in China and 60,000 in the former Soviet Union.

[22] Data sources as per Figure 2–7.

[23] South African Minerals Bureau (2000) p.8.

[24] Government of South Africa, Department of Minerals & Energy (2001) p.9.

[25] Hancock (2001).

[26] Tata Energy Research Institute (2001).

[27] Chilean Copper Commission (2001).

[28] Ibid.

[29] Ibid.

[30] National Mining Association (2001).

[31] Mining Association of Canada (2001).

[32] Ibid.

[33] IISI (2001), http://www.worldsteel.org.

[34] Ibid.

[35] International Zinc Association (2001) web page. http://www.iza.com.

[36] Ibid.

[37] Ibid.

[38] Ibid.

[39] Hancock (2001).

[40] Government of South Africa, Department of Minerals and Energy (2001) p.5.

[41] MMSD Southern Africa (2001).

[42] Ibid.

[43] Enriquez (2001).

[44] Barreto (2001).

[45] Lagos et al. (2001).

[46] Glave and Kuramoto (2001).

[47] MacDonald (2002).

[48] Ibid.

[49] Regueiro et al. (2000).

[50] Regueiro et al. (2000).

[51] Jeffrey (2001).

[52] BGR Hannover (1995), cited in Regueiro et al. (2000).

[53] See Radetzki and Tilton (1990).

[54] See Tilton (2002).

[55] Jeffrey (2001).

[56] Ibid.

[57] Ibid.

[58] Considine (1991).

[59] Moore and Tilton (1996).

[60] Considine (1991).

[61] Tilton (2002) Chapter 4.

[62] The Producer Price Index is a group of indexes that measures the average change over time in selling prices as supplied by domestic producers of goods and services. This contrasts with the Consumer Price Index, which measures price change from the purchaser's perspective. Potter and Christy (1962).

[63] Howie (2001).

CHAPTER 3

A PROFILE OF THE MINERALS SECTOR

Sustainable development requires a redefinition of roles and a strengthening of institutions dealing with economic development as well as social and environmental concerns. In the past, the key players in the minerals sector might include governments, a few companies licensed to extract minerals, and a few recognized traditional groups living in or near mineral reserves. While international organizations and financial institutions were active in aspects of minerals activities, their focus has changed over the past few decades. Other actors, including non-governmental organizations (NGOs) and consumers, have also become more involved in recent years and focused greater attention on the minerals sector. The number of constituencies and their demands are thus far more diverse today.

At every level, from the international to the local, there are constituencies who consider themselves legitimate voices in the minerals sector. At times, their claims of legitimacy can be difficult to evaluate. Central to sustainable development is the need to understand who the 'stakeholders' are, how to evaluate their legitimacy, how to ensure their accountability, and how to build their capacity. (See Box 3-1.) There is also a need to consider differing levels in capacity and differences in power among interested parties, not least because some participants lack power since they do not have the resources and information to be included in decision-making.

Industry

In the global context, the minerals industry is relatively small. The top 150 international minerals companies had a combined market capitalization of only US$224 billion at the end of September 2001 – smaller than companies such as General Electric and ExxonMobil. (See Figures 3-1 and 3-2). There is one striking difference between the mining industry and the oil and gas industry, with which it is often lumped statistically: while there are individual mine projects that are quite profitable, mining companies that do better than the average, and years that are better than others, the industry as a whole has not been doing very well. The mining industry exhibits volatile returns: over the past 25 years, it has failed to produce a long-term return that meets its cost of capital.[1]

Box 3-1. Who Is a Stakeholder?

There is a good deal of importance given to 'stakeholder process' in sustainable development. Of course, the definition of a 'stakeholder' in the minerals sector depends on the issue at hand. (See below for examples of different categories of stakeholders, from the smallest to the broadest group.) In some cases, such as local skills development, stakeholders will be concentrated in the local community but may also include company representatives, government, labour, and civil society groups. For other issues, such as the impact of energy use in the minerals sector on climate change, the stakeholder group is likely to be much larger and more globally distributed. Whatever topic is under discussion, there will be both direct and indirect stakeholders.

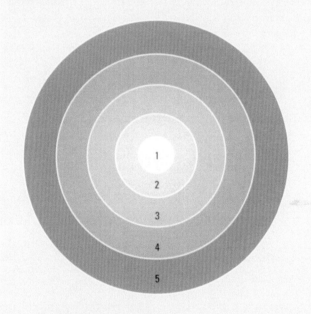

1 **Stakeholders with a veto**
Examples: Duly constituted government authorities with discretion to deny permits; landowners who own mineral rights who are under no obligation to sell.

2 **Stakeholders with a right to be compensated**
Examples: Surface owners who do not own mineral rights; injured workers; communities requiring resettlement.

3 **Stakeholders with a right to participation**
Examples: Some national indigenous agencies; local planning authorities; people entitled to participate in EIA processes.

4 **Stakeholders with a right to consultation**
Examples: Affected persons whose views must be sought; neighbours; non-decision-making government agencies.

5 **Stakeholders who should be informed**
Examples: Suppliers; the media.

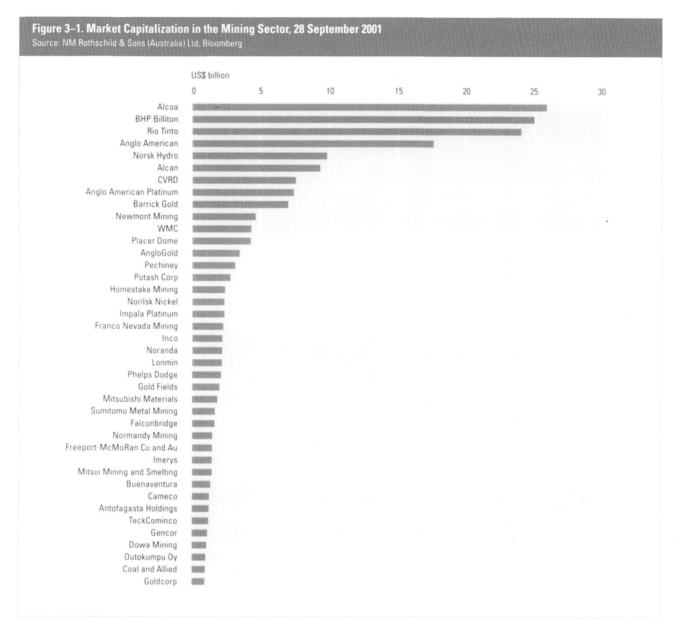

Figure 3–1. Market Capitalization in the Mining Sector, 28 September 2001
Source: NM Rothschild & Sons (Australia) Ltd, Bloomberg

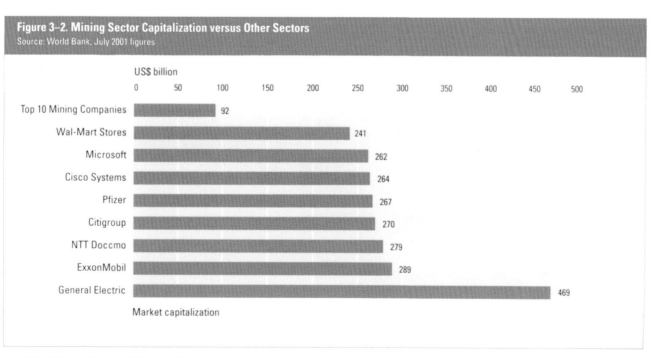

Figure 3–2. Mining Sector Capitalization versus Other Sectors
Source: World Bank, July 2001 figures

The structure of the minerals industry appears complicated and disparate. On closer examination, however, it can be shown to exhibit the characteristics of an integrated production system, with companies occupying identifiable niches and using various business strategies to reduce risk and to create opportunities for growth and upward mobility in the system.[2] (See Figure 3-3). Junior companies find new ore bodies and sell them on to the larger companies. Intermediates offer growth potential through merger among themselves or by being taken over by the largest corporations. Miners feed product to smelters and refiners, who in turn provide metals or mineral products to fabricators, and so on. Thus, in this sense, the industry is highly interdependent, both along the product supply chain and across different mineral groups.

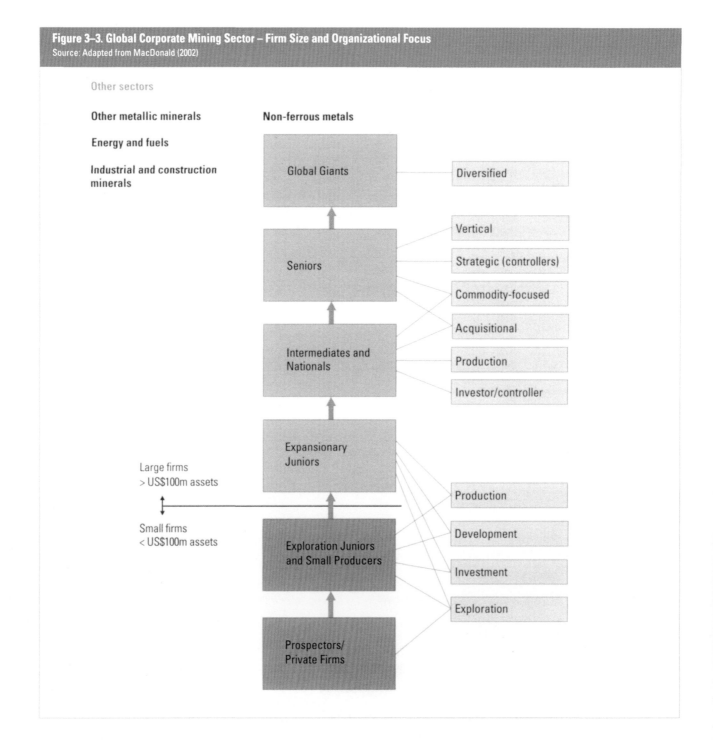

Figure 3–3. Global Corporate Mining Sector – Firm Size and Organizational Focus
Source: Adapted from MacDonald (2002)

Artisanal and small-scale mining (ASM) plays an important role in some minerals, especially gold and gemstones. The profile, potential contributions to sustainable livelihoods, and environmental impact of this segment of the minerals sector is quite different from the other players described in this chapter. ASM is described in greater detail in Chapter 13.

Throughout the 1990s, mining companies – both large and small – became more international, driven by changing regulatory structures, falling ore grades in well-established mining countries such as Canada and Australia, and the opening up of several mineral-rich developing countries to foreign investment. But the industry, despite its interdependence – from exploration through mining, metal production, smelting, fabrication, and recycling – remains fragmented, lacking a consolidated vision. This has significant implications for any collective action towards sustainable development.

The Large Multinationals

Large multinational corporations explore, mine, smelt, refine, and sell metal concentrates and metals on world markets. About 30-40 companies are in this category, although there has been increasing concentration in the last couple of years in response to low commodity prices and poor returns among the big players. (See Table 3-1.) Recent mergers include, for example, BHP and Billiton, Cominco and Teck, and the acquisition of Asarco by Grupo Mexico. The concentration of producers of metals and minerals varies significantly. (See Table 3-2.) For steel, the ten largest producers

manufacture less than 30% of global output. But for platinum and molybdenum, the ten largest account for more than 90%.

Big producers of iron ore tend to be mining companies, not steel companies, and the trend in the industry is to move away from vertical integration. BHP Billiton is currently a significant producer of steel, but it plans to sell its steel division to concentrate on mining. Kumba Resources is a spin-off from Iscor, as the South African steel company wanted to separate its manufacturing and mining activities. Iron ore producers concentrate on countries with large individual deposits, rather than on a diverse group of countries. Of the top five iron ore producers, only Rio Tinto is active in as many as three countries.

BHP Billiton and Rio Tinto are also among the main producers of coal and the major producers of coking coal for the world export market. The largest single producer is the state-owned Coal India Limited. The other two big producers are private and are totally focused on coal and related businesses.

The biggest copper producers include two big mining groups and three producers that specialize in copper and, to a lesser extent, molybdenum. Codelco operates only in Chile, but the other companies operate further afield. Although the big nickel producers derive most of their revenue from nickel, by-product revenues (including copper, cobalt, and precious metals) are significant for production derived from sulphide ores (Inco, Norilsk, and Falconbridge).

Table 3–1. World's Largest Mining and Metal Companies

Company	Home country	Sales (US$ billion)	Main activities
Alcoa	United States	23	Aluminium
Nippon Steel	Japan	22	Carbon and stainless steel
Anglo American	United Kingdom	21	Non-ferrous metals (NFMs), platinum group metals (PGMs), coal, steel, forest products, ferroalloys, diamonds
BHP Billiton	Australia	19	NFMs, PGMs, coal, steel, oil and gas, ferroalloys
Posco	South Korea	11	Carbon and stainless steel
Rio Tinto	United Kingdom	10	NFMs, PGMs, coal, iron ore, industrial minerals, diamonds
Alcan	Canada	9	Aluminium

Table 3–2. Top Five Producers of Selected Minerals and Metals

Iron Ore	Market Share (%)	Coal	Market share (%)	Copper	Market share (%)
1 CVRD (Brazil)	15.5	CIL (India)[a]	17.6	Codelco (Chile)*	12.3
2 Rio Tinto (UK)	8.8	Peabody (US)	5.0	Phelps Dodge (US)	7.8
3 BHP Billiton (Australia)	6.2	Rio Tinto (UK)	4.7	BHP Billiton (Australia)	7.0
4 Caemi (Brazil)	2.5	BHP Billiton (Australia)	4.1	Rio Tinto (UK)	6.2
5 Kumba (South Africa)	2.5	RAG (Germany)	3.2	Grupo Mexico	5.5

Nickel	Market Share (%)	Aluminium	Market share (%)	Gold	Market share (%)
1 Norilsk (Russia)	19.1	Alcoa (US)	14.4	AngloGold (South Africa)	8.3
2 Inco (Canada)	12.2	Alcan (Canada)	8.4	Barrick (Canada)	7.6
3 Falconbridge (Canada)	7.8	Russian Aluminium	7.3	Newmont (US)	6.7
4 BHP Billiton (Australia)	5.9	BHP Billiton (Australia)	4.0	Gold Fields Ltd (South Africa)	4.7
5 Eramet (France)	5.3	Pechiney (France)	3.6	Placer Dome (Canada)	3.4

[a]State-owned.
Source: CRU International (2001)

Aluminium producers tend to move in a world of their own. Of the largest aluminium companies, only BHP Billiton is a major participant in the mining of other commodity minerals. The big companies, apart from Russian Aluminium, usually have interests in smelting around the world. They are also likely to be integrated back into bauxite mining and alumina refining and forward into fabrication and marketing.

Among the multinationals, an important group is the custom smelters and refiners, usually based in Europe and Japan, which are largely focused on mineral processing. Some of these companies, such as Umicore of Belgium and Noranda of Canada, are pioneering ways to use recycled metallic materials and recover various metals from complicated multi-metal scrap.

These large multinational companies are high-profile organizations conscious of the need to have a social licence to operate. Many of them have well-developed codes of practice and ways of doing business, as well as reporting procedures that take account of a broad range of environmental and social concerns. When a company like BHP Billiton or Rio Tinto opens a new mine, there is likely to be a substantial effort to assess, minimize, and mitigate many of the environmental and social impacts, to develop an effective mine closure plan, and to foster constructive and consensual involvement with the local community.

Medium-Sized and National Players

A typical intermediate company operates several small-to medium-sized mines, possibly in a number of countries; it is also likely to be a gold producer, an industrial minerals company, or a base metal miner selling concentrates to a trader or custom smelter. For most locally and regionally traded minerals, particularly industrial minerals, the intermediates predominate. Many medium-sized processing and fabricating companies also operate mainly at a regional or national level. These companies may buy raw materials to produce metallic or non-metallic mineral products, or they may be involved further downstream in fabricating minerals or metal into products.

Juniors

Although grouped under one heading, juniors are diverse in their business strategies, risk management, financial situation, commitment to long-term positions and relationships, countries of operation, and so on. Two broad sub-groups can be identified.[3] One is involved exclusively in mineral exploration, seeking to negotiate arrangements with larger players for the development of any ore body they discover. These companies often have considerable technical expertise and business acumen and provide an essential service by discovering and evaluating the new ore bodies needed by the larger companies to replace reserves. The second group, the expansionary or producing juniors, is more ambitious and will try to hang on to an ore body they discover and gain a controlling interest in the operating mine. Also included in the junior category are the many small, often family-owned, mining companies found throughout Latin America, Asia, and parts of Europe.

Junior companies can be found in large concentration in some countries. Canada has more than 1000 junior companies (in contrast to 100 in the United States), and they are particularly active in Latin America.[4] Other major centres for junior companies include Australia, operating largely in the Pacific Rim, and Europe, operating largely in Africa.

There are intermediate and junior companies that are fully committed to the highest standards of environmental and social performance, but these are currently a minority. A majority of junior companies emphasize their mine-finding abilities and currently believe sustainable development to be a 'big company game' that has little relevance to them.[5] As a consequence, there are significant weaknesses and vulnerabilities among both the junior and intermediate companies. Two situations are of note that can lead to

undesirable outcomes and affect the image of the entire industry.

First, there are the 'promotional juniors' that focus on speculative, market-driven practices and are often guilty of activities that give the sector a bad name. Second, some of the smaller intermediate and junior producing companies are undercapitalized and short of management expertise, while at the same time under intense pressure to succeed and hence likely to take on marginal risks. With limited capacity to deal with failures or other unexpected events, there is a high risk of creating negative environmental and social situations at their operations. As such, it should be no surprise that a disproportionate number of the 'bad actors' have come from this sector in recent times. One of the major challenges facing the industry is how to ensure that the performance of this small group of companies is raised, or that their licence to operate is removed.

Consultants, Contractors, and Service Companies

The mining industry is supported by an extensive network of consultants, contractors, and service companies, which range in character from small, often highly specialized firms to large, integrated engineering and environmental organizations such as AMEC and Hatch Associates Ltd. Many aspects of the work of the mining industry are routinely assigned to the service sector, including drilling, the design and construction of new mines and, most notably, the environmental and social studies required for an environmental impact statement. In some cases mining is carried out under contract, leaving milling and the marketing of mine products to the company owning the resource. Consultants and service companies are particularly numerous and prominent in the exploration phase of the mine cycle.

The service sector can play an increasingly important role in reaching the goals of sustainable development by providing expertise in the management, engineering, environmental, and social aspects of the mining industry, which is available to all corporate interests. However, mining companies committed to sustainable development principles will need to ensure that contractors working for them, particularly those involved in activities with direct social and environmental impacts, such as drilling and construction companies, are bound by the same policies and principles of sustainable development.

Traders

The larger base-metal mines sell concentrates directly to a smelter, often within the same vertically integrated company. Smaller mines typically sell concentrate to a trader who consolidates product from several sources to create the volume and quality that is acceptable to smelters. Refined metal product may also be either sold directly to fabricators or marketed through metals traders.

In either event, trading patterns in concentrates and refined metal products among mines, smelters and refiners, and fabricators create obvious difficulties in tracking metals reliably from mine to customer. Hence, it is perhaps only the most fully integrated companies, such as aluminium firms, that currently have the potential to demonstrate that a metal has been mined, refined, and fabricated under conditions that meet sustainable development objectives.

Fabricators

Fabricators are important players in the value chain for many metals. These companies convert primary metal products such as steel slabs and copper cathodes into usable metal products in a series of cutting, shaping, forming, bending, coating, welding, and other steps. The extent of vertical integration and the number of steps varies from metal to metal and from one end-use application to another. These companies vary hugely in size and nature of business, ranging from large, fully integrated multinational producers such as Phelps Dodge, which is involved in all stages of copper production from mining to wire making, to independent subcontractors operating a few pieces of welding equipment for steel plate in a single workshop. Thus it is impossible to make any generalizations about this part of the minerals cycle.

Recyclers

Scrap merchants and recycling companies handle the collection and sorting of metal commodities for secondary production. Secondary smelters specialize in processing recycled metals. Scrap is also used as feed by the primary smelters and refiners and by the steel mills. Methods of scrap collection vary from 'mom and pop' operations with scrap metal (mostly aluminium and copper) piled in their backyard to large, sophisticated central collection and recovery centres such as those for lead-acid batteries.

The recycling business is critically important to the metals sector and for some of the non-metallic minerals. At all possible junctures, the mining companies and proponents of the sector promote the recyclability of metals as a major advantage of metals use in a more sustainable future. However, recyclability and the recycling rate are not the same. (See Chapter 11.)

State-Owned Companies

State ownership no longer accounts for a major share of world mining and metals activity, and most mining and processing is today in private hands. There has been a trend in the last 20 years towards the privatization of nationalized industries in general, of which mining has made up just a small part of the world total. Privatization examples in the minerals sector include copper producer ZCCM in Zambia, tin producer Comibol in Bolivia, copper producer Tintaya in Peru, and Karaganda Steelworks in Kazakhstan, to mention just a few.

State-owned companies are concentrated in a few countries, and in some, in only a few products. State ownership is still widespread in China, although the government is trying to encourage private ownership. In Chile, the large copper–molybdenum producer Codelco is state-owned, but most other mining and metallurgical activities are private. In some countries, the state takes a minority share in mining activities (in, for example, Papua New Guinea, Botswana, and Namibia).

In Eastern Europe and the former Soviet Union, the states have sold off most of their more attractive nationalized assets, even though some of the less profitable enterprises are still state-run so as to maintain employment. Most mining enterprises in Iran are still state-owned. In Turkey, the mining holding company Eti Holdings is a state-owned group, although a privatized mining and metallurgical sector flourishes alongside it. India still has state-owned giants such as coal producer CIL, steel producer Sail, base metals companies Hindustan Copper and Hindustan Zinc, and aluminium company Nalco; attempts at privatization have been few and far between, although a private-sector industry has sprung up alongside these companies in many areas. Various governments in the Middle East still operate mining and metallurgical companies.

Workers and Labour Unions

The modern mining industry in its best operations represents a remarkable advance from dire conditions in the past. In many parts of the world today, mine labour represents relatively high-wage work. The rates of accidents and injuries as well as occupational disease have been reduced to levels unimaginable just a few decades ago, in many cases as a result of collaborative approaches. Miners in these operations live in integrated local communities, where they and their families share the same social and educational opportunities as the society at large. When mines close, workers may have skills that are in demand elsewhere or the opportunity for training programmes to learn new job skills, along with a safety net of social benefits to support them during periods of unemployment. They are free to form and join unions, in an atmosphere that encourages management and other parts of the work force to focus on shared interests.

Even though gains have been achieved, this kind of progress is quite uneven through a global lens. Every one of the situations that were of concern earlier still exists somewhere in the world. Mine accidents that kill or disable workers are still frequent. Over 170 miners a year have died recently in the South African gold industry.[6] While statistics for China are unavailable or hard to interpret, it is known that there is a high rate of accidents in underground coal mines, and the official figures record some 10,000 fatalities a year. Smaller Bolivian tin mines are also examples of this problem. Occupational illness can result from working conditions and exposures to chemicals. Miners still live in isolation in many parts of the world, or in overcrowded 'boom towns' with few social and cultural opportunities. The predominantly male workers, linked with groups of female sex workers, have led to the rapid spread of HIV in some parts of the work force.

Significantly, the right to form free and independent unions for collective representation is still not recognized in parts of the mining world, from some of the republics of the former Soviet Union to Colombia, where threats and attacks on union officials and organizers are reported to be frequent. For example, three union leaders of the La Loma mine in northern Colombia were murdered in 2001.[7] These incidents are not restricted to the developing world but also occur in industrial countries, such as the coal miners' strike in the UK in 1984-85.[8]

World-wide, mine-related employment has been declining, with layoffs and mine closures a dominant feature in the industry in recent years. Reductions in the labour force have been dramatic as the former socialist economies have integrated into the world market-place, as previously state-owned mines have been privatized, as large companies have mechanized, and as marginal mines have closed under the relentless advance of lower prices.

Although workers and trade unions are well placed to monitor and oversee industry practices, only recently has full emphasis been placed on their role as a key partner in sustainable development. They are able to contribute to sustainable development in the work place by seeking compliance from their employer on issues such as the protection of workers' rights, equal opportunities, and worker safety. At the community level, trade unions are able to contribute to the goals of sustainable development by playing the role of ambassadors of industry interest or understanding. At the national and international levels, trade unions participate in developing global policies that promote sustainable development through active consultation with industry leaders, governments, and inter-governmental institutions.[9]

At the global level, two organizations are particularly active on labour issues in the minerals sector. The first one is the International Federation of Chemical, Energy, Mine and General Workers Unions (ICEM). As of June 2001, ICEM represented 399 industrial trade unions in 108 countries, covering 20 million workers.[10] Many of these are employed in the mining industry. A key activity of ICEM is negotiating and monitoring global agreements with multinational companies. Activities of ICEM include the promotion of workers' rights and standards for health, safety, and environmental protection. ICEM makes representations on workers' behalf to national authorities and international bodies.

The second body is the International Labour Organization (ILO), whose work on labour and social issues related to mining can be traced back 70 years to the Hours of Work (Coal Mines) Convention of 1931. Unique in the UN system because of its tripartite structure (government, employer, employee), the ILO has hosted the development of at least 19 international conventions on aspects of work place health and safety and fundamental work place rights. A recent example is the 1995 Safety and Health in Mines Convention, which has been ratified by 18 countries.[11] The ILO has also been involved in developing codes of practice and assisting national governments in implementing internationally agreed regulations on health and safety. Other areas of activity include industrial relations, employment, and small-scale mining.

A small number of ILO conventions deal with what are today recognized as 'fundamental rights'. Freedom of association and collective bargaining and freedom from discrimination and forced labour are among these. But the ILO has also developed a more specific role in relation to the mining industry through the non-binding ILO codes of practice for mining and topics relevant to mining.

Governments

Good governance includes the rule of law, effective state institutions, transparency, control of corruption, accountability in the management of public affairs, respect for human rights, and the participation of all citizens in decisions that affect their lives.[12] Governments need to be transparent, inclusive, coordinated for long-term planning, and able to act as stewards of the public interest. While there may be some debates about the most appropriate form, the need for good governance cannot be disputed.

The recent emphasis on foreign direct investment and private-sector development has not diminished the role of the state. Far from it. Governments today, from national to regional to local, are seen to be the central 'enabler' of national economic development, providing that they are transparent, efficient, and aimed at inducing growth. But weak states and institutions continue to be one of the major impediments of effective governance today and of attracting investment.

National Governments

National governments provide the overall framework of rules in which markets function and social processes take place, and they create favourable macroeconomic and political conditions for economic development. The needed conditions include, for example, a stable foundation of law based on equity, a non-distortionary policy environment, basic social services and

infrastructure, protection of the vulnerable, and protection of the environment.[13] The record of governments has thus far been mixed.

National governments play a pivotal role in the minerals sector and will be one of the most significant actors in managing the transition to sustainable development: not least because in most countries sub-surface mineral resources are owned by the state. Government is responsible for granting licences and permits, reviewing environmental and social impact assessments, planning for regional and local development, upholding environmental standards and health and safety standards, and investing and distributing revenues from mineral development to build social and human capital.[14] Normally, relevant ministries using the tools of policy, legislation, regulation, monitoring, and enforcement carry out these responsibilities. Governments also document geological information and communicate or promote it to potential investors.

In many areas of the world, however, governments lack the capacity to fulfil their duties due to scarce human and financial resources. In some cases, there is a lack of political will to meet these obligations or there is corruption, which inevitably means that the poorest peoples are excluded from sharing the potential benefits of mineral development. A further challenge arises where local goals and customs are not in alignment with stated national goals, especially where the latter have been forced into a cultural framework without adequate local consultation.

Where governments are weak or not trusted by people, there are frequently problems of credibility, which are aggravated where ministries assume multiple and potentially incompatible responsibilities. For example, a conflict of interest is seen where the same ministry is designated as manager of the sub-surface resource, promoter of mineral development, partner in some private-sector development projects at formerly state-owned mines (as occurs in a number of countries), and also regulator of environmental performance by companies. The lack of a credible institutional mechanism for demonstrating compliance with national laws, particularly environmental regulations, creates a difficult operational environment for miners with a high risk of confrontation with communities and civil society organizations. While the use of third parties to verify corporate performance may offer a short-term solution to this problem, the longer-term need is for policies, practices, and structures that create demonstrably good governance and the institutional credibility that benefits all parties.

Other Levels of Government

In some countries, such as Australia and Canada, the responsibilities just described are largely devolved to the level of the province or state. Elsewhere, it is more common that lower levels of government – regional, district, municipal, and so on – are responsible for aspects of the equitable distribution of wealth, infrastructure, environmental monitoring and enforcement, and regional and local land use and development planning.

The weakness and ineffectiveness of local governments in many countries in Africa, Asia, and Latin America can be partly explained by national economic weakness: effective local government is much more difficult without a stable and reasonably prosperous economy. Lack of resources and professional knowledge, as well as limited powers at the local level, are contributory factors. Since the late 1980s, there has been a growing recognition that the lack of democracy and accountability is a serious problem. In response, democratic reforms have been implemented at the local level in many countries. This shift in thinking from supporting government to improving governance has helped highlight the critical role of citizen groups and community organizations. It has also drawn attention to the need for a political, legal, and institutional framework that guarantees citizens civil and political rights and access to justice.

With the growing movement towards decentralization in many countries, local governments have an important role to play in the minerals sector. In some instances, they have succeeded without national support – for example, in the customary or locally approved exploitation of natural resources. Increasingly, they are assuming the responsibility for distributing revenues to local communities and for ensuring that minerals development is integrated into broader local planning. Invariably the ability of local government to perform these new roles is constrained by capacity deficits, confusion over the boundary of responsibility with central government, and lengthy bureaucratic procedures.

The Honourable Phumzile Mlambo-Ngcuka, Minister of Minerals & Energy of South Africa and Sir Robert Wilson, Chairman of Rio Tinto plc, Johannesburg, May 2001

Inter-governmental Institutions

In the minerals sector, inter-governmental or multilateral institutions have been most active in the areas of immediate relevance to security of investment, sovereign risk, and political risk assessment. The World Bank Group has been a significant player in the sector; it consists of the International Bank for Reconstruction and Development (IBRD)/ International Development Association (IDA), the International Finance Corporation (IFC), and the Multilateral Investment Guarantee Agency (MIGA), each of which plays a distinct and different role in the mining sector. IBRD/IDA provide lending and technical assistance to governments for mining sector development and reform as well as broader activities regarding environmental and social protection and overall macroeconomic management. The IFC provides loans and investment funds, while MIGA provides guarantees for specific private-sector mining operations. The World Bank is in the midst of an Extractive Industries Review to consider its role.

Other inter-governmental institutions involved with the sector include the Organisation for Economic Co-operation and Development (OECD), the UN regional economic commissions, the UN Environment Programme (UNEP), the UN Development Programme, the UN Conference on Trade and Development (UNCTAD), the World Trade Organization, the ILO, the UN High Commissioner for Refugees, and the Executive Office of the Secretary-General (through the Global Compact).

Each of these institutions has a specific role and varying capacities or resources to address issues related to the minerals sector. While many international organizations have been working to improve capacity in poor countries, their ability to help governments to do this is contingent on shrinking funds for official development assistance. Nevertheless, many of these institutions are today providing and convening important forums for debates, and are playing an increasingly active role in the development of voluntary measures. (See Table 3-3.)

Many regional governmental institutions are involved in mining sector activities. The Southern African Development Community, under its newly formed Trade, Finance, Industry and Investment Directorate, deals specifically with mining in terms of the

development and beneficiation of mineral resources consistent with broader policy objectives for the region.[15] Elsewhere, the Division of Natural Resources and Infrastructure at the Economic Commission for Latin America and the Caribbean has several mining-related programmes to determine the contribution of natural resources to sustainable development, for both large-scale and small-scale mining.[16]

Civil Society and NGOs

Civil society encompasses a wide array of organizations of different types, sizes, and functions, including not-for-profit NGOs, community-based organizations (CBOs), faith-based organizations, cooperatives, and

Table 3–3. Inter-governmental Initiatives Relevant to the Minerals Sector

Initiative	Description
Global Compact	Launched in 1999 by the Secretary-General of the UN, a commitment by a network of organizations from business, labour, and civil society to support a global set of principles for corporate social responsibility. Mechanisms for more specific sector-by-sector agreements are being explored.
Global Reporting Initiative (GRI)	Established in 1997 by the Coalition for Environmentally Responsible Economies (CERES) in partnership with UNEP to develop globally applicable guidelines through a multistakeholder process for reporting on economic, environmental, and social performance. The GRI is now developing specific guidelines for the mining sector.
ISO 14001	ISO 14001 is an internationally recognized environmental management system (EMS) standard developed by the International Organization for Standardization (ISO) in response to the 1992 Earth Summit. Approximately 30,000 companies in over 40 countries have received ISO 14001 certification and many as 300,000 companies have based their EMSs on the standard, without seeking certification.
OECD Guidelines for Multinational Enterprises	Adopted in 1976 with the objective of strengthening the basis of mutual confidence between enterprises and government authorities and promoting the economic, social, and environmental benefits of foreign direct investment and trade while minimizing the problems. A thorough review process was undertaken in 2000.
OECD Principles of Corporate Governance	Adopted in June 1999, the first multilateral effort to produce a common language of corporate governance. The principles are intended to assist both OECD and non-OECD governments evaluate and improve their own framework for corporate governance and to provide guidance and suggestions for stock exchanges, investors, corporations, and other parties that have a role in developing good corporate governance.
UNEP Declaration	The UNEP Declaration is a voluntary commitment to adopt improved sustainable production practices involving the continuous application of an integrated preventative strategy applied to processes, products, and services. In October 2000, the International Council on Metals and the Environment became a signatory to the UNEP Declaration. The Declaration is a set of high-level commitments that will need to be advanced with and through members of the International Council on Mining & Metals over time.

Source: www.unglobalcompact.org; www.un.org/esa/sustdev/viaprofiles/OECD_Guidelines.html; www.oecd.org/daf/investment/guidelines/mnetext.htm; www.iso.org; www.globalreporting.org; www.unep.org/Documents/Default.asp?DocumentID=174&ArticleID=2621

many more. Some employ thousands of people while others are run by one individual. They cover a multitude of issues and causes. NGOs and other indigenous and community organizations have become important actors in the mining sector in the past decade. In association with the media, they have become critical agents for stimulating greater corporate accountability through their power to influence public opinion and challenge government policies. Today, it is not enough for mining companies to win approval from national government for new developments: the acceptance of civil society is also necessary if the informal but all-important 'licence to operate' is to follow. This particularly applies to companies domiciled in the OECD.

The NGO movement is not homogeneous and it is misleading to talk of them as one group. It includes organizations that are global or regional, national, and local. Some NGOs have broad purposes (such as alleviation of poverty or wildlife conservation) and deal with the minerals sector only incidentally as it relates to these. Others are focused specifically on mining or even on particular mineral projects or mines. A few campaign against mining in a generic sense because of its reliance on finite resources, but most who are concerned concentrate on questions relating to the performance of specific operations or companies. A small but increasing number (such as the World Wide Fund for Nature, Conservation International, and Transparency International) work in partnership at times with industry to improve best practice, but many more prefer to campaign against corporations and to avoid working with them. Some address governments and inter-governmental institutions to argue for reform. Others work to ensure that communities and indigenous people have an effective voice. Judging from the experience of the MMSD regional processes, many NGOs are happy to engage in multistakeholder processes with industry and governments, provided that the rules of the game are clear.

NGOs concerned with this sector (or parts of it) have been attempting to develop a more unified policy. In November 2001, the Mineral Policy Center in Washington, DC, hosted an international meeting on Building a Global Mining Campaign. Participation from NGO representatives, activists, and community leaders was sought. The aim was to 'discuss the potential for a coordinated international campaign to

improve the mining industry's global performance on environmental, social, cultural and human rights issues'.[17] The intention was to develop collaboration for a campaign that would stop what participants considered to be ill-conceived or irresponsible mines.

Despite these moves, some of the dilemmas faced by NGOs will remain. Many owe their reputation and visible public identity to campaigns based on single issues. For some NGOs, making trade-offs among competing values is not a highly developed part of their agenda – at least not yet with respect to mining. (This also applies, of course, to other actors.) Many people who are not from NGOs (and some who are) raise issues concerning the accountability and transparency of NGOs. From the industry perspective, all too often the extent to which different NGOs represent different stakeholder groups is not known and is difficult to establish; who speaks for whom is a frequently heard question. It is clear that the level of internal democracy and participation in policy-making also varies dramatically. Many in the industry also question the capacity of NGOs to establish the facts of particular issue rather than to rely on secondary sources.

In reality, NGO constitutions vary. In some cases NGO leadership is elected by a broad base of members, who also participate in formulation of policy. In others, there is no membership, and leaders set any policies. Where the NGO raises funds from members, it tends to be more attuned to member priorities. Where most of the funding comes from a limited number of external sources, such as foundations or governments, there is often less accountability.[18]

Nevertheless, policies established by civil society organizations may have sufficient moral authority and public support in many regions of the world to serve as a standard for the behaviour of other organizations. Examples of this are Transparency International's principles of transparency and accountability, and the position statement on mining and associated activities in relation to protected areas produced by the IUCN World Commission on Protected Areas. (See Chapter 7.) No one can deny that NGOs are champions for change. Even the tracts that first established the very idea of sustainable development came from NGO sources.

Communities

Debates over sustainable development require equal and adequate representation of communities affected by mining. The success of a project requires an understanding of its location and social context. The involvement of civil society at the community level varies with the degree of political openness in a country. Many international and national commentators around development issues acknowledge the failure to engage local communities and affected people in development decisions and to give them the opportunity and authority to participate in the decision-making process. This issue is not confined to the minerals sector. But one of the key challenges facing it today is putting in place mechanisms to ensure that communities can effectively engage in decision-making on issues that affect them. (See Chapter 9.)

There is a great need to strengthen community-based organizations and their ability to represent their views effectively at all levels. In May 2001, partners of the former Minewatch, Partizans, and Minewatch Asia-Pacific met in London at a conference entitled Communities Addressing the Corporate Challenge: The Case of Mining. Co-funded by the Catholic Agency for Overseas Development and Christian Aid, the meeting provided a forum for discussion on the impacts of mining operations. Key issues addressed included codes of conduct for the mining industry, appropriate modes of dialogue between mining companies and communities, the role of central and local government, relationships between mineworkers and communities, and the impacts of mining on women and youth. Participants issued a London Declaration, which demanded a series of actions, including an end to all new large-scale mining projects in 'greenfield' areas of Asia, Africa, and Latin America. It also proposed that mining companies should accept complete responsibility for the impacts of their actions. The declaration called on international financing institutions to end the funding of industry-initiated mining codes.[19]

There is a potential for NGOs skilled in community development to work with various components of the mining sector. But that potential is as yet largely undeveloped. Either the sector itself will have to develop such skills or it will have to employ intermediaries in greater numbers.

Shareholders and Financial Institutions

Shareholders and financial institutions, including banks and insurance companies, all have a direct interest in the economic success of a mining venture. Of note is the range and number of mutual funds, pension funds, and similar collective investment vehicles holding shares in publicly traded mining companies. Indeed, part of the continuing consolidation in the industry is to create corporations of a size and character that appeal to managers of the larger, more influential funds.

Shareholder (equity) financing is normally the only source of funding for the junior companies involved in exploration. Expansionary junior and intermediate companies also rely heavily on equity financing to fund new operations or mine expansions.

Commercial banks are the main providers of debt financing to the minerals sector, the source of both project and corporate financing. Commercial banks provided the bulk of finance for 160 mining projects worth over US$50 billion between 1996 and 2001.[20] The multilateral financial institutions, such as the World Bank Group and the regional development banks, have a broader mandate than providing finance, but they do provide additional funds when commercial financial institutions are unwilling or unable to. This funding can also be very important in raising the level of confidence that a particular project enjoys, and can attract other sources of finance.

The World Bank has a set of detailed environmental and social guidelines for its lending activities to industry through the IFC and for insurance services offered through MIGA, as well as some specific policies on the mining sector. These are broadly applied by private lenders, export credit agencies, regional banks, and others even where no World Bank financing is involved. Banks make significant efforts to analyse risks, and many expect adherence to World Bank and International Finance Corporation guidelines as a minimum. In this respect, the standards of the multilateral banks (led by the World Bank) have become important global policy instruments. They have challenged the capacity of borrower countries to implement their requirements. Not all believe the standards are always applied, as some suggest that performance criteria for staff have tended to be related to approvals and disbursement targets rather than any sustainability criteria.[21]

Sustainable development is already of consequence to the financial institutions. In April 2001, a multistakeholder group came together in Washington for a conference hosted by MMSD, UNEP, and the World Bank Group entitled Finance, Mining and Sustainability. Key observations made during the plenary sessions included the fact that many banks and insurance companies consider a proven commitment to sustainable development by a company as a proxy for good management and hence better returns and lower risk.

Fund managers and individual investors are showing increased interest in making long-term investments in companies that are well managed and also environmentally and socially accountable. In this sense, shareholders can have a strong influence on corporate policy and behaviour. On the other hand, there is no evidence that a corporate commitment to sustainable development is of any consequence to the majority of equity investment decisions; those made seeking short-term capital gains from swings in the commodity cycles or the highly speculative junior exploration sector.

Consumers

In the context of mining and minerals, the term 'consumer' can be used to describe all users of products containing mineral commodities. This includes manufacturing companies of different sizes, service industries, and governments (through their purchase of goods) as well as private individuals.

The most influential consumers of minerals are large manufacturing companies. In terms of sustainable development, the activities of the manufacturing industry are significant in several regards: the quantity of minerals used in a product, the manner in which the product is used, the source of the components or raw materials, and to whom the product is sold. Decisions taken by leading manufacturing companies can be an important driver for change, as demonstrated in the forest products sector, though the same is yet to take place for mineral commodities. Due to the lack of interest of large metals consumers, there is currently no mechanism to pass increased social and environmental costs on to the final consumers.

Most consumers of mineral products (with the possible exception of fabricators of raw metal products) feel remote from mining and minerals processing companies. This separation between production and consumption is often a physical one, but it is also due to the complexity of many manufactured products, which may contain small quantities of many mineral commodities combined with other materials and distributed in hundreds of components. This disconnect between the producers and consumers of minerals poses serious challenges for the sector to move forward in a sustainable fashion. (See also Chapter 11.) In addition, individual consumers can also play a role in driving many low-value recycling initiatives, such as separating household waste.

Research Institutions

To meet the challenges of sustainable development, the minerals industry and others in the sector now more than ever need a steady supply of skilled professionals. The training of these professionals needs to adjust as mineral development becomes more complex and technical and as industry is asked to take on more responsibility for issues outside the usual training of mining engineers or metallurgists.[22]

A number of global research initiatives look more directly at issues relating to mining, minerals, and sustainable development. Institutions or networks are significant contributors to current knowledge of the sector. Among these are:

- *Centre for Energy, Petroleum and Mineral Law and Policy (CEPMLP)/Dundee* – This is one of the largest graduate and research institution in the field of natural resources law and policy. CEPMLP also hosts ENATRES, a global internet forum for energy and natural resources discussion, and an internet journal, which is a significant source of information.
- *Mineral Resources Forum (MRF)* – This is an internet-based system for coordination of work on the relationship between mining, minerals, and sustainable development. The aim is to bring together governments, inter-governmental entities, resource companies, other concerned organizations, and civil society for discussion and information exchange. The MRF was established as an initiative of UNCTAD in partnership with UNEP.[23]
- *Mining and Energy Research Network (MERN)* – This international collaborative research network, involving 140 research centres across the world, is based at the University of Warwick, UK. MERN's aim is to inform socially responsible decision-making in mining companies.

Endnotes

[1] MacDonald (2000).

[2] See McDonald (2000).

[3] This categorization is taken from Marshall (2001). For a detailed typology, see, for example, MacDonald (2000) or MacDonald (2002).

[4] MacDonald (2002).

[5] Ibid.

[6] Chamber of Mines of South Africa (2001).

[7] Greenhouse (2002).

[8] For detail of cases in Europe, for example, see ICFTU (2001).

[9] Presentation of Fred Higgs, Secretary General of ICEM, at the MMSD Workshop on Managing Mineral Wealth, London, 15-17 August 2001.

[10] International Federation of Chemical, Energy, Mine and General Workers Unions (ICEM) website, http://www.icem.org.

[11] Governments that ratify the convention commit to providing inspection services and the designation of a competent authority to monitor and regulate the various aspects of occupational health and safety in mines. The convention also sets out procedures for reporting and investigating disasters, accidents, and dangerous occurrences related to mines, and for compilation of the relevant statistics. Both workers' and employers' rights and responsibilities are set out. A non-binding recommendation that accompanies the convention provides more specific guidance on different sections of the convention.

[12] See, for example, Annan (2000) or World Bank (2001c).

[13] World Bank (1997).

[14] Eggert (2001).

[15] See SADC web page, http://www.sadc.int.

[16] See ECLAC, Division of Natural Resources and Infrastructure web page, http://www.eclac.cl/drni/.

[17] See Mineral Policy Center – Building a Mining Global Campaign web page, at

http://www.globalminingcampaign.com/index.html.

[18] Presentation on the Trans-national Civil Society Seminar, 2001, London School of Economics, London, 1-2 June.

[19] For the latest version of the London Declaration, see http://www.minesandcommunities.org. Christian Aid did not sign the declaration.

[20] From Mining Finance Database, published by Mining Finance Magazine (October 2001), as cited in UNEP/Standard Bank (2002).

[21] World Commission on Dams (2000).

[22] For details, see McDivitt (2002).

[23] See the Minerals Resource Forum web page, http://www.mineralresourcesforum.org.

THE NEED FOR AND AVAILABILITY OF MINERALS

The fulfilment of 'needs' is central to the definition of sustainable development. This chapter examines the ways in which different minerals can meet the needs of society or individuals. People benefit from using minerals and products made from them in a nearly infinite number of ways. In many cases the benefit is indirect, such as the power that operates a computer, and originates in burning coal or the spinning of a metal wind turbine.

People also benefit from the production of minerals - directly through jobs in mining, refining, or recycling, and indirectly through the incomes and livelihoods they derive from elaborating and selling products made in part with minerals. Any discussion of needs ends up being coupled with the question of availability: whether there are enough of some minerals physically available to continue to meet human needs and whether society will be able or willing to pay the economic, social, and environmental costs of obtaining them in usable form.

Growth in world population, together with improvements in standards of living in many countries and the development of new uses for minerals, has fuelled the pace of exploitation. This has in part been facilitated by advances in technology that allow lower-cost and more efficient extraction along with increased recycling. To balance the discussion of need, the second part of the chapter looks at availability.

The 'Need' for Minerals

One way to assess the need for minerals is to look at the benefits derived from the use of mineral products – from minerals used directly, such as zinc dietary supplements, to durable uses such as tools, bricks, and aeroplanes or non-mineral products that are made through the use of minerals (such as food produced using tractors, ploughs, and other equipment made with metal). Society today is highly dependent on mineral-related materials for energy generation and transmission, mobility and transportation, information and communication, food supply, health delivery, and countless other services. Minerals use and production is also essential in terms of the livelihoods provided through employment and income generation (see Chapter 3) and to a significant number of national economies (see Chapter 8).

The demand for mineral commodities is likely to rise with increases in population and real per capita income. Judging by the experience of industrial countries, rising income leads to increases in life expectancy and population. As development proceeds, education and health care are extended to women. For this and other reasons, the birth rate declines and population growth slows and eventually ceases. A similar trend might be expected in developing countries over the next 50-100 years. The global population in 2000 was 6.1 billion. This is projected to reach approximately 9.3 billion by 2050.[1] Most economists also believe that per capita income will rise over the next century. The difficult questions regarding the use of minerals are, how fast will income rise? How much of the growth will occur in developing countries, where the elasticity of demand for minerals is likely to be greater and focused on metals-intensive products, such as infrastructure? What are the implications for minerals and metals use of mass rural-to-urban migration?

Particularly in industrial countries, increases in demand caused by growth in population and income may in part be offset by increases in the efficiency with which mineral resources are used as a result of new technologies. Improved materials have led to reductions in the use of most mineral commodities in many applications, and the creation of new materials has led to substitution. However, increases in population and income, particularly in countries in metal-intensive phases of development, will undoubtedly have major ramifications for the demand for minerals and stimulate more efficient methods of production, use, and recycling.

If the present-day per capita use of aluminium and copper in the most industrialized countries were to be matched by the rest of the world, demand for these metals would more than quadruple. Even given that consumption data in industrial countries include mineral-related materials that are subsequently exported to developing countries, the mineral production required to support current levels of use uniformly would far exceed today's level.

Need as Demand

Even when the discussion is limited to the benefits of mineral use, there are different ways to look at need. A basic economics textbook definition of 'need' sees it as synonymous with the demand for a particular product. Individual consumers determine need by their choices in the market-place. If there are people willing to pay a price that provides an adequate return to a producer, the product is by definition 'needed'. In this view, the amount of any mineral that is needed is the amount that consumers will purchase at the prevailing price.

The problem with this strictly free-market approach is the notion that a desire plus ability to pay constitutes a need. Yet the fact that a market exists for something does not constitute adequate demonstration that a need exists for all purposes. One problem with equating need with demand is the unwillingness many have to say that someone who is obviously destitute does not need a commodity simply because he or she is unable to pay for it. From the perspective of the poorest, they may 'need' housing made from brick and concrete or a metal pot to cook in even if they cannot satisfy their demand.

Others are concerned about some having 'more than they need', consuming excessively, or the related idea that 'need' does not increase simply because demand does: demand is sensitive to consumer taste, fashion, and advertising (as seen in the current advertising campaign aimed at stimulating demand for gold). Moreover, in the absence of the 'needed' commodities, demand may be met in other ways. A free-market approach can lead to underconsumption by some and overconsumption by others because it is based on what people can afford rather than what they truly need. Finally, there are endless examples of things for which there are markets but that society prohibits, such as archaeological treasures, products made from endangered species, and chlorofluorocarbons.

The discussion of need can also be approached from an ethical perspective. This can be based on a concern that some do not have enough to live or the belief that modern consumer economies have a tendency to generate 'ever-greater and wasteful consumption'.[2] One way of addressing this is the eco-efficiency approach, which seeks increases in the ratio of economic benefits delivered by a good or service per unit of environmental impact and resource depletion. The concept of eco-sufficiency aims to ensure that there is 'enough for all' in terms of access to critical environmental resources.[3] Such a normative approach has its own difficulties, not least being who decides what is 'wasteful' and what is 'enough', and based on what criteria. (See Chapter 11.)

Any attempt to focus on what is 'wasteful' necessarily involves value judgements that will vary from one person to the next and from one region to another. For instance, is the Statue of Liberty an example of wasteful overconsumption of copper? The overall legitimacy of use is also sometimes in question. For example, some people argue that the use of gemstones for adornment is not 'needed' to meet basic human requirements or could be replaced by other materials. Similarly, some hold the view that the stockpiling of gold by central banks is subsidizing large-scale mining and environmental degradation.[4] (See Chapter 5.)

Basic Needs
Critical to any discussion of need is the goal of alleviating poverty. The Universal Declaration of Human Rights states that:

> Everyone has the right to a standard of living adequate for the health and well-being of himself and of his family, including food, clothing, housing and medical care and necessary social services, and the right to security in the event of unemployment, sickness, disability, widowhood, old age or other lack of livelihood in circumstances beyond his control.[5]

Although in many parts of the world these rights remain an aspiration, the minerals sector already plays a key role in achieving them through improving the lives of the poorest. Better access to clean water, better agricultural techniques, transportation to markets, electricity generation and transmission, and improved health care all rely on the availability of resources to buy mineral products or the services they provide. But access to these services depends on the ability of individuals and governments to pay.

Minerals can thus make an important contribution to realizing the various capital assets – natural, social, human, physical, and financial – that people draw on to build their livelihoods. Employment in the mining sector can also play an important role in providing a source of income or reducing seasonal vulnerability to joblessness.

Any attempt to calculate an individual's minimum need for mineral-related materials will ultimately involve value judgements, particularly with respect to the need for private goods. Many of the minerals that can improve the quality of life of individuals are found in communal or public goods and services, such as potable water and electricity delivery systems, public transportation and communication networks, improved health services and medical facilities, and better schools. So an ideal measure of whether basic needs are being satisfied might be made at a community level. In the meantime, as a proxy, statistics on national consumption per capita can be used to contrast countries at different levels of development. (See Chapter 3.)

Despite this important conception of the need for mineral-related materials, little research has been done to examine how much metal demand would increase if the world met some of the most basic needs of the poorest people.

Seeking a Balance Between Overconsumption and Meeting Basic Needs

The *1998 Human Development Report* from the UN Development Programme reveals that 86% of the money that goes towards personal consumption world-wide is spent by just 20% of the world's population. The wealthiest 20% also use 58% of total energy, have 74% of all telephone lines, and own 87% of all vehicles.[6] A balance has to be achieved between expanding minerals consumption in developing countries to meet basic needs for growing populations and expanding it to match current consumption levels in industrial countries. In the words of Gro Harlem Brundtland, 'It is simply impossible for the world as a whole to sustain a Western level of consumption for all. In fact if 7 billion people were to consume as much energy and resources as we do in the West today we would need 10 worlds not one to satisfy all our needs.'[7]

Some observers maintain that in order to achieve more equitable global patterns of minerals use without exceeding ecological limits, levels of use in industrial countries must be reduced. (See Chapter 11 for a discussion of resource efficiency concepts and targets.) But opinion is divided, and there are many counter-arguments and alternative solutions. For example, in terms of achieving more equitable patterns of use, there is no guarantee that limiting the consumption of the rich will necessarily enhance the consumption of the poor. Moreover, the notion of imposing limits on consumption raises ethical questions about individual freedoms as well as practical political concerns.

Furthermore, others argue that these concerns can in part be addressed by improvements in methods of production, refining, use, and recycling or by a reduction in materials use.

What is clear is that for levels of use to be optimal in terms of sustainable development, governments will need to use a package of voluntary and mandatory policy tools that take into account equity, efficiency, and environmental factors. These tools include market mechanisms, regulation, and educational campaigns. Mandatory approaches have been used to conserve scarce materials in wartime, for example, when national security was deemed to be at stake. But it is important to remember the role that markets can play in reconciling demand and supply. The real danger is when markets cannot adjust, either because they do not exist (for instance, for carbon in the atmosphere) or because they are distorted by bad policies, such as subsidies in various forms. Companies, too, will need to incorporate efficiency and other targets into their business strategies, and consumers will need to take some responsibility.[8] (See Chapter 11 for further discussion.)

Demand, Use, and Consumption

This discussion has focused more on needs met by using minerals than on needs met by producing them. In part this is because gauging the total economic benefits gained from livelihoods based on mining is even harder to determine than, say, statistics on recycling or the amount of different metals lost from use each year. It does appear that many of the key questions that sustainable development analysis might ask have not been research priorities. For example, a key question may be the elasticity of demand at very low income levels: if the world's poor had higher incomes, how would this affect demand for minerals? This has received much less attention than the behaviour of high-income consumers.

Figure 4–1 provides a simplified version of the production and use chain of aluminium. Some 573 million tonnes of aluminium have been produced since production of that metal started in the nineteenth century. There are no precise statistics on how much of that is still in use; it might be on the order of 400 million tonnes. About 25 million tonnes of aluminium enter the store of material in use each year – some from recycled materials, and some from new

Figure 4–1. Schematic of Aluminium Flows

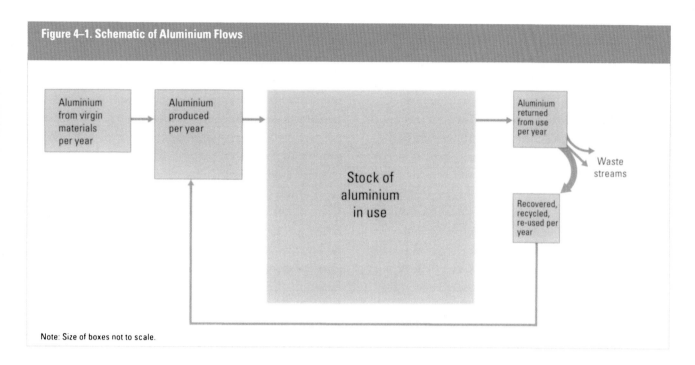

Note: Size of boxes not to scale.

production. An unknown amount of aluminium is retired from the stock in use each year, an uncertain part of which is recovered or recycled and the rest of which is lost. Some of what is 'lost' may stay out of use for a considerable time but still be potentially available for recovery if the price increases. Some is either truly lost or is too expensive to find and recover, such as ships on the ocean bottom.

Higher prices may create incentives to recover, recycle, or re-use a higher proportion of a material than that which is retired from the stock. Yet for materials such as coal, there is certainly no feasible way to recover and re-use them. This goes to the heart of the discussion about the sustainability of minerals use. Some commodities are in fact 'consumed' completely in use. But most of the gold, or copper, or aluminium ever produced is still in use and can – if materials efficiency and recycling are improved – remain so.

The Availability of Minerals

In terms of primary extraction, most minerals cannot be considered a renewable resource on any timescale of relevance to the human race.[9] Consequently, there is an extensive history of concern about minerals use and long-run availability.[10] For example, in the early 1950s the US President's Materials Policy Commission raised concern at the 'gargantuan and so far insatiable' appetite for materials and pointed to the security consequences of the depletion of domestic sources of

minerals.[11] This concern rose to a peak again in the strategic minerals debate of the late 1970s.

The debate really has three strands. One is that the world will physically 'run out' of minerals that can be located in deposits from which they are recoverable with current or reasonably foreseeable technology. A second is substitution: if society either 'runs out' physically or decides for any reason to curtail production, what would be used instead? And the third relates to cost of production: that even if there are still deposits available, the environmental, social, or financial costs of their extraction is prohibitive.

It was with the rise of environmental concern in the 1960s and 1970s that the dependence of industrial society on minerals began to be questioned, most notably in the 1972 *Limits to Growth* report. This concluded that 'if present growth trends in world population, industrialization, food production and resource depletion remain unchecked, the limits to growth will be reached sometime within the next hundred years'.[12] The first 'oil shock' of 1973-74 served to further focus public concerns on the possibility of running out of vital resources. The controversy has raged ever since, much of it negative, but it is worth noting that a major part of the thesis concerned ecosystem functions and limits, not resource scarcity. The *Limits to Growth* warned, for example, of the effects of increased carbon dioxide concentrations in the atmosphere due to human activities and the potential impact on climate. The same message is delivered today by the Intergovernmental Panel on Climate Change.[13]

Assessing the long-term availability of mineral commodities is complex and has divided opinion within academia and the mining industry for more than 30 years. The debate between those concerned about the depletion of mineral resources and those less worried about it is as relevant today as it was then. The pessimists, often scientists and engineers, are convinced that Earth simply lacks the resources to support the world's demand for mineral resources forever. They see mineral resources as a fixed stock that can be physically measured. The optimists, often economists, believe that with the help of market incentives, appropriate public policies, material substitution, recycling, and new technology, Earth can meet the world's needs far into the future. They rely on economic measures to assess availability, which reflect the opportunity costs of finding and producing mineral commodities. The best approach may be to try to combine these perspectives. Assessment of availability is further complicated when considered within the framework of sustainable development.

Physical Measures

Physical measurement is intuitively appealing. There are several approaches. At one extreme are calculations of the life expectancies of reserves (the quantities of a mineral commodity found in subsurface resources, which are both known and profitable to exploit with existing technology and prices). (See Table 4–1.) At the other extreme are calculations of the life expectancies of the whole resource base (all of a mineral commodity contained in Earth's crust). (See Table 4–2.) In between, and much easier to defend, are calculations of the life expectancies of various assessments of resources – that is, the reserves of a mineral commodity plus the quantity contained in deposits that are economic but as yet undiscovered or that are expected to become economic as a result of new technology or other developments within some foreseeable future. (See Figure 4–2.) Unfortunately, getting the correct assessment of resources is not straightforward. Reserves may be more usefully called 'working inventories', as they are subject to constant revision. For example, proven reserves of coal at the end of 1985 stood at 954 billion tonnes. Fifteen years later, despite significant extraction and consumption in the intervening years, reserves were calculated as 984 billion tonnes.[14]

Table 4–1. Life Expectancies of Identified Economic World Reserves, Selected Mineral Commodities

Mineral commodity[a]	1999 Reserves[b]	1997–99 average annual primary production[b]	Life expectancy in years, at three growth rates in primary production[c]			Average annual growth in production 1975–99 (%)
			0%	2%	5%	
Coal	987×10^9	4561.3×10^6	216	84	49	1.1
Crude Oil	1035×10^9	23.7×10^9	44	31	23	0.8
Natural Gas	5145×10^{12}	80.5×10^{12}	64	41	29	2.9
Aluminium	25×10^9	123.7×10^6	202	81	48	2.9
Copper	340×10^6	12.1×10^6	28	22	18	3.4
Iron	74×10^{12}	559.5×10^6	132	65	41	0.5
Lead	64×10^6	3070.0×10^3	21	17	14	−0.5
Nickel	46×10^6	1133.3×10^3	41	30	22	1.6
Silver	280×10^3	16.1×10^3	17	15	13	3.0
Tin	8×10^6	207.7×10^3	37	28	21	−0.5
Zinc	190×10^6	7753.3×10^3	25	20	16	1.9

[a] For metals other than aluminium, reserves are measured in terms of metal content. For aluminium, reserves are measured in terms of bauxite ore. [b] Reserves are measured in metric tonnes except for crude oil (in barrels), and natural gas (in cubic feet). [c] Life expectancy figures were calculated before reserve and average production data were rounded. As a result, the life expectancies shown in columns 4, 5, and 6 may deviate slightly from the life expectancies derived from the reserve data shown in column 2 and the annual primary production data shown in column 3.

Sources: Tilton (2002); US Bureau of Mines (1977); US Geological Survey (2000a); US Geological Survey (2000b)

Table 4–2. Life Expectancies of Resource Base, Selected Mineral Commodities

Mineral commodity[a]	Resource base (metric tonnes)[a]	1997–99 average annual primary production[b]	Life expectancy in years, at three growth rates in primary production			Average annual growth in production 1975–99 (%)[b]
			0%	2%	5%	
Coal[c]	n/a	4561.3 x 10^6	n/a	n/a	n/a	1.1
Crude Oil[c]	n/a	23.7 x 10^9	n/a	n/a	n/a	0.8
Natural Gas[c]	n/a	80.5 x 10^{12}	n/a	n/a	n/a	2.9
Aluminium	2.0 x 10^{18}	123.7 x 10^6	89.3 x 10^9	1065	444	2.9
Copper	1.5 x 10^{15}	12.1 x 10^6	124.3 x 10^6	736	313	3.4
Iron	1.4 x 10^{18}	559.5 x 10^6	2.5 x 10^9	886	373	0.5
Lead	290.0 x 10^{12}	3070.0 x 10^3	9.4 x 10^6	607	261	−0.5
Nickel	2.1 x 10^{12}	1133.3 x 10^3	1.8 x 10^6	526	229	1.6
Silver	1.8 x 10^{12}	16.1 x 10^3	111.8 x 10^6	731	311	3.0
Tin	40.8 x 10^{12}	207.7 x 10^3	196.5 x 10^6	759	322	−0.5
Zinc	2.2 x 10^{15}	7753.3 x 10^3	283.7 x 10^6	778	329	1.9

[a] The resource base for mineral commodity is calculated by multiplying its elemental abundance measured in grams per metric tonnes times the total weight (24 x 1018) in metric tonnes of Earth's crust. It reflects the quantity of that material found in the crust. [b] The figures for the 1997–99 average annual production and the annual percentage growth in production for 1975–99 are from Table 4–1 and the sources cited there. [c] Estimates of the resource base for coal, crude oil, and natural gas are not available. The US Geological Survey and other organizations do provide assessments of ultimate recoverable resources for oil, natural gas, and coal. While these are at times referred to as estimates of the resource base, they do not attempt to measure all the coal, oil, and natural gas found in Earth's crust. As a result, they are more appropriately considered as resource estimates rather than assessments of the resource base.

Sources: Table from Tilton (2002). The data on the resource base are based on information in Erickson (1973) pp.22–23 and in Lee and Yao (1970)

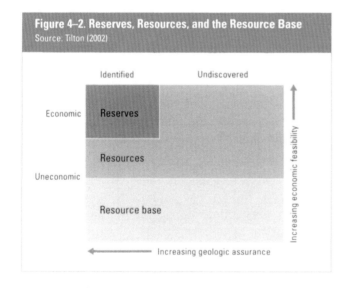

Figure 4–2. Reserves, Resources, and the Resource Base
Source: Tilton (2002)

Geologists classify elements as geochemically abundant or geochemically scarce. Eleven abundant elements, including three widely used metals – iron, aluminium, and magnesium – make up 99% of Earth's crust. The 90 or so known elements that account for the remainder may be regarded as geochemically scarce.[15] It would be easy to assume, therefore, that all elements in the first group are easy to produce whereas those in the second might be far more difficult. However, thanks to the geological processes that give rise to mineral formation, this is not always so. For example,

some of the scarcer elements, such as copper (number 28 in order of occurrence in Earth's crust), are found in large deposits at concentrations hundreds or even thousands of times greater than the crustal average.

The viability of the mining industry rests on the continued availability of minerals that have been naturally enriched by geochemical processes occurring in Earth's crust. Mineable ores of copper, zinc, and lead are all highly enriched compared with the crustal average. But a large proportion of the total mass of elements, including metals, found in Earth's crust are distributed as atomic substitutes in very low-grade minerals. The extraction and processing of these is rarely feasible. An intriguing question is, how much of the commercially important but geochemically scarce metals remains to be exploited from enriched minerals?

Copper provides a good example here. Globally, the average grade of copper ore currently mined is about 0.8%. Since, all other things being equal, higher grades are normally exploited first, the average ore grade has been falling and is expected to continue falling over time. However, geologists estimate that at some ore

Tinplate cans – crushed and ready for recycling

grade between 0.1% and 0.01% a 'mineralogical barrier' will be encountered.[16] Crossing this line could result in a staggering increase in the costs of producing copper, as different and much more energy-intensive processing techniques would need to be used. Moreover, the water required to mine copper from non-enriched crustal rock in quantities comparable to current US consumption using existing technologies would amount to something like five times the annual flow of the Mississippi River.[17] As a result, the recovery of copper from common crustal sources is currently economically and ecologically not viable.

Estimates of peak production of minerals from primary sources depend on numerous assumptions but often go well beyond the life expectancy of known reserves. For example, using certain assumptions about the role of technology, recycling, and substitution affecting copper demand and availability, it has been proposed that copper mine production will peak in about 50-60 years.[18] This contrasts with the estimate of 18-28 years for known copper reserves.

Economic Measures

Optimists point to four major problems with the fixed-stock paradigm and the estimates of long-term availability that it gives rise to. First, they argue that this approach ignores secondary production and recycling, and the fact that many mineral commodities are not destroyed after they are used. Recycling can significantly affect the rate of primary production, and hence of depletion. For example, the use of lead in the US grew by about 15% between 1970 and 1993-94.[19] Government policies regulating the recycling of car

batteries and the use of lead in paints and petrol, however, led to a fall in primary production over the same period as recycling and secondary production more than doubled.[20] But for most minerals, at least in the medium term, while the overall demand for mineral products continues to rise, the effect on primary production of increased recycling is likely to be minimal. Efforts to lower material intensity in product manufacture and design can also play a role in reducing the demand for primary extraction. (Keys to advances in recycling and materials intensity are discussed in Chapter 11.)

Second, reduction in the availability of one mineral commodity may lead to its replacement by another. Aluminium can replace copper in certain end-uses, for instance. Technologies may also be modified to accept substitutes for mineral-related materials. (See Chapters 2 and 5.) Nonetheless, the relative merits of substitution between minerals should be evaluated on a case-by-case basis, taking into account the implications for sustainable development. The same applies to situations where mineral commodities may be replaced by other materials.

Third, new sources of mineral commodities, such as from beneath Earth's crust (or, indeed, from space) may seem far-fetched today but are feasible and should certainly not be discounted.[21]

Fourth, the optimists point out, the fixed-stock paradigm ignores the critical role of new technology. New exploration technologies such as 3D seismics and hyper-spectral surveying have greatly increased the ability to find new supplies of minerals.[22] Moreover, it is conceivable that at some point in the future, new technology might allow the recovery of mineral commodities from very low-grade deposits, even deposits on the other side of the mineralogical barrier. On the other hand, it is also possible that new technology will not be sufficient to allow the complete exploitation of the lower-grade deposits still on this side of the mineralogical barrier. In this case, rising costs could eradicate demand long before the resource is entirely exploited. So the quantity of a mineral commodity yet to be exploited is largely irrelevant if the cost of extraction is prohibitively high. Economic depletion occurs before physical depletion becomes an issue.

For these reasons, proponents of the opportunity–cost approach favour an emphasis on economic measures of resource availability. Three such measures are widely recognized: the marginal costs of extraction and production, the market price of commodities, and user costs.

Marginal costs – the cost of producing one more unit of the commodity at various levels of output – focus on the production process and its impact on availability. In an important study published in 1963, H J Barnett and C Morse showed that despite considerable growth in the consumption of mineral commodities in the US, between 1870 and 1957 production costs fell by more than 75%. They attributed this dramatic reduction to the impacts of new technology, which allowed known, but previously uneconomic deposits to be exploited, permitted less scarce resources to be substituted for scarcer ones, and reduced the resources needed to produce final goods and services.[23] There were several criticisms of the study, including that it failed to consider inputs such as energy consumption in addition to labour and capital, that it ignored rising environmental costs, and that it chose 1957 as its cut-off point, whereas if the study had been extended it might have shown an increase in costs.[24] Despite these criticisms, the findings have proved robust and suggest the growing availability of mineral commodities over time.

Many mineral commodity prices in constant prices have also fallen over the past century. However, recent trends are more difficult to interpret. (See Chapter 2.) While some studies show prices continuing to fall and are optimistic about long-term mineral availability, others suggest that scarcity is now on the rise.[25] Despite the historical trend, it is unlikely that real prices can continue to decline indefinitely – so this trend will level off or possibly reverse at some stage. Reserves are sensitive to prices and to the amount of money spent on exploration. When prices have moved upwards, exploration spending has increased, and the amount of known mineral reserves has increased. Many parts of the world are still underexplored using the most modern methods.

The third economic measure is user costs – the present value of the future profits that a producer would lose as a result of increasing current output by one unit. The argument here is that the decline in future profits arises because increased production today leaves less or poorer-quality mineral deposits in the ground for future exploitation.[26] This measure under certain conditions reflects trends in the value of mineral resources in the ground. The relevant type of resources here are those that are currently just barely economic to exploit. The dearth of data on user costs makes it difficult to estimate this indicator over long periods, and the few existing studies have posted different findings. In any case, the impacts of new technology can make user costs irrelevant. For example, Sweden benefited greatly from the exploitation of its iron ore deposits to supply the European steel industry in the first half of the twentieth century. But the ability of these mines to compete was diminished by the technological leap in the 1960s that made the ocean transport of bulk commodities possible. Had Sweden decided to save these deposits in the hope of realizing higher profits in the future, it would likely not have benefited. In retrospect, the user costs of mining Swedish iron ore in the first half of the twentieth century were zero. More recently, technological breakthroughs (such as new leaching methods for copper, gold, and nickel) have changed the economics of some metals.

Despite the problems described, economic measures do permit two general conclusions. First, depletion has not resulted in scarcity of mineral commodities over the past century, despite the fact that demand for those commodities has never been higher. Second, long-term trends in availability are not fixed and can change in either direction. Just because mineral availability has increased in the past, there is no guarantee that it will continue to do so in the future. The underlying factors influencing mineral supply and demand, such as new technology and the rate of global economic growth, could change in ways that ultimately lead to economic scarcity.

Global versus Local Scarcity

The availability of minerals can also be considered in the geographical context of markets. For example, where commodities have high value per unit weight, such as gemstones and gold, they can be shipped anywhere and compete in global markets. At the other end of the spectrum are commodities with a low value-to-weight ratio, such as aggregates and sand. Transportation costs for these materials dictate they can only be sold in a local market. (See Box 4–1.) An intermediate range of materials (for example, limestone and some grades of coal) can be sold in broad regional markets but are not able to compete globally.

The metropolitan region of São Paulo is one of the fastest-growing urban areas in Brazil, with more than 17.5 million people spread over 8051 square kilometres. The metropolitan area is the country's largest consumer of gravel and sand. Between 1994 and 2000, the annual consumption of gravel in São Paulo increased from 11.8 million to 17.7 million tonnes. The region is also the country's biggest producer of gravel and sand, as it is home to 22% of national gravel reserves and 37% of the sand reserves.

Both gravel and sand are geologically available near the city. Almost all the gravel used in São Paulo is produced locally. But only about 25% of the sand is locally produced; the balance comes from sites over 100 kilometres away. This is because most of the potential reserves of gravel and sand in the metro area are no longer accessible due to urban growth. Uncontrolled expansion of housing allotments in outlying areas has resulted in land use conflicts and the shut-down of many gravel and sand quarries. The very high cost of importing gravel means that it cannot be brought in from far away, whereas the constraints on local aggregate production have made it economically viable to transport sand.

Source: Coelho (2001)

For goods sold in local markets, local scarcity may arise long before the mineral faces scarcity at the regional or global level.

Assessing Long-term Availability

The long-term availability of mineral commodities depends on the outcome of the competing forces of depletion and new technology. The rate of depletion depends on various factors, including geological and technological. Geological factors take into account the incidence and nature of mineral occurrences. The pattern of distribution will affect the rate of depletion; as depletion proceeds, lower grades of ore will be exploited. Whether the shift towards lower grades is smooth or not depends on the geochemistry of the mineral and the way in which advances in minerals processing technologies are adopted; high-pressure acid leaching (HPAL) is an example of this. If successful at the locations where it has so far been applied, HPAL could significantly change the economics of nickel recovery from certain tropical soils called laterites.

These soils contain the majority of known reserves of nickel in the world, but have not been susceptible to economic recovery until recently.

Alongside the exploitation of conventional terrestrial mineral reserves, it is important to consider other sources of minerals. It is conceivable that landfill sites may be important metal reserves in the future.[27] More knowledge about deposits that are presently uneconomic to exploit could provide useful insights on the future availability of mineral commodities.

Technology and input prices cover all the variables that affect the cost of producing mineral commodities other than geological considerations. The cost-reducing effects of new technology as well as changes in the prices of labour, capital, energy, and materials need to be taken into account. In the past, the effect of the latter on availability has been dwarfed by new technology; although this may happen again in the future, it is impossible to forecast it.

Recycling and other resource conservation measures may also reduce the need to extract minerals from the ground. The bleaker the prospects for primary production, the greater the likely role for recycling (for mineral commodities that can be recycled), and vice versa.

Conclusion

It is broadly agreed that the world is unlikely to face shortages of commercially important mineral commodities at a global level in the next half-century. The further projections go beyond that, the less certain the situation.

A key question, however, is whether it is somehow in society's interest to adopt policies to restrain or prohibit mining of some minerals because of concerns of physical scarcity. Answering this requires some consideration of how the benefits gained from the use of the mineral and metals or in terms of livelihoods can be replaced. Whether the substitute is another mineral or not, producing it will have environmental consequences.

The fixed-stock paradigm is not a sufficient basis for determining the availability of minerals: economic measures, as well as the possibility of local scarcity, must be taken into account when evaluating whether mineral resources will meet needs in the future. A vital consideration is the extent to which people are prepared to trust in new technologies to counterbalance the consequences of mineral depletion, however they may define it. Technologies affect not only the ability to gain access to mineral resources, but also new applications and substitutes for the services that minerals provide.

Although trends in minerals production and use and in the estimated resource base have reduced concerns that the world is 'running out' of minerals, the potential limits that environmental and social factors may place on mineral availability are receiving mounting attention. Developments that may limit the availability of minerals include:

• the availability of energy or the environmental effects of energy use as energy per unit output increases at lower ore grades;
• the availability of water for minerals production or the environmental impacts of using increasing amounts of water at lower ore grades;
• society's preference to use land for reasons other than mineral production, whether for biological diversity and pristine wilderness protection, cultural significance, or agriculture and food security;
• community intolerance of the impacts of the minerals industry;
• changing patterns of use; and
• ecosystem limits on the build-up of mineral products or by-products (especially metals) in the air, water, topsoil, or vegetation.

Even where concern is limited to physical factors, reduced availability can have environmental or social implications. For example, from an environmental perspective the extraction of lower-grade ores may result in an increased generation of waste. Increased scarcity may also require goods to be transported longer distances to markets, raising the environmental impacts of transportation. It may also mean mines are opened in sites that are less desirable from a social or environmental perspective. This may be particularly so where minerals are produced and sold in a local market.

Since mineral resources are non-renewable, an additional concern is the way in which the revenues gained from depletion are invested or used. These topics are at the very heart of the challenges of sustainable development and are discussed in Part III.

Endnotes

[1] Medium-variant projection of the Population Division, Department of Economic and Social Affairs, United Nations, at http://www.un.org/esa/population/demobase.
[2] This argument was put forward forcefully in Packard (1960).
[3] See, for example, Robins and Roberts (1996).
[4] Young (2000).
[5] United Nations (1948) Part 1 of Article 25.
[6] UNDP (1998) p.2.
[7] Brundtland (1994).
[8] See, for example, WBCSD (2001).
[9] This section draws heavily on Tilton (2002).
[10] The debate over resource availability can be traced back at least 200 years to the classical economists, such as Malthus, Ricardo, and Mill, though the past 30 years have been particularly active. See, for example, Meadows et al. (1972) and Meadows et al. (1992).
[11] See Packard (1960).
[12] Meadows et al. (1972).
[13] Houghton et al. (2001).
[14] British Petroleum (1986); British Petroleum (2001).
[15] Wedepohl (1995).
[16] Skinner (1976).
[17] Gordon et al. (1987).
[18] Ayres et al. (2001).
[19] The Interagency Working Group on Industrial Ecology, Material and Energy Flows as reproduced in Brown et al. (2000) p.14.
[20] See USGS, at http://minerals.usgs.gov/minerals/pubs/commodity/lead.
[21] Gertsch and Maryniak (1991).
[22] Gingerich et al. (2002).
[23] Barnett and Morse (1963).
[24] Cleveland (1991) pp.289–317; Johnson et al. (1980); Hall and Hall (1984).
[25] Slade (1982).
[26] User costs are also called Hotelling rent and scarcity rent; see Tilton (2002) Chapter 3.
[27] Ayres et al. (2001).

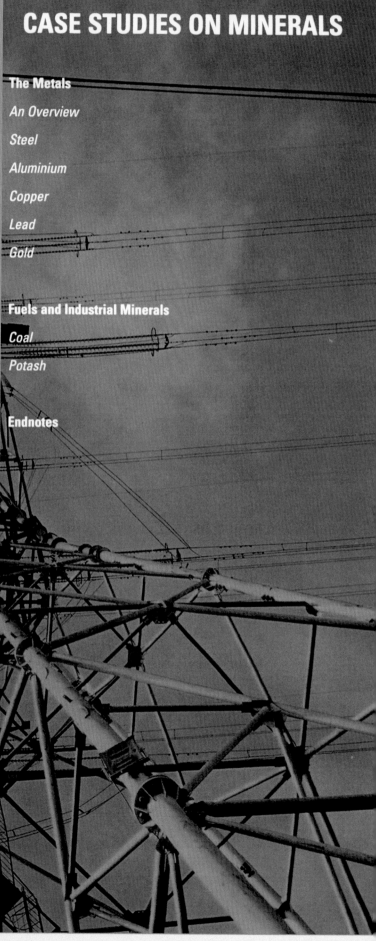

CHAPTER 5

CASE STUDIES ON MINERALS

The purpose of this chapter is to apply the general analysis developed in Chapter 4 to a range of individual minerals to see what conclusions can be drawn about need and availability. While it would be interesting and valuable to apply these methods to any mineral commodity, space and availability of data require a selection of a limited number from among the over 90 products commonly sold. While materials such as sand and gravel represent a high fraction of total mining activity, they tend to be sold in local markets, each with its own set of issues and concerns. It seemed appropriate therefore to select minerals of major economic importance that are traded in world markets.

Other minerals, such as zinc, limestone, or gemstones, would also have been very interesting. And a study of industrial clays had to be excluded for space reasons.[1] It was impossible to cover everything. The length of each section should not be taken as an indication of anything other than what is needed to express the issues and is not intended to favour or disfavour any commodity.

This includes most metals. The first section of this chapter therefore focuses on several metals, starting with an overview and then turning to specific studies of steel, aluminium, copper, lead, and gold. The second section treats a fuel mineral (coal) and an industrial mineral (potash).[2] Most of what can be said about physical availability was set out in Chapter 4, but environmental, social, and other constraints on availability will be touched on for each of these minerals.

The Metals

An Overview

By sheer volume, steel is by far the most important industrial metal. (See Table 5–1.) Steel consumption in 2000 was well over 30 times the consumption of aluminium, the second most widely used metal.[3]

Over the last 25 years, growth in demand for metals has been fastest in regions undergoing rapid development – the transition countries – which have a substantial demand for use in infrastructure, such as housing, water, and electricity supply. (See Figures 5–1 and 5–2.) The rapid growth of demand for lead in these regions reflects the growing demand for lead batteries, many of them for cars. Transition countries, in general, have a moderate level of industrialization and infrastructure, and are at the stage

Table 5–1. Production, Consumption, and Recycling of Metals					
	Steel	**Aluminium**	**Copper**	**Lead**	**Gold**
Cumulative total world production	32 billion tonnes of crude steel	573 million tonnes	409 million tonnes*	204 million tonnes*	128,000–140,000 tonnes
Recent annual world consumption	837 million tonnes	24.9 million tonnes	15.1 million tonnes	6.2 million tonnes	3948 tonnes
Consensus forecast for growth in consumption over next 10 years	0.8%	3%	2.9%	1.1%	4.3%
Share of total metal consumption derived from recycled material	US 79%, Western Europe 55%, East and SE Asia 52%, rest of western world 46%	North America 35%, Western Europe 31%, Asia 25%, world 29%	Western world 35%	US 70%, rest of western world 55%	Western world 35%

*World production from 1900–2000.
Source: CRU International; copper and lead production from USGS

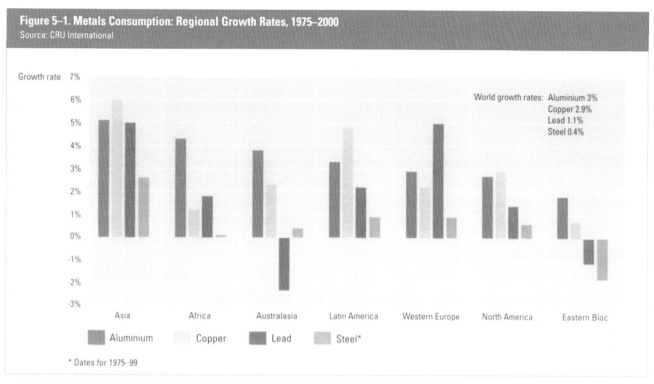

Figure 5–1. Metals Consumption: Regional Growth Rates, 1975–2000
Source: CRU International

World growth rates: Aluminium 3%
Copper 2.9%
Lead 1.1%
Steel 0.4%

Aluminium Copper Lead Steel*

* Dates for 1975–99

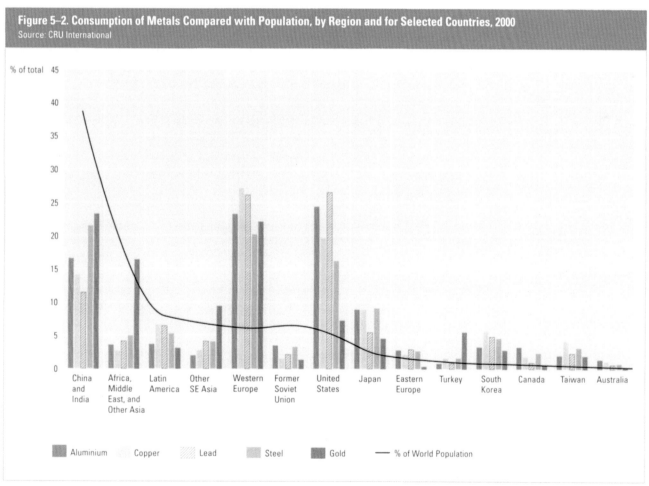

Figure 5–2. Consumption of Metals Compared with Population, by Region and for Selected Countries, 2000
Source: CRU International

Aluminium Copper Lead Steel Gold —— % of World Population

when faster growth in metal consumption can be expected. In industrial economies, demand for metals grew at rates below the world average over the last 25 years, since demand for infrastructure spending was lower.

The distribution of steel demand between the industrial and transition countries shows less disparity than in the case of the non-ferrous metals, reflecting the fact that steel is a basic industrial raw material that is essential even in the least developed countries.

Not surprisingly, given the use of metals in a wide variety of industrial and consumer applications (see Table 5–2 and Figure 5–3), there is a reasonably strong positive relationship between consumption per capita and gross domestic product (GDP) per capita. (See Chapter 2.) A significant distinction emerges between countries with per capita GDP above and below US$10,000. A large number of countries are clustered below this level, and almost all of them use less than 6 kilograms (kg) of aluminium, 5kg of copper, and 200kg of steel per capita. (See Table 5–3.) Above this cut-off point, consumption per capita rises quite rapidly because this appears to be the level at which substantial semi-fabricating industries develop to serve domestic demand as well as export markets.

It should be noted that statistics on metals use can be misleading. As consumption is measured by the

amount of metal produced and imported, it does not take account of whether products made from the metal are sold domestically or exported. Thus South Korea and Taiwan appear to have extraordinarily high metal consumption levels because they are heavily involved in metal manufacturing and are major exporters of metal products and lead batteries. Measured at the point of end-use, the real consumption of metals in these two countries would be much lower. At the same time, countries at the early stages of development do not use enough of the final product to justify local manufacture, so they import metal-intensive goods, which are not recorded in metal consumption statistics.

Recycling has an important role to play in the transitions towards sustainable development. In 2000, 15.6 million tonnes of aluminium scrap were recycled world-wide. The recycling rate is the percentage of

Table 5–2. Competing Metals or Materials in Some Large End-Use Applications

Industries	Competing metals/material
Transport: Motor vehicles	*Cast iron* and *steel* are used in the construction of motor vehicles. The need to reduce the weight of automobiles has led to the introduction of *aluminium* in engine parts and increasingly in body parts. Aluminium offers the same or better strength with lighter weight compared with steel, although the cost of aluminium per tonne (four or five times more than steel) is prohibitive. The steel industry has responded by demonstrating that cars can be built of steel and still achieve much of the weight savings associated with cars containing high proportions of aluminium. Other materials, such as *magnesium* and *engineering plastics,* are also competing for use in automotive components.
Aircraft frames	*Aluminium* won its first mass market when it was used as an alternative to *balsa-wood* in the manufacture of airframes.
Telecommunication: Cables	*Copper* lost part of this market to *optic fibres,* which are now used for new installations between major centres. Optic fibres are increasingly used in the branch connections, but copper remains the favoured material for the final connection to the end-user. *Mobile telephones* pose a new challenge, since no cabling is required.
Electrical transmission	*Aluminium* competes with *copper,* having won the market for overhead conductors. The lower resistivity of *copper,* however, makes it more effective as a conductor where space is restricted, hence its virtually unchallenged market for house wiring and power cables that are laid under ground.
Packaging	*Tinplate* was the first material to be used to make beer cans. *Aluminium* gradually made great inroads into this market, to the extent that tinplate was eliminated from this end-use in the US and to a large extent in Europe. This was a marketing triumph for the aluminium industry, which sold the concept that aluminium is recyclable (which is equally true of tinplate) and that aluminium cans are lighter and more convenient to the user. Recently, tinplate has recovered some market share, particularly in Europe. *PET* (a type of plastic) has gained market share for large containers because of convenience in use, but it cannot be conveniently recycled. *Glass* bottles can be re-used, and have traditional appeal in some countries. *Paper, plastic,* and *laminates* compete with aluminium foil in its packaging applications.

Table 5–2. Competing Metals or Materials in Some Large End-Use Applications (continued)

Industries	Competing metals/material
Construction:	
Roofing	Galvanized *steel* has always been seen as the simplest and cheapest form of metallic roofing or panelling for buildings. It tends to be replaced with better-looking or more technically efficient products as incomes rise. This market is heavily influenced by climate, tradition, and the skills of the local building trade. The selection of material depends in part on the willingness of the consumer to pay a higher price for a longer-lasting material. It also depends on the training and skill of the local building trade with each material. *Copper* is widely used in Germany and Central Europe, where snowfall is heavy. *Zinc* is traditionally favoured in France and Belgium, while the UK market prefers *lead*. Alternatives include *slate*, *tiles*, and *roofing felt*.
Window/door frames	*Aluminium* displaced *steel* and *wood* in window and door frames, but has more recently lost some market share to *plastic* window frames. The deciding factors are product design and the performance of the product when exposed to variations in temperature and climate.
Residential housing	Structural *steel* competes with *timber* in the construction of residential housing. There has been a campaign to promote steel-framed houses, especially in the US, but so far without any great success.
Heat transfer	*Aluminium* competes with copper in this sector and particularly in car radiators, where *aluminium* has been successfully promoted. Plastic plumbing tube has also taken some market share from *copper* and *brass*, chiefly on the basis of price.
Coins	*Copper alloy* coinage is threatened in some countries by *aluminium* and *zinc*, and more widely by the use of notes rather than coins. The use of *credit cards* in place of cash is also a form of substitution.
Batteries	*Lead* competes with other materials in the development of batteries for electrically powered automobiles. The lead-acid battery is bulky, has a limited capacity (and therefore range), and needs time to be recharged. Many alternative battery technologies for the motive force in electric cars are being considered, including: • solid oxide fuels cells, • hybrid fuel cell-battery combinations, • metal hydride batteries, • zinc-air batteries, and • lithium ion/polymer batteries. Fuel cells probably offer the most promising prospects, but none has yet achieved commercial acceptance compared with lead on any wide scale. Lead still dominates the market for conventional starting, lighting, and ignition batteries, the major market for lead.
Engineering	In engineering applications, the choice of materials is determined partly by tradition and familiarity, but also very much by production engineers who work on the selection of the most cost-effective and technically suitable material for components.

material becoming available for recycling each year that is recycled.

Recycling rates for building and transport applications range from 60% to 90% in various countries. The aluminium industry is working with automobile manufacturers to enable easier dismantling of aluminium components from cars in order to improve the sorting and recovery of aluminium. In 1997, over 4.4 million tonnes of scrap were used in the transport sector, and the use of aluminium in automobiles is increasing yearly.[4] The growth of packaging expected in South America, Europe, and Asia (especially China) may allow for growth in some parts of the scrap recycling industry. In the case of lead, 60–62% of refined lead production in the western world comes

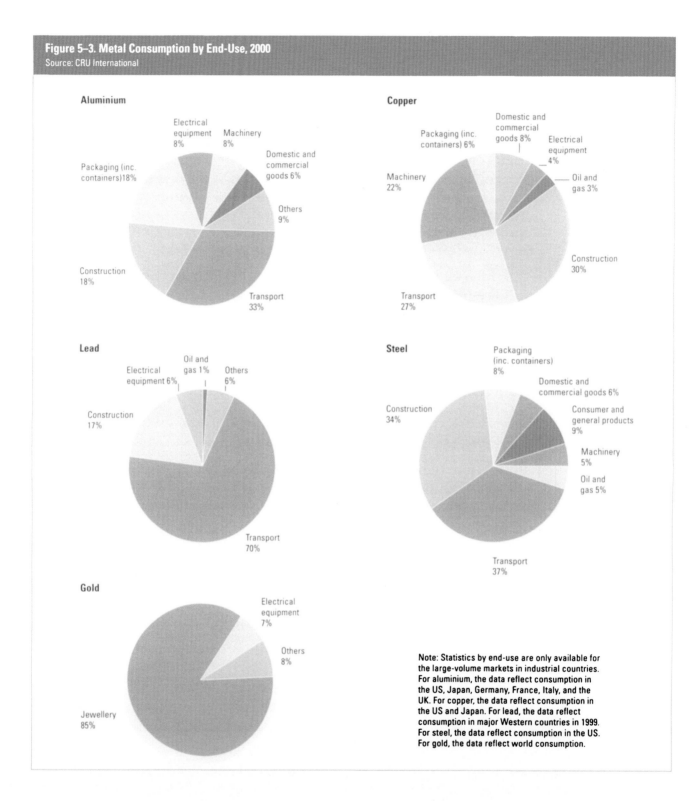

Figure 5–3. Metal Consumption by End-Use, 2000
Source: CRU International

Aluminium

Electrical equipment 8%
Machinery 8%
Domestic and commercial goods 6%
Packaging (inc. containers) 18%
Others 9%
Construction 18%
Transport 33%

Copper

Packaging (inc. containers) 6%
Domestic and commercial goods 8%
Electrical equipment 4%
Machinery 22%
Oil and gas 3%
Construction 30%
Transport 27%

Lead

Oil and gas 1%
Electrical equipment 6%
Others 6%
Construction 17%
Transport 70%

Steel

Packaging (inc. containers) 8%
Domestic and commercial goods 6%
Construction 34%
Consumer and general products 9%
Machinery 5%
Oil and gas 5%
Transport 37%

Gold

Electrical equipment 7%
Others 8%
Jewellery 85%

Note: Statistics by end-use are only available for the large-volume markets in industrial countries. For aluminium, the data reflect consumption in the US, Japan, Germany, France, Italy, and the UK. For copper, the data reflect consumption in the US and Japan. For lead, the data reflect consumption in major Western countries in 1999. For steel, the data reflect consumption in the US. For gold, the data reflect world consumption.

from recycled material. In the US, 90% of spent batteries are recycled. More than 50% of steel production in industrial nations comes from recycled materials.

Despite the rapid growth rates and large volumes consumed in Asia, especially China, on a per capita basis, most consumption still occurs in the most industrialized countries.[5] In 2000, these nations accounted for the majority of metals consumption, but only 14.6% of the world's population. Even for gold,

where it is often claimed that developing countries play a pivotal role as consumers of jewellery, per capita consumption in India is still far below that in the US or the UK. Jewellery consumption of gold ranged from 31.5 grams per capita in Dubai to 4.0 in Hong Kong, 1.5 in the US, 1.2 in the UK, 0.6 in India, and 0.1 in China. Total national consumption was 600 tonnes for India, the highest of any country reported, and 409 tonnes for the US, as against 26 for Hong Kong or 41 for Dubai.[6]

Table 5–3. Population and Consumption of Metals in Industrial and Transition Countries, Per Capita and as Share of Total Consumption, 2000

	% of World Population	Aluminium		Copper		Lead		Steel (1999)		Gold*	
		kg/head	% consumption	kg/head	% consumption	kg/head	% consumption	kg/head	% consumption	grams/head	% consumption
Industrial Countries											
United States	4.6	22.3	24.4	10.9	19.7	6.1	26.6	458.2	16.2	1.0	7.3
Canada	0.5	26.6	3.3	8.9	1.8	2.1	1.0	606.4	2.4	0.8	0.7
Western Europe	6.9	14.2	23.3	10	27.2	4	26.2	381.1	20.2	2.0	22.2
Japan	2.1	17.7	8.9	10.8	8.9	2.7	5.5	562.8	9.1	1.4	4.6
Australia	0.3	18.3	1.4	8.9	1.1	2.4	0.7	340.7	0.8	0.6	0.3
Average/Total	*14.6*	*17.8*	*61.5*	*10.3*	*58.8*	*4.4*	*60.1*	*438.4*	*48.8*	*1.5*	*35.2*
Transition Countries											
South Korea	0.8	17.6	3.3	18.4	5.7	6.6	4.9	756.8	4.6	2.3	2.9
Taiwan	0.4	22.8	2.0	28.6	4.2	6.7	2.4	1,112.30	3.2	3.5	2.0
Other S.E. Asia	7.8	1.1	2.0	0.9	2.8	0.6	4.2	68.4	4.1	0.8	9.5
Former Soviet Union	4.8	3.1	3.5	0.8	1.5	0.5	2.2	90	3.3	0.2	1.4
Turkey	1.1	3.3	0.8	3.7	1.6	0.9	0.9	188.8	1.6	3.3	5.6
Eastern Europe	1.8	6.5	2.8	3	2.1	1.8	3.0	193.5	2.7	0.1	0.4
Latin America	8.6	1.8	3.7	2	6.6	0.8	6.5	81.8	5.3	0.2	3.2
Average/Total	*25.2*	*3.1*	*18.3*	*2.5*	*24.6*	*1*	*24.2*	*128.4*	*24.7*	*0.6*	*24.9*
China and India	38.8	1.9	16.6	1	14.1	0.3	11.5	74.4	21.5	0.4	23.4
Africa, Middle East, and Other Asia	22.4	0.7	3.6	0.3	2.7	0.2	4.2	9.3	5	0.5	16.5

*Gold consumption refers to fabrication of gold only, and excludes any investment or hoarding demand.
Sources: United Nations, WBMS, IISI, CRU International

There is a consensus among forecasters that consumption of aluminium and copper will continue to grow at the historical rates of around 3%, at least over the next 5–10 years. The demand for lead is forecast to grow 1.1% annually in the next 5 years. Crude steel demand is expected to grow at between 1.8% and 2.1% per year.

Consensus forecasts are invariably based on history and a 'business as usual' approach to the future; they are often wrong. If transition and developing countries succeed in achieving a higher standard of living, barring some rather dramatic change such as development of alternatives to lead-based batteries, world consumption of lead could increase considerably. If 6 billion people in the world each consumed the 4.4kg per capita that is today typical in industrial

economies, world demand would be 26.4 million tonnes – over four times current world consumption. Renewable energy advocates have long suggested that countries without established power grids can electrify more effectively with decentralized generation based on wind or photovoltaics. This could create increased demand for batteries, which today are principally lead.

The appetite for steel in China has been driven by sustained investment in construction and infrastructure over the past decade. There remains an extremely large potential demand for cars and consumer goods among China's huge population. Increasing personal incomes and continuing investment in infrastructure could keep the total demand for steel on the rise in China for some time.

The economics of recycling is mentioned in many of the metals case studies. From a social perspective, the costs include the cost to society of acquiring landfill sites, operating them properly, and collecting and transporting material to them. In some cases this includes the costs of remediating environmental problems where disposal practices have proved inadequate. These costs are often not internalized in product prices or reflected adequately in the price of scrap materials. This has been an argument for government initiatives to encourage higher levels of recycling.

It should also be kept in mind that much recycling is done by individuals and small enterprises, or in countries where data are not well reported, and the data on their activities are often incomplete, making it very hard to define the precise rate of recycling.

Research has focused on the habits and preferences of consumers in the richest countries because that is where the biggest markets are. Little is known about what poor people use metals for – although in general terms it is clear that they have few metal products in comparison to other people. If their incomes rise, as sustainable development requires, it is hard to say what their priorities for spending those additional incomes might be, or what additional uses of metals or other minerals they would find most useful in improving their quality of life. This should be a high research priority.

Steel

The inherent qualities of steel are its strength and the ease with which it can be 'formed' or rolled into a wide variety of shapes and forms. The ability to protect steel against corrosion by zinc or tin coating has also extended the applications for steel extensively.

The mining of iron ore and the various other metals that are alloyed with steel, and the coal that is used in steel-making, together with transportation of these materials in enormous quantity and the fabrication of steel into final products, clearly makes steel the greatest direct and indirect employer of all the metals. It has been seen as a linchpin of industrialization of economies. Because modern techniques at many stages of the value chain are less labour intensive, declining employment in this industry in some regions is a major political issue, and steel has become a major focus of world trade concerns.

Steel consumption is intimately linked with overall economic development. It is, however, interesting to note that there is nothing to show that steel consumption would start to decline in industrial countries that are increasingly dependent on services rather than manufacturing. So far, it appears that steel is consumed at a marginal rate that does not decline very much with income.

In 1985 the Eastern bloc consumed 40% of the world steel total. (See Figure 5–4.) By 1995 this figure had fallen to 18%, a mark of the contrasting results achieved by the Communist and capitalist economic systems. Another major development in the world steel markets is the growth in Chinese steel consumption. This is a striking illustration of the relationship between economic development and the consumption of steel; China has become the world's largest steel-maker, something hard to imagine just a few decades ago.

Steel can be recycled easily in the same production facilities that are used to produce it from primary raw materials. The more complex steel alloys (such as stainless steel) are recycled within those alloy industries. The recycling of steel scrap plays a large and growing role in the production of steel. All steel scrap is potentially recyclable, and the main production processes depend heavily on the availability of scrap as a raw material.

In electric arc furnace (EAF) steel-making, scrap is the principal source of iron. Additional raw materials used in the EAF process are direct reduced iron/hot-briquetted iron (DRI/HBI) and pig iron. EAF steel-making has been growing as a percentage of total steel-making capacity and this is expected to continue. In many countries it has the advantages of lower capital and operating costs than blast furnaces and basic oxygen converters. The EAF process is also more environmentally acceptable.

The volume of scrap used per tonne of steel production varies from region to region, according to the penetration of the EAF process and the availability of DRI/HBI. Recent data show that in North America, 792kg of scrap were consumed per tonne of steel produced; in Western Europe, the figure was 554kg per tonne of crude steel; in East and Southeast Asia 523kg; and in other western countries 457kg. In other words, well over half the total raw material used in the production of crude steel in the western

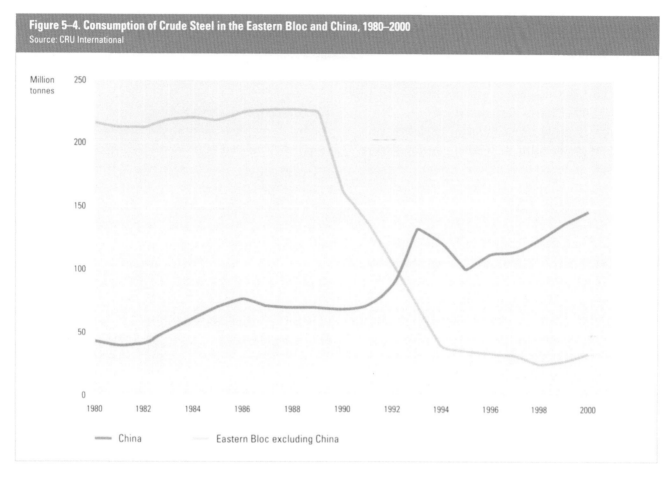

Figure 5–4. Consumption of Crude Steel in the Eastern Bloc and China, 1980–2000
Source: CRU International

world derives from scrap, and the share of scrap in total production is increasing. In Russia, China, and Eastern Europe, the figure is much lower because EAF production has so far made little progress.

Scrap is most intensively used where it is most plentiful. Transport costs constitute a major part of the delivered price, and the economics of EAF steel-making are considerably improved if the steel-maker has a good supply of local scrap. The largest sources of scrap tend to be major population centres and heavy manufacturing centres. Thus industrial economies tend to be the major generators of scrap, which is why the US has adopted EAF production most readily. Developing regions such as South and East Asia tend to have smaller quantities of obsolete scrap and therefore rely more on blast furnace production or on imports of scrap for EAF steel production.

Given the vital role of scrap in the steel-making industry and the importance of the trade in scrap to balance out local surpluses and deficits in scrap availability, governments should ensure that they do nothing that could hinder the free movement of scrap. In this regard, the provisions of the Basel Convention on the movement of hazardous waste need to be carefully

reviewed to ensure that they do not prevent steel scrap from being transported to where it can best be used.

Aluminium

Aluminium has only been produced commercially for 146 years and is still a young metal. Yet today more aluminium is produced than all other non-ferrous metals combined. There is comparatively little focus on the overconsumption of aluminium, other than consumer reaction to excessive packaging of products that is not being recovered and re-used. Relatively little is known about how people with very low incomes use aluminium, or which of their most pressing wants are unfulfilled.

Most aluminium is produced by a relatively small number of large companies; direct employment in the industry is fairly easy to determine simply by examining the payrolls of these companies. As with all minerals, the number of livelihoods that depend on this product indirectly is much harder to determine.

Production of aluminium and its ores is important to a number of national economies, such as India and Jamaica.

Aluminium's popularity is due to several specific characteristics:

- It has a high strength-to-weight ratio (which can be improved by alloying), which accounts for its use in aircraft and other forms of transport.
- Aluminium is an effective conductor of electricity.
- Aluminium can be formed by rolling down to sheet or foil with thickness of as little as 7 thousandths of a millimetre, so it can be extruded, cast, or drawn into a wide range of shapes.

Even so, there is no end-use for which aluminium is indispensable, though it is difficult to imagine another material making considerable inroads into aircraft frames. Aluminium has strong potential to be recycled in virtually all of its end-use applications, and its recycling networks and collection systems could provide a model for other large-volume metals. The volume that goes into dispersive uses – such as laminated lids of yoghurt cartons or fireworks displays – is comparatively small.

The big question surrounding the use and need for aluminium is a supply-side issue – the energy required to produce a tonne of primary aluminium (13,000–14,000 kWh). The energy requirement to recycle aluminium scrap is 5% of this. Clearly, from an energy efficiency perspective, it is best to meet growing demand with recycled material.

Community concerns at the mine site level certainly have occurred in the aluminium industry. A recent example is the Kashipur region of Orissa, India. But the most highly publicized areas of conflict over sustainable development values relate to energy use and the development of new smelters and the electrical capacity to run them, often through proposed hydroelectric development. Recent examples include the Karahnukar Hydro proposal in Iceland, a project in Orissa state in India, and a proposed project in the south of Chile.[7]

While this report is not intended to enter in depth into the climate debate, it is essential simply to note that the current concern about climate has and will focus attention on all forms of energy use, and primary aluminium smelting is a major energy user. Hydropower, especially in warm climates, may not be a carbon-neutral energy source, as found by the World Commission on Dams.[8]

The energy issue and the difference in energy consumption between primary and secondary sources drive much of the debate about aluminium to a focus on recycling.

The Recycling of Aluminium

Almost every aluminium product can be profitably recycled at the end of its useful life, without loss of metal quality or properties. In several countries, organizations have been set up specifically to promote aluminium recycling, particularly aluminium cans and foil. Many countries also have laws controlling packaging materials and recycling.

Aluminium recycling involves collecting scrap, separating it from other materials such as plastics or other metals, melting it, and casting it into a form that can be supplied as feed to a semi-fabricating process. There are two sources of aluminium scrap:

- New scrap is generated in the form of off-cuts, turnings, and saw chips in manufacturing processes. It is usually returned quickly to the supplier for reprocessing or is reprocessed by the company that generates the scrap.
- Post-consumer scrap arises when a product containing aluminium comes to the end of its life and is discarded or dismantled. This may take a few weeks (a beverage can), 10–15 years (a car), or 30–50 years (a building). Some products, notably foil and powder, are hard to recover once used.

To recycle aluminium, a collection system and reprocessing facilities are required. These will only be set up when there is a sufficient concentration of metal in use to generate scrap in large enough quantities to justify the investment. The rate of recycling for aluminium is therefore determined by the rate at which it is fabricated (in the case of new scrap) or products are discarded (in the case of old scrap). Since the use of the metal is growing, the pool of metal in use is constantly increasing, and most of this can potentially be recycled. (See Figure 5–5.)

There are major regional differences in the rate of recycling. In North America, as much as 35% of total aluminium consumption comes from secondary sources (mainly from beverage cans); in Western Europe, the figure is 31%, but in Asia it is only 25%.

In general, secondary consumption is lower in regions

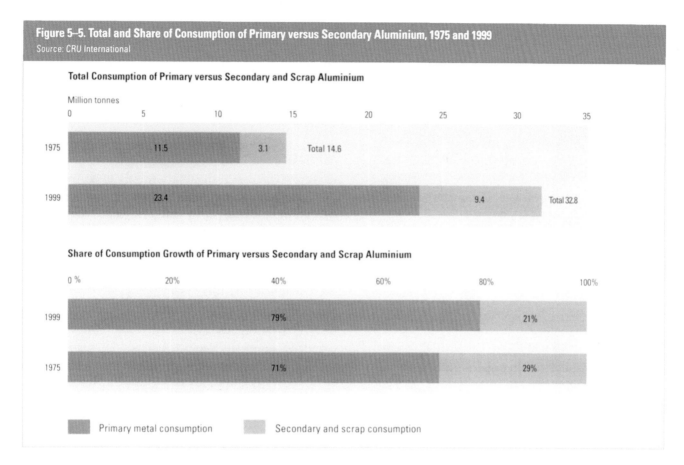

Figure 5–5. Total and Share of Consumption of Primary versus Secondary Aluminium, 1975 and 1999
Source: CRU International

Total Consumption of Primary versus Secondary and Scrap Aluminium

Million tonnes

1975: 11.5 | 3.1 — Total 14.6

1999: 23.4 | 9.4 — Total 32.8

Share of Consumption Growth of Primary versus Secondary and Scrap Aluminium

1999: 79% | 21%

1975: 71% | 29%

Primary metal consumption   Secondary and scrap consumption

where aluminium consumption has grown rapidly in recent years. Furthermore, when used to build power lines and buildings, aluminium is unlikely to return as scrap for many years. Where scrap collection is inefficient or non-existent, collection for secondary consumption remains low. Where metal consumption has been relatively high for many years, as in Western Europe or North America, and centres of consumption are more concentrated, the collection system is usually better developed. In the US, as much as 80% of the raw material used to produce can body stock consists of scrap; in Western Europe, the figure is 50%.[9]

The analysis of the economics of recycling indicates that there is a substantial (though variable) margin available to remunerate the scrap collecting chain. Companies that generate new aluminium scrap have an economic incentive to obtain cash for what would otherwise be a waste product, especially if the collection costs are small. For old scrap, the economics of collection is much more complex.

A key issue in the efficient recycling of aluminium is the way metal is used in many different alloys. Aluminium can be recycled into a more valuable product if it is sorted by alloy. It is not difficult to keep various alloys separate when it is new scrap that arises

in an industrial process. With old scrap, particularly that collected from the shredding of cars or household goods, separating the scrap by alloy is harder. While it is possible to separate the different metals contained in a car (steel, zinc, copper, and aluminium, for example), there has been no commercial process for separating the scrap by alloy. In the absence of such a process, scrap containing several different alloys can be recycled only as a foundry-grade alloy, a relatively low-value product. A recent development by Alcan Aluminium promises to make it possible to segregate shredded scrap by alloy and that others may also have developed such processes.[10]

Major Policy Issues in the Future of Aluminium Recycling
Many countries have legislation controlling packaging materials and recycling. Recycling rates are set in several states in the US for all drinks containers, while others require packaging materials to contain minimum proportions of recycled raw materials. Japan aims to recycle 70% of aluminium cans by 2000 and 80% by 2002.

The European Union Directive on Packaging and Waste requires that by 2001 member countries should have been recovering 50–60% of their used packaging, material recycling rates should have been 24–25%, and no material should be recycled at less than 15%. In practice, the aluminium can industry far exceeds these targets, though aluminium foil is recycled at generally very low rates.

Poor enforcement of regulation hinders the collection and recycling of scrap. Environmental controls are rightly imposed on the secondary smelting industry, which can cause serious pollution. But these are not effectively enforced everywhere, so the playing field is not level for those who comply. Where waste regulations do not adequately distinguish between material due for final disposal and raw material of the recycling industry, this can impose significant administrative costs.

Government intervention to increase recycling is often most effective if focused on the margin, where revenues are not quite an adequate incentive for commercial recycling. They can take different forms, from internalizing the cost of waste to producers and sellers, to instituting refundable deposits on products, and providing citizens with cheaper and more convenient collection centres.

Because of its vertical integration, and market incentives to recover material, aluminium is a fertile industry for development of more advanced concepts of product stewardship, and these do seem to be emerging.

Copper

Copper is one of the metals that has been in use longest. It has been an important material in the development of civilization because of its high ductility, malleability, thermal and electrical conductivity, and resistance to corrosion. Copper has become a major industrial metal, ranking third in quantity after steel and aluminium. Copper is very useful for power transmission and generation, building wiring, and telecommunications. It has a virtually unchallenged market for house wiring and underground power cables. The copper uses hardest to substitute may be motors and electronics. Investment in power generation and distribution and telephone systems has been a key driver of copper consumption.

As is the case with all minerals, little is known about the current uses made of copper by those in extreme poverty, or what needs they would meet with copper

products if their incomes allowed them to do so. It seems quite plausible to believe that their immediate demands might include electrification and use of more electronic products. Widespread electrification for the world's poor would undoubtedly result in increased demand for copper.

Whereas aluminium smelters often rely on hydropower, copper smelting is mostly done with pyrometallurgical techniques that can produce significant air emissions of sulphur oxides, arsenic, or other pollutants. This has long been a source of concern for local communities and other stakeholders, and increasingly stringent air quality regulations have been among the factors reducing copper smelting in places such as the US.[11] It has been an issue at smelters from Peru to Zambia.[12] Although much of the industry has made significant improvements in pollution control, and there are alternative extraction technologies gaining market share, this is still an area in which the copper industry faces a challenge to its operations worldwide.

There are two principal routes by which copper is recycled. Copper scrap free of alloying materials (including 'dirty' or contaminated alloy scrap) is refined in secondary smelters to produce pure refined copper (effectively equivalent to refined copper produced from ores and concentrates). Clean alloy scrap (of which brass scrap is a large component) is recycled by semi-fabricators into the same alloy. (See Figure 5–6.)

The supply of secondary copper is sensitive to the price of copper in the short term. Low metal prices lead to stockpiling of old scrap in the collection chain. New scrap is recycled regardless of the price. The collapse of the former Soviet Union has also had a major influence on scrap supply in Western Europe in the past decade, as large volumes of scrap were exported from Russia to Germany and other West European countries. In 2000, the Russian government took steps to restrict and finally stop this in order to retain the valuable raw material for Russian industry. The switch in Russian policy has made it harder to determine the total volume of copper recycled, since the direct use of scrap is not recorded or published in these.

While some secondary copper can be processed using some primary smelting technologies, the two are not always completely compatible. It is not always necessary to submit scrap to the full primary process.

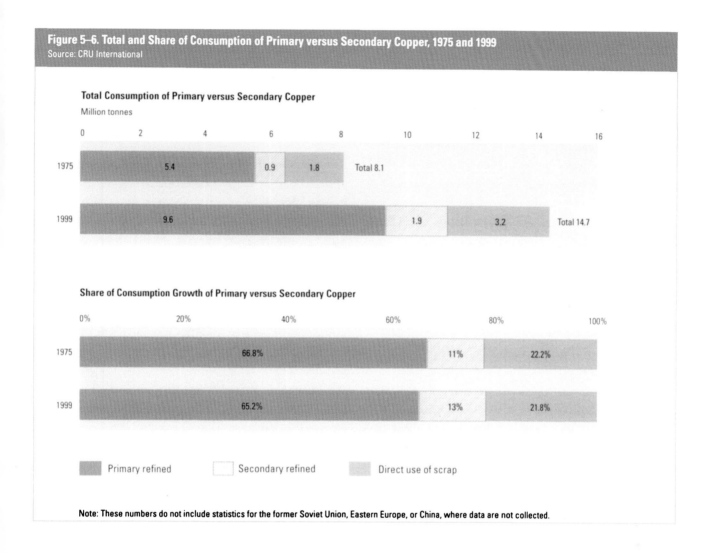

Figure 5–6. Total and Share of Consumption of Primary versus Secondary Copper, 1975 and 1999
Source: CRU International

Total Consumption of Primary versus Secondary Copper

Million tonnes

| 1975 | 5.4 | 0.9 | 1.8 | Total 8.1 |
| 1999 | 9.6 | 1.9 | 3.2 | Total 14.7 |

Share of Consumption Growth of Primary versus Secondary Copper

| 1975 | 66.8% | 11% | 22.2% |
| 1999 | 65.2% | 13% | 21.8% |

Primary refined   Secondary refined   Direct use of scrap

Note: These numbers do not include statistics for the former Soviet Union, Eastern Europe, or China, where data are not collected.

Secondary smelting costs vary according to the type of scrap purchased. High grade and pure scrap can be processed in an anode furnace and then electrolytically refined, whereas low-grade complex scrap must be smelted to produce blister copper first. In contrast to secondary smelting, the costs of the next step – refining – are less variable and directly comparable to the cost of refining primary copper.

The profitability of a secondary smelter depends largely on its ability to acquire scrap at attractive prices. Those that are able to extract other metals as well as copper (such as tin, zinc, or precious metals) may have an advantage.

The high intrinsic value of copper always ensures that old scrap has some value, unless it arises in very small quantities in locations far from any recycling facilities, or is contained in very low concentrations in other materials such as ferroalloys. New scrap is recycled promptly because it represents a ready source of cash for the plants in which it arises.

In general, copper and its alloys are easily recognized and therefore unlikely to be wasted when they become available for recycling. Very little copper is used in the form of powder or sulphate, which is dispersed and can never be recovered.

Legislation directing manufacturers to take responsibility for recycling their products at the end of their lives could increase the rate of recycling, particularly if it leads to changes in product design. Trade in some types of copper scrap may be affected by national regulations introduced as part of the Basel Convention. (See Chapter 11.)

Lead

Lead is a very corrosion-resistant, dense, ductile, and malleable blue-grey metal that has been used for at least 5000 years. In some countries, however, environmental and health issues have reduced or eliminated its use in cable sheathing, petrol additives, solder, shot, and pigments.

Lead has been used, for example, in the manufacture of water pipes since Roman times, but new piping is no longer made of this metal. In the 1960s and 1970s, there was also a market for lead in covering electric cables for insulation and for general protective purposes. Technological factors, together with the cost of lead, have caused this market to disappear except where cabling requires special protection (such as under water). Lead shot used for sporting purposes is now less popular since it has been recognized that it can accumulate on marsh lands and seashores, and can poison wildfowl and other birds that live alongside water. Lead solder has lost a market in the manufacture of food cans, because of the danger of contaminating the contents of the can. Lead was also widely used in paints, but this application has virtually ceased, at least in Europe and North America, where it is specifically banned for use in indoor applications.

The addition of tetraethyl lead to gasoline was standard in the 1960s and 1970s to improve the operation of combustion engines. This end-use has also been lost. The dispersal of lead particles in exhaust fumes is hazardous. And exhaust fumes are now cleaned to prevent other harmful emissions, through the use of catalysts containing platinum or palladium. Lead in petrol contaminates such catalysts, and was eliminated to enable them to work. (See Chapter 10.)

The result is that lead-acid batteries – the largest application in which there are to date no competitive substitutes – have become the most important end-use for this metal, accounting for about 75% of the consumption (in countries where this is measured and recorded). There are some other uses where lead may be a preferable alternative, such as radiation shielding.

Manufacturers of batteries buy refined lead and fabricate it directly into batteries for sale to car manufacturers (in the case of original equipment batteries) or the retail trade (replacement batteries). While there is some international trade in batteries and new cars containing batteries, there is less discrepancy between the location of reported consumption and the location of final consumption of the products containing lead than for other non-ferrous metals.

Demand for lead is closely linked to the demand for motor vehicles, which continues to grow world-wide. The use of lead in new and replacement batteries therefore continues to grow, and accounts for almost all

the growth in the use of lead. It was offset in the 1960s and 1970s by a gradual reduction in the size and weight of batteries required to provide starting, lighting, and ignition power for automobiles. But in the last two decades the average weight of a car battery has stabilized at about 10.5kg.[13]

The question of whether there is 'overconsumption' of lead by high-income consumers is tightly tied to the question of whether these same consumers are wastefully or excessively using motor vehicles, since lead for vehicle batteries is the dominant use of the product. It is beyond the scope of this study to consider any perverse subsidies for auto use, better and less damaging transportation alternatives, or the consequences of eventual widespread ownership of motorcars in densely populated countries like China and India.[14]

Whether there is 'underconsumption' of lead is also relatively straightforward, given its dominant role in electrical storage batteries. The question is the extent to which the ability to store electricity is a priority for people with very low incomes. (See Box 5–1.)

Box 5–1. Batteries for Decentralized Electrical Systems

In July 1997, the International Lead Zinc Research Organization, the Solar Energy Industries Association, and the Ministry of Energy and Mines of Peru signed a Memorandum of Understanding for the design and installation of pilot remote-area power supply hybrid systems to supply 24-hour electricity to remote communities. The systems incorporate solar energy, existing diesel gensets, advanced batteries to store and supply energy, and state-of-the-art power electronics.

The project, which is funded by industry and a variety of national and international governmental bodies, is due to be completed in June 2002. Its objective is to support sustainable development of rural communities in poor areas along the Amazon River in Peru, which now have little or no electricity, by providing electricity necessary to increase income-generating activities. The desired benefits include reduction in diesel fuel costs, reduction in environmental damage from exhaust and fuel spills in this environmentally sensitive area, availability of 24-hour electricity, and the enhancement of the quality of life and economic activities.

Source: ILZRO

While lead is hardly immune from the mine site, smelter, and refinery issues that are encountered in most mineral commodity chains, the most critical issues that will determine the future of this commodity have to do with lead in use, and concerns over whether it can be managed safely where it is used. The result of trends previously identified has been to limit the use of lead to applications where it can be collected and re-used or recycled without appreciable loss into the environment and where it cannot be reasonably replaced. Batteries have the advantage of being easily recycled, and provide a major source of raw materials for the lead smelting and refining industry. Dispersive uses of lead will over time be identified and prohibited. Use of the metal will be limited to applications where high and efficient rates of recovery, re-use, and recycling can be achieved.

Lead has the highest recycling rate of all industrial metals. Recycling and recovery rates for most materials in developing countries tend to be high. If dispersive uses are eliminated, as most countries are doing with leaded gasoline, most lead in use could be recovered and recycled.

Lead recycling has become an efficient but not highly profitable operation in most industrial countries. Lead is a co-product of a number of other metals, such as zinc. It is therefore inevitably produced as these minerals are mined and processed, and this availability of lead from primary production at low cost is likely to continue to limit the price of recovered or secondary lead.

Since batteries account for a high proportion of total lead use, they constitute an easily identifiable source of scrap. However, they arise not in large volumes but one by one, in the hands of individual motorists. In many countries, there is now legislation (in some form) requiring or encouraging spent batteries to be collected and re-processed. In the US, for example, people who buy a replacement battery either receive a discount for returning spent batteries or pay an extra deposit. The inherent value of lead in battery scrap is not great, however, and in the absence of other incentives, spent batteries may just be thrown away. There is a good case for creating or strengthening incentives for the individual motorist to return spent batteries, both to avoid land disposal of a potentially hazardous material and to reduce the need for primary lead production.

Many battery producers organize their own collection systems for spent batteries through garages and other retail outlets. They then have the batteries smelted back into lead by a secondary smelter. Thus battery producers are in a sense competing with the scrap collecting industry. The result is that a high proportion of spent batteries are collected and reprocessed.

Battery scrap is a valuable resource to the battery manufacturer since it arises locally and can be converted into refined metal easily. Some battery companies operate their own secondary smelting plants for this purpose.

Secondary smelting is carried out principally in dedicated secondary smelters, but some smelters, mainly in Europe, take a mixture of primary and secondary feed. There is no shortage of secondary smelting capacity, and none is expected to arise in the medium term. Some lead products, such as old lead sheet, are recycled without being smelted. They can be remelted and re-used directly.

Basel Convention regulations are a potential obstacle to the recycling of lead. (See Chapter 11.) Its objective is to prevent the movement of hazardous waste across national borders in order to prevent dumping in countries where environmental controls are weak or poorly enforced. However, it can prevent the movement of scrap, such as used batteries, that is potentially hazardous but is also a valuable resource for the recycling industry.

Gold

Gold is notable for its versatility. It is malleable and ductile, an excellent conductor of heat and electricity, immune to tarnish, and resistant to all but the strongest acids. These properties make gold very useful in a variety of industrial applications, though it is used sparingly because of its cost. It also has a role that none of the other minerals studied in this chapter performs: it is the most important mineral to be used as a store of value. Until recently, it backed most of the world's principal currencies, and it is still held as a reserve asset by many central banks. It remains the preferred store of individual wealth in many parts of the world. It is highly prized for ornament, and by far its largest current use is for jewellery, some of which has the dual purpose of ornamentation and a form of savings.

In recent years the annual demand for gold has been

around 4000 tonnes per year. Jewellery is the main driver, constituting 80% of total demand in 2000.[15] Gold has a variety of other applications, including electronics, dentistry, decorating materials such as glassware and ceramics, medals, and coins. Taken as a whole, non-jewellery use of gold has been relatively stagnant over the last 10 years, though some individual uses such as electronics have shown considerable growth. Given the cost of gold, this indicates these uses have no easy substitutes. But gold faces intense competition in almost all markets.

Use of gold for jewellery has been volatile for two main reasons – income sensitivity in industrial markets and price sensitivity in developing countries. Developing countries now constitute about two-thirds of world demand for jewellery, with about a fifth of this in the Indian subcontinent alone, where gold jewellery is of great cultural significance.[16] In a considerable part of South Asia and the Middle East, gold jewellery (and to a lesser extent bars and coins) serve as bridal dowries and a store of value.

Gold is scarce, with a very low abundance in Earth's crust.[17] In physical terms, annual production is only a fraction of most other metals. In 2000, mine production amounted to 2574 tonnes, which represented 65% of total gold consumption. Its value is sufficient that other incentives are not needed for recycling. It is certainly more highly recycled than any of the other metals considered in this study. (See Box 5–2.) Gold production has been increasing slowly over the last few decades. In the last 6000 years, over 140,000 tonnes of above ground stocks have been accumulated.[18]

Box 5–2. Why Gold Is So Interesting

MMSD received many comments on gold during the preparation of this report. There are objective reasons for this level of attention – gold issues are somewhat different than those of other metals:

- *Many livelihoods depend on gold production* – Gold often occurs in forms that can readily be identified and produced. It therefore supports many of the world's 12–15 million artisanal miners and their dependents. It also supports a disproportionate share of the employment-intensive small and medium-scale industry. Even at the large end of industry, the top 15 gold companies directly employed some 200,000 people in 1999–2000.

- *Exploration activity is concentrated heavily on gold* – In the recent peak of 1997, US$5.1 billion was spent on gold exploration, compared with base metal exploration of well under US$2 billion. To the extent communities are disturbed by exploration, the chances are good that it may be for gold.
- *There are public NGO campaigns directed specifically at gold* – Some NGOs are actively campaigning on gold-related concerns: Goldbusters, for instance, 'aims to depress the price of gold by asking governments and individuals to divest of gold investments and consumers to no longer purchase gold jewelry'. There is little parallel in the case of other commodities. There are also major public campaigns, sometimes successful, for legislation to prohibit the use of cyanide in gold mining.
- *Gold is a store of value with a continued role in the monetary system* – The US dollar is the world's principal reserve currency. The US, the world's largest gold owner, holds about 60% of its foreign reserves in gold. Many others hold substantial reserves in gold. It also is important for individual savings in many countries. Other metals do not have these functions or the controversies that go with it. Some eminent authorities expect its reserve role to continue.
- *Several highly publicized negative incidents have occurred in the gold industry* – Gold mining has had a significant share of the bad publicity received by industry in recent years.

In Tanzania, where gold exports rose from US $200,000 in 1982 to $120 million in 2000, President Mkapa noted that they 'made a deliberate and a conscious decision to make mining an engine of growth. Tanzania today is where South Africa was at the beginning of the last century.' But not all have the same view: the draft MMSD Report was criticized by Professor Philip Crowson of the University of Dundee because it 'implies that the present price of gold is somehow "right" and that development of new gold mines in developing countries should not be prejudiced. Is that really the view? To keep minerals of any type in above-ground stocks when there is no further use for them is perverse and certainly not sustainable.'

This report is not intended to be 'pro' or 'anti' gold but an attempt to reflect in as balanced a way as possible what was an exceedingly complex and passionate debate long before the MMSD Project came on the scene.

Source: Exploration expenditures from Otto (2002); Mkapa quote from Mkapa (2001); campaign quote from http://csf.colorado.edu/bioregional/apr99/0015.html

The metal is readily identifiable and rarely found in forms other than its elemental state. In some cases it occurs as free gold in veins, nuggets, or visible flakes. Since these can be used without complex recovery techniques or metallurgical processes, gold is one of the minerals that has been in use the longest.

This susceptibility to simple techniques of recovery means that production can be considerably simpler than the other minerals studied, with the possible exception of coal. While there are large gold mines, gold is mined in more individual locations and often at a much smaller scale of enterprise than is the case with iron ore or most of the base metals. As the mining industry has concentrated into a smaller number of larger enterprises, gold and coal remained among the bastions of the small and medium producer.

Gold Production as a Source of Livelihoods

After steel, aluminium, and copper, gold has the fourth highest value in terms of world metals production. It may well, however, be responsible for far more than its relative share of total mining employment. An estimated 12–15 million artisanal miners in the world support several times that number of family members. Though it is difficult to estimate the fraction of these millions of people engaged in gold mining, it is clearly very significant. It is estimated that perhaps 20% of total world gold production comes from artisanal and small-scale mining. In many countries where this is an important source of employment, the sector accounts for the majority of gold production.

Even in the formal sector, gold supports a large number of small companies. A high proportion of the well-known Canadian and Australian junior companies are in gold, which collectively employ a considerable number of people; small and medium-sized companies are frequently found in almost all gold mining regions. Even in the large end of the industry, gold is a major employer. The top 15 gold-producing companies in 1999 and 2000 employed approximately 250,000 people. (See Table 5–4.)

According to the World Gold Council, gold accounts for a significant proportion – ranging from 5% to nearly 40% – of the exports of many heavily indebted poor countries.

Gold has been central to the development of South Africa, though declines in gold employment in this industry in recent years have been a difficult problem to manage. (See Box 5–3.) In many countries where gold mining is currently important, there are at present limited options for alternative industrial activities to support economic development.

Table 5–4. Output of Top 15 Gold-Producing Companies, 1999 and 2000

	Company	Base	1999 (tonnes)	2000 (tonnes)	Employment (2000)
1	AngloGold	South Africa	215.2	225.3	77,600
2	Newmont	US	130.0	153.7	10,800
3	Gold Fields Ltd	South Africa	118.7	121.2	55,000
4	Barrick	Canada	113.8	116.4	5,500
5	Placer Dome	Canada	97.9	92.8	12,000
6	Rio Tinto	UK	92.9	84.9	5,100[a]
7	Homestake	US	74.3	68.6	na
8	Harmony	South Africa	41.4	66.8	42,600
9	Normandy	Australia	58.8	64.5	na
10	Freeport McMoran	US	74.0	59.1	7,800[b]
11	Ashanti Goldfields	Ghana	48.6	54.0	10,400
12	Durban Roodepoort	South Africa	27.7	35.7	19,111
13	Kinross	Canada	31.3	29.4	1,600
14	Buenaventura	Peru	23.6	28.5	1,800[c]
15	Newcrest	Australia	26.3	27.9	na

[a]Number of employees in Rio Tinto's gold mining interests in Kennecott Minerals (US), Kelian (Indonesia), Lihir (Papua New Guinea), Morro do Ouro (Brazil), Peak (Australia), and Rio Tinto (Zimbabwe). [b]Includes employees from the company's copper production. [c]Includes employees from the company's silver and other precious metals production.
Source: Gold Fields Mineral Services (2001); company annual reports

South Africa is the world's leading gold producer, providing nearly 17% of all newly mined gold in 2000. Its share of the total has shrunk dramatically, however, from a peak of more than 70% in the 1960s and 1970s as other producers have grown in importance and its output has fallen.

In 2000, South African gold production fell for the seventh consecutive year, dropping by 21.2 tonnes, or 4.7% from its 1999 level, to reach 428.3 tonnes. Production levels have suffered as ore grades have fallen and lower gold prices have forced the closure of less payable or profitable areas. South Africa still has more than a third of known global reserves, but much of the more accessible gold has been mined, leaving reserves that are deeper, of lower grade, and more expensive to extract, though change in operations and the exchange rate have kept many South African producers competitive. The fall in the price of gold has had a severe impact on South Africa's gold mining industry. There has been substantial restructuring, involving both company mergers and massive cuts in employment.

Employment in the gold industry has fallen drastically over the past decade, and today the mines account for just 2% of the registered labour force. From more than a half-million in the late 1980s, the number employed fell to 257,000 (including 130,000 non-South Africans) in 1998. Gold exports fell from US$6.3 billion in 1994 to an estimated US$4.4 billion in 1998. Because of gold mining's links with other sectors, however, it is estimated that for every three people working in a mine, another person is employed by industries that serve mining. In addition, on average each worker in the gold industry supports 7–10 dependents.

Source: Gold Fields Mineral Services Ltd (2001); CRU International (2001); Chamber of Mines of South Africa, personal communication (2001)

Gold may also be disproportionately important at the exploration stage. Certainly, artisanal and small-scale prospectors have been over a good part of Earth's surface. So have junior exploration companies and others with more sophisticated techniques. The western world has been spending several billion dollars per year on gold exploration – substantially more than is spent looking for copper, zinc, and nickel combined.[19]

Overconsumption of Gold?

As with all minerals, there are arguments that current levels of consumption by some consumers are excessive. In part, this is the perception that jewellery – at least in industrial countries with effective savings alternatives to holding gold – is a non-utilitarian end, despite the seemingly universal human desire to be decorated and to decorate possessions. They argue this purpose could be served by other materials that have less environmental and social impact from production.[20] They believe that people have a duty to be responsible consumers in the interest of sustainable development, and that high levels of personal gold consumption are inconsistent with that objective.

Those who feel that consumers should prefer other materials have just as much right to make that argument as the World Gold Council has to convince consumers to use more gold, though they may have fewer resources at their disposal. In May 2001, the World Gold Council, an industry-sponsored organization, launched a US$55-million campaign to 'remind consumers that gold's intrinsic value extends beyond fashionability, leading it to be revered by almost every culture for its radiance, beauty and spiritual richness'.[21] Independent of the World Gold Council, the Gold Marketing Initiative is asking gold companies producing more than 100,000 ounces a year eventually to contribute US$4 per ounce of annual production to gold promotion.[22] Since no nation seems ready to adopt eco-efficiency policies to restrain gold consumption, the jury in this case will be the world's consumers.

The other argument, which has long raged among economists without any sign of abating, is whether gold should continue to be used to back world currencies or whether this role is outmoded, with gold now a 'barbarous relic.' It is not hard to see how some have agreed with British economist John Maynard Keynes, who said 'the form of digging holes in the ground known as gold mining…not only adds nothing to the real wealth of the world but involves the disutility of labour'.[23] (Even Keynes, however, acknowledged gold had 'played its part in progress' and was an effective means of generating employment.) For Keynes, it is intuitively odd that so much human labour and capital goes into producing a product that is then often kept underground in vaults where no one does anything with it. Yet eminent economists argue that gold will have a continued role as a reserve asset 'for a long time to come'.[24]

Underconsumption of Gold?

How, besides providing livelihoods, can gold help meet

the needs of the world's poor? As in the case of lead, there is a single dominant use. Although there may be other ways in which the needs of the poor could be met by access to gold-containing products, there is one use that is most important simply in terms of quantity: gold in jewellery (and some other forms) is the store of value that in many societies has long been the principal hedge against currency depreciation for those without access to other reliable means of saving. Quite simply, if the poor had enough income enhancement to be able to save, they might very likely save in the form of gold.

This, however, can create problems for broader economic development. If these savings are not banked, they cannot back the expansion of credit and availability of capital. (See Box 5–4.) Other macroeconomic effects could also be considered undesirable: in 1998 alone, India imported more than 600 tonnes of gold, at a cost of almost US$7 billion – a big component in the soaring cost of non-oil imports.

The Future of Gold as a Reserve Asset and the Future Price of Gold

Taking into account variations since the 1960s, gold prices have been relatively stable in recent years despite their general decline. (See Figure 5–7.)

The future of gold as a reserve asset of central banks will be a major factor in the future of the market and price. But it is not the only factor. Others are the extent to which gold is still recognized and used by individuals as an inflation hedge or store of value, whether uses other than jewellery grow, and whether individual consumers decide to increase or decrease the amount of gold jewellery that they buy.

Central Bank Gold Policy

The extent to which gold still serves to stabilize the world monetary system is hotly debated, and the signs are mixed. Taken together, central banks have become net sellers of gold. The modest rise in gold prices after the events of 11 September 2001 was a clear sign – there was no flight to gold. It is also possible that gold played a role in limiting the economic crisis in Argentina in 2002.

Central banks together still hold a very substantial fraction of above-ground stocks. Much depends on

Box 5–4. The Indian Experiment With Gold Banking

India's experiment with its gold bank is an attempt to get privately held gold into the banking system, where it could be an effective source of development capital. Through the Reserve Bank of India, the government itself holds just 400 tonnes, in contrast with 12,000–13,000 tonnes thought to be in private hands. In January 1999, the government more than doubled the customs duty to try to curb the outflow of funds for gold purchases. At the same time, the finance minister set out the blueprint for a new strategy, to be implemented through a Gold Deposit Scheme to bring gold back into circulation. The intention was to reduce the country's reliance on imports and provide owners of bullion with some additional income.

The scheme also freed owners from the problems of storage, transport, and security. The depositor earned interest on an otherwise unproductive asset by lodging it with approved banks, and was also able to collateralize that asset.

An example of a typical gold deposit scheme was that launched by The State Bank of India in November 1999. An individual, family, trust, or company could deposit as little as 200g of gold, for three to seven years, in return for a gold certificate that pays tax-free interest of 3–4%. At the end of the term the certificate can be exchanged for an equivalent amount of gold, or the market value of the gold, with no capital gains tax.

The certificates are transferable, and can be used as security for a loan. Gold deposited can be withdrawn early, but with an interest penalty. Banks offering deposit schemes lend the gold to local jewellers at an interest of 9–10%, less than the cash borrowing rate. The interest spread pays for assaying, refining, paying local tax, and hedging against the risk that the bank will not be able to lend out all its gold for periods to match the deposits. Initial targets for the scheme were ambitious. The State Bank announced a goal of 100 tonnes in the first year, which would mean a saving of about US$1.2 billion in foreign exchange.

The gold deposit scheme targets households in the hope that they will take advantage of the opportunity to earn interest on their gold. The scheme is not without its obstacles, however. Most of the gold in India is in the form of jewellery, which would have to be melted down to bullion on deposit, destroying the value of the work, which is usually about 10–15% of the retail value. A more serious difficulty is that much of the gold in private hands has been bought with non-declared income, which its owners are reluctant to declare for fear of investigation by tax officials. By January 2001, the designated banks had succeeded in raising only 6179kg of gold. The State Bank of India had raised the bulk – about 5800kg, which is nowhere near what it had originally projected.

Source: World Gold Council (2001) p.17; Economic Times of India, March 20, 2001

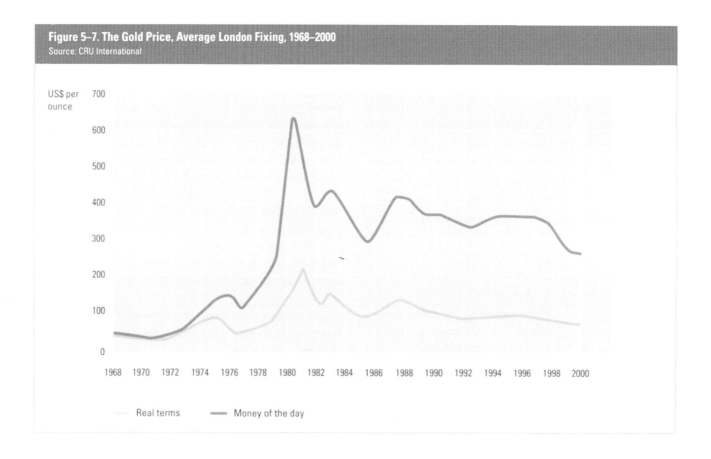

Figure 5–7. The Gold Price, Average London Fixing, 1968–2000
Source: CRU International

whether these institutions as a group are net buyers or net sellers, and on what scale. Of the 170 countries reporting to the International Monetary Fund (IMF) in the late 1990s, 70% declared some gold as part of their reserve assets. Ten countries reported that they definitely did not hold any gold; another 41 did not declare either way.[25] The US holds around three-fifths of its foreign reserves in gold. The European Union has about 27% of its reserves in gold. At current market prices, the international average is about 16%.

In the 1990s it became clear that the commitment of some governments to maintaining gold as a store of value was declining. The drop in official purchases of gold and the increase in sales indicated that some bankers thought it time to change policy. This caused concern to the gold producers and other governments. The world's key financial organizations (official institutions and the IMF) hold the equivalent of 15 years of mine output.[26] As there was no coordinated approach to gold sales by either miners or central banks, there was growing fear of a collapse of the gold price. When prices fell, much of the loss affected countries in sub-Saharan Africa. Gold mining employment in South Africa alone is said to have declined by some 300,000, in what is known there as the Gold Crisis.[27]

On 26 September 1999, the Central Bank Gold Agreement (also known as the Washington Agreement or Washington Accord) was announced.[28] A group consisting of the members of the European Monetary Union, the European Central Bank, the UK, and Switzerland, with the tacit agreement of the US Federal Reserve, the Reserve Bank of Canada, and the Bank of Japan, agreed on a programme to stabilize the gold market. Together with the IMF, these participants control well over 20,000 tonnes of gold reserves.[29] The main provisions of the agreement were a freeze on any additional lending by the signatories and a limit on gold sales to 2000 tonnes over five years, with no more than 400 tonnes to be sold in any one year. What happens at the end of the initial five-year term of the agreement in 2004 is still uncertain. As a group, central banks have not returned to the market as buyers of gold in any significant quantities and they remain sizeable net sellers. The increasing reliance on the US dollar, notably in Latin America, has been accompanied by gold sales. The emergence of currency blocs, such as in the European Union, has meant the pooling of reserves.

Future agreements affecting the gold market will be of key concern. While central banks as owners have to decide what is in their interest, these decisions are fraught with consequences for others and should be made in an atmosphere of consultation and transparency.

Availability of Gold
Total world geological resources of gold are estimated to be about 100,000 tonnes, including 15–20% in the form of by-product resources. [30] (See Table 5–5.)[31] Some of the 9000 tonnes in US resources would be recovered as by-product gold. At the current production rate, these resources would last about 25 years.

As with the other metals studied, physical availability is in the short and intermediate term less of an issue than are environmental, social, and political challenges to producing these reserves. The gold industry faces challenges at the market level, as indicated. For aluminium, energy requirements for smelting are a key issue. For copper, smelter emissions are a major problem. For gold, there are somewhat different issues.

First, given the gold industry's focus on exploration and the multiplicity of the people and companies that explore for gold, the issues of land rights will be prominent. These include the important question of acceptability to indigenous and aboriginal communities and the continued debate over what areas are or should be 'off limits' to exploration and mining.

Table 5–5. Estimated Gold Reserves and Resources (excluding some by-product reserves)		
Country	**Gold Reserves (tonnes)**	**Gold Resources (tonnes)**
South Africa	19,000	40,000
United States	5,600	6,000
Uzbekistan	5,300	6,300
Australia	4,000	4,700
Russia	3,000	3,500
Canada	1,500	3,500
Brazil	800	1,200
Other Countries	9,300	11,800
World Total*	**49,000**	**77,000**

*May be rounded.
Source: US Geological Survey, http://minerals.usgs.gov/minerals/pubs/commodity/gold/300300.pdf
(11 December 2000)

While these concerns are not unique to gold, they may be of particular importance for this commodity.

Second, the ratio of the volume of waste to the volume of product will continue to attract attention. Calculations can be done many ways, but all concur that for low-grade gold deposits, some number of tonnes of waste – and correspondingly high amounts of energy and water – may be needed to produce a relatively small and simple gold object. This will continue to strike some people as wasteful, and some of them will link this concern to the question of whether use as jewellery or bullion in bank vaults is somehow less utilitarian than the industrial uses more common for other metals.

Third, for whatever reason, a number of the highly publicized accidents and failures of recent years that have fuelled public concerns over safety and environmental protection have occurred at gold sites, from Baia Mare and Merrespruit to Summitville and Omai. Ensuring that all who are mining have the capacity for sound environmental management is a challenge for all of industry; clearly not all do.

Finally, using cyanide to extract gold is the technology of choice for larger gold companies; mercury is still the agent of choice for a large part of the artisanal sector. Both of these technologies have caused significant environmental concern. The extent to which the new cyanide code (see Chapter 10) or other steps will improve both management and perceptions, and continued progress in controlling mercury use, will both be important concerns.

Fuels and Industrial Minerals

Coal
Need and Availability
Coal has been an important energy source for centuries.[32] In 2000 it provided 24.9% of the world's primary energy requirements.[33] In addition to being used to generate electricity, coal is used directly for heating. This includes important industrial processes such as steel and cement manufacture. Coal, when processed into coke, is also important in production of iron and steel.

The types of coal may be ranked in order of increasing carbon content and decreasing moisture content:

lignite (brown coal), sub-bituminous, bituminous, and anthracite. The last three are known as 'black coal' and the last two as 'hard coal'. Most types of this mineral have specific uses. Among the hard coals, steam or energy coal is used for electricity generation or conversion into other forms of secondary energy. Although all categories of coal can be used for electricity generation, power plants have to be designed to handle specific types of this material. A plant designed to burn bituminous coal, for example, cannot burn brown coal. Coking coal is always bituminous.

Coking coal is used by the steel industry in the stage involving production of blast furnace iron. While all coking coals can be burnt in suitably designed power plants to generate electricity, the reverse is not true in that bituminous steam coals cannot all be converted into coke. An important feature of coals used by the steel industry is that they should have as low a level of ash and sulphur as possible. Coal is also used to produce liquid fuels, chemicals, polymers, and plastics.

Significant deposits of coal exist on all continents, meaning that availability at the global level is not currently a critical issue. Coal is produced in over 50 countries. Known total reserves of coal are shown in Table 5–6. In 2000, a total of 3639 million tonnes of hard coal were produced, along with 895 million tonnes of brown coal.[34] On this basis, the world has more than 200 years of coal reserves. It is important to remember that while coal production in Europe is declining rapidly, this is not true in all industrial countries. US production, for instance, increased from 710 million tonnes in 1980 to 899 million tonnes in 2000. Most important, not all types of coal are suitable for all purposes. Nor are all types found at comparable grades all over the world.

Table 5–6. Known Reserves of Coal

	Reserves (billion tonnes)	Share of total (per cent)
North America	256.5	26.1
Europe	122.0	12.4
Former Soviet Union	230.2	23.4
Asia Pacific	292.3	29.7
Rest of World	83.2	8.4

Source: BP Energy Statistics, June 2001

Like gold, coal is relatively easy to identify, and often fairly accessible to exploitation by basic technologies. This means that in many regions of the world production of coal by small and medium-scale enterprises is fairly common. For the same reasons, there is considerable small-scale and artisanal activity in several countries, notably China.

Some types of coal are traded internationally for specific uses, particularly the sub-bituminous and bituminous types. For instance, about 39% of coking coal (192 million tones) was traded internationally in 2000. In contrast, the 574 million tonnes of hard coal traded internationally represented only 16% of the total world production of this type. Due to the high moisture content of brown coal, it is uneconomic to transport this type over long distances. In the three largest coal-consuming and -producing economies (China, US, and India), over 95% of production is used domestically.

For coal that is traded by sea, the patterns of supply differ by region and by category of coal. The major suppliers of steam coal into the Pacific region are Australia, China, and Indonesia, whereas the major suppliers into the Atlantic region are South Africa, Colombia, and Russia. The major suppliers of coking coal into the Asian market are Australia and Canada, while in the Atlantic it is Australia, the US, and Canada.

Over 80% of the world's coal production is used in its country of origin. In some countries, coal is a particularly important energy source. Poland, South Africa, Australia, and China all rely on coal to produce over 75% of their electricity, since they have limited alternative fossil fuel energy sources. In many countries, coal is a key fuel for domestic heating and cooking.

Changes in the demand for coal are affected by global competition from other fossil fuels such as oil and gas. With the exception of Japan and the US, the demand for steam coal for electricity generation in many industrial countries is decreasing. In Europe, the availability of cheap natural gas has resulted in the output of coal-fired power stations being reduced and smaller, less efficient stations being closed. An additional factor affecting coal production in Europe has been the higher costs than new mines in countries such as Colombia, Australia, and Indonesia. Subsidies to support coal mining in Europe are being reduced and coal production is declining, even though imports into the major European nations are increasing.

A key area for growth in coal production is the Pacific region. Unlike in Europe, the ability to develop gas infrastructure is limited in many parts of the Pacific. As a result, coal-fired power stations are seen as being needed to meet the surge in electricity demand associated with industrial growth and rising living standards.

Factors Affecting Future Coal Use

A key factor affecting demand for coal is the technologies employed in its use. Despite an increase in the production of pig iron between 1990 and 2000, total world production of coking coal declined from 548 million tonnes to 497 million tonnes. This is partly due to an increase in the efficiency of blast furnaces, but also to more stringent environmental controls. Demand for coking coal is linked closely to pig iron output across the world.

Steel companies have introduced equipment that injects coal directly into the blast furnace as a substitute for coke. It is estimated that currently 32 million tonnes of coal are being injected into blast furnaces worldwide. Coal for injection purposes does not require coking properties. It does, however, need the same levels of chemical purity as coking coal. The technology of coke-making has developed so that poorer coking coals can be used at increasing levels in the mix of coals being fed to coke ovens. Currently this technology is used mainly in Asia and South America. These coals are often the same as those used for injection and have resulted in a second category of coking coal being established. This category is often referred to as semi-soft coal in contrast to high-quality coking coals, referred to as hard coking coals.

As with other carbon fuels, policies set by governments and producers have always had significant implications for coal use. For instance, following the oil price shocks of the 1970s, electric utilities turned from oil to coal, and by 1983 the trade in steam coal exceeded that of coking coal. Energy policy is now increasingly influenced by environmental concerns, which may have significant implications for the way in which coal is used and overall demand.

There are numerous environmental concerns relating to coal use, including emissions of polluting gases associated with iron and steel production and direct combustion for electricity generation. Technologies have been developed to address these, many of which are relatively well established in industrial countries. An example is systems to remove sulphur from flue gases in power stations (although this requires limestone to be mined). The concept of clean (or cleaner) coal technology incorporates numerous innovations that reduce emissions and use coal more efficiently. One example is fluidized bed coal combustion, which reduces emissions of nitrous oxides and leads to the efficient capture of sulphurous gases.

Emissions of carbon dioxide are now widely acknowledged as one underlying cause of global climate change and may therefore have significant effects on future coal use.[35] Coal has the highest carbon-to-hydrogen ratio of any fossil fuel and therefore produces a higher proportion of carbon dioxide than fuels such as oil or natural gas. Conventional modern coal-fired power stations operate at efficiencies of approximately 38%, compared with advanced 'combined-cycle' gas-fired plants that operate at 55% or more. Older coal-fired plants operate at much lower efficiencies. Some modifications can raise efficiencies (the conversion of the chemical energy present in coal to electricity) up to 40%. The next step in coal-fired technology is to convert coal into gaseous form and then burn it in a combined-cycle gas plant. Overall efficiency levels in the region of 50% may be achieved. Clearly, a key area of concern to industry, governments, and other actors is the transfer of these technologies to countries where coal use for electricity generation is increasing rapidly.

Obviously the contribution of coal combustion to carbon dioxide emissions needs to be evaluated alongside other sources and other gases (such as methane from reservoirs for hydroelectric power plant).[36] The Kyoto Protocol (part of the 1992 Framework Convention on Climate Change) or subsequent agreements may cause many governments to change their policies in order to create incentives for alternative energy sources. Carbon taxes and emission permits both within and between countries may affect the price of energy and thus the demand for coal. This topic is already the subject of an established debate with regard to energy policy and sustainable development. The European Union is currently one of the most sensitive markets with regard to the regulation of coal usage.

Potash

Approximately 95% of the current global consumption of potassium is used for fertilizers; the remainder is used in various industrial applications, including the manufacture of caustic potassium and other intermediate chemicals important to industry. Potash is the trade term that refers to fertilizer materials containing potassium. Potassium is essential for plant and animal life. Many soils lack sufficient quantities of available potassium for the demands of crop yield and quality. As a result, available soil potassium levels are commonly supplemented by potash fertilization to improve the nutrition of plants, particularly for sustaining production of high-yielding crop species and varieties in modern agricultural systems.[37]

95% of potash is used for fertilizers

Potassium is present in all types of rocks, but mining of potash ores is mainly restricted to two types of sedimentary deposits: deposits of marine origin that are found at depths typically ranging from 400 to more than 1000 metres below the surface, and surface brine deposits associated with saline water bodies (such as the Dead Sea, the Great Salt Lake, and China's Qarhan Lake). World resources of potassium bearing sedimentary deposits are immense and are reported to total 17 billion tonnes.[38] Of this, 8.4 billion tonnes of reserves are categorized as commercially exploitable.[39] With current annual global consumption of about 25.8 million tonnes, both economic reserves and the resource base are sufficient to meet world demand for centuries.

Potash ores situated at depth are mined mainly by conventional mechanized methods. Solution mining is used when underground extraction is no longer technically feasible. Solar evaporation of brines that naturally contain potassium is the third method of obtaining potash ore.

The processing of potash ores normally results in large volumes of waste materials, including brines, slimes containing clay, and salt tailings. The disposal of saline wastes, including the rehabilitation of land after mining, has been a key issue in the environmental management of the potash industry.[40]

World production of potassium fertilizer salts has grown significantly in the last century to meet the growing requirements of intensive agriculture. From 1998 to 2001, potash production varied in the narrow range of 25.4–25.8 million tonnes yearly, compared

with consumption of 21.9–22.8 million tonnes. In 1998 and 1999, potash usage of 11.1–11.4 million tonnes in industrial countries was only slightly higher than usage in developing countries of 10.5–10.9 million tonnes.

There are only 14 producers in the world potash market. Four countries account for three-quarters of global output: Canada, Russia, Germany, and Belarus. Canada has the largest known reserves of potassium. These extensive, consistent, and high-grade potash deposits represent more than 50% of estimated world reserves. The sizeable potash deposits in the former Soviet Union contain large amounts of ore, but these are of a type that has higher refining costs. Thailand has 10 billion tonnes of potash consisting of a mixture of ore types.

Major consuming regions, such as Asia and Latin America, will continue to depend substantially on imports, due to the resilient imbalance in the supply/demand situation and the sustained growth in demand. Exporting regions such as North America, East Europe/Central Asia, and the Near East will expand their capabilities to meet world requirements for potash in growing and emerging markets.

Four countries currently account for close to 53% of global potash usage. The US is the largest consumer, typically accounting for about 20% of the world total. China, Brazil, and India represent approximately 15%, 10%, and 7%, respectively, of world consumption. Western Europe is also an important consuming region, using about 17.5% of the total in recent years.

Potash demand is determined largely by the requirements for fertilizer production, which is forecast to reach 25 million tonnes by 2005. The most fundamental factors determining long-term demand for potash will be developments in agricultural techniques and patterns of food production to meet a growing world population. Future need for potassium fertilizers will also depend on a number of specific factors, including:

- the extent and severity of potassium deficiency in cropland,
- the introduction of new or improved crop varieties with greater potassium requirements,
- shifts in demand for agricultural products,
- the profitability of potassium fertilization to farmers,
- prices for agricultural products and other fertilizers,
- government crop production or restriction programmes, and
- weather conditions (including those associated with climate change).

The correct availability of potassium in the soil (of which fertilizer is one source) is important in plant resistance to drought, frost, and a number of diseases and pests. The element is essential for the development of the root system and fosters nitrogen fixation of leguminous crops, and it improves the size, colour, and sugar content of fruit crops. Natural reserves of soil potassium diminish with each successive crop. This withdrawal or 'soil mining' is greatly increased and accelerated by higher yields and more intensive cropping.

The decision to use potash in agriculture depends on the relationship between the cost of fertilizer and the return on yield. It also depends on the level of technology associated with the production system in question. The debate about the role of fertilizer in supplying plant nutrients is linked to concerns about the environmental and social impacts of modern agricultural production systems. In many industrial countries, there is an increasing focus on organic farming practices, which place greater emphasis on the recycling of organic matter. Even so, the International Guidelines covering organically produced foods do allow for potassium to be used where adequate crop nutrition and soil conditions cannot be achieved through the recycling of organic materials alone.[41] Potassium fertilizer (and therefore the requirement for potash mining) will continue so long as modern agricultural practices are the basis for meeting the world's food requirements.

Endnotes

[1] The industrial clays case study is available on the CD-ROM accompanying this report.

[2] Unless otherwise indicated, the data in this chapter are supplied by CRU International. Information is also provided by McCloskey Coal, Gold Fields Mineral Services, the International Iron and Steel Institute, the United Nations, the U.S. Geological Survey, and the World Bureau of Metal Statistics.

[3] In Table 5–1, aluminium consumption refers only to primary metal produced from bauxite; all scrap-based aluminium consumption is separate and in addition to this figure. Copper consumption refers to refined copper, of which 86% in the western world is produced from ore and concentrate, while 14% is produced from scrap; in addition, a large amount of scrap is recycled as alloy (notably brass). Lead consumption refers to refined lead, of which 60–62% in the western world is now produced from scrap and the remainder from ores and concentrates. In addition, a small amount of lead is recycled in the form of alloys. Steel consumption refers to carbon steel, of which over 50% is produced from scrap in the western world. In addition, stainless steel scrap is recycled as stainless steel. Production statistics are for 2000.

[4] World Aluminium Institute at http://www.world-aluminium.org/production/recycling/index.html.

[5] Defined as the US, Canada, Western Europe, Japan, Australia, and New Zealand in the statistics shown in this chapter.

[6] Data from GFMS, IMF, CRU International.

[7] For Iceland, see Norsk Hydro Ices Aluminum Smelter, Environment News Service, 4 April 2002, at http://www.corpwatch.org/news/PRT.jsp?articleid=2270; see 'World Bank in India, Car Culture Pushes Privatisation,' AidWatch, at http://www.aidwatch.org.au/news/15/10.htm; see 'Chile Green Groups Question Aluminum Plant Comment,' Planet Ark, 3 December 2001, at http://www.planetark.org/dailynewsstory.cfm/newsid/13528/story.htm.

[8] World Commission on Dams (2000).

[9] Data for secondary recovery of aluminium are much less complete than those for primary consumption. The major form of secondary production is the re-melting of scrap to produce alloy ingots. This is reasonably well recorded, but there are undoubtedly some small secondary smelters that do not report production. There are also producers of billet from scrap (with some primary additions). Production from these plants is much less well recorded in Europe. Then there is scrap that is directly re-used in semi-fabricating plants that have their own casting facilities. This scrap can arise within the plant or be bought in from scrap merchants. This recycled material is not fully recorded and in some countries is not recorded at all. Finally, some pure aluminium scrap is melted in the casthouses of primary smelters and cast into products that are sold as primary aluminium. How this metal is recorded, if at all, is uncertain. All that can be said with confidence is that the volume of aluminium recycled is greater than the volume recorded. This should be borne in mind when considering any calculations about the amount of aluminium scrap that is lost in landfills and could in theory have been recycled.

[10] The process uses laser induced optical spectroscopy. Each piece of scrap is sampled by means of a laser, identified, and then separated by alloy. If commercially proven, the process would enable much more of the value of aluminium scrap from shredded automobiles to be retained. The process is being tested by the Huron Valley Steel Corporation and is being promoted by the Auto Aluminium Alliance and the Aluminium Association; see US Department of Energy, Office of Industrial Technologies (2001); Comments of International Recycling on Draft Report.

[11] MacMillan (2000).

[12] See 'Zambian Copper Chokes Miners', Electronic Mail & Guardian, 29 January 1997, at http://www.mg.co.za/mg/news/97jan2/29jan-zamcopper.html. A list of smelters is available at

http://www.ame.com.au/smelters/cu/smelters.htm.

[13] A standard automotive SLI (Start, Light and Ignition) battery is composed largely of lead and sulfuric acid.

[14] The mobility study now being supported by the World Business Council for Sustainable Development may shed some light on these questions.

[15] Gold Fields Mineral Services Ltd. (2001). Total includes fabricated items as well as bar hoarding and net producing hedging and investment.

[16] World Gold Council (2001) p.17.

[17] Wedepohl (1995) estimates that there are 2.5 parts per billion of gold in Earth's continental crust.

[18] Gold Fields Mineral Services. Of this, some 70,000 tonnes are said to be held in the form of jewellery, and 30,000 tonnes in official institutions. Ibid.; ICMM comments on draft report.

[19] Otto (2002).

[20] See http://csf.colorado.edu/bioregional/apr99/ 0015.html and http://www.rainforestjukebox.org/ gold/platform.htm.

[21] World Gold Council, London, press release, 10 May 2001.

[22] This organization should not be confused with the Global Mining Initiative.

[23] Keynes (1936), p.129.

[24] Robert A Mundell, quoted in Gold Institute comments on MMSD draft report.

[25] World Gold Council.

[26] Ibid.

[27] Total number of employees in South African Gold Mines fell from 474,851 in 1990 to 197,537 in 2000 (Chamber of Mines of South Africa).

[28] Orellana (2001).

[29] World Gold Council, at http://www.gold.org/finalgold/gold/Gra/Pr/Wr991006.htm.

[30] This refers to gold recovered as a by-product in the mining and extractive metallurgy of other metals. The gold (or any other saleable element) is classed as a by-product if it is not the main source of revenue for the facility producing the metals concerned. The main source of by-product gold is the copper industry. Other sources include platinum producers, silver mines, and, on a very small scale, lead and zinc mines.

[31] In Table 5–5, 'reserves' refers to that part of the reserve base that could be economically extracted or produced at the time of determination. The term need not signify that extraction facilities are in place and operative. Reserves include only recoverable materials; thus terms such as 'extractable reserves' and 'recoverable reserves' are redundant and are not a part of this classification system. 'Resources' refers to that part of an identified resource that meets specified minimum physical and chemical criteria related to current mining and production practices, including those for grade, quality, thickness, and depth. The reserve base is the in-place demonstrated (measured plus indicated) resource from which reserves are estimated. It may encompass those parts of the resources that have a reasonable potential for becoming economically available within planning horizons beyond those that assume proven technology and current economics. The reserve base includes those resources that are currently economic (reserves), marginally economic (marginal reserves), and some of those that are currently subeconomic (subeconomic resources). The term 'geologic reserve' has been applied by others generally to the reserve-base category, but it also may include the inferred-reserve-base category; it is not a part of this classification system.

[32] This section is based on information provided by McCloskey Group, supplemented by information available from the World Coal Institute at http://www.wci-coal.com.

[33] British Petroleum (2001).

[34] IEA Coal information (2001).

[35] Houghton et al. (2001).

[36] Ibid.; World Commission on Dams (2000).

[37] This section is based largely on data provided by the International Fertilizer Industry Association, Paris.

[38] US Geological Survey (2000a).

[39] Measured in terms of the mass of potassium oxide.

[40] UNEP (2001b).

[41] FAO/World Health Organization (1999).

CHAPTER 6

VIABILITY OF THE MINERALS INDUSTRY

Historically, companies were expected to meet their responsibilities to their employees, their shareholders, and the regulatory authorities where they operated, which they did to a lesser or greater extent. In addressing the challenge of sustainable development, companies will have to understand and meet their newly appreciated responsibilities to these and other groups – including the national and local development arms of governments, affected communities, watchdog non-governmental organizations (NGOs), and consumers of their products. This part of *Breaking New Ground* looks at how all these different groups interact with each other and how these interactions can ease or block the path to sustainable development.

Clearly, for the transition to sustainable development to happen, the private sector needs to play an integral part in addressing the priority concerns. It needs to be convinced of the business case for private-sector involvement. But better environmental and social performance will not happen without the active engagement and support of the other key groups, whether they be government officials, union members, or community representatives. In the transition to sustainable development, all actors are at different starting points on an uncertain collaborative journey that will require ongoing adaptation and convergence at many levels in many different places. Success will be more likely with clearly defined goals, well-researched alternatives, appropriate indicators to measure progress, diffusion of technological innovation, and effective institutions to encourage appropriate actions.

First, it is useful to examine the minerals companies themselves – their reasons for adopting the sustainable development agenda and how this agenda does or does not tie in with their core business strategy, the conditions they provide for those who work for them, and their relationship with the financial institutions that support them. The focus in this chapter is largely on the major minerals and metals companies that compete for capital in global markets, operate in many countries, and produce products that are sold into global markets.

Before turning to the business case, it is important to note that mining-industry profitability falls short of most other industries. The real question facing the industry is how it can meet the minimal economic performance to remain viable in the face of mounting demands for improved environmental and social performance. Figure 6–1 demonstrates the poor financial performance of three mining sectors compared with a global index over 21 years.[1] (Share prices may not truly reflect the industry's financial performance, as they exclude dividend payments.) While individual companies may – in certain years and overall – do far better than the industry average, the statistics are salutory. However much the poor returns are a function of oversupply, cyclical factors, or plain poor management, the effect in the end is the same. There is little room in this sector to make dramatic gestures from retained earnings or profits. And for as long as this situation persists, many of the costs implicit in this report will be a struggle for individual companies

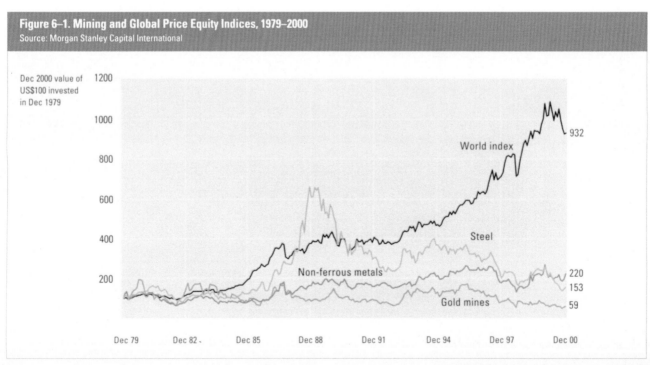

Figure 6–1. Mining and Global Price Equity Indices, 1979–2000
Source: Morgan Stanley Capital International

Dec 2000 value of US$100 invested in Dec 1979

World index — 932
Steel
Non-ferrous metals — 220
Gold mines — 153 / 59

in the sector to meet. The business case and, perhaps more significant, the political case for trying to 'raise the game' across the sector must be clear.

The Business Case for Sustainable Development

The question of how – or indeed whether – successful company strategies can integrate the concepts of sustainable development into core business practice is at the centre of this report. Is it in a company's financial interest to strive for good environmental, economic, and social performance?

The traditional discussion of a company's record on environmental and social performance was couched in terms of the problems of externalities. Many of the costs involved in improving environmental and social conditions are internal, and hence represent an additional cost to the company, but many and perhaps most of the benefits are often external. As many of the traditional benefits do not accrue directly, the company does not have an incentive to incur these extra costs. Proponents of the business case criticize this approach as being too static since it ignores the potential of companies to innovate.[2] In addition, many externalities are increasingly being internalized due to tightening legislation, consumer pressure, and the force of public opinion.

The greatest challenge to embedding sustainable development in minerals companies is this difficulty of linking it to financial success. There is a need for each company to identify more clearly the magnitude and incidence of all the costs and benefits to ensure that its actions are based on rational business interests. The business case for addressing sustainable development concerns includes numerous benefits:

• *Lower labour costs and more innovative solutions* – When corporations demonstrate a visible commitment to corporate social responsibility and corporate and employee values are in alignment, this can translate into better motivation and job satisfaction, higher productivity, more innovation and creativity among the work force, fewer union disputes, lower absenteeism, and lower labour turnover.

For instance, uranium miner Cameco has invested more than a million dollars in northern

Saskatchewan in tertiary education, training support, scholarships, school-based athletic programmes, and career information initiatives. All were designed to encourage northern aboriginal children to stay in school, pursue tertiary education, and consider occupations in the mining industry.[3]

• *Lower health costs* – A healthy environment for workers and the surrounding community improves well-being and thus productivity. Investment in social infrastructure, such as schools, hospitals, and water supplies, and in health plans and so on reduces the traditional health hazards of poverty and underdevelopment. This translates into higher productivity, reduced worker and community compensation and damage suits, lower penalties for non-compliance, and reduced costs to social services and medication.[4] The link between business performance and health and safety is clear.

At Placer Dome's Misima mine in Papua New Guinea (PNG), for example, a tripartite initiative between the mining company, the World Health Organization, and Australia's James Cook University initiated a successful campaign to eradicate the tropical disease of lymphatic filariasis – a significant public health problem – which reduced absenteeism.[5] In South Africa, HIV/AIDS programmes have been initiated by several mining companies. These include BHP Billiton's efforts at Hillside Aluminium operations, located in KwaZulu-Natal, where the prevalence of HIV among employees is 11% compared with more than 30% in surrounding communities. Anglo American at its Namakwa Sands operation in the Western Cape province has a predominantly locally recruited work force with an HIV prevalence of only 2%.[6] Over the past four years, AngloGold has been actively developing a model for an integrated HIV prevention and care programme in collaboration with the London School of Hygiene and Tropical Medicine.[7]

• *Cost savings due to cleaner production methods* – Many good environmental practices pay for themselves in cost savings and increased production. Reducing raw materials use and increasing recycling and recovery can lower production costs. Innovation and technology development can introduce new process and product efficiencies, such as the ability to treat lower-grade ore that would otherwise be classified as waste rock and to improve recovery levels of the minerals. Reducing the level of metals in the waste also reduces environmental problems. These opportunities for cost savings may not become apparent until the company is motivated by regulation or concerns about sustainability performance to examine solutions and invest in the necessary research.[8]

The benefits of this kind of practice are illustrated by projects under way at Rio Tinto's Borax operations in the US. These range from simple measures such as installation of energy-efficient lighting, efficiency in packaging, and environmental training programmes to more advanced programmes that involve ISO 14001 certification, management of solid and hazardous wastes, and reduction in carbon emissions.[9]

Although the 'pollution haven' argument has been leveled at minerals companies engaged in foreign direct investment in developing countries, many of the major multinationals argue that it is more cost-effective to install state-of-the-art clean technology rather than to retrofit older technology as environmental standards become more stringent.

- *Easier access to lenders and insurers and preferential loan and insurance rates* – Lower risks achieved through implementation of a sustainable development strategy may mean lower loan rates or insurance costs. Poor environmental performance reduces a company's access to and increases the cost of debt and equity capital, particularly in countries where legislation follows the 'polluter pays' principle.[10]

- *Lower transaction costs* – Increased transparency and dissemination of information on a project and the plans to avoid, mitigate, and minimize the negative impacts while maximizing the positive impacts will build trust among stakeholders and reduce transaction costs – in terms of management time and the length of the permitting process. The preparation and dissemination of thorough impact assessments and baseline studies, though costly, may be useful evidence in the case of future risk of liability. Community acceptance is key. Anticipating and being sensitive to problems in advance and taking appropriate preventive actions will pay dividends.

For instance, the adoption of several new environmental and community initiatives at BHP Billiton's Cerro Matoso nickel mine in Colombia

paved the way for an expansion of the operation to be approved.[11] On the negative side, poor assessment and planning for avoidance and mitigation of environmental and social impacts stopped the proposed Windy Craggy mine project in British Columbia, Canada.[12]

- *Lower closure and post-closure costs* – Development and implementation of a clear long-term and post-closure plan can lower closure costs considerably, if systems are put in place correctly from the beginning. If the plan is comprehensive and integrated, there will be less pressure to keep operating just to avoid dealing with the consequences of closure. Where site reclamation is planned from the outset, the ultimate cost is lower and the results are better. A life-cycle approach to managing the environmental and social impacts – from development through operations to closure – makes commercial sense. Poor planning incurs additional costs in relocating waste materials and dealing with watershed contamination. For example, if the acid drainage problems of the Equity Silver mine in British Columbia had been anticipated when the mine was being proposed, the project would probably never have proceeded.

The greater the time lapse between the occurrence of environmental damage and its remediation, and the greater the neglect of the social issues generated by minerals development, the greater will be the human and financial resources necessary to address the problem.[13] This translates into higher demand for financial resources at the time of closure, when the company is experiencing a reduction in revenues. Preparing for and addressing these concerns from the outset will let the company set aside the necessary funding for terminal liabilities when cash flow is strongest.

- *Improved reputation enhances market value* – A commitment to sustainable development may enhance a company's profile and reputation. This has several advantages. It may be the best way to attract the best people to mining careers, or for an individual company to get better new employees than its competitors. Externally this should lead to an improved social licence to operate: companies attempting to explore for, define, or develop deposits will be more welcome by host nations and local communities if they arrive with a clear vision of themselves as agents of sustainable development. Good relations and acceptance in the local community can reduce the time required to get government approval and lower the possibility of conflict, both of which can be very costly. On the other hand, human rights abuses and worker and community health problems – though they may not incur a penalty directly – will certainly affect the reputation and long-term value of the company. There is also a high risk as well as reputational costs associated with operating in conflict zones. Rio Tinto's Hamersley Iron, operating in Western Australia's Pilbara region, has invested heavily in the design, construction, and development of three towns, a port, a railway, roads, and associated utilities. At the request of the state, the three 'company towns' were transferred to the care of the local government. These towns are associated with a high standard of living that helps to attract and retain world-class employees for the mine.[14] The actions also reflect the outcomes of a process of agreement on obligations and mutual undertakings by the state government, Rio Tinto, and other companies concerned, as legislated through State Agreement Acts.

- *Best-practice influence on regulation* – Companies that follow best practice are much better placed than their competitors to influence how standards are set and the direction of regulatory change. If the industry leaders can adopt a set of standards based on best practice, they will have a competitive advantage when this is taken forward and incorporated in legislation addressing sustainable development issues. Best practice can help establish credibility with regulators and can aid in the move to partnerships to develop realistic, science-based regulations.

In the European Union, the metals industry has an opportunity to contribute further to the effective regulation of its products under the proposed revision of the Chemicals Policy. This can be done by the generation and provision of the best available data for the registration and risk assessment process for substances being placed on the market. The European metals industry also has a key role in ensuring the appropriate and effective development of this policy.

- *Market advantage* – Some mineral companies are finding ways to build deeper relationships with customers and believe that this will allow them to capture more value and move away from strictly being commodity sellers to providing a mix, with some service elements added. Reputation and brand value are increasingly important for companies to establish premium prices for their products.

For example, diamonds from the Ekati mine in Arctic Canada are etched with a polar bear to distinguish the product on the basis of origin. The branding has several advantages – the diamonds are marketed as coming from a source proud of its environmental and social performance, and they can be easily distinguished from conflict diamonds. The ability to establish brand awareness may be limited for minerals traded as commodities, however.

- *Ethical investors* – The rapid expansion of the ethical and socially responsible investment (SRI) movement in North America and Europe poses a new challenge for minerals companies as investors – especially pension fund managers and other large institutional funds – screen out stocks associated with unacceptable social and environmental performance. Public corporate evaluation and rating tools, such as the Dow Jones Sustainability Group Index and the Innovest Index, are becoming important influences on investment decisions. The growing trend towards 'best of class' investment by such funds potentially provides an incentive for mining companies to raise standards and achieve recognition in the investment community. Though some SRI funds operate negative screens that rule out mining companies entirely, a number of best-of-sector SRI funds have invested in the industry leaders.[15]

An example of how social responsible investment is rapidly becoming more mainstream comes from the UK, where changes to the pensions law in 2000 mean that trustees of pension funds must declare the extent to which social, environmental, or ethical considerations are taken into account in the selection, retention, and realization of investments.[16] In a survey undertaken by consultants ERM, 21 of the 25 largest UK pension funds now apply social responsibility criteria to at least part of their portfolios.[17]

In order for companies to realize the benefits of having an effective sustainable development capacity integrated thoroughly into its businesses, they need to ensure that company-wide sustainable development risks and opportunities are:

- comprehensively and systematically identified;
- understood in terms of their business significance;
- put on the table and debated, considering the company's best long-term business interests; and then
- prudently managed.

When examining the empirical evidence of the business case, there is a problem of establishing causality, which makes it difficult to draw clear conclusions.[18] Does good environmental performance lead to good financial performance? Or is it that companies in a good financial position can afford to improve their environmental performance?[19] Or are environmental and social indicators proxies for innovative and forward-thinking management, and hence better financial performance? Several mining companies have publicized particular win–win examples of better environmental and social performance going hand in hand with better financial results.[20] In addition, there are many negative examples of substantial costs incurred when environmental, social, and conflict-related issues were not given due attention (a cyanide spill at Baia Mare, Romania, for instance, and a tailings dam failure at Los Frailes, Spain). To date, no substantive empirical work on mining company financial performance has been completed that establishes a positive link with actions designed to improve sustainability performance. This should be a priority task for future research to establish evidence for the business case.

As companies begin to accept different and broader definitions of their roles, how are they equipping themselves for the new approach? As part of the MMSD process, consultants PricewaterhouseCoopers surveyed the large mining houses to provide a baseline assessment of how the mining and minerals industry is responding to the issues of sustainable development.[21] Thirty-two organizations, representing nearly US$100 billion in annual sales and over 750,000 employees, participated in the survey, with a broad commodity and global geographical distribution.

The survey found that the majority of the participating companies have taken the first critical step towards a better understanding of sustainable development by acknowledging its importance to the industry and its future. They are aware of the importance of their interaction and consultation with local stakeholders,

and of socio-economic and environmental impacts on their employees and on the local communities where they operate. Implementation of environmental management is more developed, however, than the management of social issues and wider economic impacts.

Companies are still wrestling with the concrete steps necessary to make the concepts of sustainable development operational. There are some examples of specific measures to integrate concepts into corporate practice, but most companies were far from developing a detailed vision of how to adapt to this new paradigm. Several tools were commonly used to achieve cultural change and embed sustainable development practices into organizations. (See Figure 6–2.) Most companies were still struggling to link these activities with financial success and to demonstrate a clear business case for pursuing sustainable development goals.

A number of leading mining companies are starting to put in place a range of policies and programmes that tackle different aspects of the sustainable development agenda. (See Box 6–1.) Critical questions remain about the implementation of these initiatives and the diffusion of corporate responsibility initiatives beyond the largest corporations. Through the various MMSD consultations, it was clear that most stakeholders appreciate the progress that some companies have made, but there are concerns about the continuation of 'double standards' between industrial- and developing-country operations – as well as about the continuing recalcitrance of some companies. One way of reaching beyond this is through collective business action, and the range and number of industry initiatives undertaken both nationally and globally has grown recently. (See Chapter 3.)

Sustainable Development: Enhancing Shareholder Value?

In the 1980s, global deflation and related commodity surpluses that followed from the second oil crisis led to a dramatic decline in the profitability of the mining industry.[22] With few exceptions, government-owned mining companies suffered serious losses. In many cases, far from contributing positively to the rest of the economy, they became a burden. Privatization and deregulation have since been the order of the day. Of specific influence in the mining sector was the

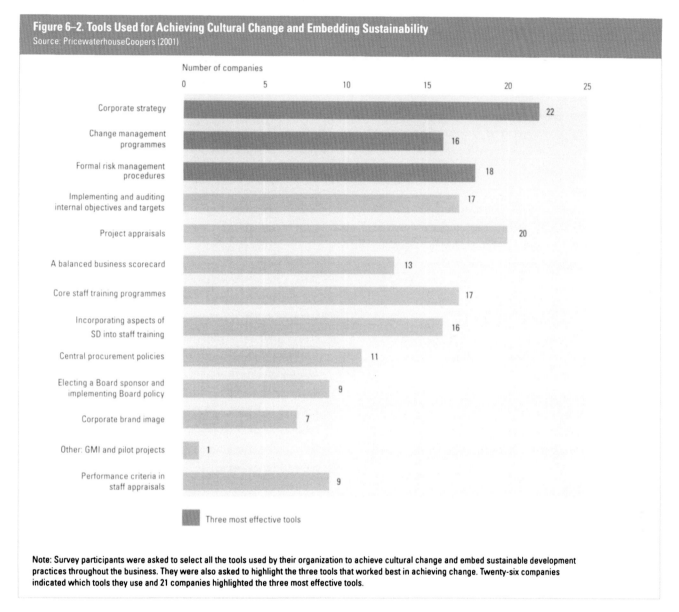

Figure 6–2. Tools Used for Achieving Cultural Change and Embedding Sustainability
Source: PricewaterhouseCoopers (2001)

Note: Survey participants were asked to select all the tools used by their organization to achieve cultural change and embed sustainable development practices throughout the business. They were also asked to highlight the three tools that worked best in achieving change. Twenty-six companies indicated which tools they use and 21 companies highlighted the three most effective tools.

tremendous exploration boom in Chile in the 1980s, which ultimately was followed by massive new investment in the industry.

Shortly after the trend towards privatization and deregulation developed, a further change occurred in the business and financial environment affecting mining companies. This was the so-called shareholder value revolution. This significant development in corporate strategic thinking in mining, as in other global industries, maintains that the principal goal of management is to increase the wealth of owners and that all other obligations are secondary. This change in the business environment gives rise to two questions of paramount importance to the debate on sustainable development:

• Does the shareholder value revolution change, for better or worse, the willingness and ability of companies in general (and specifically those engaged

in mining and minerals activities) to take account of sustainable development issues in their business decisions?

• What specific impact has the shareholder value revolution had on mining companies so far, and what is the prognosis for the future?

Contrary to initial impressions, the focus on maximizing shareholder value does not imply either a reduction in funding for environmental and social issues or a desire to minimize such costs. In fact, financial markets are becoming more alert to the potential destruction of shareholder value arising from liabilities created by inappropriate corporate behaviour towards the environment, local communities, and governments. Conversely, markets are inclined to reward companies that have established consistently high standards in this field.

It is generally recognized that a key component of

Box 6–1. Selected Mining Company Actions for Sustainable Development

For a growing number of large-scale mining multinationals, sustainable development is an umbrella concept covering health and safety, risk management, emergency preparedness, environmental management, community relations, relations with indigenous peoples, and, in some cases, human rights.

Policy development

- Developing company-wide operating policies, standards, and performance indicators for critical issues such as human rights, mine closure and rehabilitation, biodiversity, tailings management, water and energy use, and greenhouse gas emissions
- Adopting a policy of best management practices where regulations are absent and standards are not set
- Ensuring policies are long-term and cover all activities – from exploration to provision of support for sustainable community businesses following mine closure
- Developing guidelines for social, environmental, and conflict impact assessments
- Developing a remuneration policy for accidents
- Extending policy coverage to contractors and suppliers

Policy implementation

- Appointing senior management representatives and staff to implement policies
- Making compliance and corrective action part of every employee's responsibility
- Identifying and recording obligations
- Setting site and corporate performance targets for sustainability issues
- Identifying performance indicators for measuring the success of policy implementation, such as the effectiveness of contributions to neighbouring communities
- Establishing methods to evaluate social and environmental risk
- Ensuring full compliance with industry codes of conduct and legal requirements, and exceeding these where possible
- Implementing ISO 14001 or equivalent environmental management systems
- Reporting on performance at the site and corporate levels
- Monitoring, reviewing, and confirming the effectiveness of performance against company standards, targets, applicable legal requirements, technological innovation, scientific discoveries, and stakeholder expectations
- Internal and external performance assessment of current initiatives, such as company sponsorship of an external International Safety Rating System
- Developing mechanisms for public participation and community involvement

- Establishing stakeholder advisory boards
- Financing improvement programmes for sustainability issues, such as community programmes and health and safety audits
- Allocating adequate human resources to ensure that sustainability issues are given high corporate priority

Employee development

- Building environmental and social competencies by providing training on sustainability issues for employees and contractors
- Improving understanding of human rights issues
- Encouraging respect among employees for each other, and for local communities and their traditional knowledge and customs

Safety at work

- Making a commitment to reduce injuries, incidents, and occupational illnesses
- Including safety accountabilities in job descriptions
- Ensuring businesses and sites have safety management systems and safety improvement plans
- Actively seeking to prevent accidents by disseminating experiences learnt
- Ensuring high standards for incident reporting and fitness at work
- Encouraging cooperation between management and the work force on safety issues
- Supporting research and development with regards to safety, health, environmental issues, and technology to minimize impacts
- Developing and testing emergency response plans

Links with external stakeholders

- Maintaining good working relationships with local communities, regulatory agencies, businesses, government, academia, NGOs, and other affected and interested parties
- Building active partnerships in the field of humans rights, education, and biodiversity management
- Strengthening understanding of communities where companies operate and improving communication and networks with such communities
- Participating in public policy debates on sustainability issues such as climate change and recycling

Product stewardship

- Undertaking life-cycle inventories and analyses
- Promoting product stewardship
- Improving understanding and communicating risks posed by company products in the environment
- Ensuring use of company products does not harm people's health

Source: Anglo American (2001); BHP Billiton (2001); Noranda (2000); Placer Dome (2001); Rio Tinto (2000); WMC Resources (2000a); WMC Resources (2000b); PricewaterhouseCoopers (2001)

value is the net present value of a company's expected future free cash flow from its existing operations. The mining industry, particularly gold and non-ferrous metals, produces standardized homogenous commodities that are traded globally, the prices of which are set by continuous auction in a commodity market. Apart from minor differences reflecting location, all producers sell at essentially the same price, over which they have little or no control.[23] It follows from this that the only way a company can earn more than its competitors and thus improve its valuation is by reducing costs. This has led to what can only be described as an extremely strong 'cost culture' in the mining industry. This focus has been strongly reinforced by the low prices of recent years for most minerals.

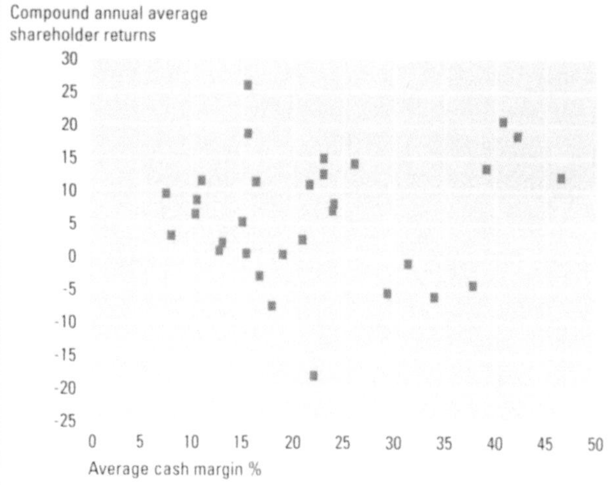

Any demand for increased expenditures on social or broader economic development programmes in the name of sustainable development appears as a direct affront to this culture. Such outlays reduce the net present value of future cash flows and therefore extinguish shareholder value. Worse, the long-term returns come in large part in intangibles (reputation and goodwill), which are hard to value now and even harder in the future. The traditional view, therefore, is that financial commitments to sustainable development – whether they take the form of direct financial payments or involve policies that are not strictly justified on competitive grounds (such as buying locally when offshore suppliers are less expensive) – are just another form of taxation. As with any tax, companies will try, within the limits of legality, to arrange their affairs so as to minimize such costs.

Fortunately this is far from the whole of the story. First and foremost, there is strong reason to doubt that the cost culture just described has served the industry well. Recent research by CRU International has found virtually no correlation between a company's cost competitiveness, as revealed by its gross operating margins, and the rate of growth of shareholder value, calculated by the total return on its common stock.[24] (See Figure 6–3 for this relationship for 50 leading mining companies over the past decade.) This suggests that the change in shareholder value is driven by a number of other factors in addition to the relationship between operating costs and prices. Among the leading possibilities are:

- *Different company-specific risks* – Estimates of net present value are based on forecasts of the future, which are inherently uncertain. Some uncertainties,

Figure 6–3. Shareholder Return versus Cash Margins (1990–2000)
Source: CRU International

like commodity prices, are common to all companies; others, specifically uncertainties relating to a mine's ability to operate, are company-specific. Faced with this, the market may value different companies on the basis of their perceived riskiness.
- *Terminal liabilities* – In many cases the ultimate liabilities of a mining company may not be clearly presented using current accounting practice and may not even be quantifiable in practice; nevertheless, the market will mark down the value of any company that it fears has potential exposure to such liabilities.
- *Capital productivity* – In many cases a low-operating-cost position is only achieved by investing large sums of capital either in the original mine or when acquiring the operation from someone else. Clearly there is a real risk that a company will invest too much capital for any given competitive position.
- *Real option value* – The ownership of a mine carries with it more than the entitlement to the free cash flow that it generates. It also confers on the owner a right to further develop the mine and exercise other real business options on terms that are not available to competitors. Such options have an independent value that is frequently recognized by the market.

Though these are not the only factors other than production costs that will affect the market's valuation of a mining company, all of them are intimately linked with sustainable development concerns, so it is useful to look at them in some detail.

First, site-specific risk: aside from commodity market risk, which is common to all, the principal risks associated with cash flow at a specific mine are geological (reserve) risk, national (macroeconomic) risk, and socio-political risk. The first of these could refer to the need to avoid mining in areas of environmental sensitivity or of cultural significance that may constrain access to specific reserves. The second has a link with sustainable development issues to the extent that they affect the national economic environment or vice versa. The third site-specific risk has a huge potential to destroy shareholder value. A classic example was provided by the Bougainville copper mine in Papua New Guinea. Initially this was a highly successful and low-cost copper and gold producer. But the mine had to be prematurely abandoned in the face of a local rebellion, which began, among other factors, when landowners complained about the social and environmental impact of the mine and which escalated into a full-blown conflict in response to the national government's heavy-handed treatment of these complaints. At a minimum, the alienation of the local community, or for that matter the regional or national government, clearly places a mining venture at risk. Funds spent to avoid or minimize that risk do not necessarily detract from shareholder value, but may in fact serve to protect and enhance it.

Terminal liabilities are a huge issue for mining companies and go right to the heart of the sustainable development debate. Major portions of these liabilities are environmental and relate to the safe closure of a mine at the end of its life. (See Chapter 10.) Current accounting practices are questionable in this regard. To quote from one corporate statement:

> We record liabilities for environmental expenditures when it is probable that obligations have been incurred and the cost can be reasonably estimated. Our estimates of these costs are based on available facts, existing technology and current laws and regulations.[25]

From this extract it appears that for liabilities to be recognized in a mining company's formal financial statement, a series of assumptions must be made – not one of which is likely to predict the outcome exactly. In particular, the technology available both for the detection of pollution and its remediation is most unlikely to remain constant. It is also very unlikely that the laws and regulations regarding such subjects will remain unchanged over long periods. This is particularly relevant in that for many large mining operations, it may be 20, 30, or even 50 years before these facilities have to be closed. The same financial report contained the following explanation of the company's accounts:

> The amounts of our liabilities for remedial activities are very difficult to estimate. This is due to factors such as the unknown extent of the remedial actions that may be required. In the case of sites not owned by us, the extent of our probable liability in proportion to the probable liability of other parties is difficult to estimate. We have other probable environmental liabilities that in our judgment cannot reasonably be estimated. Losses attributable to remediation costs are reasonably possible at other sites. We cannot currently estimate the total additional loss we may incur for these environmental liabilities, but *that loss could be substantial.* [emphasis added][26]

Terminal risks are not simply environmental. There may be liabilities to employees and to the local community. Moreover, the latter may develop over time and may be influenced by legislation that has not yet been enacted. A parallel situation is the complete inability of the nuclear industry to finance new power stations in most countries. This has arisen primarily because the markets have no idea whatsoever about the size of potential liabilities at the power station when it comes to closing down at the end of its 20–40 years of working life. In most, if not all, cases of power plant closure to date, the costs have far exceeded original estimates and the reserves that were originally destined to cover these expenses.

Another example is the wholesale destruction of shareholder value at publicly quoted steel companies in the United States. In the middle of 2000, the market capitalization of the 14 largest steel companies in the country was less than one-quarter that of a single aluminium company – Alcoa – and approximately 4% the size of Microsoft's.[27] In this industry, terminal liabilities, which are largely environmental and employee-related, have reached the point where no responsible corporation or financial institution can participate in the reorganization and rationalization that appear to be needed out of fear of attracting responsibility for such large and ultimately unquantifiable liabilities.

Faced with the extreme uncertainty that clearly exists in this field, the value that the financial markets place on a mining company's stock is going to be significantly influenced by the reputation and conduct of the company with respect to the effective management of terminal liabilities. Markets will apply significantly higher valuations to companies where they expect the potential for unpleasant surprises in this regard is low, compared with other companies that are perceived to be taking higher risks.

In terms of capital productivity, actions to lower cost were always desirable. Besides being responsive to corporate pressures, they served to improve local employment security. Low-cost mines are less likely to be closed during recessions than high-cost mines. Thus local mine management has tended to favour the substitution of capital (for which they were not usually accountable) for other inputs, including labour (for which they were accountable). As the shareholder value movement takes hold in the mining industry, this paradigm will almost certainly change. When managers are forced to consider the trade-off between capital and other inputs, chances are they will select a different, less-capital-intensive route, assuming such options are available. It is not certain, of course, that this will increase the local economic multiplier, but since the local mining community in developing countries does not generally produce sophisticated capital goods, there is no reason to suppose that it will decrease this multiplier.

Finally, real option value is particularly significant for mining companies. Most ore bodies turn out to be significantly larger than originally estimated. This happens because proving reserves is costly and there is no incentive to establish reserves that are not going to be used for 20 or more years. This means, however, that there is hidden option value present in many mining properties. Thus most mining companies have the real option to expand output at a given site by accessing additional minerals that did not form part of the original plan. Moreover, the cost of such expansions tends to be significantly less than the construction of new greenfield projects.

It is sometimes assumed that the shareholder value movement serves to discourage exploration activities because it focuses too heavily on short-term performance. This is not really the case. If a company, as a result of an exploration programme, proves reserves that either materially extend the life of a mine that is about to become exhausted or that create a new expansion opportunity at an established mine, this will be immediately discounted in the form of increased shareholder value. What the shareholder value approach does is discourage exploration for the sake of exploration, or exploration based on an ideological

Job creation and skills development can be major benefits of minerals projects

belief that a certain percentage of cash flow should, under normal circumstances, be reinvested in this activity.

Sustainable development issues clearly work to either enhance or detract from the value of real options. If environmental constraints, community opposition, or conflict over land rights make the potential expansion of a mine problematic, the value of this option to the company significantly decreases. On the other hand, if the discovery of ore extends a mine's life and pushes closure costs further into the future or it makes it easier to fund them, shareholder value will be increased.

The bottom line of this discussion is that the advent of an apparently narrower and more rigorous commitment of shareholder value does not necessarily have negative implications for sustainable development issues. On the contrary, a properly implemented switch from the cost culture to the value culture has the potential to ensure that such issues are factored into business decision-making on a more disciplined and systematic basis. It is the cost culture that is the consistent opponent of sustainable development outlays.

Many of the large international publicly quoted mining and mineral companies state that they are committed to shareholder value. They have formally embraced value-based management techniques that, in theory, encourage the recognition of such things as the risk to value posed by terminal liabilities, the value of real options, and so forth. However, this is merely the theory. In practice, certain issues and problems remain.

First, the value culture may be embraced by the corporate centre, but may not be pushed down the organization or be affecting decisions on the ground. In the bull market of the 1990s, it was easy to embrace shareholder value, as top executives' compensation was paid in highly leveraged stock options. In and of itself, this does not necessarily change behaviour. But how far down the organization have the incentives been pushed, how has the measuring and reporting system been changed, and to what extent are the employees actually using different criteria when making their decisions? If the answers are not far, not much, and not at all, then the management change is just cosmetic.

Second, the change in management culture in the mining industry is far from universal. Large, high-profile, multinational mining companies attract far more scrutiny from governments and NGOs than middle-sized and smaller companies. Moreover, new mine developments attract far more scrutiny than existing operations. When a company like Rio Tinto or BHP Billiton opens a huge new copper mine, there is likely to be a substantial effort to consider the whole range of environmental issues, develop a proper mine closure plan, deal with the local community in a constructive and consensual manner, and so on. This is far from the case when it comes to a small or medium-sized incumbent operator, possibly experiencing diminished financial capability, that is working in an old mine whose original construction and planning were far inferior to modern standards, and operating in a community where a legacy of conflict exists, possibly due to previous owners. Moreover, where a company is not publicly quoted, financial market disciplines are significantly diluted.

Third, although the traditional view is to see social costs incurred by companies in addressing social development issues as just another form of tax, this is not actually the case. Taxes are usually mandatory (though many would argue that they are sometimes negotiable in large foreign direct investment situations).[28] Corporate contributions to sustainable development, however, are not mandatory. And they should stay that way. Taking environmental issues as a case in point, the ambient conditions are totally different between the Atacama desert of northern Chile and the rainforest of Indonesia. The management of mine tailings in one of the driest places on Earth poses completely different engineering challenges and involves different risk considerations

than in one of the wettest places. Likewise, where the impact of a mine on an indigenous culture is concerned, it is clear that a 'one shoe fits all' formula is unlikely to be satisfactory.

All these caveats regarding the real-world situation today leave the following problem: rather than recognizing a social cost or obligation and building it into the financial decision-making process, the expense can be minimized or done away with altogether. Making sure that does not happen requires a government structure that:

• is transparent, not corrupt, and committed to consensual decision-making;
• has the technical capability to understand and critically evaluate the options presented by the mining company from an independent perspective; and
• is not so desperately poor that development on any terms is seen as desirable.

Unfortunately, in many cases these conditions are just not present. So what happens will largely be a function of the integrity of the company concerned and the existence of some effective international framework or safeguards applied by lenders and investors, consumers, or the public spotlight.

Minerals Companies and Their Employees

Maximizing the industry contribution to sustainable development requires industry to engage with various constituencies and stakeholders at a variety of levels: globally, nationally, and locally. Company employees are one group that has the capacity and the desire to engage with industry at each of these levels to help create the necessary framework for sustainable development, at least for workers in larger and unionized mines. This is an opportunity that should not be missed.

Job Creation
Job creation is held out as a major benefit of new mining projects and one of the industry's most convincing arguments for its contribution to sustainable development.[29] But this benefit appears to be tempered in a number of ways. Mining operations are becoming more capital intensive, generating fewer jobs. Local communities also may not benefit from the

new jobs, even though mining could create indirect employment in the local economy from services provided to the mines' employees and contractors. If there are no competitive local contractors, international contractors are brought in. Moreover, even where local people are employed, incentives for contractors to invest in training are limited by the short-term or performance-leveraged nature of their contracts. Reducing employment in current or formerly state-owned enterprises has been a priority for international institutions trying to help with the process of 'reform', especially in East Europe and the former Soviet Union. This and wider market liberalization have in many cases involved large-scale direct and indirect job losses. Bolivia, for example, saw mining industry employment fall from 73,514 in 1990 to 46,402 in 2000.[30] Similarly, in the United Kingdom 180,000 people were employed in mining in 1989 but only 70,000 by 1999.[31]

There is no 'stakeholder' more important to the future of sustainable development in the mining industry than the people who work there. And there is a strong business case for paying attention to the conditions of the work force in order to attract and retain committed employees. Numerous studies indicate that recruiting and retaining top-quality staff will be a critical source of competitive advantage in the future.[32] The large mining companies are facing a big challenge in attracting high-calibre people for a number of reasons, including fewer young people choosing mining as a career because of the perception of poor future job prospects, a negative industry image, constant moves and disruption of family life, and the poor quality of life in mining towns. In addition, the industry has done a particularly bad job to date of attracting women to work in professional jobs.

Given the great variety of circumstances of individual companies and projects at the operational level, it is hard to go beyond some general observations about companies and their employees:

• *Conditions of employment* – Good, safe, healthy, and enjoyable working conditions are the best way for companies to attract and retain human capital. Competitive remuneration, reasonable working hours, opportunities for personal career development and training, sensitivity to local culture and traditions, attention to health and safety regulations, and open and participatory management structures

are all important in providing a congenial work place and reducing absenteeism and staff turnover.
• *Local recruitment* – The best way to ensure that miners can be integrated into communities and to minimize the disruption of an influx of outsiders is to recruit workers from the community. Teck Cominco's Red Dog mine in Alaska and Placer Dome's Porgera mine in PNG are just two examples of companies already doing this.
• *Education and training* – If the company is going to attract employees who understand sustainable development issues, part of the answer will have to be mining education, which helps prepare people for the challenge. Institutions of mining education are trailing in this. They are educating for a high level of technical skills – though they are not in many cases attracting the calibre and number of students they once did. Their curriculum has changed little, and the attraction of a mining education seems to be waning fast in many parts of the world.[33] There is a need for the integration of skills across technologies as well as the incorporation of considerations of social, environmental, and conflict impacts.

The need to improve environmental management has caused many companies to recruit skilled environmental engineers and others capable of helping resolve environmental concerns. Multiskilled teams should be used in technological development. The ongoing demands of a transition to sustainable development as a model will require additional new skill-sets on the company staff. Just one example is the need for cultural skills and diplomacy training for company employees posted to new communities as well as for exploration geologists, who often make the first contact with local communities. It is also essential for management to encourage environmental and other professionals to take account of the business case for their roles in developing and deploying sound sustainable development policies.

Transferable occupational skills development could leave a valuable legacy for employees when the operation closes. Mentoring schemes for younger members of the community and courses in skills such as welding, foreign languages, and information technology software are examples of this.[34] In addition, human resources management decisions are often linked to local conditions and locations. Local management therefore has an important role in negotiations and agreements with relevant local actors.

Whether the minerals industry is building human capital depends on the rate at which the labour force gains new and useful skills and on the well-being and quality of life of those who work in the industry and their families. The quality of their livelihoods is a critical sustainable development indicator. If compensation, working conditions, and social opportunities for employees are improving, employers will be on the path of sustainable development. These are, for the most part, relatively easy to measure.

The Role of Trade Unions

The history of mine labour has often been one of deep division between labour and management and a high degree of politicization – from the Western Federation of Miners in North America to the Bolivian tin miners' syndicate, South African gold miners' unions, and the coal miners of Ukraine, Serbia, West Virginia, or England. The right to form unions for collective bargaining has often been contested, and the industry has seen bitter and bloody labour conflict, recorded in histories (such as Barron Beshoar's *Out of the Depths*), novels (Emile Zola's *Germinal*), movies, and songs.

Retrenchment as well as wider work place issues, such as wages and benefits, health and safety, and union recognition, can result in disputes between mining companies and trade unions. Indeed, several large multinationals have been accused of adopting an anti-union stance, in particular resisting collective bargaining and employee consultation over major restructuring programmes. Participation is one of the central concerns of trade unions, and trade union participation is all too often marginalized or denied.

Trade unions – even when they do not represent an entire work force – are more representative of workers than either management or NGOs. This is recognized in International Labour Organization (ILO) Conventions 87 and 98. The UN Global Compact includes adherence to these two key conventions, and yet a number of companies that have committed themselves to the Global Compact continue to deny or actively oppose the trade union rights identified there.[35] Commitment to improved participation will require that companies in the future demonstrate that they are meeting at least the minimal standards required under ILO 'core' conventions. (See Box 6–2.) These conventions are included in the ILO

Declaration, which all ILO member states have agreed to abide by, even if they have not yet ratified the eight conventions.

In addition, mining companies should observe the minimal standards laid down in ILO Convention 176 on mine safety and health and in ILO 169 on indigenous people. Although it is governments, rather than companies, that ratify ILO Conventions, there is nothing to prevent companies from freely and openly committing themselves to observing the standards laid down in these. Observance of the standards in these two treaties and the eight core ILO conventions could provide a solid rights-based foundation for company interaction with its employees and affected communities. It could, in future, be a key indicator of whether a company is seriously contributing to the social pillar of sustainable development.

The Changing Face of the Company

In the minerals sector, as elsewhere in the economy, people move around and change jobs much more than in the past, so mining communities have to deal with an ever-changing series of company representatives. At the same time, it is becoming clearer that the key to solving many problems is continuity of policy, personnel, and approach.

A high percentage of community complaints are about changing priorities – such as a promise by a company representative that a local road would be surfaced to keep dust from blowing into their houses, but the person is no longer there and the road is not surfaced.

Box 6–2. ILO Core Conventions on Workers' Rights

ILO 29	Forced or Compulsory Labour (1930)
ILO 87	Freedom of Association and Protection of the Right to Organize (1948)
ILO 98	The Application of the Principles of the Right to Organize (1949)
ILO 100	Equal Remuneration for Men and Women Workers for Work of Equal Value (1951)
ILO 105	The Abolition of Forced Labour (1957)
ILO 111	Discrimination in Respect of Employment and Occupation (1958)
ILO 138	Minimum Age for Admission to Employment (1973)
ILO 182	The Prohibition and Immediate Action for the Elimination of the Worst Forms of Child Labour (1999)

Communities do not relate to the company as an institution nearly so much as they do to company representatives as individuals. Their relationship is a personal one, which does not automatically transfer to the next person in line. People in the corporate world are so used to the people they deal with being rotated in and out of positions that they often fail to appreciate the extent to which the rest of the world does not work this way.

The same principles apply to all kinds of relationships the company has. Sustainable development requires a deeper engagement with other elements of society, which in turn requires a continuity of policy, philosophy, and approach. Unfortunately, with increasing frequency, the people the community sees as 'in charge' do not work for the mining company but for a consultant or contractor, and they know they will be with the project for only a limited time. (See Table 6–1.) In dealing with the complexity of relationships that occur around mine sites while communicating and negotiating with communities, PNG has a number of initiatives that have been successful and may be usefully deployed more widely, including community relations officers and community affairs sections.[36]

Four actions can help address the changing face of the company in the local community:

• A Community Sustainable Development Plan, produced through a multistakeholder process, should be implemented consistently over time, independent of any individuals responsible, so that if one person leaves the plan does not fall apart. (The plan is discussed in detail in Chapter 9.)
• The company should recruit people on the ground specifically for the purpose of overseeing the local development plan. This function needs to be part of the core management team, not the public relations effort.
• Local authorities or other appropriate local institutions should ensure that they provide on-going commitment and resources to play a role in designing and implementing the local development plan.
• Local authorities or other appropriate local institutions should play a facilitator role in ensuring that communities are able to play an active role in the plan.

Mine Closure

Although 88% of companies in the PricewaterhouseCoopers survey have environmental mitigation plans post-closure, only 45% have detailed socio-economic plans that are regularly reviewed and given updated costs estimates.[37] Given that the number of livelihoods in the industry has been declining and may continue to decrease, there needs to be an intense focus on what happens to mine workers after they leave the industry. If they are leaving with improved and more marketable job skills and some social safety net to protect them during the transition, this is an

Year	Phase	Principal Contact Person
1	Exploration	Junior company exploration manager
2	Development drilling	Foreman for drilling contractor
3	Feasibility studies	Transportation, water resources, environmental, social, and various other consultants
4	Permitting	Consulting firm in charge of permitting
5–6	Construction	Foremen of various construction contractors
6–20	Operation	Six different project managers who work for three different companies as the mine changes ownership
21	Closure	Environmental consultants

Table 6–1. The Face of the Company in the Community

indicator of sustainable development. In some places, workers have gained experience and skills that serve them well in other sectors. Government, companies, or unions are providing retraining programmes to equip them for new skills, transition payments to help them move to regions with more employment, and other measures designed to ease the change. In other places, however, unemployment is a heavy burden, opportunities are few, and transitional assistance is scarce or absent.

When the industry lays people off, there is a need to be clear conceptually on the lines of responsibility among companies, the worker, the union, and the state. Certainly part of the burden does belong to the state in the form of unemployment payments or other social assistance. The state receives tax revenues from the industry, which in a sense can be seen as paying for these. Just as certainly, in a sustainable development framework the company has some share of the responsibility to ensure that the human capital it helped develop is sustained. Labour unions also may have a responsibility to help workers understand their options for a transition, and individual workers have a responsibility to keep an eye on a future when the mine may close. Where a reduction of labour force is predictable, part of the solution should be integrated planning to try to ensure that there are opportunities to take advantage of the skills developed.

Improving Worker Health and Safety

Acceptable, safe, and healthy working conditions are one of the first prerequisites of a more sustainable world. The minerals industry, and mining in particular, does not have a good record in this regard. There has been significant progress in recent years, but more needs to be done to ensure the right of every miner to work without injury or illness, to learn skills that can be transferred once an operation is shut down, and to understand how to contribute to sustainable development.

Mining work has been physically demanding and often dangerous.[38] The history of explosions, rockfalls, cave-ins, rock bursts, and other accidents is a long and discouraging catalogue of large and small accidents resulting in a high number of deaths and serious injuries to miners. In addition, miners have faced occupational disease, from the coal miner's Black Lung to the hard rock miner's silicosis or the lung cancer

among uranium miners. This has been a feature not only of mining but of the downstream parts of the industry, from lead workers to beryllium workers in refining and fabrication of mineral products. Death and danger aside, miners have often lived in an isolated, often all-male environment, cut off from normal community and family life. Certainly this was the pattern of much of South African mining under apartheid. The image of the hard-drinking miner on a night in town often cloaks a much more bitter reality of isolation, loneliness, and boredom.

Today's industry in most of its operations represents a remarkable advance from these conditions. All but one of the respondents in a recent survey of the top 20 gold mining companies reported that health, safety, and sustainable communities are the most important areas of sustainable development.[39] But there is still further work required to ensure that, without exception, an individual can devote a lifetime to a mining career and emerge healthy and unharmed.

The nature of worker health and safety problems differs, depending on where a mine is located (industrial versus developing country), who is involved (large companies or small-scale miners), what products are being mined (gold or uranium versus gypsum or sandstone), what processes are used (such as underground versus opencast mining), and prevailing social and ecological conditions.[40]

Understanding the Health and Safety Effects of Mining

According to the International Labour Organization, mining is responsible for 5% of fatal accidents at work but only 1% of the world's work force.[41] The health effects of mining are not only felt in accidents – resulting in injuries and fatalities – but in longer-term health effects such as cancers and respiratory conditions.

Employment in mining also brings positive effects on health, particularly to those who may have been previously unemployed or whose job increases net earnings. Workers may experience psychological as well as health benefits associated with an increase in income and consequent improvement in living standards.

A review of published literature indicates that the main health risks faced in mines are exposure to dust, noise, heat, cold, wind, limited light, and inhalation of poisonous substances; that many accidents arise from the use of large transport or electrical or mechanical equipment; and that there are indirect negative health impacts, such as mental health conditions, stress, and job dissatisfaction. The bulk of the literature focuses on the continued burden of largely preventable health impacts that mine workers sustain, not just in their working life but also into old age.[42]

The degree and nature of risks are largely determined by the character of the mining operation. Deep underground mines may pose severe risks resulting from high blood pressure, heat exhaustion, myocardial infarction, and nervous system disorders.[43]

The health effects associated with specific minerals are often complex and interrelated and may take years to manifest. Some effects on health are more specific to certain products:

- *Coal* – Chronic diseases due to coal (and other silicates) are largely due to dust inhalation during mineral extraction. Pneumoconiosis and silicosis are the most severe outcomes related to coal dust exposure by mine workers.
- *Asbestos* – Along with coal and other silicate dusts, the dangers of mining asbestos largely relate to damage to the lungs and respiratory functioning. Resultant diseases include pneumoconiosis, asbestosis, and lung cancers, the symptoms of which may take many years to develop.
- *Uranium* – The health effects of uranium mining are also long term, sometimes manifesting themselves more than 20 years after exposure. Most studies find

the relative risks of lung cancer to be two to five times higher among uranium workers who have been exposed to higher levels of radon, or to long periods of low exposure.

In other cases, the main health risk for workers may not be the primary product mined but a by-product or some hazardous materials used in processing.

In the last half-century, there has been a significant decrease in the number of accidents, injuries, and work-related illnesses occurring at large mines in most of the world. In the US coal and non-coal sector, the average fatalities ratio (AFR) dropped from 0.234 per 100 miners a year between 1941 to 1945 to 0.029 for the period 1991 to 1995.[44] Despite this, performances differ considerably between countries. (See Figures 6–4, 6–5, and 6–6.) In South Africa, for example, despite a reduction in fatalities and injuries, the AFR for 1991–95 was 0.0988.[45] The pattern across countries is that more deaths occur in underground mining than in open-cut – a pattern that appears to be consistent over time and location.[46] (See Figure 6–7.) While fatalities and injuries in gold mining are considerably more common than in the rest of the industry, even coal mines with relatively low injury rates are prone to methane explosions, which can cause a high number of deaths.

Despite reductions in the fatality and accident rates, concern over chronic diseases such as those resulting from coal dust inhalation remain: recent studies show

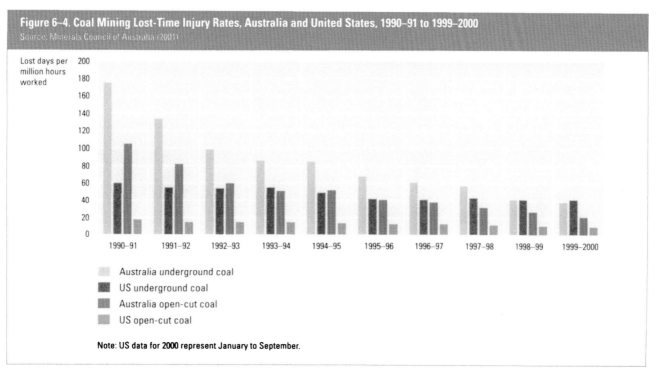

Figure 6–4. Coal Mining Lost-Time Injury Rates, Australia and United States, 1990–91 to 1999–2000
Source: Minerals Council of Australia (2001)

Lost days per million hours worked

Australia underground coal
US underground coal
Australia open-cut coal
US open-cut coal

Note: US data for 2000 represent January to September.

that up to 12% of coal miners still develop these fatal diseases.[47] In extreme cases, evidence of the detrimental health impacts of minerals may lead to calls for outright bans on mining them. For example, since 1999 the Collegium Ramazzini has called for a ban on all mining and use of asbestos, supported by international journals of occupational and environmental health.[48]

To date, workers' health has often received less attention than their safety. Moreover, the trend towards longer working hours and shift work, with mineworkers spending more time away from home, has

resulted in new health concerns. This trend is illustrated by an ILO survey in Australia, which recorded mining rosters of up to 14 days of 12-hour shifts in a row.[49] Increased fatigue, stress, and dissatisfaction among workers were observed. Families also suffered. Increases in the use of contracted labour and reduced job security also have knock-on effects on the mental health of mine workers and ex-miners. Contract workers are less likely to receive adequate health and safety training.

The impact of HIV/AIDS on the mining industry in some countries, particularly in Southern Africa, is

Figure 6–5. Fatalities in South African Mines by Mineral, 1984–2000
Source: Chamber of Mines of South Africa (2001)

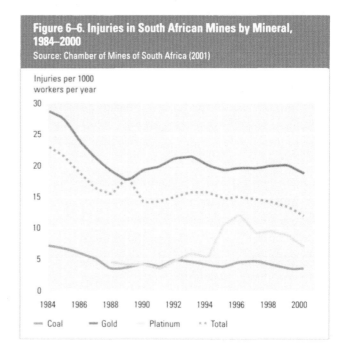

Figure 6–6. Injuries in South African Mines by Mineral, 1984–2000
Source: Chamber of Mines of South Africa (2001)

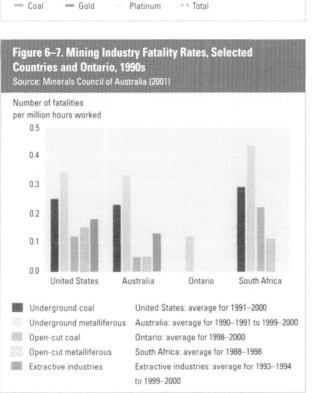

Figure 6–7. Mining Industry Fatality Rates, Selected Countries and Ontario, 1990s
Source: Minerals Council of Australia (2001)

extremely serious. In South Africa alone, 20% of coal miners and 30% of gold miners are HIV-positive, and in the next five years, 5–10% of companies' work forces will start to die.[50] (See also Chapter 9.) As illness forces workers to leave their jobs, valuable skills and experience are lost, often leading to a mismatch between human resources and labour requirements. In June 2001, the ILO adopted a Code of Practice on HIV/AIDS and the World of Work.[51] Its fundamental aim is to help safeguard decent working conditions and protect the rights and dignity of workers living with HIV/AIDS. The code provides practical guidance to governments, employers, and workers' organizations for developing national and work place HIV/AIDS policies and programmes.[52]

Initiatives to Reduce Risk and Maximize Improvements

Improvements in health and safety can be attributed to a number of factors, including increased understanding of risks and their prevention and management, laws and regulations, technology, and the health and safety culture of management and workers. An increasing number of initiatives involving different actors – workers, unions, NGOs, government, and companies – often working together for common solutions are emerging. For example, union and management activities have triggered changes in law, and governments have supported organized labour in the improvements.

Coal miners have played a unique role in improving worker health and safety, in particular through challenging companies to improve transparency of information and to provide clinics and compensation. Worker successes in this challenge date back to the 1930s and 1940s in the United Kingdom and the United States.[53] Unions have also played a major role in the development of safer conditions in mines and of health information and in sponsoring other services.

Mining companies have also been involved in programmes of worker health and safety. In the past, these mainly involved improvements in working conditions in the mines such as through safety measures to reduce injuries or air conditioning to reduce heat stress. There has been a recent initiative to harmonize safety performance reporting to enable companies to benchmark their performance against that of other companies and to find and implement best practices that lead to superior performance.[54]

To date, benchmarking has not reached broad acceptance in the industry. While a number of companies recognize the need for international benchmarking in terms of health and safety performance indicators, it is difficult to conduct meaningful analysis when most companies use different indicators and definitions. Other recent initiatives have included educational and training programmes as well as increased consideration of living and social conditions.

Laws and Regulations

At the international level, a number of ILO instruments – including conventions, codes of conduct, and recommendations – aim to improve worker health and safety in mines. ILO Convention 176, which is relevant to health and safety for the mining sector, has been ratified by 18 countries.[55] Governments ratifying this convention undertake to adopt legislation for its implementation, including the provision for inspection services and the designation of a competent authority to monitor and regulate the various aspects of occupational health and safety in mines. The treaty also sets out procedures for reporting and investigating disasters, accidents, and dangerous occurrences related to mines and for compiling relevant statistics. Both workers' and employers' rights and responsibilities are set out.

It is important to note that the convention provides a floor – the minimum safety requirement against which all changes to mine operations should be measured. The ILO recommendation on this – which is advisory – provides more specific guidance on the different sections of the convention.[56] Some of the ILO codes of practice for mining and for topics relevant to mining are even more specific.[57]

Most countries also have some form of national legislation in place that lays out measures to prevent disease and injury as well as to monitor performance. Prescriptive regulations are being reduced. New regulations highlight the responsibility and liability of mine managers, and require that they manage health and safety and provide a safe place to work. In some countries, regulation has played an important role in reducing fatalities and accidents at mines. In other countries, it has been largely ineffective, often due to a lack of enforcement.

One of the main concerns regarding laws and regulations is that indicators of disease and accidents vary among countries and sometimes among provinces within countries. Similarly, the definition of accidents can vary. In Ontario, Canada, for example, if a worker has a bad back that is considered to be related to mining activities, it is compensable, whereas in Norway, compensation will be provided only if a traumatic symptom is diagnosed as a result of the bad back.[58]

Technological Changes on Safety and Health
Improved mining equipment, methods, and technology have played an important role in reducing the risks faced by mine workers, partly through reducing the risk of human error. In the South African gold mining industry, for instance, the use of hydraulic props accounted for a reduction in accidents from 13.4 per thousand employees in 1976 to 7.7 in 1984.[59] At the Enugu mine in Nigeria, following the introduction of full mechanization, the number of mining accidents decreased by 60% between 1975 and 1980. Changes were also recorded in sickness absence indices, the most significant being the severity index, which dropped from 9.2 in 1975 to 3.0 in 1980.[60]

The effects of new technology have not been uniform, however. Some new technologies have been accompanied by new or intensified hazards – such as dust, noise, vibration, electric current, and ergonomics-related problems.[61]

A Health and Safety Culture
In addition to improvements in technology, companies attribute the reduction in the number of accidents and fatalities to the adoption of management approaches and systems for improving worker safety.

Although the health and safety discourse is widely spread among management teams, there are differing views on the extent to which this actually translates into practice. Unions sometimes report that national and management commitments do not flow down to the work place because, in reality, production pressures take priority for technical or site managers who are responsible for implementing them. Moreover, moves towards an increase in contract workers as well as an increase in shift work are less conducive to improvements. Peter Colley from the Construction, Forestry, Mining and Energy Union in Australia states that 'companies seeking to achieve good occupational

health and safety (OHS) culture need to minimize labour turnover, to have reasonable working hours, and to recognize and seek to mitigate the impact of production targets and bonuses on OHS performance.'[62]

In 1999, the Minerals Council of Australia commissioned a survey into the factors determining safety culture.[63] The survey found that in most organizations the strong focus of senior management on safety might have inadvertently eroded the focus on and responsibility for safety at lower levels. It identified several key factors – such as perceived lack of recognition for safety, rigid safety systems and procedures, and 'neutrality' towards mining dangers – that suggest mineworkers had become more complacent towards risk. This situation was exacerbated by workers experiencing and perceiving high levels of protection through hazard engineering, risk management systems, and strong leadership. The survey identified several key requirements for a sustained and positive change in safety culture, namely that:
• safety become more integrated with other business outcomes at strategic and goal-setting levels of organizations;
• responsibility for and decision-making in safety be increasingly devolved to lower levels, especially to the supervisory levels and their teams; and
• a concerted effort be made to make safety management more flexible, simpler, and team-driven.

Although there has been a movement away from paying risk premiums for unsafe work in most countries, it is still the case that pay systems based on performance rather than safety bonuses can inadvertently encourage people to work unsafely. In an effort to overcome these concerns, some companies make workers ineligible for performance bonuses if safety requirements are not met. The introduction of a safety bonus is not feasible as it may lead to workers downplaying or covering up injuries.

Some mining companies have developed safety 'core beliefs' or internal standards through social dialogue. They form part of the contract of employment and influence behaviour from the top to the bottom of an enterprise. The achievement of an effective safety culture in mining needs a sustained and visible commitment and leadership from the top, with health and safety being the responsibility of all workers, teams, and leaders in the organization. It should be accepted that improving health and safety performance is a long-term goal that requires sustained effort, resources, and commitment. Education and training in risk management and risk awareness are essential to improvements in health and safety performance at the operational level. Such training is normally a legal requirement but is often done in ways that are not plain, and the auditing of these assessments is not always transparent.[64]

The Way Forward

Though some good progress was made towards uniformity of accident reporting systems at the Minesafe Conference in Perth in September 2000 and in subsequent work of a small industry group, headed by BHP Billiton, there is a still a pressing need to get broad-based agreement on a common global reporting scheme for safety.

Even more attention has to be paid to a uniform reporting system for occupational disease in the mining sector.[65] In an effort to prevent occupational disease, benchmarking is needed to encourage best practice and to determine occupational exposure limits. The quest for uniformity in reporting is hampered by a series of obstacles. These include differences in national legislation, differences in medical surveillance, lack of standards in collection of corporate data, no standard definitions for disease and injury, and long latency of occupational disease. The International Council on Mining & Metals (ICMM) has a health advisory panel to address this issue.

A common set of standards should be developed for both accident and disease reporting through a multistakeholder process convened by ICMM with assistance from an international organization such as the ILO. Companies should not wait for governments to develop standards before developing their own.

There is clearly no single accident prevention approach. As in other sectors, the best companies are seeking a zero accident goal. A combination of different measures including legislation, education and training, technology, data collection and analysis, and above all a common vision shared by the different actors is required. Because the types of issues that predispose unsafe behaviour and their relative importance vary from mine to mine, there is no single solution to the promotion of safe behaviour. The main

strategies involve compelling, facilitating, rewarding, training, informing, and participating.

The progressive approach is not solely concerned with reducing injury and illness; it embraces a positive concept of well-being. Moreover, community health and worker health are intimately related – disease can spread quickly from and to the work place. The industry needs to be ahead of the game and to start researching the effects of trends in employment patterns before the effects are felt. There is no better example than the HIV/AIDS pandemic in Africa, where there is some leadership on the issue. But there are other issues. To give just one example, further research is needed on the impact of noise and shift work on hearing and eyesight. Research to date has largely been retrospective rather than forward-looking and participatory.

Experience shows that effective safety management on a day-to-day basis requires partnership among management, workers, and unions to identify problems, define actions, and monitor and assess performance. Safety cannot be seen as the sole responsibility of designated safety managers but as a shared responsibility of everyone.

In sum, the achievement of an effective health and safety culture in minerals operations needs a sustained and visible commitment and leadership from the top, with health and safety being the responsibility of all workers, teams, and leaders in the organization.

The Role of Technology

Technological change will continue to play a fundamental role in maintaining the profitability that is critical if the minerals industry is to contribute to sustainable development. Despite devoting far less to research and development than other sectors do, the industry has thousands of technologies currently under development.[66] These cover the whole minerals cycle, from defining and identifying new sources of minerals through to recycling. Some of the most significant are those that act as triggers for the exploitation of new types of reserves, such as the high-pressure acid leaching process (HPAL) for nickel laterites. (See Box 6–3.) For metals, more efficient means of recovery are critical if lower grades are to be mined. The introduction of solvent extraction electro-winning for copper production is one example of this.

Approximately two-thirds of the world's known nickel resources are in the form of laterites – ancient soils in tropical regions that can be up to 15 metres deep. These are relatively low-grade sources of nickel in relation to the alternative source of sulphides ores. The latter are typically found in hard rocks at depths of hundreds of metres. A new process for recovery of nickel (and the associated cobalt) from ores, called high-pressure acid leaching, has undergone significant developments in the last few years. To date, the three commercial plants using this process have operated with only limited success and have not met the claims of lower capital and operating costs. When combined with the relatively low cost of extraction of laterites, HPAL may have a significant effect on the location and nature of nickel mining in the future.

Source: Reimann et al. (1999)

One key to improving the efficiency with which a mining operation is carried out is accurate information to characterize a mineral reserve and then to manage the operation to extract it. Computer software has been developed to combine all information on a reserve (physical and engineering) into a single 3D model that can be continuously updated. In many cases this also has significant implications for safety. In South African gold mines, for instance, the rapid detection of faults and other irregularities in the ore body is critical in preventing fatalities due to collapse. Computer and satellite systems lead to the prospect of the complete automation of equipment, which has obvious implications for safety and employment.

Accurate description of a mineral reserve also leads to more efficient exploitation. At the surface, global positioning systems (based on satellites) and associated mine computer systems have a key role in controlling the equipment used so that it is more efficient. For example, such systems can avoid the inadvertent dumping of valuable material that sometimes occurs.

Source: Stewart (2000); Mining Magazine (2000)

Biotechnologies can also have a significant impact on metal recovery. In the steel industry, direct coal-based ironmaking, direct steelmaking, and thin-strip casting innovations are all driving substantial changes in costs and the structure of the industry.

Many technologies are targeted at efficient extraction of minerals from the ground in terms of energy use or ensuring full exploitation of a reserve. The increasing automation that comes through satellite and remote sensing technology is one example. (See Box 6–4.)

There have also been significant advances in the development of technologies to restore parts of ecosystems disturbed or removed as a result of mining and minerals processing.[67] The plant sciences have a significant role in this. They have even allowed the recovery of an economic crop of metals from contaminated land.[68]

New technologies based on scientific knowledge can bring new problems as they solve others – they can bring uncertain 'progress' because of their wider social and economic consequences. For instance, increased automation in the minerals sector has reduced the number of accidents but has led to changes in both the type and number of workers at any one site. Technology not specifically targeted at the mining industry, such as aviation, has enabled minerals extraction and processing in places where it would previously have been uneconomical.

Technological change is almost impossible to prevent and so it becomes increasingly important for cultural values to frame not only the application of technology in the minerals industry, but also the purpose for which it is developed. For technology to help the industry contribute to sustainable development, two goals must be kept in mind. First, technology should be integrated across the whole production process. This begins with the integration of environmental goals into production plans, which is a key aspect of a plan put forward by members of the National Mining Association in the US.[69] On the other hand, integrated technologies go far beyond reducing specific groups of impacts while maintaining or increasing technologies. Remote sensing of geological structures in the gold mining industry has implications not only for production, but also for the detection of faults, fissures, and other features that pose a danger to workers.[70] Research programmes must be funded and organized in order to achieve integration rather than single, short-term technologies.[71]

Second, technologies must be appropriate in every respect for the context in which they are deployed. This is a particular challenge for international minerals companies that often develop engineering technologies in one part of the world for application elsewhere. Assessments must be made of any technology with regard to impacts on gender equity, skills, and local capacity to solve problems relevant to the location in which it operates. Clearly, it is not just the way in which knowledge is applied that is critical. The nature of science itself and its separation from ethical considerations has prevented it from contributing optimally to sustainable development.[72]

Technology will have a key role in ensuring that current and future social and environmental costs of mining activity are internalized.[73] If better mining methods evolve, better ways to separate wastes and recycling emerge, or better ways to reduce the environmental impacts are developed, then engineering techonology – developed in an integrated and appropriate manner – can make a fundamental contribution to sustainable development.

A much larger issue is the need for research and innovation to find breakthrough technologies for multifactor improvements in eco–efficiency: the ratio of value delivered (productive output) per unit of environmental impact and resource depletion. Although the MMSD analysis did not cover this in detail, it is clear that such technologies are needed so that society can use mineral-based materials to provide a reasonable quality of life for the growing world population without jeopardizing the quality of the environment on which it depends. (See Chapter 11.) The development of such leapfrog technology is unlikely to emerge from typical, incrementally focused research and development.

The Financial Sector

One of the arguments in making the business case for sustainable development is that improved sustainability performance will result in lower risks for the financial institutions that provide debt and equity funding as well as insurance to the industry. If these institutions were able to recognize good environmental and social performance, they could reward companies with lower costs of capital and insurance premiums. Thus the financial institutions are potentially an important leverage point to improve sustainability performance. As early as 1995, a United Nations Environment Programme (UNEP) study found that more than 90

international banks were undertaking environmental financial risk assessment of borrowers and 50 of these incorporated environmental liability into loan terms.[74]

On the other hand, there is a strongly held view that financial institutions have reinforced the failings of mining companies in their lending practices by focusing largely on a project's relative cash operating costs.[75] This allows marginal or unprofitable projects to be funded and encourages operators to pursue technical economies of scale in order to spread fixed costs over a larger output level. This in turn can lead to greater environmental and social impacts as the project is scaled up. On the equity side, the market's focus on short-term performance measures (such as quarterly reports) also prevents a true assessment of the long-term profitable and sustainable mining companies.

Public financial institutions such as the International Finance Corporation (IFC) can have significant influence over how mining projects are developed because of the leverage they can bring to a project. Considering volume of equity and debt financing, the IFC is a relatively small player from a global perspective. From 1993 to 2001, the IFC financed a total of 33 mining projects through 56 transactions activities, providing US$681 million of equity and debt financing – about 18% of the total cost of these projects.[76] (On an annual basis, the mining industry invests about US$30 billion world-wide, of which less than 2% is from IFC.) However, the IFC still has quite a significant influence over how many mining projects are developed, because its environmental and social guidelines are widely accepted by many of the more responsible companies as industry standards, and because it can invest in countries that others might consider too risky. All mining projects financed by IFC must meet IFC environmental and social guidelines. Many newer IFC-financed mining projects also have local economic development components.

Another group of public financial institutions, the national export credit agencies (ECAs), are believed to be the 'quiet giants' of mining finance, though their activities have largely remained outside the public debate and they are generally unaccountable for the environmental and social consequences of their financing. Unlike most other financial institutions, many of them have failed to date to develop environmental and social guidelines and procedures to guide decision-making.[77] Notable exceptions are recent

The discovery of the Witwatersrand goldfields led to the founding of the Johannesburg Stock Exchange in 1887

thought too distant from markets, transportation, or other infrastructure.

The bitter struggles with some developing country governments, based on the perception that there was a fixed pie to be divided in some sort of 'zero sum' struggle, have pretty much subsided, at least for the moment. Although confrontational negotiations with private companies over rent capture or nationalization of mining companies have receded in recent years, host-country governments do have a stake in the outcome and will assert that vigorously through one means or another. They will take appropriate action to protect the national interest and respond to public concern if mining companies fail to meet the national expectations of economic, environmental, and social responsibilities.

guidelines developed by the US, Canadian, UK, and Australian agencies.[78] Statistics are not available on their lending to the mining sector, but it is understood to be considerably higher than all the commercial banks and multilateral institutions put together. One high-profile example is the US$2.3-billion Antamina copper and zinc mine in Peru: ECAs provided 51% of the debt finance, guaranteed a further 8%, and were part of a consortium guaranteeing a further 25%.[79]

Mining represents a very small fraction of bank lending portfolios world-wide, and probably not much more than 1% of equity investment. Equity or debt financiers may not always find the minerals sector attractive, however. As indicated at the beginning of this chapter, the rate of return on equity invested in mining, for example, has been generally low in recent years.

Over this period, market liberalization and privatization have been accompanied by a rapid opening of new areas to exploration and development, such as the former Soviet Union and Eastern Europe. Areas where foreign investment was quite limited because of broad political disapproval of government systems (South Africa and Chile, for instance) have changed governments and become attractive to investors. Legal protection and guarantees for investors, liberalized trade and investment regimes, 'reformed' mining codes, and political change have created many new opportunities for people who are looking for minerals. These trends have been helped by dramatic gains in exploration technology, which have made it much easier to locate and 'take a look' at promising geologic structures in areas that were previously

Just 25 years ago there was relatively little chance that western multinationals would be exploring or mining in Uzbekistan, Vietnam, South Africa, Argentina, Romania, Nicaragua, Chile, or a host of other countries. If, from the companies' point of view, this opening up of new areas was positive, it has had some other effects as well. One is that as it has opened up competition and helped to create the current conditions of abundant supply and sinking prices. Another is that it has encouraged companies to develop projects in areas that have relatively pristine environments but weak environmental management, indigenous groups with territorial claims that have never been effectively resolved, or local populations with immense development needs but no functioning local government. In this milieu, there have been numerous explosive conflicts over mining or exploration proposals, which have created new levels and kinds of risks for institutions that provide capital to the minerals sector. There have been some major losses for equity investors, lenders, and insurers alike.

Opponents of mining projects in some countries simply do not have other remedies. They do not have access to clear legal rights for communities, developed environmental law, administrative law capable of holding agencies to account, or functioning and reliable court systems. They have few alternatives to press their complaints. The financial institutions that support the project therefore have become a favoured venue in which complaints about social, environmental, economic, land tenure, and other issues related to projects can be heard. Not all financial institutions want or are comfortable with this role or with putting their own reputations on the line over how these issues get resolved.

NGOs and affected community groups have increasingly used both the multilateral and private commercial banks as a leverage point for changing mining practices. Friends of the Earth International and others, for example, successfully campaigned for the World Bank Group to assess its activities in the extractive industries, which has resulted in the launch of the Extractive Industries Review.[80] The annual general meetings of major banks have been disrupted by protests over the banks' involvement in mining finance. In 1999, ABN AMRO agreed to take up some NGO concerns with the mining companies to which it provided financing, particularly Freeport McMoRan in Indonesia, and to meet regularly with an NGO to discuss progress.[81] In Australia, Westpac Bank has come under pressure from several NGOs for its involvement in the controversial Jabiluka uranium mine.[82] After the cyanide spill at Baia Mare in January 2000, Dresdner Bank, which had invested US$8.5 million, became the target of an NGO campaign.[83] In July 2000, Barclays Capital was included in an NGO petition to urge strict enforcement of environmental regulations for Tiomin Resources project in Kenya.[84]

The realities from the point of view of financial institutions therefore must include:

- high transaction costs in evaluating minerals projects and associated risks;
- a growing probability that they will become the court of last resort for those dissatisfied with the project, and that their own reputation will therefore be at risk;[85]
- new and unpredictable kinds of risks, which have shown in some cases to be very real threats to project viability; and
- a quite limited flow of capital to a relatively small sector of the economy with an overall recent history of poor returns.

This has led a number of financial institutions to leave the mining sector. Although no statistics are available, it is believed that the number of institutions capable of leading a syndication for a major mining project has fallen from around 10–15 banks ten years ago to about 6–8 today.[86]

As a result of consolidation, the largest mining companies are now moving into an era where they will not be depending so much on project finance as on corporate finance. In other words, they will seek loans directly to the company on the strength of its balance sheet rather than on specific projects. This trend is reinforced by the low metal price environment, which reduces the number of new project developments. This has a number of potential consequences.

First, it may mean a lower level of outside scrutiny on whether to embark on specific projects. As it is now, a bank (or other investor) must be convinced of the merits and viability of the project. This is not possible if funds provided are not earmarked for a particular project. Second, it could take the loan decision out of the political realm: since the loan will not be (at least overtly) linked to a specific project, it will be much harder to build NGO campaigns against the loan. This again means less outside scrutiny of project decisions. And it also means that there may be additional pressure on NGOs that are concerned about projects to develop new ways and means to express those concerns. Third, if this model of borrowing becomes more attractive than project finance, there will be a growing distance between the companies big enough to avail themselves of the corporate finance alternative and those that are not. This could accelerate the trend to concentration in the industry. Nevertheless, project finance will continue to be used by medium-sized players and by the large companies to manage country/political risk.

There is what appears to be an irresistible pressure for differentiation within the minerals industry. It can begin to divide along lines of quality, based on effectively enforced common understandings about sustainable development. The industry can also begin to divide along lines simply of size: the big survive and the small starve. There is likely to be some of both, but if the division is principally based on performance, then the industry will look very different in ten years than if the split is basically just about size.

In partnership with UNEP and the World Bank, MMSD held two major workshops on mining finance. The first, in Washington in April 2001, had some 125 participants from the finance sector, the minerals industry, government, academic institutions, labour organizations, and environmental and human rights groups. The second, in Paris in January 2002, had 30 attendees from finance and insurance, the mining industry, and NGOs. It reviewed research in three key areas – indicators for public reporting, the business case for sustainably oriented management practices, and the need for clearer governance systems around the financing of mining projects. The two workshops and MMSD-commissioned research came up with several conclusions and recommendations:

• Lending institutions need to focus on a wide spectrum of indicators of long-term value of the companies they finance, including the sources of risk to that value. It is thus in their interest to be certain that these companies adhere to legal requirements and best practice in relation to the whole range of issues covered in this report.

• The consolidation among financial institutions in recent years means that there are a limited number of key institutions, which will make it easier to bring them together on a common platform.

• There is some interest in financing circles for creating effective guidelines or standards for better performance in the minerals industry built around sustainable development criteria. It is hoped that the MMSD/World Bank/UNEP process to date could be continued with the commercial lending community. What is needed is an open process that leads to clear standards that are then accepted and applied by the World Bank Group, export credit agencies, regional development banks, commercial lenders, insurers, equity investors, and other financial institutions. These need to be a set of sustainable development principles that reinforce the best of the industry itself. Clearly they would have to be open to flexible application and interpretation at the national and local level. The World Bank Group could convene a meeting of relevant institutions to discuss how a joint approach might be prepared and implemented.

• So far the various World Bank policies and guidelines have been the common standard for the financial community. They are widely used. No other broadly applicable set of norms has near this level of acceptance. Any successful strategy must therefore start by recognizing and building on these, rather than starting from scratch.

• The World Bank's Extractive Industries Review is currently under way. It is hoped that this report can be built upon by that process. The Bank needs to proceed with confidence to work with other banks, insurers, investors, and others to see whether specific common approaches can be developed within the investment community for the sector (for example, on issues such as social and environmental planning for closure and financial assurance for closure costs).

• It may be necessary to create a new process that includes World Bank entities, regional development banks, export credit agencies, investment guarantee agencies, commercial banks, insurers, and other financial institutions. Each has different practices for the participation of other stakeholders, which would need to be reconciled. The objective is to establish a mining-specific supplement to the Bank's safeguard policies.

• When the World Bank standards are used by private and public lenders in the mineral sector without Bank involvement, there are no public compliance safeguards. In the Bank, the Inspection Panel and the IFC's ombudsman deal with public complaints and compliance issues. A clear and consistent complaints system is needed for people or organizations that have grievances around the sector. (See Chapter 16.) Any agreed system of investment standards would clearly need to relate to such an entity or, in the absence of it, consider an equivalent.

• It is clear that there is enormous potential for cross-sectoral learning of financing best practice from other capital-intensive sectors, such as oil and gas or pulp and paper. This applies to sources of finance from corrupt sources as well as a host of best-practice guidelines and standards.

The Industry as Part of the Minerals Sector

A holistic approach is required to address sustainable development. This kind of integration is difficult to achieve – more difficult than improving a particular process or method. But it holds out the promise that companies that can achieve this kind of integration will be able to create durable, sustainable competitive advantages.

To meet the sustainable development imperative, companies need to go beyond their traditional responsibilities to employees, shareholders, and regulators. The transition towards sustainable development involves meaningful partnerships with local communities and government, enhanced stakeholder participation, integrated life-cycle planning, transparency, forward-looking preventive action, timely remedial action, regulatory compliance, a respect for declared 'no go' areas, and investment in the future to provide for well-being in a post-mining world.[87] These are some of the subjects of the next eight chapters.

Endnotes

[1] The figure is reprinted from Camus (2002). The data from Morgan Stanley Capital International relate to monthly price equity indices and are consistent across 23 developed markets, 28 emerging markets, and almost 6000 companies.

[2] See, for example, Porter and van der Linde (1995).

[3] Wayne Dunn and Associates (2001).

[4] Noronha (2001).

[5] Placer Dome (2001); see also http://www.wacommunity health.org.

[6] MMSD Southern Africa (2001).

[7] Elias and Taylor (2001).

[8] Grieg-Gran (2002).

[9] Borax (2001).

[10] SustainAbility (2001).

[11] BHP Billiton (2001).

[12] Young (1996).

[13] Warhurst and Noronha (2000).

[14] Case study prepared for MMSD by Rio Tinto, July 2001, 'The Contribution of Hamersley Iron to the Development of Western Australia's Pilbara Region'.

[15] Westpac in Australia has a sustainable development fund that has holdings in BHP Billiton, Alcan, and Placer Dome. YMG in Canada has invested in Noranda and Falconbridge. See Grieg-Gran (2002).

[16] *The Guardian*, London, 30 June 2000.

[17] ERM (2000).

[18] Grieg-Gran (2002).

[19] Hart and Ahuja (1996).

[20] To date, there are relatively few examples readily accessible and in the public domain that describe such win-win situations at the operational level explicitly. Some examples are found in Luzenac (2000) and in Anglo American (2001).

[21] PricewaterhouseCoopers (2001).

[22] This discussion relies heavily on personal communication with Robin G Adams of Resource Strategies, a strategy consultancy specializing in the mining, metals, and energy industries, November 2001.

[23] This applies both to upstream products like concentrates and downstream products like sheet metal; both are typically priced either on formulae that reference commodity prices or on negotiated spreads over commodity prices. The companies in question remain heavily exposed to the basic commodity market risk regardless of their degree of vertical integration.

[24] CRU International (2001).

[25] Phelps Dodge (1999).

[26] Ibid.

[27] Personal communication, Robin G Adams, Resource Strategies, November 2001.

[28] OECD (2001b).

[29] The other argument must be the essentiality of mineral products in any scenario of a more sustainable future.

[30] Bolivian Vice-Mininstry of Mining and Metalurgy, cited in Enriquez (2001).

[31] By virtue of their location often in areas remote from urban centres with few other sources of livelihood, the focus here is on mining operations. However, the reality of declining employment has occurred through the product chain (see Chapter 3 on the decline of employment in the steel industry from 1974 to 2000).

[32] SustainAbility (2001).

[33] McDevitt (2001).

[34] See, for example, Borax (2001).

[35] Personal communication, Reg Green, ICEM, 17 December 2001.

[36] Banks (2001).

[37] PricewaterhouseCoopers (2001).

[38] This section draws predominantly on the workshop co-hosted by MMSD and the London School of Hygiene and Tropical Medicine on Worker and Community Health and Safety, September 2001, and on Stephens and Ahern (2001). The latter was a review based on literature available through an international database of peer-reviewed scientific journals related to health, occupation, and environment, PUBMED; 996 peer-reviewed scientific articles published between 1965 and 2001 were downloaded.

[39] Hilson (2001b).

[40] Stephens and Ahern (2001); MMSD (2001f).

[41] ILO (2001c).

[42] Findings are based on Stephens and Ahern (2001).

[43] Stephens and Ahern (2001).

[44] Adams and Kolhos (1941); Adams and Wrenn (1941); Reese et al. (1955); MSHA (1999).

[45] Minerals Council of Australia (2001).

[46] Ibid.

[47] Stephens and Ahern (2001).

[48] Ibid.

[49] Heiler et al. (2000).

[50] World Bank–International Finance Corporation (2001).

[51] ILO (2001a).

[52] Jennings (2001).

[53] Mulcahy (1999); Derickson (1989); Derickson (1991).

[54] See http://www.hsebenchmarking.com.

[55] ILO (1995).

[56] The Recommendation is at: http://ilolex.ilo.ch:1567/scripts/convde.pl?query=R183&query1=183.

[57] ILO (1991).

[58] See http://www.wsib.on.can.

[59] Scott-Russel (1993).

[60] Asogwa (1988), as cited in Stephens and Ahern (2001).

[61] Jennings (2001).

[62] Personal communication, Peter Colley, CFMEU, August 2001.

[63] Minerals Council of Australia (1999).

[64] Extract from presentation by Norman Jennings at the workshop co-hosted by MMSD and the London School of Hygiene and Tropical Medicine on Worker and Community Health and Safety, September 2001.

[65] Based on a presentation made by David Barnes at the workshop co-hosted by MMSD and the London School of Hygiene and Tropical Medicine on Worker and Community Health and Safety, September 2001.

[66] National Research Council (forthcoming).

[67] Bell (2001).

[68] Brooks et al. (1998).

[69] US Department of Energy (2000).

[70] Stewart (2000).

[71] Ibid.

[72] Carley and Christie (2000); National Research Council (1999).

[73] Humphreys (2001a).

[74] Vaughan (1995).

[75] See for example, Crowson (2002).

[76] Personal communication, Monika Weber-Fahr, Mining Dept, IFC, February 2002.

[77] See, for example, UNEP/Standard Bank (2002).

[78] See Export Development Canada (EDC) at http://www.edc.ca/corpinfo/csr/disclosure/enhanced_e.htm#3 the UK Export Credits Guarantee Department (ECDG) at http://www.ecgd.gov.uk, the Australian Export Finance and Insurance Corporation (EFIC) at http://www.efic.gov.au/environment/environstd.asp, and the US Overseas Private Investment Corporation (OPIC) at http://www.opic.gov/.

[79] UNEP (2002).

[80] Beattie (2000).

[81] UNEP (1999); see also World Rainforest Movement (2000).

[82] See, for example Wilderness Society (2000).

[83] CEE Bankwatch Network (2000).

[84] See, for example, Global Response (2001).

[85] Rather than be associated with an environmental disaster, two financing banks of the Baia Mare project wrote off US$4 million each following the cyanide spill in January 2000; UNEP/Standard Bank (2002).

[86] Personal communication, Gerard Holden, Head of Mining Finance, Barclays Capital, February 2002.

[87] Noronha (2001).

CHAPTER 7

THE CONTROL, USE, AND MANAGEMENT OF LAND

Sustainable development, as described in Chapter 1, assumes the involvement of communities in decision-making, the observance of the principle of subsidiarity, respect for the principle of prior informed consent freely given and arrived at democratically at the local level, and a respect for cultural diversity. Perhaps nowhere is the need for dealing with the complex changes required by sustainable development more acute than in relation to decision-making around land.

Individuals may have strong opinions about how land should be used, who should use it, and who should derive benefits from it. The same land is also part of the sovereign territory of a nation-state, and governments may have different views from the occupiers about how land should be used – and who should have the right to use it.

Little surprise, then, that the discourse about land and its use for mining has been particularly contentious, because even though the global 'footprint' of mining is relatively small (mines occupy no more than a fraction of 1% of Earth's land surface – much less than forestry or agriculture, all of which also have profound impacts on communities, ecosystems, and land use) mines can only be located where there are mineral deposits. This means conflicts often tend to be not over how to conduct mining, but whether a deposit is to be mined at all. Disputes over land and mineral resource ownership have three fundamental sources: lack of recognized rights, lack of capacity (including resources), and lack of trust.

This chapter looks at the challenges posed by competing land uses, tenure and compensation regimes and the need for equitable decision-making, and focuses on three specific issues in this contentious debate that highlight its complexity: indigenous lands and mining, resettlement issues, and mining in protected areas.

Land and Society

More than 50 years ago, in *A Sand County Almanac*, American ecologist and conservationist Aldo Leopold wrote: 'The fallacy that economic determinists have tied around our collective neck and which we now need to cast off is that economics determines all land use. This is simply not true.'[1] This captures in part the nature of the problem facing developers, whether of

mining or other economic activities. A contemporary definition of economics recognizes 'economic capital' as synonymous with 'a multidimensional store of value', yet too often the earlier and more limited definition influences the decision-making process.

Looked at in terms of sustainable development, a system of land use must be based on at least three things:

• It must look at land as a multidimensional store of value capable of yielding a stream of economic, social, environmental, and cultural benefits indefinitely into the future.
• It must take a long-term view, one that does not discount the future to a point of meaninglessness.
• It must be people-centred, including more than those who 'own' the land or the mineral rights.

There is a hierarchy of ways in which those who will be affected need to be involved in making decisions about land and its use.

• *Information* – At a minimum, there are times when people should be informed of pending activities that could change the way land is used.
• *Consultation* – Anyone whose use and enjoyment of benefits from land could be affected by development has a right to be consulted; this includes those who have a vested interest in land and sites of spiritual, cultural, and natural significance. It involves ensuring that the persons consulted have access to the information necessary to develop an informed opinion, time to evaluate that information, and the ability to ask questions and get them answered.
• *Participation* – This implies a more formal process that is generally appropriate when some legally recognized interest is likely to be affected by the decision. Most environmental and socio-economic impact assessment processes fall into this category.
• *Compensation* – Discussions about compensation are appropriate when individuals or groups are required to surrender recognized legal or traditional rights for what is determined by government (through legislation, judicial decisions, or the issuance of permits, for instance) to be for the common good. Compensation may need to take more than one form: fair compensation in a cash economy may not compensate people for losses in a subsistence economy.
• *Right of veto over decisions* – Individuals or groups have the right simply to say 'no' to some land use

decisions. Some of the most difficult disputes are over the extent to which local or provincial governments, indigenous or tribal groups, or local communities claim a right to say no to development. National governments often resist such assertions. The right to say no, where it exists, is effectively coupled with the right to receive some of the economic rent from the activity.

Even if all the aspects of land use decisions are properly handled, there will be differences of opinion and the need for a decision-maker who is respected and accorded legitimacy. When there is no such individual or group, sustainable development requires attempting to create one: local communities, legal experts, and others need to develop arbitration, dispute resolution, mediation, and other appropriate mechanisms.

Land use disputes may occur throughout the chain of minerals exploration, production, processing, and use. Metal recycling plants, coal-fired power plants, lead refineries, iron foundries, and landfills leaching cadmium from discarded mobile phone batteries are not always welcome as neighbours, even by those who benefit from their products or the employment they create. But some of the most difficult land use issues are probably those related to mineral exploration and mining. This is because there is considerably more flexibility in siting downstream facilities, which tend to be located where there is already other industrial activity and where ecosystems have been altered by the multiple impacts of human activities. (See Box 7–1 on one attempt to improve performance during the exploration phase.)

There may be a widely shared perception, however, that few if any other land uses are consistent with mining. Yet mines are a temporary use of the land, which, if managed well, can revert in some cases to other uses following best-practice rehabilitation.

The first and perhaps main point of contention is that the surface rights to land are under either public or private ownership in most countries, whereas the mineral rights are generally owned solely by the state. The state then grants those rights to mining companies through concessions or permits. These are often granted as a matter of right to those who meet criteria specified by law. At this stage, in some jurisdictions, other affected parties often have no right to

Box 7–1. Environmental Excellence in Exploration

The initiative known as Environmental Excellence in Exploration, or E3, initiated by a consortium of mineral exploration companies and driven by the Prospectors and Developers Association of Canada, has been designed to help improve environmental performance throughout all phases of global minerals exploration.

By pooling company expertise and filling in gaps in knowledge, E3 will encourage sound environmental management practices by the exploration community and improved education and understanding of this by stakeholders. The initiative recognizes that exploration crews and their contractors, as the first people into an area, must be capable of creating a positive impression through the manner in which they manage and mitigate environmental impacts: failure to do so can jeopardize the licence to operate afforded to companies by the local community and others.

The E3 project will document best practices drawn from international experience. An E3 database and e-manual (which will enable rapid access by those 'on the ground'), will be available by subscription and will be continuously updated. E3 will also act as a source document to educate the public and government and non-governmental stakeholders as well as a training tool for companies and their contractors.

Source: Prospectors and Developers Association of Canada, at http://www.pdac.ca

consultation; at other localities, they wield sufficient power to stall the development. The holder of the concession or permit generally has the right to take as much of the surface as is needed to gain access to the minerals, regardless of the preference of the surface owner or occupant.

Usually there is a system for providing at least some form of compensation to the surface owner. But these systems do not always work. Most often, consent of the people who live on and make their livelihoods from the land is viewed as unnecessary, as they have no right of decision. The government therefore has generally not sought permission for the use of community land, and the rights of occupants, both formal and informal, have been abrogated. As a result of this history and recent high-profile cases of conflict, miners often find themselves cast in opposition to local communities, tribal peoples, conservationists, non-governmental organizations (NGOs), and other civil society groups promoting a range of land use outcomes that do not include mining.

Equally, while many of the issues around land use decision-making are cast in terms of the place of national sovereignty versus local community rights, the role of local politics in all of its forms should not be downplayed. Land and compensation issues are powerful campaign material and lend themselves well to manipulation designed to achieve political outcomes that ignore the realities of a local situation. Unscrupulous politicians can use any issue to unfair advantage, but few issues incite such passion as that of land rights and compensation.

Mining is therefore embedded in the context of a much broader discussion of rights and responsibilities, of political power and marginalization, of competing world views and ways of viewing land. Land access and management pose some key questions, including the following:

- *Land use planning* – What principles and practices should underpin the notion of integrated land use planning? How does mining fit into an integrated land use policy that includes the recognition of passive uses, such as conservation? What post-closure land use decisions must be made at an early stage to ensure an adequate scoping of closure issues?
- *Tenure* – What principles should govern interaction between the mining sector and communities where land is owned collectively or under traditional systems of landownership? What legal and administrative mechanisms need to be in place to establish legitimate ownership under traditional systems, and to discourage opportunistic land claims?
- *Equity* – What principles and practices should govern company negotiations for access to land that is occupied by people who do not have the capacity to defend their rights to land?
- *Compensation* – Who should be compensated, and by how much, for which kinds of uses of land? What form should this compensation take?
- *Governance* – What governance structures need to be in place to ensure that land use decisions do not harm the occupants of the land and do least harm to the environment, while still allowing development to take place when its conditions have been negotiated by all parties?

Integrated Land Use Planning

Mining presents a particular set of challenges in terms of land use. Exploration, for example, requires access to large tracts if there is to be a reasonable chance of success in finding new mineral deposits. Second, as noted earlier, there is little flexibility in locating mines.

Third, if there is to be investment in exploration and mining, there must be security of tenure. This has been a principal element of the reform of mining codes that has been a major World Bank policy initiative in the sector and has led to new legislation in many countries.[2] As William Vaughan and Michael Bourassa point out, 'what really matters is that there is a transparent, non-discriminatory system in place for the granting of mineral tenure, a judicial system which protects that mineral tenure against all third parties and the state, [and] that the holder of the mineral exploration rights has the sole and exclusive right to exploit any commercial deposit discovered'.[3] This is not to say that the right to mine is predetermined, but simply that when granted, it should fall in the first instance to the company or individual who has conducted the exploration and who then gets first right of refusal.

Gaining access to suitable land can be difficult for a number of reasons:

- Increased human populations place demand on land for many alternative uses that may be seen as inconsistent with mineral development.
- Many of the areas in which industry operates have relatively intact undisturbed ecosystems.
- Many of the suitable areas are inhabited by peoples with distinct cultures, with different views of the value and use of land, and with livelihoods tied to subsistence activities that may be disturbed by development.[4]
- Cultural differences may lead to conflict; the most common one may be the emphasis placed by traditional peoples on occupation, usufruct rights, and communal labour and ownership versus the private ownership conferred by the state through legal title held by individuals and organizations.
- For indigenous groups, the strength of social, culture, and philosophical ties to land associated with traditional activities may mean irreversible cultural impacts when mining occurs. Loss of land may engender a loss of social and spiritual integrity.

It may also seem to be part of a process that has gone on for centuries and has seen the erosion of aboriginal land rights when the dominant community identifies economic resources it wants to use.

- The community may regard land use as an intensely local issue, while the concession to exploit minerals may be granted by central government authorities that are regarded as unaccountable, and offer little or no consultation with local people. It is hard for mining companies to stay 'neutral' in such situations.
- The reality of land management is that there are multiple decisions going on all the time about the maintenance of ecosystem integrity, stable and functioning communities, and infrastructure that interact with specific land use decisions.

A fundamental dynamic here is that local people want to retain rights and systems of management while government often wants to transform or acquire greater control over local resources. It is a question of power – effectively, within local systems, people may own land, and access to it is negotiated through a mix of social as well as economic channels. People seeking land must often make formal representation to a village council. National governments may seek to undermine and override these systems, and companies have at times collaborated in this.

An integrated approach to land use management recognizes competing interests and attempts to negotiate the most appropriate course of action, bearing in mind the ecological and social limits of the area. (See Box 7–2.) In an ideal world, integrated land use planning requires, first, a solid database about current land uses and land use potential. Establishing this can be complicated by imperfect information: the mineral potential and many other values of the land – from the wildlife species that inhabit it to its support of livelihoods of local villagers – are not well known by the planners. Second, the needs and preferences of those currently based on the land need to be canvassed. Third, a negotiation or arbitration mechanism is needed that seeks to balance local, regional, and national priorities. A mechanism is also needed to compensate those affected by development or by the loss of land or land-dependent livelihoods – or to resettle those who may be displaced.

The starting point of this discussion is a clarification of the issues associated with land tenure and minerals

---

> **Box 7–2. Integrated Land Use Management in Manitoba, Canada**
>
> One example of an attempt at integrated land use management is being tested by the Government of Manitoba in Canada through the Land Access Action Plan, which is aimed at improving coordination of land use policy and regulatory proposals.
>
> The action plan is an attempt to circumvent land use conflict by minimizing the overlap of incompatible land use allocations. Key elements of the plan include the early settlement of First Nations land claims under the Treaty Land Entitlement Process and the transfer of some Crown Lands to Reserve Status for First Nations. Within 30 kilometres of a reserve, land is designated as a Community Interest Zone (CIZ). Minerals claims can be staked within the CIZ, but must be reviewed by the First Nation concerned in the adjacent reserve.
>
> Cabinet-approved regulatory and policy tools also protect other lands of high minerals potential, which are delineated as Mineral Exploration and Development Areas. Provincial Parks, Wildlife Management Areas, and Forestry Areas are subject to their own management regimes.
>
> Source: Government of the Province of Manitoba (2000)

---

tenure. In the case of mining, locking up areas of land under prospecting or mining licences – which can discourage investment in other productive activities on that land – is also a source of tension. A compensation regime needs to address the opportunity cost of not being able to work land that is taken out of the normal cycle of use through the uncertainty created by prospective mining development.

Land Tenure and Mining Law

Increasing scarcities of land, alternative land use, tenure issues, concerns over environmental protection, community involvement, artisanal mining, NGO pressure, and aboriginal land claims have all increased the transaction costs of access to land for mining. Sustainable development brings new and complex issues into the traditional negotiation of interests in mineral tenure.[5]

Land title, in the most legally binding form, is an individual property right that bestows the right to use and dispose of land, usually limited only by contemporary planning and other laws that prevent certain types of use. Beyond this owner-occupier variety of tenure, found chiefly in western industrial societies, systems become increasingly complex. In much of the world, tenure rights are based on tenancy: people obtain rights to use land through payment to a landlord in labour, cash, or crops. This system prevails in parts of the industrial as well as the developing world; share farming, for example, has become increasingly significant in US agriculture. In other places people obtain a usufruct right simply by occupying and using common land.

There are many and varied collectivist systems; these include both state collectives and villages where individuals cooperate in a communal approach to the division of land. There are also institutional forms of land tenure, in which land is owned by a private company that uses wage labour. Many tenure systems are complex combinations of these approaches, such as the *latifundio* or *hacienda* estate system commonly used for agricultural production in Latin America or the extremely complex clan-based land tenure systems found in much of the Pacific.[6] Many rural communities and indigenous groups place greater emphasis on land security than land rights. 'Security' encompasses a much broader set of rights and obligations than those bound up with formal regulations related to landownership.

A mining or exploration concession granted by a central government without local consultation, therefore, may not be simply an occasion for conflict over who wields the decision-making power, but an indication of the way in which many traditional systems of occupying land have been subordinated by formal rights-based systems of law. These formal systems have often originated in the West and are preferred by many national governments and multilateral lenders. In local communities that operate on traditional land use systems, outsiders do not have the right to show up with drill rigs without permission. When exploration companies do this – and worse, are supported by the national government – it can be a profound shock to the community. On the other hand, governments often have real concerns that a community right to say no gives priority to local wishes over those of national sovereignty, undermining the role of

government and the primacy of the nation-state.

Land tenure is often a mix of formal legal components and informally accepted normal practices that are not well protected in law. Inherited and traditional tenure systems have recently been seen as an obstacle to progress, particularly where the state or private enterprise has wanted access to traditional or communal lands. New tenure systems are then often imposed against the wishes of the occupiers and without respect for the principle of freely given prior informed consent from users of the land.

Issues of tenure often relate to conflict between what is legal and what is considered legitimate and illegitimate at the local level. Just as national law may not recognize local traditions and practices, local people may regard national law as largely irrelevant, which in fact it may be, until something like a mining project forces some kind of decision to be made. Legislation is often used selectively to legitimize the claim of one party while delegitimizing the claims of another. Equally, in many jurisdictions, awarding a mineral right or right to mine is effectively awarding a land right, because despite any legal distinctions the land is removed from other productive uses for generations, and other rights cannot be exercised during mining.

In addition, in many places institutional structures with respect to land are very weak; land title systems are confusing, unclear, and imperfect; legal compensation mechanisms may not be regarded as fair; access to justice for resolution of disputes may be illusory; native land claims may be hard to define and debatable among the various actors – even among different aboriginal or indigenous groups; and government apparatus may lack capacity, be corrupt, or simply be indifferent to the rights of local people or ethnically distinct communities or to the purposes for which protected areas were created.

For mining companies, as noted, the predominant concern with regard to land is security of minerals tenure: the ability to develop a deposit once located. Yet for other stakeholders, and in particular communities, there is no automatic 'right to mine' afforded to a company: this is something that has to be earned. Companies may also have to acquire the surface rights of a lease area by negotiation with private owners or the state, as well as rights of way and easements.[7] Law related to mineral tenure consists of rules for the allocation, maintenance, transfer, and termination of mineral rights and establishes the rights and obligations of the holder.[8]

In Latin American countries with a tradition of civil law and a *regalian* system, states have unrestricted and exclusive dominion or proprietary rights over their mines.[9] In countries with a code based on civil law, proprietorship over the land does not extend to the ownership of the minerals of the subsurface. Even if a limited private property in land is recognized in states with a socialist legal tradition, it almost never extends to minerals. In countries with a common law tradition, generally the owner of the land owns the minerals located in the subsurface.[10] However, even in many of the common law countries where mining is important, such as the United States, Canada, and Australia, a large proportion of mining occurs on lands held by the government – 'public domain' lands, 'Crown lands', or the like – where private surface occupants, if any, are usually government tenants who can be required to leave in favour of mineral development.

Market economies have tended to encourage mineral investment by providing security of tenure for mining companies. In most but not all countries, rights of tenure are generally vested in a company only after compliance with particular conditions, such as the payment of fees, submission and acceptance of a feasibility study, and compliance with technical, financial, and environmental prerequisites. To deal with these requirements, companies seek explicit rules and procedures for tenure and a minimum of bureaucratic interference.

Most countries, in the race for investment, have liberalized their mining codes – strengthening private mining rights and security of tenure, streamlining procedures, and minimizing state intervention. These changes, along with relaxed laws on the repatriation of profits and foreign ownership, have encouraged multinational players to reinvest in many countries previously ignored. The essence of the Chilean code, for example, is the reduction of discretion in the exercise of government authority, with the limitation of bureaucratic intervention at the core of its legitimacy and the provision of security of tenure and stability.[11] The Peruvian and Bolivian mining codes have unified the exploration and exploitation rights into a single concession, leaving to the investor the decision on when and how to start mining.[12]

'Montes de Oro says NO to mining and YES to life', Costa Rica

So countries have tried, often with assistance from the World Bank Group, to create legal regimes that provide more efficient administrative systems for gaining access to land for companies that meet the requisite criteria; such regimes are established to minimize uncertainty, delay, discretion, and corruption. At the same time, however, in some locations local people are increasingly restive over systems that can at any time cost them their land, sometimes without notice, and their opportunity to be heard, as well as with systems that threaten to leave them a good deal less well off.

The world's legal systems are full of provisions that recognize pre-existing traditional or legal systems where these have broad support among the public and a long history of working well and meeting social objectives. Unfortunately, in the view of many NGO commentators, mining code reform has tended to emphasize uniformity among nations and has sometimes in practice been hostile to traditional land tenure systems.[13]

There is nothing wrong with wanting the clear rules, trustworthy dispute resolution mechanisms, and prompt decision-making often required by the new codes, as long as these respect the rights of stakeholders to be involved. Until they do, it will be difficult to reach decisions that they accept and trust. A lack of trust, in turn, will undermine the security of investment that mining code reform has sought to achieve.

It is primarily the role of the state to define the rights of landowners and occupants and to ensure that the mining sector recognizes these rights in negotiating land access. It is at this stage that provisions of the mining tenure regime should come into play. For governments, the main challenge with respect to tenure is the clarification and recognition of informal but legitimate landowner/occupier relationships with the state and negotiation with the occupants of a suitable management regime for such lands.

Problems arise for a variety of reasons. One is simply that some societies have never resolved long-running conflicts. Land is claimed by indigenous people, for example, but there have been few clear settlements in which a government has recognized those claims: Voisey's Bay in Canada stands as one example. The issue may never have been a pressing one because there was little incentive to quarrel, but once there is some question about who controls a mining operation and who gets its revenues, latent conflicts can quickly escalate. Other questions relate to the building of capacity to administer such management regimes, but these are secondary to establishing the political momentum to recognize the land tenure rights of communities. Often the problem is a failure of governments to reconcile local and national interests around the development of natural resources.

For companies, explicit recognition of the right of communities to know about proposed developments and respect for the principle of prior informed consent freely given and arrived at democratically would make significant inroads into addressing the mistrust that many communities and, in particular, indigenous landowners have of mining companies. One commentator at an MMSD workshop noted that companies should always treat communities as if consent were required, so that advantage is not taken of statutes designed to oppress or remove the rights of communities.

A key question for governments and industry is the extent to which environmental or sustainability regulations will be woven into the process to obtain mineral rights, as in Venezuela, or be completely independent.[14] In the latter case, failure to meet certain operating obligations is punished by administrative sanctions rather than by cancellation of a mining right.[15] Although some Latin American countries treat mining licensing and environmental permitting as separate regimes, there is an inextricable connection between the law on use of the resource and the

regulations that lay out conditions and restrictions for that use to be sustainable.[16] Sustainable development will only be achieved with consistency of legal and regulatory instruments and rights.

Royalties and Compensation

Three types of land-related payment may accrue from mining. Two of these are designed as a return on ownership – royalties and land title payments such as rental fees. The third is compensation payments, which are simply designed to recompense the owner or occupant for property rights that he or she is required to surrender to the state or a mining company to make mining possible.

Royalties are in essence a tax paid by corporations for the right to exploit a sovereign asset – the payment is usually based on an amount per tonne or a percentage of total production or profits. Companies may also pay a land rental fee, which is a source of some contention given the other taxes levied for rights of access and exploitation.

While the state often jealously guards royalty payments, there is increasing pressure to share these with other stakeholders, particularly the community. There is often a perception in the local community that these revenues are dissipated in corruption or mismanagement, which may be the case. Promises to share the benefits locally are often broken. At the same time, many countries have a short or weak tradition of central authority and strong regional, cultural, or ethnic differences. The question of whether land use decisions (and decisions on the use of related mineral revenues) are made by the central government or by provincial or local authorities can be fundamental to the strength or even the survival of the central state. (See Chapter 8.)

Most legal systems recognize the principle of compensation: when a surface landowner's rights are taken for purposes of mineral development, the owner must be compensated for the loss. This is designed to redress in financial terms the economic impacts of a lost opportunity caused by mining, which may happen through a loss of amenity value and use, through denial of access, or as a result of damage to or conversion of land, natural and planted vegetation, or waterways to alternative uses. Yet payment for damages does not make either communities or individuals beneficiaries or material stakeholders in the project. It is designed simply to prevent a loss, not to create a benefit. Further, while a clear and comprehensive compensation policy is essential to redress the losses of those affected by mine development, the success of any such policy obviously depends on a clear definition of land tenure and rights.

The lack of clarity around compensation systems and land rights may be only one expression of a broader inequality within some societies and a reflection of unequal distributions of wealth and political power. For example, in many countries substantial numbers of people have no legal right to occupy any land. A focus on compensation to 'legal owners' leaves millions of people out of the equation.

Complying with the law is a bedrock requirement. But the law is not an instruction manual on how to do business. There may be and usually are other steps, above and beyond following the letter of the law, that are necessary to conduct business successfully. The principle of equity may mean that people need compensation or procedural rights beyond that specified by the law.

Further, a focus on compensating individuals for what are seen as removal of individual property rights may not compensate the community for collectively held interests. And where access to justice is limited, or systems of justice broadly distrusted, the individual may not have much alternative but to accept the company's offer.

In less developed areas and particularly among many indigenous groups, compensation is often regarded automatically as a benefit because it provides cash for land that was previously undeveloped or little used. In areas of subsistence farming, for example, it is not uncommon to find opportunistic planting of previously unplanted land in the hope of attracting higher compensation if the land subsequently becomes part of the mining lease area, as has reportedly happened in Fiji and at Porgera in Papua New Guinea (PNG).[17]

Compensation, even when paid to the satisfaction of the local community and others, may have unintended consequences. Bonnell, for example, found that the impact of large cash compensation payments at Porgera

had a negative impact on women and marriage.[18] Adultery, abandoned wives and children, and domestic violence became a major concern. The loss of land for food and gardening purposes also led to economic hardship for women, in particular those whose partners had left home to work in the mine.

Cash compensation for a compulsory purchase of land, the norm in some places (like Europe) when government or others are allowed to take property for public purposes, can lead to disastrous results in subsistence economies. Even where the idea is accepted, a view of what constitutes fair compensation may differ widely between traditional landowners and others. For example, an economic assessment of bequest value (the importance placed on transferring something to a future generation), option value (the value of keeping something for future use rather than using it today), or existence value (the value of knowing something is available for use, whether it is actually used or not) may not fully capture the value of land assets to indigenous groups, where loss of such assets could mean cultural demise.

While compensation is conceptually simple, it is intimately tied to issues of sovereignty: an acknowledgement of a right to compensation may be construed as a recognition of a body of other rights that the state does not care to uphold. This is particularly true when communities or individuals are informal occupants of the land with no legal status, even though they have exercised usufruct rights, in some cases for several hundred years. Even more precarious are the rights of squatters, who are using areas previously ignored by the state and private interests, but subsequently found to contain mineral wealth.

One of the principal objectives of sustainable development is betterment of the condition of the very poor. These are precisely the people who tend to have subsistence relationships with land and to lack legally protected property rights, and who therefore traditionally get moved, but not compensated. Given the thin margins on which many of these people exist, this is a serious threat to their well-being or even their survival.

Even if local communities merit sympathy and support, national governments are unlikely to give control of all, or even the majority, of any mineral revenues to the local government or community. In part, this is because the resources are perceived as belonging to all the citizens of the country, not just the few who live near them. And in part it is practical politics, because in a poor country, control over these revenues can tip the balance of power. Few politicians want their opponents to get the credit for new bridges, schools, and hospitals, or to lose control over the ability to reward local supporters and punish adversaries, or – in the most extreme cases – to recruit and equip military forces.

For companies, acknowledgement of a right to compensation creates a liability and responsibility to individuals and groups in the area of a project. Further, in areas where the social dynamic is a complex one, even meeting state requirements to compensate local communities around a mine may not satisfy the demands of all those associated with a piece of land. In some cultures, a distant ancestral tie to land in the area of a project may be sufficient grounds for serious opposition if expectations of compensation are not met, even though state law and company practice may not extend to compensation for such groups.

Part of the issue of arriving at fair compensation is that there must be some system, some neutral party or institution, that is trusted by those concerned to set compensation. It must operate according to fair and intelligible rules. If there is no such opportunity, and if the owners know that ultimately they will have to accept some offer from a company without any trusted alternative forum in which to be heard, the landowners are unlikely to feel fairly treated. They are likely to be bitter and angry about the experience, which can colour the whole future relationship between the company and the community.

In most countries, courts are supposed to fulfil this function, but in the rural areas of some countries the courts are weak. Their procedures may be arcane or incredibly slow. Equally, they may not be trusted. They are seen as agents of the company or of a national government operating in collusion with the company, or as corrupt or simply hopelessly inefficient.

A clear and comprehensive compensation policy simplifies negotiation matters for all actors. Standard policy and best practice in terms of a regulated compensation framework is exemplified by the policy for Fiji's mining sector. This distinguishes between

payments made under prospecting rights (where any damage is presumed to be caused without the use of machinery), exploration rights, and mining rights. The policy requires an initial survey of eligible occupiers and landowners and those granted usufruct rights under customary arrangements. Illegal occupants are compensated for the loss of any crops and other improvements. Other categories of compensation include loss, damage, or alteration of the natural state of the land; social and cultural disruptions; damage to the natural environment; and loss of recreation and conservation value.[19]

Estimates of minimum compensation amounts in Fiji are based on current structured pricing systems for compensable items, the application of economic instruments such as opportunity and replacement cost principles, and inflation factors.[20] In deriving compensation payments, the policy also considers past arrangements between companies and landowners and the severity of any likely impact. The policy aims to derive compensation payments that are stable, fair, transparent, and easy to administer. A rehabilitation bond is also required, which is regularly reviewed and which encourages incremental rehabilitation as mining progresses.

The policy document specifies that for the system to operate efficiently, the work of various government departments must be coordinated, which in Fiji's case has meant the appointment of a mining coordinator to the Department of Fijian Affairs. The policy also requires that the terms of compensation are captured in a socio-economic agreement with the local community. Only time will tell if the policy can be put into operation effectively in order to minimize conflict over land.

In contrast to Fiji, PNG has established a Development Forum process for addressing issues of community participation and landowner compensation. Initiated in 1988 for the Porgera mine, the forum concept was subsequently incorporated into the 1992 Mining Act, and retrospectively applied to other mining projects. The forum grew out of a Department of Minerals and Energy view that all key stakeholders should be involved in discussions concerning a potential mine from the time that the developer submits a proposal for development.

The Development Forum is a form of consultation,

not a forum for modification of the proposals for development, although this does occur to some extent. It is also not a right of veto for the various parties. Further, only those with interests within the mining leases themselves are to be involved: neighbouring or downstream parties (landowners and provincial governments, for example) are not included under this legislation.

Although the Forums are convened to discuss proposals for development, the focus to date has been on the distribution of benefits between PNG stakeholders (in terms of services, revenues, and infrastructure) from the development rather than the nature of the proposed development itself. They have generally not imposed additional constraints on the developer, and it is the national government that has conceded most at these meetings. The Development Forums have been successful at securing a greater level of community support for mine development, and further refinement of the focus of the Memoranda of Agreement could provide a greater degree of sustainable development for local communities.[21]

Although neither PNG nor Fiji has resolved all its challenges with regard to the development of the sector, both countries have made significant progress with respect to addressing what was seen by some as an obstacle to development – the collective system of landownership. Continued policy evolution has ensured that in both cases the mechanisms exist for landowners to be fully involved in making decisions about land use and deriving benefits from it.

As noted in Chapter 4, market demand and 'need' are not always the same thing because some people – often the very poor – do not participate in markets. In much the same way the property of the poor is not traded in 'mainstream' real estate markets. Nor is it always assigned an appropriate value by those used to dealing in those markets. First, as Hernando de Soto has pointed out, the market requires clear indices of title and ownership.[22] The stronger these are, the higher the value placed on the land and the more efficiently the market trades. Second, the values of the property of the poor may principally be expressed in the non-cash economy.

Since the poor often have unclear or disputable title, or even no title at all, markets are unlikely to assign much value to their holdings. Equally, property exists

Disused exploration shaft, Romania

simultaneously in at least two realities: the cash economy and the subsistence economy. The latter may well be more important than the former. If losses are compensated in the cash economy, but not in the subsistence economy, it is obvious that the compensation can never be adequate. Compensation must be evaluated on both of these scales.

Equally, the question of land value cannot be divorced from discussions of rights. The value of land is often low because land rights are not clearly identified. This often occurs with indigenous lands. Equally, mineral concessions are often passed on from one company to another, with the value realized not by the people living on the land, but by the first company to acquire the concession, which then sells promising areas to others. A large company that ultimately decides to mine the property may not consider itself responsible for very low or 'unfair' compensation that surface landowners originally received. Although this is not illegal, it may create resentment and a feeling of injustice far more costly than payment of higher compensation would have been. Thus communities that do not have the capacity to negotiate or understand how to bargain for the full value of land need greater capacity in order for fair transactions to occur.

The fundamental lesson is that following the law is a necessary but not a sufficient condition for getting results that are consistent with sustainable development and the private interests of the affected parties, including mining companies. The law is not a source of ethics. Where following the law leads to a result that would generally be regarded as unfair, continuing to push the issue without addressing that unfairness will lead to conflict.

Land, Mining, and Indigenous Peoples

The most significant presumption held by indigenous peoples is that their inalienable rights to their lands and resources override subsequent claims by conquering or dominant societies.[23] Many areas of mineral interest have traditionally been inhabited or used by indigenous peoples. Indigenous communities, peoples, and nations are those that, having a historical continuity with pre-invasion and pre-colonial societies that developed on their territories, consider themselves distinct from other sectors of the societies now prevailing in those territories or in parts of them. They are currently non-dominant sectors of society and are determined to preserve, develop, and transmit to future generations their ancestral territories and their ethnic identity as the basis of their continued existence as peoples, in accordance with their own cultural patterns, social institutions, and legal systems.[24] The association with land is fundamental for these societies; the connection is exemplified in the name of indigenous people from Argentine and Chile, *Mapuche*, which means people of the land.[25]

Indigenous peoples are a special case of public interest and community. The characteristics that set them apart in the wider society are:[26]

- *identity* – political but also bound to recognition of kin, social networks, place, and spirits;
- *territory* – land and the sustained network of social relations that are supported by it;
- *autonomy* – decisions based on communitarian consensus and indigenous perceptions;
- *participation* – acknowledgement of the right to be involved at all levels in the planning for alternative use of indigenous lands; and
- *self-determination* – the right to possess, control, manage, and develop a territory.

Sustainability is seriously challenged by actions that destroy a peoples' ability to accumulate, maintain, enhance, and transfer their wealth to future generations. Those unfamiliar with indigenous culture may mistakenly believe that mining poses minimal risks, since indigenous peoples have little income or wealth to lose and high unemployment. Yet the wealth that supports the sustainability of their culture is found in institutions, environmental knowledge, and resources, and especially in land embellished with cultural meaning. It includes access to common resources, localized prestige, secure positions within

society, culturally appropriate housing, food security, and social support and identity. Indigenous peoples invest vast amounts of time and resources in perpetuation of their culture, institutions, and social support systems.[27]

Sustainable approaches to resource development must allow for the fact that there will be some communities, indigenous ones in particular, that do not want mines on their land. Histories of exploitation, often closely associated with the quest for minerals and metals, have built a deep mistrust of mines and mining companies. Many of the long series of dispossessions of native peoples' lands by Europeans, going back at least to Columbus, were motivated by a desire to gain access to minerals. Native peoples have not forgotten this. Yet it would be unfair to lay the blame for colonialism's excesses at the door of the contemporary mining industry. The root cause of animosity is often competition for resources and disagreement over who the primary beneficiaries should be. Some communities may welcome the potential for development that mining may offer, while remaining deeply dissatisfied with a failure to be included when decisions are made to allow mining exploration and development. Dissatisfaction may as often be due to failed expectations of development or internal rifts within the community.

Control, management, and autonomy in decision-making over land are significant elements of the rights denied to many indigenous cultures. Indigenous peoples have been subject to displacement or abuse by dominant cultures; in some cases their very existence has been denied. In other cases, the potential for prospecting in such areas has been among the main reasons for displacement. Most indigenous peoples live under weak governments, with insufficient capacity, little or no legal or institutional power, and little capital. Conflicts may be sharpened by any number of institutional or legal problems and by a clear divergence of cultural attitudes. They can also be affected by national governments' fear that ceding more autonomy to indigenous or aboriginal groups threatens the political and territorial integrity of the state. Indeed, many separatist movements – including armed ones – have been based on indigenous differences with national governments. The last thing such governments may want is to provide an independent source of revenues based on mineral wealth to give economic power to those they see as opponents.

Many of the local land use issues arise from conflict about the use of customary land that is regarded as inalienable by the resident groups and that is generally communal and of great spiritual and cultural significance. Subsistence agriculture on such land provides for consumption and exchange, usually placing it at the centre of overlapping social, cultural, and economic life. Loss of land inevitably means reduced areas for gardening, which increases the dependence on imported foods and the cash economy. Community members with usufruct rights to work the land by agreement with the landowners, but who are not part of the land-owning clan eligible for compensation, may face economic ruin. For those who cannot find local alternatives to subsistence agriculture, the only option may be migration to nearby cities and the inevitable breakdown of traditional family structures centred on sharing land.

Yet it should also be borne in mind that in many cases there is an ability to progressively rehabilitate land, which can then be returned to agricultural use. Equally, concerns about 'loss of land' are often more correctly expressed as concerns about the convenience of access, proximity, or loss of investment in the improvement of a particular piece of land, through, for example, tilling and fertilizing.

Convention 169 of the International Labour Organization stands as the only international treaty dealing with indigenous peoples and land rights. It recognizes indigenous peoples' rights of ownership and possession over their lands and in particular that 'the rights of the peoples concerned to the natural resources pertaining to their lands shall be specially safeguarded' (Article 15). It also includes a provision that:

> In cases in which the State retains the ownership of mineral or subsurface resources or rights to other resources pertaining to lands, governments shall establish or maintain procedures through which they shall consult these peoples, with a view of ascertaining whether and to what degree their interests would be prejudiced, before undertaking or permitting any programmes for the exploration or exploitation of such resources pertaining to their lands.[28]

Further, under the section of the Convention dealing with land it is stated that 'Governments shall take steps as necessary to identify the lands which the peoples concerned traditionally occupy, and to guarantee effective protection of their rights of ownership and possession' and, in case where resettlement is being considered as part of a development proposal, that 'Where the relocation of these peoples is considered necessary as an exceptional measure, such relocation shall take place only with their free and informed consent'.

Similarly, the United Nations Draft Declaration on the Rights of Indigenous Peoples is categorical in its recognition of indigenous peoples' right to remain on their lands. Equally, World Bank operational guidelines (OG 4.20) are designed to mitigate the adverse effects of development for indigenous people and in particular of development projects funded by the Bank.

Building on concern over the implications of resource extraction on indigenous territories, the United Nations Office of the High Commissioner for Human Rights (OHCHR) convened a workshop in Geneva in December 2001 on the relationship between indigenous peoples, human rights, and the extractive industries that supported recognition of indigenous rights. (See Box 7–3.)

At the level of the state, the laws that define indigenous territories and the jurisdictions that promote them may not be recognized by the indigenous communities themselves, or indeed may not be put into operation by the state. States differ markedly with respect to the recognition of indigenous peoples' rights, particularly with respect to land entitlement, which in turn affects the relationship between indigenous people and mining. In Fiji and Papua New Guinea, for example, indigenous people are the majority of the population and their rights are explicit in acts and policy, including rights to compensation, respect for the principle of full and prior informed consent, and consultation related to mining proposals. In states such as Myanmar (formerly Burma), indigenous identities are not recognized in any significant way.

In the past, legal rights have been no guarantee, particularly for indigenous peoples, that their interests will be upheld. Rights are only as strong as the ability to defend them, and in many cases indigenous groups have been faced with the overwhelming might of the state and private interests, which have generally run contrary to their own.

Box 7–3. Workshop on Indigenous Peoples, Private-Sector Natural Resource, Energy, and Mining, Companies, and Human Rights, Geneva, 5–7 December 2001

The Workshop affirmed the relevance of existing and emerging international human rights norms and standards including, but not limited to, ILO Convention 169 on Indigenous and Tribal Peoples. It also affirmed the need for the full recognition of indigenous peoples' rights to their lands, territories, and natural resources, and it recognized the efforts of a number of companies to address these issues, improve dialogue, and work within a human rights framework. The Workshop further recognized the importance of economic and sustainable development for the survival and future of indigenous peoples, and, in particular, that the right to development means that indigenous peoples have the right to determine their own pace of change, consistent with their own vision of development, and that this included the right to say 'No' to proposals involving development of their lands.

The Workshop recommended among other things that states, UN system organizations, indigenous peoples, and the private sector continue to review experiences in relation to private-sector natural resource development on indigenous peoples' lands, consider best practices, and explore the links between the recognition of and respect for indigenous peoples' land rights and those successful experiences.

The Workshop recommended that states, UN system organizations, indigenous peoples, and the private sector elaborate a framework for consultation, benefit sharing, and dispute resolution in private-sector projects affecting indigenous peoples. Consultation between indigenous peoples and the private sector should be guided by respect for the principle of free, prior, informed consent of all parties concerned.

In addition to making recommendations for action by the OHCHR and governments, the Workshop recommended that private-sector resource companies continue to hold dialogues with indigenous peoples and the UN system on these matters, examine existing codes of conduct and guidelines on human rights, and participate in the Working Group on Indigenous Peoples and the Permanent Forum, as well as other relevant forums dealing with these issues. Where appropriate, indigenous peoples should provide information on arrangements they have made with the private sector, in particular mechanisms they have established for consultative processes. The Workshop invited the World Bank to adopt a policy on indigenous peoples that requires borrowers and clients to respect indigenous peoples' rights, in particular their land and resource rights and their right to free, prior, informed consent with respect to investments, loans, guarantees, and operations that may affect them.

Where legislation exists, indigenous communities may have full control over their territory except for mineral rights, which belong to the central government that grants mining concessions. Certain territories may in principle be regarded as indigenous, but not subject to the legal control of indigenous people until they comply with legal formalities that have never been concluded. In this case, economic benefits from development may flow to national treasuries to the exclusion of indigenous organizations.

The Philippines is an example of a country with a significant mining history where the issues of indigenous land use have surfaced repeatedly in relationships between various actors in the mining sector. In particular, the contemporary era highlights some of the dilemmas that confront governments in addressing the concept of free and prior informed consent.

In 1988, with an output of 35.3 tonnes, the country was ranked number nine in terms of gold production and is estimated to have the third largest gold reserves in the world.[29] The 1990s saw a decline in production due to low commodity prices, high taxation, and increasing production costs. In 1995, the Philippines Mining Act was introduced to revitalize the industry. The act specifically excludes from mining the areas occupied by indigenous cultural communities under a claim of time immemorial, except upon the free and prior informed consent of concerned individuals. To complement this protection, the Indigenous Peoples Rights Act (IPRA) was introduced in 1997. This recognizes the rights of indigenous cultural communities/indigenous peoples (ICCs/IPs) to ancestral domains that include mineral and other natural resources. Priority rights are given to ICCs/IPs in the extraction, development, or exploitation of any natural resources within their ancestral domain.[30]

The passage of IPRA was considered a blow to the mining industry. The law invoked the Constitution's recognition of ancestral domains and gave indigenous peoples control over considerable tract of lands. A study prepared by the Philippine Exporters Confederation estimated that 1.2 million hectares (53%) of areas identified in mining applications are found in areas covered by Certificates of Ancestral Land and Domain Claims. The IPRA is construed by some as violating the Constitutional maxim that wealth must be utilized and conserved for the common good.

The IPRA has been challenged on a number of bases. Indigenous peoples have claims of ownership to land and minerals by virtue of their pre-conquest rights that conflict with the state claim to ownership of minerals traced since time immemorial. These pre-existing rights effectively extinguish rights granted later by the government. Interpreted in the extreme, the IPRA could mean that an indigenous person can file a mining application and dislodge any prior vested mining rights or applications. Further, the principle recognizing indigenous peoples rights to delineate their lands is unclearly defined, as is the definition of an ancestral domain, which may mean that millions of hectares are closed to mining. Some would say that the IPRA raises questions about which authority is empowered to grant and manage minerals and mining rights: the Department of Environment and Natural Resources or the National Council on Indigenous Peoples.

Despite the intentions of the IPRA, there are still inconsistencies in the treatment of indigenous people associated with the sector in the Philippines. A spokesperson of the Subanan indigenous people visited MMSD to relate stories of resistance to an unwanted mining project in an area of the Subanan ancestral domain. The story was one of local community exclusion from their own territory by hired security forces of the mining company. Published reports about the project speak of concerted efforts to gain control over land at the expense of indigenous communities and small-scale miners, local political collusion, militarization, and human rights abuses:

> [Two] cases in the Philippines point at two widely differing companies that nonetheless have exhibited a shared disregard for local rights and wishes.
> This stands in stark contrast to the new rhetoric of sustainable mining and stakeholder accountability… seemingly so far, little practiced in the field.[31]

While these issues were raised with the office of the UN Commission for Human Rights, the statements were strongly resisted by the Supreme Timuay (traditional leader) of the Subanan of the Zamboanga Peninsula, who swore an Affidavit of Retraction that among other things expressed shock at statements made to the UN, about which neither the Siocon

Subanan Association, Inc., the Council of Elders, nor the Tribal Council had been consulted.[32] At the same time, the Subanan and the company signed a memorandum of understanding as a way to establish open communication between the parties and to develop a mechanism to address consultation, benefit-sharing, and compensation. In addition, with sponsorship from the Co-operative Development Authority of the Philippines, the company has recently championed an Accelerated Area Integrated Development programme for the establishment of the Canatuan Agro-Industrial Multipurpose consumer co-operative.

MMSD is obviously not in a position to support or refute allegations made about particular projects. It does appear clear, whatever the truth of any specific situation, that fears by local people that the interests of mining companies threaten their land tenure are common in the Philippines and some neighbouring countries, such as Indonesia. To compound this situation, the indigenous community may be divided over how to respond to potential minerals development. Indeed, one of the principal impacts of mineral activities in indigenous territories may be to promote discord and conflict within communities.

Yet mining is often the only development choice, and it may be sought after by local communities. In this respect, frustration has also been voiced with respect to the well-meaning interventions of NGOs that prefer 'western' notions of natural resource management while subordinating social concerns to those of environmental continuity and failing to recognize the internal dynamics of traditional cultures.

Where land is leased for mining, the compensation and royalty payments that accrue to landowners for land occupation and damage have brought their own dilemmas. Arguably, existing mechanisms within some traditional societies for the distribution of benefits may not be well suited to the equitable disbursement of large monetary sums; both the amount of cash payment and the choice of beneficiary are often the subject of protracted dispute. Local elites may compete to increase their wealth and power through control of compensation monies and lucrative business spin-offs from a mine. Leaders who fail to accumulate and disburse the new forms of wealth lose respect, power, and influence.

As a counter to many of the problems associated with mining on indigenous lands, the idea of prior informed consent freely given has in the past gained support as a way to deal with indigenous or aboriginal peoples. Yet putting this into practice in a meaningful way is fraught with difficulties, including:

- objections of national governments to direct consultation between mining companies and communities;
- ill-defined processes for responding to the specific needs of indigenous groups and providing information on a timescale and in a form that is amenable to traditional processes of debate, decision-making, and negotiation;
- uncertainty by industry as to appropriate behaviour with respect to indigenous communities in areas of unsettled land claims; and
- a lack of clear visions and structures recognizing the obligations of mine owners to indigenous peoples, of business incentives needed to provide more equitable treatment of indigenous communities as a norm in overseas operations, and of indigenous community capacity to negotiate and understand the risks, costs, and benefits of mining.

Ultimately in situations that are unclear, best practice would demand that mining initiatives should not take advantage of any uncertainty surrounding land issues at the expense of traditional landowners and that proposals always be negotiated in the spirit of evolving international norms concerning the rights of indigenous peoples.

The Mabo Case in Australia provides a recent example of a reversal of legal recognition of indigenous land title. In 1992, the court set aside the doctrine of *terra nullius* that failed to recognize that Australian Aboriginal communities had occupied the land prior to European colonization. The Commonwealth Native Title Act, which followed the court decision, marked a fundamental shift in the recognition of indigenous rights, so that indigenous ownership of land may be formally recognized and incorporated within Australian legal and property regimes. The management of the relationship between native title and statutory and common-law rights may now be the subject of negotiated agreements.[33]

While the process of making native title and community rights operational has been subject to criticism since the Mabo Case, it has nevertheless

allowed the negotiation of instruments such as the Yandi Land Use Agreement between the Gumala Aboriginal Corporation and Hamersley Iron Pty for the Yandigicoogina Iron Ore project.[34] This was an agreement reached by direct negotiation between the parties without the need for outside intervention. While some people emphasize that such negotiations are both time-consuming and expensive, these costs must be seen as part of the new business environment.[35]

Even though leading companies state in their public reports that they recognize the need to negotiate with indigenous communities, there is still a great deal of uncertainty around policy process and practice with regard to land access. Further, the demands of public opinion in the home countries of international companies may be at variance with what local intermediaries tell the companies are the 'traditional' or best way to get things done. Nevertheless, this is not an excuse for errant practice. If the historic patterns of mining in or near the resources claimed by indigenous peoples continue, all stakeholders face escalating costs and the whole sector faces a continued erosion of its social licence to operate in indigenous territories. The future cannot repeat the past.[36]

At an MMSD Indigenous Peoples Workshop in Quito in 2001, it was made clear that indigenous peoples are at different stages in the maturation of their interactions with mining companies. In some countries, such as Australia (where there is greater surety around sovereignty over land for some aboriginal people), aboriginal groups may, through their lands councils, be prepared to enter into negotiations on the demand for various benefits from potential projects. In Latin America and the Philippines, many groups reject mining entirely because it is seen as allied to state interests and designed to deny them their land rights and autonomy over their own affairs.

The MMSD workshop made several suggestions on addressing the relationships between indigenous peoples and the mining industry. Attendees pointed to the need to establish a mechanism for establishing an international body, run and advised by indigenous people, to create a better understanding of best practices with regard to indigenous peoples. Ultimately, success in dealing with these issues must be an integral part of any accreditation system that seeks to distinguish good from bad players. Attendees also suggested that a workable system of checks should be established for verifying that community wishes were being fairly represented at all levels.

Many factors influence the attitude of indigenous peoples towards mining projects, but perhaps the most important is the question of control. If an indigenous or aboriginal organization has clear control over its land, a legal right to at least some share of the revenues from the mineral endowment, and a right to say no or to negotiate the terms and conditions under which mining will occur from a position of power, it is more likely that a decision in favour of mining will be made.

These are certainly issues that cannot be fully resolved without government. There is only so much a community and a mining company can achieve if a government does not recognize the existence of the indigenous or aboriginal group or its right to be consulted, to receive any share of revenues, or to have any say over the lands it claims.

Many countries have simply not resolved these issues; few have resolved them fully. Where there is serious conflict between national government and indigenous groups, it is difficult for a company to succeed. The most dangerous outcome is for the company to be seen alternately as negotiating with the community to ensure it gets benefits, and then with the government to override the local community.

Industry does not have to look far for guidance on improving relationships with indigenous communities. (See, for example, Box 7–4.) There is a rich history of attempts at constructive dialogue around these issues. The Proceedings of the Canadian Aboriginal Minerals Association's conference of 1995, for example, contains an article entitled 'Guidelines For A Respectful Relationship Between The Innu Nation At Nitassinan Mineral Exploration and Development At Emish (Voisey's Bay): An Introduction To The Issues'.[37] This sets out the conditions under which negotiations about the exploration and development of Voisey's Bay should take place. There are many other examples where indigenous communities have attempted with varying success to set the conditions by which negotiations over resources development take place.

The probability of a sustainable outcome increases as each of the following 14 elements is put in play during an encounter:[38]

Box 7–4. The Red Dog Mine on Inupiat Lands, Alaska

The North West Alaska Native Association (NANA) and Regional Corporation represents the interests of about 6800 mostly Inupiat peoples of northwest Alaska in a region the size of Portugal. In 1978, Cominco had staked a claim to a previously discovered, very large zinc ore body in the DeLong mountains in NANA territory. The NANA Regional Corporation also registered a desire to select the land under the provisions of the Alaska National Interest Land Conservation Act of 1980, which recognized NANA's right to claim land, subject to prior claims. Cominco, having registered an interest before 1980, believed that this constituted a prior claim.

A long period of negotiation between NANA and Cominco resulted in an agreement in 1982 that recognizes NANA's control of the land and Cominco's right to build and operate the mine and to market the products. The agreement gives shares in the development and a priority in employment to occupants of the region, and establishes a committee with equal numbers of mining company and NANA representatives to monitor and review operations. The agreement also commits to a 4.5% royalty for the NANA corporation and an increasing share in net proceeds after Cominco's initial capital investment is repaid. Thus far it seems to be the basis of an equitable arrangement, based on well-established rights for the local communities and strong and authoritative representation from the NANA Regional Corporation.

Source: International Council on Metals and the Environment (1999)

- Sovereignty is respected and strengthened.
- The rights and access to indigenous land and nature are secured.
- At the beginning, both indigenous and non-indigenous stakeholders' presuppositions about one another are aligned with fact.
- The desired outcomes of the encounter for indigenous peoples emerge from meaningful, informed participation.
- Non-indigenous stakeholders fully and opportunely disclose to the indigenous group their plans, agreements, and financial arrangements, related to the indigenous group in a culturally appropriate manner and language. [39]
- Likewise, the non-indigenous stakeholders identify and disclose all the risks of a proposed mining endeavour. Full risk assessment means not only of

the threats posed by the loss of land but also the full range of social, economic, and environmental impacts.

- Prompt unambiguous institutional and financial arrangements are made to mitigate each risk.
- Benefit-sharing arrangements are made that step beyond compensation for damages.
- Indigenous peoples, as an informed group, have the right to approve, reject, or modify decisions affecting their livelihoods, resources, and cultural futures.
- Should restoration of a disturbed habitat prove impossible, then the non-indigenous stakeholders make provisions for an improved habitat that supports a lifestyle acceptable to indigenous peoples.
- Basic human and civil rights are protected, as specified in international conventions.[40]
- The focus of the encounter is on protecting indigenous wealth, especially the social relations that guide the sustainable use of their natural resources.
- Financial and institutional arrangements are forged that bridge the discrepancy between the multigenerational time frame of indigenous peoples and the short time frame of mining.
- A guarantor is established to assure compliance with and funding of any negotiated and mutually satisfactory agreements.

Given the uncertainties and extreme risks, it is perhaps best to extend the environmental precautionary principle approved in Rio to the impact of mining on indigenous peoples. A Precautionary Principle for Mining in or near Indigenous Peoples might read:

> Non-indigenous stakeholders in mining shall use the precautionary approach to protect the indigenous peoples and the environment that supports them. Mining cannot take place without respect for the principle of prior informed consent and participation in their self-defined indigenous development. Where there are threats of serious or irreversible damage, scientific and economic uncertainty shall not be used to postpone cost-effective measures to avoid and mitigate risks and to prevent harm to indigenous livelihoods and cultures.[41]

Resettlement Issues

The problem of mining-induced displacement and resettlement (MIDR) poses major risks to societal sustainability. The severity of these risks is encapsulated in the opening lines of the World Bank Group's policy on involuntary resettlement:

Bank experience indicates that involuntary resettlement under development projects, if unmitigated, often gives rise to severe economic, social and environmental risks: productive systems are dismantled; people face impoverishment when their productive assets or income sources are lost; people are relocated to environments where their productive skills may be less applicable and the competition for resources greater; community institutions and social networks are weakened; kin groups are dispersed; and cultural identity, traditional authority, and the potential for mutual help are diminished or lost.[42]

Displacement involves not only the physical eviction from a dwelling, but also the expropriation of productive lands and other assets to make an alternative use possible.[43] Affected peoples are those who stand to lose, as a consequence of the project, all or part of their physical and non-physical assets, including homes; communities; productive lands; resources such as forests, rangelands, fishing areas, or important cultural sites; commercial properties; tenancy; income-earning opportunities; and social and cultural networks and activities.[44] The category may also include 'host communities' when a large population is displaced onto the land of a smaller, existing host population. Rehabilitation refers to restoring the incomes, livelihoods, and social systems of those displaced to at least their pre-project level.[45]

Local resistance to MIDR is building in many places, as people and governments try to shield themselves from its transferred social and economic costs. In northwestern Peru, for instance, local farmers in the San Lorenzo valley wish to maintain the Tambo Grande area as a fertile agricultural zone rather than support plans for a large open pit copper, silver, and gold mine that would move 1600 families to new housing provided by the project.[46] This dispute is portrayed as a battle between the rights of some local communities that object to government policy and the state's need to court foreign investment for development. A report commissioned by environmental groups and Oxfam America concluded:

Mine operations would require the relocation of numerous families because portions of the mine would be excavated under the existing town. Some of the short-term impacts could be viewed as positive...however it is the long-term impacts to the community and the environment that will be most significant....The Ministry of Energy and Mines ...[has] all but decided that the project should be approved, despite the obvious negative opinions of thousands of the local citizens.[47]

In May 2001, in an effort to address the serious concerns that have arisen about the mining proposal, the government of Peru established the Tambo Grande Roundtable (*Mesa de Diálogo*). The Peruvian Ministries of Agriculture, Health, Energy and Mines are represented at this roundtable, along with local church leaders (the Archbishop of the Diocese of Piura and Tumbes), local agricultural representatives, the mayors of Piura and Tambo Grande, the Front for the Defense of Tambo Grande, and the company. The goal of the roundtable is to establish an open and transparent mechanism, to consult the people of Tambo Grande and its environs about the specific details of the environmental impact study, the possible relocation process, and the potential long-term economic benefits of the proposed mine. Based on these consultations, the roundtable will recommend whether or not a mine should be developed.

MIDR is accompanied by what displacement specialists call the resettlement effect, defined as the loss of physical and non-physical assets, including homes, communities, productive land, income-earning assets and sources, subsistence, resources, cultural sites, social structures, networks and ties, cultural identity, and mutual help mechanisms. The effect introduces well-documented risks over and above the loss of land, which may address only 10–20% of the impoverishment risks known to be associated with involuntary displacement.[48]

Displacement may have the following implications:[49]

- *Landlessness:* Land that is lost has to be reconstructed or replaced with income-generating employment to avoid impoverishment and loss of capital.
- *Joblessness:* New and sustainable job opportunities must be created. Relocation may result in loss of economic power, which may in turn lead to redundancy of skills, loss of markets, and breakdown of economic networks.
- *Homelessness:* Loss or decline in the quality of shelter is exacerbated if compensation is paid at market value rather than replacement value.
- *Marginalization:* Relocation may result in loss of social and political status if the host community regards new arrivals as strangers or inferior.
- *Food insecurity:* The loss of productive land may lead

to a decline in available nourishment, nutrition problems, and increased mortality.
- *Loss of access to common resources:* People may lose access to grazing land, fisheries, and forests, which may contribute to loss of income, employment, and recreation opportunities.
- *Loss of access to public services:* Access to health care, education, public transport, and other public services may be lost.
- *Social breakdown:* There can be an erosion of social organization, interpersonal ties, informal ties, and other forms of social capital.
- *Risks to host populations:* If the resettlement site is already populated, these people may also suffer through increased pressure on social and environmental resources.

Even when MIDR is ostensibly voluntary, there have been problems. (See Box 7–5.) Oxfam Community Aid Abroad, in the *Mining Ombudsman Report* for 2000–2001, comments that:

> In many cases brought to the Mining Ombudsman, the acquisition of land took place under what the landowners regard as duress. Some claim to have been pressured by the company or the local authorities to sign agreements that were unsatisfactory or inadequate. Others claim that they were not sufficiently informed at the time of the value of their land, or the consequences of what they were signing. There was, in other words, an absence of free and prior informed consent.[50]

Box 7–5. Rio Tinto/ PT KEM's Kelian Mine

The construction of the Kelian mine involved the loss of land at Prampus to make way for the river port at Jelmuk. Land and assets of local people were appropriated; some were compensated, but at rates deemed unfair locally. Measurements of land value and assets were regarded as unfair to the community. Displaced people experienced a dramatic drop in living standards and resettled families were in many cases provided with a house plot, but no house – though one had been promised. Further, traditional economic activities such as small-scale mining were discouraged. It is also reported that PT Kelian Equatorial Mining company, which is 90% owned by Rio, ignored human rights abuses.

Source: Oxfam Community Aid Abroad (2001)

Building new housing for villagers relocated by the Porgera mine, Papua New Guinea

In many cases, cash compensation to those who leave their homes or agricultural land has been regarded as an adequate way of dealing with displacement. But there is also a growing view that there should be a plan for an organized resettlement into new settings in which people can earn livelihoods and maintain community ties. The more marginalized a community, and the greater its material wants, the more likely it is that cash compensation will be a disaster unless it is part of a carefully thought through plan of resettlement. This is explicitly required by, for example, the World Bank Guidelines. Equally, it does not make sense to relocate people to land that is less productive or that requires input of resources that are beyond the means of the resettled. In its article 25, the Declaration of Human Rights states that 'no standards shall be diminished as a result of the relocation and compensation process'.

India has had considerable experience of dealing with displacement issues and, in terms of policy at least, has developed a unique approach to the problem. A conservative estimate of the number of people displaced due to planned development from 1950 to 1991 is about 21.3 million due to the construction of dams, mining projects, wildlife sanctuaries, and industries.[51]

In 2000 a Land Acquisition, Rehabilitation and Resettlement Bill was prepared by integrating the Land Acquisition Bill and the rehabilitation and resettlement policy. The main and most salient features of the draft bill, prepared by voluntary organizations, are as follows:

- The doctrine of eminent domain is replaced by a Principle of Trusteeship, in which government is a

trustee of the property and has a moral and legal responsibility to justify that the acquisition is for the welfare of the people.
- The term 'project-affected person' is defined to include those deprived of livelihood resources (rural artisans, traders, collectors of non-wood forest produce, and so on).
- Provision is made for providing information at different stages regarding the nature of the project, cost/benefit analysis, extent of acquisition, and displacement so that those who wish to raise objections can do so on an informed basis.
- In any public hearing on project-related matters, 50% of the participants should be women.
- Provisions are made for the payment of compensation, and payment is monitored.
- Displacement shall not take place unless the compensation is paid, an alternate land is allotted, and the rehabilitation and resettlement process is complete.

Land prices may be driven upwards by competition between companies for a particular ore body, yet communities may be compensated at a rate that reflects a statutory land valuation policy that does not accommodate price increases due to competitive bidding. When alternative land is not provided, the result may be that community members whose land is compulsorily purchased cannot afford to buy other land in the same area, leading ultimately to landlessness and migration.

The means by which to avoid grafting new, displacement-induced poverty onto pre-existing poverty are known. Forty years of studies and lessons learnt in involuntary resettlement provide a rich vein of knowledge, and reasonable guidelines and checklists have been developed. Nonetheless, attempts to restore the displaced to their former economic and social conditions have proved ineffective. Underfinancing is a key component of their failure. Although people continue to be relocated, the goal of rehabilitation remains exceedingly difficult to achieve, and the preferred goal of sustainable development – with people better off than they were before resettlement – has seldom been achieved. Underfinancing emerges from the wrong-headed notion that compensation for losses is sufficient to rehabilitate a displaced economy. Compensation by itself cannot adequately restore and improve the income levels and livelihood standards of people subjected to expropriation and forced displacement. From the operational perspective, compensation – not rehabilitation or sustainable development – becomes the goal rather than a means to help ensure a sustainable outcome.[52]

But the key question remains: Who pays for countering the resettlement effect in mining-induced displacements and resettlements? At present, mining, financiers, and governments are externalizing displacement costs onto the weakest party – the displaced.

In dealing with resettlement issues, government again has a leading role to play and several challenges to face. The Indonesian government, for example, does not fully recognize the *adat* system of land tenure that is a feature of life in some rural areas. Holders of some Contracts of Work issued by the Indonesian government have apparently been advised in the past that they need not honour or compensate local land claims, even long-standing ones.

Mechanisms need to be strengthened so that people without formal legal rights at least have access to a system that recognizes their position and levies compensation for any improvements they have made to the land. The experience in Yanacocha in Peru provides an example of people who did not have legal title, but nevertheless made an investment in the land. Most important of all is the recognition that such communities have a right to be at the negotiating table and have their views heard.

Pressures are building from many directions to regularize liabilities that until now were considered only probable and possible. It is too early, however, to expect harmonization and the emergence of a detailed industry-wide approach. One alternative may be to institute involuntary displacement and resettlement insurance to protect the involuntarily displaced, although this is probably politically premature at present.[53] In the meantime, the inability to cope with the MIDR problem is delaying projects and generating costly controversies, plunging innocent victims who find themselves 'in the way' into new poverty. And governments are inheriting the long-term costs. A MIDR Contingency Clause is proposed as an interim, on-the-ground solution. This would be an agreement that all likely MIDR risks be assessed, goals set, costs estimated, organizational arrangements proposed, and financing secured before a mining project goes forward.

If resettlement is to be undertaken, there must be a series of checks on the responsibility of the state and other actors to provide the compensation and benefits promised in negotiations with communities. In the case of dam construction, the World Commission on Dams found this to be one of the major stressors for displaced populations and intimately linked to the failure of resettlement planning.[54] While no similar studies have been done on the extent of dissatisfaction with resettlement programmes associated with mining, it is likely that unfulfilled promises will diminish trust and lead to organized resistance.

Protected Areas

The issue of access to land that coincides with protected areas has become more contentious in recent years as development interests, including mining, are pushing to realize the economic value of the resources held within these areas.[55] There is now considerable evidence regarding mining threats to protected areas.[56] A recent survey, for instance, identified 44 World Heritage Sites now affected or potentially affected by mining.[57]

In 2000, the IUCN World Conservation Congress recommended that 'IUCN's State members…prohibit by law, all exploration and extraction of mineral resources in protected areas corresponding to IUCN Protected Area Management Categories I–IV'.[58] (See Box 7–6 for a definition of these categories.) The recommendation also contains clauses calling for tight controls over any mining in Categories V and VI, exacting procedures to govern any boundary changes to permit mining, and strict regulation over any mining near a protected area. It emphasizes the need for all concerned to adopt best practice to guide every stage of the mining process.

The conservation community has been pressing major mining companies to come out in support of a moratorium on mining within World Heritage Sites and protected area categories I–IV for some time.[59] Its advocates believe that if major mining companies want their commitment to sustainable development to be taken seriously, they should respect this requirement, especially because it means restricting access to merely 6% of land.[60] The recommendation has formalized the conservation community's opinions on mining and protected areas – that they are so valuable to natural

Protected areas have a long history and are found world-wide. They are areas of land or water often dedicated to the conservation of biological diversity. However, they also often coincide with areas of outstanding natural beauty and archaeological, historical, recreational, and cultural interest. In their modern form, based upon national legislation, they began about 130 years ago. But the number and extent of protected areas has expanded rapidly in the past 30 years or so. They now cover about 10% of the world's land area (although less than 1% of the marine environment). Protected areas vary markedly from each other, particularly in their fragility, their degree of protection, and the reasons for which they were established. As a step towards consistency, the World Conservation Union–IUCN developed a system of categorizing protected areas. This system is not meant to comment on how well protected areas are being managed, but to classify protected areas according to their specific management objectives. The system has underpinned debates around 'no-go' areas for mining. The six IUCN categories are:

I.   *Strict Nature Reserve or Wilderness Areas* – for scientific purposes or wilderness protection;
II. *National Parks* – for ecosystem protection and recreation;
III. *Natural Monuments* – for conservation of specific natural features;
IV. *Habitat or Species Management Areas* – for conservation through management intervention;
V.   *Protected Landscapes or Seascapes* – for landscape protection and recreation; and
VI. *Managed Resource Protected Areas* – for the sustainable use of natural ecosystems.

Governments are responsible for their own protected areas legislation, which takes many different forms: some of it is highly prescriptive, including in some cases a ban on all forms of mining; in other cases it is much more discretionary. It is also governments that select and apply the IUCN categories to their protected areas, although they often take guidance on this from IUCN.

Some nationally important protected areas are considered of such global importance that they are also recognized under other international agreements, the most important of which are the World Heritage Convention, the Ramsar Convention on Wetlands, and the UNESCO Man and Biosphere Reserve Programme. In addition, the development of a system of protected areas is required under Article 8 of the Convention on Biological Diversity. (See also Chapter 10.)

Sources: IUCN (1994); Convention on Biological Diversity (1992); IUCN-WCPA and WCMC (1994); The World Database on Protected Areas, managed by UNEP-WCMC, http://www.unep-wcmc.org/protected_areas/index.html; Rössler (2000)

and cultural heritage they deserve to be singled out for extra protection from destructive economic development activity, and that these protected areas are simply not substitutable. While most responsible mining companies agree, in principle, that there are some areas where mining development is inconsistent with the protection of ecological, cultural, and landscape values, they have reservations over whether such areas always coincide with IUCN Protected Areas Management Categories I–IV.

But the debate cannot be solely between mining and protected areas interests. Areas within or around protected areas are often occupied by some of the financially poorest and most politically marginalized peoples. These people are the most frequent losers, whether this follows a mining development or the establishment of a protected area, as both these activities, if inappropriately managed, can restrict access to land and resources. It is not surprising, therefore, that protected areas are now at the centre of some of the more controversial debates over land access and mining.

Mining Perspectives

The major mining companies acknowledge the imperative of conserving species, habitats, and natural systems, such as watersheds, and are keen to make a positive contribution to this end. They say that their reluctance to accept existing IUCN protected area Categories I–IV as 'no-go' areas stems from a belief that protected area systems in the long run must allow for new areas to be protected, and badly managed and degraded areas to be deregulated. They also note that as long as society continues to need minerals, mining will have to continue, as will the need to gain access to more land. The access issue is made more complicated by uncertainty: society does not yet know which minerals it might need in the future, let alone where these are located. Most major mining companies feel it is enough that, in practice, they rarely seek access to protected areas with characteristics that are incompatible with mineral development activities. Moreover, not disturbing areas with unique biodiversity, landscapes, cultural, and other values is already part of the internal decision-making process for many companies, as such impacts are a source of risks and liabilities and can affect revenues, trust, and the licence to operate now and in the future.

Mining companies also argue that technological developments need to be considered – consequently the likelihood of negative impacts is gradually reducing. Modern processes of mine construction and systems of management and pollution control mean that some new mines can now operate as closed systems with minimal impact on the surrounding environment.

Companies are also quick to point out their efforts to enhance biodiversity on surrounding lands. The Arid Recovery Project in South Australia is one such example, where land held under a mining lease is being fenced off, and native species that had been wiped out are being reintroduced.[61] Post-mining rehabilitation work has helped restore land to close to its previous state. There is also considerable interest in integrated land use planning approaches that encompass a set of graded policies reflecting the varying degree of sensitivity of natural values to mining (as in the UNESCO Man and the Biosphere Programme or as advocated by the Ecosystem Approach developed by the Conference of the Parties to the Convention on Biological Diversity). There is widespread belief that the net area for biodiversity conservation and other 'natural services' could increase by applying broader processes of land use designation and innovative mechanisms, such as offsets. Meanwhile, mines under more rigorous policy and planning conditions (whereby governments would have to facilitate more equitable distribution of the benefits from mining) could provide livelihood alternatives for those living in marginal areas and possibly help to reduce exploitative pressure on protected areas.

The mining industry believes that the decision over whether or not to mine should relate to the current conservation value of the area, the current causes of degradation, the irreversibility of any impacts, and the potential for mining to make a positive contribution to conservation, if allowed.

Conservation Perspectives

Although some in the conservation community acknowledge the better-practice attitudes within the mining industry, there is concern over the lack of practical evidence of change. There is also concern that what the major players commit to will not necessarily apply to other players. Furthermore, accidents do occur even in the best-run operations, which can have enormous negative consequences if adjacent to

protected area lands. A significant tailings dam breach or cyanide spill could, for instance, threaten the viability of an entire protected area, resulting in the loss of not only biodiversity but also other natural and cultural values. (See Box 7–7.) There are also the unintended 'side effects' as a result of, for example, opening up an area for large-scale industrial processes: this can herald a rush of other applications to exploit nearby resources. Such pressures, which are the direct result of mining operations, can trigger some damaging secondary effects, due to, for example, the opening up of previously remote areas and increased population pressure, that can outlast the mining activity itself.

Mining as a land use is attractive, as it can generate large amounts of cash compared with alternative forms of economic activity around protected areas. There is recognition within the conservation community that many countries, especially the financially poorest, are desperate to boost their national income through mining, and therefore respecting the recommendation not to mine within Categories I–IV can be difficult. There is also acknowledgement that much more needs to be done to help make biodiversity and protected areas pay, by encouraging eco-tourism or trade in environmental services. There is some scepticism regarding the use of mining revenue for protected areas management and capacity building, as governments rarely allow this to happen: such finance is not sustainable, as it often dries up after closure.

At the same time, the industry's emphasis on integrated land use management is seen by some as an excuse to weaken protected areas legislation and as an effort to gain access to national parks and other areas previously excluded from minerals development. If conflict on these issues is to be avoided, and 'win–win' outcomes achieved, transparent and inclusive planning processes are essential. A good example of where this worked well is found in Manitoba, Canada: The Protected Areas Initiative involved consultations with resources industries, as well as with communities and First Nations, on proposals for protected areas establishment. As a result, since 1990, protected areas have increased from 0.5% to 8.5% of the province and an additional 5.3% has been supported by the mining industry.[62] The challenge, however, is to get such participatory consultative processes to work effectively in other parts of the work, especially where there is resistance to participatory or more inclusive cultures. There is also a great deal of suspicion around proposals to have

Box 7–7. Los Frailes – Boliden Apirsa SL Zinc, Lead, and Copper Mine, Spain

The Los Frailes zinc, lead, and copper mine in southern Spain, operated by Boliden Apirsa SL, a wholly owned subsidiary of Boliden Ltd, is some 45 kilometres northwest of Seville, near the Doñana National Park. Los Frailes is located at Aznacóllar, in the Iberian pyrite belt, and mining in the region dates back to Roman times. In 1979 Andaluza de Piritas (APIRSA) started exploitation of the Aznalcóllar open pit ore body and constructed a tailings storage facility. In 1987, APIRSA was acquired by Boliden and production continued from the Aznalcóllar open pit until 1996, when reserves were exhausted. Boliden had located another ore body, called Los Frailes, and in 1997 production from this deposit started. The same tailings storage facility was used by both companies and for both deposits.

In April 1998, Boliden Apirsa halted production after a failure of one wall of the tailings storage facility. The failure released 4.5–5 million cubic metres of tailings into the Rio Agrio and the Rio Guadiamar. The flow reached the marsh lands on the eastern edge of the Doñana National Park, 60 kilometres to the south, where it was halted by a series of rapidly constructed dikes. The tailings, which had a pH of 2-4 and contained elevated levels of copper, lead, zinc, and iron, inundated more than 2000 hectares of farmland.

The Spanish government reported that the spill caused a massive fish-kill and the destruction of many aquatic species in the river system. There was no immediate effect on the Doñana National Park, although there was concern about the contamination of the aquifer that underlies the park and the subsequent impact on bird life. Some estimate that the damage resulted in 5000 job losses in agriculture, fishing, tourism, and nature conservation. The cost of the clean-up operations – more than 16 billion pesetas (US$135.7 million) – and other financial problems forced the company to file for bankruptcy protection. Had the national and regional environment authorities not taken quick action on dike construction, large tracts of the park would certainly have been destroyed.

Source: Ramos (2000); Sassoon (1998); Mineral Resource Forum website, http://www.mineralresourcesforum.unep.ch/accidents/losfrailes.htm; Mining Technology website, http://www.mining-technology.com/projects/los_frailes

'rotating' parks that would temporarily remove some of the conditions of protected status.[63] And there is concern that some of the innovative mechanisms being proposed, such as offsets, might not create the exact array of natural and physical attributes that are found in the original protected areas they are supposed to 'replace'.

The consensus view of the conservation sector is that mining should simply not take place in protected area management Categories I–IV and in UNESCO World Heritage Sites.

The Challenges

Although the impasse over the use of IUCN Protected Areas Management Categories I–IV as 'no-go' areas remains, there have been some advances in the debate, and also a few attempts at designing decision-making criteria.[64] Particularly encouraging has been the emerging awareness within the industry and conservation groups of some of the obstacles that are blocking further consensus building on mining and protected areas and remedial action. Many of these issues were discussed at two MMSD mining and biodiversity workshops, which identified several continuing challenges.

While it is generally accepted that the IUCN categories are a good system for initial designation of protected areas, there is concern that the current system has been inconsistently interpreted and applied by governments within and between countries, and that decisions have not always been transparent and inclusive. Questions have therefore been raised over whether the 'right' protected areas fall into the 'right' categories, and whether incorrectly categorized protected areas should be reclassified. Furthermore, as the management of protected areas has often been nominal, or even absent, this has led to the degradation of values on which the original categorization was based, meaning that the protected area may be less effective than it should be. This does not mean, however, that such protected areas warrant de-designation, as only a thorough analysis of whether the lost values can be restored can draw conclusions over how 'degraded' a protected area really is. Such issues have, however, led to inevitable confusion over the role and functioning of the category system.

Many protected areas were established when scientific understanding of biodiversity was much less advanced, and the designation of parks was often based on other values and largely with disregard to local populations. Consequently, many of today's protected areas do not coincide with what is now considered 'best fit' for biodiversity, although the benefits of their continued existence are enjoyed by many. However, as science, and the knowledge it generates, is constantly evolving, so does understanding of what might be 'best' for biodiversity conservation and hence where protected areas might best be located. The biodiversity of the deep seas was previously thought to be impoverished, for instance, but recent research has found it to be more complex even than comparable terrestrial fauna, with high rates of endemism.[65] Similarly, the Caribbean was initially excluded from Conservation International's ranking exercise in 1990, but a decade later it was listed as one of the three highest ranking 'biodiversity hotspots' in the world.[66]

Although some protected areas designations may not be in tune with recent science, many still continue to maintain some ecosystem services or other critical natural or cultural values. An additional complication is that some protected areas now have significant mineral potential that was unknown when the area was originally selected for protection. This raises some difficult dilemmas. Clearly there are areas of valuable biodiversity that remain unprotected, while other areas encompassing biodiversity that is now considered less valuable remain protected. And the latter may contain valuable mineral sources and hold other natural values. What should be done where such 'older' areas continue to exist and other biodiversity areas remain unprotected? There is a great deal at stake here, as conservation interests place value on certainty and permanence in protected areas, but there could also be a great deal to gain for conservation.

There is concern that a robust and globally representative system of protected areas has not yet been achieved. Set against the ever-increasing exploitative pressures on land, achieving such a global system is proving very challenging indeed – as is the generation of resources to cover associated management and other costs.

Many protected areas do not pay for themselves and are starved of resources. Even though protected areas bring many environmental and social benefits, they also

The Ranger Uranium mine is in an enclave within the Kakadu National Park, Australia

involve costs. There are both the direct costs for their management and the opportunity costs that may arise in so far as 'economic' land uses are constrained. Keeping such areas protected is far from simple. Many are protected in name only, with a lack of capacity by the state to enforce regulations, and often a lack of political support at all levels. They are often poorly funded, which results in weak management and planning regimes. It is hardly surprising, therefore, that many protected areas are threatened in various ways by, among other things, the poverty of local populations, civil unrest and war, neglect, weak institutions, and corruption. It should be added that threats to protected areas are not a problem confined to the less developed world – planning and funding pressures of various kinds are also a reality in industrial countries.

Unless additional resources are made available, the effectiveness of protected areas will be severely diminished, and the creation of new ones deferred or cancelled – with serious implications for ecosystems and other natural and cultural values that remain underrepresented globally. Innovative mechanisms for generating adequate funding for management of protected areas by promoting alternative economic activity (such as the much promoted eco-tourism, which also carries costs and benefits) must be a key priority for these countries. The proceeds from mining could be used to fund protected areas and other conservation activities through offsets or set-asides, thus ensuring the long-term viability of such areas. However, provisions would have to be made to ensure that this funding does not evaporate post-mining. There is still much work to be done before there are sufficient levels of trust to enable this to happen, as few from the environmental side are yet convinced that the mining sector can provide benefits commensurate with the environmental costs. Yet if the mining sector is to be excluded, or encouraged to exclude itself, these potentials will not be realized.

The role of government in helping to resolve mining and protected areas issues is critical, yet it is often the weakest link, especially in developing countries. With dwindling resources, these governments are not equipped to make the sort of decisions that can lead to effective, equitable, and sustainable land use management. While bilateral contributions and those of NGOs have been critical, there is a chance that the mining industry could also contribute to conservation. Without some such support, and not only from industry, the outlook for biodiversity in these countries is bleak.

Such an approach will require a broader discussion of the integration of protected areas with buffer zones and the wider landscape, the effectiveness of protected areas management, and the way to do effective trade-offs, with an emphasis on how to ensure that local people are not undermined in the process.

There are certain activities that are likely to be acceptable to both mining and conservation interests, mainly pertaining to land under Categories V and VI and adjacent to protected areas. If successfully implemented, embarking on a short-term programme to collaborate could help build trust and confidence between the two parties, which is necessary if further dialogue and any understanding is to be achieved in the medium to longer term. However, such solutions brokered at global or national levels must be counterbalanced by the needs and interests of those usually marginalized by such discussions. The challenge lies in making fully representative decisions that are a better balance for all of society's concerns and priorities, as any solutions will most likely involve some elements of compromise on all sides. (See Box 7–8.)

Box 7–8. Huascaran National Park, Peru, and the Antamina Project

The Huascaran World Heritage Site (HNP) is located in the world's highest and most extensive tropical mountain range – it has great wilderness value and holds high levels of unique biodiversity. It also holds significant mineral deposits. Various mining projects within and outside the park, together with a number of small-scale mining activities, are exerting pressure on the area. Worried by the increasing incidence of mining, the HNP requested The Mountain Institute to provide support on mining and conservation issues – and the Huascaran Working Group (HWG) was established. The HWG's mandate was to develop a coordination strategy between the HNP, the mining companies, and other interests. Many useful lessons have been learnt by the HWG as it has moved from crisis management towards an institutionalized mechanism for communication and conflict resolution. One key lesson is never to underestimate the level of commitment, time, and resources needed for proper consultation and conflict resolution.

The HWG has been centrally involved in negotiations over the Antamina copper mine – owned by Compania Minera Antamina – which is to extract 270,000 tonnes of ore per day. Despite many constraining factors and difficult negotiations, the company agreed to relocate the main transport route from the centre of the park towards a different route that skirts the edge. They also agreed to transport the concentrate by pipeline rather than by road. This is clearly an example where, once mining had been agreed to, collaboration between the company, park management, and NGOs arrived at a reasonable compromise that has reduced negative impacts significantly.

Source: IUCN, UNESCO World Heritage Centre, and International Council on Metals and the Environment (2000)

The Way Forward

Integrated Land Use Planning

Integrated land use planning is the tool that has been developed in various forms as an aid to making the trade-offs necessary for the sustainable development of land. How it is used is ultimately a matter for governments to decide, for it has to be adapted to the physical planning system in each location. Minerals development will often be the wild card in this process because mineral deposits may not be identified when the planning process starts. The better that minerals projects are managed, the less disruptive they will be of other land use goals.

Any effective planning system needs to reconcile competing claims. These may relate to indigenous territories, compensation problems, the difficult issues of resettlement, and environmental management, among others. The process should recognize legal patterns of landownership, but also the reality of land use as it exists – including when the uses are traditional or informal – and the expectations of local communities based on those uses.

The issues go to the heart of government, and there are as many systems for dealing with them as there are jurisdictions. But the overriding conclusions of the MMSD process on this issue are that whichever system is agreed on, it should be set in law with as few discretionary powers as possible, and be as integrative, participative, and transparent as possible.

In the various workshops and discussions around the land issue, the following broad themes came to the fore for national governments to act on:

- Each should seek to have an integrated land use planning and decision-making process based on a clear definition of property rights that will satisfy local aspirations but still create an environment in which development can take place.
- All should have in place the mechanisms for equitably negotiated settlement of land claims and competing land uses; these should recognize the rights of the directly affected community to say no when there is a clear indication from a well-established collective or traditional decision-making process that the proposal has been rejected.
- All should have a statutory exploration and mining code of conduct that will incur penalties if breached.
- All should be encouraged to devise a code for interacting with indigenous groups that lays down specific and enforceable procedures, including respect for customary protocols.
- All should suspend operations that do not conform to the requirements of state and international law.
- The existence of a fair and neutral dispute resolution system is a prerequisite for getting things right. If there is no functioning court system capable of independently setting compensation and trusted by the community, such a system must be created, and some form of arbitration must be available for people to turn to if they are dissatisfied with compensation offered.

Governments can also incorporate the role of indigenous traditional knowledge when delineating sacred and heritage sites and making other plans for work on indigenous territories and can, where appropriate, provide economic development funds from royalties and public land rents.

Indigenous Peoples
One of the ideas in this area to emerge from the MMSD process came from indigenous representatives in two workshops on indigenous concerns about the minerals industries: the formation of an international body of indigenous people to study, debate, and make recommendations about whether, how, and under what circumstances minerals companies can interact productively with indigenous organizations. This would include recognition of good practice and the dissemination of information on what this involves.

The UN High Commission on Human Rights (or some other international organization as appropriate) could assist in the formation of such an international body, which could be housed within the Commission. It would convene on a regular basis around a small secretariat of indigenous experts and be comparatively low-cost, without a new institutional apparatus. It would be linked to regional organizations and should help develop principles of best practice in the relationships between indigenous peoples and the mining industry. Part of the mandate would be to establish a clear set of entry conditions to land occupied by native peoples regardless of national jurisdiction. Such a body could also play a watchdog role in calling attention to situations in which indigenous or aboriginal groups allege that they are being abused, and in establishing norms or standards for the gradual negotiation and resolution of conflicts between national and indigenous territorial claims.

Other ideas to come out of the MMSD process include:

- The need to establish an information database, including information relating broadly to indigenous territories, mining, and protected areas. Such a system would have to respect the intellectual property rights of indigenous peoples with regard to land tenure and indigenous territories and the need for confidentiality on some issues of landownership.
- The need to investigate the establishment of independent arbitration to deal with disputes

(whether this would need to be specific to indigenous peoples was not resolved).

- The need to have all states recognize the land and other rights of non-dominant groups.
- The need for each national jurisdiction to develop mechanisms for dealing with the implications of mining for indigenous peoples and other affected local communities and cultural groups in ways that are locally appropriate.
- The need for industry to deal with indigenous people as if a 'consent to mine' were needed, regardless of the law.
- The key point that corporations with a well-developed set of ethical sustainable development policies will always act on the basis of respect for the community.

Resettlement

From the outset, companies need to be creative in trying to avoid resettlement. It may be easy in some places, such as the deserts of northern Chile, to build projects without resettlement. In other cases – in much of India, for instance – it is hard to see how a significant minerals industry could be built without some resettlement.

The ideal is to create conditions of resettlement that will be voluntarily accepted by the affected peoples. But at the extreme, it is hard to maintain, for example, that a handful of people should have a veto over the future of a major project that has been accepted by the majority, any more than that one recalcitrant landowner should be allowed to prevent the building of a rail line or highway.

The MMSD baseline study suggests that conflict over resettlement proposals can be avoided in most cases by adherence to a basic set of practices. Governments should ensure that mechanisms are in place to allow:

- free and willing negotiation on the part of the community (and the host community, where there is one), including freedom from harassment or coercion and following an appropriate and extensive background study on the implications of relocation for livelihoods and culture;
- full and fair compensation of the community for loss of assets and economic opportunity;
- due consideration to the provision of alternative land of equal value and equal income-generating opportunity to the land lost;

- verification systems to ensure that these conditions have been met;
- a clearly established system for negotiation and independent arbitration on resettlement issues, including access to justice through clear, fair, and transparent means of having disputes resolved for anyone who is to be subject to resettlement;
- work with companies and NGOs to ensure that communities have the capacities and structures in place to negotiate on issues such as resettlement prior to the start of any dialogue;
- negotiations to take place with those mandated through broad support to represent the local constituency; and
- ongoing responsibility to deal with problems that occur in the resettled group as a result of the relocation, rather than 'one-off' solutions.

A reasonable starting point from a company perspective is:

- an explicit company policy that there should be no decision made at the outset of a project that results in a community being relocated without consultation or compensation and that recognizes the need to negotiate fully and openly on all related issues;
- an explicit policy that recognizes these effects of displacement and the necessity of mitigating them;
- practices to ensure that where resettlement takes place, locals are net beneficiaries by their own criteria;
- mechanisms and financing to ensure that policy and planning translates into practice;
- stakeholder involvement in decision-making – among the resettled community, the host community where there is one, and any others likely to be affected;
- an assessment of the potential alternative opportunities at the site of relocation and attention to the restoration of economic opportunities and income-earning potential;
- a proactive 'improved livelihoods' approach to the negotiation of land and resettlement issues; and
- deep involvement of affected people in design of the resettlement plan.

The industry can begin, through a lead body such as the International Council on Mining & Metals and in collaboration with other actors, documenting instances of best practice with regard to indigenous peoples. Control is a key issue: those most affected, wherever possible, should decide what is good for them.

Protected Areas

The conservation community is most closely connected with efforts to conserve protected areas, but the current system needs to be improved with the active involvement of government, the private sector, and NGOs, be it mining, agriculture, forestry, tourism, or other extractive industry interests. The various actors, as appropriate to their strengths and opportunities, need to undertake the following:

• IUCN and other conservation and development NGOs, the mining sector, and governmental organizations should establish a forum that aims to achieve consensus on 'no-go' zones for mining and protected areas, on a case-by-case basis, with a priority for World Heritage Sites.
• Some areas will be off-limits to exploration and mining activity. These should be identified through stakeholder consultation, informed by rigorous risk assessment processes, and communicated in a manner that is accessible and appropriate to all stakeholders.
• The mining sector and conservation organizations should work collaboratively to develop a package of published 'better-practice' guidance, which might be showcased at the World Parks Congress in 2003 and other relevant forums, such as the next Conference of the Parties to the Convention on Biological Biodiversity in 2004, on:
  – mining in IUCN Management Categories V and VI, dealing especially with the criteria for determining if mining is appropriate, and if so how it might best be conducted;
  – mining near protected areas, dealing with the considerations that should be addressed in deciding if mining is possible and the conditions that should then be applied to its control; and
  – 'inherited mines' in protected areas (those in existence before the area was protected).
• IUCN, in collaboration with other members of the Union and the World Commission on Protected Areas, needs to explore how to strengthen governments and protected areas agencies' capacity to improve the consistency and strengthen the application of the IUCN categories system. This might require:
  – improving the transparency of decision-making around the assignment of categories;
  – developing more detailed technical guidance regarding the application of the categories system;
  – identifying how to build the latest scientific advances into the biological assessment and the

social and economic analyses conducted for protected area category assignments;
  – encouraging governments to carry out periodic reviews of their protected areas system, which could help provide critical information on underrepresented ecosystems, which could be done in conjunction with updates of the World Protected Areas Database;
  – strengthening understanding of the opportunities that protected areas offer the mining industry, to strengthen their capacities and responsibilities for sustainable land use management, including biodiversity conservation;
  – developing a proposal to establish a system for independently certifying that a protected areas category has been correctly assigned and that the area is being managed according to its categorization; and
  – developing a set of demanding principles and strict procedures that should be applied where, for instance, a government decides to de-designate a protected area or adjust its boundaries.
• The various actors should work together on concepts and practices that can help achieve a better relationship between protected areas and other land uses, such as how to incorporate areas of known mineral potential into decision-making about new protected areas.
• Key biodiversity information institutions should undertake 'high resolution' mapping exercise that will identify the scale and extent of threats posed by mining and other sectoral activities to protected areas; it is important that such an exercise identify, where possible, overlaps between protected areas categories I–VI, World Heritage Sites, and areas of high mineral potential.
• The mining sector and conservation organizations should engaged in research and capacity-building partnerships with other sectors, notably the oil and gas industry, while ensuring that local communities' interests are also taken into account – for example, a series of case studies and best practice on innovative but not widely used mechanisms in and around protected areas, such as offsets or participatory planning processes, could be pulled together, giving examples of good and less commendable practices. This information could then lead to the development of principles to guide good practice and could help regulators set the terms for new mining projects.

Endnotes

[1] Leopold (1949).

[2] Onorato et al. (1997).

[3] Bourassa and Vaughan (1999).

[4] There are a number of mapping and other attempts to correlate areas of high mining and exploration interests with territories of indigenous communities, national parks or other protected areas, or biodiversity 'hot spots'. Since it is hard to believe that mineral deposits are concentrated in such areas, the explanation for any such disproportionate interest in these areas merits examination.

[5] Bastida (2001a).

[6] For an overview of the complexity of land tenure rights, see, for example, Toulmin and Quan (2000) p.324. See Crocombe and Meleisea (1994) p.234.

[7] Parr (2002) p.16.

[8] Bastida (2001a).

[9] In the regalian system, the state is the original owner of the minerals without considerations of who owns the surface of the land. The other system is called the accession system, in which the owner of the land is the owner of the mine as well.

[10] Quoted in Warden-Fernandez (2001).

[11] See Bastida (2001a).

[12] Ibid.

[13] See Warden-Fernandez (2001).

[14] Naito et al. (forthcoming).

[15] Williams (2001) quoted in Bastida (2001b).

[16] Bastida (2001b).

[17] McShane (2002); Banks (1994) p.40.

[18] Bonnell (2000) pp.19-87.

[19] Government of Fiji (1999) p.17.

[20] For example, the Department of Forestry and the Native Land Trust Board's rates for merchantable timber.

[21] Banks (2001).

[22] De Soto (2000) p.244.

[23] Downing et al. (2002).

[24] Definition accepted by the United Nations Working Group on Indigenous Populations, taken from Martinez Cobo (1987).

[25] Crain (2001) p.57.

[26] Echavarría and Correa (2000).

[27] Downing et al. (2002).

[28] Office of the High Commissioner for Human Rights (1991).

[29] Dalisay (1999) p.113.

[30] Cabalda et al. (2002).

[31] Forest Peoples Programme, Philippine Indigenous Peoples Links and the World Rainforest Movement (2000) p.89.

[32] Bangulot (2001).

[33] Government of Australia (1993).

[34] Senior (1998) p.14.

[35] Ibid.

[36] Downing et al. (2002).

[37] Innu Nation (1995).

[38] Downing et al. (2002).

[39] Culturally appropriate means that discussions, information-sharing, and decisions take place in the group's language and routine formats. High illiteracy of indigenous peoples often demands special methods for communication (Downing 2002).

[40] The Rio Declaration on Environment and Development, the International Convention on the Elimination of All Forms of Racial Discrimination, ILO Convention 169, Agenda 21, the OAS Declaration on the Rights of Indigenous Peoples, the UN Draft Declaration on the Rights of Indigenous Peoples, and the UN Biodiversity Convention.

[41] Downing et al. (2002).

[42] World Bank (2001d).

[43] Cernea (2000).

[44] Asian Development Bank (1998).

[45] Downing (2002).

[46] Hall (2001) p.A3.

[47] Moran (1999) p.22.

[48] Cernea (2000) pp.11-55.

[49] Downing (2002).

[50] Oxfam Community Aid Abroad (2001) p.61.

[51] Tata Energy Research Institute (2001) p.93.

[52] Ballard (2001).

[53] Downing (2002).

[54] World Commission on Dams (2000).

[55] This section is partly based on contributions from Adrian Phillips, Senior Adviser to IUCN, and Dave Richards, Senior Environment Adviser, Rio Tinto plc, and on participants' contributions from the two MMSD Mining and Biodiversity Workshops held in June and October 2001. Under Article 2 of the Convention on Biological Diversity, protected areas are classified as 'a geographically defined area which is designated or regulated and managed to achieve specific conservation objectives'.

[56] Valmik Thapar, personal communication, 2001.

[57] Rössler (2000).

[58] See http://iucn.org/amman/content/resolutions/index.html for more information.

[59] See outputs of workshop held in Gland: IUCN, UNESCO World Heritage Centre, and International Council on Metals and the Environment (2000). Also outputs of workshop held in Kew Gardens in 2000.

[60] World Heritage Sites take up less than 1%.

[61] The Arid Recovery Project, based near Roxby Downs in South Australia, is a joint conservation initiative between WMC Resources, National Parks & Wildlife SA, the University of Adelaide, and the Friends of the Arid Recovery Project. The project also aims to promote cooperation among mining, pastoralism, tourism, and conservation initiatives, while increasing public awareness of arid zone environmental issues, encouraging community involvement in conservation projects, and researching the ecology of arid zone fauna and flora. See http://www.ruralnet.net.au/~aridrp/.

[62] See http://www.gov.mb.ca/natres/pai and http://www.gov.mb.ca/itm/mrd/geo/exp-sup/min-pai.html.

[63] McNamee (1999).

[64] For decision-making criteria, see WWF (2002). The Centre for Environmental Business and Leadership of Conservation International has also been working on the protected areas issue as part of its Energy and Biodiversity Initiative.

[65] Grassle (1991).

[66] Mittermeier et al. (1998).

CHAPTER 8

MINERALS AND ECONOMIC DEVELOPMENT

Realizing the potential for mining to contribute to development in all countries where it takes place is arguably one of the greatest priorities facing the mining and minerals sector.

Mining should bring extensive economic benefits. This is particularly important for poor countries and regions that lack alternative sources of development and are otherwise unattractive to foreign investors. Provided certain conditions are met – such as an appropriate legal and policy framework, an adequate level of political stability, and well-defined property rights – foreign investors are likely to be drawn to rich mineral deposits.

In the last decade, a great deal has been done to establish enabling frameworks for mineral investment, particularly in developing countries. Much of this is due to the World Bank. This has resulted in a substantial flow of investment, creating new opportunities as well as challenges. The opportunities include hard-currency earnings in economies where they are scarce, increased government revenues, jobs, improved education and skills development, and the development of infrastructure such as roads, electricity, and telecommunications.

Although many countries have benefited greatly from minerals extraction, for a number of reasons others have failed to capitalize on the opportunities brought by mining. The ability to manage mineral wealth effectively has lagged behind the ability to attract mineral investment. A key challenge now for many countries is to develop policy frameworks to ensure that mineral wealth is captured and creates lasting benefits for local communities and the broader population. This framework must recognize that production from a specific mineral deposit has a finite lifespan; when the mine closes, it is vital that there is something to show for it in the form of improved stocks of other forms of capital.

A further challenge is for producer countries to be able to maximize the value-added from minerals. In particular, developing countries must be provided with more opportunities to do so. Markets that welcome primary products must not discriminate against products that have been further processed in the exporting country.

Minerals development creates power for those who share in it – and potentially competition for access to

it. In countries where governance is weak, this may have a corrosive effect on social and political life (sometimes associated with corruption and human rights abuses) and can exacerbate unresolved social tensions, including issues of national versus local authority. The policy framework must provide the means to ensure that various rights and interests are respected and to resolve conflicts when they arise.

This chapter examines these issues more closely – looking at the economic impact of mining at the national level, particularly in developing countries, and at the steps governments, industry, and civil society can take to ensure that mining and minerals development contribute to equitable and sustainable human development.

Minerals Production and National Economic Development

Many of the world's richest countries have benefited greatly from minerals extraction. Australia, Canada, Finland, Sweden, and the United States, for example, have all had extensive minerals industries and used them as a platform for broad-based industrial development.[1] By any standards, these are now some of the world's most successful economies: in 2001 all five were among the top ten countries in the Human Development Index prepared by the United Nations Development Programme (UNDP).[2] Moreover, in these countries minerals development seems by at least some measures to have brought benefits specifically to regions with mines. In nineteenth-century Australia, for instance, mineral exploitation brought development to the states of Victoria and Western Australia.

In more recent years, a number of developing countries can also point to minerals-led development. It is often the case that such countries are trying to leapfrog the development process and the development of governance structures in short periods of 10 to 30 years. Chile, whose copper production accounts for 35% of world output, is now among the group of 'high human development' countries (ranked 39th by UNDP).[3] Here, too, many of the rewards have been reaped locally: the mining capital of Antofagasta is relatively prosperous and over the last 20 years unemployment has fallen despite the arrival of immigrants from other regions. (See Figure 8–1.) Africa can also provide positive examples: one of the

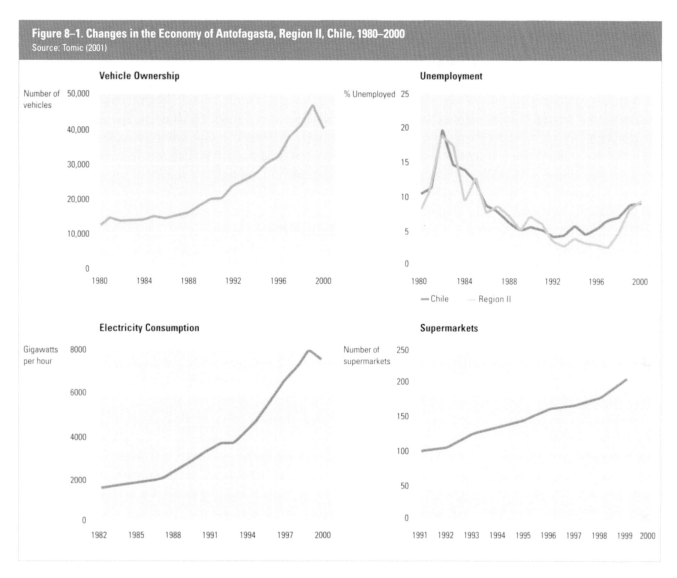

Figure 8–1. Changes in the Economy of Antofagasta, Region II, Chile, 1980–2000
Source: Tomic (2001)

most successful mining countries has been Botswana, a major producer of gem diamonds that has also had one of the world's highest economic growth rates – averaging 9% annually in 1996–99.[4] But some other countries with mineral development seem to have been considerably less successful.

There are a number of ways of deciding which countries qualify as 'mineral economies': minerals output can be set against gross domestic product (GDP), or the dependence of foreign-exchange earnings on mineral exports can be considered.[5] (See Chapter 2.) In 34 nations, mainly developing and transitional economies, exports of metals, ores, and fuels (including oil) represented 25% or more of total merchandise exports in 1999.[6] Another indication of minerals dependency is the proportion of government revenue that comes from mining. Some countries derive 30–50% of their fiscal income from a single company.

Whatever measure is used, a review of economies with significant mineral development finds countries at both the top and the bottom of UNDP's Human Development Index. Mineral wealth is clearly not a sufficient condition for successful economic development. Nor is it even a necessary one: many of the world's most successful countries in recent decades, including the newly industrializing countries of East and Southeast Asia, have had few mineral deposits. If managed effectively, however, the minerals sector has the potential to play an important role in national and local economic development.

How should a country expect to gain from the minerals sector? One of the most immediate ways should be through additional employment – both direct and indirect. Mining activity should also generate new infrastructure such as roads, railway lines, electricity supplies, schools, and hospitals that, although provided for the minerals industry and its work force, can also benefit the rest of the population. At the local level, it should contribute to the development of skills and local businesses. Meanwhile the economy as a whole can be stimulated as minerals companies forge multiple outward linkages – backwards to industries that supply goods and services, or forwards to industries that process mineral outputs. World Bank studies of mining activities around the world suggest that every dollar that a company spends on a mine generates another US$2.80 elsewhere in the economy.[7] Finally, there are more general economic benefits, including injections of hard currency that strengthen the balance of payments, along with royalty payments and corporate taxes that boost government revenues.

These and other potential benefits are by no means automatic, however. Any country that wishes to translate mineral wealth in the ground into human development for its people faces stiff challenges. These include:

- demonstrating minerals potential and attracting exploration and development investment;
- establishing an attractive investment climate and progressive minerals policies;
- developing a domestic mineral-sector infrastructure;
- creating and sustaining mineral wealth while protecting environmental quality and other social and cultural values;
- sharing the surpluses or economic rents from mineral production equitably among different levels of government, local communities, and mining companies;
- converting non-renewable resources (mineral wealth) into renewable ones by investing in physical and human capital, and doing so in a way that also helps protect the interests of future generations;
- maintaining a stable economic environment while coping with the exchange-rate impact of mineral exports, fluctuating international commodity prices, and the demands for structural adjustment; and
- dealing with the potential impact of the mining sector on crucial issues of governance, in particular corruption, regional tensions over how revenue is shared, human rights, and conflict.

These challenges are discussed at length later in this chapter.

Why do many countries seem to have fallen short of realizing the economic development potential of minerals production? There are three main schools of

thought. The first blames external market forces – and more specifically, volatile or low commodity prices. The second emphasizes internal economic stresses, arguing that a large natural resource base can cause the economy to veer off in one direction and destabilize or damage other sectors. The third argues that windfall mineral revenues tend to distort processes of economic decision-making and may foster the kind of corruption that undermines political and social institutions.

External Market Forces

World prices for mineral products have unquestionably fallen relative to the prices of manufactured goods over the past two decades. Some economists have argued that this was not inevitable – that the declines of recent years resulted from a number of random shocks and thus do not indicate a consistent, predictable trend.[8] Others, however, suggest that mineral prices dropped when production costs fell as a result of technological innovation.[9] If mining companies are selling fungible products on commodity exchanges, there is scant room to compete by offering better or innovative products. Instead, companies have little choice but to focus on being low-cost producers – by seeking operational improvements at existing operations, undertaking grassroots exploration in search of high-quality deposits, acquiring developed properties during the bottom of the mineral-price cycle, and carrying out research and development to improve production processes.

There is a related possibility that deserves some exploration. As new low-cost producers come on the market, or as older mines retool to lower costs, economic analysis would predict an exodus of mines at the other end of the curve – the high-cost, marginal producers. While this certainly does occur to some extent, the exit of high-cost or unprofitable producers tends to be slowed, perhaps for three reasons.

First, particularly where mining is an important employer and there are few alternatives, governments do not want to deal with the social and political fallout from closing mines, and therefore find ways to subsidize them. Bolivia, Ukraine, Serbia, and the United Kingdom are a few countries where miners threatened with layoffs have had a destabilizing effect on politics. In such circumstances, governments use subsidies to deflect the problems, and many of the subsidies continue years after they became established.

Sometimes they even extend to taking over mines and running them as state enterprises when private companies are no longer willing to keep them open. Examples of overt subsidies include everything from the Romanian government's years of subsidies, which finally had to be abandoned when the government ran out of money, to the current conditions in the former East Germany, the Chilean mines at Lota, and the Bolivian government's years of support of unprofitable tin mines.[10] Examples of covert subsidies are even more numerous.

Second, for multinational companies with reputations to protect – or a desire not to alienate host-country governments – it may no longer be possible simply to 'pull out' of communities without making some provision for the work force and the social, economic, and environmental dislocations associated with closure. Particularly where there has been little attention to rehabilitation or stabilization of the mine site during operations, the environmental costs of closure alone may tempt companies to stay in operation much longer than an analysis of current revenues versus current costs might dictate. There is also always a reluctance to close because it may be hard to reopen if prices improve tomorrow. Companies therefore may internally subsidize unprofitable mines. Third, banks may be unwilling to force closure as long as they can envisage at least partial servicing of their loans.

And fourth, where miners have no alternative employment, they keep mining even when mines close – formally, as in the cooperatives of Bolivia, or informally, even for minimum returns. They are therefore subsidizing production with their unpaid or only partly paid labour.

For a number of commodities, this combination of new low-cost producers and older, higher-cost producers lingering on under one form of subsidy or another may be part of the explanation for what seem to be constantly falling prices. This important issue needs additional research attention: if reluctance to bear the environmental, social, and other costs of closure and consequent overcapacity in the industry is part of the reason for dismal world mineral prices, there could be few issues more important for everyone in the sector to understand. The question of 'terminal costs' – what they are, who should pay them, and their role in a number of the industry's current problems – is considered throughout this report.

The other commodity price issue is volatility. Since the collapse of the Bretton Woods exchange rate system in the 1970s, the prices for minerals have been more volatile than those for manufactured goods. This can cause problems for mining companies, which find it more difficult to commit themselves to a steady programme of investment; for employees, whose future is rendered insecure; and for governments, whose budgets depend on taxation and rent from the minerals sector. Unpredictable prices also add to a general air of uncertainty that can discourage investment and hamper long-term economic growth.

That is the theory, anyway. Is it borne out in practice? The evidence is mixed. The World Bank says that this has not been the experience of sub-Saharan Africa, and a 1995 study found no relationship between terms-of-trade volatility and economic growth.[11] Other studies, however, suggest that uncertainty in commodity prices may indeed reduce economic growth – though the effects can be offset by good public policy and judicious use of foreign aid.

Although individual companies acting alone are often price-takers, the industry acting collectively has some ability to influence price through controlling levels of production and stocks. However, governments can do little to influence unstable world commodity prices. Although a number of mineral-producing countries have in the past banded together with commodity agreements in attempts to stabilize world prices, these efforts have had little success.

Volatility need not necessarily lead to instability if, for example, governments smooth out the variations in income using commodity loans, perhaps, or derivative-market hedges, though the consequences of potentially poorly supervised officials engaging in sophisticated and risky commodities futures plays with public moneys need to be considered before there is a rush to such solutions.[12] Another option is to establish a mineral revenue stabilization fund. When prices are high, the government can accumulate reserves to draw on when prices are lower.[13] In theory, such a fund – if insulated from political pressures – could stabilize foreign-exchange expenditures or government spending and could help dampen the oscillation of real exchange rates. Chile, for instance, has established stabilization funds for copper and petroleum as a buffer against external price shocks.[14] Botswana and Papua New Guinea (PNG) also have funds. Though the

A key challenge is to ensure that mineral wealth creates lasting benefits in host countries

subsequently to have affected other primary commodity producers in the 1970s and 1980s.[16]

The damage can be done in two main ways. First, buoyant resource industries can bid up the prices for labour and other inputs. This harms traditional export industries – their costs increase but they are unable to recoup these by raising prices, since the latter are set by world markets. (Other parts of the economy may not suffer so much. Indeed, service industries may even benefit; not only can they offset cost increases by national price increases, but they can also gather more business by providing services to the expanding export industries.) Second, natural resource exports can also damage traditional exports through the exchange rate: if booming exports cause the currency to appreciate, this too renders other exports less competitive.

Some of these stresses are inevitable in economies undergoing structural changes. Market economies constantly evolve as some sectors expand while others contract. And there need be no overall reduction of economic growth if the gains from minerals exports more than offset the losses experienced elsewhere. The effects may be felt most where governments respond to political pressure and intervene to protect vulnerable industries. This can lead to a general misallocation of resources – including tariffs, quotas, or other restrictions that will render the country less open to international trade. And the damage can be compounded if the boom in mineral exports is temporary and the country is subsequently unable to restart traditional export industries.

Chilean fund appears to have functioned well, the current evidence only relates to short-term effects. Much less is known and understood about mechanisms for long-term stabilization – an area that requires further research. Assuming that governments are confident about their ability to cope with price fluctuations, they should be able to extend this steadying influence to producers, particularly small- and medium-sized ones, by guaranteeing a local floor price for their output. Governments need to be very careful when guaranteeing 'floor prices', however, as this could lead to enormous public deficits if the government makes the wrong call. The record from other sectors is also not encouraging.

Governments can also plan for volatility on the expenditure side. They would be less exposed, for example, if they made conservative forecasts of future income and matched this with stable and predictable growth in public expenditures. Too often, for political reasons, forecasts are far too optimistic. Another option, which echoes the principle of a mineral stabilization fund, is to separate mineral revenues from other revenues and release them for spending at a steady rate.[15]

Internal Economic Stresses

Another difficulty for mineral economies is that a booming natural resource export sector can squeeze out other industries. In the Netherlands, for example, in the 1960s and 1970s a sudden increase in natural gas exports seemed to damage traditional export sectors, notably manufacturing and agriculture. What came to be known as the 'Dutch disease' also appears

Some economists argue that even successfully adjusting away from manufacturing and towards minerals exports is likely to be disadvantageous in the long term. This is because minerals production may take place in an 'economic enclave' – with fewer linkages to the rest of the economy than normal manufacturing industries. In contrast to manufacturing, mining operations necessarily have a finite life span. It is also argued that the mining industry may be less likely to exchange personnel with other industries, as the skills gained in mining are less transferable. As a result, though minerals production might create more profits in the short term, in the long term manufacturing can offer better growth prospects.[17] Nevertheless, much of this is theoretical speculation; the empirical evidence is far from conclusive. Correlation between low levels of economic development and mineral wealth should not lead to an assumption of causality. On the issue of backward and forward linkages, for example, some minerals producers indeed work in enclaves, but others may be quite well integrated with the rest of the economy. On the skills issue, there is little evidence that natural-resource-dependent economies have lower human capital accumulation than resource-poor countries.[18]

Political Economy

The third main reason put forward for the poor performance of some mineral economies is that the distortions caused by a sudden flow of mineral wealth can erode the integrity of national institutions. Some of this takes place through corruption (as discussed later in this chapter). But the arrival of mineral wealth can also cause more general shifts in economic power and influence that make the economy work less efficiently. Thus a newly rich mineral elite may use political and economic clout to fend off initiatives that work against its interests, such as using the tax revenue from mineral wealth to invest in human development or provide government support for export-oriented manufacturing. It is important to realize that disputes over mineral wealth between the central government and provinces or local communities can also be disputes over which ethnic group dominates politically. In the extreme, where there is poor governance and an inability to resolve these internal conflicts effectively, mineral revenues can be the spark that sets off open conflict, and can then be used to buy the arms to fuel it.

Another possibility is that mineral earnings can prop up inefficient governments. Some may use this money to repress dissent; others to buy off important interest groups – all of which narrows the options for political and economic change. Of course, some resource-rich states are poorly managed – suffering from ill-defined property rights, mispricing of inputs and products, poor investment decisions, wasteful spending, and a general lack of accountability. But they are hardly unique in this respect; many other countries have similar failings, and such outcomes are by no means inevitable.

Capturing Mineral Wealth

Clearly the existence of mineral deposits is no guarantee of economic development. Whether deposits turn out

to be a blessing or a curse will largely depend on governments – on the quality of their institutions, on their capacity to manage these resources well and use them to catalyse development, and on their interactions with companies, civil society, and other actors.

How much should government attempt to control mineral extraction? People in many developing countries view a mineral endowment as a finite and exhaustible 'national patrimony' and regard it as their duty to capture as much direct benefit or 'economic rent' as possible before reserves run out. In the 1960s and 1970s, some governments tried to maximize their incomes through higher taxes and royalties and by limiting the repatriation of profits. They also imposed various controls on what the corporations could import or export, and required that companies employ a certain proportion of national staff. When this did not yield the desired results, there were mandatory joint ventures with national companies, caps on the percentage of foreign ownership, and ultimately either 'creeping nationalization' through imposition of ever more burdensome requirements or even outright state seizure, sometimes followed by attempts at compensation.

By the 1980s, however, it was clear that some of these measures were not bringing the desired results. Some state mining companies, rather than contributing to the national budget, became a drain, as subsidies were required to keep them afloat. Many governments acknowledged that state ownership and public-sector management were failing to deliver anticipated social and economic benefits, and that over-regulation was discouraging investment. The 1980s also saw the onset of economic liberalization generally and a greater belief that the best option was to allow the private sector to take the lead in spearheading development. Encouraged by the World Bank and other institutions, many countries started to reform minerals sector policies. (See Table 8–1.)

In their desire to attract investors, some governments have exempted mining companies from future environmental regulation or have guaranteed fixed taxes. The Argentine National Mining Agreement, for instance, binds both the national government and the provinces not to raise most taxes on the industry for up to 30 years. In some cases governments have formalized these incentives through 'stabilization agreements' – committing themselves not to impose

Table 8–1. Mining Sector Reforms Advocated by the World Bank

From	Towards
Legal Reform	
Access to Mineral Resources: Restrictive and hostile regimes to foreign and private investment …	… an open sector with the same rules for all, grounded in the Constitution and defined by statute.
Limited access to mineral resources due to extensive state holdings …	… free access to land for mineral resources development based on first come, first served principle.
Security of Mining Title: Uncertain transition between exploration and mining licences …	… a guaranteed right for the mineral resource finder to obtain mining licence.
A restrictive right to transfer exploration and mining licences …	… free transferability without prior approval from the government.
Environmental Responsibilities: Lack of concern about environmental and social impacts …	… clear, consistent, and realistic environmental protection and social mitigation policies reflected in modern legislation and standards.
Marketing and Foreign Exchange: High barriers to imports and exports of mineral products and profit repatriation …	… marketing and foreign exchange freedoms.
Institutional Reform	
Ministry/Department of Mines: A role of the state as owner and producer of mineral products …	… a role as administrator/ regulator coordinating with other government agencies to assure policy consistency.
Mining Cadastre Office: A discretionary and opaque mining title registry largely serving the needs of state-owned companies…	…a transparent and efficient computerized licensing function with public registry and realistic budgets.
Geological Survey Institution: A focus on detailed mineral exploration …	…a focus on regional scientific and technical information with an open access policy to disseminate the information widely at nominal cost.
Mining Environmental Office: Lack of institutional attention to the environment …	…the development of baseline environmental information, sector-specific technical norms and guidelines.
State-Owned Enterprise: Creating losses stemming from economic and technical inefficiencies and uncontrolled pollution of the environment …	…the restructuring and privatization of viable operations, the orderly closure of uneconomic ones, and the application of environmental regulations equally to all.
Institutional Capacity: Demoralized, underpaid, and undertrained staff, unsupported by logistical resources …	…invigorated staff, trained in sector specifics, with better logistical support (even though still often underpaid).
Fiscal Reform	
An input- and output-based taxation regime …	…a regime based on profitability.
A taxation regime providing exemptions and holidays …	…a regime providing accounting rules adapted to the characteristics of the industry.
A mining taxation regime written into project-specific agreements	…a mining taxation regime written into a tax and/or a mining code.
An investment environment without a clear growth strategy and disconnected from international business practice …	…an investment climate that protects the interests of the country while addressing investors' and financiers' concerns.
An exclusive fiscal relation between mining company and central government...	…an acknowledgment of interests and needs of local communities to share in project benefits.

Source: Van der Veen (2000)

any new tax, royalty, environmental law, or any other regulatory burden that did not exist at the time of the investment.

Over the past decade, more than 100 countries have introduced new regulatory regimes. These clearly have had some effect: foreign direct investment (FDI) in mining has been growing at a respectable pace in recent decades, albeit somewhat slower than FDI as a whole.[19]

Not everyone accepts that this is the right approach, however – warning that countries that relax controls over mining are in danger of sacrificing social and environmental objectives. In the minerals sector, as elsewhere, there is the danger of countries competing with each other in a 'race to the bottom' – jeopardizing the prospects for sustainable development and for maintaining intergenerational equity.[20] Some argue that over time this approach works to the benefit of richer nations and the detriment of poorer ones. There is a clear need for a much more explicit understanding of where the boundary is between giving investors confidence that they will be fairly treated and not subject to some sort of regulatory confiscation, and the potential surrender of sovereignty by governments – a line that should not be crossed.

On the other hand, it is argued that standards in developing countries have actually been improving to be more closely in line with industrial-country standards. Second, many mining companies point out that it is not in their long-term interest to invest in countries with no or minimal social and environmental standards, since that increases political risk.

How, then, can governments maximize the benefits from foreign investment while minimizing social and environmental costs? One of the most important ways is for them to develop a clear policy and regulatory framework for the creation and management of mineral wealth. This should be developed through the widest possible participation, ensuring that policies reflect the interests of all stakeholders.[21] Governments should in theory be able to enshrine such requirements in legislation on environmental and social issues and on the plans and agreements reached by different parties – demanding that companies engage in prior consultation and also provide information in a clear and accessible form. They should also be able to help negotiate between mining companies and local communities. But there is clearly a long way to go: few

mining-sector structural reforms have established proper mechanisms to give local people a say in how mining activities are carried out or to enable them to partake of the benefits.

Governments should also take other steps to make the most of the gain from private-sector mining. They can stimulate investment by supporting their own minerals industry through, for example, the development of a geoscience database, appropriate training, and provision of access to particular regions of the country where there is evidence of high mineral potential. In addition to providing companies with sufficient geological information to encourage exploration, governments should aim for a non-distorting policy environment and should set mineral and other policies that define the conditions under which exploration, development, and mining occur – including land use and environmental rules. As an exploration permitting condition, governments could require companies to submit their collected geoscience data into a public database. This will facilitate more investment and the growth of a home-grown prospecting and exploration community.

One of the most basic issues is the division of the 'resource rents' between the host country and foreign investors.[22] Governments want to maximize the income from a finite natural resource. Mining companies, on the other hand, often argue that really there is little rent to capture – that international competition and price pressures drive their margins so low that they can scarcely make a profit.

Many of the crucial decisions centre on taxation – as governments attempt to gain an adequate share of the rents from mining without setting taxes so high that they scare off investors.[23] Where does the threshold of deterrence lie? One study of more than 20 countries concluded that companies are unlikely to invest if the net effective tax rate exceeds 60%.[24] Some governments, particular where the reserves are exceptionally rich, take considerably more: the government of Botswana, for one, is thought to retain up to 75% of the revenue from diamond mining.[25]

Such suggestions may give some indication of what might be desirable or feasible, but policy-makers will not be able to fall back on a generally applicable model. Instead they will have to base their decisions on local circumstances and priorities. Each country has a distinct view about the ownership of mineral rights, for example, as well as its own understanding of what constitutes fairness or equity. There are also differing views about what constitutes a fair share of rents between companies and governments.

Setting taxes high – using an intricate regime that reflects the interests of many stakeholders and takes the environment into account – may seem like the best way to maximize revenue, economic growth, and employment. But if this discourages corporations from investing or tempts them to evade payment, it could ultimately deliver less than a simpler regime would. If there is one lesson to be learned from creative tax and concession legislation, it is that no matter how it is disguised or characterized, the government 'take' is just that – funds going to government – and that above a certain level this will ward off investors no matter how it is formulated.

Over the years, governments have developed a range of methods of taxing the minerals sector. The two principal forms are corporate taxes and royalty payments. Developing countries as a whole derive around 80% of their mineral revenues from taxes on corporate profits.[26] This approach has the advantage of allowing the government to reap the benefits from profitable projects, but it also exposes the government to some of the risk, since no profits means no income. Although governments may choose to levy a standard corporate tax across all sectors, many also specifically set higher rates for minerals companies.

If the state owns the mineral rights to the land, the government may choose to charge royalties as compensation for the depletion of its assets – based on either the quantity of minerals extracted or their value. It may require these payments as periodic instalments, it may sell or auction the mineral rights at the outset, or it may use a complex combination of these methods. Governments may prefer royalties, as these provide a rapid flow of revenue, but they can lose out in the longer term if royalties discourage companies from developing marginal resources or cause them to close mines early. Foreign mining companies, on the other hand, prefer to avoid royalty payments because of the effect on their taxes in their home countries – for tax purposes, royalties are a deductible rather than a creditable item.[27] Governments, too, seem to be turning against royalties: over the past century they have been moving towards profits-based taxes: Chile,

Peru, and Zimbabwe, for example, do not charge royalties.[28]

Although corporate taxes and royalties offer the main taxation routes, there are many others, such as minimum taxes (used in Mexico and Indonesia), additional profits taxes (Mexico and Ghana), capital gains taxes (Indonesia), withholding taxes (Indonesia and all of the Southern African Development Community), and import/export duties or taxes (Indonesia), as well fuel taxes (most countries). Most countries also levy payroll taxes and various types of registration fee and stamp duties, along with different types of surface rentals, land use fees, and value-added taxes. Companies may also have to pay taxes locally, in the form of property taxes on the mine, perhaps, or via a surtax calculated as a proportion of the taxes paid to the central government.[29]

Governments and corporations of course have many other financial links. Some of the most controversial involve subsidies. In an effort to attract investment, many governments offer mining companies cheap or subsidized use of land, water, and energy. Under the 1872 US Mining Law, mineral claimants have access to federal land for an annual holding fee of US$100 per claim. If their application for title to mineral rights is subsequently approved, they pay US$2.50 or US$5 per acre, with no payments for minerals extracted beyond normal corporate taxes, and end up as outright owners of the land. Whether this is an appropriate policy is the centre of an intense and ongoing debate in the US. For some, the government is underpricing mineral resources and creating a subsidy or a 'perverse incentive' that stimulates a higher-than-optimal level of production, which in turn has a greater environmental impact. They propose a variety of royalties or other payments to insure that the government receives a higher share of the presumed economic rent. Others, on the other hand, argue that the government's total 'take' from overall taxation of mining companies in the US is not lower than the world norm, and that there is neither a subsidy nor a resultant overproduction. They also point out that the US environmental regime, whatever its flaws, is more stringent than in many other parts of the world.

Countries can increase the benefits they derive from their mineral resources through capturing more of the value-added of mineral production. To some extent this will be governed by the principle of comparative advantage. However, industrial-country governments could assist mineral economies to do more processing themselves by reducing the tariffs imposed on the import of manufactured goods. (See Box 8–1.)

Managing and Distributing Mineral Wealth

Governments that expand their mineral production rapidly also have to cope with the effects in other parts of the economy. If they are not careful they may find themselves suffering from some of the worst symptoms of the 'Dutch disease' described earlier. The important thing here is to make a realistic assessment of the prospects for minerals exploitation. If minerals have significant long-term prospects, the government may well choose to make long-term adjustments to the economy on the assumption that workers will have to move away from more traditional export industries. Nevertheless, they can also ease the pain of transition from minerals extraction by using mineral revenues temporarily to support the currency or to provide retraining for displaced workers.

Box 8–1. Tariff Barriers Impeding Industrial Development in Minerals Countries

Mineral-dependent states that want to progress to higher-value production could do so by carrying out more of the processing on their own territory. But they soon run into obstacles embedded in the world trade regime.* (See Figures below.) Although industrial countries are happy to import unprocessed minerals – such as aluminium, copper, lead, nickel, tin, and zinc – they take a very different attitude towards manufactured goods. If the same metals have been transformed into electrical wiring, say, or pots and pans, in industrial countries they may be subject to tariff and non-tariff barriers. In general, the more processed the goods are, the higher the tariff.

Trade Tariffs in the Value Chain of Internationally Traded Metals

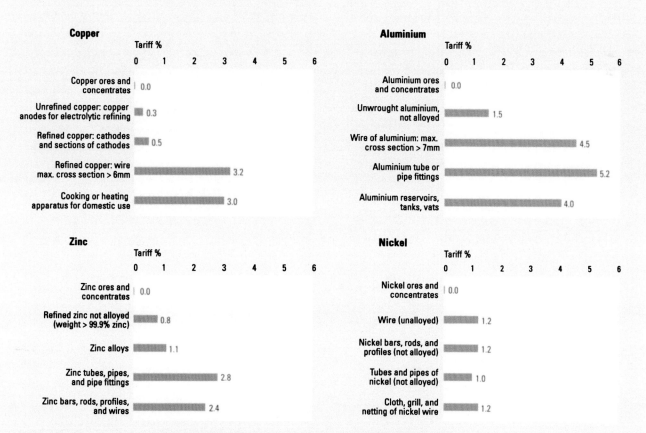

Data represent the mean import tariff for the European Union, US, Canada, Japan and Australia.

Source: UN Conference on Trade and Development, Trade Analysis and Information System

*Oxfam America (2001)

The extent to which mining operations benefit local communities has changed over time. Mining employment is in general falling in most of the world, even as output goes up. It is also becoming much more specialized. There are today far fewer semi-skilled 'pick and shovel' jobs than there once were, and it is often hard for local people to fill most of the skilled positions. In addition, it appears that a corporate strategy based on 'contracting out' or outsourcing combined with better transportation and a smaller work force means that even food and other such commodities may be increasingly supplied by foreign or at least non-local vendors. If governments and other actors want to ensure that local people gain more of the benefits from mining operations, they need to find ways of offsetting these trends.

Distributing Wealth

One of the most contentious issues is how to share mining revenues between the central government and local governments and communities in mining areas. The amount of any additional revenues from mineral development to allocate to the local level as opposed to other national purposes is a political decision within the sphere of sovereign government. Few countries with mineral development have been able to resolve this issue satisfactorily. Failure can have serious consequences for government and companies, potentially creating tension or even conflict with local communities. There can be no simple rule of thumb to deciding on the split of revenues. Much will depend on local circumstances: on the size of the surplus, for example, as well as the level of development around the mine and the needs of the local community versus the rest of the country. Governments will also have to consider local preferences: would people prefer direct payments for land use, say, or would they be happier with higher government expenditure on services?

Governments have a number of different ways of distributing benefits locally.[30] A key method is a more deliberate sharing of fiscal revenues among different levels of government and other stakeholders. In Peru, for example, the mining law (the *Canon Minero*) provides that a fixed percentage of the revenues collected from mining by the central government will be paid to regional authorities. But because of 'fiscal problems' the central government has for years delayed transfers to local governments.[31] This has become a major and bitter political controversy.

Some mining-sector reform programmes have included different types of fiscal reform, but these focused more on the type and level of taxation than on fiscal decentralization or revenue sharing. In Indonesia, the central government, which under the previous regime guarded the revenues closely at the centre, is currently embarking on a radical programme of decentralization that will pass many powers to the regions.[32] In theory, this will enable the regions to retain 80% of the revenues from mining within their boundaries. The whole process is still in a state of flux, however, and there are serious doubts about the technical capacity of local administrations to handle these new responsibilities. In reality, few countries have provisions for revenue distribution beyond the national level.

Some governments have been successful in distributing revenues, but others have been less so. In part this is a question of capacity: many simply lack the personnel or the skills to do the job well. Communication is also a problem – poor information flows among various government departments and between central and local governments often result in ignorance or a misunderstanding of local needs. Inability to distribute mining revenues effectively may also be a reflection of more general weaknesses in governance such as corruption, poor accountability, lack of transparency, and a lack of democratic decision-making processes. In addition, there are political issues – including conflicts that centre on racial and ethnic differences or on the differing agendas of central, regional, and local politicians.

A further complication for countries embarking on certain policies is that those who depend on the International Monetary Fund (IMF) may find themselves in conflict with it. Setting aside funds from a particular source of taxation and earmarking them for a specific purpose is called 'hypothecation' – a technique that runs counter to IMF policy on fiscal management and budgeting. While the IMF does not oppose revenue-sharing in principle, a mining code that provides for direct transfers of this kind may violate the host government's prior agreement with the IMF on structural adjustment loans. In theory, this could be avoided by letting local governments themselves tax the mining companies. But this is even riskier, since it would amount to a major shift in power between the centre and the regions. In some countries with unitary legal systems, local government has little or no independent power of taxation, so this step would require fundamental constitutional change. And the IMF would probably like this even less, since the Fund discourages fiscal decentralization and it could, among other things, result in an increase in total public expenditure that could stoke inflation.

There are several other models to indicate how revenues might be distributed to the local level by government, companies, and other actors. (See Chapter 9 for detailed discussion of this.) Particularly where local administration is weak, one option is for the mining companies themselves to take on some of these distribution functions. In PNG, for example, the government established an Infrastructure Tax Credit Scheme that lets the mine developer spend up to 0.75% of the value of gross sales on approved projects and have that amount considered as corporate tax already paid.[33] Most of the projects involve health and education activities, along with other services such as water supplies, roads, and policing. When identifying projects, the companies have to consult with all levels of government as well as with local communities. Although capitalizing on company skills in this way does speed up development investment in remote areas, it may also reduce the opportunities for enhancing the skills of local governments. Any such scheme should probably be transitional and involve as rapid a devolution as possible to local governance institutions. A particular shortcoming of the PNG scheme is that although it was introduced because of the lack of government capacity, it does not allow developers to get credits for capacity-building projects.

Life After Mining
In the longer term, many mineral-intensive economies must also plan for the time when minerals run out. Prudent governments will consider the best ways to use their earnings for productive investment.[34] Broadly there are two options. The first is to make investments that will produce a measurable financial return. These could include real estate or financial assets such as stocks and bonds. This is more likely in richer countries that have greater flexibility in how they use their funds and that can more easily postpone government spending. They are also likely to have larger local markets that offer greater investment opportunities – though they may also choose to invest overseas to spread their risk. The second option is to invest in assets that produce less measurable returns.

This could involve physical infrastructure, for example, as well as human development in the form of skills development and health and education services. Most poorer countries are likely to choose this approach. Companies and civil society groups can also play an important role in these investments and in ensuring that benefits are sustained at the local level. (See Chapter 9.) In some cases processing plants are constructed close to mines, and once the mine closes many of these plants continue to operate using other feed sources.

In any case, it is extremely important to recognize early in project planning that there will be terminal costs, what these will be, and how they will affect a government's obligations. Terminal costs are numerous, diverse, and sometimes very large. Examples include:
• a sudden increase in unemployment and other social costs as a region is faced with relatively high unemployment;
• the need to pay to maintain roads, telecommunications, electrical supply, or other infrastructure, which was previously done by the company; and
• the need to treat water running off the site to maintain adequate water quality downstream post-closure.

There needs to be some clear agreement on the role of national government, local government, companies, and perhaps other actors in assuming these costs. If this issue is not explicitly raised and settled at the start of a mining project, it will become difficult to deal with later as profitability falls and the company starts to look to its next opportunity. It could also lead to pressure to avoid the consequences by keeping an unprofitable operation open.

The stronger the provision is for a transition to a post-mining economy, the less political pressure there will be on government as well as companies to keep unprofitable mines open. This could lower the cost of subsidies to both of them. Since unprofitable mines may be the ones most prone to skimp on environmental controls or worker safety, it could also have other benefits.

Effective planning is a key requirement if governments are determined to manage resources in order to foster sustainable development. Mining ministries should be working with ministries of finance, planning,

environment, labour, and social affairs – all of whom
can play an important part in designing the types of
intervention that will maximize mining's positive
impact. Nowadays governments are also working more
closely with non-governmental organizations (NGOs)
and with mining companies – pooling their knowledge
and capitalizing on their different skills and experiences.
At the MMSD Workshop on Managing Mineral
Wealth, the need for participation of all stakeholders in
decision-making concerning the wider distribution of
mineral wealth was identified, as was the need for
clarification of the roles and responsibilities of different
actors.[35] The mining code of PNG provides a useful
example of a framework for decision-making based on
a Development Forum process.

Coping with Resource Depletion

Beyond considering the short- and medium-term use
of resources, governments also have to consider the
implications of the depletion of limited resources.
This has led some to propose modifications in the way
that governments account for the extractive industries'
contribution to national income. Conventional
measures of economic activity, in particular GDP, make
no allowance for the depreciation of natural capital,
whether in terms of exhaustion of minerals reserves or
general degradation of the environment. Resource
accounting methods, on the other hand, take a more
comprehensive and realistic view by drawing up
balance sheets that take into account the depreciation
of natural assets. Ultimately this could also result in
wider use of a more accurate indicator of economic
performance – green net national product or 'eco-
domestic product'.[36]

These techniques help to highlight the scarcity of
resources, warn of excessive exploitation, and permit a
more accurate assessment of the relative productivities
of different economic sectors.[37] A good example is
Botswana's Sustainable Budget Index (SBI), which
mainly focuses on recovering resource rents from
diamond extraction. This index is the ratio of
government expenditures, excluding those on health
and education, to the government's 'recurrent revenues'
– those in excess of revenues drawn from diamond
exploitation. The degree of sustainability of the
government's current expenditure can be inferred from
the SBI: a value of 1 or less indicates that government
consumption has been financed through sources other
than diamond mining, and all the revenues from

minerals have been used for public investment.[38]
A weakness of resource accounting methods is that
they may not adequately account for improvements in
technology that affect on the availability of mineral
reserves. (See Chapter 4.)

Corruption

A major obstacle to equitable distribution of mining
revenues in some countries is corruption. Some
companies in the minerals sector collude in a variety
of illicit activities, feeling obliged to – or choosing to –
bribe officials as a way to obtain licences and permits;
to acquire monopolistic power to thwart competitors;
to get preferential access to prospects, assets, or credit;
or to sway judicial decisions. Companies may make
such payments in the interests of business efficiency,
but ultimately such a system is wreaking enormous
damage – not only undermining a country's social
fabric, but also distorting the government's priorities,
undermining overall efficiency, ultimately slowing
down economic growth, and possibly leading to
instability and conflict.[39] Corruption also drains off
revenue that countries should be investing in human
development. Indeed, there seems to be a strong
positive correlation between high levels of corruption
and low levels of human development.[40]

Every country suffers from corruption to some extent.
The more mature democracies are constantly on their
guard: prominent politicians in the United Kingdom,
Germany, and France have been investigated for
accepting payments from companies that were hoping
for preferential treatment. But poorer countries are the
most vulnerable, since the opportunities – and needs –
are greater and the systems of control often laxer.
Many public officials in the poorest countries work for
very low wages, often taking other jobs to supplement
their income. So they may be sorely tempted to
supplement their incomes by demanding or accepting
bribes. At the same time, bureaucratic and management
systems may be weak. Many officials have wide powers
of discretion, allowing them to work with little or no
supervision and to make decisions with huge
implications for mining companies. Corrupt officials
also know that there is little chance of being caught,
and even less of being punished, since systems of
financial auditing are often weak or themselves
corrupt. In short, weak governance makes corruption
more prevalent.

Mining and Corruption

The most widely accepted indication of the extent of corruption internationally has been devised by a Berlin-based NGO, Transparency International (TI), which gathers the opinions of businesspeople, academics, and country analysts on the extent of corruption in 91 countries. The data are combined to produce a Corruption Perceptions Index (CPI) with ratings that range from 10 (highly clean) down to 0 (highly corrupt). Corruption appears to be especially prevalent in countries that have the highest natural resource endowments. Of 32 leading mineral-dependent countries included in the CPI, 23 score less than 5.[41] It should be noted that many of the most corrupt are oil rather than mineral producers.

Why does the minerals sector appear to be correlated with high levels of corruption? In part, this simply reflects the fact than many operations take place in poor countries where the general likelihood of corruption is greater. But the minerals sector itself has several characteristics that may be seen to further heighten the risk.[42]

- *Large capital expenditures* – Mining is highly capital-intensive. Once a company decides to go ahead, it has to commit huge sums of money to develop mines – often out of proportion to the overall wealth of the host countries. The sudden arrival of funds on this scale and the flows of royalties, taxation, and other payments present enormous temptations for underpaid or unscrupulous officials, who may be operating under information regimes that involve little transparency.
- *Extensive regulation* – Most governments understandably try to regulate the minerals sector closely, demanding that companies fulfil all kinds of conditions and obtain many different permits and approval. Governments know that mining operations, particularly those on a scale sufficiently large to interest transnational companies, have widespread impacts – economic, social, and environmental – while making heavy use of energy and transport infrastructure. They want therefore to exert a reasonable level of control. But if the people issuing the permits and certificates have wide powers of discretion, including that of delaying action, they are potentially open to taking a bribe.
- *Fixed locations* – Mining companies can only work where there are minerals, so their work sites are determined by geological conditions. Other

Diamonds will soon be certified conflict-free

enterprises faced with a difficult environment or widespread corruption might choose to establish their factories or other businesses in more congenial locations. Mining companies have less choice; when the stakes are high, officials can be in a strong position to demand bribes.

The implications of corruption – and the damage it causes – extend beyond decisions about paying bribes. Mining companies are also affected by corruption elsewhere in government. If politicians or officials divert mining revenues into their own pockets or foreign bank accounts rather than using them to invest in human development, then local people can reasonably conclude that mining brings them little benefit.

In this case, the companies may not be associated with the problem but they always suffer the consequences. As guests, mining companies need not just official permission to work but also a less tangible but equally vital 'social licence' to operate. They can only gain this – and regularly renew it – if their activities are evidently making a valuable economic and social contribution. When local people see the distribution of revenues to be unjust, they are likely to protest and even evict their guests.

Corruption among local officials can also create a governance vacuum that pulls the mining companies into taking on too many responsibilities. When administration is weak and corrupt, especially in remote areas, mining companies can easily slip into the role of surrogate government. Although this may bring short-term gains for local people, it can also store up problems for the future: corrupt officials feel under even less pressure to deliver services if they know the mining company will step in and make up for their deficiencies. This can leave a costly legacy for companies when the mine closes.

International Action Against Corruption

Aware of the extent of corruption and the corrosive damage it causes, many governments, businesses, NGOs, and international institutions have been making deliberate attempts to address the problem. The IMF, for example, restricts its operations in countries where it believes that corruption is hampering economic performance. The World Bank, too, has been determined to distance itself from corruption and has introduced sanctions on firms and governments engaged in corrupt practices: firms that have been guilty of offering bribes are banned from future World Bank–financed procurement world-wide.

Individual governments are also determined to fight corruption by domestic companies operating overseas. The United States was the first to take action – through the Foreign Corrupt Practices Act of 1977, which criminalized the bribing of foreign officials.[43] But nearly 20 years passed until other countries followed suit by signing international agreements. In 1996 the Organization of American States drew up the Inter-American Convention on Corruption, which was signed by its 21 member countries.[44] In 1997 the Organisation for Economic Co-operation and Development (OECD) produced the Convention on Combating Bribery of Foreign Public Officials in International Business Transactions. This has now been signed by 34 countries – the 29 members of the OECD and 5 others. It came into force in February 1999 and is essentially an attempt to cut off the 'supply' of bribes to foreign officials, with each country taking responsibility for the activities of domestic companies and for what happens on its own territory.[45] Companies have to maintain adequate accounting records and undergo external audits. Those found guilty of bribing foreign officials will be suspended from future public contract bids. The convention also requires governments not to allow corporations to charge bribes as a tax-deductible expense.

While the OECD convention is a major step forward, a number of grey areas remain. One that causes particular confusion is that it does not cover what are called 'facilitation payments' (also known as 'grease

payments' or 'speed money') – small sums given to officials to encourage them to carry out their normal duties more efficiently or quickly. (The US law also does not address such payments.) Home governments are thus putting mining companies in an anomalous position – ethically and legally – by allowing them to do something abroad for which they would be prosecuted at home.

Fighting Corruption at Home

Although corruption is a global problem affecting many sectors other than mining, and international resolve can help, lasting success is likely to be home-grown – through a combined effort involving governments, companies, and many civil society groups. Governments have the most important role to play in steadily reducing the opportunities for corruption as well as stepping up enforcement. They should, for example, simplify cumbersome economic and taxation regulations, demand that public institutions work in a more transparent fashion, and ensure that audit and procurement activities remain open to public scrutiny. They should also aim to limit the number of administrative decisions linked to mining and the number of people permitted to make them. Some of these procedures can be enshrined in the general tax codes or laid down in the mining code. These should establish the criteria on which decisions are made as well as covering the granting and renewal of title, the treatment of subcontractors, and compliance with international accounting standards. Enforcement of anti-corruption measures will also require an independent and effective judiciary.

Companies, too, should be playing their part, as many are already doing. A number of the major mining companies have independently drawn up codes of conduct for their employees and agents. Compliance with such codes is unfortunately sometimes another matter. Much depends on the moral leadership and the tone set by the company's senior managers. Companies also need various kinds of in-house enforcement mechanisms. These can take the form of special hotlines or channels through which employees can report infringements directly to another part of the company – the legal department, perhaps, at a regional or head office. (See Box 8–2.) One mining company is currently using ethics forms for employees to report irregularities to the company's Audit Committee, which can then discuss them in a closed session of the Board.[46]

Box 8–2. BHP Billiton's Global Business Conduct Helpline

After the 2001 merger of the Australian and South African mining companies BHP and Billiton, the company's Global Helpline, originally established in 1998, was enhanced by introducing a regional capability to address significant issues. Previously, employees could raise an issue from sites through to the corporate Melbourne-based Helpline, the Ethics Panel, and the Board. The new regional capacity will accommodate three different time zones and reflects the greater concentration of the work force in Southern Africa and South America and the reduction in the Australian work force. The Helpline offers free-call access in key global locations to provide support to employees unable to resolve issues at the local level.

During 2000/01, BHP received 300 calls from employees seeking guidance and support on work- or business-related ethical issues. Those mentioned most often included practical implementation of the company's Charter and Policy positions; information systems, including email and internet usage; and equality in employment, with a number of potentially wrongful dismissals and issues around harassment of employees. Other significant issues included clarification of travel, entertainment, and gifts policies; conflicts of interest; and use of company resources and fraud. Although a relatively small number of calls were received in relation to legal compliance, all issues were tracked and potential breaches or conflicts averted.

Source: BHP Billiton

Box 8–3. Workshop on Corruption Issues in the Mining and Minerals Sector

An MMSD workshop organized in conjunction with Transparency International identified ways of addressing corruption issues affecting the mining and minerals sector. These included:
• training at all levels in companies on how to cope with corruption issues,
• company codes of conducts designed to be relevant in the global context and the local context,
• partnerships and cooperation between companies and other stakeholders to share information and monitoring and to promote reforms aimed at reducing discretion and other incentives for corruption, and
• international mechanisms for monitoring and comparing incidents of corruption.

Source: MMSD (2001b)

One way of avoiding this kind of response is for all companies to contribute to a voluntary international register of payments by mining companies to all levels of government.

The attack on corruption will also require greater efforts from many parts of civil society. Corruption thrives in the dark, so it is vital to demand that transactions between governments and corporations take place openly. Transparency International and its national chapters, along with other NGOs, community groups, and particularly the media, can help monitor the activities of governments and corporations. Companies might instinctively prefer self-regulation, but they have a great deal to gain from external auditing, because even when they try to be transparent and disclose their payments they may be distrusted. At the same time, they and NGOs can also work with the more scrupulous public officials to help create a more open atmosphere.

One of the difficulties, of course, is that in countries where goverment is weak, civil society is also weak. (See Chapter 14.) This is a particularly acute problem in many African countries and in the more remote parts of other countries such as Indonesia, where there may be few effective civil society organizations. In order to address this, many international organizations, including those of the United Nations and the World Bank as well as many NGOs, will need to step up their efforts to strengthen both goverment and civil society.

But companies will stand a better chance of changing the general business ethos if they work with other companies – and not just those in mining – through local or national chambers of commerce or business associations. They could, for example, maintain a local database that would allow them to share information about potentially corrupt individuals and organizations. At the TI/MMSD workshop on this issue (see Box 8–3), all agreed that the key is finding a way to take joint action.

A united stand on this issue will avoid victimization of clean companies. In Indonesia, one mining company, though legally not required to do so, has voluntarily disclosed the amounts of royalties and other payments being made to the government in Jakarta. This added to public awareness but also revealed to regional administrations in mining areas just how little they were getting – as well as encouraging other groups, including the military, to demand a share of the cake.

Protecting and Promoting Human Rights

Acting either independently or in collusion with governments, mining companies have been accused of riding roughshod over local communities and respond to protests, particularly from indigenous groups, with brutality and violence. To some extent this human rights concern mirrors the issues raised in the preceding section: mining companies can only work where there are minerals, and these may be located in countries and regions where governments have regularly abused the human rights of their own citizens. This leads to charges of complicity, or at times direct or indirect responsibility, since companies have been willing to work with repressive regimes or in countries with weak governance and rule of law, such as Suharto's Indonesia, Zaire under Mobutu, or apartheid South Africa. At best, companies have expressed regret, but otherwise some have appeared to be indifferent to the human rights abuses committed all around them, regarding these as beyond their area of responsibility.

Given the scale of the investment, the fixed nature of the operation, and the long time period before an investment is recovered, mining companies need political stability. But what does that mean in this context? A traditional school of thought held that, especially in poor countries, stability was best guaranteed by dictatorship. The endless cabinet shuffling, repeated elections, or the coup–countercoup cycles seen in some countries were a great concern to investors. They felt much more comfortable – as did some in international financial institutions – with the stable figure of a 'President for Life' such as General Suharto. If the excesses of those regimes were at times distasteful, they were rationalized as a necessary step in the development process, or corporate consciences were salved by occasional symbolic statements of disapproval.

A real issue may be whether there is a broad consensus among the principal social groups that mining has a place in the national development strategy. Chile is favoured by investors, among other reasons, because it is very unlikely that the country will elect any kind of government that does not accord mining a central role in Chile's future. But in other less democratic circumstances, does too much reliance on personal connections with the 'strong man' delay the industry in the task of reaching out to all elements in society?

Does it make hostility to mining a potent political issue for the opposition?

To some extent company attitudes have mirrored those of their home governments. Particularly at the height of the cold war, many home countries were prepared to stomach human rights abuses by authoritarian regimes, provided these regime lined up on the 'correct' side. But from the late 1980s, and especially following the collapse of communism, there has been a marked shift in international attitudes. Now home-country governments see little advantage in supporting authoritarian regimes – indeed they regard them as a liability, an obstacle to secure and stable trade and investment.

Multinational corporations also have much less incentive to cooperate with authoritarian governments. Not only will they get little encouragement from their own governments, they will expose themselves to global scrutiny by the media and international NGOs. A number of high-profile companies have been targeted for their activities in overseas subsidiaries – for employing children, for example, or paying desperately low wages.[47] Mining companies may feel they are less exposed since they produce intermediate goods rather than consumer goods that are vulnerable to public boycotts. But the case of Shell in Nigeria, for example (where the company was condemned for holding its silence while the government committed human rights abuses), has demonstrated that civil society groups have become increasingly sophisticated in gathering intelligence on human rights abuses.[48] Through the internet and interested media, their findings and recommendations can define and highlight the issues in powerful ways.

Formally, the only entities bound by the 1949 Universal Declaration of Human Rights and the 1986 Declaration on the Right to Development are states, since only they have signed the corresponding covenants. Recent years, however, have seen a distinct shift in international attitudes towards human rights abuses. One important change has been a less reverent attitude towards sovereignty. People have rights regardless of their nationality and they should thus be able to call upon international protection. The United Nations, for example, is now taking a more proactive role and is more likely to countenance intervention in the most severe cases. Second, the task of protecting human rights is increasingly considered to extend beyond states, though this remains an issue of great debate. This is in part a perception of the relative erosion of state power and resources as some cede many more activities to the private sector and particularly to transnational corporations. But with power comes responsibility, and some will argue that the influence and reach of transnationals should also require from them the responsibility not just to respect but to promote human rights. A third change, which is gradually pervading many civil society groups, is the idea of rights-based development – the notion that people should be able to claim health services, say, or schooling not as a gift from a government or corporation but as a right.

This new atmosphere is presenting mining companies with difficult and complex challenges. Some of the most contentious issues concern land rights, which is addressed in Chapter 7. This section focuses on some critical human rights criticisms of mining companies: that they collude with security forces, violate labour rights, and work with 'pariah regimes'.

Security Forces
Some of the worst cases and allegations of human rights abuses have occurred when companies have relied on national security forces either to gain control over land or to defend established premises. Mineral deposits are often found in remote areas where company representatives, government officials, and security forces lack any grounding in local language and traditions, have no guidance on how to deal with claims to occupy land or continue traditional livelihoods, or feel that with no checks and balances on their actions they can behave as they wish. Today, international attention has become more focused on human rights allegations.

A prominent example of violence related to security forces in a mining area is the Grasberg gold and copper mine. This is located in the Indonesian province of Papua (formerly Irian Jaya). The government of Indonesia owns the mine, while an affiliate of the US company Freeport McMoRan Copper and Gold Inc. works the deposit. Mining in this province was always likely to be risky, given the long-running struggle for independence. The mine area has long been protected by Indonesian security forces funded by the government – at times

numbering up to 1200. Over the life of the mine, it is alleged that as many as 200 people have been killed in the area, almost all of them unarmed civilians, and there is evidence of other widespread abuses, including rape, disappearances of people, intimidation, and forced resettlement.[49] There is no evidence that the company itself had any direct involvement, but the nature of the relationship between the company and the military has suggested to some there is guilt by association or complicity.

Recently, Freeport has taken steps to promote human rights. In February 2001 it introduced a revised social, employment, and human rights policy that sets the Universal Declaration on Human Rights as the standard for all company activities. All staff and employees of the Security and Communications Relations Department are now required to sign a letter of assurance that they have neither participated in nor know of any human rights violations connected with company operations.[50]

Bolivia, too, has witnessed mining companies and security forces working in league. The use of security forces against miners led to massacres in 1942, 1949, 1965, and 1967.[51] More recently, in 1996, a dispute between an aggressive local management and radical traditional local miners escalated into hostage-taking, and a violent confrontation between workers and the security forces that left 9 people dead and 32 injured.[52]

There are always risks when securing mines in disputed areas or in areas beset with conflicts. And when there is a serious conflict and the military is brought in, they will become part of the problem. Frequently the security personnel, whether employed by the government or the company, will be outsiders, with little sympathy for local customs and traditions. When security personnel misbehave, or behave heavy-handedly, this can provoke a violent community response and further escalation of conflict.

Labour Rights and the Repression of Trade Unions
Historically, some mining companies have had a poor track record when it comes to respecting the rights of workers. Leaving aside the low pay and the appalling conditions under which miners were often obliged to work, employees were frequently subjected to violent abuse.[53] It is encouraging to see how far labour-management relations have improved among the

leaders of the industry. But this improvement has not been uniform, and the problems that remain are often found in countries with an authoritarian government.

The standards that companies should be expected to uphold are enshrined in the various conventions of the International Labour Organization (ILO), which establish the right to free association and collective bargaining. In authoritarian countries or those in conflict, however, these rights are frequently denied. The ILO standards are not even universally recognized in the more advanced countries yet, and practical observance often lags behind legal adoption.

One of the most dangerous countries for trade unions is Colombia, which usually accounts for some two-thirds of the deaths of trade union activists each year. In March 2001, two leaders of the mineworkers' union were reportedly shot dead following negotiations with Drummond Coal Company.[54] No arrests have been made to date. At times mineral companies operate in tandem with state security forces to break strikes. When 3800 workers in a Colombian labour union went on strike in 1990 at Exxon's El Cerrejón coal mine at Guajira, the President sent the army in to occupy the mine and break the strike.[55]

In some countries, miners rights are also threatened by difficult and dangerous working conditions. According to official figures, the Chinese coal industry, for example, sees around 10,000 deaths each year, although according to the International Confederation of Free Trade Unions the real figure is probably closer to 20,000, given that the authorities often hide occupational accidents.[56]

In India, bonded labour remains a concern. The Government of India ratified ILO Convention 29 concerning forced labour in 1954 and passed the Bonded Labour (Abolition) Act in 1976. Between 1976 and 2001, however, more than 280,000 bonded labourers were identified in 13 Indian states.[57] Some were involved in small-scale mines, particularly those working construction minerals. The majority have been rehabilitated under a scheme sponsored by the Central Government. Despite this effort, bonded labour may be prevalent in a few states, including in small-scale mines.[58]

'Pariah' States

Although there are signs of improvement in the human rights situation in some countries, the same cannot be said in Myanmar (formerly Burma), which is now widely considered one of the world's pariah or failing states. This country, where a military junta prevented an elected government from taking office, offers some of the starkest human rights abuses. A recent World Bank assessment concluded that a quarter of all children between the ages of 10 and 14 are working, and a UN Commission on Human Rights resolution deplored 'the deterioration of the human rights situation…including extrajudicial, summary or arbitrary executions, enforced disappearances, rape, torture, inhuman treatment, mass arrests, forced labour, forced relocation, and denial of freedom of assembly, association, expression and movement'.[59]

Myanmar has deposits of many minerals, including gemstones, tin, copper, and nickel – though mining accounts for only a small proportion of GDP. Life in the jade mines is particularly harsh and dangerous.[60] Miners, who may be forced labour, still lack basic equipment such as jackhammers, water pumps, and conveyor belts. They also light fuses with cigarettes, and pry the jade out of the ground with their bare hands. There is no safety equipment. On average miners make 50 trips up and down an open cast mine each day for a wage of around US$1, one-third of which is spent on food and water. A recent report suggests that the government has taken control of most of the mining operations that smuggle jade and gems into China and Thailand.[61] When the government took over the Yawo mining area in 1998, human rights abuses were commonplace, and according to the Karen National Union, they included extrajudicial killings, torture by beating, and looting and extortion.[62]

The international condemnation of the regime has now caused most major mining companies to leave the country. The US mining company Newmont pulled out following the US declaration of a ban on new US investments in the country.[63] And most others have declared that they will stay away: Rio Tinto, for example, announced in 1997 that it would not invest there because of the country's human rights abuses.[64] Nevertheless, at the beginning of 1999 there were thought to be nine foreign companies with major investments in Myanmar.[65] Some were from other countries in the region, while others were 'junior' companies from Australia and Canada.

One concern is that the companies with the greatest commitment to human rights and the most reputation to protect pull out of pariah or failing states early, while foreign mining and other types of investment continue in the form of less recognizable companies whose provenance and ownership are difficult or impossible to trace. This is analogous to the 'drift netters' in the Pacific, who behind layers of intermediary corporate vehicles continue practices almost universally condemned.

A Fresh Commitment to Human Rights

Over the past ten years the world has given greater attention to human rights. States that tolerate human rights abuses in or outside their boundaries are increasingly considered internationally unacceptable. This has been reflected in the policies of the UN and other international agencies, and in 1999 the UN Secretary-General launched a Global Compact that called on industry to 'support and respect the protection of international human rights within their sphere of influence and to make sure that they are not complicit in human rights abuses'.[66]

National governments have also been using their convening power and diplomatic 'good offices' to establish the norms they expect companies to follow. The Voluntary Principles on Security and Human Rights announced by the US and UK governments in December 2000 set forth guidelines on risk assessment and relations with state security forces as well as private security providers for extractive sector companies operating internationally. Two mining companies joined five oil companies, human rights NGOs, and corporate responsibility groups in developing and welcoming the public launch of the principles. Since the launch, the companies involved in the process have been working on implementing the principles in their operations. To this end, the two governments organized visits to Nigeria and Indonesia in late 2001/early 2002. The governments have also been working on outreach towards other potential participants. The Dutch government joined in late 2001 and several other companies are considering whether to become involved in the process.[67]

These principles have helped clarify company responsibilities with respect to security forces as they operate in conflict zones and other regions beset by violence and human rights abuses. Although the principles were drafted collectively by major companies, human rights NGOs, and corporate responsibility groups (together with the US and UK governments), they have been criticized for not so far including governments, companies, and NGOs based in the developing world. While the Voluntary Principles are gaining recognition as the emerging global standard on the specific issues they address, it remains to be determined how inclusive the process will become and how effective over time the principles can be in altering the conduct of companies and their relationships with security forces on the ground.

Many NGOs have been establishing standards they would expect companies to follow, such as Amnesty International's Human Rights Guidelines for Companies and the Australian NGOs' Principles for the Conduct of Company Operations within the Minerals Industry.[68]

In this changing international atmosphere, companies too have started to formalize their commitment to human rights. Most realize that they can no longer ignore the social and political realities in the countries where they operate, or shelter behind the excuse of following 'local standards' – especially when these are the standards of remote areas of Indonesia, the Democratic Republic of Congo, or Colombia. In some cases the mining companies, such as Rio Tinto and Freeport-McMoRan, have their own codes of conduct on rights matters or have tried to incorporate the principles of the Universal Declaration of Human Rights into their business principles and internal guidelines.[69]

But it is one thing to have guidelines and codes of conduct and another to enforce them. Many regional business units of major mining companies seem to enjoy a high degree of autonomy, and it is unclear how subject they are to guidance and decision-making at the head office. This is not to say there are problems – rather, in the absence of evidence to the contrary, someone somewhere will assume the worst. And there is always some concern that the most unpleasant tasks, which would bring the harshest criticism, are delegated to local intermediaries under some form of 'don't ask, don't tell'. As a result, some mining companies are demanding that each year their employees sign statements about not violating human rights, the content of which is subject to independent verification.

The Impact of Conflict

The last decade has seen widespread civil violence in 15 of the world's 20 least developed nations, many of which are home to some of the most commercially desirable and underexploited mineral veins.[70] According to a World Bank study, 'countries which have a substantial share of their income (GDP) coming from the export of primary commodities are dramatically more at risk of conflict', in particular during periods of economic decline.[71] For the mineral sector, conflict is becoming increasingly important, not least because important minerals are located in politically unstable areas of the world.

At the same time, mining itself can also serve as a focus for conflict – particularly if the rewards are not equitably shared. Another aggravating factor is large-scale in-migration, which causes resentment among the current residents. Mining companies themselves thus have a critical role to play in conflict prevention. Disruption can also occur when mines are closed and thousands of people suddenly find themselves out of work. (See Chapter 9.) Understanding and addressing these issues is essential to the success of a mining operation.

Conflict in and around mining operations usually stems from poor governance. Operating often in areas far from capital cities and media attention, government and company officials may have little understanding of the customs and traditions of those living around the mines and lack the capacity to deal with a new and complex environment. These areas may also harbour secessionist movements, as happened in Aceh and Papua in Indonesia and in Bougainville in PNG. (See Box 8–4.) In short, even though mineral exploitation has the potential to bring economic benefits that can lead to peaceful progress, it can also heighten existing tensions or provoke additional grievances.

Furthermore, mineral exploitation can provide a source of funds to sustain outbreaks of violence. In 1999, for example, it was alleged that South African mining tycoon Billy Rautenbach was bankrolling the Kabila government's side in the civil war in the Democratic Republic of the Congo. The South African government accused Rautenbach of siphoning profits from exploitation of Congolese cobalt and copper mining to reimburse the Mugabe government for Zimbabwe's involvement in the Congo war.[72] And in

---

Box 8–4. Land Ownership versus Mineral Rights

When the original mining leases and agreements for the Panguna copper mine on Bougainville island were established in 1967, Papua New Guinea was an Australian colony. The leases for mining, tailings disposal, and road access were negotiated between the Australian administration and Bougainville Copper Pty Ltd (BCP). Most of the land in question was in customary ownership, but the Administration 'owned' the mineral rights. Resentment grew due to the lack of consultation over exploration and mining plans and perceived inadequate consideration for the landowners. This led to threats of secession in 1969.

During the following years, opposition to exploration continued and in some instances the Administration used force to obtain access to land. Many Bougainvilleans believed that they should be allowed to decide when and how development of their resources should proceed without interference from the Australians or other Papua New Guineans. All these factors contributed to the emergence of Bougainvillean nationalism. In 1974 the secessionist movement reached a crisis point, with fervent opposition to the newly formed national government and mainland Papua New Guineans.

In the same year, the PNG government renegotiated the terms of the 1967 agreement, which was now enacted as the Mining (Bougainville Copper Agreement) Act. This full-scale renegotiation was in part due to the pressure brought to bear by two Bougainvillean politicians and was finally precipitated by the substantial profits made by the company in 1973. However, neither the province nor the landowners were invited to take part and the new deal did little to appease the province or the landowners, whose grievances festered.

During the period 1974-76, the newly formulated mineral policy framework attempted to deal with the Bougainvillean grievances, agreeing that all mineral revenues from Panguna would be returned to Bougainville, and that a provincial government be established which would effectively have a veto over any further mining development in the province. However, the distribution of cash benefits from the mine did little to reduce the resentment towards the national government and the company over the following years. While Bougainville's income at this time exceeded that of other provinces, the complexities around the distribution of this wealth, questions of land and mineral ownership, political autonomy and unresolved historic legacies configured to exacerbate tensions.

In 1989, the mine became the focal point of a rebellion and secession movement led by the Bougainville Revolutionary Army. Many possible causes for the rebellion were cited, with the Panguna copper mine of central importance among them. Some of the mine-related factors that contributed to the rebellion include compensation and benefit-sharing issues, land availability, and environmental impacts. The Panguna Mine closed and has never reopened.

Source: AGA (1989), Denoon (2000), O'Faircheallaigh (1984)

---

several other African countries – notably Angola, Sierra Leone, and Liberia – the trade in diamonds has financed the activities of various rebel movements.

In Angola, for instance, the rebel movement UNITA is thought to have earned US$3.7 billion in 1992–97 from these 'blood' or 'conflict diamonds', which it used to finance its continuing struggle against the government. In 1998 the United Nations placed an embargo on 'all diamonds from Angola that do not pass through official state channels'. Despite this, around US$1.2 million worth of diamonds continues to be smuggled out of Angola every day.[73] Not all now come from UNITA, which has lost much of its mining capacity; nevertheless UNITA still accounts for around 25% of the illegal diamonds leaving Angola.[74]

Diamonds have also financed armed struggles in Sierra Leone. The rebel Revolutionary United Front may now be disarming, but thanks to mining in the Kono area they are continuing to stockpile their wealth. Sierra Leone does have a system of certification, but many gems are never seen by official eyes, and corrupt dealers continue to buy the diamonds.[75] In response to the problems relating to armed conflict, the Kimberley Process is developing a global system for certification of diamonds. (See Chapter 11.)

In other cases, armed conflict can deter rather than encourage mining investment. A 2001 survey of the mining industry looked at why companies over the previous five years had refrained or withdrawn from otherwise sound investments. Some 78% of respondents indicated that a key factor in the decision was political instability – and in particular, armed conflict.[76] This concern is understandable. Companies know that widespread violence disrupts markets, destroys infrastructure, threatens ownership rights, and breaks supply chains. They also fear for the safety of their workers, who may be kidnapped or killed. And if they stay there, they expose themselves to accusations of complicity in the violence or of fuelling or even causing civil war, and subsequently risk the wrath of popular protest, legal action, stock divestment campaigns, and consumer boycotts.

Countries that need funds from multinational corporations will only be able to attract them if they have achieved some degree of peace and stability. But they will need to be vigilant about avoiding future conflicts – strengthening the quality of governance and

honouring commitments to distribute and share mineral revenues fairly among the populations. Conflict prevention strategies can also benefit from cooperation with the private sector, donor agencies, NGOs, and other institutions.

The Way Forward

Attracting Investment

As governments and international institutions continue to adopt legal and institutional changes designed to provide a framework to encourage mineral investment, there is a need to focus on appropriate principles and boundaries for the process. Investors have a legitimate interest in protection against arbitrary government action, but governments should not contract away essential elements of their sovereignty in a rush to attract investment. To do so will result in a downward spiral of conditions and terms – to the long-term detriment of all. To address these issues:

- inter-governmental groups such as the World Mines Ministers, Asia Pacific Economic Cooperation, and others could work to develop statements of principle about appropriate terms for concessions, stabilization agreements, or legislative frameworks;
- the way to strike the right balance between attracting investment and the rights of affected peoples needs further investigation;
- UNDP, the UN Conference on Trade and Development (UNCTAD), and other United Nations organizations need to provide further policy guidance and capacity building in this area; and
- all parties must encourage a clear public debate on a definition of principles that balance fair protection for investors with a fair return to host governments, including calculations of all revenue and indirect payments.

Experience suggests that the best results occur when all government departments are involved – the objective should be to arrive at fair trade-offs within governments as well as between governments and investing parties.

Global Markets

Tariff and non-tariff barriers currently discourage mineral-producing countries from developing downstream linkages from their minerals industries.

- Consistent with the principles behind the new trade round, the major consuming countries should take action to lower barriers to free trade not just in raw mineral commodities but in more elaborated goods made from those minerals.
- In preparation for future trade negotiations, there is a need for a much more comprehensive and rigorous study of tariff and non-tariff barriers that may hinder developing countries from incorporating more value-added into the kinds of mineral-based products they sell in world markets.

Managing and Distributing Mineral Wealth

A universal formula for the distribution of wealth within countries is clearly inappropriate. The choice of formula should be determined by each nation according to domestic priorities and political systems. However, central control of all mineral revenues is unlikely to be appropriate. A proportion of benefits needs to be distributed through local administrative structures to enable them to take advantages of the opportunities presented by mineral development and to prepare for the transition to a post-mineral economy.

There tends to be a lack of capacity at different levels to manage the challenge of mineral development, particularly in poor countries. To address these challenges:

- International organizations like the World Bank, UNDP, and UNCTAD should continue to promote study and discussion of wealth distribution issues, including the distribution of returns from mining industry taxes and royalties, in their dialogues with governments, with a view to a better spread of resources to lower levels of government and to communities.
- As some already are, companies should be sensitive to the effects of their procurement policies and should aim through them to build capacity in and around the mines.
- As suggested at the MMSD Workshop on Managing Mineral Wealth, an international database of good practices at the national level could be maintained.
- Experience differs in the use of mineral stabilization funds to overcome the price cycles in the sector. Further research is needed into the use of such funds to deal with the problem.

Governments should consider further:

- developing long-term strategic plans for the management of mineral wealth that include appropriate levels and methods of capturing the rent from minerals and distributing revenue, the creation of various forms of capital, and planning for the effects of mine closure at both local and macro level; and
- developing measures, including commodity loans and fiscal restraint, to prevent undue stress on public finance resulting from mineral price volatility.

Transparency in the Management of Mineral Wealth

To enable free political debate about how mineral wealth is managed:

- governments and companies should more widely adopt the practice of open publication of the basic information about how much wealth is generated, the amounts of revenue received by all government departments, and how that money is spent;
- industry organizations should consider, possibly in partnership with an international organization such as the World Bank Group, taking the initiative to establish an international and public register of all payments by mining companies to governments at all levels; and
- NGO 'watchdog' organizations could bring pressure to ensure that open publication regarding mineral wealth is realized.

Combating Corruption

Corruption poses a serious threat to sustainable development, and international concerted action is needed to combat it. The minerals sector should consider more widespread adoption of the following measures:

- individual company codes of ethics, aimed at both company employees and contractors, with requirements for employee and contractor sign-offs, plus employee support mechanisms such as internal help lines to report irregularities;
- action by industry organizations working with organizations such as Transparency International to establish common industry-wide guidance;
- government adoption of national legislation to put the OECD anti-corruption convention into effect (recognizing that the complex issue of 'facilitation payments' is not yet covered) – there is no reason for this convention to be confined to OECD members; and
- government collaboration with other sectors, NGOs,

and Chambers of Commerce to move as a block to disclose all payments at a national level.

Promoting and Protecting Human Rights

Good practice in human rights need to spread. Initiatives suggested include:

- company/industry-wide human rights guidelines with employee sign-off and support mechanisms, and extension to all local contractors;
- corporate social reporting or disclosure on human rights indicators;
- cooperation by industry bodies as the Global Reporting Initiative develops mining-specific guidelines;
- company adherence to the Voluntary Principles on Human Rights and Security;
- third-party monitoring and verification of company practices concerning human rights;
- international organization and company lobbying of governments to adhere to some form of human rights code, including relevant ILO Conventions and global agreements between companies and unions; and
- more research on clearer human rights indicators and measures of compliance for governments, companies, and civil society.

Preventing Conflict

Many companies continuously assess political risk so as to avoid conflict. Nevertheless, more needs to be done to prevent mineral-related and other conflict. In the MMSD workshop on this issue, it was suggested that companies should:

- conduct detailed research prior to investment decisions where there is a risk of conflict – if the conditions for maintaining human rights and other relevant policies do not exist or if avoiding conflict is difficult because of political conditions, investment should not follow;
- on the basis of the conflict impact assessment and involving relevant stakeholders, determine what conflict prevention or social investment strategy should be implemented;
- cooperate with conflict-prevention NGOs to build capacity in and around mine sites to prevent conflict;
- cooperate with others to support and provide input to conflict-prevention work more broadly in the country, including devising local economic development programmes and strengthening the

capacity of local businesses; and
- support the study of and dissemination of information about the Kimberly Process of diamond certification as a potential model for use elsewhere in the sector.

Companies, NGOs, and international organizations should continue researching the relationship between the private sector and conflict and developing appropriate tools to manage this.

Endnotes

[1] See the mining cluster studies in Buitelaar (2001).

[2] UNDP (2001).

[3] Ibid.

[4] See Lamont (2001).

[5] Eggert (2001).

[6] Ibid.

[7] Weber-Fahr et al. (2001) p.10.

[8] World Bank (2000a) pp.103-32.

[9] Eggert (2001).

[10] See, among others, USGS International Minerals Statistics and Information website, at http://minerals.usgs.gov/minerals/pubs/country; Ministry of Economic Development of Bolivia website, at http://desarrollo.gov.bo; Ministry of Economy, Mining and Energy of Chile website, at http://www.minecon.cl.

[11] See World Bank (2000a) pp.103-32; Sachs and Warner (1995).

[12] Ibid.

[13] See, among others, Auty and Mikesell (1998); Mitchell et al. (1996).

[14] Tomic (2001).

[15] Daniel (1992).

[16] Eggert (2001).

[17] See, for example: Hirschman (1958); Seers (1959); Baldwin (1966).

[18] Sachs and Warner (1995).

[19] Ostensson (1997).

[20] Third World Network-Africa (2001), electronic source (forwarded email).

[21] Loayza (2001).

[22] See Eggert (2001) for a detailed discussion of resource rents.

[23] Brewer (2001).

[24] Otto et al. (2000).

[25] There are considerable economic profits (or rents) to be gained from diamond mining in Botswana due to the unique richness of the resources. There is therefore more rent to be captured.

[26] Cawood (2001).

[27] Sunley and Baunsgaard (2001).

[28] Cawood (2001).

[29] Otto et al. (2000).

[30] McPhail (2001).

[31] Pasco-Font (2001).

[32] MMSD (2001a).

[33] Marshall (2001).

[34] Hannesson (2001a).

[35] MMSD (2001a).

[36] Green net national product is long established but rarely calculated or published due to a lack of consensus among national accountants on how to measure the depreciation of different forms of capital (that is, buildings, machinery, and natural capital).

[37] Hamilton and Lutz (1996).

[38] Lange (2000).

[39] Marshall (2001).

[40] Schloss (2000).

[41] See Transparency International website, http://www.transparency.org/.

[42] This discussion is drawn from Marshall (2001).

[43] Marshall (2001).

[44] Organization of American States (1996).

[45] OECD (1997).

[46] MMSD Workshop on Human Rights, Berlin, 16 September 2001.

[47] Handelsman (2001).

[48] Ibid.

[49] Ballard (2001).

[50] Freeport-McMoran Copper and Gold Inc, USA, personal communication. See also Freeport's website at http://www.fcx.com for information about the company's human rights and other social programmes.

[51] Handelsman (2001).

[52] Organization of American States, Inter-America Commission on Human Rights (1997), cited in Handelsman (2001).

[53] See as an example Barron (1957).

[54] Handelsman (2001).

[55] Ibid.

[56] ICFTU (2001) p.98.

[57] Government of India (2001) p.93.

[58] Tata Energy Research Institute (2001).

[59] World Bank (1999); United Nations Commission on Human Rights (2001).

[60] This section is based on Müller (1997).

[61] Handelsman (2001).

[62] Karen National Union (1998).

[63] Moody (2000).

[64] Ibid.

[65] Ibid.

[66] Annan (1999).

[67] Government of United States of America – Department of State (2001).

[68] Amnesty International (2001); Australian Asia-Pacific Mining Network (1998).

[69] Ballard (2001).

[70] UNDP (2000) p.36; World Bank (2000b) p.170.

[71] Collier (2000) p.7.

[72] Powell (1999).

[73] Angola Peace Monitor (2001).

[74] Ibid.

[75] BBC News (2001).

[76] PricewaterhouseCoopers (2001).

CHAPTER 9

LOCAL COMMUNITIES AND MINES

Mineral development can create new communities and bring wealth to those already in existence, but it can also cause considerable disruption. New projects can bring jobs, business activities, roads, schools, and health clinics to remote and previously impoverished areas, but the benefits may be unevenly shared, and for some they may be poor recompense for the loss of existing livelihoods and the damage to their environment and culture. If communities feel they are being unfairly treated or inadequately compensated, mining can lead to social tension and sometimes to violent conflict. (See Chapter 8.)

Mining's interaction with local communities has changed over time. With the dramatic decline in the costs of transporting bulk materials and the emergence of multinational companies as major players, mines can now be located far from where the ores are processed. At the same time, they have become larger and more technically complex, bringing a decrease in employment and an increase in the skill levels required of workers. In many countries, mines have tended to become specialist enclaves, isolated from other sectors of the economy. The premier example of this is 'fly-in, fly-out' operations based on long-distance commuting. This invariably means that the communities living nearby gain less in terms of jobs, business opportunities, and the multiplier effects.

Exploration increasingly occurs in remote regions with little or no development. By nature of their remoteness, the areas to be explored are frequently ones where the title to land is disputed or unacknowledged and where local government lacks the capacity to provide essential services or to mediate between mining companies and local communities. A consequence is the potential for mining companies to wield too much power in the local context. Traditional cultures may have difficulty coping with vast industrial operations and the influx of outsiders. A growing appreciation of the intrinsic value of traditional cultures has heightened awareness of these issues. All these trends have significantly changed the balance of costs and benefits at the community level and have contributed to a rethinking of mine–community relations.

In addition, all mines have a finite life span, and it is difficult to sustain the direct benefits they bring to communities in terms of wages and improved welfare after mine closure. The infrastructure that develops with a mine may be scaled down or neglected when the mine closes unless provision has been made for maintenance and upkeep well in advance. Communities are particularly vulnerable where linkages with other sectors of the economy are weak.

There is an inherent tension between local and national rights to mineral wealth and the other benefits brought about by mining. That people living near mines or adversely affected by them should be compensated for any inconvenience, hardship, or loss of opportunity suffered is generally not disputed. The question is, should they receive a larger share of the benefits? If so, how should that share be determined? The rationale for local communities to receive a greater share of the benefits is clear: first, for communities to accept mining on their doorstep, they must see some realizable benefits over and above being compensated for loss or other impacts. Second, for mining to contribute to the goals of sustainable development at the community level, it must provide a net benefit to the affected community. Sustainable development requires an equitable sharing of benefits; if there is obvious inequity, there will be strife, which impedes the development process. The question is therefore more appropriately, how should the share of benefits received by communities be decided? This is discussed later in the chapter.

Sustainable Development at the Community Level

At the local level, sustainable development is about meeting locally defined social, environmental, and economic goals over the long term. Interactions between the mine and community should add to the physical, financial, human, and information resources available – not detract from them. (See Table 9–1.) The challenge is to ensure that the effect of interactions are regarded as positive by those affected locally as well as by the promoters of the project, and that communities develop in ways that are consistent with their own vision. This may be realized through, for example, the provision of social services, income, or skills development. Enhancing community values presents a particular challenge, given the often intense social change brought about by mining and the potential influx of outsiders.

Table 9–1. Means for Sustainable Development at the Community Level

Resources – quantity, quality, access to them, and realizable value

Physical resources
• Land, natural resources, and environmental services
• Productive equipment to make use of these services
• Infrastructure (especially safe and secure shelter, water supply and sanitation, education, energy, transport, communications)

Financial resources
• Income
• Savings, investments, and credit

Human resources
• Health, safety, and security
• Skills, knowledge, and qualifications
• Jobs and other economic strategies such as migration/remittances and subsistence activities

Information
• Information about technical/policy/market opportunities and obligations
• Information about change

Community values and knowledge
• Shared values, norms, goals, and aspirations for sustainable development
• Community knowledge of society, environment, and economy and their interaction
• Associated social traditions (history, culture, religion)

Community institutions
• Community governance institutions, mechanisms, rules, and sanctions – for participation in problem and opportunity assessment/ debate/ communication/ consensus/ conflict management/ decisions/ self-help/ joint work/ learning and innovation/ social security/ cost–benefit sharing/ vigilance and monitoring/ accountability
• Legitimacy and reputation of the community and its institutions
• Trust, leadership, membership, management of community groups, federations, networks
• Internal relations/partnerships within the community, such as gender/ethnic relations
• Relations/partnerships with other communities, actors, and service providers
• Other means to seize opportunities, manage risk, and improve resilience

Individual and community powers
• To negotiate with bureaucracy and private sector
• To influence politics, policy, laws, and instruments
• To influence market conditions
• To plan/control developments and activities in the vicinity
• To express community needs, ideas, and choices

Individual and community rights
• To claim, receive, defend, transform, and trade material and financial assets
• To information
• To representation and engagement in processes (political, policy, legal, market)
• To development and self-determination

Key factors: Community coherence, diversity, equity, stability, resilience, options, pace

Power differentials can leave a sense of helplessness when communities confront the potential for change induced by large, powerful external companies. The problems are most acute where local government capacity or other forms of local representation are lacking and where community rights are not enforced by the central government. Ensuring that mechanisms are in place to enable local communities to play effective roles in decision-making is one of the greatest challenges in mining's ability to contribute to sustainable development at the local level.

Whatever is agreed to (or not, as the case may be), minerals activities must ensure that the basic rights of the individual and communities affected are upheld and not infringed. These may include the right to control and use land; to clean water, a safe environment, and a livelihood; to be free from intimidation and violence; and to be fairly compensated for loss. Such rights may be enshrined in the national law or based on and expressed through a range of international human rights instruments and agreements. (See Chapter 8). Moreover, all groups have a right to development, and the interests of the most vulnerable groups – the poor and the marginalized – need to be identified and protected. Reconciling the various rights and responsibilities in different governance environments to the satisfaction of those concerned is perhaps one of the most difficult challenges.

Having the right processes in place to reach outcomes acceptable to as broad a range of community members and other stakeholders as possible is the way forward. Such processes have to be within the confines of available resources and capacity as communities themselves work towards sustainable development.

Gains and Losses at the Local Level

It is important to acknowledge the different categories of community involved in or affected by mining operations:

- *Occupational communities* – households or families who derive all or most of their income from mining.
- *Residential communities* – households or families who live within the geographical area affected by mining. They may live in close proximity or many miles away, such as on a river polluted by mine tailings. These communities fall into two types: those in existence before the mine was built and those that have developed as a result of the mining operations.
- *Indigenous communities* – households or families with an ancient and cultural attachment to the land where mining occurs or has an impact.

These three categories are not mutually exclusive, of course. Indigenous communities may work in a mine, and therefore be occupational communities too, while long-distance commuting, as is the case in fly-in, fly-out operations and operations that rely on migrant labour, may mean that occupational communities do not live near the mine. (This chapter does not deal with occupational communities formed by artisanal or small-scale miners.)

In occupational communities, people must have the means to survive and prosper, either in the same place or elsewhere, once mining ceases. Issues such as the transfer of skills and future employment must therefore be addressed. In residential communities, minimizing the environmental footprint of mining will be a priority, and thus access to information about potential impacts as well as the power to influence decisions will be important.

Indigenous people present a special case of community. As well as having specific social needs, in many countries they are the poorest and most marginalized

in society.[1] Indigenous communities have traditionally been based on very distinct systems of decision-making, social and political institutions, and systems of wealth generation and distribution. Additionally, indigenous culture, whose value has commonly gone unacknowledged, is often closely associated with natural resources that have social, economic, and spiritual significance. Many of the differences between indigenous cultures and wider society have been poorly understood. Moreover, development involving minerals and other natural resources has been the cause of displacement and victimization, made easier by poor protection of indigenous peoples' rights to their land. The injustices of the past and present have engendered a deep mistrust of outsiders – in this case, governments and mining companies.[2]

The goals of sustainable development will differ among indigenous communities. For some it may mean that their attachment to their land and culture survives the upheavals caused by mineral development. Others may be ready to abandon subsistence activities and explore the opportunity to benefit from, for example, improved housing, health care, and education. Either way, it is crucial for the survival of indigenous communities that their rights and culture are respected.

The nature of the mining operation – including its size, life span, and type of mineral being extracted – will influence the interactions between mining and the community and the means available for working towards sustainable development. The more recently established operations are more likely to use environmentally friendly technologies and be more sensitive to social concerns. The characteristics of mining operations tend to differ regionally (see Chapter 3), which also affects the nature of interactions.

The stage of the mining operation is another important determinant of effects:

- The exploration stage is of comparatively low economic impact but is critical since it is often the first encounter between the community and mining company. Encounters can be sporadic but extend over long periods of time as different companies undertake exploration activities in a locality. This is the stage at which the relationship between the community and mining company (or industry) is set up, which, depending on how it is managed, can result in either positive or negative perceptions of the industry for a long time, including the later stages of mine development and operation.

- The construction phase, although relatively brief, is probably of greatest impact in the short term and has long-term implications. It potentially brings a boom in jobs but can also cause considerable physical and social upheaval, opening up remote areas through the development of infrastructure and stimulating migration to the area.
- The production phase has the longest-term impacts – bringing, for example, income and infrastructure, but also negative and often unintended repercussions.
- The impact of the closure phase depends largely on the degree of forward planning and the available means to sustain benefits, such as institutional capacity and financial resources.

The actual impacts experienced and the perceptions of the community will depend on the pre-existing situation, the process of community engagement and capacity-building, the role of governments, and other social changes. The credibility or trust in the government as well as attitudes towards private or foreign capital will affect a community's attitude towards a mining project.[3] The relationship between the mine and community can also dramatically change at any stage of the mining life cycle due to unintended events such as accidents and social conflict, or due to changes external to the mining operation.

This chapter focuses mainly on the production and closure phases. The dynamics of the interaction at the exploration stage are quite distinct from these later stages of development.[4]

An Economic Perspective

Communities can receive compensation and substantial flows of revenue when a large mine is established, which can act as an important catalyst for change and growth. For areas previously peripheral to the cash economy, these monetary flows can transform the economic and social basis of communities. The types of payments and the way they are used are key to mining's ability to contribute to sustainable development at the community level.

As noted in Chapter 7, losses suffered by communities in homes, land, or access to other sources of livelihood should be compensated. However, there are many problems with compensation systems. They may, for example, address property values recognized by the legal system much better than they deal with informal occupation of land or the loss of traditional subsistence livelihoods. Many actors now recognize that cash for people with little prior experience of cash economies may leave them worse off in the long run, as it may lead to social tension or investments that yield few long-term gains. Experience shows that social tensions resulting from compensation agreements made at the beginning of an operation are likely to continue throughout the life of the mine.

The closer countries are to the source of mineral wealth, the further away they often seem to be from capturing many of the benefits. This paradox is often repeated within countries, with the regions that are rich in minerals losing out, in economic terms, to those that are not. In many instances, communities do not receive a share of the equity of mining operations since their surface rights to land do not translate into rights over minerals. Though often hampered by the low governmental capacity or the lack of political will, a key challenge is to ensure that an agreed proportion of revenues is redistributed locally.

Mining often provides local communities with jobs, which may enable those in subsistence to join the cash economy. Others who already had paid work may find themselves better off, since in many countries mining pays relatively higher wages. Particularly in developing countries, wages may increase through localization schemes or through moving local employees into higher positions within a company by way of corporate training. Counter to this, however, modern mines tend to have much higher levels of productivity than older mines, employing small but highly skilled work forces. A recent study in Chile found that the number of mine workers with higher education rose from 26% in 1990 to 36% in 1996 (compared with 14% for other sectors).[5]

In some regions, mining provides the bulk of job opportunities. The Grasberg copper and gold mine in West Papua, employing 14,000 people, provides a dramatic example: the number of indirect jobs created as a result of Freeport's mining activities is estimated at 75,000.[6] Elsewhere, with the exception of the construction phase, many mines no longer generate significant numbers of local jobs. In Peru, a GRADE study showed that the local sources of employment are very limited, and that much labour is imported.[7]

A smaller number of employees means that the multiplier effect has declined relative to historical levels.

Retrenchment is a current concern for mines all over the world, and some regions have been severely hit. Until recently, for example, Romanian mines were government-owned and received huge subsidies. With the liberalization of the economy, the government closed 178 uneconomic mines with 83,000 miners – resulting in a sharp economic decline in mining regions.[8] While workers could find work in different mines, it may involve uprooting their families; other mine workers could be employed in alternative activities, as many have developed transferable skills through education and training.

Another important source of economic benefits to communities, particularly where mining is the main activity, is the input services provided to mining operations. Companies are increasingly required to assist local business development, to outsource services, and to give preference to local businesses. However, increased demand may cause the prices of goods and services to rise locally. Moreover, the concentration of economic activity centred around the mine often increases the community's dependence on the mining operation, making it vulnerable to downsizing or other changes and exacerbating the power imbalance. On the other hand, since the company may also depend on the community for employees and services, a well-organized community can potentially make numerous demands on the company.

A Social Perspective

It is difficult to separate the economic impacts of mining operations from the social impacts. Many social problems are direct consequences of poverty, and if mining helps a community become prosperous, it may also help it tackle social ills such as malnutrition, illiteracy, and poor health. On the other hand, mining activities may cause economic hardship – by polluting rivers and damaging fish stocks, for instance, or by appropriating grazing land and forestry resources. This, in turn, may exacerbate existing social problems or create new ones.

If the revenues from mining are not equitably shared, this aggravates inequalities within communities. For example, a social audit of the Grasberg mine showed that the worsening inequalities in income distribution favour young adults, modifying their position and prestige vis-à-vis their elders and affecting traditional social structures.[9] If people in a community perceive the revenues of mining to be unfairly shared, this can result in social tension and even violent conflict within the community or between the community and the mining company or government.

Relocation

The displacement of settled communities can be a significant cause of resentment and conflict associated with large-scale mineral development. Communities may lose their land, and thus their livelihoods, disrupting also community institutions and power relations. Entire communities may be forced to shift into purpose-built settlements, into areas without adequate resources. They may be left near the mine, where they may bear the brunt of pollution and contamination. Involuntary resettlement can be particularly disastrous for indigenous communities with strong cultural and spiritual ties to the lands who may find it difficult to survive when these are broken. (The resettlement of communities is also discussed in Chapter 7, as are the difficulties faced by communities without legally recognized land tenure.)

As with compensation payments, some of the issues associated with relocation may take years to surface. Where houses built with permanent materials replace traditional homes, for instance, communities may not have the skills required to maintain them, and companies may be reluctant to become involved in the process. Increasing household sizes may place pressure on relocation housing; young people may demand an equivalent dwelling when they marry.

Migration

One of the most significant impacts of mining activity is the migration of people into a mine area, particularly where the mine represents the single most important economic activity. For example, at the Grasberg mine the local population increased from under 1000 in 1973 to between 100,000 and 110,000 in 1999.[10] Similarly, the population of the squatter settlements around Porgera in Papua New Guinea (PNG), which opened in 1990, has grown from 4000 to over 18,000.[11] With this influx of newcomers, disputes may arise over land and the sharing of benefits. (These were among the factors that led to violent uprisings at Grasberg in the 1970s and the 1990s.)

Sudden increases in population can also lead to pressures on land, water, and other resources as well as bringing problems of sanitation and waste disposal. In San Ramon in Bolivia, for instance, migration led to an increase in land and housing prices and the saturation of public services, including schools. Among the corrective measures taken, the mining company is making extra tax contributions to improve the local school system.[12] And population increases create difficulties in determining the level of facilities required, particularly when the population rises substantially after the initial resettlement planning.

Migration effects may extend far beyond the immediate vicinity of the mine. Improved infrastructure can also bring an influx of settlers. For instance, it is estimated that the 80-metre-wide, 890-kilometre-long transportation corridor built from the Atlantic Ocean to the Carajas mine in Brazil created an area of influence of 300,000 square kilometres.[13] From a social perspective, such an influx can lead to the build-up of a large mass of people with weak links into society as a whole and a disruptive influence on local social control, leadership, and lifestyles. From the corporate and state perspective, these migrants may be seen as representing an increased security risk and may effectively dilute the value of benefits provided to the host communities.[14]

Infrastructure Improvements
There can be significant infrastructure improvements with the construction of a large mine.[15] Most mining operations of any size are served by airstrips, roads, water supplies, sanitation systems, and electricity. If these are restricted to use by the company, and designed solely for company objectives, they may be of little relevance to anyone else. With some advance planning and a willingness to consult with the community, however, these can bring lasting benefits at little or no added cost. And the development of infrastructure may facilitate other forms of economic activity, such as tourism.

Health
In terms of community health, a basic paradox arises. Resources available locally for health services typically increase markedly with the advent of mine development as companies develop facilities for employees and their families. Moreover, employment and increased living standards can bring important nutritional and psychological benefits, and hence better health standards. But these may not necessarily translate

Traditional indigenous housing near the Kumtor Gold Mine, Kyrgyzstan

into overall improvements in community health if the facilities are not made available to the broader community or if the introduction of new diseases and health risks associated with the mine are taken into account. Relatively isolated communities, including indigenous peoples, may be particularly vulnerable to diseases brought by miners, such as influenza, malaria, and HIV/AIDS. Abandoning traditional subsistence lifestyles of hunting and fishing, and instead buying food from outside, could lead to a nutritionally poorer diet.

A key issue is sustaining health services and benefits in the community after mine closure, which might depend on the approach taken during the life of the mine. Training local health paraprofessionals, for example, might provide higher benefits in the long term than importing contract doctors.

Another constraint is the complexity of causal effects for certain diseases. In some developing countries, it is often difficult to confirm a relationship between mining and the spread of already prevalent diseases such as malaria and HIV/AIDS. (See Box 9–1.)

Finally, some of the detrimental health effects of mining on communities may surface years after mining has ceased. An example of this is found in South Africa, where communities near an asbestos mine that closed in 1968 registered higher incidences of lung diseases several years after the operation ended.[16]

Education
As with health, access to educational services and facilities can improve dramatically for communities close to or around large mines, particularly for mines

In Southern Africa, there is a general belief that the spread of HIV/AIDS is a particular problem within mining projects, due mainly although by no means solely to a migrant labour system in which workers spend months away from their spouses, often living in single-sex hostels with a high prevalence of sex workers. One difficulty in assessing this relationship is the lack of uniformity in statistical evidence. For example, a research report on HIV/AIDS undertaken by ING Barings concluded that mining will be the most affected sector in South Africa, followed closely by transportation and storage. The researchers predicted that about 27% of mineworkers will die of AIDS by 2005. In contrast, a project undertaken by the South African National Union of Mineworkers and a number of mining companies found that the incidence of sexually transmitted diseases is higher in townships than in mining communities. What is evident is that findings differ significantly depending on the population surveyed, since the spread of HIV/AIDS is not uniform through Southern Africa.

Another difficulty in data collection is the lack of acknowledgement of the disease by those infected and their families. This can be attributed to a number of factors, including cultural taboos on the open discussion of sex, the stigma associated with the disease, and a lack of awareness about the link between AIDS and other diseases. Since AIDS manifests itself in the form of other diseases such as tuberculosis and pneumonia, poor health is often attributed to these illnesses rather than AIDS.

Sources: Business Day, 28 December 1999, cited in Elias and Taylor (2001); Ndubula (2001)

in remote areas of developing countries. The mining company is often involved in the provision of educational facilities – either directly or indirectly through the redistribution of revenues by the state or through innovative means such as the tax credit scheme in PNG.[17] Other increases in educational opportunities come through scholarships. These can come in the form of corporate support or through trust funds or foundations, such as the Inti Raymi Foundation in Bolivia, which sponsors educational projects, and the Rio Tinto Aboriginal Foundation in Australia.[18] Even though the opportunity to receive income through direct or indirect employment in the mine can act as a disincentive for schooling, education is one of the most significant and lasting benefits that a community can derive from a large mine.

For different reasons – including the recent trend towards streamlining of mining operations to improve efficiency, and the recognition that companies could not provide long-term funding – there has been a tendency to move away from providing services such as housing, schools, and health care for mineworkers and their families, except in remote regions. The privatization of previously state-owned mining companies has accentuated this trend, though declines in social provisions could also result from the continued operation of financially non-viable state-owned mines.[19] In Guyana, the privatization of the Linden bauxite mine brought with it a desire on the part of the new owners to be relieved of the responsibility for most of these services.[20]

Social Change

The social benefits of minerals development must be seen in the context of the many social problems associated with large-scale mining operations. These mines may be accompanied by the widespread availability and consumption of alcohol, an increase in gambling, the introduction of or increase in prostitution, and a widely perceived breakdown in law and order. Violence, alcohol-induced and domestic, may increase. And, as at the Porgera mine, migrants may encourage traditional forms of violence such as tribal fighting. Of course, many of these processes of social change may be under way already and mining may simply accelerate them. These problems are not restricted to pre-existing communities. Male-dominated mining camps, such as those found in South Africa, often attract prostitutes and may lead to high levels of sexually transmitted diseases. In an effort to overcome some of these problems, mine accommodations are being improved. In South Africa, in areas where the work force can be drawn locally, there is a trend away from single-sex hostels to family accommodation.[21]

Mining activities often involve social tension within affected existing communities. There can be differences of opinion within a community about a whole range of issues. While some welcome a new mine, others may oppose it. While some are satisfied with compensation packages on offer, others will wish for more. While some are reluctant to countenance any change, others will eagerly embrace new business opportunities. Such is the case in Canada, where the small Innu population is currently struggling to come to terms with plans to mine Voisey's Bay nickel deposits in Labrador.[22]

Options for Women

Women account for approximately 70% of the world's poor, lacking not only in income but also in access to resources, services, and opportunities in the economy and society.[23] Mining operations are often perceived as widening gender disparities within communities. Women tend to bear a disproportionate share of the social costs and receive an inadequate share of the benefits. Since women often play an important role in reducing poverty at the household and community level, and have the right to equality, this problem deserves serious attention.

In occupational communities, women are more often spouses of mine employees, and are therefore passive recipients of benefits. There are few job opportunities for women in mining communities. Despite the recent development of proactive policies by some labour unions, governments, and companies, mining remains a male-dominated sector. In a number of countries, this is in part due to legislation prohibiting women from working underground, a ban based on contested evidence that such work endangers women's health.[24] In some countries, such as South Africa, such discriminatory laws have been repealed, but few women have taken up this opportunity for employment. In 2000, women made up only 2.3% of the work force in the South African mining industry, mainly in jobs traditionally their domain, such as clerical, catering, nursing, adult education, and human resources.[25] Men continue to dominate mine-related work. Similar imbalances exist elsewhere.[26]

In some countries, a greater number of women used to work in mining, but their participation in the work force decreased due to increasing mechanization and the resulting bans on female labour. In India, for example, from 1900 to 1935 women accounted for over 30% of the work force in open cast mining in the Eastern Indian collieries, whereas today they represent approximately 6% of total employment in mining and quarrying in the region.[27] At the international level, a number of International Labour Organization (ILO) conventions have restrictions for women's involvement in shift work and in underground mines. These include the 1919 Convention on Night Work and the 1935 Convention on Underground Work, although ILO is no longer actively seeking ratification of the latter.[28]

Increasing female employment at mine sites would bring direct benefits to women and children by increasing their incomes. It could also contribute to a 'normalization' of mining communities, helping to mitigate many of the social ills, such as alcoholism and prostitution, found in some occupational communities. Clearly, strategies need to be developed for integrating women into the sector. But they need to be realistic: the trend in the mining sector today is towards downsizing the work force.

Change brought on by minerals development can also contribute to an erosion of women's traditional socio-cultural roles. Men involved in mining are well placed to enhance their social position through their access to employment and business opportunities. As landowners, they may also receive a higher proportion of benefits in compensation and royalties. As traditional lifestyles are eroded, the contribution of women to subsistence production may also become less appreciated in a new cash economy.[29] Particular attention needs to be paid to the potential impacts on women's land rights, status, identity, and assets.

The lack of job opportunities for women in mines is aggravated by other limiting factors, including the relative isolation of many mine sites, the absence of local markets to support other economic activities, a lack of credit facilities, and insecure tenure, with the provision of homes often being dependent on the employment of spouses. And since women are often responsible for subsistence activities, as farmers, herders, and agriculturists, they are likely to be disproportionately affected by any negative environmental consequences of mining. Further, women face not only the burden of subsistence production on land degraded by mining developments, they may also lose assistance in this task, as the men go to the mines.[30]

The lives of women in areas hosting migrant workers have been shaped by the sector for generations. In the communities of migrant workers and fly-in, fly-out operations, women are left at home to play a crucial role in maintaining the household economy – supporting families, managing the land, and often receiving only a portion of the wages. Increased incidences of domestic violence and marital breakups can result from the greater stress on family life, with men spending large amounts of time away. In some cases, women may pick up sexually transmitted diseases from partners home on leave. Cases of sexual abuse of indigenous women and girls linked to mining operations are common, though not often discussed. For instance, an independent inquiry into employees at a Rio Tinto mine in Borneo found 'cases where local Dayak women and girls had been raped or coerced into having sex'.[31] Following these allegations, Rio Tinto worked with a local NGO and the Indonesian Human Rights Commission (*Komnasham*) to determine the facts in an open and transparent forum. The company has also engaged *Komnasham* to help raise awareness of human rights issues at the operation.[32]

This is not to say that women do not benefit from mining. The provision of services such as water and electricity in occupational communities will reduce the time spent on chores such as walking long distances in search of potable water or firewood for fuel. There are also benefits from improved nutrition and access to medical services, and from the move away from the provision of single-sex hostels towards family dwelling units in some countries – with facilities such as schools in the settlements. These improvements in living standards can have a spill-over effect on gender equity through, for example, enabling mineworkers to send both boys and girls to school. In this respect, however, women are vulnerable to recent changes in the mining sector, including privatization, downsizing, and retrenchment.

Women can also benefit from community programmes within mining communities. Unless gender issues are considered from the outset, however, existing disparities can be reflected in the distribution of benefits. For example, research undertaken by MMSD Southern Africa found that in a community irrigation scheme sponsored by a mining company in Zimbabwe, only 20% of plot holders were women, and these tended to be already powerful landowners.[33] The inequity stemmed from a government policy that plot holders had to have an annual income of Z\$600 (US\$226, in 1990 figures) as well as land in dry fields to exchange with the previous owner of the plot now under irrigation. As land in Zimbabwe is inherited along the male line, the criteria basically excluded single women and widows. Clearly, since women are largely responsible for food security, this particular scheme would have more impact on poverty alleviation if more women had plots of land.

A Cultural and Political Perspective

Mineral development often changes the balance of power within communities. This can be exacerbated by mining companies being unaware of or choosing to ignore traditional decision-making bodies and negotiating with individuals who do not have the trust or support of their own community. Companies have been criticized for using 'divide and rule' tactics, which can seriously undermine the social cohesion of indigenous and other communities.[34]

Large flows of money at the local level can encourage bribery and other forms of corruption, undermining the potential for communities to receive a fair share of the revenues from mining for longer-term investment. This may damage the social fabric and lead to conflicts. (See Chapter 8.)

Conflict in and around mining operations usually stems from poor governance. It is also more likely to take place where the distribution of mineral revenues and benefits are non-existent or perceived to be unjust, or where the community opposes and actively resists any mining activity on their land. Companies or even central governments may have little understanding of the customs and traditions of those living in and around the mines, and may therefore be insensitive in their dealings with local communities, potentially fuelling further conflict. It has been suggested that in a number of cases of conflict involving local communities and mining interests, radical environmental NGOs (often headquartered in a foreign country) have been involved whose primary aim is to contribute to tension in the community through misinformation and fear-mongering.[35]

In some cases, human rights abuses by police or security forces acting in the interests of the company may occur. A number of complaints recently brought to the Community Aid Abroad Mining Ombudsman concerned Australian companies operating in various developing countries who had been removing people, sometimes violently, from their land or homes. In some instances their houses, mining equipment, or other assets have been destroyed.[36]

Mining activities can cause considerable disruption to local cultures, especially when the operations occur, as is increasingly the case, in areas occupied by indigenous people who have had little contact with the outside world. While some of the 'western' values imported by the mining company and its workers may be admirable or suitable, this is by no means always the case. Cultural clashes may occur, with deep-reaching destabilizing effects on traditional ways of life.

Often the very activity of mining and its accompanying infrastructure can strike at the heart of indigenous culture. For example, the construction of the infrastructure for the proposed Voisey's Bay project in northern Labrador is likely to threaten the migration of caribou. Caribou cows with their calves tend to avoid noisy areas such as roads and pipelines. The herds are therefore likely to be cut off from some of the best habitat for food and growth, potentially damaging their health and productivity. The pattern of extended seasonal migration to hunt for caribou is central to the subsistence of the Innu people and incompatible with full-time wage labour, and caribou play a crucial part in the social, cultural, and spiritual beliefs of the Innu.[37]

Some local cultural traditions and practices decline, or their significance alters, which may be particularly lamented by older members of communities. In many cases traditions may have already been in decline as a symptom of general modernization. At some locations, companies may deliberately intervene and try to support cultural institutions or events. At the Red Dog mine in Alaska, indigenous peoples have negotiated flexible working hours to accommodate their needs to return to their communities to hunt and fish, with a Subsistence Committee that plays an important role in environmental protection. One of the committee's first tasks was to select a route for the 85-kilometre road from the mine site to the port that would largely avoid important caribou migration paths, fish spawning areas, and waterfowl nesting sites.[38]

A related cultural issue is that of geographic boundaries between groups. Borders that may have been fluid may become more precise and fixed as they become critical to obtaining benefits from a development. This can lead to the recognition of some rights to the exclusion of others. A group with traditional rights to hunt in an area, for instance, may not have this recognized in the distribution of benefits from a mine if there are groups with a more complete set of rights (such as residence) to the area.

An Environmental Perspective

Much of the environmental damage caused by mining affects local communities, most significantly in terms of their livelihoods and health. Environmental health problems may become evident not just close to the mine, but some distance away.

Overburden, waste rock, tailings dams, buildings, roads, airstrips, and so on – as well as immigration of population and increased human activity – all create considerable change in local environments. (See Chapter 10.) This may lead to loss of biological diversity, including plants and animals important to peoples' livelihoods, such as cultivated land or pasture for livestock. The changes may affect land used by indigenous people for hunting and gathering, shift cultivation, or adversely affect forests that yield timber and a wide range of non-timber forest products such as game, resins, dyes, vegetables, and medicinal plants. The destruction of habitats fostering traditional herbal and medicinal plants can also weaken indigenous people's autonomy and identity, not to mention their health. Noise from mining operations can be a problem for nearby settlements. For example, the heavy vehicle traffic around mining operations can also disturb surrounding ecosystems and climates.

In dry climates, dust from mining operations, traffic, and waste impoundments can be extremely problematic. If dust suppression methods are not rigorously applied, fine particles can easily be inhaled. At times the dust may contain deleterious substances, such as metals. A common complaint, for example, is clothes getting covered with dust while they dry. In extreme cases, the dust can cause respiratory distress.

Problems caused by dust pollution are also of concern in the smelting phase of mining. In a study in Mexico, researchers assessed the level of lead exposure in children aged 6–9 attending three primary schools who lived near a lead smelter. They concluded that soil and dust ingestion and inhalation were the main routes of exposure, and that environmental contamination resulted in an increased body burden of lead, suggesting that children living in the vicinity of the smelter complex were at high risk for adverse effects of lead.[39]

Mining operations often require vast quantities of water. This can create a number of changes in the supply and quality of water for other uses. Besides damaging biodiversity, water depletion may also destroy or reduce fish stock, depriving local people of a vital source of food and, possibly, livelihood. Mining operations can contaminate surface and groundwater through acid drainage, chronic leaks from waste impoundments, or direct disposal of waste in water bodies. Water contamination can result in important pollution legacies years after mining operations cease. (See Chapter 10.) Domestic uses of contaminated water for cooking, drinking, swimming, and washing can have health impacts. The contamination of water may contribute to the build-up of toxic chemicals in fish and in those who consume the fish.

Other changes in water systems can greatly affect communities, particularly when large amounts of waste are dumped in rivers or along shorelines. Rivers can widen and become impossible to cross, for example, or become shallower and difficult to navigate. Riverbank land can also flood and be lost. Bays and shorelines can be altered, as happened in Chanaral, Chile, where an artificial beach was created by mine waste smothering port installations and ocean fauna, affecting local fishing patterns.[40] And in Bougainville, local communities believe that an increase in malaria throughout the province was caused by an increase in the area of marshland created by mine tailings blocking river tributaries.[41]

Another environmental impact of mining is an unintentional one: mine-related accidents of various kinds. Such accidents can have serious consequences for communities. For example, in 1998 a truck delivering to a mine in Kyrgyzstan spilled two tonnes of sodium cyanide into the Barskoon River. It was alleged that more than 1000 people who drank the affected water were hospitalized.[42] The company claimed that the numbers were inaccurate, and that ill effects were caused by the chemicals used by the government to treat the spill. One of the most publicized accidents occurred in the Philippines in 1996, when the concrete plug sealing a drainage tunnel at the Marcopper mine burst. Up to 4 million tonnes of mine tailings poured into the Boac River. A month later, a UN team declared the river biologically dead. Besides destroying all aquatic life, the spill affected more than 20,000 villagers who lived along the riverbank.[43]

Maximizing Mining's Contribution to Communities

If mining operations are to help communities work towards sustainable development, the communities need to be able to participate effectively in the decision-making processes for establishing and running the operations, in order to avoid or minimize potential problems. Moreover, the relationships between the community and other actors, including the company and government, need to be ones of collaboration, trust, and respect. It is obvious that the benefits brought and enabled by mining must be maximized and the negative effects avoided or mitigated. Furthermore, the benefits need to be shared equitably within communities and sustained after the life of the mine. The actions of companies and governments need to reflect cultural sensitivity and relevance.

Evidence gathered during the MMSD Project shows that while many examples of good practice exist, the current situation often falls far short of these goals: local communities all too often do not participate in decision-making or in guiding the impacts of mining, bear a disproportionate share of the costs of mineral development without adequate compensation, and receive an inappropriately small share of the economic and social benefits.

The complexity and diversity of communities presents a particular challenge, as do trends towards downsizing in the industry, increased technology, reduced direct employment, and weaker economic linkages. Another is ensuring that the goals and means of achieving sustainable development are defined by the community. Perhaps the greatest challenge, in light of the power imbalances, is determining who is responsible and accountable for realizing developmental choices and outcomes at the community level, and how this accountability is best administered.

Widespread community demands for relevant, direct, and sustained benefits from mineral wealth are a relatively recent phenomenon, so frequently neither government institutions nor companies or communities themselves have been properly equipped to respond to them. Governance structures, particularly in developing countries, are often inadequate to ensure that communities receive a fair share of the benefits

that could be put to equitable and sustainable use.
If governance structures are weak and unrepresentative,
so too generally is the legal framework regarding
citizens' rights and the protection of the public good.
(See also Chapter 14.) This challenge cannot realistically
be met by individual companies acting alone.

Matters are complicated in the short term by the
process of decentralization occurring in some
countries. Local governments are becoming important
actors as they take on many of the roles previously left
to central government. Yet in many developing
countries local governments are weak and ineffective;
others are unrepresentative. Agreements negotiated
solely between them and a mining company may not
be recognized as legitimate by local people. At an
administrative level, local governments often do not
have the capacity for effective management of the
collection and distribution of revenue, let alone the
capacity to respond to issues such as the need for an
integrated land use policy with a long-term perspective.

As became evident in the MMSD workshops on
managing mineral wealth, in such situations
communities often turn to the operating companies,
which have found themselves providing development
services to obtain or to maintain their social licence to
operate. Traditionally, these services tend to have been
provided in a paternalistic manner, leading to
dependence on the company and a situation in which
benefits cannot be sustained when the mine closes.

A new relationship is beginning to emerge, based on
recognition of the rights of communities and the need
for community participation in decision-making.
Moreover, new initiatives seek to avoid the company
assuming the role and responsibilities of government,
but rather focus on improving the capacity of local
government and other local institutions to deliver
mine-derived benefits over the long term. It is
increasingly recognized that non-governmental
organizations (NGOs) and other civil society groups
can also act as independent mediators, facilitating the
flow of information to and from communities and
implementing actions in partnership with companies
and government. This approach centres on establishing
a formal relationship with local people and their
representatives and being guided by their needs and
priorities – in effect, trying to work well with formal
and informal local governance structures.

The work undertaken by Business Partners for
Development (BPD) provides useful lessons on local
partnerships. This project-based initiative studies,
supports, and promotes strategic examples of
partnerships involving business, civil society, and
government working together for the development of
communities. The Natural Resources Cluster of BPD -
co-convened by BP Amoco, WMC Resources, CARE
International, and the World Bank Group - has five
pilot projects to develop guidelines, systems, and
structures for dealing with community issues and
mitigating risk by optimizing development impact on
host communities.[44]

There is much talk about the potential costs of
sustainable development. At the local level, however,
working towards sustainable development need not
imply increased costs. It is often about doing things in
a better way rather than doing more. It requires
investing more time in proactive processes, but often
less on physical investments. Mistakes that are made
should be shared and used as a basis for learning rather
than ignored.

The remainder of this chapter suggests mechanisms for
maximizing mining's contribution to communities,
including mechanisms for redistributing revenues from
the national to the local level, promoting the role of
women, providing services and infrastructure to local
communities, maximizing local employment and the
contracting of local businesses, developing skills and
diversifying the economic base, resolving conflicts,
planning for mine closure, and ensuring the capacity of
a community to participate effectively in decision-
making.

Revenue Distribution and Use

Traditionally, all taxes and royalties from mining
operations have gone to the central government, and
the only benefits from equity that communities could
expect to receive were those that trickled down
through central government spending. This is not to
say that money has not been used to the benefit of
communities when collected at the national level
through, for example, the establishment of funds or
investment in services such as education.

In many countries, this is now changing, and
negotiations and agreements increasingly include
communities and regional or local authorities receiving

a share of the revenue. A proportion of rents should, of course, continue to go to central government to ensure that the benefits from the mining of national resources are distributed equitably throughout the country. The amount going to a local administrative structure should be part of an agreement involving the central government. (See also Chapter 8.)

Recently, attempts have been made to redistribute some of the benefits to the local level through changes in policy and legislation; such changes have taken place in a range of countries, including Bolivia, Canada, Colombia, Indonesia, the Philippines, PNG, South Africa, and Venezuela. In the Philippines, for instance, mineral royalties prior to 1995 went directly to central government, which generally failed to distribute a significant share to the provinces. Following a new mining law in 1995, local governments benefit in three ways: 40% of the excise tax goes to them and they can impose a real estate tax on mining companies, which must donate 1% of their operating costs to a social development plan that is used in local communities.[45] Changes such as these have achieved varying degrees of success. In some cases implementation is hindered by the vagueness of policy. In the Southern African Development Community (SADC), for example, most member countries' mineral policy reforms are not explicit in terms of the relationship between mining projects and communities near mine sites.[46]

Even where policy is explicit, bureaucracy may hamper reform where, for example, numerous government ministries remain responsible for decisions. In the case in South Africa, although the government has embarked on policy and legal reform, weak local governance and complex fiscal disbursement mechanisms at the national level have made it difficult for communities to obtain funds. The Public Finance Management Act of 1999 governs disbursement of funds to municipalities. It requires agreement and consultation from the Ministries of Finance and of Provincial and Local Government before the Minister of Minerals and Energy determines that any community or local government may receive a payment from mining royalties. The act specifies that the funds disbursed to municipalities should be paid into a Local Economic Development Fund administered by the national Department of Provincial and Local Government.[47]

In some cases the capacity to implement policy reform simply does not exist. In others, a lack of institutional capacity and transparency at the local level may constrain the development impacts of revenues directed to local administrations. Such attempts do not always fail, but they may be hampered by certain weaknesses. (See Box 9–2.) In Peru, there is legal provision for the distribution of revenues to the

Box 9–2. The Mineral Development Fund, Ghana

Mining companies in Ghana produce gold, diamonds, manganese, and bauxite, and they pay the government both a corporate tax (at 35%) and royalties that range from 3% to 12%, depending on profitability in a given year. In addition, they give the government a 10% equity stake. This revenue all goes to the central government, however, since mineral ownership in Ghana is vested in the President.

As a way to redistribute some of this income, the government in 1993 established a Mineral Development Fund. This is replenished by 20% of the mining royalty payments (which in 2000 corresponded to 8% of the government's total mineral revenues). Half of the fund goes to the Mines and Geological Survey Department and the Minerals Commission to support special projects. The rest is distributed in the mining areas for projects to mitigate the effects of mining – 25% via the district assemblies and the rest to communities.

Although most people agree with the principle of the fund, there is considerable dissatisfaction with the way it is working. The mining sector institutions say that the monies are often delayed, which affects their budget planning. The district assemblies also complain of delays, and argue that they should get a larger share since the traditional authorities are not using the money to benefit the communities. The communities say that the funds are useful but inadequate. The companies welcome the fund since it takes some of the pressure off them, but also say the traditional leaders are misusing the money.

The fund clearly has a number of weaknesses. It has no formal legal backing and does not seem to be making a visible social contribution. At an MMSD Workshop on Managing Mineral Wealth, it was suggested that to move forward the fund should be covered by an Act of Parliament and supervised by a board of trustees. Also its objectives should be more clearly defined to include the creation of alternative livelihoods, and the companies should take an active part in supervising use of the money from the fund.

Source: Mate (1998); Manu (2001)

regional and local levels, but until recently regional governments received no information on how much revenue they were to obtain, and mining revenues were not being returned to the mining area by national governments.[48]

In some countries, local administrations are by-passed and the money is distributed directly to communities. Several mineral-rich countries and regions have established investment funds whose purpose is to spread some of the wealth derived from mineral operations across a broad swath of the population. One of the more successful has been the Alaska Fund established in 1976 – 25% of all oil and gas revenues in the state were deposited in the fund. The money there cannot be withdrawn, and since it was established the fund has grown to over US$25 million. A dividend scheme ensures that every citizen of Alaska receives an annual cheque, amounting at present to around US$2000.[49] Needless to say, this fund is extremely popular.

In Australia, Northern Land Council exploration licence agreements usually provide for traditional Aboriginal owners to achieve an equity position of around 5% in any project developed as a result of exploration on their land. There may also be provisions for the developer to help owners increase their equity if mining proceeds through, for example, an interest-free loan or an issue of equity financed from royalty income foregone by traditional owners.[50] (See Chapter 7 for land use agreements and impact benefit agreements.)

Ideally, revenue distribution should be decided through equitable decision-making structures involving representatives of the affected stakeholder groups. A successful example is the Development Forum in PNG, which is based on a participatory approach to decision-making – involving government, company, and local community representatives. The Development Forum concept was incorporated into the 1992 Mining Act. The outcomes took the form of three Memoranda of Agreement among the landowners, the provincial governments, and the national government. They cover issues such as the provision of infrastructure, the delivery of government services, local staffing, the breakdown of royalty payments, funding commitments, and the provision of equity for local communities and provincial governments. To date, the Development Forum has functioned well and has been instrumental in achieving a higher level of participation by local communities.

It has also secured a greater level of community support for mine development. Further refinement of the memoranda could provide a greater focus on sustainable development for local communities.[51]

A further challenge relates to the way in which benefits are best distributed within communities. Once a mine starts operating, the range of economic and social influences begin to play out in an uneven way between and across communities. Past experience has shown that there may be winners and losers within communities. Even traditional decision-making procedures, such as public negotiations between kinfolk, may be ill-equipped to deal with the influx of large sums of money. New structures and guidelines may be required to handle the distribution and sustainable use of compensation and other monies. Communities can bear some responsibility as to whether inequalities are strengthened or weakened. For instance, Aboriginal organizations in Australia have sought changes to Queensland's Aboriginal Land Act 1991, which, by creating a hierarchy among categories of people in terms of the nature of their affiliation to land, increases the possibility that royalty payments will exacerbate inequalities in indigenous communities affected by mining.[52] At the same time, Marpuna community members on Cape York have sought to develop structures to distribute equitably royalty from a new mine on their land, regardless of the provisions of the Aboriginal Land Act.[53]

In many respects, the central issue is less about how much is received than about how it is used – how should this revenue best be spent to contribute to sustainable development? In PNG, for example, the bulk of compensation is paid in cash, and ample evidence suggests that much of the revenue is spent or invested outside the area. Researchers looking at Porgera estimated that just 5–10% of compensation payments were invested, 20–25% went into business developments (most of which quickly failed), and 65–75% had been used (or redistributed and then used) within Porgera or distributed to people outside the area.[54] Much of the cash flowing to individuals is distributed widely among community members. While this helps spread the economic benefits of the mine, smaller amounts of cash are likely to be used quickly, which works against the longer-term accumulation of assets there.

The incorporation of mining into local and regional development plans can assist in sustaining benefits and ensuring a diversified resource base. Where such a plan does not exist, it should be developed through some form of multistakeholder forum. If government capacity is lacking, an NGO or other independent third party should be responsible for administering the work. The plan should be revised and assessed at predefined intervals throughout the life of the mining operation.

In summary, the redistribution of wealth from national to community level can be facilitated through policy and legal reform. Ideally, the share of revenue received by the community should be determined through a democratic process and incorporated into initial agreements between governments and mining companies. The design of policy, regulations, and agreements must reflect the capacity to implement them. In the short term, where there is insufficient government capacity to distribute revenue, the best option is to take a collaborative approach, where companies and NGOs work with government and at the same time build local administrative capacity. In the long term, the aim should be that a local administrative structure take over the role of redistribution. Alternatively, revenue can be redistributed directly to communities through equity payments or investment funds.

Gender Disparities

The impact of mining on women has been exacerbated by the failure to identify them as a distinct group of stakeholders in the planning and operation of mine sites and to establish trusted means of communication. This clearly needs to be redressed. One difficulty is the emphasis on consulting and channelling information to community leaders, who are invariably male.

Local women undertake rehabilitation work at the Vryheid Coronation Colliery, South Africa

Women's interests are typically subsumed into wider interests. Field research undertaken at an operation in Zimbabwe for MMSD Southern Africa's Gender and the Mining Community Report highlighted difficult relationships between the mine management and women living in the mining community. Although channels of communication existed, the women felt threatened by the presence of men throughout the hierarchy. Women were also reluctant to speak up and raise concerns in case they jeopardized the employment conditions of their spouses. The perception of poor communication was not shared by the mine authorities.[55]

Mining can provide an opportunity for reducing gender disparities through direct and indirect employment and through access to project services. During the operational phase, women can benefit from a parallel process of encouraging diversification in the local economy and skills development. This would also help to cushion the shock of current downsizing.

National and international organizations have adopted gender-specific policies. For example, the SADC Heads of Government Declaration on Gender states that 'the integration and mainstreaming of gender issues into the SADC Programme of Action and Community Building Initiative is key to the sustainable development of the SADC region'.[56] Similarly, the SADC Women in Mining Trust's area-wide commitment to achieving gender equality provides an enabling environment for setting targets and achieving substantive change towards greater women's participation in the regional mining sector.[57] The challenge is to translate policy into practice.

In some cases, conscious efforts are made by companies to address the needs of women. For example, in Zambia companies provide neo-natal health care for women in occupational communities.[58] In La Oroya, Peru, the *mineras* (miners' wives) broke the cycle of unemployment and poverty by starting small businesses, following the establishment of a community bank that lends money to women.[59] Such efforts need to be replicated where possible.

To conclude, mining has the potential to act as a catalyst for the improvement of women's economic and social situations. Gender considerations need to be mainstreamed so that the effects of mining projects on women and opportunities provided by them are fully considered:

- Governments need to develop national gender-specific policies to, for example, encourage appropriate access to credit and landownership for women. NGOs and companies will need to play a role in translating these into practice.
- Companies should also develop gender-specific policies, including recruitment and skills-development strategies for women, which could be developed in partnership with governments, trade unions, and NGOs.
- The formation of loose associations, cooperatives, and savings clubs among women could be encouraged and resourced by companies, government, and NGOs.
- The basis for legislation restricting women's work in mines needs to be examined using current scientific evidence, and legislation should be amended accordingly.
- Women should be given the opportunity to be fully involved in decisions concerning the interaction of the mine with their community. Gender-sensitive channels of communication between women and mine personnel need to be in place. Female employment at all levels can assist in this, as can the sensitization to gender issues of male employees and both men and women within the community. The way to achieve this should be determined on a case-by-case basis and guided by the women in the affected community.
- Specific measures should be put in place to monitor and evaluate the gender performance of operations during the different phases of mine life through to post-closure.
- Finally, there is a dearth of literature on women and large-scale mining settlements. Further research is needed to address the concerns of women affected by mining.

Projects, Funds, and Foundations

During the past decade, many mining companies – often in collaboration with governments or other groups – have established programmes to ensure that communities share the benefits of mineral development. These have been set up prior to the opening of a mine or in reaction to dissent among affected communities or to criticism from NGOs and others.

At Porgera, the company employs more than 100 community development workers.[60] At the Antamina

mine in Peru, the company has developed a Sustainable Development Plan with the UN Development Programme, which is thought to be the first of its kind within the industry.[61] The plan is still in its early stages, with recognition of the need to be realistic about capacity requirements.

Where provincial and local government capacity is too weak to deliver services such as roads, health, and education, infrastructure tax credits have proved a useful instrument. The Bolivia Mining Code, for example, permits companies to invest in community infrastructure and to offset this against tax liabilities.[62] At the MMSD Workshop on Managing Mineral Wealth, concern was expressed that infrastructure tax credits may undermine government capacity and may not be an ideal long-term solution.

Companies have often used foundations to address governance issues, particularly with respect to corporate social investments. Some foundations rely entirely on company money; the more successful ones have been able to attract interest from external donors. This is important for ensuring independence and for the sustainability of foundations after the mines close. The nature and success of foundations vary considerably, however. (See Box 9–3 for two examples.)

The lessons from the experiences to date of several tax credit schemes, funds, and foundations are clear:

- These are useful mechanisms for ensuring that communities derive benefits both during and after a mine's life.
- Companies should ensure that their financial contributions to foundations are fixed and transparent. Ideally, funding should not detract from government spending.
- Where foundations, trust funds, and infrastructure tax credits are used as an alternative to redistribution of benefits through government, this should be made explicit.
- Foundations and funds should be managed by an independent structure to ensure trust and institutional sustainability, or at a minimum should be overseen by a board of directors representative of the different stakeholder groups. In the medium to long term, alternative financing mechanisms would strengthen the likelihood of the funds being sustained. Ideally, governments or NGOs should take primary responsibility.

In Namibia, the Rossing mining company created the Rossing Foundation in 1979. The foundation is overseen by an independent Board of Trustees and is financed through donations from the earnings of the Rossing Mine. The company contributes 3% of its net earnings to the foundation, and by 1996 it had invested US$25 million. It is estimated that more than 15% of Namibians have benefited from the activities of the foundation.

The Rossing Foundation's principal objective is to improve the living conditions of Namibians through activities such as informal education and training, a library network, and assistance to self-support programmes in the rural communities, particularly in the artisanal sector. The policy is to create projects principally in regions where Rossing employees were recruited.

The activities of the foundation have grown enormously since 1990, and it is now an internationally accepted organization that between 1994 and 1996 administered US$10 million from other donors, including the World Bank, the European Community, and the US Agency for International Development. Strategic areas of investment are in line with government policy and accepted by the community. Key to the foundation's success is a bottom-up, participatory approach to decision-making and the priority given to the development of trust among all participants.

In Bolivia, the Inti Raymi Foundation, set up in 1991 by the Inti Raymi Corporation, also attempts to facilitate development in the region surrounding a mine and characterized by poverty. It supports development of the region through training and education and through support to agricultural production, housing and water supply, reforestation, health, infrastructure, and artisanal activities. Although in relative terms the efforts to maintain a good relationship between the company and the community are considered to be positive, a number of problems have been identified:

• There is a lack of information and transparency on the part of the company and foundation.
• Communities have not been involved in decision-making processes and, as a result, several projects have failed.
• The staff at the foundation changes frequently.
• The company uses its investments in the foundation to reduce tax payments, so the state is subsidizing the foundation.

Source: McMahon (1997)

• Mechanisms should be designed in a way that bolsters rather than undermines government capacity.
• Effective community participation in decision-making and throughout all stages of the project is essential to the success of sponsored projects.

Supporting Small Local Businesses

A number of companies have adopted preferential procurement policies towards local suppliers and distributors. Many of these are increasingly enforced through provisions in national policies and legislation concerning foreign direct investment through, for example, joint ventures, partnerships, and outsourcing as a way of localizing multiplier effects.

For instance, in 1998 Hamersley Iron (a subsidiary of Rio Tinto) opened a mine at Yandicoogina, in Western Australia. The mine is on lands to which various Aboriginal peoples of the Banyjima, Yinhawangka, and Hyiyaparli language groups have Native Title claims. Prior to establishing the mine, Hamersley entered into lengthy negotiations with the Gumala Aboriginal Corporation, which was expressly established to represent Aboriginal interests. The result was the Yandicoogina Land Use Agreement, signed in 1997. Negotiations took 18 months, and an external mediator was used throughout.[63]

The agreement provides the Aboriginal peoples with benefits of more than A$60 million (US$46 million) over 20 years in the form of long-lasting community development, training, employment, and business opportunities. Gumala Enterprises Pty Ltd (GEPL), the business arm of the Gumala Aboriginal Corporation, launched three new enterprises after signing the agreement – an earthworks business, a catering and servicing company, and a business hiring equipment and fuel supplies. The first two are operating successfully, and have contracts with Hamersley and other major employers in the area. GEPL now employs 100 people and has significant Aboriginal representation.[64]

Similarly, in an effort to promote local economic development, AngloGold has implemented a programme for small enterprise development in South Africa. The company sources a substantial proportion of purchases from small firms, awarding tenders on a competitive basis. At each operation, outsourcing opportunities are organized through Small Business

Committees, which provide a platform to receive and generate new business ideas and to screen new business proposals. AngloGold also provides non-mine opportunities to small businesses. Associated with this quest is a package of assistance that includes services such as management and technical assistance, venture capital, loan finance, bridging finance, loan facilitation, and joint ventures.[65]

In conclusion, supporting local businesses provides an important means of benefiting communities and building human and financial resources. Preferential procurement policies towards local suppliers and distributors should be incorporated into mining agreements and company policy. Local procurement should be accompanied by skills development and, ideally, the identification of additional economic activities, in order to reduce the community's dependence on the mine.

Employment and Skills Development

One way that projects can contribute to sustainable development is by building human capital through direct training and education of the work force. As the industry has moved to smaller and more specialized labour forces, there are concerns that opportunities for a large number of semi-skilled jobs may further decrease, with yet fewer employment opportunities for local people. While it is still possible to hire and train individuals, it may take some hard targets to which managers are held accountable to increase the percentage of local labour as training programmes qualify them for work. At Escondida mine, 80% of the 2000 permanent staff have been hired locally.[66] As with the support to local businesses, this requirement is increasingly stipulated in national law and policy.

Better still is to provide employees with the opportunity to become shareholders in the company. In South Africa, for example, Employee Share Ownership Participation Schemes are seen as important vehicles for the participation of employees in the management of existing mining companies.[67]

The Red Dog mine in Alaska provides another example. It is the largest zinc mine in the world, operating under a lease with NANA Regional Corp, Inc., an Alaskan native corporation. The mine is located in Alaska's Northwest Arctic Borough, which has a population of around 6800, mostly Inupiat peoples, known as shareholders. The mine is the principal industry in the borough. The Red Dog Operating Agreement includes commitments to provide training and employment for NANA shareholders. It also stipulates that NANA will receive an increasing share of profits over the 40-year life of the mine.[68] Currently, Red Dog and its major contractors employ 630 people, of whom 62% are NANA shareholders. The original agreement forecast that 100% of employees would be NANA shareholders by 2001, but it has been difficult to find enough skilled employees in such a sparsely populated region. To encourage NANA shareholders to work in the mine, the company has introduced flexible working hours so that people can still find time for hunting, berry-picking, and other subsistence or traditional activities during Alaska's brief summer months. While NANA strives to improve educational standards in the borough, Teck Cominco, the parent company, has provided training and scholarships to students interested in pursuing a career in the mining industry.[69]

Employment of local people is often constrained by a shortage of skills within a community – large mining operations should be seen as significant opportunities for workers and other members of local communities to develop skills. In many countries, legislative provisions govern requirements for skills development in companies.

In South Africa, private-sector human resource development initiatives have broadened the scope beyond the technical skills development of individuals and entrepreneurs to include training programmes for young people and women.[70] In 1999, the Escondida mine in Chile established a specialist training centre, the Centro Técnico Escondida (CTE), that helps develop the occupational skills required in mining and heavy industry. CTE offers multi-year apprenticeships in areas of key industrial need; hundreds of workers, from both the Escondida mine and others, have benefited from its programmes.[71]

A number of conclusions can be drawn. The employment of local people is essential and should be incorporated into mining agreements and company policy. If skill levels in the local community are not sufficient at the outset, a staged approach to employment may be necessary, complemented by skills training.

For employment schemes to have long-term success with indigenous, tribal, and other marginalized communities, it is essential that specific language and cultural requirements be accommodated. Local people should be trained and given the opportunity to hold senior managerial positions, not just the lowest-paid manual jobs. There should also be cultural awareness programmes, not just for mine managers but for all employees, particularly if there is a prevalent culture of racism against local employees.

Skills training should not be limited to workers but should be extended to the community as a whole. The design of programmes should consider the need for alternative economic activities to support the community during and after the life of the mine. Skills development should be linked to educational trusts to ensure that opportunities continue after the mine closes.

Retrenchment

Some initiatives are more directly geared towards the concerns of workers who lose their jobs, in terms of providing psychological support and helping them develop skills or seek new employment. One example is the Care retrenchment project in Southern Africa. Between 1990 and 2000, 360,000 mineworkers lost their jobs.[72] This has had a major impact on mining communities, especially in remote areas and among communities that have been almost entirely dependent on the income from mining. The impact of retrenchment can be far-reaching, as each migrant mineworker usually supports many dependents at home.

Against this background, the Care Project was launched in 1999. In April, Placer Dome Inc purchased 50% of the South Deep mine in South Africa. For the mine to be economically viable, major retrenchment and modernization were required. This involved laying off 35% of the work force (2560 workers) over four months. The Care Project was set up to help retrenched mineworkers develop new skills and find jobs elsewhere. Its initial aim was to provide support and assistance so that 70% of retrenched employees (or a nominated family member) would become economically active by the end of 2001. The project also sought to help develop infrastructure and expertise to run an HIV/AIDS programme.[73]

Traditionally, mining companies provided retrenched employees with a small cash severance and a three-

month training period. The company initially provided this package, but it was deemed inadequate. A team of over 20 trained field workers met one-on-one with retrenched employees and their families to counsel and advise on project benefits. In addition to providing skills and vocational training, the project also seeks to enhance the institutional capacity of the Mineworkers Development Agency and The Employment Bureau of Africa. Geographically, the Care Project covers rural communities in Mozambique, Lesotho, and Eastern Cape Province in South Africa, where most workers and retrenchees live.[74]

Though it may be too early to assess the impact of the Care Project, the challenges facing it are not unique in rural development. Any process to enable retrenched people (or nominated family members) to create their own jobs or find an alternative one is likely to be fraught with constraints, such as dispersed or unavailable markets, infrastructure, and cultural barriers.

An alternative to seeking new forms of employment in home communities is for retrenched workers to work in other mines. A particularly interesting initiative of the Misima Mineworkers Union has been to establish a joint venture with Placements Ltd (an Australia-based recruitment agency) to find employment for Misima workers.[75] Its rate of success is not yet clear; initiatives of this kind may also be restricted by local procurement policies.

In summary, efforts to assist retrenched workers will be of limited success if initiated only when retrenchment is a reality. Some companies are now finding that the best approach is to discuss these issues frankly and openly with their employees and others in the local community, as this allows all the actors to use their knowledge and judgement to make the best decisions they can, which may ease the shock of closure and retrenchment. Skills development and savings schemes should be geared to maximizing the possibilities of workers finding alternative sources of employment or returning to their previous employment. Workers should also be involved in designing assistance schemes relevant to their needs.

Conflict and Dispute Resolution

Disputes and conflict between communities and mining companies, government, or other actors, as well as within communities, can be largely avoided if the interactions between the mine and community start on the right basis and are managed appropriately.

Conflicts and tensions may arise and they should preferably be resolved through open dialogue among all stakeholders. In some cases, not all the parties are willing to enter into dialogue, or the dialogue is perceived to be conducted under unreasonable conditions. When the situation reaches an impasse, it may require the intervention of a third party to avoid escalation, such as a lengthy legal action or possibly violent confrontation.[76]

An example of third-party intervention is provided by the Oxfam Community Aid Abroad Mining Ombudsman, established in February 2000. Its aims include assisting communities in developing countries where basic human rights are threatened by the actions of Australia-based mining companies, by raising their cases directly with the companies concerned in Australia to get a fair, negotiated resolution; assisting communities to understand their rights; and helping ensure that the Australian mining industry operates in a way that protects the basic rights of landowners and affected communities.[77] The Ombudsman receives complaints from communities and landowners through the organization's networks in Asia, the Pacific, Africa, and Latin America. All claims are validated through on-site investigations and then taken to the company concerned, for initial response and resolution. The Mining Ombudsman may or may not mediate the negotiation process leading to resolution.

Although each case is unique, the grievances of landowners and affected communities can be loosely grouped into four areas: loss of land, loss of individual and collective sustainable livelihoods, degradation of the environmental and natural resources, and human rights abuses. In nearly all cases, the root problem lies in the denial of some basic economic, social, or civil rights of the affected groups or individuals. This is particularly so where government does not adequately respect these rights.[78] (See Chapter 14 on dispute resolution.)

Disputes may also arise within or between communities as a result of the changes brought about by mining, such as the changing balance of wealth and power of individuals or subgroups. A recent study at the Porgera mine in PNG suggests resolving

Some mining companies in southern Africa are undertaking community-wide HIV/AIDS prevention and management programmes

community conflict through increasing intergroup cohesion and trust. When 'connections' are reinforced – such as shared values and aspirations or membership of groups, like churches and youth groups – people find ways of tolerating differences and working together on common problems. It also suggests how impacts from mines can be managed to encourage rather than discourage community cohesion, through, for example, the development of cross-community enterprises that depend on each other for success or the investment of revenues in services, and funds that benefit the community as a whole.[79] Finally, the study demonstrates that improving understanding and the ability to identify how mining activities affect conflict dynamics will help everyone recognize appropriate options to reinforce community stability.

Community Health Initiatives
Traditionally, companies have provided health services to employees and their families, such as hospitals and health care centres with modern equipment and professional, often expatriate, staff. Particularly in poor communities, such infrastructure has generally reflected an inadequate understanding of local needs and expectations, as well as a lack of consideration for its ability to be sustained after the mine closes. Furthermore, beyond work-related diseases, there have been few endeavours to prevent diseases that affect the wider community, such as sexually transmitted diseases or malaria, or to consider the broader well-being of the community. On the whole, company involvement in community health issues has been reactive rather than pre-emptive.

Although traditional approaches still prevail, a number of companies are taking steps to reflect better the needs of local communities in the design of health care and to assist in the provision of health services to local communities more broadly. In October 2001, for example, Anglo American won the Commonwealth Award in recognition of its exemplary work in prevention and management strategies in relation to HIV/AIDS and malaria in South Africa.[80] Such approaches are essential to addressing sustainable development in a comprehensive manner. This is particularly so where mining may contribute to the spread of a disease or where a disease is prevalent among mine workers and the local community, as in the case of HIV/AIDS in Southern Africa.[81] In addition to accidents or the spread of diseases, the effect of the mining operation on broader community well-being needs to be addressed – including its psychological impacts as well as changes in diets and lifestyle brought about by mining.

Communities, too, can take the initiative. One example of local community-initiated action, concerning the harmful effects of the manufacture of a mineral product, is a study of blood lead levels of Nicaraguan children living near a battery factory. In response to requests by parents in Managua, whose neighbourhood bordered this plant, 97 children were tested for blood lead, as were 30 children in a neighbourhood without an obvious source of environmental lead. Children living near the battery factory were found to be at increased risk of lead poisoning, and this enabled the parents to petition the government to control the factory emissions and to improve appropriate health services, with the resultant closure of the factory.[82]

For companies, there is a strong business case for more of a pre-emptive approach; not only can this enhance reputation and improve relations with the local community, it can also save money. For example, the benefits of implementing child survival services at a private mining company in Peru were described in one study. Despite considerable outlays for medical services, few children under age 5 were vaccinated and half of their illnesses went untreated. Following a study demonstrating these shortcomings, the company hired additional staff to provide integrated maternal-child preventive health care and family planning, and contracted for intensive training and periodic on-site supervision. In less than two years, vaccination coverage reached 75% and virtually all children under age 1 were enrolled in growth monitoring.

Prescriptions were reduced by 24%, including a 67% drop in anti-microbials.[83]

Similar changes have occurred in the way in which the mining industry, with other actors, approaches the problem of HIV/AIDS in Southern Africa. Rather than discriminating against workers with the disease, proactive attempts are being made to prevent its spread and to support employees and family members with the disease. (See Box 9–4.)

For companies, useful lessons can be learnt from the oil and gas sector. In June 2000, the International Association of Oil & Gas Producers issued 'Strategic Health Management: Principles and Guidelines for the Oil & Gas Industry' (SHM). Its purpose is to 'provide a basis for incorporating work force and community health considerations systematically into project planning and management'.[84] The guidelines describe the main elements necessary to develop, implement,

---

Box 9–4. A Change in Direction: HIV/AIDS Initiatives in Southern Africa

In 1985 the Chamber of Mines of South Africa introduced an HIV/AIDS test for foreign workers, and those who were HIV-positive were sent back to their countries of origin. Following this, an agreement was signed between the Chamber and the National Union of Mineworkers (NUM) of South Africa to solve the problem of discrimination in testing. NUM's approach was to call for changes allowing miners to stay with their families, as well as promoting awareness of the risks that miners face in the working environment. In particular, the following recommendations were made:

- to develop housing, thereby improving the living conditions of miners and their families;
- to reduce the number of sex workers in the working environment;
- to inform the mining community of the different risks they face; and
- to combine forces in addressing HIV/AIDS rather than allow the current competition among companies to be seen as the most efficient way to tackle the problem.

Despite these improvements, more needs to be done to tackle the spread of the disease and to develop effective means of caring for those infected. For example, there is a need for improved collaboration between mining companies and other actors as well as other sectors to avoid duplication and to encourage an exchange of ideas.

Source: Ndubula (2001)

---

and maintain a strategic health management system. SHM is intended to facilitate cooperative interaction among industry groups, host governments, the local health care system, community representatives, and other stakeholders. Its key messages are that industry cooperation on health is beneficial, that industry can help host governments fulfil their responsibilities, that primary health care can have the greatest impact, and that lasting improvements can be achieved through early stakeholder involvement and consultation. The success of this initiative to date is difficult to measure. Some mining companies are now taking on a broader role in community health programmes by working in partnership with other stakeholders. One example of this is the World Alliance for Community Health, formed in 1999 by five mining companies to promote the development and implementation of community health projects and the World Health Organization (WHO).[85] To facilitate and to earn recognition for its projects, the World Alliance entered into a Cooperation Agreement with WHO under which members could seek to have a community health project designated as 'WHO-approved', based on meeting certain criteria. The agreement provided a list of issues to be addressed in project plans. The emphasis is on partnerships, capacity building, and programme sustainability. The latter was not seen as an absolute requirement, but each project had to be seen to be working towards that goal, with communities or governments eventually taking over the programmes.

While the World Alliance has attracted genuine interest from health professionals and corporate sustainability personnel, only four projects have been developed for approval by WHO to date, and no new members have been found. One limiting factor may be the strict focus on the very high standards of partnership and sustainability. Moreover, in the absence of industry policies and best-practice guidelines in this area, no measures exist to drive progress in the implementation of community health policies and programmes.

Although still in the early stages of formation, the Global Health Initiative of the World Economic Forum (WEF) may provide an opportunity for stimulating large-scale action by mining companies on broader health concerns. It was announced in January 2001 with the objective of stimulating large-scale corporate action in the fight against TB, malaria, and HIV/AIDS. Member companies were invited to participate in an initial meeting in Geneva in March,

when working groups were set up on best practices, resource opportunities, and advocacy. In July 2001, WEF staff and a task force with representatives from the mining, aluminium, and oil and gas industries defined the overall objectives and a work programme. For the Global Health Initiative to succeed, it was agreed that private-sector CEOs would have to be engaged in a meaningful way, so that they would provide active support for the participation of their business units in community health programmes.[86]

WHO is the leader in initiatives such as the Lymphatic Filariasis Alliance, Roll Back Malaria, STOP TB, and UNAIDS. Each of these is based on partnerships with other organizations and seeks to promote projects around the world. There are a few examples of companies working with these global programmes at individual mining locations, but the opportunity exists for many more sites to become involved in a mutually advantageous manner in the future.[87]

Several ways to move forward on community health are clear from experiences to date:

- In areas where diseases such as HIV/AIDS or malaria are rife, the project assessment process should consider these issues at an early stage, and be oriented to recommending measures to deal with any problems. These should consist of education measures for the affected population, which includes but cannot be limited to workers.
- Industry policy and best-practice guidelines should be developed to drive progress in the implementation of community health policies and programmes.
- The planning and delivery of health programmes around mine sites should be based on a partnership approach, with a strong role for the local community in their design and implementation.
- Programmes should include capacity-building as a short-term objective.
- Particularly in the longer term, government should take lead responsibility for the continuation of health programmes. Where government capacity is lacking, independent trust funds may be developed and managed by local institutions or other independent organizations to ensure the sustainability of the programme.
- At a company level, comprehensive health policies and programmes for employees and dependents should be put in place.

Mine Closure

When a mine closes, the impact is often more dramatic than it would be for other kinds of industrial plants, as mines frequently constitute a larger proportion of the local economy. In the classic remote mining town, closing the mine often meant closing the town as well. The remoteness of many mining operations often means that there are few or no alternative employment opportunities. In the past, the environmental dimensions of mine closure were given priority. (See Chapter 10.) It is increasingly realized that the social and economic dimensions of closure planning are equally important.

In richer societies, where employment levels and resources are relatively abundant, recently there have been efforts to mitigate these effects. Government or company-sponsored retraining programmes, union contracts calling for retraining, severance pay and relocation benefits, and targeted efforts at development of alternative employment bases have all become more frequent. Even in the richest countries, while there are examples of former mining communities succeeding in new endeavours such as tourism, it is not uncommon to find depressed former mining towns or even 'ghost towns'.

In societies with less wealth and fewer alternative forms of employment, mine closure can be very traumatic. And when the problem affects a whole mining region – perhaps because of a fall in commodity prices – it can have serious political repercussions, as seen in tin mine closures in Bolivia, coal mine closures in parts of the former Soviet Union, and retrenchment in the South African gold industry, to name but three of many examples. A government that is highly dependent on its minerals economy is likely to face resource shortages just when the demand for its assistance is at the highest level.

From this perspective, mine closure planning needs to include a plan for the transition to the post-mining economy. In concept, it is clear what needs to be done: the planning and development of any mining project needs to be aimed at creating durable benefits on a number of scales:

- The infrastructure in place needs to be useful for something besides mining. During the mine's life, the capacity to maintain that infrastructure needs to be developed in the local community, along with an enduring base of economic resources to pay for

maintenance. This means not only the physical infrastructure of roads, water supply, electricity, and telecommunications, but the social infrastructure of health care providers, teachers, and government. The health, education, skills levels, and employability of local people must be greater than when the project started.

- There needs to be development of other economic bases besides mining. Although it may not be possible to match the best years of mine operation, it is realistic to aim for sustainable ongoing economic activity at levels that substantially exceed those in place before the project – ideally, diversified and providing a broad range of employment opportunities.
- The capacity of the local community to understand and manage residual environmental concerns needs to be in place when the physical closure plan for the mine is implemented.
- For some communities, the ability to continue previous subsistence activities to some extent while the mine is in operation could reduce the detrimental impact of closure.

These are achievable objectives. What is required is a clear understanding of the roles and responsibilities of various actors and the right process for cooperation among them. The mining company has a major responsibility for achieving these results, but it cannot achieve them alone. Communities need to own this process and organize themselves accordingly.

The mineral wealth that government captures during the mine life must be managed in ways that develop long-term benefits for the community. Among other things, it needs to be used to develop government and local capacity to manage infrastructure, education, health, and other systems. A major challenge is the limited capacity for this kind of planning and financial assurance, particularly in smaller companies and in government. A clear theme that emerged from the Mine Closure Workshop hosted by the World Bank Group in March 2000 was the universally reported difficulty for local authorities to take on responsibility for social services and infrastructure when mines close or are privatized.[88]

Currently operating mines may be influenced by decisions taken decades ago. In general, the longer a mine has operated, the more difficult it may be to make dramatic changes. In existing mines, the issue of sustaining benefits often only becomes a major concern when mine closure approaches. The greatest degree of flexibility is with new mines, which can explore all options fully with minimum constraints, even though comprehensive planning for mine closure is not always part of pre-mine planning for many new and proposed mines. Government policies, where they exist, are often restricted to the physical environmental aspects of mine closure.

There are examples of companies working with district and local administrations or institutions to develop plans to plot out viable long-term sustainable socio-economic development. An example of this is the Porgera District Plan in PNG. The company aims to provide additional resources and capacity for local administrative structures and to establish durable economic, social, and administrative institutions and activities. A Porgera Management Team will be responsible for developing and implementing the plan, in addition to communicating with local stakeholder groups. A series of rolling five-year sectoral plans cover health, education, infrastructure, justice, primary industry, and services. Each of these will be developed with local community input, including specific goals for the period. Internal and external monitoring, auditing, and evaluation will be central to the plan. This case has the advantage of working through existing frameworks, as District Plans are meant to be prepared in any case. What is new is the formal structure, the management team, and the resources of the mining company.[89]

At both Ramu and Ok Tedi in PNG, companies have decided to promote similar objectives through foundations. Both seek to direct funding from mine benefits, government sources, and possibly external donors through an independent institution that is jointly managed by the mining company and various local, provincial, and national government agencies. The aim is for coordinated local-level development planning, with a specific focus on the delivery of long-term sustainable benefits. These foundations seek to work around the lack of capacity at local and provincial level, introducing new institutions (in contrast to the Porgera Plan).[90] Trust funds are also increasingly being used for the up-keep of infrastructure post-mine.

The Sullivan mine in Kimberley, British Columbia, in Canada provides a good case of planning for mine

closure. The mine is fortunate in its location in a relatively prosperous area of outstanding natural beauty with reasonably strong economic linkages. Kimberley also has a well-organized and stable community with good local representative structures. While the challenges faced are thus far less than may be found in other areas, the process and the lessons learnt are useful. (See Box 9–5.)[91]

In conclusion, a strategy for mine closure needs to be an integral part of mine development and operational planning. It will need to be revised throughout the life of the mine to reflect, among other things, changes in community expectations, economic activities, and the increasing capacity and changing responsibilities of certain actors. Planning for closure will be particularly difficult at the beginning of a mine's life, but at a minimum consideration needs to be given to ensuring that the mechanisms, institutions, and processes created to distribute benefits will be sustainable in the long term. For example, economic alternatives need to be considered at the outset, as does the ownership of processes and outcomes. The following elements are essential to any strategy:
- leadership and commitment on the part of all actors;
- capacity-building;
- identification and establishment of economic activities for communities post-mine, including pre-existing activities and those related to the mining activity as well as non-mineral-related activities such as tourism and agricultural services; and
- mechanisms to ensure essential services can be sustained post-closure.

Fly-in, Fly-out Operations
The discussion of fly-in, fly-out operations is perhaps most relevant in relation to mine closure. Fly-in, fly-out operations were first set up in Canada at Asbestos Hill, Quebec, in 1972 and now exist in a number of countries, such as Australia and Canada. Under this system, remote mineral deposits are mined without developing traditional mining towns, and workers are brought in from outside. This invariably means that communities near the mine gain relatively little in terms of jobs, business opportunities, and the multiplier effect, and the system may place a strain on the families of mine workers. Yet communities are also protected from some of the negative consequences of mining, such as exposure to the problems of a 'boom town' environment, a mass influx of people, or environmental

Box 9–5. Sullivan Mine in Kimberley, British Columbia, Canada

The settlement around the Kimberley mine was originally established as a mining camp and developed over 90 years into a city with a population of 7000. A great deal of infrastructure and recreational and social development occurred because of the mine. On average, the mine has employed around 1000 people, although the work force was considerably smaller at the time of closure, in December 2001.

The community established an Economic Development Office to consider post-mine economic sustainability strategies and began looking for industrial partners to develop the area. Planning began 20 years before closure. Economic diversification was undertaken through various initiatives: development of an industrial site, a plan for developing tourism, one resort golf course and a second one under construction on lands acquired from the mining company, and a residential development plan done with the hope that taxes from it would cover revenue loss from the mine.

About 400 people lost their jobs when the mine closed. A transition committee has been established to assist workers. The lessons learnt from this experience are that preparing workers for redundancy cannot start too early but is likely to be met with general apathy at first. When a mine has been operating for a long time, it may be difficult for the workers and community to come to terms with the fact that it may actually close.

The experience demonstrates that when planning for sustaining economic benefits, the community must be aware of the need to plan for closure and be willing to sustain itself, and the local political will to do so must exist. In this case, the role of individual leadership has been key.

It has also underlined the important role of government, particularly in providing supportive policies and regulations and in assisting with the implementation of programmes. Although the government was largely supportive, some policies and regulations were found to be counter-productive, leading to difficulties in implementing some programmes. For example, around the mine, 'brownfield sites' were no longer available due to provisions in contaminated sites regulations, agricultural land reserves were off-limits to development, the environmental assessment process was lengthy, taxes were high relative to competing jurisdictions, and the economic rents received by the government were not invested locally.

The company was also seen to play an important role in providing financial support for certain projects and providing land at a reduced rate. However, the company has been criticized for its past resistance to other forms of industrial activities and the resultant missed opportunities.

The involvement of community groups was considered particularly important, given that they are remaining in Kimberley now that the mine has closed. What remains to be seen is how well the community is able to adapt from being a mining community to one based on service industries.

Source: Based on presentation by Dave Parker, Teck-Cominco, at the Managing Mineral Wealth Workshop, August 2001, and on discussion at Sullivan Roundtable Workshop co-hosted by Teck-Cominco and the World Bank, Kimberley, November 2001

concerns. Moreover, it could be argued that fly-in, fly-out operations are less disruptive as no new mining settlements are created. Without doubt, fly-in, fly-out operations have the potential to decrease conflict arising over the use of resources or interactions between the community and 'outsiders', and to lessen the likelihood of abandoned post-mine communities.[92]

In some cases, residential communities may resist the proposal of a fly-in, fly-out operation if they feel it will reduce opportunities for community members to be employed or to provide services to the mining operation and mining town.

Community Participation in Decision-making
Historically, governments have formulated mineral development policies without consultation with communities, and companies have negotiated directly with central government. Yet some examples of effective community participation are beginning to emerge, such as the extensive community consultation involved in the drafting of the recent minerals policy in South Africa.[93] At the local level, public consultation has traditionally been limited to communicating certain aspects of projects to affected communities or dealing with complaints. Only recently has it been applied by regulation as a formal process to integrate public input into a social impact assessment (SIA) process and to identify public concerns.

Practical experience has demonstrated to companies that there are significant benefits to good consultation at the local level. Perhaps the most important for a mining project is that the process helps foster genuine relationships with mutual respect, shared concerns, and shared objectives among the community, company, and other actors.

Decision-making needs to recognize the rights of communities to representation and engagement in processes that affect them, and bases the interaction between the mining project and the community on the values, goals, and aspirations of the community affected. For example, the community may be less concerned with traditional measures of benefits such as income and employment and more concerned with social well-being and the impact of mining on cultural values and local institutions. An absence of community decision-making is likely to result in ineffective or inappropriate arrangements for the distribution of benefits, or in institutions that are not able to sustain the benefits after mining ceases.

The control over their own futures that such participation in decision-making engenders is particularly crucial to the sustainability and survival of indigenous communities. (See Box 9–6.) Much needs to be done to ensure this at both the local and national level. For example, one attendee at the MMSD Indigenous Peoples Workshop in Quito explained that in Ecuador, to mobilize themselves effectively around issues, indigenous people have had to organize at all levels, particularly nationally. While the Ecuadorian Constitution may appear to uphold and respect their collective rights, decisions are continually made on their behalf without their involvement.

Box 9–6. Participation in Decision-making in Indigenous Communities

MMSD held a preparatory workshop in Quito that was designed to address a range of issues associated with the relationship of indigenous peoples to the mining, minerals, and metals sector. This workshop was convened to provide a forum for indigenous people and those working with indigenous communities in an advocacy capacity to discuss issues of trust, relationships, and capacity building in preparation for a multistakeholder workshop on these issues in Perth, Australia. The Quito meeting was attended by indigenous participants from South America, North America, Australia, the Philippines, and Kyrgyzstan.

Two main themes emerged from the workshop. First, indigenous communities have different levels of interest, ability, and preparation in terms of negotiations with those wanting to mine on their lands. Second, there was considerable discussion of

the need to establish an international body run by and for indigenous people that would assess corporate and project performance with respect to the treatment of and negotiation with indigenous communities. This was seen as a positive approach to recognizing best practice where it is identified and making such information available to indigenous communities considering mining projects.

The multistakeholder follow-up workshop in Perth was attended by indigenous people and those working on these issues from government, industry, and civil society. Three themes provided a focus for discussions: the challenges faced in building rights, the capacity of indigenous communities and others, and the essential components of building relationships between indigenous peoples and other stakeholders.

The indigenous attendees recognized that indigenous rights to land and empowerment must be respected by all stakeholders if there is to be progress towards a sustainable future. At present, indigenous rights in most jurisdictions convey limited rights upon the affected communities and traditional landowners. Many attendees felt that indigenous rights had a low priority. It was also clearly stated that 'talking the talk' with respect to indigenous rights is commendable at the CEO and ministerial levels, but ways must be found to translate this into tangible advances at the local level.

Harmonized international standards for dealing with indigenous peoples across the entire spectrum of mining operations was seen as essential. Equally, communities need to develop leadership and capacity internally, while governments need to provide the necessary education opportunities so that both this and future generations can fully assess the challenges and opportunities provided by mining and the exploitation of minerals and metals.

At a session attended solely by indigenous peoples, participants recommended that an international, regionally representative indigenous peoples body be established as part of the immediate MMSD standard-setting process. This group could monitor the elaboration of international standards and ensure the effective participation of indigenous peoples in standard setting and implementation. Participants also urged the international mining industry and governments to acknowledge and accept that necessary financial and other resources will be required by this body, and to make a commitment to identifying funding for this work.

Source: MMSD Preparatory Workshop on 'Legacy Issues, Indigenous Peoples Rights, Exploration and Mining on Indigenous Lands, Impacts and Benefits Agreements', 27–28 September 2001, Quito, Ecuador; Multistakeholder Indigenous Peoples Workshop, 4–6 February 2002, Perth, Australia

Companies that wish to foster genuine participatory relationships with the community need to do so with understanding and sensitivity. Communities often feel powerless in the face of large mining corporations and may have heard enough negative stories to be cynical regarding what they can achieve through participation.

To overcome such difficulties, the mining company needs to be willing to have a genuine two-way dialogue with the community. It needs to be transparent in its communications from the outset and throughout the life of the mine, and to listen to and respond appropriately to the issues raised by the community. Communities should be updated at regular intervals or whenever there is a change, such as an expansion or contraction of mining activities. The process of communication needs to be established in such a way that it does not intimidate local people. (Overuse of technical language, for instance, can form an instant barrier to communication.) Different forms of participation should be acknowledged and valued. Issues such as availability of transport, child care, and the timing and location of meetings are also critically important to enable a cross-section of the community to participate.[94] Access to information about the project is key. (See also Chapter 12.)

The community itself may need help in building the capacity required for full participation in decision-making. Programmes aimed at capacity building need to be planned jointly with local leaders. Funds for such programmes should be controlled locally wherever possible: local control of finances encourages organizations to develop administrative and managerial skills. In order to encourage participation, which can be very time-consuming on the part of individual members of the community, people need to know that they are acquiring skills that can be integrated into the economy after the project is complete.[95]

Currently one of the biggest areas of debate is the extent to which consultation implies some degree of shared decision-making. While mining companies increasingly recognize that communities and NGOs should be involved in defining mitigation measures or social development projects, sharing decision-making on core management issues is not easily accepted. Regardless of the comfort level in companies, however, communities and interest groups will question the validity of consultation processes unless and until their concerns are seen to affect decisions about projects.[96]

Moving towards participation rather than consultation will ultimately mean that local communities are directly involved in the decision-making process through, for instance, representation on the Board of Directors. This may not be an immediate possibility, but it should be a longer-term goal.

At the local level, developing the democratic process through multistakeholder forums can provide an effective means of facilitating community awareness, capacity-building, and community involvement.[97] Inclusive, multistakeholder processes run by independent parties will reduce the power differential and avoid the sense of helplessness felt by many communities. The Development Forum in PNG described earlier provides a useful example at the national level. At the local level, Community Development Forums provide a good model.[98] They require democracy to work most effectively, but companies with the assistance of NGOs and other actors should try to implement them even in the absence of a democratic government. The underlying assumption, however, must be that there is explicit commitment to the process on the part of all actors such that they have joint ownership. (See Table 9–2.)

Improved Social Impact Assessment

Social impact assessment is currently the most widely applied tool used to address the impact and mitigation of social issues associated with mine development.[99] Developed originally in the 1970s in response to the requirements of environmental regulations, it did not

Table 9–2. Roles and Responsibilities in Community Development Forums

Community	Own the process
Company	Commit to process and contribute funds
Government	Establish regulatory framework and requirements for process, and contribute funds
Local government	Help companies in region to develop common strategies for interventions Request community participation Ensure national-level framework reflects expectations of community
Donors	Assist in funding where national government is not supportive

emerge as a significant component within environmental impact assessment (EIA) until the 1990s. Until then, it was part of an EIA process that served to evaluate whether a project met the test of 'do-no-harm/acceptable impacts'.[100]

Since SIA introduces knowledge about the social implications of an activity into the planning, decision-making, and management process associated with it, it has unofficially become the mechanism for predicting and interpreting the implications of development for communities. Recently, as community issues have received increasing attention, SIA has become more significant and certainly more necessary, if not always more effective.

An underlying tension that cuts across all of the issues associated with SIA is the difference between its potential (currently realized in a small percentage of projects) and its general use. The difference can be extreme. At one end, SIA is a dynamic, inclusive, ongoing process of integrating knowledge on potential social impacts into decision-making and management practices; at the other, it is a static, one-shot technocratic assessment undertaken to gain project approval or financing, with little or no follow-through.

The important issue is to understand how SIA might assist companies and other actors in meeting the challenges of sustainable development. This tool is so far rarely used in its wider capacity to aid the management of the social impacts of mining on an ongoing basis through the life of a project and to help plan for closure and beyond. The potential exists for SIA to provide information and understanding that can be applied to achieve durable net benefits for people affected by mining operations.

A particular challenge to conducting SIA is the need to incorporate cultural norms, realities, and subjective perceptions into what is otherwise (in terms of the overall EIA process) considered a logical, technical, and scientific process. The findings of the landmark Berger Inquiry in Alberta in 1974–78 were repeated recently at the Voisey's Bay Hearings.[101] The potential for SIA to contribute to sustainable development goals is there. The question is how to frame the decision-making process once the facts are available:

> The implication for the inquiry, and for SIA, was that the proposed pipeline project had to be

evaluated...in terms of the vision of the people whose communities it would affect. The question was better cast in terms of whether the project would help or hinder the realization of that vision. Where the technical model of SIA focused on economic well-being as measured by income and employment, the political model emphasized social well-being, self-determination, and the centrality of cultural values and social institutions.[102]

Industry best practice continues to evolve, and the current model, used by a few companies, is to engage in a process of continuous dialogue and consultation with the community and other stakeholders as plans for the project advance and the SIA is prepared. A high level of interaction is maintained; community needs and concerns are discussed and, wherever possible, built into the mine development plan. Despite the effectiveness of this approach, it is not uniformly popular with the industry because of a perceived loss of control over timing and costs.

Other constraints hold SIA back from realizing its full potential. First and foremost, in spite of the existence of a number of good guidelines on SIA, there is no widely recognized standard that is referred to and used consistently. One of the most persistent problems is that none of the parties to the process are necessarily aware of what should be done for a responsible SIA in a given situation. Low expectations on the part of one party (government regulators, company, community, or consultants) can result in reduced quality.

Under current procedures for conducting SIA, there are real and perceived difficulties with achieving objectivity. SIAs are normally carried out by consultants who work on behalf of, and by implication act in the interests of, their client – the company proposing the project. The company prepares studies to support its proposal for a mine development, and the state, responsible for assessing the report, is in conflict by being the owner of the resource, the proponent and beneficiary of resource development, and also the regulator. The challenge is to ensure that SIAs accurately reflect the views of all stakeholders, particularly of local people. Ideally, the SIA should be endorsed by the community and by government.

Due diligence investigations on the outcomes of SIA are few and far between. It is essentially unknown for the state to review projects after giving approvals based on SIA. With the exception of the World Bank Group, few financial institutions requesting SIA, social management, and development plans have any social staff. They often depend on outside consultants to carry out audits and reviews.

It is also extremely rare for monitoring programmes to be set up to assess social impacts in communities. If developed effectively, social monitoring programmes can significantly enhance the ability of all stakeholders to contribute more effectively to sustainable development. At the moment, there is a lack of data on the flows of costs and benefits from mining to local communities. Some mines contain a requirement for social monitoring, but this is rarely done effectively.

Social monitoring programmes should be developed directly from social impact assessments, and should put in place the systematic management systems to implement the process, with responsibilities, budgets, monitoring schedules, implementation plans, and so on. Local people should be involved in defining and monitoring their key social indicators. An independent professional should be appointed to oversee the monitoring process. (See also Chapter 7.)

In conclusion, there is urgent need for common, standard, best-practice SIA guidelines for use in the mining industry. The experience of applied practitioners, with input from stakeholder groups, is possibly the most credible base for developing such guidance. The absence of standard guidelines gives the mining industry a chance to show leadership in developing and adopting SIA standards, which might become accepted in the various regulatory regimes where the companies are active.

More generally, SIA provides an opportunity to plan how a minerals development project can best support sustainable development and the community's vision of the future:

• Sustainable development calls for appropriate methodologies of information acquisition and presentation and a move from SIA to integrated impact assessment (IIA).
• SIA should become a dynamic, ongoing process of integrating knowledge on potential social impacts into decision-making and management practices and should lay the foundation for a Community Sustainable Development Plan.

• A community-level resource inventory could be compiled as part of the SIA process, including data on demographics, land-carrying capacity, water availability, and so on. This would help mining companies inform communities of the potential impacts of minerals development.
• Communities should be involved in continuous dialogue during the preparation of an SIA. Meeting legal requirements for public participation and information is necessary, but where these are inadequate to develop a shared vision, other processes should be considered.
• SIAs should be endorsed by the local community as well as by government.
• Social monitoring needs to become an integral part of SIA and to involve local communities as well as independent experts.

The Way Forward

Few areas present a greater challenge than the relationship between mining companies and local communities. Many stakeholders are directly involved – local management, employees and their families, other local inhabitants, local government, labour unions, and so on. Others are indirectly involved – for example, acting on behalf of local community interests with varying degrees of local representation. Issues of 'who represents whom' arise and disparities in the capacity of actors are key. Each operation, be it a mine or a plant, and the community around it are unique. The priorities and approaches taken will differ. What is good practice in one case may not be applicable elsewhere. As in other areas, the best is good and the worst is appalling. The legacy of abuse and mistrust is clear. Mining and local communities has to be an area of particular focus.

The approach taken here is to discuss a series of steps in the relationship between a community and a minerals project, culminating in the establishment of a Community Sustainable Development Plan (CSDP) at each mine.

Company–Community Engagement

The first contact between the community and a company is critical, and there are many factors to consider. The time frame for decision-making in communities is different from that in companies. Many communities operate by building a high degree of consensus, which may take time. If 'gatekeepers' are needed, for reasons of language or local knowledge, there should at least be several of them with ties to different parts of the community. An outside interest seeking to engage the community, such as a company, should develop multiple and diverse entry points to ensure that all elements are approached and consulted.

Integrated Impact Assessment for Sustainable Development

SIA should be coupled with EIA to enable a transition to integrated impact assessment. IIA should be universal for new projects and should include a community-level resource inventory as well as examine the whole spectrum of sustainable development issues, in addition to those required by legislation. IIA should become an inclusive, dynamic, ongoing process of integrating knowledge on potential impacts into decision-making and management practices. It should be endorsed by the local community and government, and entail independent monitoring of impacts. Ideally, the IIA should lay the foundation for a CSDP.

Community Sustainable Development Plan

MMSD suggests that based on the findings of IIAs, companies should ensure that, where appropriate, a CSDP is put in place at individual mines. CSDPs will not be appropriate for all mining operations, particularly where they are operating on a very small scale or where mining constitutes only a small proportion of local economic activity. Moreover, at the many sites where community plans already exist, this suggestion may involve reviewing and improving existing plans rather than developing new ones. The CSDP should provide the fundamental framework for relationships among the company, the community, the government, and any other relevant parties throughout the project life and into post-closure. MMSD suggests it be designed through consultation that begins during the IIA. Experience suggests that a multistakeholder forum administered by an independent party can help ensure the effective involvement of all actors. This must at a minimum include the community (through its local government or some other legitimate body), the national government, and the company. The CSDP should be based on the community's concept of how its interactions with the mine can best contribute to achieving its social, environmental, and economic goals, and should be grounded in the willingness and ability of the company and national government to contribute to and support those goals.

The roles and responsibilities of each actor should be specified, as well as the most appropriate means of achieving the community's goals. These include consideration of a range of issues, such as:
- the redistribution of revenue from central government;
- tax credit schemes, funds, and foundations;
- disparities, such the impact on women and families;
- skills development;
- institution strengthening;
- preferential procurement policies towards local suppliers and distributors;
- conflict or dispute resolution;
- social and cultural values; and
- mine closure.

The plan will need to evolve and be amended over the life of the mine. Short-, medium-, and long-term approaches may be adopted. In the short term, for example, with insufficient government capacity to distribute revenue, the best option may be to take a collaborative approach, where companies and NGOs work with government while building local administrative capacity. In the long term, the aim should be for a local administrative structure to take over implementation of the plan.

Independent mechanisms for monitoring and evaluation, including clear and agreed indicators of performance, need to be incorporated into the CSDP. Ideally, it should be backed up by a memorandum of understanding signed by all participants, including national and local government, so that responsibilities are formally recognized and delivered.

Community meeting for the Lihir gold mine, PNG

Roles and Responsibilities

Many factors need to be in place for mining to contribute to sustainable development at the community level. As a starting point, all actors need to have:

- a commitment to sustainable development at the local level;
- a commitment to effective community participation in decision-making;
- a belief in open communication among actors;
- a commitment to proactive rather than reactive approaches;
- respect for independent evaluation and monitoring systems; and
- a willingness to share responsibility and collaborate with others.

Working out the boundaries of rights and responsibilities is the challenge; the precise roles of the various actors will depend on local circumstances.

Companies

Companies should not have to assume the role of government at the local level. Much of the responsibility should lie with government; in some cases they are already taking on this agenda, but in others they clearly are not. It may be difficult for a company to avoid taking a leadership role in establishing a Community Sustainable Development Plan. In the long term, however, companies should focus attention on ensuring that the project works constructively alongside national and local government development programmes and helping the community work towards sustainable development. A phased approach may be necessary. Where government capacity is insufficient, it may be better to work with NGOs, churches, or other institutions than for a company to try to do everything itself.

Government

Governments have the primary responsibility in the national context for ensuring that the rights of all citizens are respected. Equally, they are charged with ensuring that the nation prospers while communities gain from development that takes place on their land or in their local vicinity. Governments should take the lead in setting policy and standards to ensure sustainable development takes place at the local level, including developing systems for project monitoring and evaluation, and to protect citizens from any kind of abuse. Local authorities need to be capable of formulating and executing plans for the development of social and physical infrastructure.

Non-governmental and Other Independent Organizations

NGOs, particularly international ones, should further develop internal policies to provide guidance for community engagement. Often the interests of communities may be different from those engaged in advocacy around development and environment issues. Experience suggests that the different roles NGOs play – be it in community development or advocacy and dispute reconciliation around community issues – need to be differentiated and clear. NGOs that get involved directly in community issues should endeavour to respect different community perspectives towards proposed development, including those not in support of their agenda, and to communicate with all elements in the community. At the local level, NGOs should work on building the capacity to articulate local perspectives and to determine that the full range of development options are available to communities.

International and Bilateral Development Agencies

International agencies such as the World Bank, the United Nations Development Programme, and the bilateral development agencies have a unique position of influence and responsibility, particularly in harmonizing the standards by which communities are treated and in bringing influence to bear on public- and private-sector concerns with these standards.

These agencies could well move towards integrated impact assessment for sustainable development in projects in which they are involved, and develop broadly applicable guidelines for such processes. They could also consolidate their experience and assist in the development of Community Sustainable Development Plans, including integrated mine closure plans, particularly in countries where they have experience and projects. They could also continue to fund capacity-building exercises for communities and state institutions.

Endnotes

1 InterPress Service (1994).

2 Howard (1988) p.258.

3 Joyce and MacFarlane (2001).

4 See Thomson and Joyce (1997).

5 Emsley (2001).

6 See Freeport-McMoRan Copper Gold Inc. website, at http://www.fcx.com/mr/fast-facts/ff-econimpact.htm.

7 Pasco-Font (2001).

8 Van der Veen (2001).

9 Labat-Anderson Inc. (1997).

10 MMSD (2001c).

11 Fraser (2001).

12 Loayza et al. (2001) p.12.

13 McMahon (1997) emphasizes the fact that many of the problems would have been greatly reduced if the federal government has not given fiscal and credit incentives to induce in-migration.

14 Banks (2001) p.43.

15 McMahon (1997).

16 See http://www.icem.org/update/upd2002/upd02-02.html for more information.

17 Banks (2001).

18 Inti Raymi in International Development Research Council (2001) Chapter 2, Part 2, p.12.

19 See Kenny (2000).

20 McMahon (1997).

21 Musvoto (2001).

22 Conference organized by MiningWatch in 1999.

23 UNDP (1999b).

24 Ranchod (2001). According to the South African Medical Research Council, there is no information to support the need for a blanket ban. There appears to be little documented information available about the real risks involved in women working underground.

25 South Africa National Union of Mineworkers Gender Policy (1998).

26 Scheyvens and Lagisa (1998).

27 Earlier data adapted from figures in Lahiri-Dutt (1998).

28 ILO Conventions quoted in Lahiri-Dutt (2000) p.7.

29 Scheyvens and Lagisa (1998) p.61.

30 Emberson-Bain (1994).

31 Dodd (2000). Also see Whiteman & Mamen (2002).

32 Rio Tinto, personal communication (2002).

33 Musvoto (2001).

34 Norwatch (1999).

35 Prospectors and Developers Association of Canada, personal communication (2002).

36 Oxfam Community Aid Abroad (2001).

37 Heathcote (undated).

38 Horswill et al. (1999).

39 Vargas et al. (2001), cited in Stephens and Ahern (2001).

40 Castilla (1983).

41 Applied Geology Associates (1989).

42 International University of Kyrgyzstan (1999).

43 Coumans (1999b).

44 For more information, see http://www.bpdweb.org.

45 Ramos (2001).

46 Choshi (2001).

47 Ibid.

48 Aste (2001).

49 Hannesson (2001b).

50 O'Faircheallaigh (1995) pp.2–5.

51 Banks (2001).

52 O'Faircheallaigh (1996).

53 Holden and O'Faircheallaigh (1995).

54 Banks (2001) p.42.

55 Musvoto (2001).

56 Southern African Development Community (1997).

57 See http://www.mbendi.co.za/orgs/cp7d.htm/.

58 Kangwa (2001).

59 Musvoto (2001).

60 Placer Dorne Asia Pacific (1999).

61 Botts (2001).

62 McPhail (2001).

63 Rio Tinto (2001).

64 Ibid.

65 Anglogold (1998) cited in Choshi (2001).

66 See IDRC website at http://www.idrc.ca/mpri/.

67 Choshi (2001) p.24.

68 Horswill (2001).

69 Ibid.

70 Choshi (2001).

71 See http://www.escondida.cl.

72 Government of South Africa, Department of Minerals and Energy (2001).

73 Dunn (2001); Choshi (2001).

74 Ibid.

75 See http://forests.org/archive/png/onmoremo.htm/.

76 Oxfam Community Aid Abroad (2001).

77 Ibid.

78 Ibid.

79 Anderson et al. (2001).

80 See also Appendix of Brehaut (2001) for examples of community health programmes undertaken by companies in partnership with other actors.

81 Ndubula (2001).

82 Morales et al. (1998) cited in Stephens and Ahern (2001).

83 Foreit et al. (1991) cited in Stephens and Ahern (2001).

84 Brehaut (2001).

85 Extracted from Brehaut (2001). For more information see http://www.wacommunityhealth.org.

86 Brehaut (2001).

87 Ibid.

88 Khanna (2000).

89 Banks (2001) p.45.

90 Ibid., p.73.

91 The mine has only recently closed, so the full effects of closure are not yet known.

92 See also Storey and Shrimpton (1995).

93 See Mineral and Energy Policy Centre (2001).

94 CSIRO Minerals (2001).

95 Gibson (2001a).

96 Joyce and MacFarlane (2001).

[97] This suggestion is based on the report-back from a breakout group at the MMSD Managing Mineral Wealth Workshop, London, 15–17 August 2001.

[98] Ibid.

[99] This section is based on Joyce and MacFarlane (2001).

[100] Gibson (2000) cited in Joyce and MacFarlane (2001).

[101] A landmark event in the establishment of SIA was the inquiry by Chief Justice Thomas Berger into the proposed MacKenzie Valley gas pipeline, from the Beaufort Sea, Yukon Territory, to Edmonton, Alberta (1974–78). This was the first time that social impacts had been formally considered in project decision-making and led to the recommendation that the project be postponed for at least ten years to allow sufficient time for land claims to be settled and programmes and institutions set up to support the native population. See Berger (1983) and Gamble (1978) for more information, both cited in Joyce and McFarlane (2001).

[102] Cited in Joyce and McFarlane (2001) (references in the original omitted).

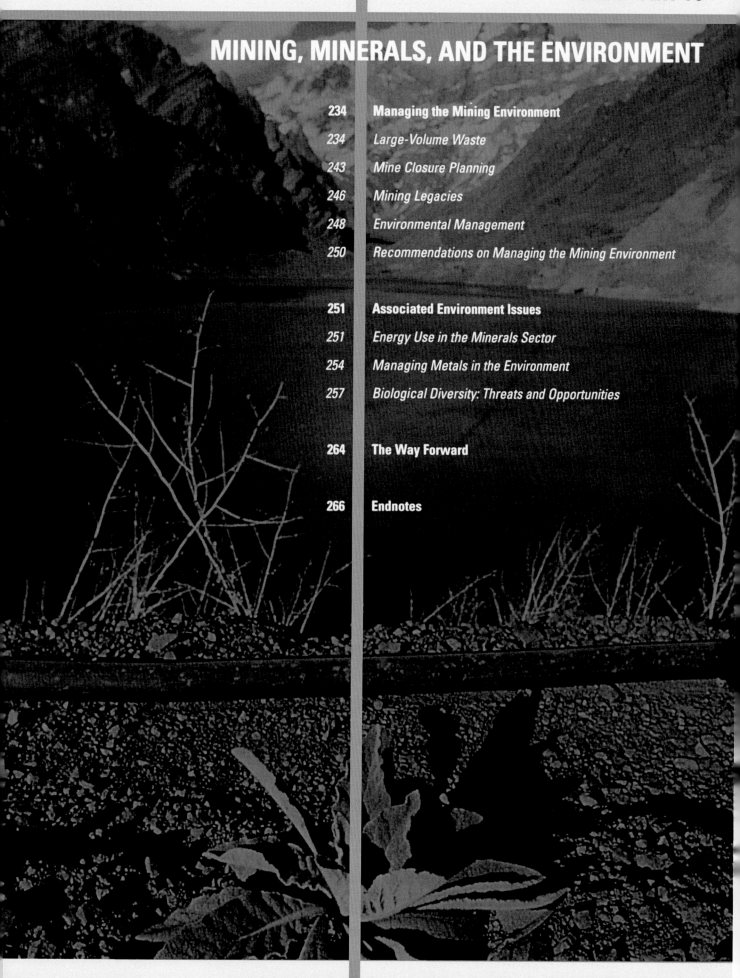

CHAPTER 10

MINING, MINERALS, AND THE ENVIRONMENT

One of the ideas at the heart of sustainable development is that of 'capital formation'. In this report, five main forms of capital are discussed: natural, manufactured, human, social, and financial. In theory, determining whether the world is on the path of sustainable development is measured by the net gain or loss in the total of these capital stocks over time. There is as yet no common currency between all the forms of capital, so the judgement is bound to be subjective.

Many people hold the view that natural 'capital' should not be used at a rate that exceeds the capacity for replenishment or that reduces environmental quality, regardless of whether in the process other capital stocks are increased.[1] Others believe that when natural capital is reduced, the conditions for sustainable development may still be met so long as other forms of capital, such as manufactured and human capital, increase.[2] This is the debate over 'hard' versus 'soft' views of sustainable development described in Chapter 1.

There is obviously change in nature even without human activity; ecosystems are not static. The 'hard' view of sustainable development does not demand that ecosystems be unchanged, or that humans not alter them, but instead that some limits on that alteration be observed, to keep change within the ability of ecosystems to self-correct. This is a difficult position for this sector to live by if it includes resources laid down over geological time. Thus all depends on what is considered to be 'critical natural capital' that has to be maintained to keep the system in balance, and that must therefore not be traded for improvements in other capital stocks.

Part of the problem is that the make-up of natural systems and how they work – let alone their resilience to perturbation – is not well understood. This in turn leads to the idea of precaution, but that too brings methodological problems – how precautionary is enough?

It is hard to argue that mineral extraction, processing, and use generally benefits the local ecosystems concerned or makes them more productive. There may be a few cases when such direct benefits do occur, such as the mining of areas previously degraded that in the process reclaims them, or rare species of bats surviving because old mine tunnels replace habitat

humans have destroyed. Indeed, part of the flora of the Cornish peninsula in the UK owes its presence to the mining that has gone on there since Roman times. But these are exceptions.

Taking a wider view, it can be argued that the use of metals, say, in the production of sewage pipes reduces the impact of people on their environment in our cities and in many other places. It is possible to imagine wood pipes – but at what cost to the forest? The arguments will no doubt continue.

Overall, the ability of local ecosystems to provide biological benefits has often been seriously impaired by mining and mineral processing. In the most modern mines, smelters, refineries, recycling centres, and landfills, there may be a considerable reduction in the damage done to natural capital per unit of output versus the past. But growing demand for minerals also means that total output is higher and so in absolute terms the damage function may be increasing. It is not known because it has never been measured for a nation, let alone the world.

'Best practice' in environmental management has a long way to go before it reaches the last operation. And then the best operations still have some impact, although their contribution is smaller per unit of output and no doubt will be reduced further. The worst are still bad from an absolute environmental point of view, but progress is apparent. For example, the best modern surface coal operations may leave behind sites at which casual observers may not even realize that mining has occurred. However, it is hard to contest that past mining methods have led to environmental damage that will take a very long time, if ever, for nature to repair.

In some of the world's famous mining regions, it is hard to accept that there has been some kind of gain that offsets the obvious loss of natural capital. Potosi, in Bolivia, has been mined for five centuries, producing a phenomenal amount of silver but at a great human, cultural, and environmental cost. Bolivia is still a poor country today, and the region around Potosi is one of the poorest in the nation, though mining still provides some of the better livelihoods for local people.[3] The legacy of colonial buildings is a World Heritage site that attracts some tourism, but the built or human capital that would compensate in some way for the losses must be largely found elsewhere.

When evaluating the undoubted environmental impacts of the minerals industry, the first question to ask is whether the impact is within the self-correcting capacity of the ecosystem. Is the duration of the impact short-term or long-term, and if it is long-term, is it reversible or irreversible? Second, is it worth it in terms of some other 'capital accumulation'? These bigger questions are touched on throughout this report. They cannot be answered in any rigorous way, as the metrics for doing so are not available. Thus this chapter is not about taking stock of the overall position but about how to reduce impacts, wherever they occur, to a minimum. Even so, much has had to be excluded.

Since it is obviously impossible to catalogue all the environmental impacts that may occur as a result of some aspect of the minerals chain, this chapter will focus on the issues that are widespread – that occur world-wide or with great frequency – and that have long-term implications. Some impacts that may meet these criteria are not included, however.

The use and management of cyanide in the gold industry will not be dealt with because during the MMSD Project, there has been a major discussion on this issue promoted by the UN Environment Programme (UNEP), which led to the development of a Cyanide Code (described later in this chapter). Most of what can be said on that issue was said by the parties to that debate and there is little that can be added.[4] The radiological and other downstream impacts of mining uranium are also excluded because they relate to a limited class of minerals, and the issues, while important, are complex and were beyond the chosen scope of MMSD.

Finally, issues related to water are only included where associated with other impacts such as acid drainage. This is partly because water consumption in minerals production, while an important impact, ends when operations end and thus does not present a long-term liability. But it is also because weighing up competing water demand issues was beyond the project's scope. Note, however, that some regional reports have gone further on this question because the competition for water imposes critical developmental constraints.[5]

This chapter covers seven principal areas of discussion where the impacts are serious and long-term and thus most likely to be considered impairment of the natural capital base:

For many, waste rock dumps are the main visual impact of mining

- large-volume waste,
- mine closure planning,
- mining legacies,
- environmental management,
- energy use in the minerals sector,
- managing metals in the environment, and
- threats to biological diversity

The first step towards managing and mitigating the negative environmental impacts of mining involves identifying where responsibilities lie. Results of the MMSD research and consultation suggest that such responsibilities should be shared far more broadly, particularly since civil society will perceive impacts in different ways depending how much they benefit and how much they individually shoulder the costs. At the moment, however, it is rarely local people who have the power to decide whether the trade-offs are worthwhile.

The majority of the content, views, and recommendations contained in the following section, Managing the Mining Environment, were developed based on the working papers prepared for MMSD on large volume waste, mine closure, and abandoned mines; the proceedings of the workshop held to discuss these topics; and comments received from an independent review committee and workshop participants.[6] These background papers document some of the existing best practice guidelines, including those developed by the International Council on Metals and the Environment (ICME)/UN Environment Programme (UNEP), the Mining Association of Canada, Australian Minerals and Energy Environment Foundation, and the Chamber of Mines of South Africa.

Managing the Mining Environment

Large-Volume Waste

Large-scale mining operations inevitably produce a great deal of waste. One of the most important environmental considerations at any mine is how to manage these large volumes of waste so as to minimize the long-term impacts and maximize any long-term benefits. On land, the physical footprints of waste disposal facilities are often significant, and these operations are rarely designed for a beneficial end-use. When they occupy land that was previously productive as wildlife habitat, farmland, and so on, it may be a very long time before the previous level of productivity is achieved if they are not rehabilitated adequately.

In addition to loss of productivity, these wastes can have a profound effect on the surrounding ecosystems. Where they are not physically stable, erosion or catastrophic failure may result in severe or long-term impacts. Where they are not chemically stable, they can serve as a more or less permanent source of pollutants to natural water systems. These impacts can have lasting environmental and socio-economic consequences and be extremely difficult and costly to address through remedial measures.

This is perhaps the principal reason for the widespread belief that mining, unlike many other land uses, is a permanent commitment of land. The visible evidence that land has in fact been rendered sterile and unproductive through past mining activities is such a powerful message that it is unlikely to be changed by anything short of a concerted effort at rehabilitating the worst of these sites.

In recent years, there have been significant advances in best practice in the environmental management of mine sites. This includes the introduction of operating procedures that have improved the methods of waste disposal and rehabilitation methods that reduce the likelihood of long-term impacts. But in the majority of cases there is still a long way to go before a mine can be seen as contributing to ecosystem improvement.

The volume of mine waste produced depends on the geological characteristics of the ore body, the type of mining (underground versus open pit), and the mineral being mined as well as the size of the operation.

Mine wastes are produced in a number of different categories, including:

- *overburden* – the soil and rock that must be removed to gain access to a mineral resource;
- *waste rock* – rock that does not contain enough mineral to be of economic interest;
- *tailings* – a residual slurry of ground-up ore that remains after minerals have been largely extracted; and
- *heap leach spent ore* – the rock remaining in a heap leach facility after the recovery of the minerals.

A key factor in deciding on the location of mine waste disposal facilities is cost. The cheapest option is often to deposit waste as close as possible to the mine site, or in a location where it can be transported by gravity. Selection is also heavily affected by climate: the options are very different for Escondida in the Chilean desert, where it almost never rains, and Grasberg or Batu Hijau in Papua (formerly Irian Jaya), where annual precipitation may total 8–11 metres.[7] Mining engineers also have to take into account the topography, hydrology, and geological characteristics of an area. The options may be different where there is a high risk of earthquakes. Other considerations include local communities, existing land use, protected areas, and biodiversity.

These decisions can have an enormous impact on the future of local people, who will have to live with the consequences long after the mine is closed and the company has gone. A company on its own simply does not have the information about local ecosystems or the details of local social and economic life that qualifies it to make these decisions unilaterally. This underlines the importance of consulting closely with local governments and communities while planning and constructing waste disposal facilities.

Land Disposal

The most common place to dispose of mine waste is on land. A variety of methods are used, which depend among other things on the type of waste.

- *Overburden and Waste Rock*

Overburden and waste rock are typically broken up sufficiently to be moved to the allocated disposal site, where the material is usually dumped and any excess is bulldozed over the edge, forming slopes at the natural angle of repose. The most important considerations are to produce stable slopes and control the flow of water in and around the waste so as to minimize erosion, protect the structure, and try to prevent infiltration. The most pervasive problem associated with waste dumps is acid drainage, an issue considered in greater detail later. Where precipitation rates are high, there needs to be particular care to ensure the physical stability of waste rock facilities, as they can fail with catastrophic consequences.

In some climates, too little water can be a problem and the surface of the facility may require regular wetting to reduce the generation of dust. Wetting is not a practical long-term solution and, at the time of closure, a permanent method of rehabilitation needs to be established. In some climates this can take the form of a vegetative cover, while in more arid regions it may be necessary to form a crust on the surface.

- *Tailings*

Tailings are the finely ground host rock from which the desired mineral values have been largely extracted using chemical reagents. This residue takes the form of a slurry that is at least half water and can be transported by pipeline. Tailings are usually discharged into storage facilities and retained by dams or embankments constructed of the tailings themselves, mine waste, or earth or rock fill. (See Figure 10–1.) When the tailings are discharged into the facility, the solid fraction settles – forming a beach enabling the slurry water to be decanted and discharged or recycled. As tailings are deposited they are often used to increase the height of the tailings embankment.

Given that tailings storage facilities usually contain residual chemical and elevated levels of metals, it is vital to ensure their chemical and physical stability. These structures are prone to seepage, which can result in the contamination of the ground and surface water and, in the worse cases, can fail catastrophically – an issue considered in greater detail later. Because tailings are made up of fine particles, when dry they can be a source of serious dust problems: in the Bay of Chañaral in Chile, there is a real concern about lead-rich mine tailings that blow over the local town.[8] In Gauteng, South Africa, old tailings storage facilities generate dust that can be blown over several kilometres. During the dry months the dust is overpowering, and local people are forced to tape up their windows and doors in an effort to keep it out.[9]

Mining often takes place in areas where water is scarce. In these regions, the consumption of water for mineral processing can have a severe impact on aquifers. At some mine sites the tailings may be thickened prior to disposal and the liquid re-used in the processing circuit. In many cases this has the added benefit of recycling process chemicals. Water may also be decanted from the storage facility and recycled to the processing plant. Any recycling of tailings water reduces the discharge to the surrounding environment and the potential for negative impacts.

Tailings may also be thickened to improve the method of disposal. Conventional tailings are 30–50% solids, while 'thickened tailings' are 55–75% and 'paste tailings' are over 75% solids. Thickened tailings can be stored with minimal water retention, creating a more stable structure both physically and chemically, while paste tailings can be used to backfill underground mines.

- *Heap Leach Spent Ore*

A third type of waste deposited on land is the residue of heap leaching. Here the crushed ore is placed on a membrane-lined 'pad' and irrigated with the appropriate reagent – cyanide in the case of gold or silver, and sulphuric acid in the case of copper or uranium. (See Box 10–1 for information on a new cyanide management code.) The leach solutions are then collected in channels around the pad and pumped to the processing plant. (See Figure 10–2.) The effluent is then re-charged with reagent and re-used.

The goal is to operate a closed system that does not discharge any of the solution into the natural water systems. However, all liners leak to some extent, and current best practice is to build the pads with multiple liners and to incorporate systems for leak detection.[10]

After recovery of the metals from the ore, the heap is rinsed to remove any remaining chemicals. Even after rinsing, however, some of the chemicals and elevated levels of metals may remain, so the facilities need to be designed to control surface drainage to prevent erosion, seepage, or failure.

While overburden, waste rock, tailings, and spent heap leach facilities display some issues in common, each type of waste has its own separate set of concerns. By mixing some of these waste products, it may be possible to compensate for the problems associated with each: waste rock is porous and prone to acid

Figure 10–1. Tailings Dam Geometry Definitions
Source: Martin et al. (2001)

Upstream Method of Tailings Dam Construction

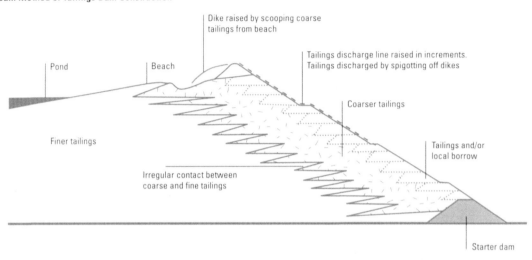

Downstream Method of Tailings Dam Construction

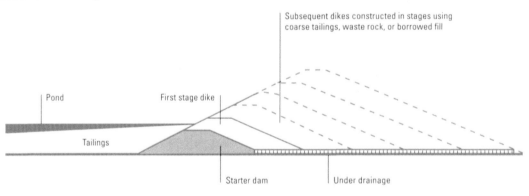

Centreline Method of Tailings Dam Construction

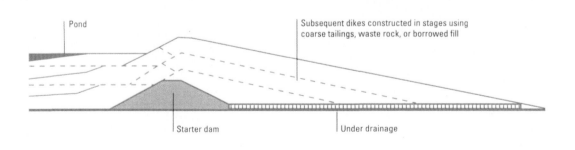

Box 10–1. International Cyanide Management Code

At the present time, there is no economically viable, environmentally sound alternative to using the reagent cyanide in the production of gold. Cyanide is also an hazardous chemical that requires careful management.

To address public concerns about cyanide use and management, UNEP and the International Council on Metals and the Environment (ICME) co-hosted a two-day multistakeholder workshop in May 2000. Participants confirmed the importance of a Code of Practice 'to drive improved performance in mining through high standards of technology, management and control to provide the public with confidence that their concerns were being addressed'. The Code's mission statement is 'to assist the global gold mining industry in improving cyanide management, thereby minimizing risks to workers, communities and the environment'.

Developed by a committee of 14 participants from large and small gold producers, the financial sector, environmental groups, governments from industrial and developing countries, labour, and chemical suppliers with broad public consultation, the code sets out nine principles, each with specific Standards of Practice to protect workers, the environment, and the public. The principles address responsible production, safe transport, proper handling and storage, operations, the need for decommissioning plans, worker safety, emergency response strategies and capabilities, training, and public dialogue. At present, an adoptive institution is being sought for the code, and a third-party audit has been planned but not yet started. Mechanisms are still being developed with respect to loss of certification, dispute resolution, and periodic updating.

For further information, see http://www.cyanidecode.org and http://www.mineralresourcesforum.org/cyanide

generation, while tailings are very fine and prone to instability. One idea is that the co-disposal of these two wastes could create storage facilities that are both chemically and physically more stable. (See Box 10–2.) The International Network for Acid Prevention (INAP) has embarked on sponsored research to investigate various aspects of co-disposal. These include constructing facilities for the co-disposal of waste rock and tailings and the use of co-disposal to construct covers for waste rock retention facilities.

Mine wastes are occasionally seen as a resource and may be suitable as aggregates for road construction and

Box 10–2. Co-disposal

Co-disposal mixes waste rock with tailings. This has the advantage of filling in the gaps between the particles of waste rocks. If consolidation characteristics are right, this excludes some of the air, thereby reducing the potential for acid drainage and also reducing dust problems with wind-borne tailings. The total amount of land needed for disposal is reduced, less water is used, and the deposits can provide a better substrate for growth of vegetation and other biota. However, this kind of 'co-disposal' also carries risks. If the proportion of tailings is too high, the deposit will be physically unstable; if it is too low, air and water can penetrate more easily, leading to increased dangers of acid rock drainage. Co-disposal is currently mainly used in the coal mine sector, particularly in Australia.

Sources: Van Zyl et al. (2002); discussions at MMSD Vancouver workshop, 2001; http://www.inap.com.au/inap/homepage.nsf

Figure 10–2. A Heap Leach Facility
Source: Adapted from IAEA (1993)

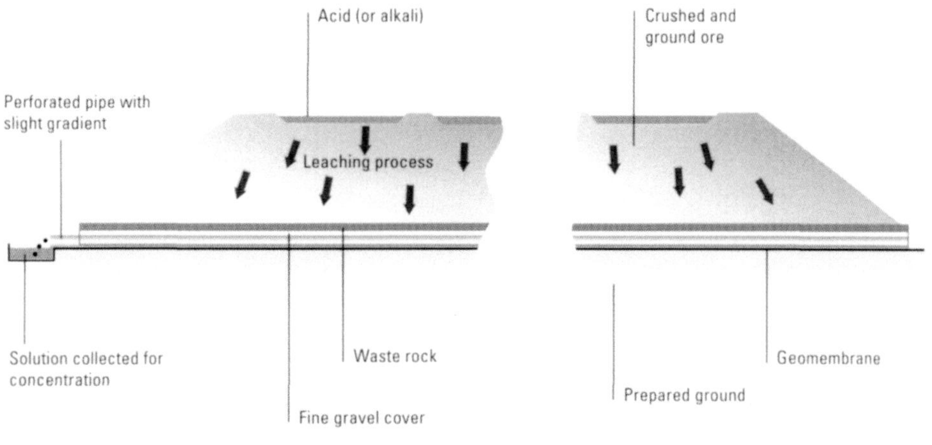

building materials. A number of projects are looking at a range of end-uses. However, the volume of wastes is so great it is hard to see more than a small fraction of them being used in this way. They should also be used with care, especially in the construction industry, as contaminants in the waste have sometimes caused long-term problems.

Backfilling mine waste into underground workings or open pits has certain advantages and disadvantages. The main advantages are the reduction in the use of land and the stabilization of underground workings. However, the increase in the volume of waste when excavated means that it is not possible to backfill all the material removed. As a result, only around 60% can be returned and the rest placed in surface disposal facilities.

Backfilling open pits during operations is only possible where there are separate pits or an elongated pit. Double-handling of waste materials is rarely economically feasible, and environmental problems can occur during the temporary storage of the waste. However, the environmental impacts of a partially backfilled open pit may be considerably greater than a surface storage facility. Some critics argue that the companies reject backfilling without sufficiently serious analysis, and this may at times be true.

Waste may also be disposed of under water in either natural or artificial lakes or flooded open pits. (See Box 10–3.)

Acid Drainage

The most serious and pervasive environmental problem related to mining is acid drainage (AD).[11] AD occurs in many major mining regions, particularly

---

Box 10–3. Lake Disposal

Lake disposal can be used for waste rock, as the lack of exposure to bacterial action and oxygen reduces acid drainage. It needs to take into account the chemical composition of the waste, however, and artificial structures have to be carefully monitored. Some pits expose acid-producing rocks, and adding more acid-producing rocks can alter water quality and lake biota dramatically.

Source: http://www.nrcan.gc.ca/mets/mend/

---

those with temperate rainfall, and regional studies show that it is a widespread problem.[12] Where it does occur it can have a serious impact on the productivity of ecosystems. AD can be a long-term problem and may result in a reduction in natural capital.

Acid generation begins in the circumneutral pH range when iron sulphide minerals are exposed to, and react with, oxygen and water. This is a process that occurs in nature, and there are cases where it has reached problem levels without any help from humans. But by exposing these materials and breaking them up, mining can greatly accelerate the rate at which these reactions take place. Other factors that influence the oxidation of sulphide minerals are temperature, acidity levels (pH), ferric/ferrous iron equilibrium, and microbiological activity, especially in the form of *Thiobacillus ferrooxidans*. Mining exposes sulphide-rich materials in the walls of open pits, mine tunnels, waste rock, tailings, and so on. AD is of less concern where mines exploit oxidized ore bodies. Because these deposits are less numerous and seem to be exploited more readily than sulphide deposits, some argue that the problem will increase as industry exhausts the oxide sites.[13]

AD is characterized by depressed pH values and elevated concentrations of dissolved heavy metals; the sulphuric acid easily dissolves metals such as iron, copper, aluminium, and lead. One of the most serious aspects of acid drainage is its persistence in the environment. An acid-generating mine has the potential for long-term, severe impacts on surface and ground water and aquatic life. Once the process of acid generation has started, it is extremely difficult to stop. The combination of acidity and dissolved contaminants is known to kill most forms of aquatic life, rendering streams nearly sterile and making water unfit for human consumption.[14]

AD is not a problem at every mine, even in sulphide-rich zones. In some circumstances the reaction may be inhibited by a lack of water or oxygen. In others the surrounding soils may have 'buffering' qualities that help neutralize the acid.[15] But in some cases metals and sulphates may still be mobilized even though acid conditions do not appear.

In some cases the problems may be evident from the outset and steadily increase during the life of the mine. In others, AD may only appear after the mine has closed and the company has left the area. Once started, however, the process can endure for centuries or even millennia. For example, acid generation in the Rio Tinto mining district in Spain is believed to have been caused by Roman or perhaps even Phoenician miners.[16]

• *Treatment*
Dealing with AD effectively is very difficult. There are known management methods to minimize the problem. Effective mine design can keep water away from acid-generating materials and help prevent AD from occurring. But in many cases this is not adequate to prevent it altogether.

AD can be treated actively or passively. Active treatment involves installing a water treatment plant. Here the AD is first dosed with lime to neutralize the acid and then passed through settling tanks to remove the sediment and particulate metals. The costs involved in operating a treatment plant can be high and require constant maintenance and attention.

The goal of passive treatment is to develop a self-operating system that can treat the effluent without constant human intervention. An example would be passing the water through an artificial wetland in which organic matter, bacteria, and algae work together to filter, adsorb, absorb, and precipitate out the heavy metal ions and reduce the acidity.[17]

So far no one has designed a passive system that will operate indefinitely without human intervention. It is therefore not free of ongoing costs. Treatment will be needed not just during the mine life, but indefinitely into the future. A number of research initiatives and programmes are currently aimed at the prevention and control of acid drainage. The best known of these are Mine Environment Neutral Drainage and INAP.[18]

• *Sustainable Development and Acid Drainage*
There could be a debate about the extent to which the reduction in natural capital represented by AD can be outweighed by the addition to human capital. The debate could become even more complex if it focused on who has the right to make those trade-offs – governments of developing countries, the more environmentally focused North, or those who can speak for the next generation. The legislature in Wisconsin in the United States has taken the dramatic unilateral step of requiring – as a condition of issuing a mine permit – verification that one or more sulphide

mining operations have been undertaken in full compliance with pertinent environmental laws and without causing any 'significant environmental pollution' before issuing a new mining permit. (See Box 10–4.) More than 50 mines have been studied in an effort to find a site that can be shown to comply with these requirements; all have been rejected. Failure to show that there is any site that can meet these criteria could have serious consequences for the future of the mining industry, in Wisconsin and elsewhere.

The science that allows prediction of the occurrence of AD in advance is imperfect and is oriented more towards a range of probabilities than precise answers. In addition, the science that is available is not always used, particularly when regulatory authorities lack the capacity or the understanding to ask the right questions and demand the best answers. The debate largely takes place out of public view because the issues are thought to be too technical for the public to understand, because the regulatory process occurs in an environment without a tradition of public participation, because the issues are cloaked in scientific jargon, and perhaps because the benefits may come now while the costs will come later, which puts a premium on optimism. The trade-offs among competing criteria are therefore not made consciously, explicitly, or transparently.

Box 10–4. Wisconsin Legislation on Mining

The law requires the Wisconsin Department of Natural Resources to make two key determinations before issuing a mining permit:
• that a mining operation has operated in a sulphide ore body that, together with the host rock, has a net acid-generating potential in the United States or Canada for at least ten years without pollution of the groundwater or surface water from acid drainage at the tailings site or at the mine site or from the release of heavy metals, and
• that a mining operation that operated in a sulphide ore body that, together with the host rock, had a net acid generating potential in the United States or Canada has been closed for at least ten years without pollution of the groundwater or surface water from acid drainage at the tailings site or at the mine site or from the release of heavy metals.

Source: State of Wisconsin (1997); Wisconsin Statute 293.50. The Mining Moratorium Law

Waste Storage Failures

Any human activity that involves shifting large volumes of rock, cyanide, acid, and other hazardous reagents will inevitably be subject to accidents. Accidents have occurred throughout the chain of mineral production and use, though there has been enormous progress in the best companies in reducing the frequency. This does not mean that more cannot be done. Accidents that occur later in the minerals cycle, at smelters and refineries, are discussed to some extent in Chapter 6. This section addresses accidents at mine sites and focuses on those with serious and potentially long-term environmental consequences.

At the global level, the greatest single concern is the failure of tailings storage facilities.[19] Although it is difficult to arrive at total numbers, given different monitoring and reporting systems, one estimate suggests that there are 3500 tailings storage facilities in active use and many thousands of others that are closed, at least some of which could still pose serious risks.[20] Since 1975, tailings storage facility failures have accounted for around three-quarters of major mining-related environmental incidents.[21] Major accidents seem to occur on average once a year, but there are many other smaller events that fall beneath the threshold of government reporting requirements.[22]

As a specific example of this, in 1996 Rio Tinto initiated a two-year review into the disposal of mine waste at 75 sites world-wide. The review included a desktop study of all sites followed by inspections at 26 sites. The results of the survey showed that in the ten years prior to the survey, there had been a total of 16 structural failures (21% of the sites), 10 of which involved tailings and 5 involved waste dumps. In addition, 10 facilities were classified as 'high hazard' under the Western Australian criteria.[23]

The failure of tailings storage facilities can have devastating consequences.[24] In 1965, an earthquake in Chile destroyed 11 facilities, one of which released 2.4 million cubic metres of tailings that ran 12 kilometres downstream – burying the town of El Cobre and killing 300 people.[25] Such incidents naturally provoke fear and anger, but even the threat of failure can cause severe anxiety to the local population. Major incidents also bring calls for tighter regulation. In Chile, the El Cobre failure resulted in new regulations for tailings storage facilities. In the United States, the Buffalo Creek disaster overcame years of industry opposition

and led to the enactment of national environmental standards for coal mines.[26] The list is a long one and includes incidents other than tailings failures, but the connections between highly publicized accidents, of which tailings failures are the most frequent, and new and tighter regulations is inescapable.

As indicated earlier, the location of large tailings storage facilities is a land use decision with what are effectively permanent consequences. If the facility is a hazard, this risk does not always end when the mine closes. If the facility is badly sited, designed, or constructed, rains, floods, or earthquakes can cause failure long after operations cease.

• *Why Do Tailings Storage Facilities Fail?*

The main problem is that tailings storage facilities are built over long periods. Often the embankment is constructed from the waste itself. Unlike water storage dams, which are usually built in one operation and can then be given a rigorous final inspection, tailings storage facilities are built continuously, possibly over the many years of the mine's life. This means quality control is much more difficult. During this time the ownership or management may have changed, and there will have been considerable turnover in staff. So even if the original design parameters were sound, they may be lost, they may not be followed with sufficient care, or the originally planned height may be exceeded. Meanwhile, the properties of the tailings may also have changed as the mine enters new ore zones or as processing technology is adjusted.

The leading large international companies usually employ qualified consultants, send their staff to international meetings, and keep abreast of developments in design. This is not to say that there are never errors at the outset, resulting from poor site selection or flaws in design. But these at least can be minimized if companies follow the latest best practice and use an independent design review committee.

The most serious problems affect big and small companies alike. Organizations are notoriously poor at ensuring quality management over long periods of time. It is surprising how often there is no single responsible person in charge of the facility. Having a competent person in charge with clear authority is an absolute requirement for safety; too often it is absent. Someone with the correct training is needed to ensure that the company carries out any necessary adjustments in design as conditions change.[27] But even good personnel have problems managing if they do not know the original assumptions on which the dam was designed, so that they can tell if these are exceeded. Too frequently the original design parameters are forgotten and the people managing the facility are no longer clearly aware of the limits they are supposed to observe. The level of on-site expertise usually falls once the project receives a permit and commences normal operations.

In principle, even the smaller companies should be monitored by lenders, governments, and local communities. But these external agents rarely provide effective oversight. Insurance companies have a clear interest in better practice in this area, but are often deterred from conducting their own reviews by the cost. Governments, too, pay most attention to the early stages – ensuring perhaps that there are suitable regulations about initial design but making few stipulations about ongoing stewardship.[28] In any case, governments rarely have sufficient skilled staff to monitor conditions or step in when problems arise. Under these circumstances inspection can be more dangerous than inattention, since it will give the management a false sense of security.[29]

Finally, both companies and local administrations frequently fail to ensure effective risk assessment and emergency planning. This includes measures to ensure the protection of both the settled local communities and also any informal squatters who may have been drawn to the area by the mine.

• *Best Practice for Tailings Storage Facilities*
Tailings storage facilities require not just good design but also close, consistent, routine attention over a long period. Those in charge need to be well trained and aware that they are being monitored, otherwise their performance is likely to deteriorate. This close surveillance is difficult to achieve, particularly in remote locations.

The first priority should be to ensure that all designs are based on the highest design standards possible. One option would be to have an international system of certification for designers, or at least some formal pronouncement by engineering bodies as to the minimum qualifications for undertaking such a task.

Companies should also establish a second layer of protection elsewhere in the system, probably at company headquarters through geo-technical review boards.[30] This would ensure periodic review and audit of safety conditions, including a thorough review of the original design, any new factors that might require adjustments, and an assessment of how the management system is being implemented in the field.

The third layer of protection should be external and involve governments, local communities, and insurers. Governments should be able to ensure frequent inspection by adequately qualified people. Some countries already have this capacity, but others do not.

Neither the first nor the second layer of protection will be fully effective if appropriate instrumentation is not incorporated into the facility from the beginning.

Marine Disposal

Though most mining waste is deposited on land, some companies discharge waste rock or tailings in the sea at depths varying from the shoreline to the deep sea. The greatest known impacts of this practice appear to be found in shallower waters.

Shoreline or surface-water disposal typically occurs where depths are less than 20–30 metres. This is the zone of highest biological productivity, and impacts can be severe. The waste increases water turbidity and smothers the organisms that live on the seabed. The sediment may also get washed up on the shore.

Shallow-water disposal generally involves releasing tailings from submerged pipelines into fjords, sea channels, and coastal seas at depths of between 30 and several hundred metres. In Canada, the Island Copper mine and the Kitsault mine have deposited tailings at such depths in sheltered fjords, and these appear to have remained mostly at the intended deposition area.[31]

Due to the problems associated with shoreline or shallow-water tailings disposal, greater interest has recently been shown in deep-sea tailings disposal. This involves depositing wastes below the maximum depth of the surface mix layer, the euphotic zone (the depth reached by only 1% of the photosynthetically active light) and the upwelling zone, on the assumption that the waste will not be re-mobilized in the surface water.[32] When the waste is discharged from the pipeline, it continues to flow downwards, eventually settling on the sea floor at perhaps 1000 metres or deeper. (See Box 10–5.)

Pipelines have the same risks of accidents under the water as they do on land. At Newmont's Minahasa Raya gold mine in Indonesia, for example, the tailings are piped out 800 metres from the shore to a depth of 82 metres.[33] But the pipe has broken more than once and released tailings to the surface, which is said to have caused a serious loss of fishing resources and destroyed some of the surrounding coral reefs.[34]

Box 10–5. Marine Disposal from the Misima Mine in Papua New Guinea

One example of deep-sea marine disposal of tailings is found at the Misima open-pit gold and sliver mine in Papua New Guinea (PNG) – a joint enterprise between Placer Dome Inc (80%) and a state-owned company. Mining began there in 1989 and ended in 2001, though processing of stockpiled ore will continue for another four years.

The company has disposed of overburden and waste rock (around 53 million tonnes in total) and tailings (15,000 tonnes per day) in the sea. This option was chosen following five years of environmental investigations as well as extensive consultation with landowners and the government. After the tailings are washed with fresh water in thickeners, they are mixed with sea water and de-aerated before being discharged into the sea, via pipeline, at a depth of 112 metres. The depth of the sea floor in the area of deposition is 1000–1500 metres.

So far, this method of disposal appears to have had relatively little environmental impact. A systematic review carried out since 1993, using direct observation, acoustic sensing, and analysis of water samples, indicates no permanent damage to the marine environment. Tailings appear to have stayed in place and, after five years of deposition, bacteria and meiobenthos had recolonized the sediment.

Nevertheless, it is still too early to come to final conclusions. The Misima operation is still 'young', and there is relatively little research on the long-term effects of such methods on tropical marine areas. Moreover, the current information has been funded entirely by the company and has yet to be verified by independent research.

Source: Van Zyl et al. (2002); Jones and Jones (2001)

Deep-sea disposal remains a controversial option, however, and there is little agreement on or evidence about its long-term effects. Some industry studies suggest that the risks are minimal and that within several years of closure the sea floor can be recolonized by benthic fauna.[35] Other research suggests that deep-sea ecosystems might be more complex and biodiverse than comparable terrestrial fauna.[36] Relatively little is known about deep-sea ecosystems and the interaction among marine species at different depths.

In some circumstances deep-sea marine disposal might be an option deserving serious consideration – when the mineral deposits are on islands that have little spare land, when available space is at risk of flooding, or when the stability of land disposal facilities is uncertain because of high rainfall or seismicity. Nevertheless, since relatively little is known about the long-term environmental implications of deep-sea marine disposal, many observers are demanding that this option be considered only after far more extensive and rigorous scientific investigation. And in light of some of the tailings pipe failures that have occurred, the problem of how to get the tailings into deeper water without undue risks to shallower near-shore environments would have to be addressed.

Riverine Disposal

Even more controversial than marine disposal is the practice of disposal of waste rock and tailings into river systems. In this case, however, a good deal is already known about the impacts, and almost all of this experience is negative. Miners have tipped waste into rivers throughout history, and at numerous sites the legacy of riverine disposal will endure for a very long time.

There are only three currently operating large mines where international companies use rivers for waste disposal. These are the Ok Tedi copper and gold mine in Papua New Guinea (see Box 10–6), Placer Dome's Porgera gold mine in PNG, and Freeport's Grasberg copper and gold mine in Papua (formerly Irian Jaya), Indonesia.[37] Riverine disposal is also currently used by many small-scale and artisanal miners around the world, by a number of small or medium companies, and at an unknown number of sites in Russia and China. The main advantage of riverine disposal is that it is cheap and convenient, and it may also appear less hazardous than constructing a tailings storage facility, especially in high-rainfall areas with little stable land and a risk of seismicity. In the case of Ok Tedi, the

Box 10–6. Riverine Disposal from the Ok Tedi Mine in Papua New Guinea

The riverine disposal of tailings and waste rock at Ok Tedi gold and copper mine in PNG is highly controversial. It has involved lengthy legal disputes and there have been extensive efforts by downstream communities to close the mine. The company that held a majority share in the mine, BHP Billiton, decided to withdraw from the project because it no longer wished to be associated with this method of waste disposal. (The socio-economic impacts of this project are considered in Chapter 14.)

The original proposal included two stable waste dumps and a conventional tailings storage facility. During the early stages of construction, a massive landslide destroyed the site of the tailings storage facility. To keep production on schedule, an interim tailings scheme was approved that allowed for the retention of 25% of the tailings, the remainder being released into the Ok Tedi river. An alternative site for a tailings storage facility was never identified, and the construction of a permanent waste disposal facility was deferred. At present, approximately 80,000 tonnes of tailings and 120,000 tonnes of waste rock are discharged daily into the Ok Tedi. Waste material has reached the Fly River, into which the Ok Tedi flows.

The Ok Tedi mine has led to a four- to fivefold increase in the suspended sediment concentrations in the Fly River. This exceeds the sediment transport capacity of the river system, resulting in the build-up of sediment in the river bed in the Ok Tedi and middle Fly River, which in turn has increased the incidence and severity of overbank flooding. The flooding has resulted in the deposition of mine waste and abraded waste rock on the flood plains, causing the die-back of vegetation. The area affected by 'die-back' increased from 18 square kilometres in 1992 to about 480 square kilometres in 2000. A risk assessment carried out by the company stated that the area ultimately susceptible to die-back induced by mining ranges from 1278 to 2725 square kilometres.

Dredging has been attempted along part of the Ok Tedi river bed in an effort to reduce the impacts of the flooding. This has reduced the frequency of flooding, but the problems of vegetation dieback continue.

Source: Van Zyl et al. (2002); Kirsch (2002)

government of Papua New Guinea accepted this option because the only alternative was to shut the mine – with severe economic implications.[38]

Riverine disposal has caused many types of environmental damage. These include a change in the morphology or physical form of rivers and an increased risk of flooding, resulting in the die-back of vegetation and damage to the aquatic ecosystems. The finer sediments can also have impacts further downstream when they reach estuaries or deltas. In Chile, 150 million tonnes of mine sediments disposed of in the Salado River from the El Salvador mine have created a new 3.6-square-kilometre beach many kilometres downstream in the Bay of Chañaral.[39]

These impacts may have serious consequences for communities downstream – particularly for people's health. As well as changing the physical character of the river, mine wastes may also increase the levels of minerals and process chemicals to the water. Overbank flooding may increase the incidence of malaria. Local people may find their livelihoods affected if deposits reduce the potential for fishing or cultivating riverside gardens.

There has been a long and often bitter debate over whether in some circumstances riverine disposal might be acceptable. Some companies and governments argue that it should be accepted if the alternative is to have no mining at all. Other companies have stated that they will no longer consider riverine disposal an option.

Mine Closure Planning

For a mine to contribute positively to sustainable development, closure objectives and impacts must be considered from project inception. The closure plan defines a vision of the end result of the process and sets concrete objectives to implement that vision. This forms an overall framework to guide all of the actions and decisions taken during the mine's life.

Critical to this goal is ensuring that the full benefits of the project, including revenues and expertise, are used to develop the region in a way that will survive after the closure of the mine. To achieve this, a mine closure plan that incorporates both physical rehabilitation and socio-economic stability should be an integral part of the project life cycle and designed to ensure that:
• future public health and safety are not compromised;
• environmental resources are not subject to physical and chemical deterioration;
• the after-use of the site is beneficial and sustainable in the long term;

- any adverse socio-economic impacts are minimized; and
- all socio-economic benefits are maximized.

At the time of mine decommissioning and closure, not only should physical environmental rehabilitation be completed in a satisfactory manner, but the community should have been developed to maintain a sustainable existence.

Closure planning was first used as an environmental tool but was quickly expanded to include socio-economic issues.[40] Best-practice planning for closure involves integrating the closure design for the entire mine area, identifying the timing of the planning process, and considering issues that relate to specific disposal methods and post-mine economic and community activities, as well as financial planning.

There are significant costs when a mineral project closes. Workers may be unemployed or need to pay to relocate somewhere they can get a job. Someone needs to pay to keep the roads open or the schools running. Someone needs to pay to close the mine shafts, remove hazardous reagents from the site for safe disposal, stabilize the slopes, rehabilitate the facilities, and ensure that long-term environmental and social problems are minimized.

If there is no understanding in advance as to who will be responsible for what, and no planning for the day of closure, many of the benefits of development will be lost. This has clearly happened in many instances in the past, and these negative post-mining conditions have contributed to the industry's current public reputation.

If mine closure comes with little advance warning, the company will no longer have any revenues from which to fund anything. Government revenues are also likely to be affected, the local economy depressed, and individuals out of work.[41] The result is that no one can afford to do much. Public services fall apart, the benefits of infrastructure are lost, and the community is dislocated. Many companies in the past kept the results of operations and consideration of closing confidential as proprietary business information. Some of them are now starting to believe that the more open this discussion is, the more it allows other economic actors such as government, workers, and local businesses to make rational plans for their own future. This lets them rely more on their own resources and foresight and

means they may turn less to the company to solve problems.

Unemployed mine and minerals processing workers have destabilized numerous governments over the years, including in Bolivia, the Ukraine, and Serbia. They have been a major political factor even where governments did not fall, in countries such as the UK, South Africa, and Germany. As a result, governments often subsidize mining operations to keep them open. This may be in the form of open subsidies to unprofitable state enterprises, such as the payments that nearly exhausted Romania, the years of Bolivian subsidy of the tin industry, or the mines at Lota in the south of Chile.

Companies have their own reasons for wanting to keep mines open even after they have stopped being good performers. Some of this may simply result from a hope that prices will improve if the company just continues long enough. Additionally, many of the reasons may have to do with accounting rules, balance-sheet pressures and the effect on a company already in the economic doldrums of having to write off assets or recognize costs. But some of it also has to do with a lack of clarity about what the company will be expected to pay when it closes and a desire not to press the issue unduly. Some of the high-profile issues on which the industry is currently being criticized are controversial precisely because some feel that the companies are not paying their fair share of long-term liabilities at closure. (See the discussion of Marcopper and Ok Tedi in Chapter 14.)

A framework for closure agreed at the outset could significantly ease these problems for government, companies, and communities. That would make it easier to preserve the social and economic benefits of development and to avoid long-term charges against the natural capital account. It might also remove some of the excess production and help to stabilize commodity prices.

Closure Planning Today

The modern concept of closure planning is based on the following key considerations:

- *Pollution prevention* – It is cheaper to prevent problems than to try to fix them later. If a company has an obligation to deliver the site in a specified condition at the end of the mine life, it will create strong incentives for pollution prevention during the whole life of the mine.

- *Changing expectations* – Companies can reduce the risks of the rules of the game changing midstream by entering into a binding agreement on the end results they need to achieve. This makes costs more predictable, and they can be recognized on balance sheets.[42]
- *Continuity* – Mines get bought and sold, companies merge or are acquired, and management changes. The ultimate objective must be to develop an understanding about what the site will be like at the end of mining, in a form that will survive all these events, and not depend on the good intentions of individual managers who are likely to have moved on by the time closure occurs.
- *Financial surety* – Given that many mine closures have occurred as a result of poor market conditions, low profitability, or even bankruptcy, there is a need for some kind of financial surety to make certain that closure costs are funded. To ensure that the funds are available for these closure activities, the company is generally required to post a financial surety or bond.[43]
- *Public participation* – Some form of public consultation process is required that allows for dialogue over the long-term issues and end-use of the site.

Post-Closure Costs

Sometimes there will be ongoing costs that have to be paid after closure occurs. One of a number of examples is the cost of operating a water treatment plant to abate acid drainage, as described earlier. But decisions on mining projects have to be made long in advance of this point, on imperfect knowledge, and usually based on probabilities rather than a clearly known outcome. This provides decision-makers and the public with three alternatives, all of which are highly unpalatable to at least some actors. First, there could be a decision that the risks are too high and mining will just not be permitted. Second, there could be a decision that the risks are acceptable and the project will proceed. If the company cannot be induced to pay whatever long-term liabilities result, society will assume them. And third, government could set a guarantee or bond requirement sufficiently high to cope with identified future problems.

This latter method of funding has proved quite effective in some countries, though it has failed in others. Bonding is a government function, and it is hard to know how to proceed when a government does not want to take that role. A number of governments in the developing world have chosen, at least to this point, not to follow that route:

- Even if multinationals can post bonds, many local companies do not have the resources, and in many cases these smaller local companies provide more employment than the big ones.
- Effective closure planning requires considerable skill and capacity on the part of both government and companies, and this is sometimes not available.
- Many developing countries have recently undertaken comprehensive review and revision of mining legislation to attract foreign investment, and this is seen as a backward step and an economic disadvantage in competition for investment with other countries that have no such requirements.
- Effective planning requires considerable flexibility to develop appropriate solutions to site-specific problems. This implies discretion in government officials, which is seen as a disincentive to investment and a source in some places of potential corruption.

Although the polluter pays principle requires the company to pay the costs, this does not necessarily mean that the company should itself maintain the site in perpetuity. Perhaps the best solutions are those where the company pays a local institution to take the responsibility. This does not imply that the company should necessarily be absolved of all responsibility if things do not go according to plan. There are now private companies emerging that will assume the liability for ongoing site maintenance for a fee.

There is a clear need to integrate the accounting profession into any discussions of long-term financial arrangements to ensure that accounting rules do not drive companies away from best practice.

The primary responsibility for mine closure lies with companies and the governments that regulate them. But this responsibility should also extend to the lenders. Neither private lenders nor multilateral lending or funding agencies have given this matter sufficient attention, perhaps in part because closure will not occur until long after their loans have been repaid.

One way forward could be the promotion of Community Sustainable Development Plans as a part of the project process. (See Chapter 9.) These would involve local communities, national governments, and companies working out their respective roles and obligations during the project life and at closure.

In addition, there is a role for accounting professionals to improve handling of these issues. There should be a review of the accounting and tax treatment afforded closure costs, to ensure that if negative balance sheet implications of proper approaches to closure or awkward tax consequences are a disincentive to best practice, these issues are identified and dealt with.

The TRAC programme (Transfer Risk and Accelerate Closure) is a risk-based, fixed-price approach used in South Africa and the US in which the mining company enters into a fixed-price contract for the purpose of transferring the risks and responsibilities for mine closure to a contractor.[44] This may be a helpful model in some circumstances.

Mining Legacies

The environmental issues of current and prospective mining operations are daunting enough. But in many ways far more troubling are some of the continuing effects of mining and smelting that occurred over past decades, centuries, or even millennia. These sites have proved that some impacts can be long term and that society is still paying the price for natural capital stocks that have been drawn down by past generations.

It is impossible to estimate how many former mining sites exist around the world or how many of these carry environmental risks. For one thing, there is no clear way to define a former mine site. Using a fairly inclusive definition, it has been estimated that in the US there are more than 500,000 abandoned hard rock mine sites.[45] Certainly not all of them present environmental problems. In the UK, most of the problems are related to tin mining in the counties of Devon and Cornwall, where there are some 1700 abandoned mine workings, most of them very small, that continue to affect the water in some 400 kilometres of classified rivers.[46] In most countries with a long history of mining, there are relatively few data on former mines or their environmental legacy, though there is enough information to know that problems are widespread.[47]

Given the uncertainty about the numbers and the state of abandoned mines, it is impossible to estimate with any precision what it would cost to rehabilitate them. Moreover, the cost depends very much on what 'rehabilitation' consists of and to what standard it is pursued. Information available from sites with serious problems that have been investigated suggest daunting sums. Since 1980 the US has had a 'Superfund' programme administered by the Environmental Protection Agency to locate, investigate, and clean up the worst hazardous waste sites, a number of which are the result of mining, smelting, or refining minerals. In the Clark's Fork River region of Montana , for example, where gold and silver mining started in the late nineteenth century and continued until the early 1950s, rehabilitation measures have been roughly estimated at US$1 billion.[48] The Summitville mine in Colorado is likely to cost some US$225 million to clean up, and the Yerington copper mine in Nevada, around US$200 million. The US-based Mineral Policy Center, a non-governmental organization (NGO), suggests that it will cost US$50–60 billion to clean up abandoned mine sites in the US alone.[49]

Paying for the Legacy

One way to create a credit in the current natural capital account would be to deal with the worst environmental problems at abandoned mine sites. Improving these sites could create benefits, which could offset or perhaps even exceed any deficits attributable to current operations. And at some of these sites even a relatively small investment can have a big environmental payback.

It would clearly be in the interest of the industry to get this done. These sites are effectively advertising against the industry. In some places, they are highly visible and effective advertising. It might be that a dollar spent in reducing the amount of this kind of advertising might be more effective than one spent on promoting positive corporate image.

The issue is who will pay the costs. Good economic policy suggests that identifiable environmental costs be internalized on one principal condition: that all other companies have to do the same. If a company fails to obey the law, penalties should be used to make it comply. At the other end of the spectrum, the only prospect for cleaning up a historic mine site is with public funds.

Between these clear cases, there is a wide range of intermediate scenarios based on how long ago the mine was abandoned, whether the laws applicable at the time were complied with, who owns the site now, and the succession of companies operating it. (See Table 10–1.) In some cases of US litigation, such as the Smuggler Superfund proceedings, millions of dollars have turned on whether a modern company is the successor in interest to a firm that operated a particular mine many decades ago.

It may still be difficult to make the polluter pay even for recent mining operations. In industrial and developing countries, there are sometimes quite different attitudes and values towards past liabilities for environmental damage.

This raises the question of the source of public funds. One option is to take the money from general government funds. This might be equitable if most of the minerals were used within national borders – and assuming that the use of mineral products is distributed roughly according to the payment of taxes. On the other hand, many poor countries, including ones with significant adverse legacies, cannot afford this.

Alternative ways of generating a fund for abandoned mine work are discussed in Chapter 16.

Priorities for Action

Clearly, far too little is known about the extent of mining's environmental legacy or what it would cost to remedy the problems. But these uncertainties are no excuse for inaction. The worst sites have already been identified: they are fairly hard to miss. There is plenty of work to be done while the parameters at the less blatant sites are debated.

The first global priority must be for the public authorities to identify and register abandoned mines and assess the risk they pose. Given the scale of the problem and the limited capacities of public agencies, they will need to establish priorities – the registration process, for example, would need to be set beyond some agreed threshold of mine size. They would also have to concentrate the immediately available resources at the most dangerous sites, where clean-up will offer the greatest benefits.

The second priority at the national and international levels should be to develop new funding mechanisms that will be sufficiently robust and sustainable to tackle problems that will be a burden on future generations.

Table 10–1. Possible Allocation of Responsibility for Dealing with Mining Legacies	
Scenario	**Responsibility**
Ancient mine workings	Rehabilitation with public funds
Historic mine with no identifiable owner	Rehabilitation with public funds
Mine closed and former operator can be identified, but no longer owns the site	Former owner could be liable or rehabilitation could be a public responsibility
Mine closed but former owner still owns the site	Owner/operator is responsible for preventing damage to neighbouring property and controlling hazards
Mine is still operating	Owner/operator is responsible through an agreed closure plan
Operating mine early in project life	Owner/operator is responsible through an agreed closure plan
Permits granted but no operations have yet started	Costs fully internalized to the extent current scientific and technical understanding permit
Mine has not yet received necessary permits	Costs fully internalized to the extent current scientific and technical understanding permit

Environmental Management

Environmental Impact Assessment

Environmental impact assessment (EIA) is perhaps the most widely used tool of environmental management in the minerals sector. This is due in part to people in the minerals sector and in the World Bank who have been instrumental in spreading its use. Even in its origins, social and economic factors tended to creep into this environmental exercise. This is now being deliberately promoted with the development and integration of tools such as social impact assessment (SIA) and cost–benefit analysis into the EIA process.

The need for EIAs is well established, and they are now mandatory for most large-scale development projects. (See Box 10–7.) However, their implementation is often poor. One of the core problems is that the international community has yet to set firm technical standards on, for example, gathering baseline hydrological data, assessing archaeological remains, predicting acid drainage, or identifying key flora and fauna. This uncertainty allows EIAs to drift down to the lowest common denominator. It also discourages professional excellence. Reputable consultants who insist on sound

methodology in carrying out such assessments find it difficult to compete on price with people who are willing to take short cuts – especially if regulators are not sufficiently well informed to be able to reject substandard work.

Environmental impact assessment has proved a successful tool and has been expanded to include social concerns – sometimes within the EIA process, sometimes in a separate SIA. There is now considerable interest in ensuring that other issues, like the potential for spreading HIV/AIDS or for local economic development, are included in the assessment. An integrated impact assessment should incorporate analysis of all relevant variables in a single coordinated process. (See Chapter 9.)

Environmental Management Systems

To gain the full benefits of an EIA, it should become part of an environmental management system (EMS) that seeks to integrate environmental responsibilities into everyday management practices through changes to organizational structure, responsibilities, procedures, processes, and resources. An EMS provides a structured method for company management and the regulating authority to have awareness and control of the performance of a project that can be applied at all stages of the life cycle – from identification of a deposit to mine closure. The stages in an environmental management system cycle are:
- organizational commitment,
- environmental policy,
- socio-economic impact assessment,
- environmental impact assessment,
- community consultation,
- objectives and targets,
- environmental management plan,
- documentation and environmental manual,
- operational control and emergency procedures,
- training,
- emissions and performance monitoring,
- environmental and compliance audits, and
- reviews.

The EMS is a repetitive cycle, with each stage being continuously revisited and improved on each visit. Although it is designed as a tool for the company, an effective system provides an easy way for the regulatory authority to check compliance. The responsibility for setting up and running an EMS lies with the company.

> **Box 10–7. EIA Leads to Mining Refusal in South Africa**
>
> The eastern shores of St. Lucia Lake in South Africa contain valuable reserves of titanium, and in the 1970s and 1980s the government granted mining rights to Richards Bay Minerals. In addition, this area of forested dunes is a valuable source of biological diversity. In 1986 it was designated as a wetland area of international importance within the International Convention on Wetlands.
>
> Between 1989 and 1993 the post-apartheid government in South Africa undertook an environmental impact assessment. The research was entrusted to over 50 scientists and other experts and was presented in the form of individual reports that were commented on by the various stakeholders. A Review Panel was charged with using this information to determine whether mining would be compatible with nature conservation and tourism. As a result of this rigorous exercise, mining permission was refused and in 1999 the area was declared a World Heritage Site. Not all believe that this was the 'right' decision, given South Africa's current economic situation.
>
> Source: Porter (2000); King (2000)

Compliance with the EIA can be monitored through an EMS.

Best Practice

The mining industry operates in a highly dynamic business climate that increasingly demands successful adaptation to changes in social values and public expectations of corporate behaviour. At the corporate level, respect for both the physical and social environment is now considered to be an essential element of good business practice. (See Box 10–8.) Most major mining companies are committed to the continuous improvement of their environmental and social performance, often going beyond the legal requirements to include voluntary industry codes of practice and management systems.

At the international level, for example, ICME established an Environmental Charter that was developed and endorsed by its members. The charter originally encompassed environmental stewardship and product stewardship. Following consultation with its stakeholders, ICME adopted a Sustainable Development Charter. At the national level, in 1996 the Minerals Council of Australia launched a Code for Environmental Management on behalf of the Australian minerals industry. This code was reviewed in 1999 and has recently been revised. (See Chapter 14.)

At the 'local' level, the method and level of interaction between the company, the regulatory authorities, and the community can be critical to the success of the project. At the Lisheen mine in Ireland the company, Anglo American, spent five years collecting baseline data and communicating with the relevant groups in order to design a project that was acceptable to all and met the legislative requirements. (See Box 10–9.)

Box 10-8. What Is Best Practice?

The concept of best practice dominates discussion of improving environmental performance in the mining industry and making decisions on waste management options and mine closure more inclusive. Unless the meaning of best practice is agreed on, however, the term is meaningless and its use is often misleading. Best practice may be defined as the methods and techniques that have proved to lead to successful outcomes through their application, but different interest groups will almost certainly have different views of what constitutes 'success'.

Box 10–9. The Lisheen Zinc/Lead Mine in Ireland

Before construction could start on the Lisheen mine the company had to obtain a planning permit, an Integrated Pollution Control (IPC) Licence, and a mining lease. They also had to convince the local community and the regulatory authorities that a mine at Lisheen would bring considerable benefit to the region and not cause any environmental damage. The mine is located in the rural heartland of Ireland.

The main areas of concern were the deposition of tailings and the potential contamination of the groundwater. It was agreed that 51% of the tailings would be mixed with cement and used as backfill underground, while the remaining 49% would be deposited in a fully lined tailing storage facility located on a peat bog. The company also undertook to sink replacement boreholes for the farmers. Before granting the IPC Licence, the authorities required the company to lodge a bond worth in excess of US$16 million to pay for closure and rehabilitation costs.

The company decided to adopt a policy of transparency, and held meetings and consulted some 20 local groups. As a result, the company received positive support from the local communities and the licences were granted without the need for a public hearing.

Source: MEM (1998); Stokes and Derham (2000)

However, this level of commitment is often due to the personality of one individual and the continuity may be broken when that person leaves the project.

In addition, many international organizations, such as the UN, the World Bank Group, the World Health Organization, and financial institutions now have their own operating guidelines that include environmental and social issues. However, there does need to be a push for higher standards in the production of an EIA and for the incorporation of the EIA into an EMS. This will make a major contribution not just to better practices in mining, but also to sustainable development generally.

Risk Assessment and Emergency Response

Risk assessment and management are becoming increasingly important in the development of a mining project, where the uncertainties associated with environmental (and social) prediction are potentially higher than those of other industrial sectors. The process of risk management incorporates many different elements: from the initial identification and analysis of potential risks to the evaluation of tolerability and the identification of potential risk reduction options through to recommendations regarding the selection, implementation, and monitoring of appropriate control and reduction measures.

Although risk assessment has a wide application in the mining industry, there would be little value in investing in detailed risk analysis if the potential outcomes did not influence development or operational decision-making. Recent catastrophic failures of a number of tailings storage facilities have shown that in many cases the response bodies, the community, and the companies were not fully prepared to deal with such emergencies. In response UNEP has published an Awareness and Preparedness for Emergencies at a Local Level handbook for mining (known as APELL).[50] This publication is aimed at improving emergency preparedness in the mining industry, particularly in relation to potentially affected communities. It looks at a number of hazards and risks and identifies ten steps required to prepare adequately for an emergency.

Recommendations on Managing the Mining Environment
These recommendations should be read in conjunction with those in Chapter 16, which contains the integrated Agenda for Change.

- *Large-volume waste* – The International Council on Mining & Metals (ICMM) and other appropriate convenors such as UNEP should initiate a process for developing guidance for the disposal of overburden, waste rock, and tailings and the retention of water. This should be incorporated into the industry Sustainable Development Protocol proposed in Chapter 16. The views of all stakeholders should be solicited from the outset for the design of this process. Long-term and short-term risk assessment and financial considerations should be included.
- *Land disposal* – The mining industry should re-examine its land disposal practices to include alternative uses for waste, and the long-term future of the site. An integrated approach should be taken to water management, including water supply, dewatering activities, tailings, and heap leach water management.
- *Management of tailings facilities* – The industry should establish a method of international certification for the designers of tailings storage facilities.

Governments and funding agencies should require regular independent audits of all tailings storage facilities and establish a method of implementing the findings of the audit.
- *Marine disposal* – Industry, governments, and NGOs should agree on a programme of independent research to assess the risks of marine and, in particular, deep-sea disposal of mine waste. A shared and reliable information base on which optimal decisions can be made is required.
- *Riverine disposal* – A clear commitment by industry and governments to avoid this practice in any future projects would set a standard that would begin to penetrate to the smaller companies and remoter regions where this is still accepted practice. Whether that is done in the context of a protocol process or otherwise, industry is more likely to accept this idea if it gains confidence that other options will be looked at on their merits.
- *Consultation* – Before a mine proposal is accepted, all concerned – especially the local community – should be consulted on the proposed development. (See Chapter 9.)
- *Capacity* – A source of technical expertise and advice must be made available to government, insurers, communities, companies, and others to ensure that they can build their capacity for best practice.
- *Monitoring* – Industry, government, and other stakeholders should establish the best method of conducting environmental and socio-economic monitoring and of incorporating the results into the management of environmental and socio-economic impacts.
- *Legislation* – Industry, government, and other stakeholders, perhaps under UNEP auspices, should prepare best practice guidelines for all aspects of environmental and social issues. These guidelines should include, but not be limited to, mine closure in the context of sustainable development, acid drainage, tailings management, and risk assessment and emergency planning.
- *Lenders* – All lenders, including funding agencies and multilateral banks, should encourage more rigour in dealing with closure issues in mining proposals. This should include a well-developed closure plan that identifies the resources that will be required and a system of independent review.
- *Abandoned sites* – The industry should cooperate with international organizations and bilateral donors to develop an inventory for abandoned mines and identify sites for priority action.

• *Funding mechanism* —A funding mechanism should be developed to pay for remedial action programmes at abandoned sites. Alternative funding mechanisms are discussed in Chapter 16.

Associated Environmental Issues

Energy Use in the Minerals Sector

Responsibilities in the Minerals Sector
The current level and pattern of energy use is a critical factor affecting global environmental conditions. Climate change is a central concern for sustainable development. It has the potential to cause major impacts on the productivity of ecosystems and is hard to reverse once established.

Current scientific data indicate that human activities have modified the global climate over and above what may be associated with the fluctuations caused by natural cycles. The signing of the Framework Convention on Climate Change in 1992 was a turning point in public and inter-governmental awareness of this potential. Since then, mounting scientific evidence shows that a root cause of global climate change is gases emitted from the burning of fossil fuels and other sources, such as the release of methane gases from agriculture and oil and gas production.[51] It is widely acknowledged that developing countries will have the least capacity to adapt to a climate change.

Responsibilities for these problems are shared among the public and private sectors. Governments, industry, and the public in the most industrialized countries play a key role in both contributing to global energy use and providing policies for addressing the resulting problems. Currently, some companies in the oil and gas industry (such as BP and Royal Dutch Shell) are addressing this issue and have reaped financial benefits from proactively establishing greenhouse gas reduction programmes.

There are many reasons why the minerals sector is particularly implicated in the aspects of potential global environmental change that are related to energy use:

• Production of mineral commodities from primary sources involves the movement and processing of large volumes of material, all of which requires a source of energy.

• Many finished products that depend on mineral commodities to function consume considerable amounts of energy, such as motor vehicles and electronic goods.
• Due to its energy requirements, the mining and minerals industry may influence decisions about investment in power sources.
• Several mineral commodities, most notably coal, are used as fuels.

The last of these reasons is of profound importance for sustainable development and has already been the subject of a critical debate among NGOs, industry, academics, and energy policy specialists. Despite its importance, this issue is beyond the scope of this report for two reasons. First, in the limited time available, involvement in these issues was beyond project resources. Second, there were already a number of participatory processes, some of them larger than MMSD, looking at these specific issues, and it was unclear that MMSD could add anything significant to the ongoing debates.

Although it is sometimes said that 4–7% of global energy demand comes from 'mining', the boundaries are not sufficiently defined to determine an accurate universal figure.[52] The best estimates relate to individual mineral commodities, but even then the figure depends on where and how they are produced. Estimates of use of energy through the whole minerals cycle are even harder to develop.

Figure 10–3 illustrates some of the variation among countries in the importance of electricity consumption in different minerals industry sectors. Total electricity consumption in mining and quarrying by countries in the Organisation for Economic Co-operation and Development (104,000 gigawatt-hours) is comparable to that of rail (89,000 gigawatt-hours).[53] Electricity is, of course, only one of many forms of energy used in these industries. Put together, the five minerals industry divisions used 11.3 million tonnes of diesel in 1998, which is only 4% of the total used in road transport (286 million tonnes).

The impact of electricity production on climate change depends to a significant extent on the source of the power for electricity; if electricity is primarily produced in coal-fired plants, then the impact is greater than if it comes from some renewable sources.[54]

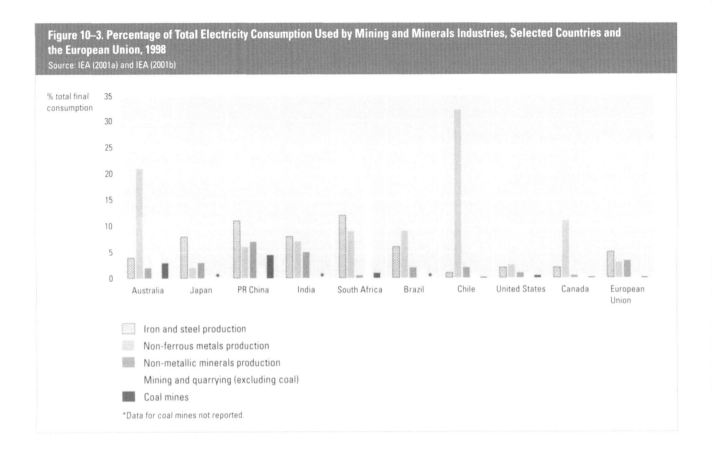

Figure 10–3. Percentage of Total Electricity Consumption Used by Mining and Minerals Industries, Selected Countries and the European Union, 1998
Source: IEA (2001a) and IEA (2001b)

Iron and steel production
Non-ferrous metals production
Non-metallic minerals production
Mining and quarrying (excluding coal)
Coal mines

*Data for coal mines not reported.

Energy Efficiency in the Production of Mineral Commodities
The minerals sector has a critical interest in reducing its use of energy per unit output, because of obvious implications for production costs. Depending on the specific operation in question, energy costs for different unit operations vary considerably in relation to total operating costs. For minerals processing, it may be up to one-quarter of the total. (See Table 10–2.) Considering the whole process of making primary aluminium, expenditure on energy may account for one-third of the total cost of production.[55]

During the twentieth century, the sector achieved dramatic advances in energy efficiency by means of technological innovation. Over the last 50 years, for instance, the amount of energy required to produce 1 tonne of primary aluminium has decreased by 40%.[56] Motors and pumps used for minerals extraction have become more efficient. The target is not, however, just to increase the efficiency with which energy from any one source is used. A key priority is to reduce direct and indirect releases of greenhouse gases. Mitigation options vary between different sectors of the industry. In the case of aluminium, iron, and steel, there is a

diverse set of emission sources, including both power generation and process-oriented ones. Security of supply is a critical issue to consider in the selection of energy sources.

The future role of technology in reducing emissions within minerals businesses is discussed in Chapter 6. There are, however, a large number of options for increasing the efficiency of current production processes. These range from relatively straightforward updates of portable mine site equipment (see Box 10–10) to those that depend on significant long-term capital investment and policy changes affecting the industry (see Box 10–11).

The price of energy may increase as a result of commitments made at government level under the Kyoto Protocol (part of the Framework Convention on Climate Change). This may be either because of the switch to low-carbon energy sources or because of the need to pay carbon taxes or purchase emission permits. Energy price increases could mean that pressures to cut costs in the minerals sector may become even greater in the future. Cost increases could range from 10%

Table 10–2. Estimates of Energy Costs as a Share of Total Operating Costs, Selected Ore Mining Operations (based on US price data for 1999)

Type of operation	Detail	Size of operation (tonnes per day[a])	Percentage of operating costs		
			Fuel	Electricity	Total
		Ore output			
Surface mine	Stripping ratio 1:1	1000	0.3	6.4	7
	Stripping ratio 8:1	8000	2.1	8.7	11
Underground mine	Room and pillar adit	8000	nd	nd	6
	Room and pillar shaft	8000	nd	nd	5
		Feed input			
Hydrometallurgical mill	Cyanide leach mill	2000	nd	nd	27
Flotation mill	one concentrate product	1000	0.0	27.5	28
	three concentrate products	8000	0.0	28.4	28

[a]Estimates are only approximate as they are based on only one group of theoretical models for mine costs. nd: not determined

Source: Schumacher (1999), with the help of additional decoding by O Schumacher

Box 10–10. Cost and Energy Savings from Basic Technology Application

The Blue Circle Aggregates Lithonia Quarry in Georgia, US, produces 1 million tonnes per year of aggregate and manufactures sand for construction and road building. Based on an assessment conducted by the George Institute of Technology, the quarry implemented a series of motor system upgrades, which reduced the energy use of 4 million kilowatt-hours by 6.2% and cut the electricity demand of 500 kilowatts by 16%. This saved the company US$21,000 per year.

The greatest energy savings resulted from reducing the capacity of three large water pumps and changing the source from which they drew water. A second modification was simply to physically lower another pump by 25 metres. This particular upgrade had a simple payback of 1.5 years. A third innovation was to replace four motors with more efficient versions once they reached burnout. It is predicted that this will have an average payback period of about 2.4 years.

Source: US Department of Energy (1999)

Box 10–11. Energy Efficiency in India's Primary Aluminium Sector

Although aluminium production accounts for only 0.5% of the value of output within the manufacturing sector, it is one of the most energy-intensive industries in India. In 1993, its share in total fuels consumed was 2.6%. Energy costs in this sector are the highest of all manufacturing sectors in India, from 35% of total production costs upwards. Aluminium demand is expected to increase to 1.06 million tonnes in 2006–07. In order to sustain competitiveness for both internal and export markets, retrofitting and efficiency improvements have been undertaken, based on state-of-the-art technology. Despite this, a detailed study of the productivity of the aluminium industry in India has estimated that energy-saving potentials of 20–40% could be achieved at some alumina manufacturing plants. At the smelting stage (conversion of alumina to aluminium), energy-saving potentials range from 16% to 30%. The barriers to energy efficiency concern access to capital, lack of information on the savings and benefits of the required technologies, and national policy changes affecting the industry.

Source: Lawrence Berkeley National Laboratory; Schumacher and Sathaye (1999) p.31

to 50%, and may have a major impact on mining company cost structures and competitiveness.[57] This will produce winners and losers, since companies that increase their energy efficiency most rapidly will gain a competitive edge. There will also be shifts at the international level. Companies mining in the most industrialized countries will feel the impact first under the Kyoto Protocol, while those working in many developing countries will not be subject to limits for the next decade or so.

For the extraction of metal ores, one of the greatest challenges for energy efficiency is that of declining grade. Lower grades inevitably require greater amounts of material to be moved per unit of product. In this context, it is important to acknowledge that the amount of metal in recyclable materials is often greater than the ores currently being mined. Key challenges to advancing recycling for mineral commodities are discussed in Chapter 11. Once collected and sorted, the production of scrap metals often requires a fraction of the energy used in production from primary sources.

Making the Use of Mineral Commodities More Energy-Efficient

As highlighted in Chapter 2, mineral commodities are fundamental components of numerous products, and thus play a significant role in global energy use by enabling the existence of a product in the first place and by making products more or less energy-efficient.

The energy efficiency of products has significant implications for the amount and type of metal used. The way in which mineral commodities are used also has significant implications for their re-use. Product design for recycling, re-manufacture, or extended product life has significant implications for energy use. Clearly, product designers, recyclers, and manufacturers need to work together much more effectively to exploit the business opportunities provided by this. Manufacturing processes can be substantially improved in order to avoid waste material being generated (whether or not it is then recycled).

In some cases, greater energy efficiency for some products may result in the use of greater amounts of a mineral commodity. (See Chapter 11.) Increased emphasis on efficiency in the use of electricity is likely to increase the demand for copper, as more efficient

electric motors have a higher amount of copper winding.[58] Energy efficiency can be increased through the use and application of metals – such as the use of zinc in increasing the durability of steel through corrosion protection and the better energy efficiency of electrical equipment achieved by increasing mass or volume.

Recommendations on Energy Use

- Initiate a global advisory body to address the lack of comprehensive, consistent, and regular data on energy use in the mining and minerals industry and the role of recycling. This body should make recommendations to all minerals and mining trade groups publicly available. It should assess the best means of making non-proprietary, audited data concerning energy use in the minerals sector available to the public.
- Convene a task force to report on the implications of climate change policies for the safety and security of mining and minerals processing operations.

Managing Metals in the Environment

A number of metals are of great environmental concern because of their potential chemical toxicity. These concerns extend to metalloids – non-metallic elements, such as arsenic, that in some respects behave like metals. Indeed, the toxic properties of many metals and metalloids have been exploited in the design of pesticides or antiseptics. For many people, the fear of harm is as important as the damage they know has been caused. This is a significant issue with respect to risk communication and may have social and economic consequences. For example, the value of land is depreciated if there is a risk of contamination. It is therefore possible to argue that metals and metalloids can reduce natural capital not only through their toxic action and persistance, but also by their presence at concentrations that cause unease.

Many opinions are rooted in the catalogue of infamous incidents where metals and metalloids have, beyond reasonable doubt, caused serious human health effects. One such case was the debilitating bone disease called *Itai itai* ('cry of pain') that broke out among people in the lower part of the Jinzu river basin in Japan. While the nutritional status of the people was an important factor in determining the magnitude of the disease outbreak, a significant underlying cause was cadmium discharged to the river from a lead-zinc mine. River water was used to irrigate rice crops, which accumulated high concentrations of this element. Consumption of the rice was an important cadmium exposure route for the people of the area.[59]

There are numerous other cases of concern. Among these are arsenic as a by-product of copper production in some parts of the world, and the effects of mercury on artisanal and small-scale gold miners. (See Chapter 13.) Concerns are, of course, not just restricted to sites of metals production. The use of lead in gasoline and paint (now phased out in many countries), which caused concentrations of this metal in blood to exceed health guidelines, is another example. The mercury pollution caused by discharges from a chemicals factory at Minamata, Japan, resulted in a shift in public perceptions of this element. Manufacturing processes, recycling, and waste disposal can be equally contentious because of the contamination they may cause. This includes occupational exposure, such as the respiratory diseases affecting workers involved in the processing of beryllium ores and production of the various chemical forms of this element.[60]

In many cases, the actual detection of toxic effects may not be relevant; it is the presence of a metal or metalloid above a threshold for the health of humans or ecosystems that causes the alarm or is used to cause alarm. As with all chemical hazards, demonstrating actual harm beyond reasonable doubt, and setting the thresholds, is an entirely separate and formidable task. Managing metals in the environment must involve dealing with scientific uncertainty and deciding on appropriate levels of precaution. This is not just the realm of scientists and politicians. Perceptions of the benefits of use of a metal, the merits of alternative materials, and the likelihood of mismanagement are fundamental determinants of the chance of harm. They also affect the willingness to act.

A key feature of most contamination and pollution incidents is that responsibilities for harm are poorly defined and slow to be taken up. This is often the case with the use of metals and metalloids, which can be released into the environment at all stages of the so-called minerals cycle. For instance, are mining companies responsible for the ultimate environmental fate of the materials they produce? Should recyclers accept a share of responsibility equal to the proportion of world demand that they supply? Clearly, the

Taking fish samples for heavy metal analysis in the Fly River, downstream from Ok Tedi copper mine, PNG

problem is ensuring that all actors in the minerals sector clearly allocate and share responsibilities for managing the risk of harm.

Allocating responsibilities is no easy task. First and foremost, this is because metals and metalloids are naturally ubiquitous both above and below Earth's surface.[61] This is particularly true for mining areas, where ores have been present at or near the surface for millions of years. Furthermore, the absolute concentrations of any metal or metalloid are usually less important, in terms of the risk of harm, than the chemical and physical form in which it is present. Not all forms are bioavailable, and some forms may become more stable over time. However, some fear that the reverse is also true and promote the idea of 'chemical time bombs'.[62] Some metals have truly global cycles, and human modification of the environment (such as through acidification and climate change) can alter their behaviour without additional releases by humans. At the local and regional level, land use change can be equally important. The case of mercury in the Brazilian Amazon exemplifies this. Here evidence now shows that mercury concentrations in soils are greater than can be attributed solely to gold mining.[63]

Progress in the Management of Metals

The world has steadily learnt more about the environmental chemistry of metals and metalloids.[64] Today's greater understanding has been the basis of a number of global initiatives to manage the production and use of these elements, including international forums on the safety and management of chemicals. Metals have also been the subject of international agreements, including the 1998 Heavy Metals Protocol of the Convention on Long-Range Transboundary Air Pollution (an international agreement that governs emissions and uses of lead, cadmium, and mercury) and the 2001 International Convention on the Control of Harmful Antifouling Systems (which controls the use of tributyltin on ships). An important part of all these efforts is maintaining up-to-date information systems. The International Union of Geological Sciences and UNESCO are making a global contribution to this with the International Geochemical Mapping Project. The International Council on Metals and the Environment (now ICMM) has played a role in encouraging work in the scientific community on assessing the risks to the health of ecosystems and humans associated with the production of these elements.

These, and a number of national efforts, have helped reduce some of the most harmful emissions. For example, the dispersion of arsenic has dropped significantly over the last two decades. In 1983, an estimated 10,000–15,000 tonnes were being released in Europe, the United States, Canada, and the Soviet Union.[65] But by the mid-1990s the total had fallen to around 3500 tonnes for the world as a whole.[66]

These gains have not been evenly shared, however. While, many people in industrial countries benefit from reduced risk of exposure, there are still severe problems in many developing countries. These often relate to the legacies of contaminated mining sites, as in Southern Africa.[67] Acid drainage and the generation of mining wastes, discussed elsewhere in this chapter, are means by which some of this continues. The transport of materials also poses serious hazards, as demonstrated by the spillage of mercury on its way from Yanacocha mine in Peru.[68] Landfill sites containing batteries and electronic equipment continue to affect aquifers world-wide.

Strategies for Managing Responsibilities More Effectively
The list of technical requirements for managing the risk of harm caused by metals and metalloids is unending. For the mining and minerals industry, these relate mainly to acid discharges and atmospheric emissions. This section discusses strategies for managing metals in the environment more effectively; the focus here is on prevention rather than clean-up.

While there is a continuing role for penalties and incentives to reduce metal emissions, additional strategies are emerging to manage the risk of harm more effectively. The most recent is the growing interest in product-oriented public policy, particularly in Europe; the general usefulness and success of such a policy will have to be evaluated over time. One advantage of this policy is that it takes into account the entire supply chain, from extraction through processing and use to (if necessary) disposal. This 'cradle-to-grave approach', also known as life-cycle analysis, is discussed further in Chapter 11.

The precautionary principle (see Chapter 1) must lie at the heart of the management of metals and metalloids for sustainable development. Those advocating or exercising precaution in the light of uncertainty must do so on the basis of transparent and wide debate. Workers and communities are often simply unaware of the harm that may be caused or the possible impacts of a precautionary policy on their livelihood. It is important to appreciate that harm may be caused by exceptional cases of the mismanagement of products or materials (such as illicit dumping, transport disaster, or failure of a waste facility) rather than when policies and strategies of governments and businesses go according to plan.

There is clearly pressure on dispersive uses of metals, namely uses that put these metals into the environment in ways where they cannot be recalled, recovered, or recycled. Examples of dispersive uses that have been or are in the process of being phased out are many: lead in gasoline and paint, arsenic and mercury in fungicides, cadmium as a dye. These pressures come from two directions. First, there is the environmental concern that their presence in the biosphere will have negative effects on human health or on plants or animals. Second, there is the growing demand for stewardship over metals in use for reasons of resource recovery. Caught between these demands, the remaining dispersive uses will increasingly be questioned.

This approach should not be followed for all metals and metalloids without wider considerations. Many elements that are potentially toxic at high concentrations are also essential nutrients. Removing them completely from the environment would entail supplements in the human diet to replace them. This can be illustrated by the growing awareness of the dangers of zinc deficiency.[69] The approach so often followed with synthetic organic pollutants, for example, of recognizing no lower threshold of human health effects and assuming 'the lower the better' for environmental concentrations is not appropriate for elements that are ubiquitous in Earth and necessary for many forms of life.

Recommendations on Metals in the Environment

- ICMM should identify the priority areas of uncertainty regarding the contribution of the mining and minerals industry to the global cycle of potentially toxic elements. It should seek to initiate collaboration between industry associations, international agencies, and academia to ensure that such knowledge is generated and effectively communicated to all interested parties. The aim should be to establish links between specific sources and the likelihood of human health impacts or effects on ecosystem function.

- All industries associated with the metals life cycle must work together more effectively to ensure that data are available in order to undertake risk assessments for the uses of their products and by-products in society. This should be part of their product stewardship activities. Industry associations should play an active role in facilitating this.

Biological Diversity: Threats and Opportunities

Biological diversity (or biodiversity) is a critical part of our natural capital endowment. Defined by the UN Convention on Biological Diversity (CBD) as 'the variability of all organisms from all sources…and the ecological complexes of which they are part…[including] diversity within species, between species and of ecosystems', it is an abstract concept.[70] (See Box 10–12.) Biodiversity issues have been overlooked frequently in planning and decision-making, and the term has often been interpreted too crudely as the sum total of living things and the ecological processes associated with them. But it is much more than just 'goods' and 'services'. Biodiversity – and its inherent variation – fuels living organisms' ability to adapt (or to be adapted by an human intervention, such as plant breeding) within an ever-shifting environment. It is therefore best understood as the living world's capacity to change – variability – and the wealth of biological forms and processes that

---

Box 10–12. The Principal International Framework for Action on Biodiversity

The UN Convention on Biological Diversity is a key instrument of the global programme for sustainable development. It represents a concerted attempt to provide a legally binding policy framework for biodiversity based on international consensus. Now ratified by more than 180 countries, it provides the minerals sector with a politically sound basis for engaging in constructive dialogue and partnerships with the biodiversity community.

The CBD has three key objectives:
- the conservation of biological diversity,
- the sustainable use of its components, and
- the fair and equitable sharing of the benefits arising out of the utilization of genetic resources.

The CBD translates these guiding objectives into a series of Articles that contain substantive provisions on in-situ and ex-situ conservation of biodiversity; the provision of incentives for the conservation and sustainable use of biodiversity; research and training; public awareness and education; assessment of the biodiversity impacts of projects and minimization of adverse impacts on biodiversity; regulation of access to genetic resources; access to and transfer of technology; and the provision of financial resources. Most of these provisions are equally applicable at a mine site, to a government department's work programme, or at international level. Thus the CBD provides governments, NGOs, and the private sector with a most useful conceptual framework.

The CBD has established institutional arrangements for its further development and monitoring of progress. The key institutions include the Conference of the Parties, which meets biannually; the Subsidiary Body on Scientific Technical and Technological Advice; and a Secretariat. Industry bodies can attend CBD-related meetings as observers.

Other relevant legislation at international, regional, and national levels that needs to be taken into consideration includes the RAMSAR Convention on Wetlands of International Importance and the World Heritage Convention.

Source: The Convention on Biological Diversity (1992). For the definition of biodiversity see Article 2 of the Convention. See also Secretariat of the Convention on Biological Diversity (2001)

---

derive as a result – variety. Biodiversity is therefore found everywhere, albeit in different concentrations and configurations.

Biodiversity's critical value lies in the choices or options that it supports, for both present and future benefits – whether this relates to the alternative food sources it provides, to the range of bio-chemicals and processes that underpin modern and traditional medicinal products, or to the way it increases the resilience of the biosphere's myriad natural processes, from pollination to watershed protection. Humans are all somehow dependent on biodiversity, so its loss is likely to affect everyone. But those most likely to suffer the consequences of biodiversity loss are indigenous peoples' or rural dwellers, many of whom continue to remain directly dependent on wild habitats and natural ecosystem services for their entire livelihood needs, whether by choice or through lack of alternatives.[71]

In the past, trade-offs between human activities and biodiversity were made unconsciously – some land was set aside for strict protection, irrespective of impacts on local populations, and the rest was converted to other uses, irrespective of any biodiversity loss.[72] Today the context of operations has changed dramatically. Escalating populations and consumption needs are placing ever-greater demands on land and natural resources; protected areas – which have been the principal biodiversity conservation instruments – unable to withstand these mounting pressures suffer regular encroachments, whether through agriculture, forestry, fishing, or mining-related activities. It is clear that protecting these areas will not conserve biodiversity if the rest of the land base is poorly managed. Thus the focus of attention must fall as much on addressing all three objectives of the CBD, or biodiversity's 'triple bottom line' – conservation of biodiversity, sustainable use of its components, and equitable sharing of the benefits arising from its use – as on all three dimensions of biodiversity (ecosystems, species, and genes). The CBD framework can therefore help link biodiversity much more effectively to the economic and social dimensions of sustainable development.

Encroachments into protected areas have, however, raised many controversial debates related to land access and ownership (see Chapter 7) and what is considered 'best' for biodiversity conservation. Community conservation has been promoted as an alternative – and complementary – approach on lands held outside or adjacent to protected areas. But there are many policy and institutional issues constraining its wider adoption. On the more technological side there is ex-situ conservation, which focuses on the collection and storage of specimens in gene banks, zoos, or botanical gardens. There is much the mining sector could do to support such approaches further, in concert with other sectors, in addition to mitigation of their direct impacts on all biodiversity wherever it is found.

Clearly, much more still needs to be done if such biodiversity is to be maintained. Although the CBD demonstrates a growing commitment towards the cause, its implementation is constrained by, among other things, a serious lack of resources, inappropriate economic tools and incentives, and insufficient capacity, especially in developing countries. The minerals sector has a key role to play in biodiversity maintenance, given that some mining ventures can eliminate entire ecosystems and all their endemic species and that its activities are increasingly prolific in relatively undisturbed high-biodiversity-value areas.[73] Lasting success, however, will depend on coherent remedial actions of all sectors, including economic planning, agriculture, fishing, energy, infrastructure, and tourism. It will also depend on wealthier consumers' understanding of the social and ecological impact of their consumption patterns.

Identifying Areas of Valuable Biodiversity

Not all areas are of equal biodiversity conservation concern. Thus any 'intrusive' sector, be it agriculture, mining, commercial logging, or infrastructure, must be informed on the specific locations of zones of greatest biodiversity value or most critical conservation concern, so that appropriate mitigation measures can be taken. Biologists and the conservation sector invest heavily in such identification and priority-setting exercises, and at the global level there are now various descriptions of global biodiversity priority areas based on different approaches such as hotspots, endemic bird areas, important plant areas, and eco-regions.[74] Some of these coincide with protected areas; others do not. The conservation sector has, however, singled out protected areas (IUCN Management Categories I–IV) and UNESCO World Heritage Sites as areas to be avoided by the mining sector at all costs. This recommendation has raised many difficult dilemmas. (See Chapter 7 for more detailed information on mining and protected areas.)

While such priority-setting exercises are a useful first approximation, they are not always spatially coincident, and they use different proxies for biodiversity, making it difficult for outsiders to know which to give priority to. Scientists disagree about which proxies to adopt, mainly because biodiversity per se cannot in all its complexity be quantified by any known all-embracing measure, and knowledge of it is constantly evolving. Given that everyone has different interests in and understanding of biodiversity, whether any chosen proxy is the 'right' one is always open to debate. For instance, aspects of biodiversity that have compelling value to one group may mean little or nothing to another: a hunter-gatherer's view of which plants warrant conservation may vary markedly to that of a western botanist or a specialist in traditional Chinese medicine. Selection of proxies is therefore predicated on value judgments and scientific assumptions about which facets of biodiversity matter more than others.[75]

Global mapping exercises have also proved too coarse a resolution for use in local land use planning or zoning. At the same time, valuable information that is available at the site-specific level has often not been systematically catalogued or peer-reviewed and is not therefore accessible to decision-makers. Innovative mechanisms, such as the use of the internet, for peer review of such data and for ensuring that it remains within the host institution's memory are necessary, especially given the rapid decline in the availability of resources for systematics and ethnobiological survey activities.

Progress in presenting more coherent and up-to-date thinking on priority biodiversity conservation areas and methodologies for their identification and assessment have also been seriously hampered by progressive underinvestment by the public sector in a number of related research areas, particularly in systematics and taxonomy (the identification and enumeration of different species). Only 1.7 million species have yet been named out of a possible 20–100 million.[76] Existing taxonomic expertise is also skewed towards certain groups such as mammals rather than invertebrates or the plant kingdom. Links between western and indigenous classification and assessment mechanisms are weak as well. Governments in both industrial and developing countries have lost interest in such activities and are at times openly sceptical about their importance. Perhaps there is some cause for scepticism – especially in the developing-country

context where other demands on already scarce resources are intense – but it may also stem from inappropriate previous public support for this discipline.

The consequence is that many scientific institutions that previously housed invaluable expertise, herbaria, or zoological collections have run short of finance, and irreplaceable knowledge and data have been lost. Such information gaps produce uncertainty, and it is impossible to draw conclusions about what is being lost – or the consequences. At the same time, the funding and execution of survey, research, and publication on biodiversity has been largely taken over by international NGOs, multilateral agencies, and the private sector. (See Box 10–13.) While such institutions should continue to play a key role in these activities, they need strong central coordination and independent peer review. Otherwise, individual agendas are likely to dominate, reducing the objectivity of science.

How Mining Affects Biodiversity

Measuring the impacts of mining and biodiversity – and defining their effects and implications – also presents certain challenges, for reasons similar to those described in the preceding section. When assessing impacts on biodiversity, the key question is, Which proxy is best, as not all species are of equal value? Some species will increase, others will decrease, and some will not change at all following mining disturbance (assuming the entire ecosystem is not being removed). And peoples' perceptions of the effects of these changes will also vary. The proxies most commonly selected are rare, endemic, or threatened species, or protected areas, and there are good reasons why these are chosen. But they are by no means representative of all biodiversity. In conducting biodiversity impact assessments and drawing conclusions about their implications, it helps to articulate clearly which proxy was chosen and why. There also needs to be thorough analysis of whether or not the 'new' combination is better, worse, or unchanged, and for whom.

The mining and minerals sector is not necessarily the most important influence on biodiversity in a particular region. Figures released by the National Parks and Wildlife Service in Australia suggest that mining was responsible for 1.1% of presumed extinctions of endangered plant species, compared with

Partnerships between companies and research institutions could provide some interesting new opportunities for biological and ethno-biological research. When companies explore for minerals they are often entering pristine regions, unexplored by science. Given the current public funding crisis, there is clearly potential for greater cooperation between researchers and mining companies – not just for providing financial resources but for the necessary access and infrastructure that rigorous survey and research activities require. While the time frames may not always coincide, especially at the exploration stage, the potential should not be rejected.

An interesting example for such industry support to science is a series of studies funded by PT Freeport Indonesia (a subsidiary of Freeport-McMoRan Copper and Gold Inc. and Rio Tinto plc) during the 1990s in the company's area of activity near the Lorenz National Park in Indonesia. A highly controversial mine by many accounts, this operation has managed to make a major international contribution to increasing understanding of the flora of New Guinea through the collection of materials of poorly known species and of species new to science. About 5600 plant collections now form the basis of the database of 9500 collections. Eight papers have been published describing new species, and the total number of species estimated from the region is 8400, with 500 or more occurring at over 3000 metres. Of the estimated species in the area, probably fewer than 40% are found in Kew Gardens' collections.

None of this valuable information would have been created if not for the support of PT Freeport Indonesia. Many will certainly argue that this simply cannot offset the mine's social and environmental impacts. Certainly the trade-offs have been enormous, and the benefits of biological information generated are small in comparison. Still, there are some opportunities here that, even in apparently adverse circumstances, could yield collateral benefits to science if suitably pursued.

Source: Dr Robert Johns, Herbarium, Royal Botanic Gardens, Kew

38.2% attributed to grazing and 49.4% to agriculture.[77] Nevertheless, mining does almost always have an impact on biodiversity; in some cases the effects can be huge and, where global extinctions are at stake, they can be irreversible. Surface mining often results in total clearance of vegetation and topsoil, often leading to accelerated desertification, and while better-managed operations make provisions for rehabilitation, mining impacts can be more far-reaching than those of other sectors.[78] There is a great deal of detailed published material on the impacts of mining on biodiversity and natural ecosystems, including Conservation International's Guide to Responsible Large-scale Mining, IUCN and the World Wide Fund for Nature's review of mining and forest degradation in Metals from the Forest, the Minerals Policy Center's review of the damage hardrock mining has done to US aquatic ecosystems, and the Australian Minerals and Energy Environment Foundation's contribution to the MMSD project, not to mention the many relevant academic and company-sponsored papers.[79]

Generally, the greatest risks to biodiversity are when mining ventures enter relatively remote and undisturbed areas. The very act of building access roads for exploration purposes brings significant risks to biodiversity – as the raised expectations of potential large-scale benefits often trigger rapid in-migration. Large-scale biodiversity loss occurs as colonizers must clear land for settlement and farming and take out economically valuable wild species to supplement their income or for food. (See Box 10–14.) Sometimes new people and activities in an area can also bring in alien pests and diseases that have hugely detrimental effects. It is worth noting that this may all be at its most intense before mining starts and before any major mining company is on the scene, and activities are frequently ungoverned and unregulated. In cases where the mine does not get developed, such activities frequently continue unabated, as there are few alternative livelihood sources to fall back on.

'Junior' exploration companies – which may not be involved in mining at all – do a great deal of the world's exploration. In areas of emerging mineral interest, there may be many such companies on the scene. Given that grassroots exploration is high-risk and capital-intensive, with finance often hard to get, success can depend on speed: getting in, getting results, and getting out, with a minimum number of days of drill crews in the field. It may also depend on not letting competitors know what is being surveyed or where. This can present distinct challenges for mitigating negative impacts, as dealing effectively with intense bursts of mineral interest, where multiple actors are moving quickly and into remote areas far from government scrutiny, is a daunting task. Furthermore, instituting evaluation and permitting processes can lead

Box 10–14. Coltan and the Conservation Crisis

Until relatively recently, few people had heard of columbite-tantalite ore or 'coltan', which contains the rare metals tantalum and niobium that are widely used in the manufacture of capacitors for electronic devices. (See Chapter 11.) Between 1997 and 2000 the price of coltan rose from US$100 to US$800 per kilo. Significant deposits of this ore are found in the east of the Democratic Republic of the Congo, where it is easy to extract from shallow pits using picks and shovels.

The result has been a modern-day 'gold rush' into this region. This has triggered a dramatic decline in the wildlife population, notably of the Grauer's gorilla, which has been hunted for food and for trade. Recent evidence suggests that over the past five years the gorilla population has dropped by 80–90%, and the animal is soon likely to be classified as critically endangered.

This well-publicized case has dramatized the need to find ways of conserving biodiversity in the face of economic pressures. On a good day a miner can produce a kilogram of ore a day worth around US$80 – in a region where most people live on 20 cents a day. It is unrealistic to expect people to forgo income on this scale. The only solution must be to find ways of paying individuals or countries for conserving such areas. The Global Environment Facility has provided some help in the support of biodiversity, and UNEP has a Great Apes Survival Project, but such efforts have not yet had much impact in this area.

Source: Harden (2001); Redmond (2001)

to costly delays. Despite these challenges, there have been some attempts to implement good practice in exploration – as in the Asarco Ltd Camp Caiman Gold Project in French Guiana.[80] There is clearly an urgent need to create the conditions whereby good practice in exploration becomes more widely adopted.

Mining processes themselves also have serious implications. Clearing vegetation, shifting large quantities of soil, extracting large volumes of water, and disposing of waste on land or through water systems often lead to soil erosion and sedimentation and the alteration of the flow of watercourses. This can change the spawning grounds of fish and the habitats of bottom-dwelling creatures. Acid drainage, as described earlier, may be the most widespread negative impact on aquatic species. Such effects can instigate

extinctions, or they can restrict access to species that local communities depend on, such as snails, mushrooms, medicinal plants, and so on. Local extinctions can be caused by any sectoral activity, but there is one group of plants that is likely to go extinct as a result of mining activity alone. These plants – metallophytes – grow in areas where soils are heavily loaded with metals, and are often of very restricted distribution. They often grow on or very near mining deposits, hence mining activities can easily obliterate them, resulting in the loss of a potentially valuable resource.

Mining can sometimes boost some aspects of biodiversity. This can happen through the creation of new habitats or even from disturbance. Abandoned mineshafts, for example, serve as sanctuaries for many of North America's largest populations of bats. Sand and gravel pits in the UK have attracted many varieties of wildlife. Many of these benefits may have been random or accidental, but some companies are now making concerted efforts to enhance habitats, which may help to enhance biodiversity. Others have taken steps to protect certain species during the mining process. Viceroy Gold Corporation of British Columbia, for instance, helped The Nature Conservancy create a 150,000-acre Desert Tortoise reserve as a mitigation measure for California's third largest gold mine.[81] If all companies made the effort to identify habitat needs critical for the survival of species of concern, to protect them during their operations, and to enhance them wherever possible, there could be many more biodiversity success stories.

Abandoned mine sites are generally seen as a liability, as they are often a major source of pollution. However, they sometimes offer some interesting biodiversity phenomena. If a former mining area and surrounding tailings are naturally recolonized by vegetation, the unwanted legacy can become a resource base of unique genetic materials and plant and animal behaviour. The study of these organisms and their colonization behaviour and evolution observable on former mine sites can enhance closure and rehabilitation strategies. Their cataloguing and conservation is a priority. This is to be done not only prior to mining activity but also throughout a mine's life since these plants and animals have revealed a remarkable adaptive capacity to changing metal environments.

Others have taken care to encourage flora and fauna as part of the process of rehabilitation of mine sites.[82] Here the best practice is usually to introduce native species that are able to survive in that environment. Well-intentioned attempts to revegetate sites disturbed by mining have been a source of introduction of exotic species that have had many deleterious effects on native plants and the ecosystem. In some cases, however, local communities have asked companies to revegetate with non-native species that might yield better livelihood benefits, such as pine trees for fuel or timber. Even where a species is requested by the local population, careful assessments should be carried out to understand and avoid other potential negative effects.

There are also a number of interesting examples of a new use being found for an abandoned mine that has significantly enhanced biodiversity and local livelihoods. These include the BHP Billiton mine in the Cape in South Africa, where the company has supported the opening of the 700-hectare West Coast Fossil Park with both fossils and wildlife to attract tourists.[83] In Cornwall in the UK, a former china clay quarry is now the site of the spectacular Eden Project, which includes one of the world's largest greenhouses.[84] Other good examples of mine closure include rehabilitation of the bauxite mines in Western Australia by Alcoa, which was listed on UNEP's Global 500 Roll of Honour for its achievements.[85]

Managing Biodiversity

Some of the larger mining companies have begun to take steps towards addressing biodiversity issues. Many have formulated biodiversity policies; some have followed this up with innovative actions within planning, design, and operating management. (See Box 10–15.) Evidence of such remedial actions is encouraging, but still they remain largely restricted to a few major players, and even within this group, some are doing much more than others. Adopting 'biodiversity-friendly' practices remains hugely challenging, especially for smaller companies and peripheral players. This is partly because governments, while perhaps committed on paper to biodiversity, have found it difficult to create the incentives and apply the necessary regulations that could encourage all players, from the individual miner to the large company and the other economic sectors, to conserve biodiversity.

Box 10–15. Balancing Biodiversity Conservation with Economic Development

Since 1986, Rio Tinto and its subsidiary QIT Madagascar Minerals S.A. (QMM) have been assessing the potential for a 50–60 year ilmenite (titanium dioxide) mine near Fort Dauphin in southeastern Madagascar. The project is potentially the most important in the industrial history of the island – a US$350-million investment with US$20 million in annual revenue predicted for the state, including mining royalties, of which 70% is to be returned to the region. Together with the possible 30% local employment commitment, it appears that the project has the potential to bring some economic benefits to the region.

However, the mineral deposit is located on or near remnant fragments of a unique littoral ecosystem that contains several endemic species. Elsewhere, these forests have been largely degraded or removed, so the sections, while patchy, have gained conservationists' attention. They raised serious concerns about the proposed mine, and requested a two-year moratorium during which alternative development options, such as eco-tourism, were to be explored. But no significant eco-tourism developments materialized.

QMM commissioned a team of specialists to undertake various social and environmental baseline studies – perhaps one of the lengthiest such exercises ever conducted in the mining industry. This information was summarized and presented as a social and environmental impact assessment (SEIA). Some of the basic assumptions in the SEIA have been questioned, however – such as the speed at which forest will be depleted. Conservation International believes that a significant slowing of forest reduction could also be achieved in the absence of the mine. Overall, however, the SEIA has certainly covered new ground in linking both social and environmental issues, and in tackling biodiversity issues explicitly.

The SEIA concluded that the forest fragments are already under pressure for charcoal and building materials, and that given current depletion rates, and without any new planting of fast-growing species, the remaining forest would be destroyed within the next 20–40 years. These facts and predictions were key in the pro-mining argument – that is, that the forests would disappear anyway and the mine could help reduce local dependence on forest resources. QMM has proposed various activities that would help offset further impacts, such as planting of various fast-growing species to provide a sustainable alternative source of fuel and timber. Various tests have been conducted to identify the most suitable species, as there are distinct ecological constraints, such as the thin and fragile topsoil, as well as social challenges regarding the management

---

of these forests. QMM also intends to protect almost 1000 hectares of littoral forest remnants in three or four conservation blocks, rehabilitate all wetland areas and about 600 hectares of native forest, and establish monitoring procedures for the forest. These are encouraging steps, but while the plantations are likely to offset some of the demands it is unlikely that, given the intense pressures, they can offset them all. Additional planting, in concert with governmental efforts to tackle root causes of forest loss, will be necessary for more lasting and widespread success.

Some observers continue to believe mining is simply not a viable option here, so all mitigation attempts will be inappropriate. The social and environmental plans are ambitious and the constraining factors great. If the mine goes ahead – currently it is in its feasibility study stage – there is no guarantee that they can be overcome. QMM intends to invest in a Regional Planning Process, but, as experience from all over the world shows, these do not always meet their original expectations. However, QMM seems determined to try and get it right. Their significant social and environmental investment in the project seems to be indicative of a genuine intention to implement a considered and responsible project. If the mine does go ahead, it should provide some valuable lessons and, if the various programmes are successful, perhaps it will set some precedents for other companies.

Sources: QMM S.A. (2001); Porter et al. (2001); Nostromo Research (2001)

In principle, mining companies should be operating according to planning decisions and biodiversity criteria set by governments and should be monitored by appropriate agencies. In practice, few governments – especially in developing countries – have the necessary capacity, even though they may have ratified the CBD and developed a National Biodiversity Action Plan. The onus falls instead either on the companies themselves or on conservation organizations. It is therefore far too easy for companies and organizations to exploit this vacuum and implement measures they consider best fit.

In some cases governments have introduced appropriate laws and regulations but have not enforced them because they have no capacity to do so. Despite various biodiversity planning processes required under the CBD, there is frequently insufficient information on the status of biodiversity on the ground. As a result, they find it difficult to make informed decisions on trade-offs – on alternative uses for the same land.

But there are also issues of power balance within administrations. Since the extractive industries bring in revenue and employment, the voices in the Ministry of Mines arguing for mining are usually stronger than those in other ministries arguing for the protection of biodiversity. For this to change, there needs to be much stronger incentive to act on biodiversity, which often means additional financial resources.

One area causing great concern is the weakness of environmental impact assessments. As indicated earlier, these are now required for most large-scale industrial projects, including mining. But they generally afford doubtful protection – using the term 'biodiversity' very loosely and giving little indication of how it is to be interpreted. The recent report commissioned by the International Association of Impact Assessment has gone some way towards addressing the integration of biodiversity into EIA systems, but further work is needed.[86] Often the EIA is not carried out until after detailed exploration or even development drilling, by which time the site can be covered by a network of roads, making it impossible to establish true baseline data. It is essential that at least rapid biodiversity surveys be carried out prior to this stage.[87] Clearer international standards for EIA practice need to be developed in a variety of areas to begin to make EIA a more effective tool of environmental management.

The weakness of governments tends to put the burden for managing biodiversity on NGOs and particularly on international conservation organizations. While these may act as a line of defence for biodiversity, they cannot really claim to act on behalf of civil society in general, especially when they are based in industrial countries. NGOs often claim to speak 'on behalf of' those who will suffer from a loss of biodiversity, in much the same way that companies will speak 'on behalf of' those who have most to gain economically. Thus far, unfortunately, there have been too few well-informed and empowered local organizations willing or able to take appropriate decisions.

Recommendations on Biological Diversity
These recommendations are based on discussions at two MMSD Mining and Biodiversity Workshops in October and June 2000:[88]

- *Strengthen government capacity to manage biodiversity, especially in developing countries* – The CBD presents a challenging agenda for action, especially in terms of managing the trade-offs between poverty reduction and biodiversity conservation. At the national level, the CBD should provide the necessary framework within which economic sectors could operate. However, more resources and a strong political commitment are needed if enabling policy, institutional, and regulatory mechanisms are to be developed successfully. Without strong government inputs, governance falls to the private sector or NGOs.

- *Develop tools for more inclusive and integrated land use planning, especially in developing countries* – Rigorous analytical tools for weighing up the social, ecological, and economic costs and benefits of different land use options and for arrangements that support participatory decision-making processes on land use need to be developed to support better-informed and more inclusive decision-making processes. This work should also build on existing relevant concepts, such as UNESCO's Man and Biosphere Reserve or the Ecosystem Approach of the CBD. Tools development must happen in parallel with strengthening the capacity of and incentives for developing-country governments and civil society groups to participate in land use planning. (See also Chapter 7.)

- *Address funding shortfalls for biophysical science* – If rigorous decision-making on biodiversity and conservation is to continue, and if conflicts are to be minimized, governments – especially in industrial countries – must acknowledge true responsibility in this scientific area. There are many opportunities for mining companies (and the private sector in general) to stimulate and contribute towards research partnerships on biodiversity conservation, such as through contributing to taxonomy in remote areas. But private funding alone cannot solve the rapid decline in independent scientific capacity – hence the urgent call to governments to reverse this decline.

- *Improve access and coherence of information on biodiversity priorities* – Relevant conservation organizations, academic institutions, the mining industry, and other key sectors (such as energy) need to work towards establishing user-friendly, regularly updated and linked information systems on global and local biodiversity priority areas as a matter of priority. Holding a workshop on 'Information for Conservation' could be a first step forward. In order to improve coherence, it is particularly important to

achieve some level of consensus between specialists on which proxies are best used for biodiversity, and why. Such work could also feed into biodiversity indicators development for EIA.

- *Articulate and enhance biodiversity better practice within the mining industry* – There have been no industry-wide attempts to articulate the industry's biodiversity principles. The mining companies, through ICMM and in collaboration with conservation specialists and organizations representing local community interests, should work towards producing a series of guiding principles on mining and biodiversity for the different stages of the mine cycle, along with appropriate training manuals. This could involve, among other things, multistakeholder reviews of better practice, workshops, and lessons learnt analyses from existing cases. If considered appropriate, such principles could eventually become 'codes of practice'.

The Way Forward

All the environmental issues raised in this chapter pose complex problems that test the capacities of mining companies, governments, NGOs, and civil society. This is partly because of the inherent complexity of technical and ecological processes whose outcomes are difficult to predict. It includes envisaging the quality of water in a lake that will not be filled for decades, for example, or the likely stability of a tailings storage facility in the event of a once-in-a-lifetime storm or seismic event. Some of them also require close attention over a long period of time; something it is hard for any organization to achieve.

Companies can help strengthen society's ability to solve environmental problems of all kinds. For example, mining company expertise in the rehabilitation of disturbed lands has often been useful to other industries with less experience. Companies can support capacity building on environmental issues by providing access to information and the funds to make this information more readily available, by supporting stronger school and university curricula and helping educate their own future employees, and by developing important new skills and perspectives in their current managers, professionals, and workers.

This chapter has focused on a series of priority environmental areas for the minerals sector. They are not the only ones, but they are among the most pressing – and the ones where the consequences are greatest. Industry is not yet at the point of providing a net positive contribution to the natural capital, whatever its contribution to other forms of capital. There is, however, undoubted progress towards better recognition of environmental problems and their effective management.

There are some clear dilemmas. Employment in the sector, especially in mining, is highest in smaller enterprises, which are financially the weakest and often have the least capacity to deal with complex new and continuing challenges. There is a concern that pressure for environmental progress may threaten a large number of livelihoods. Those whose livelihoods are threatened will not receive the environmental message well if they see it as unsympathetic to their problems and hostile to their immediate and long-term interests. The only way they are likely to embrace change is if it is coupled with opportunity. Perhaps this is an affirmation of the principles of sustainable development: there will be little progress in one dimension unless there is progress in all.

Another dilemma is that of the level playing field. Resistance to taking on greater environmental costs is much less when companies perceive that everyone is taking on the same costs. On the other hand, when they are selling in a global market, the requirement for cost internalization for everyone is a daunting task. All companies need to face consistent guidelines for environmental management if the mining industry is to avoid a 'race to the bottom'.

It is important to acknowledge that not all governments are ready to promote the more stringent environmental management of the industry. In poorer countries, governments may have other priorities and may fear that higher standards (and direct costs) may drive the industry away. In many cases progress towards better environmental management is at a rate that the economy can absorb or is instigated by international loans or aid.

Governments of industrial countries where mining takes place generally have sophisticated regulatory systems that can cover most eventualities, or they can draw on extensive local expertise as required. But the situation is quite different in developing countries, where small and overstretched government departments can be called on to make rapid decisions

Thlaspi caerulescens, a hyperaccumulator of zinc, nickel and cadmium, growing on zinc mine waste in Belgium. Shoots can contain up to 5% zinc

on the basis of relatively little information or technical knowledge. To help fill that gap, MMSD proposes the establishment of a Sustainable Development Support Facility to provide technical support, on request, to governments, insurers, lenders, or companies in order to help them build their capacity and to ensure that there is a viable, meaningful system of external inspection and the resources to fund it. This facility can be used as a source of information and advice on such issues as:

- integrating the local community and civil society into decision-making,
- development of detailed technical criteria for EIAs and supporting studies,
- the review and approval of designs for tailings storage facilities,
- inspections of tailings facilities,
- prediction and control of acid drainage,
- development of standards and procedures for mine closure planning,
- risk assessment and emergency responses,
- development of techniques to survey abandoned mines and set priorities on remediation, and
- rehabilitation plans for abandoned mine sites.

Details of the proposed Sustainable Development Support Facility are provided in Chapter 14.

It is also important to address the problem of how to manage exploration better, most especially how to deal with the in-rush of exploration companies (or sometimes artisanal miners) when an area suddenly becomes 'hot'. A great deal of damage can be done to biodiversity and other values before there is a proposal to mine anything, or even where no mining ever occurs. Examining how to undertake exploration effectively should be a focus for research funding. Perhaps industry associations in the countries important in exploration, and those governments, could take a lead in the establishment of a modest research project to better understand some of the more well-known case studies.

Endnotes

[1] UNDP/UNEP/World Bank/WRI (2000) p.389.

[2] Pearce et al. (1994).

[3] Centro de Estudios y Proyectos SRL and Netherlands Embassy (1999).

[4] See http://www.cyanidecode.org.

[5] Ashton et al. (2001).

[6] All of this material is collected in Van Zyl et al. (2002), which covers many of these issues in more detail than space here allows.

[7] Phelps (2000).

[8] Van Zyl et al. (2002).

[9] Mokopanele (2001).

[10] Cale (1997).

[11] Mitchell (2000).

[12] Ashton et al. (2001).

[13] Mitchell (2000).

[14] Ashton et al. (2001).

[15] See for example Ashton et al. (2001) p.308.

[16] Mitchell (2000).

[17] Colorado School of Mines website, at http://www.mines.edu/fs_home/jhoran/ch126/amd.htm.

[18] Details of these initiatives are provided in Van Zyl et al. (2002), at http://www.mend2000@gc.ca, and at http://www.inap.com.au.

[19] UNEP (1996).

[20] Martin et al. (2001); see also Mining Association of Canada (1998).

[21] UNEP (2000).

[22] ICOLD (2001).

[23] Richards (2000).

[24] Ibid.

[25] Castillo (1998).

[26] In 1972, at Buffalo Creek, West Virginia, in the United States, 125 people died in a coal waste rock failure. See Antenna website at http://www.antenna.nl/wise/uranium/mdaf.html.

[27] Martin et al. (2001).

[28] Ibid.

[29] ICOLD (2001).

[30] Martin et al. (2001).

[31] Ellis et al. (1995).

[32] NSR Consultants (2001) Overview of Deep Sea Tailing Placement for BHP Minerals.

[33] Data from the Newmont website at http://www.newmont-indonesiaoperations.com/html/environmental_issues_nmr.html.

[34] Data from http://www.jatam.org/std/inggris/english.html.

[35] Ellis and Robertson (1999).

[36] Grassle (1991).

[37] Van Zyl et al. (2001).

[38] Sassoon (2000) pp.108–09.

[39] Castilla (1983).

[40] Ricks (1994).

[41] The Summitville mine closed on less than a week's notice. The company declared bankruptcy (leaving unpaid a large local tax bill), laid off the workers, and stopped vital environmental maintenance at the mine.

[42] Danielson and Nixon (2000).

[43] Miller (1998).

[44] UNEP/Standard Bank (2002) p.46.

[45] Lyon et al. (1993).

[46] Sol et al. (1999).

[47] See, for example, Ashton et al. (2001).

[48] Bob Fox, of US EPA Montana, personnel communication, January 2002.

[49] Mineral Policy Center (1993).

[50] UNEP (2001).

[51] Houghton et al. (2001).

[52] Lovins et al. (2002).

[53] IEA (2001).

[54] According to the World Commission on Dams (2000), significant greenhouse emissions may also arise from reservoirs associated with hydroelectric power plant.

[55] ICF (2000) p.78.

[56] Ibid.

[57] Lovins et al. (2002).

[58] Ibid.

[59] International Programme on Chemical Safety (1992).

[60] International Programme on Chemical Safety (1990).

[61] Thornton (1995) p.103.

[62] Lacerda and Salomons (1998).

[63] Roulet et al. (1999)

[64] Nriagu (1996).

[65] Nriagu and Pacyna (1988).

[66] Pacyna and Pacyna (2001).

[67] MMSD Southern Africa (2001).

[68] Compliance Advisor Ombudsman (2000) p.57.

[69] See http://www.zinc-health.org or http://www.izincg.ucdavis.edu.

[70] Convention on Biological Diversity (1992).

[71] Koziell (2001).

[72] IIED (1994).

[73] A recent mapping exercise by Conservation International indicated that areas where mining and mineral exploration are active and where mineral potential is highest show a high degree of overlap with those areas where biodiversity 'value', however defined, is considered greatest.

[74] Hotspots are areas characterized by both high levels of endemism and high levels of threat; see Myers et al. (2000). Endemic bird areas contain two bird species that have a breeding range of less than 50,000 sq. km; see ICBP (1992). Ecoregions are large units of land or water with distinct climate, ecological features, and plant and animal communities. They are considered to be some of the richest, rarest, and most endangered areas, and hence of critical conservation concern; see http://nationalgeographic.com/wildworld (a WWF initiative called Global 200).

[75] Vermuelen and Koziell (forthcoming).

[76] May (1998).

[77] Leigh and Briggs (1992).

[78] IUCN (2002).

[79] Rosenfeld Sweeting and Clarke (2000); IUCN and WWF (1999); Lloyd et al. (in prep.); Minerals Policy Center (1997). See also Cooke (1999).

[80] IUCN, UNESCO World Heritage Centre, and ICME (2001).

[81] See http://ceres.ca.gov/biodiv/newsletter/v2n4/mining_company_reclaims_biodiversity.html.

[82] Jenkin (2000).

[83] See http://www.billiton.com/newsite/html/annual/98/HSEPolicy.htm and http://www.indabadailynews.co.za/tuesday/article04.html.

[84] See http://www.edenproject.com/.

[85] See http://www.alcoa.com.au/environment/miner.shtml.

[86] The International Association of Impact Assessment has developed a Proposed Conceptual and Procedural Framework for the Integration of Biological Diversity Considerations within National Systems for Impact Assessment.

[87] See outputs of workshop held in Gland: International Union for the Conservation of Nature, UNESCO World Heritage Centre, and International Council on Metals and the Environment (2000).

[88] See the minutes on the CD-ROM accompanying this report.

AN INTEGRATED APPROACH TO USING MINERALS

For the minerals sector to contribute fully to sustainable development, the use of its products must be considered along with mining, mineral, and metal processing activities.[1] *Agenda 21*, the blueprint for action agreed to at the Earth Summit in 1992, acknowledged the importance of taking the whole product life cycle into account. It drew attention to the need to focus public policy on 'the demand for natural resources…and…the efficient use of those resources consistent with the goal of minimizing depletion and reducing pollution'.[2] In the mining and minerals sector, taking such a 'cradle to grave' approach is particularly challenging because there is little connection between the production and use of mineral commodities. Even if mineral users realize that the material in their hands originated in a mine, they are generally unaware of its geographical origin or how it became incorporated into a product. The diversity of the sector – as well as the vast and ever-increasing range of applications for mineral commodities – adds to this challenge. (See Chapter 2.)

Like other stages along the minerals cycle, the use of mineral commodities has implications for the economic, social, and environmental dimensions of sustainable development. These materials play an important role in meeting basic human needs and in enabling modern society to function effectively (see Chapter 4), but as noted throughout this report, there are environmental costs or health risks associated with their use.

Until now, much of the concern, policy, and regulation regarding the use of mineral commodities has focused on environmental issues, on health risks associated with use, and on physical measures of the long-run availability of mineral resources. A number of conceptual tools aimed at increasing the efficiency of minerals use and calculating optimal levels of use have been developed to this end. But the social and economic dimensions of current use and of potential future changes are generally not given equal consideration. An integrated or life-cycle approach to using minerals includes all dimensions of sustainable development. This is a particular challenge for the whole minerals sector, including mining companies. A PricewaterhouseCoopers survey of 32 mining companies undertaken for MMSD found that only 68% of respondents suggested that life-cycle issues were part of their company's understanding of sustainable development. (In contrast, 97% of them

considered the impact of mining on people and local communities to be part of sustainable development.)[3]

To ensure that the level and patterns of use of mineral commodities are better aligned with sustainable development, stronger linkages need to be made between production and use. Integrated approaches – including market-based instruments, appropriate regulation, and more effective supply chain management – are key to this. Responsibilities for reducing the negative impacts as well as associated costs need to be shared among actors and along the value chain (all the activities in the minerals cycle). This applies to costs incurred not just in use but throughout the whole chain.

To address concerns about equity of access to mineral resources, 'wasteful' use, and environmental impacts, the use of primary sources of mineral commodities must be managed more effectively through, for example, recycling, better product design, and re-manufacture. Yet decisions to reduce dependence on primary sources (those produced from the natural resource stock) need to consider the impacts on, for instance, people whose livelihoods depend on extracting such resources.

The environmental and health impacts of the use of different mineral products need to be understood. Responsibilities for this can again be better apportioned in the context of a life-cycle approach. Where mineral products have potential risks associated with their use, the precautionary principle should apply.

Connecting Production with Use

Despite the strength of opinion concerning the performance of the mining and mineral processing industry, most people have little or no idea about the origin of mineral-related materials or how they are produced. Environmentally motivated consumers who buy a new vehicle or electrical appliance are more likely to be interested in energy efficiency and pollution potential than in any effects of resource extraction. This bias is reflected in eco-labelling schemes for products containing metals, such as refrigerators and washing machines, as the labels (perhaps sensibly) tend to concentrate on energy efficiency.

Traditionally, mining companies have been separated from direct contact with intermediate and final consumers by the way in which mineral commodities are traded. (See Chapter 2.) Attempts to address this have started through dialogue initiated by various commodity associations with companies downstream in the value chain. But from the perspective of the user, most mineral commodities are at least as anonymous as other materials, including glass and plastics. The contrast between the mineral and oil industries is striking. Unlike the former, the fuel products of the latter are usually associated with a logo that is identifiable all the way back to exploration. The metals in many products are likely to originate from numerous parts of the world, often remote from where they are used. And one product or batch of products could include metals from many different mining operations as well as from recycled sources. For most products, minerals from different sources can be used interchangeably. Furthermore, mineral-related materials often form a small, albeit important, component of the finished product. The product itself has impacts (such as through energy use) that may be greater and easier to quantify than those at the point of mineral production.

Although the value chain for locally traded mineral products may not be as complex as globally traded ones, even at this scale there are often multiple suppliers and a mixing of materials from different sources. The main exception to this is where quarrying is undertaken to develop a particular item of infrastructure, such as a road or railway.

Supply Chain Management
The link between the production and use of mineral commodities can be improved through more effective management of the supply chain (the parts of the value chain upstream of the operation under consideration). Strengthening the relationships among companies within the chain can help one company exert influence on others or improve business practices between them and thus reduce negative effects.

The need to address the connections among firms is increased by the current trend to outsource jobs as a means of reducing costs, which gives rise to increasingly complex interdependencies between firms. Globalization is also leading to new relationships among companies in any one supply chain.[4] In the last decade, there have been numerous cases of companies

Innovative incentives are required to encourage better recycling

exerting pressure on upstream suppliers of materials to improve performance. Examples include the environmental and social standards set by large buyers of forest products and textiles.[5]

The introduction of such supply-chain measures flows in part from the growing need for companies close to the consumer to take responsibility for both upstream and downstream impacts. The management of downstream impacts – embodied in the notion of extended producer responsibility – has been driven in part by 'take-back' and other environmental legislation.

Until recently, most manufacturers were concerned largely only with the environmental performance of their most immediate suppliers rather than conditions of supply further up the chain. However, two recent high-profile campaigns have raised awareness about the conditions of extraction in certain locations that has led to pressure on producers to certify the origin of their raw materials.

Concerns about coltan mining in the Democratic Republic of Congo (DRC), including the financing of armed conflict in the region, the harm being inflicted on protected areas and on certain animal species, and the health impacts of extraction, have led to the World Conservation Union and other groups calling for buyers to avoid this source.[6] Even though DRC is a relatively small source of tantalum, distinguishing coltan from this source has become important for many actors along the value chain.

Similarly, concern over the use of diamonds to finance the activities of various rebel movements in countries such as Sierra Leone and Angola has led other diamond producers and manufacturers, with assistance from third parties, to certify the origin of their diamonds. (See Box 11–1.)

These cases also demonstrate how the reputation of one part of the value chain can become tarnished by the action of another. What remains to be established is the extent to which this type of pressure could work for mineral commodities more broadly. For example, the Kimberley Process for diamond certification relates to armed conflict in a specific region and not the whole process of diamond production. In addition, the non-industrial uses of diamonds are associated with strong emotions that are not found concerning many other mineral commodities. Currently, there is no commonly accepted system for manufacturers and other users of mineral-related materials to assess the overall performance of the mining and processing stages. This is partly because impacts of different mineral reserves or means of production are hard to describe, much less measure. Although it is difficult to trace a mineral from a particular mine through to the shop shelf, interest is gathering in the potential for a more broad-reaching system of verification for the minerals sector, similar to schemes in other sectors. In the forestry sector, for example, the certification schemes administered by the Forest Stewardship Council (FSC) and others have been adopted by a number of buyers as a requirement for doing business.[7]

A number of ways of managing the supply chain are being developed for the minerals sector at the regional or company level. This includes models being developed by universities and other organizations to help companies manage supply chains so as to reduce overall the environmental impacts of their products. In Australia, the World Wide Fund for Nature is building on its experience with the FSC and investigating the feasibility of a system of independent certification on the environmental and social management performance of mine sites in the South Pacific.[8] Certification can help reassure downstream users that a certain standard is being met, or can distinguish between different levels of performance. Still, there remain considerable challenges in applying this to the complex and diverse supply chains for mineral commodities. At the same time, it should be noted that some companies are already attempting to distinguish their mineral products on environmental criteria: in

Box 11–1. Evolution of a Diamond Certification System

Certification schemes are increasingly being developed and used to secure 'a chain of custody' between producer and final end-use markets. In the diamond industry, certification has been introduced to deal with the problem of conflict diamonds to ensure a system is in place that can audit and verify by country of origin the passage of diamonds from mine extraction through to their entry into the legitimate diamond economy.

Growing concern over the links between armed conflict and the diamond trade has led to an emerging consensus among governments, non-governmental organizations (NGOs), the UN, and the industry about the need to introduce a coordinated system of regulation and self-regulation to address this problem. The Kimberley process embodies this approach by seeking to establish a minimum level of acceptable international standards for national certification schemes for the import and export of rough diamonds. It also aims to systematize the exchange of information on transactions between importers and exporters.

Specifically, the proposed scheme involves:

- a certificate of origin for each shipment of rough diamonds, with agreed minimum standards of information present;
- an accredited office to handle the import and export of rough diamonds;
- internal regulatory controls designed to eliminate the presence of conflict diamonds;
- the establishment of an international statistical database recording and analysing the production, export, and import data for rough diamonds;
- the establishment of a Kimberley Process Secretariat;
- the establishment of an effective monitoring mechanism; and
- the issuing of warranties by the diamond trade that are independently verified by auditors with government oversight.

While measures like these to distinguish legitimate stones and prevent the illegal diamond trade are widely endorsed, including a recent Conflict Diamond Bill passed by the US House of Representatives in December 2001, questions remain over the efficacy of such measures to combat illicit diamond smuggling and the strength of compliance, verification, and monitoring systems. There are also concerns over the ability to implement a workable system that takes into account the different control and export regimes of producer countries. Though some issues must still be resolved, it is hoped that the process will be launched in November 2002. Following further endorsement by the UN General Assembly, it is proposed that the agreement be strengthened through a UN Security Council resolution in 2003.

Source: Personal communication, Alex Yearsley, Global Witness, February 2002; Global Witness (2000); MMSD (2001e)

Brazil, the Plantar company is promoting 'green' pig iron smelted with charcoal originating from forests certified by the FSC.[9]

The complexity of the value chains for mineral commodities may mean that in many cases pressure for performance verification from institutions financing mining operations will prove more effective than downstream supply pressures. (See Chapter 6.)

There are additional challenges associated with using supply chain pressures to drive environmental or social improvements in the sector:

- Standards set by large multinational companies and their customers may not be sensitive to the interests of smaller producers or their ability to conform. The setting of standards may therefore have a negative impact on small producers by excluding them from certain markets.[10]
- Dialogue will need to be developed among groups that may traditionally have regarded themselves as remote from one another along the value chain.
- There is also a need to share the costs and benefits of improved performance. In the timber sector, for example, it has often been those at the beginning of the value chain that bear the cost of improvements, while buyers reap the financial benefits.[11]

Product Stewardship
The term 'product stewardship' describes the shared responsibility that those with control over the life cycle of a product – including producers, manufacturers, retailers, users, recyclers, and waste managers – have for any costs associated with negative impacts and for reducing these impacts. Product stewardship is borne of the belief that without serious commitment from parts of the value chain, significant progress cannot be made towards managing products in accordance with sustainable development.[12] This overlaps with the notion of 'extended producer responsibility', which so far has been largely focused on the responsibilities of individual manufacturers for products at the end of their life.[13] This provides a useful way for government and other actors to devise tools and incentives and to assign responsibilities for waste prevention and appropriate product design, and to further encourage recycling, re-manufacture, or re-use.[14]

To date, product stewardship initiatives undertaken by companies producing or using mineral commodities have focused mainly on the end of a product's life. (See Box 11–2.)

Box 11–2. Examples of Product Stewardship Activities

Collect NiCad is a non-profit association that represents European producers and importers of nickel-cadmium batteries as well as manufacturers that use batteries in their products. Collect NiCad runs a scheme to support and promote the development of collection and recycling programmes for spent batteries as an alternative to disposal in landfills. This involves collection of data on battery recycling and research on economic instruments to achieve better recovery rates. The work of Collect NiCad contributed to the recovery of 521 tonnes of the 1994 tonnes of cadmium used in Western Europe in 2000 (representing over 340 million batteries).

Collect NiCad hopes that its success will stop a proposal to ban NiCad batteries within the European Union (EU) by 2008. The scheme also hopes to benefit from the proposed Waste Electronic and Electrical Equipment Directive in Europe, which will make it easier to collect batteries from electronic products.

In resource efficiency terms, the main benefit of the scheme is the increased responsibility of industry for take-back, which should encourage innovation in battery design, collection, and recycling. On the other hand, it is important that the capacity to recycle is not used as the sole basis for decisions that simply increase the number of batteries in use without taking into account other environmental effects and alternative materials.

A similar initiative is managed by industry through the Rechargeable Battery Recycling Corporation in the United States and the Battery Association of Japan.

In 1984, Canadian-based metal producer Noranda acquired Micro Metallics Corporation (MMC), a supplier of recyclable materials based in San Jose, California. MMC offers secure processing of high-grade electronic scrap, including scrap from production of integrated circuits, circuit boards, and components salvaged from end-of-life electronic equipment. Noranda subsequently built a similar facility in East Providence, Rhode Island.

Noranda started a strategic alliance with global IT company Hewlett-Packard (HP). HP was a pioneer in asset recovery from obsolete electronic products but was unable to achieve an ambitious goal of eliminating waste. HP and MMC have worked since 1997 to increase materials recovery, expand the volume of material processed, and reduce costs at an HP facility in Roseville, California, that is now operated by MMC. HP sources material resulting from its own production processes and markets recovered components, while MMC sources external feeds and markets recovered materials. The Roseville facility extends Noranda's recycling activities to include a wide range of end-of-life electronic products. The cost of processing the low-grade mixture of metallic and non-metallic materials still exceeds the value of the recovered materials. Noranda smelts the copper and precious metals fraction in Canada. All other materials recovered are sold in the US.

In 2001, HP launched its Planet Partners programme, offering a recycling service to all US consumers of HP or other electronic products. HP and Noranda built a facility for this in LaVergne, Tennessee.

Source: http://www.collectnicad.org/index_flash.html; personal communication, L. Surges, Noranda

Mineral commodity associations have begun to encourage dialogue among companies along the value chain with the aim of improving product stewardship, including health and safety concerns about production processes. They have played a role in facilitating the exchange of information on good practice. In addition, several of them are working to assess the implications for human health of the use of certain mineral commodities. For instance, the Nickel Development Institute and the Nickel Producers Environmental Research Association are working with other organizations to increase understanding of the allergic contact dermatitis that is associated with prolonged skin contact with certain nickel-containing products.

Through engagement with stakeholders from outside industry, the Non-Ferrous Metals Consultative Forum on Sustainable Development is working towards more effective stewardship of this group of metals and their uses. (See Box 11–3.) Although the product stewardship activities of the forum are currently general in scope, the effective implementation of these suggestions presents a considerable challenge for all involved in the life cycle of non-ferrous metal products. The forum is seeking to identify real product stewardship issues to be resolved and to work towards addressing these on a pilot basis. Similar processes are needed to encourage and understand the implications of product stewardship for other mineral commodities.

Box 11–3. Non-Ferrous Metals Consultative Forum on Sustainable Development

In September 2000, the member countries of three International Non-Ferrous Metals Study Groups organized the first Non-Ferrous Metals Consultative Forum on Sustainable Development. The forum was convened to build on the outcomes of a Workshop on Sustainable Development held in London in November 1999. The workshop had identified the need for activities that promote the production, use, re-use, and recycling of efficient, effective, durable, and environmentally sound materials. The forum then identified action items that could be achieved with support from governments, multilateral institutions, industry, and NGOs. Participants were given the task of developing the components of an action plan and its implementation, for consideration by member countries of the Study Groups and others. The plan included product stewardship programmes for non-ferrous metals, the promotion of recycling by better design of products and collection schemes, product design to ensure correct use and lowest risk of harm to human health or the environment, and open and transparent mechanisms to improve communication among stakeholders.

To address these and other issues, three multistakeholder Working Groups were established:
- Production of Non-Ferrous Metals (addressing sustainable development drivers and community engagement);
- Product Stewardship (addressing a product stewardship scheme for the non-ferrous metals industry and recycling technology transfer); and
- Science, Research, and Development (addressing sustainable development initiatives, risk assessment, life-cycle assessment, and science networking).

Each Working Group is co-chaired by representatives from government, industry, and civil society. Secretariat support is provided by the Study Groups. Currently, 13 countries (including the EU), 15 industry associations, 25 companies, 15 NGOs and academics, and 3 international organizations are actively participating in the groups.

Source: http://www.nfmsd.org

To arrive at a balanced system, industry must also extend product stewardship principles to include choices between materials, including from where and how they are obtained. Information needs to be freely available to interested parties in a way that allows dialogue and feedback. (The need for reporting is discussed in Chapter 12.)

Life-Cycle Assessment

Life-cycle assessment (LCA) involves measurement and appraisal of the environmental impacts of products from the beginning to the end of their life. It is a tool for supporting decisions concerning the reduction of these impacts and making them more transparent. LCA has been developed and promoted by the UN Environment Programme/Society for Environmental Toxicology and Chemistry (UNEP/SETAC) Life Cycle Initiative, and the methods involved have been standardized under the ISO 14000 series.[15]

LCA use has been motivated by three main drivers thus far. One has been public policy, requiring firms to assess their products or to justify the materials and production processes that they use. The second pressure has come from market competition in cases where substitution between materials has been possible. Third has been companies seeking to improve the efficiency and reduce the environmental impacts of their production processes. As a result, LCA methodology is increasingly being used by some firms and trade associations. Evaluation of the quality and scope of these is, however, difficult because the information is not always readily available to the public.

These pressures are likely to increase in the future and to lead to the integration of decisions about the use and means of production of mineral products. LCA also has a wide set of broader potential applications, including helping governments to develop product-related policy and assisting NGOs concerned with the social and economic impacts of products and the materials and methods by which they are made.

At an MMSD Workshop on LCA held in New York in August 2001, a number of possible uses of LCA for the minerals sector were considered: [16]
- to look at the environmental impacts in both mineral-producing and mineral-using economies, including the differences in the environmental burdens carried by industrial and developing countries;
- to help metal fabricators and manufacturers using mineral commodities understand the life cycle of mined products;
- to enhance the quality of supply chain management;
- to aid policy development, such as the Integrated Product Policy proposed by the European Union;[17]
- to support recycling initiatives, including the siting

of facilities such as secondary smelters; and
- to determine which ore body to exploit using which technology.

The MMSD workshop identified several challenges that must be overcome, however, in applying LCA to minerals and mineral-related commodities if it is to be an effective tool. First, although LCA is based on scientific understanding, it incorporates a number of value judgements. For example, the selection of environmental impact parameters to be considered will affect the assessment of the product or process. For minerals and metals, there is uncertainty over the specification and integration of impact categories, the relative importance of different environmental impacts, and the boundaries of impacts over both time and space. Metals do not degrade, for example, so it is not appropriate to express the eco-toxicity of metals in terms of persistence, which is how a standard LCA works. A further constraint is that eco-toxicity is highly dependent on metal specification, but LCAs often provide just a total emission (not differentiating between, for example, metallic and organically bound metal with different toxicities). The International Council on Mining & Metals (ICMM) is starting work with UNEP/SETAC and other organizations on improving the LCA methodologies related to metals.

A second set of difficulties relates to the lack of information and data available to undertake a mineral-specific LCA. This is compounded by the complexity of the value chain associated with mineral commodities. Finally, LCA only delivers an understanding of the potential environmental impacts. So for decision-making both within and outside the minerals industry, LCA should be only one component in a 'toolbox' required to make decisions in line with sustainable development objectives. It may be appropriate to assess social and economic impacts alongside an LCA, or after it has been completed.

Much more consideration should be given to the meaningful participation in LCA of all groups with an interest in decision-making about a product, process, or service. This includes those in developing and minerals-producing countries. It should go far beyond being a product defence tool for existing applications of metals, in which internal and non-attributable data are used. LCA calculations must be transparent and incorporate the viewpoints of all stakeholders. When applied to production processes, this tool must not be

---

---

used to unduly favour the modern manufacturing plants in some countries. Economic and social considerations should be taken into account in the wider decision-making process.

LCA can inform policy development and become integral to the regulatory process itself. The notion of integrated product policy involves a shift in emphasis in environmental policy from solely evaluating wastes and emissions during manufacturing to consideration of the total environmental impacts caused by a product. The proposed EU Integrated Product Policy suggests that LCA is one part of the generation and collation of information on the environmental impacts of products. In many cases, it is the use phase of products that is a significant source of impacts.

It has also allowed consideration of the service life of products as well as the extent to which their component materials can be recycled. LCA initiated by industry has improved the quality of information available and thus facilitated a more holistic, realistic view of environmental objectives for sustainable development and the policies to achieve them.

Yet there are reservations about LCA's role in the policy development arena. This is partly because of the lack of consistent methodologies and data sets. But more fundamentally, LCA is a purely environmental decision-making tool, and therefore has only a limited role to play in assessing how a product performs from an integrated sustainable development perspective.

Pricing to Reflect True Costs

In a well-functioning market economy, the price paid for a mineral commodity – as for any other good or service – should reflect the full marginal costs of both production and use. For the minerals sector, as for many others, this is currently not the case. In particular, the prices paid by users of mineral commodities do not reflect the environmental and social costs incurred at all stages of the mineral cycle, including environmental damage and social disruption in mining as well as pollution from processing and waste following use. There are many reasons why markets largely fail to reflect such costs, and many potential responses.[18] Ultimately what is required is a framework of regulations, property rights, liability regimes, and market incentives that will lead producers, traders, and end-users of mineral

commodities to 'internalize' these environmental and social damages in their economic decisions. An important first step is to improve information on the extent and nature of these non-market costs, so that private and public decision-makers can craft appropriate responses.

Sufficiency, Efficiency, and Use

Concerns over Material Throughputs

In recent years, there have been growing calls by environmentalists for a reduction in the material throughputs that are demanded by many national economies, particularly in industrial countries.[19] (See Chapter 2 for data on production and use.) Numerous concepts have been developed in order to highlight current levels of dependence on natural resource throughputs, their link to economic output, and geographical imbalances in resource use. (See Table 11–1.) They apply to products, people, or countries. The statistics that arise from some are striking. For instance, the Wuppertal Institute has estimated that 1kg of copper carries an 'ecological rucksack' of 500kg of natural resources (including water and air) that are used and transformed during its life.[20] Similarly, in order to meet the global environmental and equity targets derived from the concept of environmental space, Friends of the Earth Europe proposes that the use of aluminium (which it classes as a non-renewable raw material) per European resident will need to be cut by 90% over the next half-century.[21] Calls such as this challenge all associated with the mineral cycle: mining and minerals processing companies, governments (in both producing and consuming regions), manufacturers, those involved in the recycling industry, and others.

The measures, principles, and targets in Table 11–1 are mostly based on the view that current levels of dependence on natural resources are – or soon will be – exceeding Earth's carrying capacity in the biophysical sense. For at least some aspects of mining and minerals processing, such as their contribution to climate change, the concern is sufficient to be a matter of government policy. (See Chapter 10.) But other concerns are far more controversial. For example, many argue that the mass of wastes associated with minerals production is not an accurate guide to the resultant environmental effects, as these depend on their characteristics and how they are managed. On the

Table 11–1. Measures, Principles, and Targets for Resource Efficiency That Could be Applied to Mineral Commodities

Name	Origin(s)	Measure
Environmental Space[a]	Friends of the Earth Europe; Wuppertal Institute (Germany)	The amount of natural resources that can be used per capita without exceeding the carrying capacity of the planet or impinging on the rights of all members of present or future generations to have a equitable access to these resources.
Ecological Rucksack	F Schmidt-Bleek, Wuppertal Institute	Total weight of natural material that is disturbed in its natural setting or is 'carried' in order to generate a product, minus the weight of the product itself.
Material Intensity Per Unit Service	F Schmidt-Bleek, Wuppertal Institute	Material input (including that associated with energy transformation) per total unit of services delivered by a product over its useful life span.
Ecological Footprint	W Rees, University of British Columbia (Canada)	The area of land and water required to produce the resources used, and to assimilate the wastes produced, by an individual or population at a specified material standard of living.
Total Material Requirement[b]	World Resources Institute (WRI)	The sum of total material input, including hidden or indirect flows caused by economic activity within a country.
		Principle
The Natural Step	K H Robert and other Swedish scientists	Stability with regard to human influence on the 'ecosphere', fair use of resources with respect to meeting human needs.
		Targets
Environmental Space	Friends of the Earth Europe; Wuppertal Institute	A series of targets for the reduction in resource throughputs (per capita) in Europe, based on the Environmental Space measure, to be achieved by 2010 and 2030.
Factor Four	EU von Weizsäcker (Wuppertal Institute) and A. Lovins	Industrial countries should use energy, water, materials, and mobility four times as efficiently so as to increase wealth in developing countries by a factor of four without additional resource use, and stabilize wealth in industrial countries while reducing resource use by a factor of four.
Factor Ten	F Schmidt-Bleek, Wuppertal Institute	The industrial world must achieve a ten-fold increase in material and energy resource productivity in the next 30–50 years.

[a]Preceded by the 'eco-scope' concept, promoted by the Dutch government and developed by other Dutch organizations.   [b]One of a group of measures for materials cycles developed by World Resources Institute
Source: http://www.foeeurope.org/sustainability/foeapproach/espace/t-frame-espace.htm; http://www.factor10-institute.org; Wackernagel and Rees (1996); Matthews (2000); von Weizsäcker et al. (1997)

other hand, the mass of waste is at least a good indicator for a significant part of the environmental burden (the energy requirement for the excavation, transport, and disposal of the mining wastes).

Targets for resource efficiency are closely related to the vision that there should be reduced dependence on throughputs of materials in the economy, and greater focus on the services that they provide. A Worldwatch Institute publication summarizes this:

Recognizing the problems caused by depending on materials is the first step in making the leap to a rational, sustainable materials economy.... Societies that learn to shed their attachment to things and to focus instead on delivering what people actually need might be remembered 100 years from now as creators of the most durable civilization in history.[22]

Obviously the intensity of use of mineral commodities can change as a result of factors unrelated to resource efficiency.[23] Patterns of use for mineral-related materials depend on the stage of development – particularly in terms of infrastructure requirements. The World Resources Institute has examined materials flows in a group of industrial countries (Netherlands, Japan, Austria, Germany, and the US) over the last 25

years.[24] The results show that overall resource use and outputs of waste to the environment in these countries are increasing in absolute terms. The rate of increase has, however, been less than that of economic growth, due in part to changes in the intensity of use of materials. But WRI's findings do indicate that if impacts are to be reduced, greater efforts towards resource efficiency in industrial countries are required.

Resource efficiency can be increased in numerous ways, some of which may be ranked according to their relative environmental impact.[25] (Table 11–2.) Others, such as substitution between materials, do not fit easily

Table 11–2. A Materials Efficiency Hierarchy Applied to Mineral Commodities

Class	Practice	Benefits	Status with regard to mineral commodities
Recovery	Recycling	Avoids primary resource extraction and associated environmental impacts	Subject of a long-established industry. Dispersion and complexity of old scrap a key limitation. Also price largely determined by that of the equivalent primary material.
Extended Product Life	Product and component re-manufacture	Avoids manufacturing new products and resource use for recycling	Undertaken for some product groups (such as vehicle parts), but re-manufacture for other groups (such as electronics) a key challenge, given the rate of technological change.
	Repair and re-use	More service from each product, reducing resource use per unit of service	
Increased Intensity of Product Use	More intensive product use	Reduces resource use per unit of service	Materials science being used to make products more durable (metals, construction minerals).
	Product sharing/ lending/leasing	Reduces number of items produced and may assist those who could not otherwise afford use of the product	
Avoidance of Use	Product redefinition, service rather than product	Cuts resource use per unit of service	Policies to prevent use for resource efficiency motives largely un-adopted. Some metals banned due to certain views on their inherent toxicity, or the risk of harm associated with their use in products or upon disposal.
	Voluntary simplicity/ self-sufficiency	Avoids product purchase	
	Redesign of systems (buildings, urban planning, transport)	Could eliminate groups of products and wastes	

Source: Adapted from Young (2000)

into this order. But the substitution of one mineral commodity for another is often controversial and must be based on rigorous life-cycle assessment, as well as tools to evaluate the social and economic implications.

In pure resource efficiency terms, the benefits of recycling are clear, as noted by the US Geological Survey: 'One metric tonne of electronic scrap contains more gold than that recovered from 17 tonnes of gold ore.'[26] But across all the metals, recycling may not be the answer. It is important to consider associated costs, such as the environmental costs of transporting recycled products or even, some would argue, the loss of employment in production from avoidance of use.

In effect there are complex trade-offs that have to be weighed together. In the end they can only be resolved by public policy decisions and even then they will be complex because they have implications for the trade rules and international relations. MMSD has not attempted to go into these complex issues in any depth. But some key points have emerged in the MMSD discussions around the issue:

- Mining, minerals processing, metals fabrication, and recycling provide an important source of livelihoods that support whole communities and national economies. They have to be considered in the policy mix.
- Concerns about long-run availability must be dealt with alongside questions of present human need – questions of equity in availability matter. The capacity of the environment to accept wastes is also an important consideration that may increasingly affect decisions on the use of mineral resources. (See Chapter 4.)
- Mandated change – if it is to be enforced (and be enforceable under the current trade rules) – must be implemented over a time frame sufficient to enable producer countries to adapt.
- The use of metals may have implications for the efficiency of other materials and energy use (and vice versa). For instance, reducing the amount of copper used in an electric motor may make it less energy-efficient. (See Box 11–4.) Optimized resource efficiency requires careful analysis.

Given these considerations, it is important to determine how businesses and governments can respond most appropriately to resource efficiency considerations and the associated targets.

> **Box 11–4. Energy Efficiency Linked to Greater Copper Use**
>
> Although electricity suppliers may purchase less copper for generators, this should be more than offset by electricity-saving devices that use more copper. The main opportunities to market more copper to help save electricity include:
>
> - *motors* – the most efficient models use at least 20% more copper per kW than old ones;
> - *interior distribution wiring* – increasing wire diameter cuts resistive losses, so in a new installation the extra copper typically pays for itself in less than a year and it can even make sense to retrofit;
> - *pipes* – since friction falls in a pipe as diameter increases, there is a strong economic incentive to specify larger pipes;
> - *heat exchangers* – increasing the surface area of heat-exchangers also increases capacity; and
> - *lighting* – retrofitting old fluorescent lighting systems with more energy-efficient systems typically involves replacing aluminium with copper wiring.
>
> Source: Lovins et al. (2002)

Business Responses

The overall framework for business responses to concerns about resource efficiency is 'eco-efficiency' – increasing the ratio of economic benefits delivered by a good or service per unit of environmental impact and resource use.[27] The World Business Council for Sustainable Development (WBCSD), which coined this term, has suggested a series of principles for businesses aiming to increase their eco-efficiency. (See Table 11–3.)

The business case for eco-efficiency has been outlined by numerous organizations, including WBCSD, the Rocky Mountain Institute (RMI), and The Natural Step. These groups provide examples of how businesses have succeeded in achieving radically more efficient use of natural resources while maintaining a profit.[28]

RMI has promoted a strategic framework, under the title of 'natural capitalism', of far-reaching innovation.[29] The approach calls for major shifts in business practices so as to acknowledge the true economic value of services derived from the natural environment. The concept is rooted in the notion that the most efficient and therefore profitable industrial processes should be regarded as those that are integrated in a way that has inputs and outputs (including wastes) flowing continuously.

Table 11–3. WBCSD Eco-efficiency Principles, with Key Considerations Regarding Mineral Commodities

Eco-efficiency principle	Key consideration for mineral commodities
Reduce the material intensity of goods and services	The amount of waste material associated with mining and minerals processing is as important a consideration as the amount of material actually used in a product.
Reduce the energy intensity of goods and services	Primary and recycled sources of some mineral commodities require very different amounts of energy; the quantity of energy used should inform decisions on primary versus recycled material. The use of some metals may increase the efficiency of a product by making the product lighter (aluminium versus steel in cars) or more energy-efficient (such as use of more copper in wiring or motors).
Reduce the dispersion of any toxic materials	This should include not only toxic releases associated with product manufacture, use, and disposal but also toxic materials associated with mining and minerals processing operations.
Enhance the 'recyclability' of materials	All metals are 100% recyclable in theory: the key is in the economics of recycling and a thorough assessment of the environmental and social benefits and drawbacks.
Maximize the sustainable use of renewable resources	Although mineral resources are not renewable, metals and other mineral commodities in products are not always easily substitutable with other materials.
Extend the durability of products Increase the service intensity of goods and services	The durability of products can be enhanced by the use of mineral commodities – for example, by means of specialized metal alloys or industrial minerals to coat paper. Durability is not always an appropriate criterion, such as where it decreases the potential for recycling. Instead, durability and service intensity should give priority to the design of products for re-manufacture and easy maintenance.

Source: Principles from WBCSD (1996)

Over the last few decades, competition and other commercial pressures have lead to significant changes in the resource efficiency of products, including the processes by which they are made. In the US, for example, aluminium cans on average now weigh more than 40% less than in 1985.[30] And an office building that needed 100,000 tonnes of steel 30 years ago can now be built with no more than 35,000 tonnes because of improvements in steel technology and architectural design.[31] Efficiency gains have also been made by the development of new materials, including advanced metal alloys. Nonetheless, there are enormous opportunities for improvement.

Government Responses
In 1997, the governments of the world called for consideration of increased resource efficiency by a factor of 4 to 10 over the next two to three decades.[32] Individual governments of some industrial countries have made commitments for resource efficiency in

addition to waste recovery targets. In 2001, the UK government noted that 'greater resource productivity offers significant benefits not only to the environment but also to business. New methods which make use of fewer resources and minimize waste point the way to an economy that will in the future be radically different from the resource intensive, and often hugely wasteful, economies of the past.'[33] Local governments also play a key role in deciding on specific priorities and goals for resource efficiency.

Governments have a role in setting the policy framework within which businesses pursue resource efficiency for mineral commodities. The practice of eco-efficiency can be either facilitated or blocked by the environmental and product policies of national governments. The Organisation for Economic Co-operation and Development (OECD) has assessed the implications of eco-efficiency for national policy among its members and found that policy instruments that increase incentives for firms to identify and act on environmental-commercial synergies are key.[34] Within governments, there is a need for better integration among departments so that appropriate resource efficiency policies can be complementary and effectively implemented.[35]

The introduction of market-based instruments can provide an effective and cost-efficient means of stimulating innovation in resource efficiency as well as in reducing other costs throughout the life cycle. In some cases, they may be preferable to conventional 'command-and-control' regulations that rely on uniform standards and provide no incentive to go beyond compliance. Governments are increasingly using such incentives to achieve environmental and social goals. An example of a simple market-based tool is the deposit refund on aluminium cans to encourage recycling in some parts of the US, Canada, and Australia. Although the prime motive for many of these schemes is waste management, they could feasibly be extended to consider the costs of production. Creating the incentives for innovation of recycling and re-manufacture is critical.

A wider role of government is that of education and public information-sharing. Governments need to provide information to companies, the public, and others on resource use, on options for reducing it in line with sustainable development objectives, and on existing resource efficiency activities such as recycling. (See Chapter 12.)

Public authorities at all levels have a key role to play in practising resource efficiency for mineral commodities. In the most industrialized parts of the world, it is estimated that government activities alone are responsible for up to 15% of gross domestic product, thereby having a significant potential to stimulate market demand for products designed with resource efficiency in mind.[36] In mining-related sectors this can be even higher. The parallel WBCSD study on cement estimates that some 40% of total demand is public procurement.[37] Procurement policies based on environmental considerations are already a reality for governments in a number of countries in Europe and North America.

The ultimate challenge for all stakeholders is to develop an extended sense of responsibility for the way they use mineral resources.

Keys to Advances in Recycling

There have been economic incentives to recycle mineral commodities for many hundreds of years. The recycling industry is presently an important source of livelihoods world-wide, as well as an important component in the supply of many mineral commodities. This is especially the case for metals, which are often promoted as being infinitely recyclable. The current extent and nature of recycling for mineral commodities is discussed further in Chapter 2.

From a sustainable development perspective, the recycling of any material is far from a panacea. It is associated with many of the same trade-offs between environmental and social factors that concern the extraction and processing of primary resources. Consequently, there will be an optimum recycling rate for any mineral product that can feasibly be recycled.

Appropriate Public Policy

The role of public policy is key, not only in creating incentives for recycling but also in facilitating, improving, and encouraging the collection, transport, and trade of metals and other mineral commodities before and after recycling. This report does not go into this well-worked area of public policy, particularly in the case of the OECD countries. Suffice it to say, incentives for recycling need to be considered in product design, along with means by which users can avoid disposal costs and processors can show a positive return on capital employed. Increasingly regulations, such as take-back laws, are being used to achieve higher recovery rates. The principal groups of products that are the focus of take-back laws are vehicles, packaging, and domestic electronic goods. (See Box 11–5.) In the EU, the proposed Waste Electrical and Electronic Equipment Directive is designed to make manufacturers responsible for taking back and recycling products.[38] A supplementary Electric and Electronic Equipment Directive is also being drafted that aims to integrate environmental considerations into products at the design stage.[39]

In some countries, tax incentives encourage the use of recycled rather than virgin material. An example of this is the UK tax on the production of aggregates, which exempts recycled material.[40] In the United States, there are numerous examples of how public policy at the national and local level has encouraged the development of an aggregates recycling industry.[41]

Box 11–5. Recycling Home Appliances in Japan

The Law for Recycling of Specified Home Appliances, enforced in Japan in 2001, introduces a series of responsibilities to be shared among the owner, the retailer, and the manufacturer. These responsibilities can be summarized as follows:

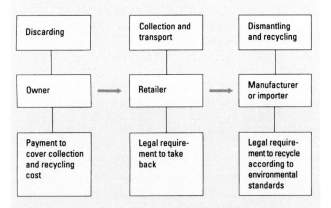

To ensure that appliances are returned to the retailer and not dumped, the law is supported by a waste disposal law with stringent penalties.

Appliances covered by the law include televisions, refrigerators, washing machines, and air conditioners. Approximately 20 million units are disposed of every year, totalling 600,000–700,000 tonnes. Metals are an important component of all these products. For instance, according to Toshiba, steel, aluminium, and copper constituted three-quarters of the mass of air conditioners it produced between 1990 and 1995. Prior to the new law, local governments had processed 40% of these appliances in the domestic waste stream, while private businesses dealt with the remainder. Although some metal recovery took place, many appliances ended up in landfills. The new scheme means that recycling is undertaken entirely by the private sector.

The law was driven by a scarcity of disposal sites in Japan and by government policy concerning resource efficiency. It illustrates how waste management and resource efficiency considerations can be brought together in a single policy instrument based on shared responsibilities for products. Moreover, pressure to reduce the cost for the owner to return an appliance for recycling creates some motive for design for recycling.

Sources: Development Bank of Japan (2001)

These include grants, incentives for collection, and reduced fees for permits to set up recycling facilities.

Public policy in one region has to be balanced with the impacts in another. The Basel Convention demonstrates the problem, in this case of balancing the hazards of dumping toxic waste products outside the industrial world with the potential for recycling in developing economies. (See Box 11–6.)

Finally, environmental standards for other concerns (such as air pollution) can limit the economic feasibility of recycling activities. For example, in the US the costly administrative requirements and pollution abatement technology required by environmental regulations have been cited as factors underlying a dramatic reduction in secondary copper smelting and ingot-making capacity.[42]

Overall, the direction of the recycling economy is clear. It is growing. The drivers are clear too. The principal concern is energy efficiency, and within that climate change mitigation is all-important. But also resource availability in some instances and other environmental considerations are important too. Options for safe disposal, toxicity, and even visual impact can be important. Not all agree where it will end. Industrial ecologist Robert Ayres, who developed a global model of copper supply and demand for the MMSD, concludes that it will be significant indeed. Based on scenarios for copper availability (defined in terms of depletion of the physical stock of copper ores), Ayres argues that recycling will become the dominant source of copper at some point in the twenty-first century.[43] He concludes: 'Best of all…would be an evolutionary transformation of the primary producers from an extract, refine and sell industry to a true service industry which treats each of the metals as a capital asset rather than as a commodity.'[44]

Information and Decision-Making Frameworks

To make policy decisions on recycling, decision-makers need to know how much is currently available for recycling and what proportion of this is actually being recycled. Both statistics are difficult to determine and are often not collected in any systematic way. This is further complicated by the lack of information about the service life of different mineral products before recycling.

Source: Cosbey (2001); Johnstone (1998); Subramanian (1997); Hoffmann and Wilson (2000)

<table>
<tr><td>

</td></tr>
</table>

Box 11–6. The Basel Convention: Implications for Metals Recycling in Developing Countries

The Basel Convention on the Transboundary Movement of Hazardous Wastes and Their Disposal entered into force in 1992. As of April 2002, there were 150 parties to the agreement. The treaty was motivated by cases in the 1970s and 1980s of illicit trade in toxic substances that receiving countries did not have the capacity to manage. The convention has three principal objectives:

- to reduce the generation of hazardous wastes globally,
- to minimize transboundary movements of hazardous wastes, and
- to ensure that there is prior informed consent from the recipient country before export takes place.

Hazardous wastes are defined according to lists of characteristics (such as toxicity), constituents (such as mercury), and origins (such as the pharmaceutical industry). Much metal-bearing waste may be included on the basis of contaminants and associated materials (such as toxic metals).

Since ratification, the requirements of the convention relating to the regulation and monitoring of trade have been extended to include bans on the export of certain materials. In 1992 the Conference of the Parties decided to prohibit the export of hazardous wastes for final disposal between Annex VII countries (OECD, the European Union, and Liechtenstein) and other countries. More recently, this has been extended to material intended for recycling, and in 1995 an amendment was passed to incorporate these bans into the text of the convention. The latest amendment has not yet come into force, and legal uncertainties lead some to question whether it ever will. On the other hand, some Parties to the Convention have created national export and import bans in response to the 1995 decision.

The overall impacts of these bans on the capacity of developing countries to source recycled metals are not clear. Some argue that they will have serious impacts on the economies and industrial growth of these countries. Others believe that the wastes most likely to be affected by the ban do not constitute an important part of the international trade in non-ferrous metal-bearing wastes and scrap, and that changes in the relative amounts of waste generated in developing and industrial countries could mean that the ban is likely to affect a declining proportion of potential trade.

There is, however, a need for the Parties to the Basel Convention to consider the effects of such a ban on the livelihoods supported by metals recycling in developing countries as well as the contribution of recycling to these national economies.

Bans on the import of metal-bearing waste are likely to encourage and enhance the collection and recuperation of domestically generated scrap. From an environmental perspective, it is therefore important that the requirements for technical and financial cooperation in the environmentally sound management of wastes laid out in the original convention are fulfilled. The regional centres envisaged and set up to help implement the training and technology transfer aspects of the convention have a key role in this.

Life-cycle analysis can be used to aid decision-making based on environmental factors for recycling. By undertaking an LCA, it is possible to:

- compare the environmental performance of different recycling scenarios, including energy provision and transport considerations;
- compare the relative environmental impacts of recycling versus primary extraction (although this depends crucially on how they are weighted);
- compare the environmental performance of different recycling technologies;
- develop products that can be recycled at lower cost;
- determine appropriate and effective collection mechanisms; and
- develop better routes for access to financing.[45]

To determine the rates and forms of recycling versus primary production that can best contribute to sustainable development, however, an integrated approach that goes far beyond environmental considerations is required.[46]

Technology

Technological advances are key to increasing the rate of recycling for mineral commodities.[47] This is particularly so for the recycling of metals once they have been used in products. Whereas the waste arising from production of metal shapes such as wire and tube ('new scrap') is always likely to be recycled because of the ease of retrieval, collecting waste from used products ('old scrap') depends on technologies for efficient recovery. Although advanced technologies for separating many metals from products such as cars and electronics have been developed in some parts of the world, there is a need to ensure that they are more widely available. The sorting and identification of alloys and composite materials is critical. For instance, Huron Valley Steel in the US has developed a laser technology for separating aluminium alloys from scrap that cannot be recycled by a single process.[48] New chemical technologies will have a role in aiding better recovery of by-product metals, such as zinc from dust produced during steel manufacture.

Considering that the price of recycled metal is set according to the price of metals from primary sources, producers of these materials from each source are effectively in competition. The principal effect of downward trends in metal prices to date is on the potential for increased recycling of material from used products.[49] New technologies for recycling play a crucial role in maintaining the competitiveness of all industries involved in the recycling process. And as indicated, governments have a role in creating the climate in which the necessary investment can occur.

Product designers and managers, together with regulators, have a role to play in developing systems for recycling (such as product take-back schemes) above and beyond new engineering solutions for processing wastes. The question of where to allocate and direct funding for research and development into recycling technologies needs to be addressed by companies in the minerals sector as well as by governments.

Re-manufacture and Re-use

Complementing recycling, re-manufacture and re-use can help slow the growth in demand for primary mineral commodities. Re-manufacture refers to the process of product disassembly, whereby parts are cleaned, repaired or replaced, and then re-assembled to sound working condition.[50] Re-use involves extending the life of a product through maintenance or re-conditioning. From an environmental perspective, re-use and re-manufacture may have advantages over recycling in that in many (but not all) cases, more of the energy and capital cost embodied in a mineral product can be conserved. By comparison, recycling requires a product to be broken down to its constituent materials before they can be used again.

Many products containing metals are already re-manufactured after first use, including some types of computers, photocopiers, automotive components,

tyres, refrigeration compressors, and printer toner cartridges. The US Environmental Protection Agency has estimated that approximately 480,000 people are employed in re-manufacture of all products in the United States.[51] For some products, the vast proportion can be re-manufactured because of the way they are designed. Xerox Corporation, for example, claims that 90% of its office equipment can be re-manufactured if the appropriate facilities for doing so are available.[52]

Caterpillar, the mining equipment manufacturer, states that it rebuilds trucks and excavators once or twice to extend their life.[53] And it re-manufactures engines, transmissions, and hydraulic components as many as three or four times. Despite these encouraging signs from individual companies, few policies are targeted at using re-manufacture as a way of encouraging resource efficiency.

Consumer purchasing trends in many countries pose serious challenges to the design and demand for re-manufacture and re-use. For example, consumers are increasingly concerned with owning the 'latest' hi-tech equipment. The fast rate of technological advance in hi-tech equipment combined with a high turnover of what is deemed 'fashionable' has increased the rate of disposal of such goods and reduced the demand for re-use. This problem must, however, be balanced with the potential energy efficiency of advanced products on the market.

Regulation and End-use

Some people believe that from a sustainable development perspective, the costs associated with using certain mineral commodities outweigh the benefits. This may be the case if, for example, they consider the health risks associated with use to be unacceptable or subject to uncertainty. (See discussion of metals in the environment in Chapter 10.)

It is primarily a government responsibility to balance the uncertainties regarding the potentially negative impacts resulting from the use of a mineral commodity with the merits of allowing it onto the marketplace. Governments should, however, undertake this task in a transparent manner – with the full participation of all interests. Industry possesses (or at least has some capacity to generate) much of the scientific information required for the regulation of end-uses.

The proposed revision of the EU Chemicals Policy has addressed this by placing new responsibilities on industry to provide information about the nature of substances being placed on the market. (See Box 11–7.)

National governments have an important role to play in ensuring the safety of material products placed on the market. In some cases this involves the ban of specific uses. The decision to ban the end-use of a certain mineral commodity (or a substance based on it) must, however, be founded on a thorough and

transparent risk assessment. Furthermore, the relative merits of substitutes or alternatives must also be considered from the point of view of sustainable development. Rigorous life-cycle assessment is also key to this, despite the fact that it involves only environmental considerations. An example of the consequence of failing to take such an approach is demonstrated by the ban on metal cans for beverages in Denmark. (See Box 11–8.) In the EU, policy developments that restrict certain uses of metals remain controversial because of differing viewpoints on the implementation of the precautionary principle with regard to the risk they pose and the relative merits of alternatives.[54]

While the precautionary principle involves prudence where impacts are unknown or uncertain, it is important to realize that 'scientific certainty' is not a well-defined goal. In most cases, this level of certainty is unlikely to be achieved to the satisfaction of all people. As a result, the risks and benefits of permitting use of a particular mineral commodity will always require careful balancing.

Governments should take steps to ensure that decisions concerning end-use are not based on scientific knowledge that has been unduly influenced by the

---

Box 11–7. Regulating Chemicals in the European Union: New Responsibilities for Industry

In 1998 the European Commission reviewed its chemicals policy and concluded that there was a lack of knowledge about the properties and uses of chemical substances already on the market and that existing mechanisms to assess the risk posed by the introduction of new substances were limited. The response to the review has been a proposed Chemicals Strategy. This aims to place all substances produced or imported at over 1 tonne per year per manufacturer under one system for centralized registration. Metals and metallic compounds are included in this. Industry, including users of chemicals downstream in the value chain, is responsible for supplying information about chemicals and their uses. Substances of high concern will require authorization for specific uses.

Eurométaux, the European non-ferrous metals industry association, has proposed that thorough risk assessment should be used to evaluate and manage substances placed on the market. In addition, the particular characteristics of metals should be considered, including their natural cycling and their combination in the form of alloys. Non-governmental groups representing environmental and consumer interests are calling to expand the number of chemicals requiring authorization (as opposed to registration). They also call for tighter deadlines for the provision of data by industry and ultimately a ban on various hazardous chemicals by 2020.

Agreement needs to be reached between industry and regulators on the extent of the risk assessments proposed and the balance of responsibility for the cost of carrying them out. Collaboration is required between industry and government to define the need for assessments, their level of detail, and appropriate ways of meeting the costs.

Source: Commission of the European Communities (2001b); Eurométaux (2001)

Box 11–8. Ban on Metal Use: The Danish 'Can Ban'

In 1989, the Danish government introduced a system obliging Danish producers of beer and carbonated soft drinks to use refillable or re-usable bottles. This included a general ban on the use of metal cans. The Danish Environmental Protection Agency did an LCA as a basis for this policy. The LCA has been criticized for failing to meet internationally agreed standards for this procedure, such as those of the ISO 14040 series. The Danish government was taken to the European Court of Justice (ECJ) by the European Commission for infringement of the EU Packaging Directive and for preventing the free movement of goods on the basis of what it regards as a flawed environmental justification, and the ban is therefore likely be rejected by the ECJ. Can manufacturers have opposed the Danish policy as it has considerable implications for markets access, which is a critical issue in the European Union.

Source: Legislation or rule n° 124, 27/02/1989, modified by rule n° 583, 24/06/1996, and rule n° 300, 30/04/1997; ENDS Magazine (2001)

values and priorities of the particular groups that have funded it. To address this, governments themselves can help by commissioning collaborative research of the highest standards of rigour and openness.

The Way Forward

Connecting the production and use of mineral-related materials is critical to ensuring that the minerals sector contributes optimally to sustainable development. The necessary integration of the value chain is a two-way process: users of mineral commodities have a key role in influencing the way in which these materials are produced, and producers have an interest – some would say a responsibility – to ensure that mineral commodities are used in a manner that is eco-efficient.

Current resource efficiency concepts (as far as they go) argue for a reduced dependence on physical quantities of mineral resources, with particular emphasis on the energy needed to extract and refine them. Many argue for a greater emphasis on maximizing the services that these resources provide. One starting point could be for different groups to work together to produce scenarios of how needs for mineral commodities are likely to be met in the future, including the balance of supply between primary and secondary sources.

The industrial countries where the greatest proportion of mineral commodities are currently used are taking the lead in resource efficiency. But much more needs to be done to ensure that developing countries are not disadvantaged or excluded from the associated benefits by way of limits to the free flow of technologies and ideas. Recycling, re-manufacture, and re-use – some of the means by which the efficiency of use can be improved dramatically – are only just starting to become part of effective public policy. The next stage, involving product design for providing the same services but with greatly increased resource efficiency, is in its infancy, but no one need doubt the revolution has begun. This presents challenges not only for designers and technologists within companies, but also for governments to create incentives so that those who improve performance can be rewarded.

The efficiency with which mineral commodities are used needs to be considered alongside questions of sufficiency of access to these materials. This means ensuring equitable access to the resources (both in

terms of affordability and local availability) and the livelihoods currently gained from producing them.

Collaboration Throughout the Value Chain

Collaboration between individual companies throughout the value chain is an important part of the way forward for an integrated approach to using minerals. This can take two forms. First, companies can explore business opportunities inherent in forming partnerships throughout the value chain. They can learn from those that are already doing so. New business relationships among minerals producers, manufacturers, retailers, recyclers, and customers are forming and will grow where there is a policy framework that rewards innovation. Companies can and should communicate their sustainable development policies to their suppliers, contractors, partners, and customers and encourage similar practice along the value chain.

Second, companies throughout the value chain need to work collectively to provide information on uses of these materials and their effects. Commodity associations have a particularly important role to play in compiling, standardizing, and disseminating information on supply chains for the benefit of their members, consumers, government, and the public. If the information and advice they give is to be trusted by non-industry actors, there may be a need for independent advice or peer review.

Life-Cycle Assessment

The mining and minerals industry has started to engage in the development of LCA as one element of a holistic approach to decision-making for sustainable development. This work is essential to making informed choices on alternative materials. But more needs to be done to build trust. Some specialist NGOs and academics have a significant role to play in reviewing the different sources of information and helping to build confidence in the conclusions drawn.

The International Council on Mining & Metals and the individual commodity associations should continue to be actively involved in disseminating information on the usefulness and interpretation of LCA. Efforts should be coordinated and lessons learnt from experiences in other sectors. To generate useful comparative material, the mining industry needs to build consensus on definitions of assessment boundaries, allocation procedures to be used, and approaches to aggregation over space and time.

A specific focus on LCA and metal recyclers is needed. The recycling industry associations could do more to facilitate access to recyclers, bring them on board in the data-gathering process through outreach and education, and build consensus within this part of the minerals industry.

The UNEP/SETAC Life Cycle Initiative should continue to address the methodological shortcomings of applying LCA to the minerals sector. This can be enhanced if representatives from all parts of the minerals sector provide input. The Life Cycle Inventory element of this initiative should become a forum for the assimilation of data on mining and minerals processing, particularly for use by downstream industries.

The MMSD LCA Workshop concluded that the impact categories included in LCA need to be reviewed, as they currently do not reflect adequately the performance of the minerals industry. In particular, salinity, land use, and water management need to be investigated as potential additions to the existing categories. Also, data are needed on eco-toxicity, resource depletion, and other impact categories. The industry should continue to make publicly available the LCA data collected and take steps to generate the additional data required.

Further research needs to determine what tools other than LCA can be used to incorporate an understanding of the 'social performance' of the system, using the work of the Life Cycle Management element of the UNEP/SETAC Initiative.

Product Stewardship

As in other sectors (such as the timber and chemicals industries), it may be appropriate to begin a Product Stewardship Initiative that would enable all actors in the value chain to exercise their joint responsibility to provide information on the safe use, transport, recycling, and disposal of their products. Such an initiative could result in information on the best way to use the product in a particular application to minimize risk, information on prolonging service life, and advice on recycling and final disposal. The initiative could build on the work already undertaken by the

'Cash for Scrap Metal' – a metal merchant in London

commodity associations and the Non-Ferrous Metals Consultative Forum on Sustainable Development.

In short, the minerals and metals industries need to collaborate further with regulatory authorities, downstream users, and other groups to develop sound, scientifically based means to ensure safe use, re-use, and eventual disposal of its products.

Recycling

If the aim is to know what happens to the different mineral commodities, the industry associations, recycling trade organizations (such as the Bureau of International Recycling), and multilateral organizations (including OECD, the UN Conference on Trade and Development, UNEP, and the World Customs Organization) could collaborate to develop public systems for the systematic monitoring of trade flows in scrap and secondary materials. An appropriate funding mechanism for this will need to be developed.

Governments clearly need to continue to identify the incentives and disincentives for recycling and for innovative design in metals use and develop policies for them. They should continue to work with industry associations and other bodies to develop national strategies for recycling mineral commodities and extending product life, with measurable targets. These may include collection networks, infrastructure, and investment in recycling technologies. Policy initiatives need to be coherent so that one policy does not contradict another in promoting recycling. Provisions for helping to manage any negative social or economic consequences may also be needed.

Governments of industrial countries that are currently working to promote resource efficiency could assist developing countries through technology transfer and demonstration models for recycling, although no one should doubt the importance of the informal economy in recycling in many poor economies.

As part of an overall product stewardship initiative, ICMM could work with the recycling trade associations to compile a database of good-practice examples of recycling across regions (both nationally and internationally) and across mineral commodities.

The precise effect of the Basel Convention on trade in scrap metals needs to be clarified by the metals recycling industry. This relates particularly to the implications of prohibition of the export of recyclable materials from industrial to developing countries. Parties to the Convention and the various working groups must consider how limits on scrap metal exports will affect wider sustainable development criteria. In particular, there needs to be greater clarity regarding the definition of 'environmentally sound management' of material controlled by the convention. Practical ways to enable developing countries to implement this by means of recycling need to be identified.

Risk Assessment and Policy

The industry needs to work with regulatory authorities to ensure that risk assessments for the use of metals can properly inform regulation and materials selection. The relevant industry associations should have input, together with other stakeholders, into the development of national- and regional-level government policy to ensure that the assessments are adequate and fair. For this to happen, the information needs to be provided in a transparent and open way.

Agenda for Further Analysis

Some commentators pointed out that MMSD's process and its subsequent analysis focused more heavily on the extraction end of the industry than on metals and minerals use. This necessarily meant that many important topics have been given less treatment than they deserve. Topics for additional analysis, undertaken

in the same spirit as much of the analysis in this report, might include:

- examining innovation in product development to permit the production of finished goods with less material input and the substitution of more abundant for less abundant mineral commodities;
- examining how public policy, including procurement policy, helps, hinders, or affects the transaction costs in recycling, and the operation of incentives in an integrated approach to maximize resource use efficiency;
- examining ways to advance LCA methodologies and other product-oriented tools to clarify appropriate recycling approaches, recognize the value of materials that can be recycled repeatedly, and define data requirements to support scientifically sound and transparent decision-making;
- assessing how to ensure that the various initiatives to develop indicator sets converge and that they are consistent, academically rigorous, and extend their application into product use areas;
- examining the environmental costs, health and safety issues, and legacy issues associated with the use and disposal of metals and minerals;
- developing the business case relating to use and recycling of metals and minerals;
- assessing internal and external drivers facing companies in developing an integrated approach to materials management and analysis of the necessary management practice and tools to implement such an approach;
- assessing the impact of industry procurement policies on small- and medium-size enterprises and local supply networks; and
- reviewing the responsibilities of the industry towards the characterization of hazard and risk and the communication of assessment.

Endnotes

1 In this context, 'use' is meant to describe the service derived from primary mineral commodities (refined metals, raw processed industrial and construction minerals) in products handled by industry, government, and the public. For the purpose of this chapter, use includes re-use.

2 United Nations (1992) Chapter 4.3.

3 PricewaterhouseCoopers (2001).

4 Gereffi et al. (2001).

5 Roberts (2000).

6 The World Conservation Union News Release 19 March 2001, http://www.iucn.org/info_and_news/press/coltan.html; MMSD telephone interviews with five electronics manufacturers, November 2001. Coltan is the common name for the mineral columbite-tantalite, a primary source of the metal tantalum, which is used in capacitors in many electronic goods, including mobile phones.

7 Bass, Thornber et al. (2001).

8 Rae and Rouse (2001) p.33.

9 http://www.plantar.com.br. Accessed December 2001.

10 Roberts (2000).

11 Bass, Thornber et al. (2001).

12 http://www.epa.gov/epr/about/index.html.

13 The concept of Extended Producer Responsibility was first coined in 1990 by Swedish environmental economist Thomas Lindhquist.

14 OECD (2001a) p.161.

15 http://www.unepie.org/pc/sustain/lca/lca.htm.

16 MMSD (2001d) p.55.

17 Commission of the European Communities (2001a).

18 See, for example, Baumol and Oates (1988); Cornes and Sandler (1996); Portney and Stavins (2000).

19 Young (2000) p.290; Jackson (1996) p.218.

20 Schmidt-Bleek (1999).

21 http://www.foeeurope.org/sustainability/foeapproach/espace/t-frame-espace.htm.

22 Gardner and Sampat (1998) p.24.

23 Radetzki and Tilton (1990).

24 Matthews (2000) p.138.

25 Johnstone (2001).

26 US Geological Survey (2001) p.4.

27 Five Winds International (2001).

28 See World Business Council for Sustainable Development, http://www.wbcsd.org/projects/pr_ecoefficiency.htm; Hawken et al. (1999); The Natural Step, http://www.naturalstep.org.

29 Hawken et al. (1999) p.396.

30 http://www.world-aluminium.org/applications/packaging/cans.html.

31 Womack and Jones (1996) p.316.

32 Paragraph 28, United Nations Special Session of the General Assembly to Review and Appraise the Implementation of Agenda 21, New York, 23–27 June 1997, at http://www.un.org/documents/ga/res/spec/aress19-2.htm.

33 Blair (2001).

34 OECD (2001d) p.74.

35 OECD (2001c) pp.265-72.

36 http://www.unepie.org/pc/sustain/design/green-proc.htm.

37 WBCSD (2002 in print).

38 Commission of the European Communities (2000).

39 Commission of the European Communities (2001c).

40 Part of the UK Government Finance Act 2001 (which came into effect on 1 April 2002).

41 Wilburn and Goonan (1998).

42 Jolly (2000).

43 Ayres et al. (2001).

44 Ibid., p.87.

45 MMSD (2001b).

46 Quinkertz et al. (2001).

47 Tilton (1999).

48 See US Department of Energy, Office of Industrial Technologies (2001).

49 Tilton (1999).

50 Definition from The Remanufacturing Industries Council, at http://www.reman.org/frfaqust.htm#1. Accessed November 2001.

51 US EPA (1998).

52 http://www.xerox.com.

53 Correspondence from Caterpillar Global Mining, 15 October 2001.

54 For example, the End of Life Vehicles Directive and the proposed Waste Electrical and Electronic Equipment Directives include bans on certain uses of metals.

CHAPTER 12

ACCESS TO INFORMATION

Information flow is essential in a sustainable stakeholder society. Information comes in different forms and is of variable quality. Information about a company and its operations is used by a range of actors, such as communities, investors, employees, lenders, suppliers, and customers, often through appropriate accounting and reporting procedures based on defined indicators and measurement techniques. Within the industry, information is used by management to monitor performance efficiency and the impacts of operations. At the exploration phase, accurate geoscientific data and maps are crucial.

Corporate reporting covers many different strands. Environmental reporting may include energy and materials accounting, environmental impact assessment, product evaluation, environmental auditing and measurement, and reporting of toxic emissions among others. Reporting is only one method of disclosure. The importance of the general media and its use by corporations, governments, and civil society for highlighting issues, informing the public, or campaigning cannot be underestimated.

The central question is, to what extent is the concept of sustainable development affecting the production, access to, need for, and flow of information in association with the mining and metals sector? Further, if availability of information has increased and systems for its dissemination have multiplied, to what extent is this moving society towards more equitable, open, and effective negotiated solutions to problems in this sector? This chapter considers basic information needs in the sector and the challenges faced by those involved with or affected by mining.

Information's Key Role

Nobel laureate Amartya Sen has pointed out that famine has rarely taken place in a country with a democratic government and a free press.[1] This underlines the intrinsic value of information as an enabling tool within society. Access to information is broadly accepted as essential in a democracy. Information helps the different players in an economy perform efficiently and effectively. It helps individuals and organizations establish, understand, and question policies, practices, and regulations; communicate needs and concerns; and obtain and defend fundamental rights to resources. Information is also a core

component and a driver of globalization. One facet of this is the growth in communications over the internet and the use of web-based methods for transmitting complex information.

Information is also an important tool for education and empowerment. For example, employees need information to exercise their rights and to contribute safely and productively to the progress of the enterprise. Industry needs information to educate employees and management about changing trends, health, and safety and about constraints and opportunities within corporations. Industry also needs information from employees about work-place safety, improved efficiency, and many other areas of mutual interest. Companies and other stakeholders stress the need for environmental information prior to deciding whether or not to mine.

Communities have particularly acute information needs relative to other stakeholders at all stages of the minerals cycle because of the power imbalances between communities and other actors. Communities, for example, find it difficult to press for change and accountability without reliable, valid, and timely information. Non-governmental organizations (NGOs) and civil society groups also need information to educate others about the activities of mining projects, companies, and governments. If campaigning organizations do not have access to good-quality information, their effectiveness can be reduced.

The provision and use of information are not value-free. The production, disclosure, distribution, and use of information carry with them a series of political, economic, legal, and social implications and responsibilities – both for those who provide it and for those who use it. Further, information is not communication. Good communication depends on many factors, including the levels of education and training of the recipient, cultural beliefs and practices, and the financial constraints of the providers and the recipients of information.

The ability to block access to information is also a powerful political and economic tool. Any discussion of the concepts and norms that might underpin the production, disclosure, and dissemination of information raises some fundamental questions for the sector. As historian Howard Zinn noted: 'The chief problem in historical [and journalistic] honesty is not outright lying. It is omission or de-emphasis of important data. The definition of "important" of course depend on one's values.'[2]

The use (or abuse) of information based on 'the facts' is always value-dependent. Individuals and organizations have vested interests in the outcomes set in play by the information they disclose. The challenge, in part, is to develop an information-sharing system that acknowledges a diversity of 'truths' and that separates these from facts. As pointed out by Sharon Beder, who writes on corporate communications and information in the global era and its use to influence the environmental debate:

> A [reporter] must have values, priorities (conscious or otherwise), must filter facts, must report subjectively.…The reality and the determined denial of reality surrounding the issue of media freedom, verges on the surreal and is easily as bizarre as any primitive religious dogma, belief in a flat earth or faith in a kindly Fuehrer plotting global conquest.[3]

Further, there is a lack of trust among the actors in this sector, which colours how they receive information. People have moved from the naivety of a 'tell me' world to one in which they ask not only to be told, but to be shown and involved, and to have the evidence verified. The constant demand for verification is in part a testimony to a well-founded lack of trust.

Trust is sometimes said to be irrelevant to the process of reaching equitable decisions on resource development – agreement can be a mercenary transaction, and it is more important that the parties involved have fulfilled their objectives. Others, however, may view trust as a form of social capital, as people may reach their objectives faster if there is some measure of trust.[4] In some cases, it may be impossible to build equity without trust.

If society demands that corporations, governments, NGOs, and others disclose truthfully and to the fullest extent possible the detail of their activities, then there must be an understanding not only of what constitutes 'truth' for each actor (their value systems and principles), but also the details of their production, use, and dissemination of information – what, when, how, why, and to whom.

Governments and companies are being held to ever-higher standards of accountability, transparency, and

openness by citizens and shareholders. Increasingly, it is expected that other communities of interest, such as NGOs, will perform to the same standards demanded of governments, companies, and multilateral organizations. NGOs and other civil society organizations have exactly the same responsibilities to use information equitably and fairly as governments and companies – and this responsibility has not always been exercised.

Systems for the production, dissemination, use, and revision of information are open to abuse. They must be rigorous and robust enough to ensure that abuse and misuse of information do not prevent or diminish the ability to build sustainable economies and livelihoods.

Clearly there is a business case to be made for improved corporate disclosure within a sustainable development framework. Some companies are now finding that moving towards full disclosure, far from leaving them exposed to greater risk of negative interactions with stakeholders, has reduced transaction costs and led to more positive ways to resolve problems.[5] The involvement of stakeholders can often increase the information base on key social issues in a time- and cost-effective manner. The use, for example, of traditional ecological knowledge in the case of indigenous communities can provide companies with a sound knowledge about existing community/ environment relationships for baseline studies. In addition, secrecy does not build trust.

There is a strong business case to be made for free and open access to information. Once a company has established the fundamentals of improved sustainability performance, then increased trust, reduced transaction costs, better feedback, reduced risks, more effective resource use, and increased reputational value all arise through communicating this effectively to others.

Basic Information Needs

Stakeholders in the minerals and metals sectors need information throughout the discovery, construction, exploitation, refining, processing, use, and disposal or recycling stages of operations. The requirement for information at all scales is immense. The need for information varies according to the scale of the operations. The exploration stage, for example, relies heavily on the provision of good-quality geological, geophysical, and geochemical information from governments. New technologies in satellite imagery and information technology are also revolutionizing the exploration process. Companies rely on constantly evolving databases and enhancements of the mining cadastre. Information needs fall into several main categories: technical, regulatory, financial, local environmental and social, and performance monitoring. Geographical information systems and software such as Geosoft are also crucial to exploration.

Production increasingly relies on sophisticated systems to produce information for technical processes and for the management and monitoring systems to improve the operation of facilities with respect to labour, energy use, health and safety, and environmental considerations, particularly regarding hazardous chemicals release and the disposal and re-use of materials. Requirements for environmental information also increasingly cover understanding of local biodiversity.

States require information to establish regulations that set standards and norms, and to improve policy decision-making processes. The maintenance of current databases on exploration activities, tenements, permitting, and closure planning is a key function of national and regional governments, while land use planning in general depends on the collection of key land use and other types of data. There is also a requirement to make the particular legal regime more explicit to others.

Economic and financial information is vital for the trading and marketing of minerals commodities and for predictions about market behaviour and future commodity prices. Security regulators and exchanges also require information from companies.

To complement the technical information directly related to finding, exploiting, using, and disposing of mineral resources, there is a growing requirement for local environmental, social, and economic information that may be affected by or have impacts on a project. There is also a vital need to provide communities with the capacity and the information to participate knowledgeably in decision-making around minerals projects. Triple bottom-line approaches anticipate that companies will report publicly on their environmental and social performance in a manner that is accountable

and transparent and that allows for appropriate participation.

Information is also a key to monitoring performance of companies and states with regard to human rights, worker health and safety, and development. If communities and regions consent to mining, there must be ways to verify that the promised benefits do materialize. Employees also need access to information in the work place to help them monitor performance.

One thing is certain: technology is central. Web-based technologies will continue to evolve, increasing the quality and complexity of information that can be transmitted about a project. Software applications, for example, now allow 'walk-through' 3-D representations of complex architectures such as an open-pit mine and the surrounding facilities, giving communities a very real sense of what a proposed mine might look like. Such advances in technology certainly enhance the ability of communities to participate effectively in decision-making and to comment on proposals. However, the digital divide means that many of these technologies are generally not available to all the stakeholders. This may be one area where some simple and cost-effective remedies, such as providing access to such technologies in the areas of proposed mines, would enhance the quality of participation for stakeholders in poor areas or countries. Yet it is also clear that access to information in itself is not sufficient – people must also be given the ability, through the political system, to use this information.

Key Challenges

The challenge is to design and improve policies, procedures, processes, and institutions to deal effectively with societies' growing demand for information as technology is providing more information than ever before, though often in a highly random and uncoordinated fashion. Equally, rational systems that would allow the sector to operate effectively are needed – not systems of excessive generation or duplication of information and the financial burden that this entails. Cost issues, although dismissed by many as irrelevant, are a central challenge to all the actors.

A related and equally important issue is the protection of the intellectual property of the private and public sectors, of communities, and of others. Confidentiality, when breached, can have costly financial and social implications, particularly where it affects corporate competitive advantage or when it threatens the personal and employment security of workers who report malpractice or other wrongdoing.

Shareholders, employees, and stakeholders all want to know more about how corporations conduct their business, and there is a growing recognition that reputation can no longer be maintained through a culture of secrecy.[6] Getting to grips with the information explosion and managing it to meet specific ends is a challenge for all. This section looks at seven key components of addressing this challenge.

Evening classes for mine workers are a useful means of information provision

Building Trust and Balance

Empowerment is key to building trust and yet it is often fraught with difficulties. In some jurisdictions, giving access to certain types of information can compromise the personal security of recipients. In others, governments do not want disclosure, and act to suppress information and control its flow. Corporations and employees may also seek to place unnecessary controls on information for a variety of reasons. As a consequence, mistrust among stakeholders is often widespread.

In any circumstance, information can be manufactured, misused, and concealed. Corporations may also complain that while they are held to the highest standards of accountability and performance with regard to disclosure of information, the same does not apply to some of their critics. There is a clear lack of trust in research that has been generated by industry, which is often regarded as partial and designed to highlight the benefits of a project while concealing or at least playing down any potential negative impacts. Independent verification by suitably designated bodies that include representatives of various stakeholder groups can go some way towards overcoming the lack of trust in this area.

In addition, claims to representativeness on all sides may not be legitimate. Some reports criticizing companies may not be verifiable, and their authors may not be held accountable. Last but not least, there is also a significant mistrust of globalization by some sections of society, which may in turn be reflected in attitudes towards large corporations in general.

Dealing with Uncertainty and Risk

Mistrust breeds uncertainty, which translates into risk in the market-place. Disclosure carries risks for corporations and other actors – from NGOs to communities – which need to take into account the legal and therefore financial implications when they release or comment on any information. The rights and power to litigate can be open to abuse. Sometimes even when information can be verified and accounted for, its dissemination can have unintended consequences. The provider of the information can quite easily stand accused of biased reporting, resulting in legal action.

The selective use of information is a problem that all sides encounter. Depending on the jurisdiction and the circumstances, the burden of proof may lie with the informant or the objector. In either case, if there are no clear rules around the need to disclose information and the need to be accountable for objections to the substance of any disclosure, the consequences can be far-reaching and costly for all sides.

Establishing Equity

Communities and other civil society actors may feel powerless since they do not have the financial and political resources to produce the kind of information that corporations and governments can produce. Due to the power imbalance, it is important that the processes of information-gathering are transparent and that the rules are clear to all parties, along with the procedures for appeal. In terms of social justice, information gathered and disseminated in an equitable fashion enhances the rights of those involved or affected.

Building Capacity

The issue of capacity deficit and imbalance needs to be addressed. Civil society groups and individuals may lack the resources to address issues, to participate meaningfully in protracted debates, and to verify information. Similarly, people in developing countries may not have access to the internet or the means to pursue their rights, where they exist, with respect to information – the right to know and to prior informed consent. At the same time, small companies often argue that while they can be held to the same performance principles as the global giants, they cannot respond in the same way. They lack, for example, resources for communications campaigns. It is not just a case of building structural capacity, however, but also of building the cognitive capacity within society to process information in an increasingly information-rich world.

Building Quality

There is an important question of information quality that has to be addressed in the case of data around project proposals and operations. The case for well-qualified third-party professionals supported by understanding of community needs on information is clear. Companies and governments have to build capacity both internally and externally to improve the quality of assessment data. This does not mean having a number for everything; it might mean, for example, gathering good qualitative genealogical data through tribal stories.

Building Effective Systems and Mechanisms

Governance around information generation is often poor. Governments have been slow to implement the recommendations of such regional instruments as the 1998 Convention on Access to Information, Public Participation in Decision-making and Access to Justice (known as the Aarhus Convention), while international systems for information exchange and action around mining issues are few, although growing.[7] Clear mechanisms for the handling and transfer of information between stakeholders are often missing. Corporations complain that there are too many regulations and reporting requirements, as well as duplication, calling for a rationalization of the reporting system. Civil society representatives criticize the lack of transparency on the part of companies and the state, and note that neither the state nor the private sector has the authority to decide for others how much information they should have – that NGOs and communities will decide for themselves what is useful to know.

There are weaknesses in current systems in the following areas:

- *Comparability* – Where regulation exists and is monitored, for example on corporate disclosure and reporting, it is difficult to compare reports and information effectively, and to distinguish leaders from laggards.
- *Verification* – In terms of information quality, many questions arise. Is the science good – that is, measurable, verifiable, repeatable, and relevant? Is the information timely, reliable, and targeted?
- *Cost* – While it is recognized that policies, systems, procedures, and institutions are required, the private sector is unlikely to be able to bear the full cost of improved systems alone.
- *Acknowledgement of leadership* – Industry leaders at all scales, whether small, medium, or large companies, report and often do so to a good standard, yet they are commonly singled out for criticism because of their higher profile – while the laggards get off free. Leadership should not result in competitive and reputational disadvantage. It would help to have mechanisms in place to verify corporate performance.

Addressing Stakeholder Concerns

All these challenges pose significant obstacles to charting a transition to sustainable development in the minerals sector based on stakeholder-inclusive concepts. (See Box 12–1.) While the extent to which business decisions should be informed by stakeholders in wider society is often hotly debated, failure to address stakeholder concerns has been costly to the mining industry, and individual companies have suffered significantly from stakeholder reaction to errant and ill-received operational and business practices.

Existing Mechanisms, Standards, and Initiatives

Global Agreements

An enormous number of recent initiatives in the area of information access have implications for the mining and minerals sector. Much of the current focus in the national and international policy arenas is a result of

Box 12–1. Two MMSD Workshops on Information

Two MMSD workshops brought together participants from the North and the South to discuss key issues in relation to information access in the minerals sector. A March 2001 meeting in Toronto was designed to construct a work plan for MMSD to target some key areas in which baseline research could be commissioned. Themes that emerged during the discussion were civil society's lack of trust of the industry, the need for industry to have a rational and cost-effective system of public reporting, concerns that not all of the information needed by civil society to comment on project proposals and be involved in decision-making is being disclosed, and a concern by industry that civil society organizations often did not perform to the same standards of accountability as industry and governments. The attendees suggested that background papers be commissioned on systems for making information available to stakeholders, the role of governments in information dissemination, corporate communication standards, practices and issues, community information needs, and a gap analysis of current information practices.

In December 2001, a Vancouver workshop provided the opportunity to discuss these background papers and to explore an agenda for change in the way that information is currently viewed and handled by the sector. Recurrent themes were that information often fails to flow to communities in a timely and transparent fashion, that disclosure practices often fall short of current best practice, and that one-size-fits-all systems of public reporting or a global reporting standard would be an extremely difficult initiative to develop. The distinct nature of specific mines, projects, companies, locations, and communities means that a different mix of indicators, metrics, and evaluations is needed. One effective way of scoping the need for information around any project is to ask the community what they need to know in considering project proposals. Again the need to build trust, even if this involves industry owning up to past mistakes, came through strongly. It is because stakeholders, particularly in communities, do not trust companies and governments that they press for such a high volume of information and verification about projects.

Source: MMSD (2001h)

networks to share information on sustainable development, particularly between non-governmental and private-sector actors.[8]

The most far-reaching and explicit refinement in this regard is the Aarhus Convention of the UN Economic Commission for Europe. Article 7 states that:

> Each Party shall make appropriate practical and/or other provisions for the public to participate during the preparation of plans and programmes relating to the environment, within a transparent and fair framework, having provided the necessary information to the public.[9]

In brief, the convention binds states and public authorities to make environmental information publicly available within a framework determined by national legislation, within a specific period from the time a request is received, and without the need to state with what interest a request is made. It encourages parties to establish national inventories of inputs, releases, and transfers for a variety of substances, products, and processes, including resources, energy, and water use, along with the impacts of on-site and off-site treatment and disposal plants. In particular, the Aarhus Convention focuses on people affected by the environmental impacts of development and their right to information that will help them mitigate such impacts. The treaty has been criticized for its many exceptions to the general rule to disclose information – exceptions that are based on public security, national defence, and international relations.

Regional Agreements

In 1996, the Council of the Organisation for Economic Co-operation and Development recommended that its member countries 'take steps to establish, as appropriate, implement and make publicly available a pollutant release and transfer register (PRTR) system' and that 'the results of a PRTR should be made accessible to all affected and interested parties on a timely and regular basis'.[10] The actual implementation of this principle is the matter of further national legislation by individual states.

Other regional initiatives that seek to implement the information principles of the Rio Earth Summit include the Inter-American Strategy for the Promotion of Public Participation in Decision-making for Sustainable Development, by the members of the Organization of American States.[11]

principle 10 of the Rio Declaration on Environment and Development, which among other things recognizes the need to facilitate access to information at the national level. Likewise, chapter 40 of *Agenda 21*, the blueprint for sustainability agreed to in Rio, emphasizes the need for establishing and coordinating

Within the European Union (EU), an emphasis on environmental information is provided by Council Directive 313/90/EEC.[12] As a specific norm on environmental permitting, Council Directive 61/96/EC on Integrated Pollution Prevention and Control regulates access to environmental information in the course of the permitting process and during operation.[13] Further, EU Council Directive 337/85/EEC and its amendments, on environmental impact assessment (EIA), refers to participation rights in decision-making regarding individual administrative procedures with respect to development consents within a group of listed activities.[14]

Multilateral Codes of Practice

The World Bank Group requires environmental and social impact assessments of proposed projects, as well as Resettlement Plans and Indigenous Peoples Development Plans where appropriate. (These guidelines are currently the subject of the Bank's Extractive Industries Review for the mining sector.) Under the current disclosure policy, the external release of some information may be precluded in individual cases when the content, wording, or timing of the disclosure is deemed detrimental to the interests of the World Bank Group, a member country, or its staff. The International Finance Corporation (IFC) has guidelines that presume in favour of disclosure, although there are numerous exceptions, especially where the information is deemed to be materially harmful to the business and competitive interests of IFC clients. IFC senior management also have discretionary power that is loosely defined, further enabling case-by-case non-disclosure of certain information.[15] The International Bank for Reconstruction and Development and the International Development Association have similar conditions for information disclosure.

Under US law, all Executive Directors of US nationality at the World Bank and regional multilateral development banks are required to abstain or vote against any proposed action with significant impacts on human environment if it has not received an appropriate environmental assessment (and a Resettlement Plan and Indigenous Peoples Development Plan, as needed), or if the assessment has not been available to the Executive Directors and the public for 120 days before a vote.[16]

For the United Nations Environment Programme (UNEP), the United Nations Berlin Guidelines (of 1991) and the Environmental Guidelines for Mining Operations published in 1994 have information dissemination as a key component. The latter specifies that states, regulators, and companies should 'ensure that the decision maker(s) and the community are fully informed of the nature of the development, its impacts on the environment and the nature of the mitigating measure proposed as a component of good operational management'.[17] Further, UNEP's Awareness and Preparedness for Emergencies at the Local Level and the 1997 Benchmark Survey on company environmental reporting further extend the emphasis on information and disclosure.[18] And the Dublin Declaration of 16 October 2000 (through UNEP) commits to building a state-of-the-art environmental internet portal for public access.[19]

In many cases, international organizations set their own internal criteria for the dissemination and use of information, and these become by default the international standard. Examples include the World Bank's array of guidelines and the various standards set by the International Labour Organization, UNEP, and the European Commission, among others, which have implications for information access and use. It is noticeable that discussion of disclosure around environmental issues is far more advanced than that around social issues.

National Legislation

Most national governments have statutory provisions for information access in several areas, particularly on the environment and increasingly with regard to social concerns through the social impact assessment (SIA) process. In addition, regulatory regimes can drive the behaviour of companies listed on the stock markets in Australia, Canada, the UK, and the US. The initiatives of the securities regulators can also bring about greater clarity, credibility, and transparency among the junior and intermediate mining companies. Canada's National Instrument 43-101 was developed to ensure clarity, objectivity, and truth in reporting. The move towards web-based reporting to regulators can improve access and transparency. National environmental provisions are discussed here to illustrate government's role in the facilitation of access to information.

In Chile, environmental impact assessment is obligatory under the law, and there is a section on Community Participation in the Process of Evaluation of Environmental Impact under Regulation No. 30, enacted on 3 April 1997. An excerpt from the Environmental Impact Statement, including a description of the principal adverse environmental effects of the project, must be published in the Official Gazette and in a regional or national newspaper of general circulation within ten business days following its submission to Conama (National Environmental Commission) or the corresponding Corema (Regional Environmental Commission). Community organizations and individuals directly affected by mining projects have 60 business days to submit their observations on the Environmental Impact Statement. Legal entities must consider these opinions when issuing a verdict on an application to develop a project.[20]

In the United States, the National Environmental Policy Act of 1969 (Section 4332) includes provisions for reporting on the environmental impacts and implications of a proposal. This is complemented by provisions to make such information available to the public under the relevant provisions of the Freedom of Information Act. The Emergency Planning and Community Right-to-Know Act passed in 1986 requires businesses and local governments to report to state and local governments the locations and quantities of chemicals stored on-site. This was followed by mandatory public disclosure through the Toxics Release Inventory (TRI), providing communities with information about potentially hazardous chemicals and their use.[21] In 1991, facilities were also required to indicate the amounts of chemicals that are recycled, used for energy recovery, and treated on-site.[22]

In May 1997, the US Environmental Protection Agency added seven new industry sectors to the TRI: metal mines, coal mines, electrical utilities that combust coal or oil, commercial hazardous waste treatment facilities, chemical wholesalers, petroleum bulk terminals and plants, and solvent recovery services.[23] These sectors need to report activities such as the release of toxic substances into the environment and their transfer off-site for treatment or disposal. (In May 1998, the National Mining Association filed a lawsuit challenging this ruling that added the mining industry to the universe of facilities subject to section

313 of the Emergency Planning and Community Right-to-Know Act; the case is still under review.)[24]

In Australia, the National Environmental Protection Measure contains provisions for a National Pollutant Inventory (NPI). There are also provisions for internet access to the NPI database; production of annual CD-ROMs to be circulated to local libraries, to universities and educational institutions, and to state, territory, and local governments; and publication of reports summarizing NPI information. The information is to be made freely available to the public in plain English and includes links to other relevant databases and users of the information.[25]

The Canadian Environmental Assessment Act of 1992, c. 37 55 (1), has a registry of environmental assessment reports and provisions for public access. This system shifts the burden of enforcing reporting obligations to the respective government agencies. Canada also has its own National Pollutant Release Inventory, which companies are obliged to report to under the Canadian Environmental Protection Act of 1999.[26]

Voluntary Initiatives

Several voluntary initiatives seek to standardize the way in which corporations disclose information. Although there is still some way to go within the sector before a harmonized and standardized set of reporting guidelines is available, there are currently some promising opportunities to move forward on this issue.

The Global Reporting Initiative (GRI) was convened in 1997 by the Coalition for Environmentally Responsible Economies (CERES) 'to make sustainability reporting as routine and credible as financial reporting in terms of comparability, rigour and verifiability' through 'designing, disseminating and promoting standardized reporting practices, core measurements and customized sector specific measurements'.[27] UNEP has partnered with CERES in supporting GRI activities. The June 2000 GRI Sustainability Reporting Guidelines suggest reports should include a CEO statement, key indicators, a profile of the reporting entity, policies, organization and management systems, management performance, operational and product performance, and a sustainability overview. MMSD's work with GRI aimed at building a picture of the necessary conditions for a set of sector-specific harmonized guidelines for the mining sector. (See Box 12–2.) GRI will become an independent international institution in 2002.

Other systems, such as ISO 14001 from the International Organization for Standardization, have disclosure as an outcome of the auditing and management systems. The ISO addresses internal environmental management systems. Certain items within the ISO 14000 series of standards refer in general terms to external communications as part of an organization's environmental management systems.

Evolving out of the move towards improved environmental and social reporting are the notions of constructive obligations (wherein environmental obligations are derived from good business practice)

and equitable obligations – the duty to use the same reporting criteria in developing and industrial countries even when domestic law does not require it.

Several organizations are compiling systems for measuring sustainability performance based on a rating index, including private concerns such as Sustainable Asset Management, based in Switzerland.[28] The Dow Jones Index seeks to chart sustainability performance in the belief that this is more than a way to simply manage environmental risk but is becoming a proxy for good management in the wider sense.[29] Such systems are still evolving, but hold promise.

The World Resources Institute, the Environmental Management and Law Association in Budapest, and Corporacion PARTICIPA in Santiago are also collaborating on an initiative to improve policy and decision-making processes by establishing common global practices for access to information, participation, and justice in environmental decision-making.[30] The initiative seeks to raise awareness of issues and to build the capacity of public interest groups to assert their rights to information.

Corporate Best Practice

Corporate practice and behaviour on information access issues are evolving rapidly, and current best practice for the sector does indicate some ways forward. It includes the following approaches:[31]

- *Multi-parameter reporting* – This describes the company's economic, environmental, and social performance, also known as triple bottom-line or sustainability reporting.
- *Independent verification of environmental reports* – Since there are unresolved problems in measuring and verifying reports other than financial ones, a number of leading companies are experimenting with a process of independent verification.
- *Continuous community consultation* – This is an essential component in bridging the information and trust gap. A number of companies have adopted the policy and practice of continuous community consultation, from the first phase of exploration through to mine closure and beyond.
- *Community involvement in environmental management and community development* – This can be accomplished through a community-based environmental or social development monitoring

---

Box 12–2. The Global Reporting Initiative's Work on Indicators

MMSD worked with the Global Reporting Initiative to address some questions about establishing a broad set of public reporting criteria, based on indicators. Indicators are clearly a source of information, and the selection and aggregation of indicators is a sensitive issue, yet a vital one in trying to set up a fair and open public reporting system.

During 2001, the GRI and MMSD jointly convened an advisory panel to determine a work plan and the issues that should be addressed. The first step was the establishment of a 'straw dog' – a surrogate set of reporting indicators designed to act as a stimulus for discussion of the issues and problems involved in trying to adapt generic reporting guidelines to the mining sector. The 'straw dog' was based on a scoping study of more than 15 corporate reports from the mining sector and the comments of the Advisory Panel.

The 'straw dog' indicators, posted on the GRI website, are not meant to be exhaustive but rather to provide a starting point for discussion. GRI is interested in determining whether such a 'list' approach accurately captures the key indicators of sustainability for the sector and if there are any significant gaps that need to be addressed in defining a public reporting standard. While standardization of indicators for public reporting is a common cry, the point was made in MMSD-commissioned research that 'off the shelf' packages of indicators will fail to capture the kinds of information that communities want access to or the most important information about projects (Warhurst, 2002, p.113).

group that has access to and preferably participates in environmental sampling, review of results, and recommendations to improve measurement and management systems. Examples of this type of community–company collaboration include the northern Saskatchewan programme of Cameco in Canada and the community environmental group created around San Marcos by Antamina in Peru.[32]

- *Transparency of feasibility studies* – The EIA process is rapidly becoming substantially transparent in all jurisdictions, while the accompanying feasibility study remains largely company-confidential. Companies are under increasing pressure to ensure that local companies benefit from resource development. The experience of Diavik in Canada illustrates that disclosing the distribution of revenues can be a positive step to take to alleviate pressures.[33]

- *Open book reporting* – This can include areas still lagging behind in transparency, such as health, safety, and environmental reporting; closure and reclamation work reporting; and continuous reporting of not only positive aspects but also negative developments of a mine or project. A few large firms have started to use this 'open book' reporting of incidents to create corporate legitimacy.

- *The 'business case' for best practices in information disclosure* – Companies have a vested interest in providing clear, reliable, timely, and credible information on their performance. Some of the benefits may reduce transaction costs with other stakeholders and increase credit for transparency and accountability; the systematic organization of a reporting framework may reveal a great deal about the corporation and indicate areas of improvement. A strong business case can be made for the move towards a clear and comparable system of public reporting on economic, financial, social, and environmental issues.

Corporations are also guided in disclosure practice by the codes of their respective associations and governing bodies, such as the Sustainable Development Charter of the International Council on Mining & Metals or the Minerals Council of Australia's Code for Environmental Management.[34] (See Chapter 14.)

Initiatives by Other Private-Sector Actors

Private-sector actors, such as the major software and hardware providers, have played a significant role in the establishment of information standards used in the industry and will continue to be key with regard to the evolution of information technology. Microsoft programs, for example, are the default international standard for the format of much information.

Equally, the rapidly evolving mobile phone and satellite communications industries have implications for the mining and metals sector, making it much easier to disseminate complex information in a timely manner. As the prices of such technology decrease, there is a greater likelihood that they will be available to an increasing number of actors, although the digital divide between the North and South is at present still highly conspicuous, putting the poorer actors in these regions at a disadvantage. Advancing technologies, including solar-powered radio communications and other devices, have considerable potential.

Challenges for Specific Components of the Mining Sector

National Governments and Regulators

Governments have responsibilities to other stakeholders as regulators, but also as providers of the information necessary for a viable sector. At the exploration stage, for example, governments have a responsibility, capacity allowing, to maintain and provide adequate geoscience data for exploration purposes, including surface and subsurface geology, geochemical, and geophysical data.

The processes for establishing the norms and standards of information generation and transfer, the regulatory system to ensure conformity to these standards, the opportunities for reaction in the public domain, and the freedom to participate without fear of reprisal are largely the responsibility of the state, with the cooperation of other actors.

Within many developing countries, liberalization of mining codes has often neglected the interaction between communities and companies. Equally, the state plays a conflicting role as regulator and facilitator and may be subject to competing demands from different stakeholders. Additionally, most governments – industrial and developing – are struggling to come to terms with a globalized economy, rapidly changing information technologies, a more enlightened and demanding citizenry, and competition for mobile foreign investment, among other pressures. Many lack the capacity to act as facilitator or regulator, while in some countries corruption is common in state agencies. (See Chapter 8.) All these factors affect and are affected by the flow of information.

Government's role in pursuing mining and minerals development as a viable development alternative – as described in earlier chapters – includes establishing an institutional framework for gaining access to mineral resources, setting up effective and efficient legal systems, levying appropriate taxes, and designing an environmental regulatory system to prevent and control environmental impacts from mining activities. All these elements rely on the provision and exchange of information if they are to be established within the boundary conditions for sustainable development.[35]

In addition, provision needs to be made for public participation in the decision-making processes around the development of the sector. The Inter-American Strategy for the Promotion of Public Participation in Decision-Making for Sustainable Development has recognized the need for government to take a lead in providing the conditions for civil society to participate in resource use decision-making by providing adequate information and mechanisms at all levels of government.[36]

Public participation in planning and decision-making is a growing but still contested area of interaction between stakeholders around mining projects. This phenomenon – variously called public participation, citizen involvement, stakeholder engagement, indigenous peoples' rights, local community concerns, NGO intervention, access to information, and access to justice – will probably become even more central to sustainable development of mineral economies in the twenty-first century.

The factors behind this public participation 'explosion' include democratization trends since 1989, the adoption of the new paradigm of sustainable development, the international environmental movement, international financial organization requirements, human rights regimes, organizations of indigenous peoples and local communities, and technology – particularly the information-exchange capabilities of the internet.

To develop a baseline and an analysis of this issue, MMSD partnered with the Academic Advisory Group

(AAG) of the Section on Energy and Resources Law of the International Bar Association (IBA), the world's largest association of lawyers and legal associations. The AAG conducted a two-year study (1999–2001) of public participation in mining and resources development.[37] An MMSD and IBA workshop was held in May 2001.

It was suggested at the workshop that legal instruments are growing in recognition as a key element of public participation and that there is a definite trend towards contractual or quasi-contractual arrangements to satisfy (if not control) public participation and public benefit interests.[38] In Canada, for example, participation law is changing the way Canadian mining and resources government agencies, companies, and stakeholders operate. But, with the exception of First Nations, the laws have only created a partial bridge to real empowerment so far.

The emerging issues in public participation include regulatory reform, the need for empirical and comparative studies, the unevenness of public participation in practice in different countries, and the extent to which it is more than 'just politics'.

New international and national laws and practices are injecting this 'human dimension' into resources planning, financing, licensing, operating, and closure on a global scale. Two areas exemplify this trend:

- *Indigenous peoples* – Expropriation of indigenous peoples' lands and resources for national development – often without their consent or even consultation – is a serious problem. International law now requires, at a minimum, indigenous participation in resources development on traditional lands.
- *Protected areas* – There are a number of legal instruments relating to information and decision-making regarding protected areas. Three of the most important are the 1972 Convention for the Protection of the World Cultural and Natural Heritage, the 1971 Ramsar Convention on Wetlands of International Importance, and the 1992 Convention on Biological Diversity.

The mining and minerals industry's response to public participation should not be reactive or limited to government regulatory models. Companies have an interest in public participation processes that work, and if following the legal minimum will not create effective results, something more may be in order. Increasingly, the industry itself is creating new bilateral 'contract-based' arrangements that address the diverse social, economic, and environmental issues that arise in planning and developing new projects. These private-sector models of public participation may be necessary to supplement the prevailing public regulatory models where those are not adequate to create a sound basis for company interaction with communities and other stakeholders.

Four examples are:
- 'participation agreements' between Diavik, a diamond mining company, and Northwest Territories aboriginal peoples in Canada;
- 'local agreements' between the Flambeau open pit mine and government and community representatives in the US;
- 'future act agreements' between Rio Tinto and aboriginal groups in Australia; and
- the 'corporate social investment programme' of Richards Bay Minerals with local community and cultural heritage interests in South Africa.

Corporations

Information flows around the mining industry are complex and governed by the type of company, the stage in the mine cycle (exploration, feasibility, production, and so on), the location of the head office and the project, and the stakeholder group to which the information is directed.

For corporations, issues centre on obtaining information to enable effective economic and financial management of the business, including compliance with regulatory requirements. In addition to the regulations set out by the stock exchange and securities commissions regarding information disclosure, companies are also required to report on core corporate and head office functions. They also need to report to other authorities, such as environmental or fiscal bodies, where exploration or mine operations are located.

Increasingly, triple bottom-line thinking is encouraging companies to think more in terms of ethics and values, although regulation is still the primary driver for corporate disclosure of information.[39] Other corporate information pathways involve communications

between companies, among industry professionals, and with financial institutions. Disclosure is an ongoing process and a particular requirement of the junior sector during the exploration phase. Most information is generally available from press releases or annual and other reports. Without question, the most complete disclosure of a mine project comes with the presentation of an environmental impact statement during the permitting process for new mines. Differences exist between junior companies (which do exploration only) and the major companies that have operating mines. Regulatory disclosure is heavily influenced by the concept of materiality, which recognizes that anything likely to affect the value of decision-making around a project, prospect, or company is material and should be disclosed. The Toronto Stock Exchange acknowledges that materiality will vary with company size, since what is material to a small company will be insignificant to a large one. In the words of one corporate interviewee:

> There is a dynamic there that exists between a group that sees a benefit in releasing as much info as possible (partly to be clear to their shareholders, but also to create excitement) and a group that sees information flow as only necessary to meet regulatory approval, or such material goods such that there is an upside in the Profits: Earnings relationships.[40]

The junior sector desperately wants stakeholders to understand that it faces a dilemma: the costs of being a public company in an era of heightened information, disclosure, and regulatory demands is, some complain, undermining the capacity to perform their core functions – the discovery and delineation of mineral resources. Equally, for other juniors, restricted financing may mean that there is less attention to information issues in favour of other expenditures, which may create problems in the future.

There is also considerable disagreement about what reporting and disclosure should look like, since there is an incredible variation in standards and depth among voluntary reporting initiatives. The Stratos Group in Canada recently surveyed 35 companies (including 5 mining and minerals companies and 2 aluminium and steel companies).[41] Company reports were rated in terms of numerous criteria grouped into 10 categories:
- context and coverage (2 criteria);
- leadership and direction (3 criteria);

- policies, organization, and management systems (9 criteria);
- stakeholder relations (2 criteria);
- environmental performance (10 criteria);
- economic performance (7 criteria);
- social performance (8 criteria);
- integrated performance indicators (3 criteria);
- extending influence up and downstream (5 criteria); and
- trust, accountability, and accessibility (3 criteria).

Mining company reports scored an average of 58 points out of 156 against an overall average score of 55 and a maximum of 68 points for all sectors. The most effective reports demonstrated clearly that 'the reporting organization is managing its business using the performance indicators on which it reports'.[42]

Disclosure issues are particularly acute in the developing world, and here the mining sector faces its biggest test – applying the same standards of practice and performance, of ethics and behaviour, that would be applied in the corporation's home country. There are also several key areas in which many companies have been reluctant to disclose information:

- Many exploration groups would prefer to say as little as possible about their activities in order to avoid attracting the attention of 'anti-mining activists'.
- Among mine operators, there is wide concern that releasing information on environmental performance, particularly on water quality, air emissions, and solid wastes, would provide anti-mining groups with ammunition to use against the company, though this seems to be unfounded. In Canada, both Placer Dome and Noranda talk of labouring extensively over the decision to release all environmental data for their mines and anticipating negative comments.[43] Both companies report that to date, however, nothing untoward has happened. The only noticeable effect has been an end to requests from NGOs for such information. Yet for others this does not ring true – the posting of Toxic Release Inventory data on the internet in the US has brought widespread criticism of emissions practices, yet it is argued by some that this is because these data have been misunderstood and misrepresented by anti-mining entities.
- Companies are particularly concerned with maintaining competitive commercial advantage, which usually translates into keeping certain

technical expertise and intellectual property confidential. Two areas most frequently mentioned in this regard are geological information that would allow the company to find new ore reserves and process technology that would improve the efficiency or profitability of mine operations.

Clearly there is a need to restrict some information that is fundamental to the competitive advantage of a company, but the nature of this information is an area for negotiation between corporate and other actors. Restricting information about practices that gain a competitive advantage but that would be unacceptable under broadly held standards of practice is untenable.

Equally, the costs of information production and dissemination are extremely high, and it is not enough for other actors simply to ask for more and more information with little regard for cost. Balancing costs with value is a responsibility for all actors.

Communities often seek information on payments by corporations to other entities and in particular to government. In the long run, public disclosure of such payments must lead to a harmonized system of taxes as everybody becomes aware of the negotiated settlements of tax and other liabilities between governments and corporations in each jurisdiction. In some respects, this could be regarded as eating into the competitive advantage of a country as others try to attract investment. Nevertheless, balancing this, it is recognized that there is also a clear need to have transparency in all transactions between corporations and states, and that a most effective way to achieve this is to make payments public knowledge.

Beyond these issues, there are some general principles about information disclosure that most companies currently subscribe to:
- avoidance of disclosure during the reconnaissance phase of exploration and until a land position is firmly established;
- reluctance to engage the local community in full dialogue and consultation over the potential for a mine until late in the process of discovery and evaluation in order to avoid building false expectations, since most projects fail;
- confidentiality around the feasibility study, although all companies do not subscribe to this and, indeed, there is a measure of ambiguity about how the feasibility study is handled with financial analysts

and others; and

- keeping detailed information on the production costs of operating mines confidential, as companies believe possible release of these data could affect their long-term contracts with suppliers.

Labour

Labour has particular needs for information, as indicated, in terms of worker health and safety, other conditions of employment (including wages), opportunities for skills enhancement, and the options facing workers at mine closure, among other issues. There is clearly a need for a two-way process of access to information and a need for mechanisms that enable information to reach employers from workers.

The work force is the corporation's most valuable asset in achieving its productivity targets in a safe, sustainable, and appropriate manner. In this respect, workers must be ensured strong corporate management and ethics systems, whereby workers will not be victimized for calling attention to issues or practices the ending of which may adversely affect the bottom line in the short term but that in the long term are unsustainable.

Communities

Communities need information to participate in making informed decisions about mining activities. Yet simply providing information does not ensure that a message will be understood in a community or that the information will be disseminated widely. People's comprehension of information may be affected by, among other things, how the information is communicated, an individual's ability to obtain and use information, and the prior relationship between industry and the community. The National Research Council in the US recognizes several rationales for responding to community information needs:[44]

- Community members who are informed and involved in a project can become project proponents, reducing the potential for future conflict and reducing the risk of investment.[45]
- If community members are informed, there is a greater likelihood that potential issues will be identified at an early stage in the mine life cycle, allowing the company to respond to concerns, provided that the original information is true and verifiable.

- When community members are informed of mining development, local needs and strengths can be identified. Strengths and information can be leveraged, and local opportunities for growth can be pursued.

Notwithstanding the capacity issues that relate to communities, it is also worth noting that communities, when treated with respect, openness, and fairness, should respond in kind, with timely transmission of agreed information to companies and others where this information has relevance to project decision-making. Communities and civil society in general need access not only to public reports but also, on request, to the information that lies behind a report.

A number of factors will affect the way different members of the community understand or use information, such as gender (see Box 12–3), economic status, type of community, and literacy. Often there is a difference between expert and public assessments of risks and benefits. Community members may assess new developments or risks in the context of their everyday experiences, without necessarily being aware of specialized knowledge.[46]

With regard to company interactions with communities, exploration groups in general feel comfortable talking to local stakeholders about the process of exploration and the economic benefits of mining.[47] An exploration team often feels that it has to 'sell' the positive aspects of mining to bring the local community on side with the company in support of the project. Of course, there is a fine balancing between 'selling' a project and falling prey to misunderstandings developed from unrealistic expectations.

During the later stages of exploration and feasibility studies, all companies describe a concerted effort to communicate the benefits and opportunities that a new mine might bring to the local community or surrounding district.[48] Many companies appear to approach this phase with an assumption that the mine will become a positive experience for all and that there is a need to inform and educate the local population about this reality. Others, though a minority in the ranks of both junior and major companies, take a more pragmatic approach. They talk of the need to help the community understand what will happen if a mine is developed and the importance of identifying potential vulnerabilities, recognizing cultural sensitivities, and

Box 12–3. Information and Gender Considerations at Voisey's Bay, Canada

With the discovery of considerable mineral wealth in the Voisey's Bay region of northern Labrador, the Voisey's Bay Nickel Company (VBNC) set out to undertake an environmental impact assessment. At the outset of this process the VBNC asserted that the 'proponent shall also explain how it has used feminist research to identify how the Undertaking will affect women differently than men'. The participation of women in the consultation was limited to the public processes.

After two years of consultation, the company failed to document how the mining development could potentially affect the lives of women in surrounding communities. The Tongamiut Inuit Annait Ad Hoc Committee on Aboriginal Women (TIA) responded by drafting gender equality provisions for the Labrador Inuit Association to include in its impact-and-benefits negotiations with VBNC. The TIA was later informed that the company had rejected their proposed provisions, but the committee had no sense of the dynamics surrounding the negotiations, nor any details on why these provisions were rejected. They were thus denied the opportunity to negotiate alternative wording or have some provisions included at the expense of others. In response, TIA noted:

> As primary caregivers...women end up coping with the results and effects of development decisions made by men. They may, in fact, bear the brunt of these impacts. Limited and impoverished information gathering for the EIS will result in inadequate mitigative and monitoring programmes. Women and their organizations, which receive very little financial support from governments or industry, will be left to pick up the pieces. If there are to be positive changes for women in our communities, women must be able to voice their own perceptions...and demand full participation in the planning, decision-making and evaluating process of this development.

Source: Archibald and Carnkovich (1999); Tongamiut Inuit Annait Ad Hoc Committee on Aboriginal Women and Mining in Labrador (1997)

carefully matching expectations to the economic potential of the resource.

Indigenous communities have a particular need for the provision of good and timely information that is set in contexts that can be understood locally. Again, trust must be established at an early stage through open dialogue. A systematic approach based on advice from community members should be established so that technical information can be translated and communicated in an appropriate manner. Some

companies are already leading with approaches that include participatory techniques for describing the minerals exploitation process and the local implications for indigenous communities. Local advice is essential if effective communications are to be established with indigenous communities.

One example of a proactive approach to advising others on consulting with indigenous peoples has been provided by the Nishnawbe Aski Nation (NAN), Land and Resources/Economic Development Unit, which – in response to companies exploring on their lands in search of diamonds without prior consent – has published a guide to consultation for use by explorationists. The guide details the correct procedure to follow in negotiating access with local communities. (See Figure 12-1.)

Finally, it should also be remembered that companies and others collect information on communities. Again there is the need for well-established systems of governance that will protect sensitive information, particularly when community members speak in confidence on specific issues.

NGOs and Other Civil Society Actors

NGOs vary widely in their approach to the mining and metals sector. Development NGOs have been more willing to work with companies and governments on issues relating to the siting and operation of mining and metals processing facilities in terms of social and environmental performance. Companies, NGOs, and communities have benefited from such collaborative approaches.

The role of advocacy NGOs and other civil society organizations involved with the sector, on the other hand, has often been ambivalent and contentious. While companies argue for a rationalization of information disclosure systems, NGOs, community-based organizations, and others argue that they need access to all the information and that they will then decide what is useful. Indeed, there is a great deal of suspicion about decisions on disclosure that are left entirely in the hands of governments or companies. The NGO community has been extremely vocal and highly skilled when opposing aspects of particular mining projects or the industry in general. The industry is disillusioned by a seeming failure of

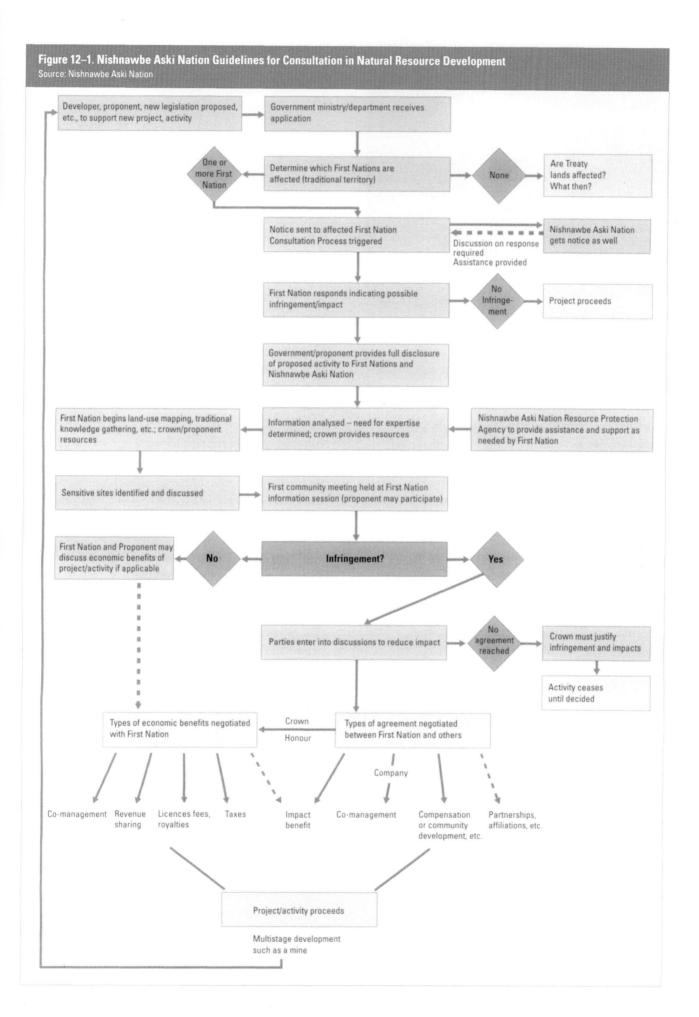

Figure 12–1. Nishnawbe Aski Nation Guidelines for Consultation in Natural Resource Development
Source: Nishnawbe Aski Nation

Local and national government representatives presenting the Environment Plan for the Lihir gold mine, PNG

governance and frustrated that regulators do not regulate the information flows from other stakeholders effectively.[49]

Despite their reservations, mining companies both large and small are coming to realize that they must engage broadly with these stakeholders. The reality is that not responding and not getting involved is damaging in and of itself. In an interview one industry respondent stated that 'the Catch-22 is exposed: if you don't give out information, your silence is assumed to be some sort of guilt. If you do give out information, it is corrupted from its original spirit and used against you there too'.[50] Ultimately, NGOs and other groups can be as bad at handling information as companies or anyone else; good information may be used ineffectively. On the other hand, civil society organizations may, for example, only reveal partial information about a project, company, or circumstance in order to make a political point, when standards of corporate disclosure would demand that all information is put on the table so that other stakeholders can make up their own minds.

There are obviously unresolved issues that currently interfere with proactive relations between mining companies and these stakeholders, not least of which are the counterproductive perceptions created by the entrenching of positions on the many sides of the mining debate.

The Way Forward

Given that the mining industry does not enjoy the

trust that it should, the need for good, verifiable information is paramount. All actors are involved. Some things can be rectified immediately, and others will take extensive and long-term negotiation within a framework that is also trusted. Progress demands a focus not just on what information people want, but the processes through which it is generated. The fundamental importance of multistakeholder initiatives as the new way to address pressing sustainable development issues should also be stressed.

Governments

Governments continue to be responsible for setting norms and standards and for regulating industry's adherence to them. The culture of disclosure differs not only between the industrial and developing worlds but also within industrial countries. Desirable norms – as seen by the more liberal jurisdictions – include:

• All levels of government having legal and regulatory provisions permitting citizens free access to any information in government possession for which there is not a valid and publicly stated reason for non-disclosure. Mechanisms need to back this up, such as contact points established for the regular exchange of information with civil society. An example would be public information repositories in communities where mineral projects are proposed.

• Government agencies and civil society organizations having established clear and agreed procedures for requesting, receiving, and disseminating information, including opportunities for the public to identify the information they need for effective and responsible participation in the decision-making process.

• Government agencies – after consulting civil society organizations – having performance indicators to measure the effectiveness of information and communications programmes. They should be responsive to user opinions about problems.

• Government proponents of projects having a complete information and communication strategy for the various phases of major projects. The best strategies extend to monitoring, auditing, and reporting. Comments from the public are sought and considered.

• Government and civil society having expanded the availability of information technology to grassroots organizations and rural and remote communities so as to ensure that information arrives in the form appropriate to the intended recipients, at the appropriate time.

- Information being used as a 'levelling' tool to ensure that all affected groups have adequate knowledge and can participate effectively on a fair basis with decision-makers. This can include a tremendous effort in situations where there is illiteracy and a language barrier. For example, the various impact statement processes are of little use if local people have no conception of what is proposed. Here, in particular, it is essential that communication happens. It is not enough to have baseline information that is accurate, science-based where appropriate, and verifiable if no one can understand it. These data also often need to reflect traditional knowledge perspectives where relevant, and must be available to communities and others as part of the process of verification.
- Government supporting research into ways of fostering public participation in decision-making, opening up access to information, and defining and fostering stakeholder rights.

Thus the challenge of governments is to find ways to improve the communications aspects of all mineral-related activities. It only needs the will to do this, as all manner of precedent and tools are available.

Companies

Out of the MMSD process, a set of clear best bets has emerged around the information issue:

- Corporations should work with the Global Reporting Initiative or other international bodies to harmonize public reporting. Trust will follow if what is reported in the public domain conforms to a broadly agreed set of reporting standards. The GRI is currently taking the lead with respect to compiling sector-specific guidelines for public reporting, and increased collaboration between the sector and GRI would be beneficial. There is a role for the International Council on Mining & Metals and other organizations such as the Prospectors and Developers Association of Canada in bringing the experience of companies and associations to bear on the formulation of sector-specific guidelines for the mining and metals industry.
- There is also a need for a standard for information management compliance that can be independently verified. Two ISO standards provide a potential

framework for such a standard. The quality and environmental standards, already used by many mining, minerals, and metals companies, involve a process of defining policies and procedures for a management system, which is independently audited against the standard. Deficiencies and non-conformances are identified, and corrective or preventative actions are taken. Compliance is certified, and the performance is continually measured, with a view to improvement.

- An industry Sustainable Development Protocol (see Chapter 16) could, and probably should, establish benchmarks for public reporting practice based on verifiable criteria. This could draw on experience from other sectors and the best in the sector itself.
- The private finance community should take a stronger role in encouraging best practice in public disclosure. This does not imply that the finance sector should police the minerals sector, but that lenders in particular, through rigorous attention to internationally accepted norms, should demand best-practice performance as part of the management of risk. Loan checklists, for example, should include the project's information policy and disclosure strategy. The ethical investment community should include reporting issues in its criteria for ranking companies.
- Corporations should work to create a culture that sees fair and equitable dissemination of information as desirable. To do this there needs to be a clear policy that distinguishes proprietary information, which the company's commercial interest requires be confidential, from other types of information that should be publicly available. This requires a clear move away from systems in which all company information is presumed secret and multiple internal reviews and permissions are necessary to divulge anything.
- Public information strategies in such things as permitting and EIA processes must be based on achieving the company's goal for effective communication, not simply following legal requirements as a checklist. If the company wants to communicate effectively to local people, it must move beyond compliance to a strategy that is focused on broader objectives. For example, experience shows that even where the law does not require it, information provided at the local level needs to be given in the language of those who are supposed to be its key beneficiaries. Facilities need to be provided for those who take a different view to be heard too. If there is significant local illiteracy, other tools appropriate to the community should be

devised. Equally, the company needs to have a way
to listen effectively to communications given in the
local language.

Labour
Workers have specific information rights and needs.
Among labour concerns are likely to be plans and
provisions for the eventual closure of any facility.
The best ones have mechanisms for sharing this
information and having a candid two-way dialogue on
the subject.

• Companies need specific policies, consistent with
  emerging international norms, for providing
  information to workers and getting information
  from workers. Global agreements would be one
  mechanism to enable this. Organized labour has an
  important role to play in coordinating the
  establishment of standards with recognized industry
  bodies and governments, while also advising
  individual companies on appropriate policies.
• Labour agreements should address the exchange
  of information between workers and their
  organizations and companies.

Communities
Communication goes both ways: it is about listening as
much as it is about providing information. A few
fundamental principles of community consultation
seem clear:[51]

• Communities have the right to be informed of
  development before a project begins, indeed before
  any irrevocable commitment to that project has
  been made.
• Communities have the right to seek multiple sources
  of information. There is no single account of
  minerals development that is 'objective', as
  development often has many unintended
  consequences. People cannot foresee all eventualities,
  and all accounts provide a different lens on the
  foreseeable future.
• Communities operate on very different time scales
  for taking decisions. The communication process
  should not be compressed by arbitrary time limits
  established by the company's decision deadlines or
  the government's legal requirements.
• Communities have the right to seek information
  from sources that they trust, at the same time as they

evaluate information from those they do not. But
systematic approaches to the production and use of
information must be mindful of the potential for
unnecessary delay through unproductive duplication
of information from multiple sources.

NGOs and Civil Society
The emerging norms on information disclosure and
access are equally applicable to NGOs and other civil
society groups in the minerals sector:

• NGOs and others should have systems of
  governance that will ensure they can perform to the
  same standards of transparency, accountability, and
  legitimacy demanded of other stakeholders.
• Information is the currency with which many
  NGOs do their work. The more confidence there is
  in that currency, the more effective they will be.
  Thus the best NGOs have clear and understood
  procedures for evaluating information before they
  act on it.
• NGOs should work with other stakeholders to
  define best practice in public disclosure. It is not
  enough to simply ask for 'all information' to be
  made available in a public reporting format.
  Cost and efficiency considerations require that
  information production and dissemination are
  conducted in a rational manner. Information
  production also needs to pass the tests of usefulness,
  adequacy, timeliness, appropriateness, and
  effectiveness.
• Many NGOs also recognize that they are in a
  unique position within society. Because of their past
  record, they have enormous powers of influence.
  Through their scrutiny, they have provided a check
  on the excesses of governments and corporations.
  The work of NGOs is thus viewed as altruistic and
  morally commendable, which means they are
  afforded considerable trust by civil society. To hold
  on to that trust, they too have to ensure that it is
  not abused through the dissemination of information
  that cannot be substantiated or that is selective in its
  interpretation. Full and frank disclosure, even when
  the information does not support the message or
  the agenda, is the policy of the best – as is the need
  to speak out when others in the sector are clearly
  wrong.
• NGOs could well develop a code of practice around
  information production and use. The integration of
  such a code would have several benefits, including

the strengthening of trust in their own organizations by other stakeholders.

International and Multilateral Actions
In the international arena, the following actions found a wide measure of support in the workshops and consultations:

- Establishment of an international base of data on mining and minerals, including data on several key areas where people want to learn from each others' efforts. The information should be described in a fashion that does not assume expert knowledge and that respects the need for confidentiality in some areas and the intellectual property rights of others. The database could be housed in existing international organizations or in industry associations. It might include information about:
  - legislation, regulations, policy, guidelines, and voluntary codes;
  - royalties and taxes;
  - mining fundamentals, including types of deposits, metals, and markets;
  - payments made by companies to government;
  - payments received by governments from companies;
  - terms of impacts and benefits agreements;
  - EIA, SIA, and conflict impact assessment guidelines and practice;
  - corporate public reports and other relevant information; and
  - consultation procedures.
  Such a database is seen as a resource for communities, governments, companies, and others and could be established with the cooperation of existing government and university institutions as well as civil society organizations, could be housed with an inter-governmental body such as UNEP, and could be financed through a trust fund, through fees from users (graduated according to category), or through multilateral donor and industry support.
- Establishment (through a body such as the GRI) of criteria for a harmonized public reporting system that would include verification, which is agreed to by a multistakeholder process. Although such a system would of necessity be voluntary, as no international legal mechanisms exist to enforce it, more research could be conducted to explore whether and how an appropriate regulatory regime

might work or be established.
- Development of a wide-ranging and binding set of principles on reporting to communities at mine sites, in particular during and after accidents.
- Establishment of an international multistakeholder panel to address the implications of instruments such as the Aarhus Convention and mechanisms for implementation at an industry level.
- An international focus on systems for financing improved access to information and in particular to look at questions of capacity versus needs and North/South issues of information access.
- Creation of mechanisms for greater collaboration among corporations, governments, and civil society on access issues that facilitate capacity building for governments and communities.
- Development of systems of accountability that ensure that principles and practices aimed at high environmental and social performance and outlined in corporate reports are consistent with the principles by which a company is managed.

Endnotes

[1] Amartya Sen as cited in Lash (2001) p.586.

[2] Howard Zinn as quoted in Beder (1997) p.288.

[3] Beder (1997).

[4] See, for example, Fukuyama (1996).

[5] Anecdotal evidence based on informal discussions with corporate sustainability leaders. Work needs to be done to confirm these general reflections.

[6] Zadek et al. (1997) p.239.

[7] United Nations Environment and Human Settlement Division (1998).

[8] Fulop and Kiss (2001) p.45.

[9] United Nations Environment and Human Settlement Division (1998).

[10] OECD (1996).

[11] Organization of American States (2000).

[12] The EU Directive on freedom of access to information on the environment. See http://europa.eu.int/servlet/portail/RenderServlet?search=DocNumber&lg=en&nb.

[13] The EU Directive on pollution prevention and control. See http://europa.eu.int/servlet/portail/RenderServlet?search=DocNumber&lg=en&nb.

[14] The EU Directive on the assessment of the effects of certain public and private projects on the environment. See http://europa.eu.int/servlet/portail/RenderServlet?search=DocNumber&lg=en&nb

[15] Fulop and Kiss (2001) p.45.

[16] In 1989, the US Congress passed into law the Pelosi amendment (U.S. Code Title 22, Chapter 7, Section 262m), a step towards ensuring proper administration of the environmental assessment process at the World Bank and at all regional multilateral development banks.

[17] UNEP-UNDESA (1994) p.19.

[18] UNEP (1988).

[19] UNEP-Infoterra Network (2000).

[20] Government of Chile (1997).

[21] The Emergency Planning & Community Right-To-Know Act (EPCRA) was passed by Congress as part of the Superfund Amendments and Reauthorization Act of 1986 (SARA). As a result, EPCRA is also referred to as SARA Title III. The Toxics Release Inventory is a publicly available EPA database that contains information on toxic chemical releases and other waste management activities reported annually by certain covered industry groups as well as federal facilities. This inventory was established under the Emergency Planning and Community Right-to-Know Act of 1986 and expanded by the Pollution Prevention Act of 1990. See http://www.epa.gov/tri/.

[22] See http://www.epa.gov/tri/.

[23] Ibid.

[24] See Fulop and Kiss (2001) for a discussion of the legal challenge mounted by the NMA.

[25] See Environment Australia-National Pollutant Inventory website, http://www.npi.gov.au/.

[26] See Environment Canada-National Pollutant Release Inventory website, http://www.ec.gc.ca/pdb/npri/.

[27] Global Reporting Initiative (1999).

[28] See Sustainable Asset Management website, http://www.sam-group.com/.

[29] See Dow Jones Sustainability Indexes website, http://www.sustainability-index.com/.

[30] World Resource Institute (2001) p.4.

[31] Thomson and MacDonald (2001).

[32] Comeco (2001); Compania Minera Antamina (2001).

[33] Diavik-Diamonds Mines Inc. (2000).

[34] See ICMM (2001).

[35] Rosenfeld Sweeting and Clark (2000).

[36] Organization of American States (2000).

[37] Zillman, Lucas, and Pring (2002).

[38] Pring (2001) p.22.

[39] Elkington (1998) p.407; Thomson and MacDonald (2001) p.32.

[40] Thomson and MacDonald (2001) p.32.

[41] Stratos Inc. (2002) p.4.

[42] Ibid., p.iii.

[43] Thomson and MacDonald (2001).

[44] National Research Council (1996).

[45] Rosenfeld Sweeting and Clark (2000).

[46] Powell and Leiss (1997).

[47] Thomson and MacDonald (2001).

[48] Ibid.

[49] Ibid.

[50] Ibid.

[51] Gibson (2001b) p.18.

CHAPTER 13

ARTISANAL AND SMALL-SCALE MINING

Most attention in the mining industry is focused on large companies, but in many parts of the world, particularly in developing countries, minerals are extracted by artisanal and small-scale mining (ASM) – by people working with simple tools and equipment, usually in the informal sector, outside the legal and regulatory framework. The vast majority are very poor, exploiting marginal deposits in harsh and often dangerous conditions – and with considerable impact on the environment.

ASM is a livelihoods strategy adopted primarily in rural areas. In many cases, mining represents the most promising, if not the only, income opportunity available. However, ASM activities are often viewed negatively by governments, large companies, environmentalists, and others. Concerns range from the use of child labour and the potential for environmental damage (particularly through the use of mercury in gold mining) to the use of ASM revenue to finance conflicts, the social disruption and conflict sometimes caused by 'rush' operations, the high incidence of prostitution, and the spread of HIV/AIDS where migrant workers are involved.

At the extreme, governments consider the sector illegal and attempt to ban it through different means. In many cases (since ASM falls outside the regulatory framework), they simply neglect it, thereby allowing negative social and environmental impacts to be aggravated. In only a few cases has this part of the mining sector been supported and regulated successfully. The relationship between large companies and small-scale miners is poorly understood and often troubled, with mutual mistrust and sometimes conflict. Large companies may consider small-scale miners as 'trespassers', while small-scale miners may see the granting of a concession to a large company as depriving them of their land and livelihoods. Although examples of more positive relationships are beginning to emerge, accusations are still made that governments and large mining companies, sometimes in collusion, forcibly evict small-scale miners from their land.

The relative contribution of ASM to sustainable development depends on the priorities accorded to different objectives. In terms of meeting the world's need for minerals, large companies currently dominate overall. For some minerals – such as emeralds and tungsten – virtually all production is from ASM. From an economic perspective, most resources can be mined far more efficiently and intensively using large-scale mining methods, and in terms of environmental damage, small-scale mining generally has a greater impact per unit of output. From a livelihoods perspective, ASM often provides the only means of obtaining income and is therefore important. Yet for many people it never provides more than a subsistence wage, so its actual contribution is often limited.

In the short to medium term, whatever the contribution – whether positive or negative – at the poorer end of the spectrum ASM activities will continue for at least as long as poverty drives them. Moreover, the rights of individuals to secure a livelihood must be respected, as must the objectives of meeting basic needs and maximizing economic well-being. It is therefore essential that efforts be made to maximize the benefits brought by small-scale mining and to avoid or mitigate the costs. Attempts to achieve this are constrained by a number of factors. Some of these, such as the lack of government and community capacity, apply to larger companies as well. Others are specific to ASM, such as poor access to finance and a lack of collective capacity, particularly for artisanal mining with operations at an individual or household level.

In the longer term, however, many ASM activities are likely to disappear naturally if progress towards sustainable development is made since alternative, more attractive employment options for small-scale miners will become available. This is not to say that some forms of ASM will not persist, particularly those undertaken seasonally on a low-intensity scale or those that are formalized and managed in a collective way where the nature of deposits lend themselves to smaller-scale activities.

This chapter provides an overview of artisanal and small-scale mining in developing countries and the social, environmental, and economic issues associated with it. ASM's relationships with government, large-scale mining, and international institutions are discussed. Examples of initiatives aimed at improving or supporting ASM, including its contribution at the national and local level, and at reducing its environmental impact are given. But no one issue pertaining to ASM can be dealt with in isolation. Any attempts to introduce change – for example, to reduce the environmental impact of ASM or to phase out child labour – must be accompanied by awareness-building and the provision of immediate incentives. These may come in the form of tangible economic or health benefits or alternative livelihood opportunities. Efforts must also consider the broader objectives of sustainable rural development.

The chapter is based on a summary of a global report on ASM commissioned by MMSD. In addition the chapter draws on 18 country studies commissioned by MMSD (on Bolivia, Brazil, Burkina Faso, China, Ecuador, Ghana, India, Indonesia, Malawi, Mali, Mozambique, Papua New Guinea, Peru, Philippines, South Africa, Tanzania, Zambia, Zimbabwe) as well as the outputs of a regional and global workshop hosted by MMSD. The country studies provide a more detailed understanding of the legal status of artisanal and small-scale miners; the status, role, and importance of ASM in a country; specific support activities for the sector; and interactions between small-scale miners and large exploration and mining companies.

Characteristics and Products of ASM

There is as yet no widely accepted definition of artisanal and small-scale mining. The term can be used to cover a broad spectrum of activities – from the army-run Hpakant jade mines in Myanmar, for example, to individual *garimpeiros* panning for gold in remote regions of the Brazilian Amazon, as well as former state mining company workers or laid-off private-company employees who have organized themselves into cooperatives.[1] At the other end of the scale, particularly in industrial countries, are many quite sophisticated industrialized small-scale mining activities. This chapter largely focuses on artisanal and small-scale mining in developing countries that use the most basic methods for extraction and processing.

The broadest distinction – and the one followed here – is between artisanal mining, which may involve only individuals or families and is purely manual, and small-scale mining, which is more extensive and usually more mechanized. Another distinction is in the nature of miners' rights to the land. In some instances, small-scale miners have legal title to the land that they work, which is recognized by the state and others. In other cases, they work land they have traditionally inhabited but without any recognition of land rights from the state, or they may be working the land informally and regarded as illegal squatters by local and state authorities. Of the two groups, artisanal miners are

'Quimbalete' – a small-scale mining amalgamation mill in Peru

more likely to be working without legal mining title.

But artisanal and small-scale miners also share many characteristics, broadly speaking:

- They exploit marginal or small deposits.
- They lack capital.
- They are labour-intensive, with low rates of recovery.
- They have poor access to markets and support services.
- They have low standards of safety and health.
- They have a significant impact on the environment.

Who Are Artisanal and Small-scale Miners?

Most of these miners – men, women, or children – are rural and poor. In such countries as Bolivia, Colombia, Indonesia, Mali, the Philippines, and Zimbabwe, they often come from communities that have a long tradition of small-scale mining. But they are not necessarily involved in this full-time. Artisanal miners often work seasonally: in Malawi, for instance, subsistence farmers mine gemstones in the dry season when there is less agricultural work. People may also take up mining as a last resort during periods of economic recession – as has happened in Bolivia, Peru, Venezuela, and Zimbabwe. Many other people can suddenly be drawn into mining following the discovery of new mineral reserves, as with gold or diamond 'rushes' during which thousands of people hope to make their fortunes. Examples of this include Serra Pelada in Brazil (gold), Mt. Kare in Papua New Guinea (gold), Ilakakain in Madagascar (sapphire), and Nambija in Ecuador (gold). ASM activities can also follow environmental shocks, as occurred in Southern Ecuador following the 1985 El Niño.

Since there is no clear definition of ASM, and because many of these miners work casually or informally, it is impossible to arrive at a total number of artisanal and small-scale miners.[2] Recent research suggests that throughout the world small-scale mining involves on the order of 13 million people directly, mainly in developing countries, and that it affects the livelihoods of a further 80–100 million.[3] The important point is that the number of people employed in ASM is very large.

In the future, the number of people working in ASM in certain regions could well rise as economies falter. In Zimbabwe and other parts of Southern Africa, for instance, the number is expected to triple over the next ten years.[4] The number of miners also fluctuates with the international demand – and thus price – for a particular mineral. For example, the global increase in the use of mobile phones recently contributed to a surge of informal mining activity for coltan (the mineral columbite-tantalite is a primary source for the metal tantalum, which is used in capacitors) in the Democratic Republic of Congo. (See Chapter 10.)

Artisanal and small-scale mining also contributes to the livelihoods of people other than miners, their dependants, and the local economy. Many miners do not complete the processing themselves but instead sell the ore to intermediaries, who concentrate it and transport the products to market.

Women Miners

Women play a relatively small part in large-scale mining but are frequently involved in smaller-scale operations. In Bolivia, for example, women account for around 40% of the ASM work force; in Madagascar, Mali, and Zimbabwe, the proportion is 50%; and in Guinea, the figure is 75%.[5] Moreover, women may be predominant in particular parts of the industry: in the Gaoua region of Burkina Faso, for example, the exploitation and selling of gold has traditionally been a female-only activity.[6] Table 13–1, based on MMSD-commissioned studies, summarizes the extent of women's involvement in selected countries. Women are engaged in most aspects of mining except usually the handling of mechanized equipment, which tends to be reserved for men. They are also indirectly involved through ancillary activities such as the supply of food, drink, tools, and equipment, as well as in trading gold and gemstones.[7]

In some cases, particularly in Africa, women own mines or processing plants. Frequently, these enterprises are better managed than those run by men, even though women find it more difficult to get financial, legal, or technical support.[8] In the case of bank loans,

Table 13–1. Women and Children Directly Employed in Artisanal and Small-scale Mining in Selected Countries				
Country	Number of Women	Women as Share of Work Force	Number of Children	Children as Share of Work Force
Bolivia	15,500	22%	–	–
Burkina Faso	45,000–85,000	45%	–	–
Ecuador	6,200	7%	4,600	5%
Ghana	89,500	45%	–	–
India	33,500	7%	–	–
Indonesia	10,900	10%	2,180	2%
Malawi	4,000	10%		
Mali	100,000	50%	–	–
Mozambique	18,000*	30%*	*	*
Papua New Guinea	12,000	20%	18,000	30%
Philippines	46,400	25%	9,300	5%
South Africa	500	5%	–	–
Tanzania	143,000	26%	>3,000	–
Zambia	9,000	30%	–	–
Zimbabwe	153,000	<50%	–	–

*Estimate is for women and children.   – indicates no information available
Source: MMSD country studies

this is because women find it harder to offer collateral and may lack the education that would help them deal with formal lending institutions.[9] But they also face various forms of prejudice – official or popular. In seeking finance, they may find male bankers who disapprove of women engaging in business.[10] And they also come up against traditional obstacles. In Zambia, for example, one of Africa's most prominent women mine owners reported: 'People believe that a woman should not venture near a gemstone mine because the spirits of the stones would be disturbed and the stones will burrow deeper into the earth. I fought all that superstition, obtained a prospecting licence, and here I am.'[11]

A distinct advantage of having female members of the household involved in mining is that they are more likely than men to spend their incomes on maintaining their families – investing in, for example, food, schooling, clothing, or agriculture. Men are more likely to spend their wages on gambling, alcohol, and prostitutes.[12] When women are engaged in mining as members of a mining household, however, they have less control over expenditures, as the income is still likely to be managed by men.[13]

Child Labour

Artisanal and small-scale mining also involves significant numbers of children – an issue that received international attention in the 1990s following press reports of child labour in coal mines in Colombia.[14] It is difficult to say how many children are working in mines, although MMSD country studies did come up with estimates in a few cases, as indicated in Table 13–1.

Child labour, in mining as in other forms of work, is rooted in poverty. Children work in the mines to help their parents, and to supplement the family income in order to buy basic goods such as clothing and food. Since much of the work is physically hard, they may not be fully involved at first. Typically children increase the scope of their activities as they grow older: from the age of three, some might start washing gold, while from age six they could be breaking rocks with hammers or washing ore. From nine onwards, however, children can be found labouring underground and doing much the same work as adults. Where small size is an advantage, younger children may also work underground.

Working long hours under arduous conditions is difficult enough for adults. It takes an even more serious toll on the soft bones and growing bodies of children. Young children are also especially vulnerable to physical and chemical hazards. In Peru, for example, children as young as six are exposed to the mercury used in gold extraction.[15] Beyond this they also suffer psychological and social disadvantages and may sacrifice future prospects. Some child mineworkers do not go to school, while others do so erratically – hampering their education and ultimately reinforcing the cycle of poverty. Parents may be unaware of the immediate risks and long-term disadvantages, though in such situations of extreme hardship they are usually more preoccupied with day-to-day survival than with their children's future prospects.

Child labour is illegal in most countries. The ages of prohibition vary from country to country and from one occupation to another, but all governments try to exclude young children from mines. In 1999 the International Labour Organization (ILO) adopted Convention 182 on the 'Worst Forms of Child Labour' – and working in mines is one of these forms.[16] This convention had been ratified by 113 countries by the end of 2001, yet many children continue to work in mines or in processing activities.[17]

What Does ASM Produce?

Artisanal and small-scale miners extract a broad range of minerals. In many countries, most of them produce gold, which has the advantage of being relatively simple to extract, refine, and transport. In Ecuador and Ghana, for example, gold accounts for two-thirds of their production of minerals; in the Philippines, it accounts for 90% and in Peru, almost 100%.[18]

Many miners extract gems and precious stones, such as diamonds, sapphires, and garnets; these are easy to process, transport, and sell – legally or illegally. For others, as in Bolivia, the main opportunities may lie with other metals, including silver and zinc. In China, small-scale miners work with over 20 minerals, but the majority mine coal (46%) and construction materials (44%) that they sell in local markets.[19] In India, the range is even more diverse, involving more than 40 different minerals.[20]

As in the modern part of the mining sector, the decision on what to mine is based on many different factors, including the quality and accessibility of the ore and market prices. There is also something of a division of labour: the larger enterprises prefer deposits that allow them to profit from mechanization and economies of scale – so they favour seams that are wide and uniform even if these require working underground or shifting large quantities of overburden. This leaves a niche for miners who work on a smaller scale, are more flexible, and can exploit irregular ore bodies and steep, dipping seams. However, conflict over ore bodies may arise, for example, where a large deposit has a particularly high-grade section close to the surface that would help a large-scale operation offset set-up costs, as it may also appear attractive to small-scale miners.

As the large companies do, artisanal and small-scale miners weigh production costs against market prices. But since they do not have either the capital or the time to invest in exploration or geological studies, they rely more on local knowledge and experience. And once they find a likely deposit, they will start to exploit it immediately.

The form of mining will depend on the location of the ore: whether it has to be mined underground, can be reached via an open hole in the ground, or is available as an alluvial deposit in rivers or streams. In each case, the tools and techniques used are normally fairly rudimentary – extracting with pickaxes and shovels, and sluicing and panning with simple equipment. Small-scale miners also carry out any subsequent processing with materials that are simple to use and cheap, such as mercury or cyanide. Although they may use less sophisticated processing methods, these miners can recover quite high proportions of minerals from ore by repetitive reworking and scavenging. (See Box 13–1.)

The often large numbers of people involved in ASM means that on a national scale total production can be significant – in some cases equalling or exceeding that of large mines. According to the ILO, in recent years artisanal and small-scale mining accounted for 15–20% of the world's non-fuel mineral production.[21]

The importance of small-scale mining for different minerals varies between country and sector. It accounts for the vast proportion of gemstones (90–100% in

---

Box 13–1. Repetitive Scavenging and Mineral Recovery

Though small-scale miners use low levels of technology, mineral recovery is often boosted by unplanned repetitive scavenging. In the first stage of recovery, miners pick out the higher-grade ore by hand, leaving the lower-grade ore as mine-fill. But even this low-grade ore may be used eventually: the same or other miners may return to it later, if more attractive alternatives are not available, since it will not need drilling or blasting. Sooner or later, any ore that provides a living will be exploited by some means or other.

The second opportunity for retrieving ore takes place at the processing plant, when more low-grade material is picked out before feeding the ore into the plant. After processing, the 'tailings' will be dumped along with the low-grade ore. Again, little of this residue tends to be wasted. Women and children frequently rework these dumps until nothing is left.

Recovery is also increased by sequential processing. In the case of gold, for example, artisanal or small-scale miners may recover only around 50% of the metal at the first stage by amalgamation with mercury. But they can also accumulate the tailings and later sell them or process them with cyanide. Artisanal cyanidization may not be very efficient either, recovering around 70% of the remaining gold, but this process too can be repeated, leading to overall recovery rates of close to 100%.

Source: Hentschel et al. (2001)

---

most countries) and diamonds (80–100% in countries that are not major producers).[22] In China, ASM produces 75% of the bauxite.[23] In Indonesia, the total production of tin by small-scale miners equals that of large-scale production.[24] And in Ghana ASM is estimated to produce 60–70% of the diamonds.[25] Table 13–2 provides estimates for the total and proportional production of different minerals by ASM in various countries, along with estimates of the number of workers involved.

Environmental Impact

The numerous environmental impacts of ASM are perhaps of greatest concern to many observers in the mining sector:
- mercury pollution,
- cyanide pollution,

Table 13-2. Artisanal and Small-scale Mining Employment and Production in Selected Countries

	Number of Workers (thousands)	Minerals (proportion of ASM miners, where available)	Annual Production (in thousands tonnes unless otherwise indicated)	Proportion of National Production from ASM
Bolivia	72	Base metals 54%, gold 45%	Gold – 12 tonnes Silver – 433 tonnes Zinc – 149 Tin – 12	All minerals – 27%
Brazil	Small-scale miners, 67; *garimpeiros,*' up to 300–400	Small-scale miners: construction and building materials 84%; *garimpeiros:* gold 73%, diamonds 11%, cassiterite 10%	–	–
Burkina Faso	100–200	Gold, phosphates, limestone, kaolin, clay, construction materials	Gold – 513 kilograms	Gold – 46% of all gold production
China	3,000–15,000	Coal 46%, construction and building materials 44%, iron, gold, base metals, agricultural minerals	Coal – 475,590 Limestone – 161,300 Iron – 68,120 Gold – 21 tonnes	–
Ecuador	92	Gold 65%, construction materials 23%, pumice 6%	Gold – 4 tonnes Pumice – 172	–
Ghana	200	Gold 67%, diamonds 30%	Gold – 107 ounces Diamonds – 558,241 carats	All minerals – 17%, Diamonds – 60–70%
India	500	Iron ore 23%, manganese 10%, copper 6%, limestone and building materials, bauxite, galena and sphalerite, phosphates	–	–
Indonesia	109	Gold 55%, coal 18%, tin 18%, clay, carving stone, diamonds	Gold – 30 tonnes Coal – 4000 Tin – 42 Diamonds – 33,600 carats	–
Malawi	40	Lime 12% coal, gemstones, bricks, sand, clay	Lime – 3.250 Coal – 44	
Mali	200	Gold, diamonds, semi-precious stones	Gold – 1.7 tonnes	Gold – 6%
Mozambique	60	Gold, gemstones	Gold – 360–480 kilograms	
Papua New Guinea	50–60	Gold 90%	Gold – 1860 kilograms	–
Peru	30	Gold	Gold – 15 tonnes +	Gold – 16%

Table 13–2. Artisanal and Small-scale Mining Employment and Production in Selected Countries (continued)				
	Number of Workers (thousands)	Minerals (proportion of ASM miners, where available)	Annual Production (in thousands tonnes unless otherwise indicated)	Proportion of National Production from ASM
Philippines	185	Gold 89%, sand and gravel 7%, industrial minerals 4%	Gold – 17 tonnes	–
South Africa	10	Gold, diamonds, gemstones, kaolin, limestone, coal, dimension stones, salt, sand, silver, talc	–	–
Tanzania	550	Gemstones 54%, gold 4%, lime, salt, aggregates 5%, gypsum, dimension stones, diamonds, sand	Gemstones – 48 tonnes Gold – 720 kilograms Salt – 97 Limestone – 120 Gypsum – 9 Diamonds – 93,205 carats	–
Zambia	30	Gemstones (particularly emeralds), lead, limestone, dimension stones, quartz, sand, silver	–	–
Zimbabwe	350	Gold, tantalite	–	–

*Brazilian term for artisanal miners
Source: MMSD Global and Country ASM Reports. In addition, data for Brazil are taken from Barreto (2001)

- direct dumping of tailings and effluents into rivers,
- threats from improperly constructed tailings dams,
- river damage in alluvial areas,
- river siltation,
- erosion damage and deforestation, and
- landscape destruction.

Some view these as unacceptable and as sufficient reason to ban many forms of artisanal and small-scale mining.

It is certainly true that small-scale miners tend to do more damage to the environment than those working in modern mining enterprises – with a greater environmental cost per unit of output.[26] A lack of awareness – particularly of the less visible or long-term environmental impacts of activities – combined with a lack of information about affordable methods to reduce impacts and a lack of obvious incentives to change all contribute to this problem. (Since their operations are often subsistence activities, small-scale

miners tend to focus more on immediate concerns than the long-term consequences of their activities.) This is compounded by the fact that in many cases, governments do not attempt to control these activities, which fall outside the regulatory framework, or they lack the capacity to monitor or control them, as the activities often occur in remote and inaccessible locations.

The activity of greatest concern for many is the use of mercury by gold miners – at the risk of their own health and that of others. This process may involve grinding the ore so as to free the gold, and then adding mercury, which combines with the gold to form an amalgam that is denser than the residual material and can be separated off as a 'cake'. The miners then heat this cake to distil – or simply burn off – the mercury as a vapour, leaving a residue of gold. Mercury is extremely toxic, so this is a dangerous process not just for the operators but for anyone in the vicinity. Inappropriate use of mercury often arises due to a lack of knowledge of the process. For example, in parts of Africa there is a rudimentary understanding that mercury has something to do with gold recovery, but little idea of what, so a 'just chuck some in and hope for the best' approach is taken. In Papua New Guinea, as in other countries, where even the simplest equipment is often unaffordable, miners just burn the amalgam in their huts, sometimes on the blades of knives used to prepare food. They may even deliberately sit downwind of the fumes in order to keep warm.[27]

In the Philippines, miners discharge mercury into rivers where the chemical characteristics of the water are highly favourable to its accumulation in the food chain.[28] Elsewhere the activity is still dangerous but the environmental risk can be less. Gold miners also use mercury in Amazonia, for example, but here there is already a considerable amount of mercury in the soil, so the high mercury concentrations observed in fish are probably due primarily to eroded soil washed down by tributaries of the Amazon.[29] Moreover, the chemical characteristics of rivers within Amazonia seem to control the extent to which mercury accumulates in the aquatic food chain.[30]

Hazards to Health

Small-scale miners often operate in hazardous working conditions. According to the ILO, the five major health risks associated with ASM are exposure to dust (silicosis); exposure to mercury and other chemicals; the effects of noise and vibration; the effects of poor ventilation (heat, humidity, lack of oxygen); and the effects of overexertion, inadequate work space, and inappropriate equipment.[31] Although the health risks of mining are similar for both sexes, there can be additional hazards for women miners, especially if they come into contact with chemicals that present a health risk to foetuses or breast-feeding infants. Children are particularly vulnerable. The mine sites can also be breeding grounds for waterborne diseases such as malaria and bilharzia.

In addition, there are many accidents in artisanal and small-scale mining. The five most frequently cited causes are rock falls and subsidence, lack of ventilation, misuse of explosives, lack of knowledge and training, and obsolete and poorly maintained equipment.[32]

For a number of reasons, the health and safety risks to which small-scale miners are exposed can be significantly greater than for large-scale mining. Most obviously, the informal and unregulated nature of ASM means that it usually operates beyond the scope of legislation or enforcement on health and safety issues.[33] Some of the risks are the result of poor equipment. Self-employed artisanal miners can choose for themselves what safety measures to take. But even simple items such as helmets, boots, gloves, and dust masks represent a costly investment with no immediate return. Moreover, some miners have introduced more mechanized equipment or techniques without the complementary safety measures. Often these individuals are not aware of the risks they are running. If they have previously worked in large mines, they are more likely to use safety equipment. Otherwise they are likely to know very little about these issues.

There is also a poor flow of information in the other direction: artisanal and small-scale miners are slow to report illnesses or accidents if they fear they will be exposed to official sanctions or interventions that will damage their livelihoods.

The dangerous environment extends beyond the mines. Those engaged in ASM are already some of the poorest people and are therefore likely to have inadequate sanitation, with little access to clean water or basic health care. These problems are likely to be even worse where miners have converged around a freshly discovered deposit or settled in unorganized camps. Such remote and temporary settlements are unlikely to have public health facilities – and apart from harbouring diseases related to poor sanitation, they can also be breeding grounds for crime, prostitution, and sexually transmitted diseases. In remote areas, health care services may already be limited and a long way from the mining location, and access may be very difficult, especially at certain times of year. There is also often poor awareness of mining-related health issues in rural health services, such as recognition of mercury poisoning and appropriate treatments.

Many of these 'boom towns' develop haphazardly with little or no planning. As a result, working and living areas often overlap; miners frequently build houses at the mine entrance, for example, to protect the property. Similar overlap is common in local businesses: general stores will sell groceries alongside chemicals, and restaurants may combine serving food with 'complementary services' like buying and burning amalgam. In some circumstances, the living quarters can be more dangerous than the mines. In Peru, for example, where amalgam may be burnt almost anywhere, mercury poisoning can be higher among women and children than among men, who spend much of their day in the only uncontaminated area – the mine.[34]

Although such settlements may ultimately be recognized as regular villages and towns – and qualify for sanitation and public health facilities – this can take years or even decades. Meanwhile, a whole generation of children will have been exposed to multiple disease threats, including malaria, cholera, tuberculosis, bilharzia, and other parasitic and infectious diseases. And HIV/AIDS may have had time to become epidemic.

Social Issues

ASM can be an important aspect of rural livelihoods.[35] Most of this form of mining takes place in remote rural areas. Here it can provide a means of survival for the miners and stimulate demand for locally produced goods and services – food, tools, equipment, housing, and various types of infrastructure. But where ASM has taken place over an extended period of time, its contribution tends to be limited to supplementing existing livelihoods.

Many of the social issues facing communities affected by small-scale mining are similar to those associated with large-scale mining. In some cases, there is a major issue of change in social order where a move from subsistence agriculture to ASM occurs. The local environmental damage caused by ASM can also aggravate economic hardship and cause ill health. In addition, ASM can be disruptive – particularly when it takes the form of a sudden 'rush'. Some of this is linked to in-migration: when large numbers of new people arrive, they can come into conflict with local residents, sometimes provoking violence and introducing new social and health problems. But other problems can arise when local people are attracted by glittering opportunities, real or imagined, that cause them to desert their farms. This is even more likely when the mineral concerned becomes a parallel local currency, as gold does. When the rush is over and mining activities have subsided, local people may

conclude that they have seen few lasting benefits: most of the profits will have disappeared, while the social and environmental damage persists.

In extreme cases, small-scale miners have been accused of killing local people in order to gain access to mining land. This happened to Yanomami Indians who live in the forest on the border with Venezuela. They are the largest of Brazil's tribal groups and have managed to maintain their traditional way of life. At least 10,000 members of this tribal group live across the border in the southern part of Venezuela, on lands rich in mineral resources. Following the illegal entry of thousands of gold prospectors into Yanomami lands in 1987, some 1500 Yanomami were estimated to have died from violence and disease. Since 1990 there have been several government attempts to remove illegal gold prospectors from the area, and in November 1991 the Venezuelan government signed a decree officially demarcating 9.4 million hectares of land as the Yanomami Indian reserve. It appears, however, that the re-entry of Brazilian miners into Yanomami lands as well as brutal killings of villagers continue in both Brazil and Venezuela.[36]

Relationships with Others in the Mining Sector

Governments

As noted earlier, artisanal and small-scale miners work largely in the 'informal sector'. This serves as a serious impediment to improving the sector's contribution to sustainable development. It implies that their businesses are not registered – they operate beyond government supervision and thus do not strive to follow health and safety regulations or meet environmental standards. Nor do they receive any formal support. ASM enterprises do not normally pay royalties to the state or taxes on profits. They may also lack official rights to exploit a particular deposit – working without mining title or any kind of contract with the owner of the concession, which makes them vulnerable to eviction. In these circumstances, informality also shades into illegality. In many countries, over 50% of small-scale miners are thought to operate illegally.[37]

In some cases, ASM workers operate informally as a matter of choice. There are often strong financial incentives for avoiding regulation and participation in the formal sector. Registering their business may be a tortuous and expensive process – costly in both time (it often takes years to become registered) and money and offering limited advantages. Moreover, in the remote areas where they work, the national government or local authority generally lacks the capacity to regulate or support such disparate activities. In many cases, however, governments choose not to recognize ASM activities and may even enforce bans on them. This may be the case if land rights are not recognized or if the health, safety, environmental, and social costs of ASM are perceived as too high relative to the benefits. A recent example of this is in China, where the government ordered the closure of all small-scale coal mines on the grounds that they posed excessive safety risks. (See Box 13–2.)

Informality and illegality extend to the marketing of products. Here there are clearly some disadvantages. The lack of formal protection increases the risk that the miners will be exploited by intermediaries or traders, and they will rarely get fair prices. It also encourages criminality in the commodities chain.

Since the products enter the supply chain informally, they can also be diverted into illicit channels and are frequently smuggled. In countries where the

government is officially the monopoly buyer of mineral products such as precious metals and gemstones, traders can usually make more by smuggling the items out of the country and selling on international markets. These products can also be used to launder money. In Central and South America, for example, drug traffickers often buy gold from informal miners and then declare the metal to be part of the output from a formal mine.[38] Another illegal use for these products is to finance rebel activities – as with the 'blood diamonds' in Angola, for example (see Chapter 8), and the mining of jade in Afghanistan. In these cases, the links between informality and illegality tend to be self-reinforcing. Governments that wish to stamp out such illegal activities often try to suppress small-scale mining, though this may simply have the effect of further marginalizing these workers – and driving them straight into the arms of smugglers and traffickers.

Even where they have tried, few governments have had much success in supporting artisanal and small-scale miners or in controlling their impact on the environment and society – finding it difficult to monitor activities that are mostly informal, often illegal, and frequently distant from urban centres of authority. Governments that have tried to ban the use of mercury, for instance, or to shut down ASM operations have generally failed. When the miners have no other source of income, they will usually find ways to evade controls and carry on working.

The lack of government success in controlling ASM activities has in part been due to a tendency for regulatory frameworks to be control-oriented, with few obvious benefits or incentives for miners. Artisanal and small-scale miners will only formalize and register their operations if they see some real advantages to doing so. And they will only stop mining if alternative, more attractive sources of income are available. Thus those who register might gain access to technologies and services, along with training for health and safety and for environmental management. They could also get financial assistance, as well as information on prices and access to markets – which would make them less reliant on intermediaries for the sale of their products and enable them to get better prices.

But government officials also need incentives for action. Many at present do not consider it worth the effort, especially where land rights are not recognized

Box 13–2. China's Dangerous Small-Scale Coal Mines

China's small-scale coal mines, which employ roughly 2.5 million people, are among the world's most dangerous. Official statistics suggest that around 6000 people die each year – though there are probably thousands more unreported deaths in illegal operations.

In June 2001, the central government issued a State Order to shut all the country's small mines immediately – citing their bad record on health and safety and their environmental pollution. This would also serve to remove a supply of coal that was undercutting the viability of larger state mines.

Closing these mines in remote areas without providing alternative employment will cause considerable hardship and is unlikely to be successful. Given previous experience, the most probable outcome is that many of these mines will continue to operate, but now illegally. In Hunan province in central China, for example, the government has closed some mines as many as 20 times.

Source: Gunson and Yue Jian (2001)

A small-scale mining district support centre in Tarkwa, Ghana

and it is difficult to grant legal title. Other officials may actually prefer the status quo, especially if they are corrupt and ASM is giving them ample opportunities to smuggle or launder money.

Nevertheless, for most governments there should be advantages to regulating artisanal and small-scale mining. Those that want to attract foreign investment in large-scale mining, for instance, will find it simpler if small-scale mining is already well regulated. Social problems and community conflicts associated with ASM can also be reduced. And there should be fiscal incentives. One would be a reduction in smuggling. This is particularly important for countries that produce precious metals or gemstones. If this sector is largely informal, it risks being 'captured' by warlords or cartels from neighbouring countries, allowing most of the output to slip across the border, along with the associated profits and potential foreign-exchange earnings. If, on the other hand, informal miners can sell their output in regular local markets at a fair price (that is higher or equal to what they are able to get by illicit trading), the profits will stay within the country and subsequent exports will earn foreign exchange. Indeed, the fiscal situation is even more advantageous with ASM production than with large-scale mining corporations, which often repatriate profits to foreign investors. In some circumstances, regulations will also provide tax revenues.

Tanzania liberalized its minerals markets in the 1980s – licensing private gold and gemstone dealers and thus offering new legal channels for ASM sales. Between 1989 and 1997 the number of mineral dealers' licences increased from 17 to 2000. This, along with efforts to

encourage local investment in mining, resulted in a steep increase in mining activity, mostly in ASM: between 1990 and 1995 the number of registered claims increased from 1998 to 4123. This also boosted total mineral exports, which between 1989 and 2000 rose from $16 million to $184 million.[39] It should be noted that more recently, three large-scale gold mines have begun operations in Tanzania, accounting for a large part of the increase in production and exports. By contrast, in nearby Madagascar virtually all the country's $400 million worth of gemstones are still exported illegally.[40]

Less obvious but equally important considerations for government are the role that ASM has in rural development. This is particularly critical in light of the difficulties of rural poverty and mass migration to the cities being experienced in most countries with ASM. Moreover, the significant problems associated with this type of mining are likely to worsen if ignored, with implications for broader society.

Large Mining Companies

The relationship between large mining companies and smaller-scale operators has often been characterized by tension and mistrust. Because of the problems associated with ASM, the fact that these miners' traditional rights to land are often not legally recognized, and the potential benefits from large, organized mining operations, governments may be quick to ignore or 'clear out' artisanal and small-scale miners in favour of large companies. In these cases, legal entitlements are granted to the large companies, and the traditional miners are often forced into illegality. In some cases, a legitimate process of resettlement and compensation is undertaken to allow large-scale mining to take place. But in others, government intervention or even police involvement to enforce company entitlements is used. This obviously leads to resistance and resentment, and even to serious conflicts. To some extent, this is because the miners are competing for the same resources. Sometimes this is no coincidence – mining and exploration companies use artisanal and small-scale miners as unpaid 'geologists', exploring wherever there is ASM activity. On the other hand, small-scale miners have often congregated around a larger-scale mine, taking advantage of the better access and perhaps re-mining some of the larger company's waste.

Once operations have started, some companies have tried to keep small-scale miners at bay and to build systems of security. Others have found that building constructive relationships works better than trying to shut small-scale miners down and hope the 'problem' disappears – through, for example, finding alternative employment, setting aside areas for them to mine, and providing other forms of assistance.

Still, cases of conflict between large mining companies and small-scale miners, sometimes involving government, abound. One example of this is the reported attempt by the Brazilian state mining company, CVRD, to evict a group of small-scale miners from a concession in Serra Leste. The local miners are alleged to have taken seven employees of the mining company hostage until their demands were met.[41] Similarly, in Suriname conflict emerged between villagers and Golden Star Resources (GSR) over access to the region's gold reserves. According to a special assessment team assembled by the Organization of American States, 'from the perspective of the small-scale miners…these deposits represent a lifetime of employment. From the perspective of GSR, however,…mak[ing] available parts of their concessions to small-scale miners may not be realistic from an economic perspective.'[42]

Conflicts sometimes occur in situations where it is difficult to ascertain the legality of occupation and claims to the land, what policies of resettlement or relocation are applied, and whether rights have been violated or abused. In part this may be because of the difficulty that artisanal miners have articulating their views effectively to authorities or to world media, and the difficulty that company officials, finance institutions, governments, NGOs, or others have in establishing the facts of events occurring in distant mining regions.

A recent controversial case involves the alleged eviction of small-scale miners from a site in the Bulyanhulu mining area of Tanzania. A Tanzanian environmental NGO has alleged that in 1996, Tanzanian police, acting to assert mining rights claimed by Kahama Mining Corporation Limited, displaced or evicted a large number of small miners (the group suggests 400,000) and their families from the site.[43] Eventually the rights to the site were acquired by Barrick Gold, well after the events allegedly occurred, which began to develop a mining project.

Subsequent allegations, which if true would be very serious, included the charge that some small-scale miners had died or been killed in the earlier eviction process. There have been a number of attempts to determine the validity of these allegations. One of these was by the Multilateral Investment Guarantee Agency (MIGA), an arm of the World Bank, which had insured part of Barrick Gold's interest in the project since the company had received a $56.3-million MIGA guarantee for its investment in an underground gold, silver, and copper mine.[44] The results of MIGA's investigation were described in a September 2001 press release:

> The Multilateral Investment Guarantee Agency said today that the so-called 'new' evidence it has received relating to deaths that allegedly took place in 1996 at the Bulyanhulu mine in Tanzania during a government operation to fill illegal mining shafts provides no evidence of wrongdoing on the part of either the Tanzanian government or Barrick Gold Corporation of Canada.[45]

MIGA also asserted that 'Amnesty International, the Tanzanian government, the Canadian High Commissioner, and many others investigated the allegations and consistently found that they could not be substantiated'.[46]

These investigations have not satisfied the NGOs that raised this issue, however, and they continue to press for further investigation.[47] The issue was further complicated by an allegation that 'Tanzanian police have carried out arrests and searches of witnesses, government critics and researchers to silence those who have been raising the allegations in that country'.[48] And in April 2002, MIGA announced that the 'IFC/MIGA Office of the Compliance Advisor/Ombudsman (CAO) has received a complaint from LEAT, a Tanzanian NGO and has decided to make a preliminary assessment of the complaint'.[49]

MMSD has not investigated this case itself and has nothing to add to the record of documentation already in existence. But whatever the outcome, this clearly illustrates the kind of issues that increasingly are presented to lenders, governments, civil society organizations, and companies, as well as the lack of any mechanism trusted by all that can reach a result that will stay undisturbed.

Companies have often been ill equipped to build good

relationships with small-scale miners. Difficulties are compounded by a lack of government presence or support for this part of the mining sector. The link between ASM activities and large-scale mining operations means that small-scale miners need to be treated with consideration to avoid serious problems between the two groups. As discussed later in the chapter, there are several examples of proactive measures being taken by companies to better relations.

International, Donor, and Non-governmental Organizations

The importance of artisanal and small-scale mining and the difficulties that governments have had in addressing it have increasingly been recognized at the international level and by individual donor governments. ASM has been the focus of a number of international meetings. In 1995, for example, the World Bank held a major conference in Washington on artisanal mining, and in 1999 the ILO held a Tripartite Meeting on social and labour issues in small-scale mining. ASM issues have also been considered in meetings of the Mines Ministers of the Americas and of the Union Économique Monetaire Ouest-Africaine.[50] The focus of these discussions has gradually sharpened and moved from definitional and legal issues, and purely technical assistance, towards policies that consider assistance to artisanal and small-scale miners as part of overall strategies for poverty alleviation and building sustainable livelihoods.

A few bilateral agencies currently have programmes of assistance for ASM. Germany, for example, finances programmes in Colombia, Ghana, and Zimbabwe, and the United Kingdom is looking at a model scheme of assistance for small-scale miners. The UK's Department for International Development (DfID) is also undertaking research on ASM issues. At the multilateral level, the most important initiative began in March 2001 when a group of donors launched the Communities and Small-Scale Mining (CASM) initiative.[51] CASM's mission is to enhance the developmental impact of ground- and policy-level work in the artisanal and small-scale mining sector, both at the grass-roots and policy level, in ways that will directly contribute to reducing poverty and realizing sustainable development in communities affected by or involved in ASM in developing countries. It intends to achieve this by providing a forum to facilitate communication and coordination between miners, communities, donors, governments, industry, and other stakeholders and by actively

promoting the sharing of knowledge, lessons learnt, good practices, and policies. CASM is housed in the World Bank and chaired by the DfID. Although there have been similar attempts to address ASM in the past, prior to CASM few agencies recognized the important role that artisanal and small-scale mining plays in rural livelihood strategies. Continued and increased support is needed in order to have a real impact.

A number of international and local non-governmental organizations (NGOs), such as the Intermediate Technology Development Group (ITDG) in Zimbabwe and the Mineral and Energy Policy Centre in South Africa, are actively undertaking research, training, and support work for artisanal and small-scale miners.[52] Such organizations also play an important role as independent facilitators.

Maximizing the Contribution of ASM to Sustainable Development

Artisanal and small-scale mining is critically important for many poor communities, providing temporary or full-time work and offering potentially the only source of income, though it also has many serious social and environmental implications, as indicated. The challenge now is to capitalize on the livelihood opportunities while ensuring that ASM also contributes to other goals of sustainable development, particularly to rural development.

Achieving this depends to some extent on the nature of the mining. With better organization and training, a degree of mechanization, and an integrated approach to livelihood strategies, small-scale mining communities in some instances should be able to pursue mining activities while co-existing productively with larger enterprises. The situation for individual artisanal miners, however, is more difficult. Here the aim should be to develop other employment opportunities for them either in the small-scale sector or elsewhere. In the case of mining camps that suddenly spring up as a result of newly discovered deposits, the priority should be to integrate the mining operations with existing local economic activities and strengthen the miners' relationship with neighbouring communities.

Broadly speaking, with respect to sustainable development, the short- and medium-term goals of artisanal and small-scale mining should include:
- where applicable or feasible, encouraging alternative economic activities;

- encouraging a contribution to poverty alleviation and local economic development through ensuring that revenues are invested in ways that bring sustained benefits;
- adopting a gender-sensitive approach that gives particular emphasis to the role of women;
- ending child labour in mining through providing viable alternatives;
- avoiding or mitigating negative environmental and social impacts as well as impacts on human health;
- encouraging 'fair trade' markets for mining products;
- increasing the ability of individual enterprises and ASM in general to make a better contribution to sustainable development;
- developing the collective capacity of miners to contribute to sustainable development; and
- ensuring good relationships between miners and other stakeholders.

The remainder of this chapter discusses ways of working towards these goals.

Supporting Rural Development

In the past, most efforts on ASM have focused on the mining operations themselves – trying to improve productivity and environmental performance and to regularize their legal status – but these have often helped only a few select operations or entrepreneurs rather than whole communities.

A better approach is to take into account the existing socio-economic system and consider how mining can best contribute to poverty reduction and sustainable development in the context of holistic local or regional development. In the case of longer-term or seasonal operations in small-scale mining, the main priorities will be finding better ways of integrating them into the rest of the economy and encouraging mining communities to invest their revenues in other forms of economic activity as well as in communal services such as schools and health centres (while recognizing the need to ensure that government does not abrogate its responsibilities as a provider of public services). (See Box 13–3.)

The UN Department for Economic and Social Affairs has developed a sustainable livelihoods approach for artisanal mining communities. This is currently being implemented as a pilot scheme in Ethiopia, Ghana, Guinea, and Mali.[53] The main policy recommendations are:

> **Box 13–3. Diversification for Small-scale Miners in Mali**
>
> In 1997, a large open-cast mine entered production at Sadiola in western Mali. The major shareholders were AngloGold and a Canadian company, IAMGold; the minor shareholders were the International Finance Corporation and the government of Mali. Sadiola was already a traditional artisanal gold mining area. After the mine began operating, environmental concerns led to a decision to resettle the inhabitants of two adjacent villages, Sadiola and Farabakouta, to sites a couple of kilometres away.
>
> To compensate local communities, the mining company introduced the Sadiola Gold Mining Project. This had several objectives: to help artisanal miners, to promote community development, and to diversify the local economy. Activities started with a public consultation with traditional groups and local NGOs in order to identify target groups and potential partners.
>
> On the mining side, this resulted in the creation of the Sadiola Mining Cooperative and a programme of technical assistance to the gold miners – including geological studies and the identification and testing of mining equipment. On the community side, it led to the creation of a community development fund and support for a school, a health centre, and a learning centre for adults. Environmental work included improvement of mine sites through the planting of fruit trees. The project also supported small enterprises such as bakeries, woodwork shops, jewellers, metalwork shops, and, specifically for women, market gardening and businesses making dyes and soaps. In all, the project has affected some 500 people in four villages and has stimulated local entrepreneurial activity and purchasing power.
>
> Interestingly, the number of people engaged in ASM at the Sadiola site is declining rapidly because of the better commercial opportunities provided by trading with workers in the large mine. This illustrates the links between ASM and poverty – as soon as something better turns up, people will take it.
>
> Source: Keita (2001)

- *Poverty eradication* – Policies on poverty eradication should be included in national policy-making for all sectors, including minerals.
- *ASM as a starting point* – ASM should serve as both a catalyst and an anchor for other productive activities, stimulating complementary and alternative productive ventures.
- *A focus on people* – The organizational capability of the local community should be strengthened.

- *Building on enterprise* – Instead of hands-on state intervention, which has rarely been successful, governments should encourage private initiatives, especially micro-enterprises or cooperatives, that can provide better local services.

Assisting Women in Mining

Although women play a central role in many small-scale mining operations, they have frequently been by-passed by programmes of assistance. Future programmes will need to focus more sharply on gender issues – looking for ways to give women more power in their communities and their households.

A good starting point for this kind of work is a women's mining association. The Southern African Development Community, for example, has the Southern African Women in Mining Trust. Founded in Zambia in 1997, the trust now has chapters in a number of other countries, including Angola, Botswana, Democratic Republic of Congo, Kenya, Mozambique, Namibia, Swaziland, Tanzania, and Zimbabwe. Its main objectives include lobbying for support of women in mining, training women in environmentally sound mining methods, establishing revolving loan funds, and facilitating the marketing of members' products.[54] Another example is the Tanzanian Women Miners' Association. This is establishing a centre that rents mining equipment and tools as well as a lapidary and jewellery production unit. It also has a training centre that focuses on environmentally sustainable mining and processing methods, health and safety issues, and the rehabilitation of ecologically sensitive mining areas.[55]

Eliminating Child Labour in Mines

No children should be working in mines, so the objective must be to eliminate child labour, and immediate measures must be put in place to bring this about. In the interim, it is important to try to reduce the dangers and to improve the conditions for children currently involved in mining. The ILO is one of the leaders in the field through its International Programme on the Elimination of Child Labour (IPEC). On the southern coast of Peru, in the artisanal gold-mining community of Santa Filomena, for example, IPEC has a programme run by the Peruvian NGO Cooperacción. Started in 1998, the first two phases are now complete: the local population has identified alternatives for child labour in mining, and

children no longer carry minerals. It is expected that in the future children will be withdrawn from mining here altogether.[56] The ILO is also working in the Philippines to provide education and vocational training to children withdrawn from gold mining.

Protecting the Environment

As noted earlier, artisanal and small-scale miners often use excavation and extraction techniques that are harmful to their own health and to the environment.[57] But given the scattered and informal nature of much of this activity, governments are unlikely to be able to raise standards immediately simply through legislation and enforcement. A more realistic approach is to raise awareness of the risks and to demonstrate less dangerous alternatives that are appropriate to local circumstances – social, cultural, and economic – and that allow mining communities to make better-informed choices.

A first step should be to alert people to the dangers – to themselves, their children, and the environment in general – of, for example, using mercury to extract gold and to encourage them to use a simple method to capture the mercury vapour. In Papua New Guinea, the Department of Mining, with the support of AusAid, has started an outreach programme that includes demonstrating safer ways of burning amalgam. One option is to use empty fish tins. These cans are widely available and can be fashioned into simple retorts that can be used to recycle the mercury.[58]

Another option is to introduce alternative forms of gold extraction that do not involve mercury at all. In South Africa, the government's mineral technology research body, Mintek, has developed a new Minataur process. This involves treating the ore with hydrochloric acid in the presence of sodium hypochlorite and then using sodium metabisulphate or oxalic acid to precipitate the gold out as a concentrate that is 99.5% fine gold powder. This has the key advantage of avoiding the use of mercury or cyanide through the use of simple equipment.[59] For miners to take up a new process like this, there must be immediate and obvious financial or time-saving benefits. Miners also need to understand and trust the new technology.

Meanwhile, governments also have to develop appropriate and enforceable legislation that will draw

ASM into national programmes for environmental protection.[60] When governments deal with large-scale enterprises, one of the first requirements is an environmental impact assessment (EIA) and a corresponding environmental management plan. But this is expensive and far beyond the reach of most small-scale miners, who at best will try to comply by contracting low-quality environmental consultants or, more likely, continue to operate illegally. In these circumstances, one solution is to bring small-scale miners together to produce a collective EIA – on the assumption that small-scale mining enterprises in an ecologically homogenous zone will have similar environmental impacts and therefore could use identical environmental management plans.

In Ecuador, for example, a local NGO, CENDA, has worked with 100,000 or so artisanal miners in the southern part of the country and a government agency to develop a collective solution: Plan ECO+. This involves technical assistance to miners along with a host of social programmes – including providing meals for miners' children, improving water supplies, and promoting alternative sources of work. The government accepted this idea as a pilot project, and between 1996 and 1999 the miners adopted more than 200 individual environmental measures. When the project ended, the government incorporated the concept in its regular mining environmental legislation as 'joint environmental studies'.[61] Several other countries have since implemented or are evaluating similar models.

Better Markets for ASM Products

Mining communities in the ASM sector typically have to sell their products, either refined ore or metal, as quickly as they can – and usually get low prices. Those working further along the chain – traders, intermediaries, and manufacturers – tend to make higher profits. This imbalance is likely to be even greater when the miners are working illegally and are effectively selling black market goods. There are a number of ways in which the profits retained by mining communities can be increased.

One way to retain more of the profits is for mining communities to establish processing industries of their own. (See Table 13–4 for some opportunities to do this.) They might be able to take some of these steps while still in the informal sector, but they would stand

Table 13–4. Opportunities for Processing ASM Products	
ASM product	**Potential local transformations**
Gold	Jewellery, coins, medals
Gemstones	Cutting and polishing (lapidary), jewellery
Coal	Coke
Dimension stone[a]	Tiles and slabs
Non-metallic minerals	Bricks, ceramics, paint, and so on

[a] Material capable of being cut to size

a better chance of getting access to capital and to government services in the formal sector. Governments that want to promote such enterprises will need to simplify the requirements for establishing a small business.

Government, companies, international agencies, and other actors should also be able to offer some guidance on suitable businesses to develop. There is no reason why miners should also make good jewellers, and most experiments that have encouraged them in this direction have failed. So such businesses will need to be established by other people, or miners will need to be encouraged to engage in activities that better complement their existing skills.

Another priority should be to make it easier to divert ASM raw materials to existing manufacturing enterprises. In Bolivia, for example, small-scale miners produce gold on legally granted concessions, but tend not to declare or pay tax on their output. As a result, Bolivian jewellers who want to operate legally have often found it simpler to use imported gold. In order to help the jewellery industry, the Bolivian government has therefore established a system of 'autodeclaration' for gold purchased from the informal market. Jewellers who wish to export their products simply have to include the value of locally bought gold as a deductible cost and they can then export the products exempt from value-added tax.[62] This has helped make the industry more competitive internationally, and has also formalized at least one part of the production chain.

Direct links with the growing 'fair trade' movement in

industrial countries could also help achieve better prices for ASM output. Consumers in richer countries are becoming increasingly concerned that the goods they buy – including jewellery – may have been produced under exploitative conditions and possibly with child labour, may have had unacceptable levels of environmental impacts, or may have played a role in fuelling conflict. In response, a number of NGO trading companies are now prepared to pay a premium for guarantees of ethically and environmentally sound production and have established direct links with small-scale producers in developing countries.

A German NGO, Fair Trade e.V., for instance, has established links with many ethically approved producers – including a women's diamond cooperative in Lesotho, cooperatives producing gold and jewellery in Bolivia, cooperatives producing platinum and other metals in South Africa, and gem producers in Madagascar and Tanzania.[63] For producers to qualify for these marketing channels, they have to work within a democratic framework – typically cooperatives – and must be committed to high environmental and labour standards. Producers benefit in a number of ways. First, they get better and more stable prices because selling directly cuts out various layers of intermediate trader and opens up new markets. Second, they get a guaranteed market. Third, they get more money to invest in improving local social and environmental conditions.

Access to Finance and Credit

Most artisanal and small-scale miners would like to step up to higher levels of productivity and output by mechanizing more of their activities and developing new reserves. But few are able to gain the necessary capital: banks are wary of ASM producers, who are usually in the informal sector, work in rural areas, and lack acceptable forms of collateral. Even bankers who do lend to such individuals regard these as high-risk loans and charge correspondingly high interest rates – which can render many sound projects non-viable.

A number of international donors have identified the lack of credit as a bottleneck and have supported small-scale credit programmes for mining and other enterprises, often as part of projects for raising levels of technology and productivity. These programmes have yielded a number of lessons. One of the most important is to ensure that the lending is sustainable.

The lending institution has to be able to make its decisions independently and charge interest rates sufficiently high to cover inflation and operating costs – including loan losses – and also have enough clients to permit economies of scale. The best strategy is to ensure that loans are combined with the borrowers' own savings, and to start with small loans and then move on to larger ones that become part of a longer-term relationship. Donors also need to sustain their links – helping build the capacity of lending institutions and maintaining an interest in their control and supervision.

Finance for small-scale mining need not, however, be confined to banking and credit schemes. Funds can come from a range of more specialist institutions, such as exploration funds or mining development banks. Other ways of channelling finance to miners include leasing equipment, selling shares, and establishing joint ventures.

Associations for Artisanal and Small-scale Miners

When governments are developing policies for formal-sector activities, they usually consult a relevant trade association that can represent the interests of the sector as a whole. This is difficult in the case of ASM, which normally lacks any sort of organized representative structure. Some NGOs, governments, and international donors have therefore tried to encourage the creation of such groups, whether as cooperatives, enterprises, or other associations. This has not always been successful, and artisanal and small-scale miners have often resisted joining cooperatives for mining operations. They have been happier to work in groups when it comes to getting finance, marketing, pooling equipment, or collecting by-products. Even where associations have been welcomed, however, difficulties have sometimes arisen in transferring the management of the cooperative to the small-scale miners and in ensuring its continuing financial viability. (See Box 13–4.)

A further possibility is to arrange for the trade association for larger mining enterprises, usually the Chamber of Mines, to represent the interests of artisanal and small-scale miners by having ASM groups as associate members. This would have many advantages, including assisting informal miners to join the formal sector, as well as offering a channel through which the government and other bodies could communicate with and support ASM. Many Chambers

Box 13–4. A Problematic Mining Project in Zimbabwe

The Shamva Mining Centre in Zimbabwe was established in 1989, originally to support 43 small-scale gold miners in the Shamva area northeast of Harare. This was a joint initiative between the Ministry of Mines, the Intermediate Technology Development Group, the Small-Scale Miners' Association of Zimbabwe (SSMAZ), and donors. The centre was to provide a milling facility for the miners and offer training on mining, health and safety, and environmentally sustainable mining methods.

By 1995 the centre had proved so popular that more than 150 miners from a radius of 200 kilometres were using it. They paid fees for the milling that were directly related to the price at which the gold was bought by the reserve bank. By using this service, miners were able to increase their incomes, sometimes by as much as 30%.

Nevertheless, the centre was running into problems. One was a lack of capacity to meet the growing needs of local miners. The SSMAZ responded by requiring miners to bring at least 10 tonnes at a time for processing – effectively excluding the smallest operators. However, the worst difficulties emerged in 1999. The centre decided it could continue without external assistance but did not succeed in replacing the ITDG-appointed manager and soon ran into financial problems. In January 2001 the Executive Committee decided to lease the centre to a local miner, and since then it has operated at well below capacity. This experience raises doubts about the advisability of putting such projects in the hands of producers' associations rather than more experienced commercial managers who can provide an efficient and competitively priced service.

Source: Mugova (2001)

of Mines would not welcome this kind of collaboration, however, because large-scale enterprises often have a strong aversion to ASM. Until recently, for example, the Zimbabwe Chamber of Mines was in the forefront in condemning artisanal and small-scale miners for their impact on the environment.[64] Nevertheless, there are promising signs of change. The South African Chamber of Mines is currently exploring ways of accommodating the interests of these miners – helping with the formation of ASM associations that could then become associate members of the Chamber.[65]

The lack of local ASM associations is mirrored at the

international level. At different times, there have been various ASM-related networks and communication, but these have typically been through specialist journals or channels established by NGOs. Modern communications technology, and particularly the internet, has created other options, though these too operate at the level of general information and research about the sector. They include FACOME, which promotes collaboration and communication on issues related to mercury in the Amazon (at www.facome.uqam.ca), and Redminera.com, which is concerned with mining in general, including ASM. For donors and other institutions, an important development has been the Communities and Small-Scale Mining initiative mentioned earlier. Thus far, however, there is no evidence that miners themselves are able to take much advantage of internet-based linking. This is not surprising, given their scattered locations, though the situation could change with the spread of mobile and satellite-based systems.

Improving Relationships

Between Large- and Small-scale Mining
In recent years, the attitude of some of the larger companies towards small-scale mining operations has begun to change. As they have become more sensitive to criticism of their activities, they have begun to pay greater attention to their relationships with those near mines – including artisanal and small-scale miners. They also see the business case for doing so.

The large mining companies can gain from greater cooperation. For example, in the near term, it will help to avoid tension and potential conflict with local miners. In the longer term, if they have developed a more stable relationship with miners and the community as a whole – and have supported community development – then local people are more likely to take greater care of the site after the mine has closed and less likely to restart mining in rehabilitated areas or in waste facilities, for which the mining company may still retain environmental liability.

Artisanal and small-scale miners also gain from good relationships with mining companies. The company can, for instance, buy their ore, provide laboratory services, or help them to develop clean and productive small concentration plants. Companies can also help with such issues as health and safety, and can provide technical assistance on the use of explosives along with geological information and legal advice. However, there needs to be a clear business case for this on the part of the company.

Building this kind of relationship requires considerable sensitivity and patience and has to start from the first phases of exploration. Companies should endeavour to understand the needs, perspectives, and concerns of small-scale miners and respect their rights to secure a livelihood. While the right of large companies to protect their assets should be respected, companies should try to avoid using forms of harassment against small-scale miners. The companies have to facilitate an early process of dialogue and participation, not just with ASM leaders but also with other members of ASM communities – signing agreements, where necessary, with all the miners in the group. Such agreements should be based on an honest assessment of what the company can and cannot do for ASM. The most difficult negotiations may be with indigenous groups, whose laws, land rights, and ownership of natural resources may not be formally recognized. Governments can help foster these dialogues, but only to a limited extent, since small-scale miners are also frequently at odds with local officials. Where necessary, NGOs or other local institutions could play the role of independent facilitators.

Fortunately, there are a number of positive examples of cooperation between larger enterprises and small-scale miners. The experience of AngloGold in the Sadiola area of Mali was described earlier; the relationship between Placer Dome and local miners in Las Cristinas in Venezuela is also noteworthy. (See Box 13–5.)

With Governments

Governments should acknowledge and provide appropriate support to ASM. Consistent and well-integrated policies need to be developed that contribute to four strategic objectives: alleviating poverty and contributing to integrated rural development, avoiding or minimizing environmental and health impacts, achieving a productive business climate, and stabilizing government revenue. There needs to be consistent regulation and legislation for large- and small-scale mining.

Priority areas for action should include the following:

Box 13–5. Placer Dome and Small-scale Miners in Venezuela

One of South America's most important gold mining areas is Km 88 in southeastern Venezuela – an area that has attracted many artisanal miners. In 1990, the government gave exploration and development rights for the Las Cristinas deposit in Km 88 to the Canadian company Placer Dome. To make way for the new mine, it had to resettle some 2800 small-scale miners but did not compensate them by offering other mining areas. So when the government left, the miners simply returned and resumed operations, leading to tensions between the miners, the company, and local authorities.

Facing the prospect of social unrest, the company initially followed a path of 'passive accommodation', allowing the miners free access to certain areas. Then it moved to a 'constructive engagement' phase by offering technical and other assistance. The miners organized themselves with a representative committee and began to introduce better mining methods and to reduce the use of mercury.

Ultimately, harmonious relations were established not only with the miners but also with the surrounding communities, who were able to serve as a stabilizing force that prevented new small-scale miners from working the concession. This effort by Placer Dome, which has now sold its interest in the mine, is recognized as one of the best examples of a company developing good relations with informal miners.

Source: Davidson (1998); Wood (2001)

- *Building appropriate legal and regulatory frameworks* – These should be transparent, consistent, and non-discriminatory, and should offer people easy access to mining titles and legal channels for production. They should be developed with participation from small-scale miners to ensure their needs and priorities are reflected. At the same time, the capacity of government needs to be boosted to ensure compliance and the ability to penalize infractions.
- *Offering incentives for regularization* – These could include tax allowances for new enterprises, exemptions from import duties on equipment or supplies, access to finance, and assistance with exports.
- *Creating necessary services* – Government should organize services that meet miners' real needs – legal, organizational, technical, and health and safety.

They can also encourage ASM to develop its own services by supporting the formation of associations or cooperatives.

- *Ensuring coherent administration* – The government will need to make sure that all the ministries involved – finance, mining, and environment – coordinate their policies. These departments also need to work closely with regional and local governments. Indeed, governments should try to decentralize as many activities as possible to ensure that they mesh with other strategies for promoting rural development.

All these policies will apply to ongoing mining operations. But governments also need to deal with 'rush' events. Few governments currently have the legal or administrative ability to control these situations.

It remains true that most governments are unlikely to have the capacity to support and regulate artisanal and small-scale mining. Although this will differ from country to country, government cannot be solely relied upon and will need to collaborate with NGOs, donors, industry, and other actors.

The Way Forward

Given the complexity of issues surrounding artisanal and small-scale mining, a coordinated and collaborative approach is required to improve ASM's contribution to sustainable development, involving all levels of government, industry, and civil society. The approach taken should be appropriate to local social, cultural, and economic circumstances.

- *Governments, donors, and NGOs* should continue to recognize the importance of ASM and focus on improving the livelihoods of those involved as well as reducing its impacts as part of integrated rural development. ASM activities should also be incorporated in relevant regional and local development programmes.
- *Governments* have a principal role to play. They need to develop an appropriate, consistent, and transparent policy and regulatory framework that focuses on both the facilitation and management of ASM. For the framework to be effective, they need to ensure that sufficient financial and regulatory incentives exist for small-scale miners to formalize their activities. It is also important that any framework

recognizes the linkages between large-scale mining and ASM, and that there is coherence in policy, regulation, and legislation for the whole spectrum of mining activities.

- *Donors and international organizations* should increasingly work together through such efforts as the Communities and Small-Scale Mining initiative to disseminate examples of best practice, facilitate communication and cooperation, and implement pilot projects geared towards helping those involved in ASM activities to contribute to sustainable development.
- *More large mining companies* could engage directly with artisanal and small-scale miners and ASM communities near a mine, helping them to work in a more sustainable fashion and, where necessary, to find alternative employment.
- Many more in *the mining industry* could recognize ASM as part of the minerals sector and find ways to support it, for example through the provision of technical advice, support of the CASM initiative, or collaboration with national governments and NGOs. A key incentive for the mining industry to help small-scale miners is reputation protection. Civil society often does not differentiate between large- and small-scale mining, so social and environmental problems in the ASM sector can rebound on the industry as a whole.
- *Small-scale miners* need to be alerted to the effects of their activities and encouraged to take measures to mitigate or reduce the negative impacts. Where possible, this should be enforced through government intervention. In practice, new measures will need to be financially attractive to miners if they are to adopt them. In particular, they need to be informed about the dangers of mercury amalgamation and helped to adopt appropriate techniques for using mercury more safely in the short term, although ultimately its use should be stopped. Although raising awareness is primarily the responsibility of government, all actors can assist in this effort.
- *International and bilateral organizations, governments, and NGOs* must continue to develop outreach programmes to ensure that parents fully appreciate the hazards faced by children engaged in small-scale mining. These programmes must provide children with livelihood opportunities that ultimately eliminate the need for child labour.
- *Governments, donors, international organizations, and companies* could do more to assist in the formation of

ASM associations and work with them to raise standards.

- *Research institutions* should increasingly focus on the development and implementation of viable solutions to the well-documented problems in ASM. Research should be directed at learning from existing experience and successes in ASM, in community development, and even in large-scale mining operations that could be incorporated within ASM initiatives.

Endnotes

[1] Levy and Scott-Clark (2001); Veiga and Hinton (2002).

[2] See, for example, Gunson and Yue Jian (2001) for a discussion of the difficulty of making these estimates.

[3] ILO (1999b).

[4] Drechsler (2001).

[5] United Nations Economic and Social Council (1996).

[6] Gueye (2001).

[7] ILO (1999b).

[8] Ibid.

[9] World Bank (2001a).

[10] ILO (1999b).

[11] AllAfrica.com (2001).

[12] UNDP (1999a) p.17.

[13] ILO (1999b).

[14] Hentschel et al. (2001).

[15] ILO (2001d).

[16] ILO (1999a).

[17] Ibid.

[18] Hentschel et al. (2001) p.12.

[19] Gunson and Yue Jian (2001).

[20] Chakravorty (2001).

[21] ILO (1999b).

[22] Ibid., p.4.

[23] Gunson and Yue Jian (2001) p.8.

[24] Aspinall (2001).

[25] Hilson (2001a).

[26] This section draws on Wotruba et al. (1998); McMahon et al. (1999); Hentschel (1998); IENIM (1996).

[27] Hentschel et al. (2001).

[28] Appleton et al. (1999).

[29] Lodenius and Malm (1998); Roulet et al. (1999).

[30] Silva-Forsberg et al. (1999).

[31] ILO (1999b).

[32] Ibid.

[33] Hentschel et al. (2001).

[34] Ibid.

[35] This section draws on Labonne (1997) and on Labonne and Gilman (1999).

[36] Amnesty International (1993).

[37] ILO (1999b).

[38] Hentschel et al. (2001).

[39] Drechsler (2001).

[40] Hentschel et al. (2001).

[41] Rosenfeld Sweeting and Clark (2000) p.54.

[42] Unit for the Promotion of Democracy-Organization of American States (1997) p.114.

[43] Lawyers' Environmental Action Team, at http://www.leat.or.tz/active/buly.

[44] MIGA website, at http://www.miga.org/screens/projects/guarant/regions/ssa/Barrick.htm.

[45] MIGA Statement on Bulyanhulu Mine in Tanzania, 26 September 2001, at http://www.miga.org/screens/news/press/092601.htm.

[46] Ibid.; see also Hutchinson (2001).

[47] Letter to National Post from Lawyers' Environmental Action Team, 9 January 2002, at http://www.leat.or.tz/about/pr/2002.01.09.national.post.php.

[48] Statement by Mining Watch Canada and the Council of Canadians, at http://www.miningwatch.ca/publications/NP_response.html.

[49] MIGA website, 4 April 2002, at http://www.miga.org/screens/projects/guarant/regions/ssa/Bulyanhulu.htm.

[50] Hentschel et al. (2001).

[51] See CASM (2001).

[52] Drechsler (2001).

[53] Hentschel et al. (2001).

[54] Southern African Women in Mining Trust (2000) p.11.

[55] World Bank (2001b) p.2.

[56] For more detail see OIT/IPEC and AECI (2000).

[57] This section draws on Priester and Hruschka (1996) and on Fundación MEDMIN (in press).

[58] Susapu and Crispin (2001).

[59] Mining Industry Associations of Southern Africa (2001). For a description of the Minataur process in general, see MINTEK (2001).

[60] For further discussion on regulation and environmental instruments for ASM, see Lagos et al. (2001).

[61] Mamadou (1995).

[62] Hentschel et al. (2001).

[63] Ibid.

[64] Drechsler (2001).

[65] Ibid.

CHAPTER 14

SECTOR GOVERNANCE: ROLES, RESPONSIBILITIES, AND INSTRUMENTS FOR CHANGE

Achieving effective governance is a major challenge facing the mining and minerals sector and is a key to dealing effectively with many of the issues discussed in previous chapters. Sustainable development requires understanding and redefining the roles, rights, and responsibilities of all the actors – governments, companies, labour unions, international institutions, communities, and non-governmental organizations (NGOs) – and introducing new instruments for change.

Though there have been areas where governance of the minerals sector has significantly improved, prevailing governance structures continue to reflect imbalances in power among different actors and in the priorities given to their interests at the national and international levels. Minerals development has in the past been the province of the investor, who was often foreign.

A transition to sustainable development requires more symmetry in establishing the rules of the game and a more equitable distribution of rights and responsibilities, as well as risks and benefits, among different actors. Moves to provide clear rules and predictable results for mining investors and lenders should proceed hand in hand with similar rules and fair processes to deal with concerns such as national interest, community issues, and environmental management.

Government has a central and unavoidable role to play in improving governance for sustainable development. Government provides incentives, passes laws, adopts regulations, decides what kinds of cases can be brought in courts, and enforces laws, all of which are core governance activities. Another key role for governments is enabling, organizing, or participating in multistakeholder processes for policy reform. All of these and other activities constitute a framework that has enormous impact on whether and how various minerals activities occur.

As one observer has noted: 'The 1990s saw a remarkable regulatory transformation in the developing economies. Nation after nation adopted a new mining code and amended their related laws in an effort to become globally more competitive. The reform process was driven by a realization that exploration and mining activities are not well suited to government-managed development and that to attract private sector

investment, the regulatory environment must be conducive to investors' needs.'[1] New or modified mining policies and legislation were adopted in more than 100 countries. These changes demonstrated quite clearly just how responsive the sector is to the governance framework: they stimulated international interest in minerals as well as investment in countries where it was previously minimal. The reforms were for the most part explicitly undertaken to promote foreign investment and to create a stable and attractive fiscal and regulatory climate. They institutionalized liberal economic policies for mining and other investments, creating a more competitive international arena.

Whether this legal and institutional reform will result in a renewed flow of investment when economic conditions in the industry improve, and whether this in turn will catalyse sustainable development, remains to be seen. This 'first generation' of reforms dealt mainly with the concerns of investors, who in many cases are now enmeshed in problems that were not so thoroughly addressed by the reform movement, as described in earlier chapters. Can these problems be addressed successfully by a 'second generation' of reforms that meet the challenges of sustainable development?

Minerals investment has unquestionably created real opportunities and benefits for some people in some areas of the world. It has also increased the adverse impacts and risks for others. Some of the opportunities have been lost due to lack of adequate governance structures to resolve conflicts or through lack of government capacity to manage them, corruption, or damaging power struggles and conflicts over who 'owns' the asset and who 'controls' or shares in the revenue. Governments may provide clear enabling legislation and strong policies in one area, but these are devalued by failure to address the rest. Complementary and essential areas of policy may be just emerging, hobbled by unclear or antiquated laws, with unclear lines of authority and few resources.

In the most successful economies, the state's role as facilitator of investment is balanced by its role, for example, as regulator – establishing laws and policies that provide for regional land use planning, ameliorate environmental and social impacts, or take advantage of the opportunity to develop roads, schools, and better health care. Relatively well resourced states may also provide a social safety net that cushions the impact of change – such as the move away from a subsistence to a cash economy, or closure of a mine – on those most in need.

To improve their ability to fulfil their roles, governments must be given support and assistance in eliminating the asymmetries in policy and legislation, in strengthening capacity, and in building a policy framework capable of turning investment into sustainable development. This will take time. It will highlight the importance of supplementary instruments of governance not to replace the state role, but to deal effectively with immediate and pressing problems while governments find the ways to respond more effectively.

This chapter focuses on the roles of different actors in various instruments – such as regulations, market-based mechanisms, and voluntary initiatives – to promote change. It closes with a discussion of the main governance challenges currently facing the minerals sector.

National Policy Framework

Legislation
Law has always been and will continue to be a key part of the governance framework for the mining sector.[2] Effectively implemented, law is a leveller: it generates consistent incentives for responsible behaviour of all companies and other actors, regardless of their size. It implements the will of the majority while protecting the rights of minorities. The application of law is rarely simple. Laws alone achieve nothing without effective and capable administrative agencies to administer them, or effective access to a functioning court system to enforce and protest the rights they create. Law can also be a tool for the powerful in some countries, helping one group to the exclusion of others. Getting the right balance for the distribution of risks and opportunities, and of costs and benefits, taxes all policy-makers.

National government provides the legislative framework for the minerals industry, and national or sub-national legislation is the route through which most legal rights and obligations attach to companies and the many others with whom they must deal. For regulators, a clear-cut and enforceable framework is essential to control the activities of the industry effectively. For citizens, the framework protects them against the risk of loss of livelihoods or property, or unfair and arbitrary treatment, and gives them opportunities to seek to improve their position. For industry, it is important to have a regulatory system that is stable, transparent, and appropriate to the conditions of the country. National law provides the basic framework for determining the distribution of economic wealth. It can even reduce power imbalances between companies and communities. Legal rights to land, to information, and to compensation enhance communities' negotiating powers. Legally enforceable rights and effective access to justice can help build trust by reducing the fear that compromise inevitably means a win by the more powerful party.

Law must be understood in context. It is never the total answer to how societies govern themselves. If it were, society would be in a continual state of litigation. Negotiated cultural norms, customary usage of business and trade, traditional ways of doing things, rules observed by cultural groups that precede the creation of the nation-state, and the influence of religious doctrines are extremely important to how things get done. Law has different levels of importance in different societies. In some – perhaps the United States – law has achieved a dominant position in the way things are done. Some countries or societies are to a large extent governed by customary law. In others – remote traditional villages with infrequent contact with central authorities – the affairs of society are governed by rules well understood locally but not necessarily incorporated into national legislation. In many countries, effective implementation and enforcement of law is currently little more than a desirable goal.

An exploration or mining company that is domiciled where law is paramount may find itself operating in a traditional society. The company may see itself as entitled to rely on the national laws that create the conditions for its investment, whereas communities who do not fully recognize those national laws and receive a disproportionate share of the risks without a compensating share of the benefits may see it as a 'licence for theft'. National government may see the company as an instrument for extending the authority of its laws and institutions into areas where they are weak. Local people may regard this as an imposition that undermines customary or other systems of local authority. To prevent conflict in such situations, operation within the national legal framework and a good understanding of and respect for local systems are both required.

The range of legislative systems in different countries has resulted in a diversity of methods for allocating the rights and responsibilities for these issues among mining, investment, planning, environment, and other laws. No two countries possess exactly the same framework. Each nation needs to assess the level of legislation generic to all industries and how much should be specific to the mining industry. In addition, the arrangements for administration and enforcement tend to be complex because the division of responsibilities among different government departments and national, provincial (or state), and local levels of government is seldom straightforward. There is no one ideal system.

Mining Legislation
A mining act is the principal regulatory instrument governing mineral exploration and production activities in most regimes. It defines both the rights and the obligations of the mining title-holder and the power of government officers. The government's first role is to regulate the sector at all levels, including domestic exploration and exploitation or extraction, as well as primary mineral processing.[3]

Mining acts or associated rules and regulations typically state that the holder of an exploration or mining licence must comply with all other relevant laws; some include provisions, such as environmental or social requirements, that go beyond the traditional province of mining law. For example, many mining acts require one or all of the following: an environmental and social impact assessment/statement, an environmental management plan, a rehabilitation programme, or a rehabilitation or restoration fund. Many of the environmental clauses contained in mining acts overlap with environmental legislation, though the latter are usually generic to all activities and contain a more precise description of the requirements. There is a growing trend for countries to draft specific environmental regulations for the mining sector.

Many mining acts also provide for 'regulatory stabilization' in one form or another: a guarantee that the investor will not be subject to new or changed

requirements, such as higher taxes or new environmental laws, planning requirements, or other future legislation.[4] Even where these are not explicitly stated in legislation, countries have in some cases been willing to agree to project-specific contractual 'stabilization agreements'. Although these may encourage investors, they are also controversial, as they may bind the hands of government in terms of dealing with changing social demands and circumstances of development for decades into the future.

Another kind of mining-specific legislation is mine closure planning laws, also referred to as reclamation or rehabilitation laws. These are the norm in Australia, Canada, and the US.[5] Typically they require the development of a plan, with some form of public participation, specifying the environmental conditions to be achieved at the site at the end of the mine's life, and a financial guarantee assuring that the company will meet those objectives. South Africa also has such a law. Few other developing countries have closure laws, although some are starting to appear, and they generally do not require the financial guarantee. Although these have played important roles in improving performance in industry, their administration requires considerable capacity.

The World Bank has had a key role in helping governments reform their mining codes. It has made loans for legal and institutional strengthening to attract investment, with the idea that increased revenues will provide a source of funds for loan repayment. Though this reform addresses environmental concerns and, occasionally, social issues, it has largely focused on meeting the concerns of investors and lenders, not least because foreign direct investment is an important source of capital for economic development in poor countries. This activity and project-specific support by Bank group entities such as the International Finance Corporation (IFC) and Multilateral Investment Guarantee Agency (MIGA) for new mines in countries where investment has been facilitated by the reform process have attracted criticism from many NGOs. They argue that the outcomes of the reforms are biased towards needs of industry at the expense of community concerns. Since a 'second generation' of reform to deal with these problems might not generate obvious streams of revenue for loan repayment, it is unclear how to finance it.

Other National Legislation

Many important issues relevant to the minerals sector are found in other legislation. Investment laws, for example, set out the basic conditions of security for foreign investment and other important issues such as the ability to repatriate profits. Investors want to know that there are transparent, non-discriminatory systems for the granting of mineral tenure; that a judicial system protects mineral tenure against all third parties and the state; that the holder of the mineral exploration rights has the sole and exclusive right to exploit any commercial deposit discovered; that the applicable taxation laws are fair and reasonable; that the producer has the right to sell any product produced on the free market; and that the producer has the right to freely convert profits to other currencies and to repatriate capital.[6]

Tax laws vary widely, but are highly relevant to mining investment. (See Chapter 8.) A major question previously mentioned is often tax stability – the degree of protection that a company has from future government decisions to raise taxes.

Business law sets out the basic framework for the pursuit of profit at the national level, governing the relationships between owners (such as shareholders) and managers (often directors) of businesses. It sets out the basic rules that govern how the interests of financial stakeholders are protected and financial risk allocated.

Labour law provides the basic framework for the protection of workers in the minerals sector. It deals with issues like terms of employment, job security, dismissal, and the rights of injured workers. It also deals with the rights of trade unions and the issues of health and safety and child labour.

Land law deals with land tenure – the acquisition, disposal, use, protection, and management of land. Some aspects of this are discussed in Chapter 7.

Planning laws create a framework for local or regional land use and economic planning issues, and for the coordination necessary to ensure that infrastructure needs can be met in an effective manner. They may also be a basis for planning regarding social needs such as medical care, education, and housing.

Environmental law is increasingly important to minerals activities in almost all countries. Countries frequently start by enacting a law to provide for environmental impact assessment, the most common tool of environmental management in national legislation. This may be accompanied by a 'framework law' establishing the national environmental authority and allocating responsibilities among government agencies. In many developing countries, international treaties such as the Convention on Biological Diversity have provided direction for national law.

As systems of environmental law mature, they tend to add legislation for water pollution control, air pollution, solid waste, and the handling and disposal of toxic substances, all of which are highly relevant to the minerals industries. Other areas that apply to the minerals sector include water resources law covering use of surface and ground water. The pace at which many developing countries have adopted legislation, inspired by international conventions, internal political demands, and foreign examples, has been rapid and may have grown faster than the infrastructure necessary to make it work effectively.

The tensions over environmental law in the minerals industries are many. Three most salient are the extent to which environmental statutes can be used simply to stop development of projects rather than focusing more on improving the management of their impacts; the extent to which companies can be held liable later for environmental problems arising from activities that were legal when they were conducted; and the administration of environmental laws by an environmental agency versus a sectoral agency, such as a mining or natural resource ministry.

International Conventions

International agreements in the form of new conventions or protocols to existing conventions have been adopted in many areas relevant to sustainable development. Most of these address specific global or regional issues. Although conventions are meant to be legally binding, most have no mechanism for ensuring compliance. Conventions are intended to oblige governments to pass national legislation to implement their commitment, but many of them are not integrated into national policy due to a lack of resources, political will, or the power of enforcement. There are also non-legally binding 'soft law' declarations setting international policy objectives and norms for government action in a range of areas. Broader sets of international statements to which governments subscribe, such as the Rio Principles, attempt to codify basic values that should underlie individual and collective action.

The number of international conventions has increased significantly in recent years, dealing with an ever-widening range of issues. (See Table 14–1.) Conventions today cover biodiversity and protected areas, and most recently climate change, but also pollution and waste issues such as hazardous chemicals and the disposal of waste. (See Chapter 10.) The International Labour Organization (ILO) core conventions (see Chapter 6) and others provide for the protection of workers, women, and children. A number of international instruments (such as the Rio Declaration) recognize public rights to information or participation in decision-making. (See Chapter 12.)

There is currently no international governance regime or statement of principles for mining or mineral resources, which stands in stark contrast to renewable resources such as agriculture, fisheries, marine resources, and forestry.[7] Some NGOs consider this as a gap. Part of the explanation for it may be that the exploitation of mineral resources does not lend itself as readily to international standards or principles as other resources do because of the number of minerals and their uses, the wide variety in methods of extraction, and the differences in physical environments and climates where mining takes place. But arguably the most significant issue is one of jurisdiction and national sovereignty. The few international regimes for mining that do exist apply only to areas beyond national jurisdictions. However, arguably, similar differences exist in the case of marine, forestry, and other resources for which international principles or governance regimes have already been formulated.

Table 14–1. Key International Agreements of Relevance to the Mining Industry

Instrument	Relevance to the Mining Industry
Aarhus Convention, 1998	Establishes rights to access to information, public participation in decision-making, and access to justice.
Convention on Combating Bribery of Foreign Public Officials in International Business Transactions, Organisation for Economic Co-operation and Development (OECD), 1997	Requires international cooperation in the effort to combat corruption.
ILO Safety and Health in Mines Convention, 1995	Establishes the principle of national action on the improvement of working conditions in the mining industry.
Biological Diversity Convention, 1992	Aims to conserve biodiversity and ensure an equitable distribution of benefits from its use; implemented through national biodiversity strategies and plans.
Framework Convention on Climate Change, 1992	Seeks to limit changes in the global climate by controlling emissions of greenhouse gases, notably through the 1997 Kyoto Protocol, and is leading to a range of national measures such as carbon/energy taxes.
Basel Convention on the Trade in Hazardous Wastes, 1989	Prohibits all transboundary movements of hazardous wastes for recycling and recovery, affecting the trade in scrap metals.
Indigenous and Tribal Peoples Convention, 1989	Provides basic rights for indigenous and tribal peoples, including respect for their traditions and property.
Montreal Protocol on Ozone Depleting Substances, 1987	Forces changes to fire protection and refrigeration practices, especially in the deep gold mining in South Africa.
World Heritage Convention, 1972	Protects natural or cultural values.

Another factor may be the size of the global mining industry in comparison with other development activities, since the level of capitalization is relatively small. There may be less impetus for broader action.

Other Instruments

Command-and-control legislation, accompanied by a threat of punishment and a penalty, is not the only effective way of promoting change. Prescriptive legislation can be costly to implement and requires an appropriately trained enforcement team, extensive and regular monitoring of operations, analytical and data evaluation support, and an effective judicial system to administer fines and penalties.

Increasingly, it is recognized that it is useful to improve standards by appealing to the self-interest of those most directly involved. A new generation of policy thinking ties instruments to the characteristics of the societies where they will be implemented. For example, laws intended to enforce the eradication of child labour in small-scale mining need to be accompanied by strategies for poverty elimination that provide economic alternatives.

Government authorities are now using a variety of other regulatory approaches that are incentive-based. However, none of these alternatives used alone is able to address all situations. In practice, a mixture of instruments is now advocated in order to provide the most suitable response to national needs. Among these are performance targets, market-based instruments, and negotiated or voluntary agreements. In many cases, these require collaboration between the community and NGOs as well as relevant government agencies and the company.

Prescriptive versus Non-Prescriptive Legislation

Prescriptive legislation provides absolute values or standards, set by the relevant government department or agency, that have to be met at all times. They are relatively simple to put in place and provide a measured response to the question of compliance. While prescriptive legislation can be highly successful in certain areas such as pollution reduction, there are also disadvantages in this approach. Because of differences in ore bodies, climate, local resources of concern, and other factors, large minerals operations lack the degree of standardization present in other sectors such as manufacturing. Standardized

requirements, an integral part of a prescriptive system, may result in reduced efficiency – underprotection at some sites and unnecessary overprotection at others. Standardized solutions do not necessarily deliver the optimum environmental or economic performance. There are also significant capacity problems with adoption of numerical norms, such as the water and air criteria that have been developed in such detail in the industrial economies. Measuring pollutants in waste streams or general environmental media at parts per million or parts per billion levels requires skilled personnel using expensive and specialized equipment, often in laboratories, which many developing countries lack.

In contrast, non-prescriptive legislation relies on the operator identifying the issues and making the management commitments to deal with them. This provides the opportunity to develop the process and procedures and to identify suitable standards on a site-by-site or case-by-case basis to be built into the overall management of the operation. This approach is more flexible to deal with many social and environmental issues that tend not to fit any one model.

On the other hand, non-prescriptive regulation can provide the operator with the opportunity of understating or hiding issues that may be socially or environmentally critical. Ill-defined standards are difficult to measure and open to individual interpretation. It also means that compliance or non-compliance often is unclear, leaving the regulating agency unsure of its role.

Standards and Criteria

Standards are an essential tool for a regulator who wishes to use (at least in part) a command-and-control or prescriptive approach. They are also used for market-based instruments and voluntary agreements. Standards should be used with caution. Many of them are established using little science and a great deal of guesswork. A government may base its standards on those of another country with little or no reference to existing domestic conditions. The best standards are the product of local multistakeholder processes, with a degree of international comparability, and follow internationally agreed norms in their development.

Performance Targets

Performance targets are part of a carrot-and-stick approach. They enable the regulator to use a non-prescriptive approach, particularly on environmental performance. They are based on the local environment and the most appropriate technology, and are expected to show a gradual but continuous improvement. The choice is left to the operator, who is assumed to have sufficient expertise to make sound, well-informed decisions. They differ from quality objectives in that they try to define the behaviour of industrial operations rather than its impacts. Such an approach assumes that there is an effective regulatory and enforcement system in place and that legal recourse, in cases of non-compliance, is feasible. Independent monitors, trusted by the government, the operator, and the community, are needed to monitor compliance.

While there are statements of intent in many government policy documents and provisions in minerals agreements on areas such as local employment targets, business spin-offs, and infrastructure, the use of social performance targets generally lags behind environmental ones.

Market-based Instruments

Market-based instruments are increasingly favoured because they can harness competition to drive better performance and because they are more economically efficient than 'one size fits all' or command-and-control systems. They can, when properly applied, produce a desired outcome at lower cost than regulation by encouraging innovation and continuous improvement, by finding solutions suitable for local situations, and by reducing enforcement and administrative costs. They are often used in regulatory regimes as a way to provide funds for the regulatory agency or as an incentive to improve environmental and social management. Fees or charges can be levied for a number of stages in the regulatory process, such as the submission of a social and environmental impact statement or the issuing of an environmental permit. These fees are usually set at a fixed rate regardless of the social and environmental implications of the project and provide no incentive for a company to improve its performance.

Governments have long used tax incentives as a tool of public policy. These can take a wide variety of forms, depending on the national tax code and the objectives being sought. For example, tax incentives can be used to reduce the cost of an environmentally related expenditure or to encourage reductions of emissions or waste generation. In the mining sector, they can also play a role in encouraging technological adaptation towards more efficient and sustainable processes.

Because tax incentives can be costly and may distort investment decisions, many governments have recently reduced rather than increased the tax incentives they offer. But instead of lowering costs to business, some governments have begun to increase costs by taxing environmentally undesirable activities. The Scandinavian countries, in particular, have introduced several taxes, primarily related to the use of energy.[8] Over the long term, such 'green' taxes may be offset by cuts in traditional taxes, such as income or payroll taxes, as part of an effort to shift the tax burden from 'goods' to 'bads'.

Voluntary Agreements

Voluntary agreements, covenants, and other instruments sometimes described as self- or co-regulatory are finding an increasingly important place in the regulatory system. The advantage is the high degree of flexibility they provide, allowing companies to find the most cost-effective solutions for each individual case. The disadvantage is their inability to ensure that all companies comply (enforcement mechanisms are rarely built into voluntary agreements) and the fact that non-signatory parties are not bound by the agreements. Nevertheless, efforts such as MEND (Mine Environment Neutral Drainage) in Canada and the Responsible Care Program in the chemicals industry demonstrate that sector-wide voluntary programmes can produce impressive results in some areas.[8] (Voluntary initiatives are discussed further later in this chapter.)

Financial Surety

Government is usually ultimately responsible for the cost of dealing with the social and environmental problems created by the abandonment of a mine site. As a result, it is becoming common practice for some form of financial surety or rehabilitation bond to be established prior to project approval. This provision is designed to guarantee performance and to cover both the technical and financial failure of a mine operator to meet the full obligations at the time of closure or in the event of an unplanned closure. (See Chapter 10.) Governments establish financial sureties in order to protect the environment and avoid the costs of cleaning up orphaned sites. However, the cost of a surety can be significant and could deter a potential mining investor. In addition, it is important to note that in the forestry sector, for example, the means used for long-term financial surety are highly vulnerable to politically motivated misuse or to corruption (such as long-term hidden funds).[10] Smaller or thinly capitalized companies often have difficulty with surety requirements. It is therefore necessary for the government to have a good understanding of the issues involved in the design and application of a financial surety policy.

For some mine operators, the amount of financial surety is established during project negotiations based on information in the environmental impact statement and is an estimate of the closure and rehabilitation costs. Another method is for the mine operator to be charged a levy on every tonne of rock or ore mined or processed or on every tonne of concentrate or metal produced. The financial surety should be available to either the mine operator or the relevant regulatory authority, to pay for rehabilitation. If the mine operator defaults, the money remains in the hands of the regulatory authority. Thus, the funds from the guarantee should be separate and not reachable by creditors in the case of bankruptcy or business failure. Once all stages of rehabilitation have been completed, including a passive care programme, the remaining funds may be returned to the mine operator. Whichever method is used to establish a financial surety, it is essential that it is regularly assessed, as part of the environmental management of the project, and increased or decreased as necessary. In some countries, contributions to a financial surety are tax-deductible.

Enforcement

While all instruments promoting behavioural change need data collection and monitoring, those based on specified requirements require an effective and regular enforcement mechanism to ensure their success. Traditionally, a mining or an environmental inspectorate has been charged with monitoring and enforcement. Today, the increasingly complex legislative requirements call for new approaches to enforcement as well as training and institutional strengthening to support the more conventional functions of the enforcement agency. Close liaison between various government departments is essential. Practical resource allocation increasingly favours a division of functions, with, for example, the environmental agency responsible for establishing policies, law, and standards,

while the mining department undertakes management and enforcement.

In countries with a federal government structure, it is common for enforcement to be delegated to the provincial (state) or local government. While the central government maintains the overall control and management of the project, the regional government, which is often more in touch with the local situation, is responsible for the day-to-day monitoring and direct liaison with the company and local community. Some countries have elected to place a full-time enforcement officer at each major project who, with proper training, can work closely with the company to ensure compliance while improving cooperation and consultation with all levels of government and the local community. Others have deliberately rotated officers to keep them from becoming too close to company management.

Whatever arrangement is adopted, compliance with environmental standards and legislation may be ensured by mechanisms such as imposing civil liability on mining operators, compulsory insurance or payment into a guarantee fund to pay for damages and compensation, financial surety, and incentive measures to maintain social and environmental standards in the absence of specific regulations. All these measures require some degree of inspection and enforcement by the competent authorities, and fines or sanctions of sufficient importance to discourage non-compliance.

Government agencies are also starting to use consulting services in enforcement. In Western Australia, for example, evaluation of the assessment reports is now being handled by accredited assessors rather than by the government agencies directly. A key new role for the agencies is now checking the credentials of assessors. In addition, there are calls from some quarters for independent roles in enforcement that could be taken up by NGOs.

Litigation

Depending on national laws, litigation is available to individuals acting alone or in class action, to private organizations, and to governments. Lawsuits can take many forms, including private-versus-private litigation (for example, where industrial activity imposes 'unreasonable' costs on neighbouring communities); government-versus-private litigation, as a means of enforcing statutory obligations; and private-versus-government action, in which individuals or groups seek a judicial order to compel a government to act in accordance with its constitutional or statutory duties (though this does not apply to all countries). In addition, in some countries courts can help to clarify responsibilities on, for example, whether a particular level of government has the authority to address a particular issue.

Litigation can provide clarity and an enforceable outcome. Because it is expensive and time-consuming, however, and often tends to exacerbate and formalize conflict among the litigating parties, it is normally only pursued where non-confrontational modes of resolving the dispute are not possible or have failed. The extent to which private parties have access to litigation, including right of standing and intervention, depends in part on national statutory provisions.

Responsibility without accountability is a hollow prospect, and providing for effective access to justice is fundamental to accountability. In many countries, even where claimants have serious, valid complaints as a result of environmental, health, or human rights aspects of mining activities, their national court systems do not necessarily afford them clear or speedy remedies. Other countries may have corrupt court systems or systems where legal actions associated with human rights abuses by public agencies cannot be pursued. More significant perhaps, lack of access to trained lawyers or effective financial assistance for legal representation may put justice through the courts beyond the reach of many citizens. In South Africa, for example, the Legal Aid Board, faced with a financial crisis, ceased providing funding for all but a very few personal injury claims in 1999. In a series of actions beginning in 1997, more than 7500 South Africans, assisted by public funding from the Legal Services Commission, claimed damages for personal injuries in UK courts against Cape plc, at one time the world's largest asbestos mining company. An 'in principle' agreement on an out-of-court settlement worth £21 million was reached in December 2001.[11]

In the face of such barriers, there have been a growing number of cases against parent companies of mining (and other resource companies) in recent years: in UK courts over operations in South Africa and Namibia, in Australian courts over the Ok Tedi mine in Papua New Guinea (PNG), and in US courts over operations

in Papua (formerly Irian Jaya) and Colombia.[12] They have resulted in a variety of rulings, with a limited record of success for the claimants. Although some of this litigation may be motivated by nothing more complex than the fact that getting access to courts in western industrial countries is easier, that they award higher damages, or that they reflect values different from host-country governments, it also reflects weak systems of governance in some host countries. A major factor in bringing this litigation is that there is sometimes nowhere else to take these complaints.

Bringing a claim over community-level problems in Africa, Asia, or Latin America before British or Australian court systems is not the ideal way to proceed. But if there is no other option, the pressure to open up these or similar forums to numerous increasingly complex disputes will be high. Without clear and effective methods of expressing grievances within an ordered system of governance, they will emerge as they often do now – before institutions that are not well equipped to handle them, in social protest movements, in media campaigns, and with no clear mechanism for demanding that some kind of action be taken where it may be sorely needed.

Key Challenges for National Legal Systems

Environmental issues are far from the only area where there is conflict or uncertainty over national legal requirements. Many of the problems are complex and depend heavily on national circumstances. The areas where attention is needed, as identified in previous chapters, include – in addition to environment – management for sustainable development, land rights, revenue sharing, access to information, and public participation. This is the agenda for a 'second generation' of reform of legal and institutional structures in the minerals sector. It may be that not all of these elements are important everywhere, or that this list may need to be supplemented, but these are core issues. Governments need to make a concerted effort to find ways forward on them in consultation with other stakeholders.

Management for Sustainable Development

A framework for the relationship between the minerals investor and the host-country government is essential. But so is a framework for the interaction of these parties with others who have a vital interest in the outcome. Such a framework probably has at a minimum three elements, which should link with and support each other:

- a good system of integrated impact assessment early in a project that includes thorough attention to all relevant environmental issues, but that also includes the relevant economic and social factors that will be affected by any development;
- a provision for developing a Community Sustainable Development Plan, in consultation with all who may be affected, to create a vision of the economic, social, and environmental future and to identify how to achieve the objectives; and
- a requirement for developing an integrated closure plan, defined at the earliest possible stage, that identifies the desired environmental, social, and economic results at and beyond the point of closure and that assigns responsibilities for achieving those objectives.

Land Rights Regimes

In many countries, minerals belong to the state, which can grant concessions to others to search for and develop them. Where this happens, affected owners should in principle be compensated for any losses, such as having to leave their land. But particularly where people depend heavily on subsistence activities, a cash award of 'fair market value' for a small agricultural holding may not be adequate to live on, even if invested. Other lost values, such as the use of communal lands, may not be compensated at all. People understandably also resist the loss of the only social and community ties they know. In addition, many people in developing countries have no recognized legal title to the land they occupy and may therefore not be compensated at all. Where an owner does not think an offer adequate, the courts may be far away or expensive to gain access to, take years to hear a plea, or simply not be trusted. Where displacement or resettlement of people is proposed, the issues become even more difficult.[13]

The solution of a decree in court ordering legal or informal occupants to leave with compensation they do not accept or no compensation at all, followed by police or military action to evict them, may lead to violence and continued conflict through the life of any project. It is increasingly unacceptable to companies worried about their reputations, to lenders and investors, and to much of national and world opinion, led by campaigning NGOs inside and outside the host country.

International governance: United Nations, New York

Indigenous, Aboriginal, and Traditional Land Claims

There are relatively few situations in which indigenous, aboriginal, and traditional land claims have been resolved to the satisfaction of all. In many places there is at best an uneasy status quo. National governments believe they have settled the issue by constitutional provisions and legislation, much of which reserves all mineral rights and revenues to the state even when the right of local populations to own or control the surface and its resources is acknowledged. Indigenous, aboriginal, and traditional occupants in many cases have not agreed to these legal provisions, and do not acknowledge the right of the government to grant concessions in the territory they regard as rightfully theirs. At the extreme, governments do not acknowledge the existence of indigenous or aboriginal peoples or any distinct cultural identity and rights. And these communities in turn may give little recognition to the government or its claimed prerogatives. Asserting a claim through an exploration or mining concession in these circumstances is almost bound to lead to conflict.

Sharing of Revenues

The local community and local government will experience a great increase in the demand for all kinds of services from water, waste disposal, and law enforcement to education and housing. Without some share of the revenues, local government will be marginalized and dependent on what the company may choose to do. And development opportunities will certainly be lost if government is unwilling to spend to help extend and complement the transportation, education, or health care facilities that the industry may build. There is no universal formula for how to do this, and the result should likely depend on a number of factors such as whether the local community is a few dozen households or hundreds of thousands of people. This issue cannot be solved without government leadership. The message is that whatever the ultimate formula, national government cannot simply ignore the issue.

Access to Information, Public Participation, and Access to Justice

The right to participate in decision-making and to have access to needed information are key elements for any framework for sustainable development. Without clearly established laws and administrative procedures to give these rights substance, the ability to capture the benefits of development is very likely to be lost.

Lenders, Investors, and Customers

Criteria for lending can prescribe sustainable development-related conditions for the provision of funds to companies for new projects or ongoing operations. These types of criteria would either have to be adopted by the lending agency itself or imposed on it by legislation at the national level. Public pressure could help lead such a change. For public institutions, broad stakeholder support would probably be required if the criteria were to significantly alter or constrain the lending institution's activities. (See Chapter 6.)

Central to current practice in this area are the various guidelines, policies, and directives used by the World Bank Group in its lending decisions. These are applied not only when the IFC makes a loan or MIGA guarantees it. They are almost universally used as a guideline by private commercial banks even where there is no World Bank Group involvement in a project. They are also referred to frequently by insurers, export credit agencies, national investment guarantee authorities, and others important to minerals finance. The Extractive Industries Review currently being sponsored by the Bank is therefore of broad importance, as any proposals it makes for significant changes could have widespread effects.

Criteria for lending are used by both private and public lending agencies. Even aside from the World Bank policies, many private lenders (such as chartered banks) already account for social and environmental factors in assessing the risk related to a potential loan.

Some have gone further and are starting to explore the utility of more comprehensive sustainable development–related risk factors. This trend could be extended to account more explicitly for sustainability factors in a particular sector such as mining and minerals. Public lending agencies such as multilateral national development banks and, to a lesser extent, export credit agencies already account for a range of public policy considerations that are not directly related to their own expected rate-of-return when determining how to dispense funds (such as meeting job creation objectives). Dialogue with lenders over these criteria and future direction in their application was a major focus of MMSD activities.[14]

Sustainability criteria or principles for investment are used to set out conditions for the investment of funds by institutional investors in equity or debt markets. Criteria vary, but often include requirements for a commitment to environmental awareness and accountability, an ongoing process of improvement and dialogue, and comprehensive, systematic public reporting. Experience to date indicates that both pressure from shareholder coalitions and investment opportunities associated with good corporate performance on sustainability criteria can encourage publicly traded companies to change their behaviour. It is also important for the financial community to be open and transparent in its dealings and screening methodologies.

There are many examples of 'sustainability' criteria – such as green funds and socially responsible or ethical funds – initiated by financial services and investment sectors, sometimes in collaboration with social or environmental interest groups. (An example is the Dow Jones Sustainability Index, which ranks publicly traded companies against a set of sustainability criteria.) Many of these have no or very few minerals companies in their portfolio. Social and environmental criteria are also increasingly used by insurers active in the minerals sector. In addition, some large consumers of mineral products are becoming aware of the potential impacts of environmental and social factors in their supply chains.

Terminal Liabilities: A Long-term Challenge

A key governance challenge in the minerals sector is the issue of closure costs or long-term liabilities.

Closure costs can be significant. They may include the expenses of relocating or retraining the work force, maintenance of schools and other infrastructure, environmental remediation, and the long-term treatment of acid drainage from the site. At many mine sites, and especially where governance is weak, there may be no clear agreement on who should be responsible for these various costs – government, the company, the local community, unions, or individuals. As the time for closure approaches, questions over responsibility arise and opportunities for positive solutions decrease. This is most extreme where closure results from a lack of profitability. Without prior agreement, such as bonding, it is likely that no one will have set aside the funds required.

Sustainable development requires a long-term approach to decision-making. Investment in long-term, durable solutions is unlikely to be made unless the company, the government, and others take responsibility for closure costs and regard them as part of the costs of mining. All too often there is the assumption that someone else will pay – in the future.

The lack of acknowledgement of closure costs is exacerbated by the accounting treatment they receive, as the costs may look small when discounted at 6–8% or more over 30 years. There should be a serious look at the balance-sheet treatment these anticipated liabilities receive and how company accountants and auditors view them.

The lack of clarity on this issue can also provide an incentive to all parties to delay closure because they fear the outcome of negotiations. When closure occurs, there is sometimes a justified concern that costs simply will not get paid: the company and the government may never agree on who should pay what, or one party may not have sufficient funds. Moreover, they will have a joint interest in minimizing the bill.

This concern is heightened by a number of recent controversial end-of-life cases. (See Box 14–1.) In Papua New Guinea, one condition of BHP Billiton's withdrawal from the Ok Tedi mine was that there would be a process of informed consent. Consultation was conducted by Ok Tedi Mining Limited and the PNG government with the affected villages in the Western Province so that, in formally agreeing to the mine continuing for its full life, villagers understood that the mine's continuing

operation would result in significant environmental impacts.[15] The Melanesian Peace Foundation was commissioned two years ago by the company to help the local communities develop negotiation skills. To date, Mine Continuation Agreements have been signed with more than 90% of affected villages. In these agreements, Ok Tedi and its shareholders are released from all demands and claims associated with future environmental impacts. This arrangement has met with considerable opposition. Four landowner leaders wrote a letter to PNG Members of Parliament, warning that if legislation setting the scene for BHP Billiton's liability-free exit from Ok Tedi passed, they would shut down the mine.[16] The PNG Parliament passed the OK Tedi Mine Continuation Bill in December 2001.

The Ok Tedi and Marcopper cases raise many important questions regarding liability for past decisions. In the case of Ok Tedi, regarded as a national asset by PNG's Prime Minister Sir Mekere Morauta, the government has prevented the mine being closed, which would clearly be the best solution for the prevention of further environmental damage. The government fears that closing the mine would devastate the national economy and ruin communities.[17] The establishment of a fund management company in Singapore has raised questions for many, particularly community members. In the case of legacy issues, it is incumbent on companies and governments to be entirely transparent about their dealings and respond to the serious questions raised by stakeholders if trust is to be built and maintained.

At Marcopper, Placer Dome was a minority shareholder in the operating company, Marcopper Mining. Questions are still being raised by critics about the conditions of the company's withdrawal from a project that used a system of tailings disposal deemed unacceptable in its home country of Canada. The company believes that it has exceeded its contractual liability by paying for the clean-up, which is still being completed. However, local actors and others continue to worry about the long-term implications of the project, still dogged by reports of seriously unsafe and leaking tailings storage facilities and the possibility of a repeat of the 1996 spill.

These two cases demonstrate the importance of factoring closure costs in from the time a mine opens and not developing a project if the environmental or social costs are likely to be prohibitively expensive.

Box 14–1. Terminal Liabilities: The Cases of Ok Tedi and Marcopper

The mining of gold and copper from Mt. Fubilan in the Star Mountains adjacent to the Ok Tedi River in Papua New Guinea began in 1984. The approved proposals incorporated two stable waste dumps and a conventional tailings storage facility, but a landslide destroyed the facility site. An interim tailings disposal scheme was approved that retained 25% of the tailings but released the rest into the Ok Tedi River. Following unsuccessful attempts to identify a suitable storage site, the PNG government approved the deferral of the construction of permanent waste retention facilities until 1990. A further agreement in 1990 allowed for the disposal of all the tailings and a large portion of waste rock from the failing dumps into the Ok Tedi, with considerable impact on the environment. (See Chapter 10 for further information on these impacts.) Because of its revenue-generating potential and provision of employment in a region with poor development, the mine has been actively supported by the government of PNG.

It is estimated that 73,500 people live in the Ok Tedi/Fly River drainage area with a subsistence lifestyle based on traditional gardening and hunting. Inundation of the floodplains has meant a loss of land, especially in the Ok Tedi area, and elevated sediment levels have severely reduced the fish population in the Ok Tedi.

Growing opposition to the waste disposal culminated in legal action against the operating company, BHP, and an agreement to pay damages to landowners in 1997. In 2001, the newly merged BHP Billiton sought to close the mine rather than face further environmental litigation over mine waste polluting the river system, but this was opposed by minority partners Inmet Corp. of Canada and the PNG government, because the mine accounts for 10% of GNP and 20% of total exports. Despite the fact the PNG government as regulator had stated that the mine would not be closed, BHP Billiton negotiated with other shareholders for this to occur because it felt that it had no alternative.

The net result is that BHP Billiton is terminating its involvement with the project. In the words of its Managing Director, Ok Tedi is 'not compatible with our environmental values and the company should never have become involved'. BHP Billiton has made a commitment not to become involved in new mines with riverine tailings disposal. Under the withdrawal plan, BHP Billiton will transfer its 52% stake in Ok Tedi Mining Limited to a specially established Singapore-based Programme Company called the PNG Sustainable Development Programme, to be used for sustainable development purposes in PNG for up to 40 years. Outlining the main elements of the agreement, BHP Billiton said that the new company had clearly defined corporate rules for decision-making, distribution of funds, and public reporting. BHP Billiton would give financial support to the new company for three years. Another aspect of the BHP Billiton's exit arrangements requires that full cash provisioning for mine closure be made by all shareholders between now and then, including a proportional contribution from the Programme Company to ensure responsible mine closure at Ok Tedi.

In the Philippines, the Marcopper Mine on Marinduque Island was permitted in 1968. The mine was 39.9% owned by Placer Dome. Initially tailings were stored in an impoundment north of the Taipan open pit. In 1975 Marcopper shifted to near-shore disposal of tailings into the shallow waters of Calancan Bay. Between 1975 and 1990 an estimated 200–300 million tonnes of tailings were discharged. In 1991, production shifted to the San Antonio open pit, and tailings disposal was shifted into the old Taipan pit. This method of disposal involved plugging a dewatering tunnel that had drained the open pit.

In March 1996, the plug in the drainage adit failed catastrophically, releasing an estimated 1.5–3 million cubic meters of tailings into the Makulapnit River, Boac River, and eventually the ocean west of the island, 26 kilometres from the open pit. A UN investigation blamed the spill on poor environmental stewardship by the management of the mine.

In 1997, Placer Dome divested its shares in Marcopper and refuted the claim that it had responsibility for the spill, as it was a 39.9% shareholder in the mine and not the operator. Nevertheless, the company agreed to clean up the Boac River and compensate affected villagers. The clean-up included installing a temporary plug in the adit, building berms to prevent further overbank flooding, and the dredging of a channel in the Boac River to catch tailings washed downstream. Placer Dome spent about US$50 million to clean up the Boac River and retired a US$20-million loan that Marcopper owed the Asian Development Bank.

Sources: Ok Tedi from Pintz (1984); King (1997); Regan (2001); Banks and Ballard (1997), Fitzgerald (1999), and personal communications with BHP Billiton, February 2002; Marcopper from Plumlee et al. (2000), Coumans (1999a), and Robinson (2001)

They also demonstrate the importance of ensuring that open and transparent processes for dealing with closure are in place, along with clear processes of dispute resolution when conflicts arise. Ok Tedi is a subject about which much has been said and written. (See Box 14–2.)

Box 14–2. An Alternative View on Terminal Liabilities

According to some observers, despite criticism dating from the outset of the Ok Tedi project BHP and Ok Tedi Mining Limited failed to implement tailings containment that would have prevented the devastation of two rivers. Indigenous petitions and protests were discredited and indigenous political campaigns carried out both domestically and abroad were ignored by the mining company and the government. What policy initiatives might help prevent another Ok Tedi?

• Indigenous people should have veto power over projects affecting their land and livelihoods.

• Independent social and environmental monitoring is required to evaluate mining and other large-scale resource extraction projects.

• Where appropriate, indigenous environmental knowledge should be incorporated into environmental impact assessments and monitoring.

• There is an urgent need for full disclosure of environmental information and more effective communication between mining projects and affected communities regarding impacts.

• Corporations must provide just and reasonable compensation for their impact. Valuations should take local cultural values into account.

• Mechanisms for dispute resolution at a variety of levels must be supported, including the courts.

• There is an urgent need for international legal precedents based on recognized standards and norms and for greater specificity of standards for environmental human rights.

Mining companies need to assess their responsibilities in terms of longer time frames commensurate with the longevity of their environmental impacts – at least 50 years in the case of the Ok Tedi mine, for example. Most important, no new ore bodies should be exploited until tested and reliable strategies for tailings containment are identified. This means that some ore bodies will be off-limits to development in the near future and perhaps even permanently if no effective means of tailings disposal is available.

Source: Kirsch (2001)

Improving Industry Performance

The minerals industry operates in a business climate that is increasingly demanding successful adaptation to changes in social values and public expectations of corporate behaviour. At the corporate level, respect for social and environment standards is often now considered an essential element of good business practice. (See Chapter 6.) Many companies in the minerals sector are committed to the continuous improvement of their social and environmental performance, in some cases including involvement in voluntary initiatives. A voluntary initiative is one not required by law – but this does not mean that its requirements are always non-binding on those who voluntarily subscribe to it.[18]

A wide range of instruments can be classified as voluntary. These include company-specific and industry-wide codes and policies, reporting norms, management systems, procurement requirements, and agreements between government and industry, between company and community, or between company and NGO.

There are complex linkages between voluntary initiatives and domestic law. For example, many commentators emphasize the need for a strong underlying regulatory regime to encourage the development of, participation in, and continued evolution of effective voluntary initiatives. Government measures might be necessary to create the appropriate incentives for compliance.[19] Initiatives may be better at improving the performance of the best than in dealing with the poorest performers. But there is also the possibility that through widespread acceptance and application, voluntary initiatives take on some authoritative status of their own as 'best practice' or even, in common law legal systems, a possible standard of care with legal consequences.

Governments, NGOs, and businesses retain a healthy scepticism about the potential efficacy of voluntary initiatives for addressing 'difficult' measures of performance. This scepticism stems in part from a reluctance to depart from the perceived certainty of outcome that is associated with regulatory approaches. It also relates to the lack of assurance of performance gains and unclear public accountabilities in a number of international and national voluntary programmes. In response to all these concerns and to lessons learnt from voluntary initiatives in other sectors, there is growing recognition of the need for involvement of non-industry stakeholders, transparent design processes, clear measures of performance, and good accountability mechanisms.

While there is increasing recognition that voluntary initiatives can supplement existing legal regimes, many concerns have been raised about them. Some have to do with the vast number of these instruments being developed – more than 100 in eco-tourism alone. NGOs and academics worry about their capacity to track and influence all relevant initiatives to ensure they embody high standards and are applied as intended. A growing number of businesses also maintain that there are too many voluntary initiatives, some of which are duplicative. They worry that continued rapid proliferation may lead to confusion that, in turn, may dilute the effectiveness of any given voluntary initiative in reassuring stakeholders. On the other hand, there is no denying that voluntary initiatives can be as effective as, but less cumbersome and costly than, regulations.

Policy, Codes, and Guidelines

Some mining companies have adopted corporate policies, demonstrating their commitment to improved performance and sending a clear signal throughout the organization that sustainable development is a corporate priority. These policies are designed to promote the integration of social and environmental concerns into all aspects of corporate activity, from exploration to the closure of a mining project, and are given the same treatment as economic considerations.

In some cases the underlying principles of these corporate social and environmental policies have been adopted and incorporated into a common framework by mining associations for application on an industry-wide basis at international and national level. The Australian Minerals Industry Code for Environmental Management (see Box 14–3) and guidelines on the environment and on participation formulated by the South African Chamber of Mines provide two examples. The Minerals Association of Canada also has draft principles in its Towards Sustainable Mining Initiative; as of 2000, there are mandatory reporting requirements for members.

The Australian code has already had important national

Box 14–3. Australian Minerals Council Code

In 1996 the Minerals Council of Australia launched a Code for Environmental Management on behalf of the Australian minerals industry. The code is recognized by the UN Environment Programme (UNEP) as one of the most comprehensive voluntary codes devised for the mining industry and the only one to require disclosure of environmental performance. The code is reviewed periodically to ensure it remains relevant to the needs of communities, industry, and regulators.

The code does not seek to replace regulation but to provide a framework of principles and processes aimed at encouraging signatories to improve existing levels of performance, from exploration to mine closure. Signatories represented by the Minerals Council of Australia account for 90% of Australia's mineral production, though this does not include the vast majority of small and medium-sized companies. A number of major companies are applying the code to their operations world-wide and have integrated code reporting requirements with other environmental management systems, such as ISO14001. To date, over 40 public environmental reports have been published. Other signatories are yet to fully implement the code to cover all operations and have signed on as their Australian or Asia-Pacific operations.

A defining feature of the code is that its implementation is adaptable to the size, scale, and environment of each mining operation. The voluntary nature and the absence of prescriptive or standard-setting requirements seeks to encourage creativity among companies to develop solutions to their own environmental issues. This level of flexibility is recognized by the Australian minerals industry as an essential driver for change across a diverse industry. Conversely, this is also regarded by some NGOs as an excuse for enacting minimal change.

The objectives for the code are underpinned by a set of elements and activities, including cultural and social objectives, with primary emphasis given to environmental management priorities. But the lack of explicit recognition of social priorities such as human rights, particularly in relation to off-shore activities of Australian mining companies, has attracted some NGO criticism. The translation of code principles into practice has also generated debate on issues of implementation, where ingrained corporate culture and the absence of governance systems to monitor compliance effectively have been identified as areas that need to be addressed, particularly if performance is to be achieved in different cultural and community settings. Incorporating these concerns is an essential part of the code's regular review process.

The code was reviewed in 1999, involving further consultation with all interested parties. The operation of the code was streamlined, and its environmental management focus was placed within a broader sustainable development context. The revised code, launched in 2000, emphasizes the importance of verification of performance and includes a self-assessment protocol to monitor and analyse industry implementation. The next review, which will commence in late 2002, will address the issue of developing enhanced governance structures, including entry criteria and sanctions for non-compliance, as well as a strengthened approach to external verification of code implementation. The code will also evolve to incorporate the social dimension.

Source: Wells (2001), Personal Communication with Minerals Council of Australia (2002)

impacts in terms of providing open access to reporting and a forum for addressing stakeholder concerns appropriate to community expectations for the industry. It has been used as a model for a codified framework in Ghana, and interest has been expressed by a number of other countries. It has also helped inform the international debate on the role of voluntary industry-led initiatives and is among the leading models that could provide a basis for a similar framework on a global scale. A principles-based framework could provide the flexibility and variation required to reflect the differences among the countries and regions.

At the international level, the International Council on Mining & Metals (ICMM) has a Sustainable Development Charter, endorsed by its members, that is an international code of conduct for the mining and metals industry. It was developed in response to constituency pressure to broaden the mandate to cover sustainable development issues more comprehensively. The current charter has 32 management principles covering environmental management, product stewardship, community responsibility, ethical business practices, and public reporting. Decisions about how to implement the code are left to individual companies. The charter was not developed by industry alone. A task force of member companies of the International Council on Metals and the Environment (ICME), the predecessor of ICMM, prepared the first draft in 1999. With the assistance of the World Bank, ICME convened a multistakeholder workshop to review the draft and to comment on subsequent versions.

There is no empirical evidence that the charter – formally adopted only within the last year – has yet had direct impact on company performance. Member companies are not required to adhere to it, and it does not provide for verification or public reporting. Only a relatively small portion of the industry, mainly the largest international and national companies, has actively supported the charter, and much work remains to be done for it to gain universal understanding and application. Nevertheless, it may represent the basis for the development of a more detailed set of norms and management framework guidelines for the mining and metals sector. (See Chapter 16.)

Certification Schemes

Organizations or companies can seek certification to demonstrate that their activities, products, or services meet the requirements of a particular recognized standard. Certification schemes can be product-related (such as eco-label certification programmes), process-related (management system certification schemes such as European Eco-Management and Audit Scheme and ISO 14001), or site-related (certification of greenhouse-gas-emission reductions associated with a particular project). While some standards allow companies to self-declare or self-determine their conformity with the requirements (companies can, for example, declare that they have met the requirements of ISO 14001), many management systems and product standards require independent verification to provide a level of assurance to interested stakeholders.

Certification by an independent third party is usually perceived to be most credible, although this can entail significant costs to the company seeking certification. This is the model used by the Forest Stewardship Council, which accredits certification bodies to conduct audits of company sustainable forest management practices. Companies will usually pursue third-party certification to a given standard only if there is an adequate business case supporting the decision. A high level of consumer understanding of what certification to a particular standard means is essential for the success of such programmes.

A company must decide to seek certification in order to initiate the process. Usually the standard-setting body will establish the certification requirements and infrastructure. One approach would be to ensure that communities and NGOs are interviewed as part of the certification process. Certification bodies either accredit or directly conduct certification audits. Certifiers and auditors of adherence need to be trained specifically for the purpose and to be subject to some form of oversight. For example, the chemical industry's Responsible Care Program sets out the frequency of verification audits and dictates the composition of the verification team. It also requires that the verification team include a community representative as a full team member. While research has indicated that the rate of improvement of Responsible Care firms is slower than non-participants, it also shows that the overall performance standards of the chemical industry have improved since the inception of Responsible Care.[20]

Based on lessons from other sectors, a number of observations can be made about certification for the minerals sector.[21] First, it is important to identify the users (consumers, investors, lenders, insurers, or others), as this has implications for the design of the certification scheme. Second, the boundaries of a certification scheme need to be explicitly set. A cut-off point could be the individual mine-site or operation, which has the benefit of simplicity and control. However, certification of mining companies, combined with performance checks of individual mining operations, might be appropriate for equity investors. Specific dispensations could be made in the certification process for small operations.

Third, mineral processing and the manufacturing chain are very diverse and it would be extremely difficult to include them under a single certification scheme. Where processing or trade in minerals involves a high-profile, high-value, niche product, however, and where there are obvious environmental or social issues that might concern consumers, a post-extraction certification scheme might be appropriate. Such product labelling for consumer reassurance would involve extra requirements (such as a chain-of-custody certification) and may not be practical for many products with complex chains.

Fourth, the costs of certification depend on the type and level of standard, the costs of accreditation, and the needs for consultation and transparency. Experience from other sectors indicates that certification may have inequitable effects: it is often granted to the larger, richer groups, while others experience various forms of discrimination (based on costs or because local norms and practices are not recognized by standards). They also may tend to reflect the values of industrial-country institutions with resources to participate actively in their development more than the values of developing-country stakeholders. They may emphasize the environment pillar of sustainable development more than the economic or social pillars. Although certification schemes need to build on best practice, this must not only mean the practices of bigger, richer, 'scientific' enterprises. Many other traditions need to be incorporated, and poorer countries and producers need help to participate.

In the minerals sector, few examples exist of attempts to develop certification programmes. The Kimberley Process on international diamond certification provides one useful example for a specific product. And in Australia, the World Wide Fund for Nature is investigating the feasibility of a system of independent certification on the environmental and social management performance of mine sites in the South Pacific. (See Chapter 11.) It is possible to envisage a time where certain minerals products (such as diamonds) and most large-scale mineral operations are certified.

Corporate Reporting

Many mining companies now prepare annual reports describing their environmental (and sometimes social or sustainable development) performance. While reports are often a requirement of any voluntary code or charter to which a company is a signatory, public reporting is also seen as a method of enhancing a company's reputation. Reporting is also a valuable internal tool, as it provides a comprehensive assessment of the company's operations, and challenges managers, engineers, and others to address the sustainable development issue.

Voluntary social reporting in the mining industry is a recent phenomenon and occurs infrequently and inconsistently. Social performance is a key ingredient in assuring a company's licence to operate and supports the company's ability to deliver high-quality environmental and economic performance. While there is some agreement on measures for certain dimensions of social performance, they are not as well developed to date. Social reporting provides an opportunity for the presentation of corporate social policy and provisions, measurement against social performance indicators, and the systematic analysis of corporate community involvement. Considerable focus needs to be given to defining useful metrics for the measurement of social performance that can be easily reflected in reporting.

There is no consistent or harmonized approach towards the format or level of detail these reports should contain, and companies have total discretion in publishing what they wish. In response to this, the Global Reporting Initiative (GRI) produced a framework for reporting that promotes comparability between reporting organizations while recognizing the practical considerations of collecting and presenting information across diverse groups.[22] (See Chapter 12.) The GRI is currently addressing sector-specific guidelines for the minerals industry.

A consistent system of reporting guidelines needs to be developed for the minerals sector. A balance must be struck between the need for consistency to allow comparison and the need for flexibility to meet the different information needs of local stakeholders. The system will only work well if there is trust in the transparency and accountability of those doing the reporting and it has support of a broad cross-spectrum of actors.

International Institutions and Guidelines

A number of international organizations, such as the World Bank Group and the United Nations, have produced guidelines that are relevant or specific to the mining industry. In the case of the former, the guidelines are designed to apply to all Bank Group-funded projects, although they are often used as a benchmark for other projects. Guidelines produced by agencies such as UNEP and the World Health Organization (WHO) are more generic in nature and are intended to provide world-wide reference points:

- The World Bank Group approved the *Pollution Prevention and Abatement Handbook* in July 1998 (published in 1999), which replaces the 1988 *Environmental Guidelines*. It contains a number of industry-sector guidelines that specifically relate to the mining sector.
- The World Bank Group, through the Environment Division of the IFC, has also produced a good-practice manual, *Doing Better Business Through Effective Public Consultation and Disclosure*. This

provides the policy and procedural framework to deal with the need for and benefits of consultation with people affected by IFC projects. It is designed to reflect the IFC's private-sector mandate and project cycle and is modelled on the World Bank's revised environmental and social policies.

- The United Nations, through UNEP, has produced a series of guidelines relevant to the mining sector. These include *Monitoring Industrial Emissions and Wastes, Environmental Management of Nickel Production,* and *Environmental Aspects of Selected Non-Ferrous Metals Ore Mining.*[23]
- In 1996 WHO produced a revised version of *Guidelines for Drinking-water Quality, Health Criteria and Other Supporting Information,* with an addendum in 1998.
- Amnesty International has developed a set of human rights principles, based on international standards, to help companies develop their role in situations of human rights violations or where there is the potential for such violations.
- The UK and US governments have developed Voluntary Principles on Security and Human Rights for companies in the extractive and energy sectors.

Guidelines have limited utility without systems designed to ensure their effective application and to resolve disputes over their applications. The World Bank has also developed some dispute resolution mechanisms, including an Inspection Panel that has a process for complaints about World Bank-financed projects. This does not often apply to the mineral sector, since much of the Bank's involvement in minerals projects is through the IFC and the MIGA, which deal with the private sector. There was a long dispute over the extent to which these bodies should apply the guidelines, and what remedies would be available if they did not. Bank management has now made it clear that the guidelines do apply to the Bank's private-sector activities, and established a system, an office of the Compliance Advisor/Ombudsman, which now has pending before it a number of mining-related complaints.[24] There have also been experiments with a number of private dispute resolution mechanisms. One of the most notable has been the Mining Ombudsman project run by Oxfam Community Aid Abroad in Australia. (See Chapter 9.)

Stakeholder Engagement

There is a good deal of importance given to 'stakeholder process' in sustainable development. The interest in stakeholder processes comes fundamentally from two considerations. First, globalization means that, to an unprecedented extent, people in different parts of the world share interests. There is often no existing government or other structure that can bring them together to discuss how to deal with their common interests or resolve their differences. Second, even within countries governments may not be capable of serving as brokers to resolve differences or promote shared opportunities effectively. This is particularly true in poor countries, where governments may simply lack the resources or legal structures to foster joint decision-making. It is also true in countries experiencing conflict, particularly where government is seen as allied with one side.

Stakeholder processes therefore have two main purposes: to try to get the right people together to share information and make decisions, and to ensure that there is joint ownership of any decisions reached. Even where the result is not completely satisfactory to particular interest groups, they are likely to accept it – or at least not try to resist it – if they have participated in a process they regard as fair and have achieved at least some of their objectives.

In any situation with conflicting interests, there are those who will seek common ground and those who think their interests are best served by staying apart. Since stakeholder processes are almost always voluntary, if they are to make progress they need to be sufficiently attractive that a 'critical mass' of people see their interests better served by participating.

Stakeholder processes are most effective where there is a relative balance of power among those involved. The influence of different stakeholders will depend on a number of factors, including the strength of their interest in the outcome, their legal rights, their access to external support, or their ability to block the outcome. Globalization has made it easier for people to block or frustrate implementation of decisions they disagree with; they can, for example, trigger international campaigns through the internet, put pressure on banks or export credit agencies, or assert complaints at companies' annual meetings.

Where there are great disparities in capacity and access to those with decision-making power, those who feel at a disadvantage are likely to be reluctant to participate unless some sort of rules of engagement can be developed to redress the imbalance. Getting over this hurdle can be very difficult. From one perspective, those with the most power are seen as wanting to rush into discussions in which they will clearly have the upper hand. From the other, there is an impatience to get to substantive discussion. Conducting these preliminary negotiations through a skilled intermediary trusted by all enhances the opportunity for success. Processes will also need to have sufficient flexibility to be able to adapt to changing priorities and capacities.

Some interest groups – often those who are politically marginalized or lack economic resources – do not have very well defined ways of representing their interests through acknowledged, legitimate leadership. This presents a challenge for sector governance for sustainable development. Entering into a consultation or shared decision-making process with any constituency requires an appraisal of those who set themselves up as spokespersons or 'gatekeepers' for interaction. While it may seem easier to approach the group through gatekeepers, this can cause problems unless it is clear that the group has unequivocally appointed them to that role.

Some people make their living as intermediaries. The harder a group is for outsiders to understand or interact with, the more prominent this role is likely to be. Gatekeepers may also misrepresent the community. They may sometimes serve their own interests as much as the interests of the group they are representing. Generally, they represent only some subset of the community: in addition to personal motives of power or economics, they may wish to maintain their exclusive roles to ensure that the interest of the subgroup they represent dominates in any dealings with outsiders.

At a particular mine site, the host-country governments, the multinational company, and the NGO may each appoint a different community gatekeeper to confer legitimacy. This can result in local communities being polarized to serve outside interests, and conflict within the local community may ensue. When an outside group seeks to consult or interact with a particular community, it is important that the contacts are not limited to professional gatekeepers.

In conclusion, the right of groups to select their own representatives and leadership should be respected. The twin dimensions of proven or accepted primary identity with the group concerned, and accountability to that group, are important. The more broad-based, transparent, and democratic the process of selection, the greater credibility and legitimacy the representatives will have.

Capacity Building

Many of the issues discussed in this report relate to poor governance or to the need to build the capacity to cope with the dynamics of an increasingly complex and interdependent world. Weak governance results from many factors, including lack of resources and capacity, lack of specialized personnel, power imbalances, lack of political will, lack of coordination and integration, or lack of representation of stakeholders in decision-making. Problems of capacity apply to differing degrees to all actors.

It is especially important to focus on strengthening the capacity of national and local governments to design and enforce regulations. Building on efforts by the World Bank Group and the UN Conference on Trade and Development, international institutions and bilateral donors could devote more resources to capacity building for developing countries and local communities. The capacity of communities can be improved through providing platforms where they can learn from and communicate with each other. UN bodies, NGOs, and industry trade associations can play active roles in this process. Developing the capacity of local government is a key, often overlooked priority. Companies need to ensure that effective sustainable development capacity is integrated thoroughly into their businesses. The development of a company sustainable development policy will assist in achieving this.

Capacity can also be strengthened through voluntary collaboration between different actors. Collaboration builds on complementary competencies, where each sector contributes resources and skills for the common good. The work undertaken by Business Partners for Development provides useful examples of the benefits of collaboration at the local level.

In some cases, existing governance structures fail due

to bureaucracy, dictatorship, lack of accountability and transparency, or corruption. At the extreme, poor governance can go hand in hand with abuses of human rights and conflict. As one way to strengthen institutions, companies – individually and collectively – can take voluntary measures to ensure that at a minimum they do not encourage poor governance in countries where they operate. International organizations and NGOs can play an important role in assisting in the development of these measures. (See Chapter 8.)

The Way Forward

The issue of governance has been emphasized throughout this report. In the context of sustainable development, it is not enough to talk of the triple bottom line or the reconciliation of social, environmental, and economic factors without some idea of how that can take place over time in a myriad of circumstances. For good governance to work, there will need to be clarity and consistency in how the responsibility for minerals and sustainable development is understood and shared locally, nationally, and globally. Agreed standards and benchmarks will need to be established, together with agreed mechanisms to deal with the legacy of past mining operations and the future effects of today's activities. To achieve this, effective and trusted forums for stakeholder engagement are required. These need to ensure that those with most at stake, especially the most vulnerable groups, are able to participate in appropriate ways. The way things get done is very culture-specific. One size does not fit all.

Efforts are needed to avoid the proliferation of competing schemes – norms, standards, guidelines, and criteria for the minerals sector. No one's system will work if everyone is developing something different. There is a need to work with interested organizations to build on existing and well-functioning initiatives and to collaborate on the ones that overlap.

Stakeholder processes should be developed where appropriate to try to get the right people together to share information and make decisions, and to ensure that there is joint ownership of the decisions reached. Efforts should be made to ensure that the process does not favour any particular group and that stakeholder groups are fairly represented.

Different actors continue to rely on the state to define the needed boundary conditions for the roles, rights, and responsibilities of the various players who operate within its boundaries. Companies may be granted a legal licence to operate. But when the law is not arrived at in an open and democratic way, or when it is outdated for today's circumstance, or when it is not enforced equitably, it is helpful to have a set of norms for 'sector governance' that are applied to different actors regardless of the location of the operations. Chapter 1 laid out such a set of governance principles that should be followed by the different actors if progress is to be made:

- Support representative democracy, including participatory decision-making.
- Encourage free enterprise within a system of clear and fair rules and incentives.
- Avoid excessive concentration of power through appropriate checks and balances.
- Ensure transparency through providing all stakeholders with access to relevant and accurate information.
- Ensure accountability for decisions and actions, which are based on comprehensive and reliable analysis.
- Encourage cooperation in order to build trust and shared goals and values.
- Ensure that decisions are made at the appropriate level, adhering to the principle of subsidiarity where possible.

While these can be improved upon and elaborated further, the point is clear. There have to be some guiding rules if sustainable development is to follow. MMSD did not set out to negotiate such a set of principles but attempted to lay out the ones that seem to have come up most frequently in the course of the study. More work is required to achieve consensus on some guiding principles.

Strengthening the National Policy Framework

This report suggests that governments should take the lead in setting standards to ensure sustainable development takes place at the national and local level. Of course, this is not always easy to achieve; nor do governments always have the power to choose. In addition, many issues remain contested, such as the so-called Washington consensus, which assumes that liberal economic reforms should be universally applied.

Regardless of the difficulties, there is no substitute for government intervention of one kind or another. With the wide array of instruments available, this need not always mean regulations. As a starting point:

- Countries with significant mineral development could consider a comprehensive review of their legal frameworks and their impacts on sustainable development. While the review should be respectful of the need for investment, it should focus on how to turn this investment into opportunities for sustainable development. This review would be most beneficial if it were not an internal process within government but an open discussion that involves all of the key actors in industry, labour, and civil society.
- The government bodies responsible for managing the impacts of minerals development – social, economic, and environmental – must have adequate resources. A complement to any review of national legislation could be a review of the resources available to the various state departments charged with managing mineral wealth and turning investment into opportunities for long-term development. This will require analysis of the ability of government at all levels to use project revenues effectively for development purposes. This review could be carried out in a manner in which relevant stakeholders at the national level could forward their views.
- The subject matter of sustainable development is distributed throughout government in a sometimes awkward way – from local communities to provincial or state government, national government, and even the United Nations. The mechanisms for cooperation across ministerial or departmental boundaries at these various levels are often inadequate. Sustainable development will suffer until these are found.
- Individual governments should develop or strengthen the policy and regulatory framework relating to the minerals sector at all stages of the life cycle to ensure that social and environmental issues are properly considered along with investment and economic development objectives. Three key and interrelated elements of this framework were previously identified: integrated impact assessment, Community Sustainable Development Plans, and integrated planning for closure. Governments should also ensure effective participation by stakeholders, build linkages among governance structures at different levels and between departments to improve

coherency, and strengthen capacity.

- Individual governments should ensure that effective enforcement provisions are in place. Where there is insufficient capacity, alternative instruments based on voluntary processes should be considered (for example, between management, labour, and communities).

- This report identifies the need to find methods of capturing the benefits of financial surety. Major companies, environmental organizations, governments, and others that want to move forward on this issue share an interest in solving them. Some suggestions are to:

  – develop administrative procedures to come up with plans within a reasonable amount of time, and ensure that guarantees would be ended when the plan is complied with – the World Bank and UNEP could be a source of advice;

  – adopt a collective approach among countries through regional bodies to take this issue out of the realm of competition for investment; and

  – recognize that financial surety is not an effective way of managing artisanal miners and those at the very smallest scale of production – different approaches should be developed for them, and the guarantee applied only to those above some cut-off point.

Improving Industry Performance

While an individual organization such as a company should pursue policies consistent with sustainable development to improve performance, collective action can also help provide incentives. A variety of initiatives are already being facilitated through national mining associations, commodity associations, or global bodies such as the International Council on Mining & Metals.

A Declaration on Sustainable Development embodying a commitment to a Sustainable Development Protocol is the next step along this path. The Declaration and Protocol are intended to complement, not replace, other priorities and initiatives identified at other points in this report. They are designed to simplify the current multiple codes and sources of guidance by providing a way to bring these together over time into one document and one management system. They should build on the recently adopted Sustainable Development Charter of the ICMM. The first step

Participatory processes are essential for ensuring joint ownership of decisions

could be review of that charter, based on the findings and conclusions of this report.

The process of developing a Declaration – and then a Protocol – for the sector could take place in three phases. (See Chapter 16.) While ICMM might have a key role in developing the language of the Declaration and Protocol, including guidelines, codes of practice, and principles, from the outset these should be in a form that allows non-member companies – small, large, and intermediate – to subscribe to them.

It is suggested that the Declaration call for an immediate set of commitments that could be adopted by individual companies to demonstrate willingness and to have some requirements in place while the Protocol is developed. One alternative would be to declare adherence to existing guidelines, codes, conventions, and laws that can provide guidance for companies. While many elements for such a list have been proposed, there is a need to consider the practicality of achieving an initial commitment in a reasonable amount of time. The preliminary list of principles should be small enough in number so that companies can understand and apply them. A limited number that best serve the purposes of the Declaration have been identified. (See Box 14–4.) They are principles already contained in existing initiatives that:

- can be applied world-wide,
- have been developed through recognized international processes,
- preferably have received a commitment from at least one minerals company,
- reflect an understanding of the need for a partnership approach,

- Rio Declaration
- The United Nations Global Compact
- Environmental, social, and economic guidelines on corporate reporting that have been developed within the Global Reporting Initiative
- OECD Guidelines for Multinational Enterprises
- World Bank Group's Operational Guidelines, including, but not limited to, those on Environmental Assessment, Involuntary Resettlement, Indigenous Peoples, and Projects in Disputed Areas.
- OECD Convention on Combating Bribery of Foreign Officials
- ILO Convention 98 on the Right to Organize and Collective Bargaining; ILO Convention 169 Concerning Indigenous and Tribal Peoples in Independent Countries; ILO Convention 176 on Safety and Health in Mines and ILO Recommendation 183, which accompanies it
- Voluntary Principles on Security and Human Rights

- reflect a balance of industry-specific and general considerations, and
- relate to factors important to the way financial markets evaluate risk.

The Declaration should also provide for a company commitment to adopt and comply with national or regional industry codes of conduct where they exist. For example, companies operating in Australia should initially comply with the Australian Minerals Industry Code, and companies in Canada with the Mining Association of Canada's environmental policy.

An Emergency Response Capability
When accidents occur, their impacts are immensely magnified when there is no effective capacity to deal with them promptly, decisively, and effectively. Uncertainty, lack of knowledge, and inaccurate information may cause as much public concern as the accident itself. An international Emergency Response Facility, supported in part by industry and with appropriate involvement of other stakeholders, could play a significant role. It could mobilize world-class experts who could supplement government capacity to assess, respond to, and control accidents and emergencies, or to make sure that threatened emergencies do not happen. This approach could assure the public that the best possible advice was available to responsible officials. This function might not need ongoing staff beyond a coordinator but could rely on an 'as needed' basis on experts from consulting firms, universities, governments, companies, or other institutions, including NGOs. Preventing or just minimizing the impact of one incident could achieve considerable direct and indirect savings.

A Sustainable Development Support Facility
The complex and demanding tasks of proper management of the minerals sector may tax available expertise and capacity of government and other actors, particularly where countries do not have a great deal of prior experience with such operations. It may be very useful to group all existing aid players to coordinate and target efforts.

This could be centred in a Sustainable Development Support Facility that could be supported by one or more sources of concessionary funds, with a commitment long enough to give it a chance to prove its worth, and could be administered by the World Bank Group as a trust fund. It could help governments, NGOs, UN bodies, trade unions, or other appropriate organizations committed to cooperative approaches to sustainable development to build the capacity of applicants and others to raise performance and standards in the minerals sector.

This would, in effect, be a fund available for technical assistance relevant to the goal of sustainable development. It would need a small secretariat set up regionally or globally and based in existing organizations.

Lenders and Investors
The MMSD process continuously found that many actors believe institutional investors and lenders should aim to increase their use of 'sustainability' criteria in informing investment and lending decisions. Criteria could be extended to account more specifically for certain sectors, including the minerals sector.

Commercial lenders could require that an effective dispute resolution mechanism be available to affected people and organizations as a condition of loans. If the proposed industry Declaration and Protocol are adopted, commercial lenders could support it as a means to the better management of risk. It could be recognized appropriately in credit decisions.

The insurance industry could also follow the development of the proposed industry Declaration and Protocol carefully – perhaps participating in its design – to maximize these business opportunities. If the Declaration and Protocol emerge as effective tools for managing risk, the insurance industry could recognize this appropriately in the products it offers to companies that adopt the Protocol, or in the rates it charges them.

In addition, the insurance industry is keen to prevent accidents and emergencies. It could participate in the design of the proposed emergency response capability and in defining its tasks to ensure maximum business benefits. Companies could also consider whether these benefits are sufficient to merit financial support from the insurance industry, in the way that this industry has supported other collective risk-reduction organizations in the past.

Equity investors may want to evaluate the extent to which company participation in the proposed Declaration and Protocol are likely to be relevant to investors' risks and share value.

International Organizations and Donor Governments

Since capacity building is key, international organizations such as the World Bank Group and donor governments should give greater priority to funding for and capacity-building efforts of national governments and communities in selected areas indicated in this report, such as the Communities and Small-Scale Mining initiative. Their efforts could help to harmonize the standards of mineral operations in host countries and to ensure that standards incorporate the goals of sustainable development. They could work with member governments and others to develop benchmarks for capacity building.

International organizations such as the World Bank and the UN could continue to facilitate national and international stakeholder processes for information-sharing and decision-making. In addition, organizations with research capacity such as the World Bank, the UN, research institutions, and NGOs could also synthesize cross-sectoral and transnational learning for public dissemination.

NGOs and Other Independent Practitioners

NGOs and other independent practitioners could assist in capacity building and in facilitating company-funded development at both the national and local levels; play a role in designing and participating in stakeholder processes; continue to lobby at all levels for effective participation by stakeholders; and act as 'watchdogs' – independent arbitrators or monitors. They could also enhance their effectiveness by developing internal policies for sustainable development and management systems to implement them. This could include, where appropriate, published standards for investigation of claims – similar to those now used by several human rights organizations – to enhance the impact of their campaigns.

A Complaints and Dispute Resolution Mechanism

Companies should have a serious interest in endorsing fair, reasonable ways (through a form of mediation/conciliation system) for people with grievances to get the attention of management, and to seek some kind of solution. Lack of such a mechanism drives people with grievances to other measures, many of which can present much higher levels of risk for all.

A mechanism must not conflict with national jurisdiction or existing processes – rather, it should reinforce them in positive ways. But when a group feels aggrieved by a foreign investor or an interest group, it should be able to be heard in a setting that has rules of evidence and procedures.

A dispute resolution mechanism should bring parties together, in a neutral forum, to work out a mutually acceptable facilitated settlement. The elements of the mechanism are envisioned as similar to the methods and procedures of an ombudsman, such as the IFC's Compliance Advisor/Ombudsman or the Mining Ombudsman project that has been operated by Community Aid Abroad in Australia.

The principal elements of this mechanism are described in Chapter 16. In each region or locality, an independent organization would be contracted to operate the complaints and dispute resolution mechanism. A balanced Board would periodically issue public reports of its activities and the overall process. It can establish rules for the conduct of the process, and amend them as necessary based on stakeholder feedback.

Endnotes

[1] Otto (2002).

[2] A good part of the discussion in the legislation sections is drawn from United Nations (2002).

[3] A good deal of information, mostly written from an industry perspective, about legislation of all types that affects mining is available through the Rocky Mountain Mineral Law Foundation, at http://www.rmmlf.org.

[4] A list of some countries providing tax stabilization is given in Table 4 of Otto (2002).

[5] Danielson and Nixon (2000).

[6] Bourassa and Vaughan (1999); Parr (2002).

[7] The discussion on the lack of international governance regimes for the minerals sector is drawn from Dalupan (2001).

[8] See, for example, http://www.vyh.fi/eng/environ/econinst/econotax.htm.

[9] See http:// www.nrcan.gc.ca/mets/mend.

[10] Bass and Hearne (1997).

[11] See Meeran (2002).

[12] For an overview on Papua, see Ward (2001); Greenhouse (2002).

[13] See Downing (2002).

[14] MMSD (2001g); MMSD (2002).

[15] Personal communications with BHP Billiton, February 2002.

[16] O'Neill (2001).

[17] Regan (2001).

[18] MMSD did considerable research on voluntary initiatives; see Greene et al. (2001); MMSD (2001e).

[19] Palmer (2001).

[20] King and Lenox (2000).

[21] Bass et al. (2001).

[22] Global Reporting Initiative (2000).

[23] UNEP/UNIDO 1996, TR27; UNEP 1993, TR15; UNEP/ILO 1991, TR5., cited in United Nations (2002).

[24] See http://www.tomoye.com/simplify/cao/ev.php.

PART IV

RESPONSES AND RECOMMENDATIONS

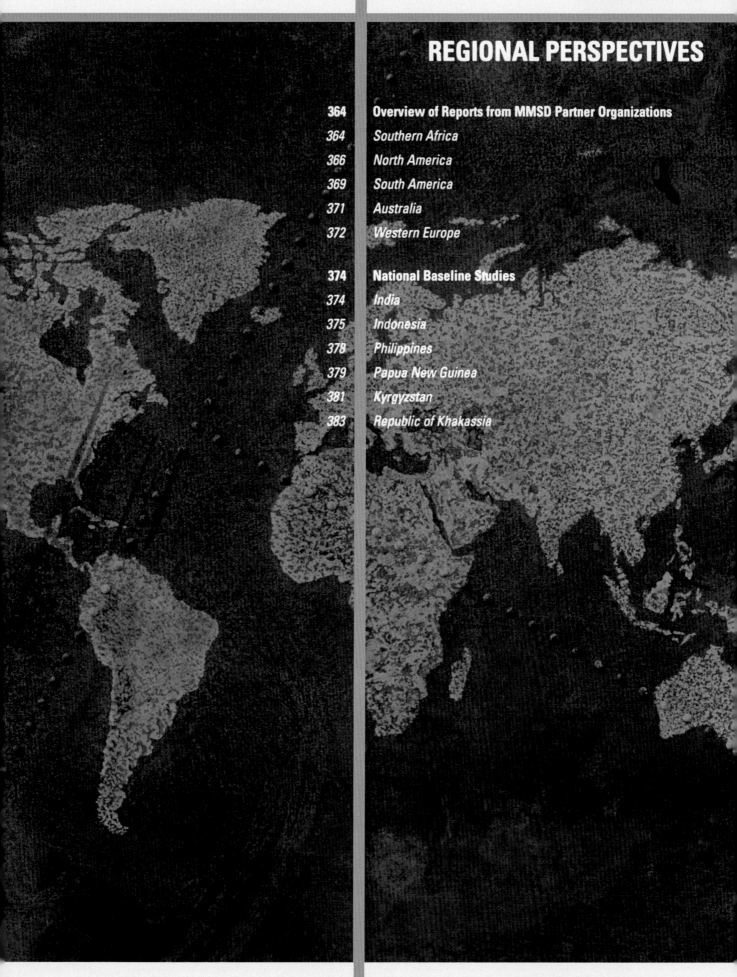

CHAPTER 15

REGIONAL PERSPECTIVES

The minerals sector often has a uniquely local profile. While a large copper mine or a small gold mine may look similar in different parts of the world, the technical, management, social, political, and environmental skills that need to be applied to operate in different localities will result in a different type of project in each case. Mine localities – with different histories, cultures, and environments – have great bearing on the way mining and processing are viewed and the way a project is implemented and managed at the local level.

This diversity cannot be captured and reflected effectively from an office in London or by those who have not lived and worked with mining in these localities. The MMSD Project was therefore critically and substantively informed by diverse research and stakeholder engagement that was undertaken by the project's regional and national partners in various parts of the world.

The perspectives brought to bear in the regional discussions derive in part from locally specific factors, but are also strongly influenced by the place of the region in global and regional economies. Some people might debate the value of gold mining, for example, but for the Southern African region it is a key source of employment and foreign exchange earnings and thus an essential component of local and national economies. In many areas within these regions, mining may be the only viable form of economic activity, and mine closures cause considerable hardship where unemployment may already be unacceptably high. Regional priorities differ in other ways: while the transmission of HIV/AIDS by migrant labour forces working in the mining industry is of significant concern in South Africa, it does not register as such in North America or Australia.

The implications of the North–South divide come through clearly in some of the regional work. Some governments and private companies may view with suspicion calls to change operating standards and practices to a sustainable development norm that only addresses the concerns of affluent industrial countries. In some cases, governments and industry may see the evolving sustainable development agenda driven by industrial nations as creating barriers to entry for minerals and metals commodities originating in the South. And technology, information, and capacity gaps between North and South may mean that timescales

and approaches to putting sustainable development into practice may be very different.

Due to space constraints, this chapter can provide only an overview of the considerable work undertaken at national and regional levels. In the case of the regions, the executive summaries were provided by the regional partners; fuller reports, with much more detail than can be included here, are available from the partner organizations. In other cases, summaries have been integrated directly from the baseline studies and background papers.

The themes that run throughout the regional work mirror those at the global level – capacity and governance, equity and transparency, the economics and mining, and so on. Within this complex of issues, it is clear that the potential solutions and courses of action are often local in nature; strategies for community involvement in decision-making, for example, may be quite different in South Africa, North America, and India. Thus implementing the recommendations in *Breaking New Ground* will understandably require different tools and approaches, and will proceed at different paces, in various regions of the world.

Overview of Reports from MMSD Partner Organizations

Southern Africa
In Southern Africa, the MMSD Partner was the University of Witwatersrand in Johannesburg and the Council for Scientific and Industrial Research in Stellenbosch.

Despite the prevailing economic pressures on the mining industry, the mining sector in the 12 mainland SADC countries directly employed 2.3% of the region's total available work force, which was estimated at 68 million in 1999. Employment in the sector increased to 2 million in 2000, not including informal miners. Although these figures do not account for the millions of people who are dependent on miners' incomes for their livelihoods, they do emphasize the importance of the mining sector as a source of employment.

Today, despite recent adverse economic developments

and depressed commodity prices for many metals and mineral products, mining and its associated industries continue to form the cornerstone of the economies of most Southern African countries.

The wealth generated by the mining and minerals industry has not always been used to rehabilitate environmental degradation caused by mining nor to benefit the communities affected by the industry. In spite of this, current trends in the mining and minerals sector indicate that it can contribute to the region's move towards sustainable development. The industry remains a most significant factor in the region's future development.

Small-scale mining is an important source of income for many people in the region and is likely to grow in importance. For most small-scale miners, however, poverty and lack of skills are major constraints to changing subsistence activities into more profitable ventures. In addition, the cumulative environmental impact of the growing small-scale mining sector is increasing due to a lack of awareness and the inability to implement environmentally friendly technologies and management programmes. This activity is usually wasteful of non-renewable resources and hazardous to human and environmental health. However, it has the potential to give disadvantaged groups economic power and to enrich nations by virtue of its low investment costs and the short lag time from discovery to production.

The mining industry has shaped the lives of women in rural Southern Africa for many generations. Rural economies are impoverished by the loss of labour to the mines. The poverty is intensified when male workers in particular are retrenched and return to the rural community, which has become dependent on their wages. The important role women play in the rural economy while the men leave to work in the mines is a key feature of the mining industry. Positive results have been achieved by multistakeholder initiatives that aim to reduce the impact of retrenchment on communities, especially in areas providing labour.

HIV/AIDS is arguably the most significant threat to sustainable development in Southern Africa. A decade ago, HIV/AIDS was regarded primarily as a health crisis. Today, it is clear that the disease is a development crisis. The economic implications are dire: loss of

productivity, loss of the benefits of education and training, and the diversion of resources from investment to health, orphan care, and funerals.

The mining and minerals industry has been a key player in the fight against HIV/AIDS, providing a substantial proportion (and sometimes almost all) of the initiative and effort in the region. However, neither the responsibility nor the capacity rests with one stakeholder group, and positive signs of cooperation between various stakeholders are emerging in the region.

The Southern African region is rich in natural resources, including minerals. But future regional growth and development may be constrained by the increasing scarcity of one of the most critical resources – fresh water. Water pollution caused by mining activities is a significant problem in several countries in the region.

In November 2000, at a Multistakeholder Meeting in Johannesburg, stakeholders identified five key areas for research. The five key areas were:
- small-scale mining and sustainable development in Southern Africa;
- HIV/AIDS, the mining and minerals sector, and sustainable development in Southern Africa;
- social issues within the mining and minerals sector in Southern Africa;
- mining, minerals, the biophysical environment, and the transition to sustainable development in Southern Africa; and
- mining, minerals, economic development, and the transition to sustainable development in Southern Africa.

At the various meetings, certain overarching issues were given priority by stakeholders. These issues have to be addressed if progress towards sustainable development is to be achieved, and they appear as cross-cutting issues in the recommendations. There is not sufficient space here to relate all 42 specific recommendations for action, which are detailed in the final report; some of the key points are as follows:

Poverty alleviation – In a region where the average daily income is just above US$2, it is to be expected that poverty alleviation is a critical issue. The most important way in which poverty can be alleviated is through the involvement of all stakeholders. The processes include education, policy-making, and facilitation of the means of avoiding increased poverty, such as the establishment of medical benefit schemes. Job creation and capacity building are recommended as essential to poverty alleviation, and specific emphasis is placed on the small-scale sector of the economy.

Job creation – Unemployment rates throughout the region are high and exacerbate poverty and its attendant ills. The minerals sector, on the one hand, contributes to this situation through resettlement, downscaling, closure, and retrenchments. On the other hand, the sector can do much to alleviate the problem. The recommendations envisage job creation through education, by providing opportunities for development in local communities and by stimulating the growth of the small-scale mining and agricultural sectors.

Capacity building and skills training – A lack of skills and capacity are prevalent in the Southern Africa region, presenting a challenge in the move towards sustainable development. The recommendations envisage capacity building by a variety of means: education, government policy, self-regulation within a stakeholder group, and consultative and collaborative approaches. An imperative in the move to sustainable development is multistakeholder cooperation. This is an aspect of the majority of recommendations, and is epitomized in the recommendation that proposes cooperation across a broad spectrum of activities by all stakeholders to deal with the threat of HIV/AIDS.

Governance – If the wealth generated by the mineral sector is to be managed sustainably and shared equitably between all stakeholders, good governance is required. Government policies determine whether such an enabling environment exists. However, governance is not just the responsibility of the state but of all stakeholders, and the benefits accruing from good governance affect all stakeholders. The recommendations address the unsustainable practice of child labour and the situation of marginalized and disempowered sectors of the community, such as women, resettled communities, and people infected with HIV/AIDS. Good governance as a factor in regional cooperation is addressed, as is protection of the natural environment. The equitable distribution of the rents from minerals exploitation is ensured by good governance.

Gender Equity – In a region where the majority of the

population are poor, women are among the poorest. Culturally, historically, and economically they are also disempowered and form a significant marginalized group. The recommendations address all these issues, and urge women to take steps to address their own situations. The main thrust of the recommendations is the empowerment of women, because equity will flow from this. Empowerment in education, employment, and opportunities to obtain these needs to be accompanied by recognition of women's status as legitimate stakeholders by others.

Stakeholders expressed reservations that the research and subsequent recommendations would end up where many initiatives had ended up before – gathering dust on shelves. An urgent request was made that structures should be put in place that could implement the recommendations of the MMSD Southern Africa process. Such structures would not only be needed to implement recommendations, but also to coordinate the move towards sustainable development across the region. Greater regional cooperation was stressed as an essential element of a successful transition to sustainable development.

It is noted that the World Summit on Sustainable Development will be held in South Africa and that mining in the region will also develop within the framework of the New African Initiative for 'Millennium Africa' proposed by President Thabo Mbeki of South Africa.

North America
The MMSD Partner Organization in North America was the International Institute for Sustainable Development based in Winnipeg and Ottawa, working with the Mining Life Cycle Center, MacKay School of Mines, at the University of Nevada at Reno. Participants in MMSD North America established five tasks to be completed in meeting MMSD objectives.

First, work was commissioned to develop a comprehensive profile of the mining/minerals industry and to describe the contributions over time (positive and negative) of mining and minerals from the perspective of sustainability. Because different interests view the contribution of the mining/minerals industry differently, effort was put into describing the various interests (industry, indigenous people, mining-dependent communities, government, labour, non-governmental organizations (NGOs)) as well as their sense of that contribution as it has evolved through the past century.

Task 2 was the creation of four scenarios that looked forward in time at a range of possible futures. The implications of each scenario were identified, not only for the industry but also for other stakeholder interests. Task 3 turned to the operational level, where the objective was to develop practical guidance for assessing a project's contribution to sustainability, resulting in an assessment framework in the form of Seven Questions to Sustainability. The applications span from early appraisal through planning, financing and insuring, licensing and approvals, internal corporate reviews, corporate reporting, and external reviews. Tasks 4 and 5 involved the proposal of an action plan that would see the momentum initiated through MMSD North America continued and the synthesis of the results into the regional report.

Work on the profile showed that the mining/minerals industry in North America is best described as an integrated production system consisting of interdependent firms that range in size from small to large. Successfully aligning activities of this complex production system with the concept of sustainability will only be possible through the involvement of all parts in designing and implementing the needed steps for change. Furthermore, there are significant differences in the US and Canadian mining sectors. These differences too must be carefully accounted for.

Major uncertainties facing the industry were identified, and the two most dominant uncertainties – future variations in societal values and performance of the economy – were chosen as the basis of a logical framework for developing four distinctly different scenarios. (See Box 15–1.)

The assessment framework developed by MMSD North America asked seven key questions that should be considered in assessing whether a proposed project's or operation's contribution to sustainability is positive over the long term:

• *Engagement* – Are processes of engagement committed to, designed, and implemented that ensure all affected communities of interest, including vulnerable or disadvantaged sub-populations (by reason of, for example, minority status, gender,

---

> **Box 15–1. Four Scenarios Developed for the Mining and Minerals Sector in North America**
>
> • In the New Horizons scenario, there is a coincidence of strong economic conditions and a high level of trust and respect characterizing overall societal values. For the most part, this same trust and respect is found among mining- and minerals-related communities of interest. Vision and change are guided through collaborative activity involving many communities of interest interacting in a constructive way. Confidence in the future is high.
> • In the Phoenix Rising scenario, difficult economic conditions serve to drive innovation. At the same time, respectful social values further facilitate positive change. The overall result is that difficult times give way to more encouraging conditions, like a phoenix rising.
> • In the Perfect Storm scenario, depressed economic conditions coincide with fractious social conditions. Here the spiral is down with little hope of reversing the trend. With this juxtaposition of unfortunate conditions, the Perfect Storm is inevitable.
> • The dominant force in the Money Divides scenario is an excess of money. However, rather than serving as a positive force, industry arrogance and societal divisions increase. Government stands back and watches Money Divide.

ethnicity, or poverty), have the opportunity to participate in the decisions that influence their own future? And are the processes understood, agreed on by implicated communities of interest, and consistent with the legal, institutional, and cultural characteristics of the community and country where the project or operation is located?
• *People* – Will the project or operation lead directly or indirectly to maintenance of people's well-being, preferably an improvement during the life of the project/operation and after it closes?
• *Environment* – Will the project or operation lead directly or indirectly to the maintenance or strengthening of the integrity of biophysical systems so that they can continue in post-closure to provide the needed support for the well-being of people and other life forms?
• *Economy* – Is the financial health of the project/company assured and will the project or operation contribute (through planning, evaluations, decision-making, and action) to the long-term viability of the local, regional, and global economy in ways that will help ensure sufficiency for all and provide specific opportunities for the less advantaged?
• *Traditional and non-market activities* – Will the project

or operation contribute to the long-term viability of traditional and non-market activities in the implicated community and region?

- *Institutional Arrangements and Governance* – Are the institutional arrangements and systems of governance in place that can provide confidence that the capacity of government, companies, communities, and residents to address project or operation consequences is in place or will be built? And will this capacity continue to evolve and exist through the full life cycle, including post-closure?
- *Overall Integrated Assessment and Continuous Learning* – Has an overall evaluation been made and is a system in place for periodic re-evaluation based on, at the project level, consideration of all reasonable alternative configurations (including the no-go option in the initial evaluation); at the overarching strategic level, consideration of all reasonable alternatives for supplying the commodity and the services it provides for meeting society's needs; and a synthesis of all the factors raised in this list of questions, leading to an overall judgement that the contribution to people and ecosystems will be net positive in the long term?

An 'ideal answer' to each of the seven questions is also offered, along with example objectives, indicators, and specific measurements that provide the data and information base needed to answer the questions. In applying the framework, values come into play and there isn't necessarily a unique or 'right' answer to the seven questions.

In acting on the results of any assessment, a company, community, or government will inevitably have to weigh certain trade-offs. In doing so, the rules governing such trade-offs along with fair processes for their application need to be established. However, the starting point for all of this is the identification of the considerations that are fed into the decision-making process.

The Action Plan for Change developed in the final regional report derived from the North America regional process identified ten key points:

- *Addressing the Legacy* – A comprehensive strategy should be developed with all communities of interest to address the legacy issue. In Canada, the lead for this falls to a current multi-interest initiative of the Intergovernmental Working Group on Mining.

The discussion should be expanded to encompass Canada, the US, and Mexico.

- *Taking Preventative Action* – A broadly accepted approach to current projects should be designed and implemented that will give confidence that acceptable post-closure outcomes will be achieved and that commitments made will be fulfilled. The initiative should encompass Mexico, the US, and Canada.
- *Assessing for Sustainability* – Further development of the Seven Questions to Sustainability approach to assessing the contribution of an operation or project to sustainability should be undertaken initially through a series of pilot tests. Pilots should span both industrial and developing country examples of activities across the mine-project life cycle. Multi-interest Work Groups, led by the most appropriate actor, should be maintained and, following completion of several of the pilots, reconvened by the appropriate body.
- *Encouraging Success* – Mechanisms should be developed by which communities of interest can encourage good performance and discourage bad performance among their peers (within companies, across the industry, across NGOs, across governments). Leadership for this initiative should be assumed by the Northwest Mining Association (US) and the Prospectors and Developers Association of Canada, acting collaboratively with a number of organizations, including the Mining Association of Canada, Canadian Institute for Mining and Metallurgy, the National Mining Association (US), the Society for Mining, Metallurgy and Exploration, Inc. (US), and NGOs in both the US and Canada.
- *Addressing Disputes* – An effective suite of mechanisms for dispute resolution applicable at the project/operation level of the mining and minerals industry should be designed and implemented. The Dialogue Forum (Centre for Dialogue at Simon Fraser University in Vancouver BC) has offered to facilitate this exercise.
- *Encouraging Recycling* – A North American recycling policy regime should be designed and implemented that effectively encourages recycling of metals and minerals while controlling the movement of hazardous waste. The lead for this initiative should be put to a partnership of environmental NGOs and industry in collaboration with the North American Commission for Environmental Cooperation and governments.
- *Addressing Equity* – Capacity needs to be created for

identifying the mining/minerals-related distribution of costs, benefits, and risks accruing to various communities of interest and for creating mechanisms for ensuring that the distribution is fair and equitable.

- *Adjusting the Current Financial, Business, Economic Model* – The economic model that is currently taught in mining and business schools and used by mining companies, the financial services industry, and government needs adjustment so that it is more effective in its treatment of ecological and social liabilities, costs, benefits, and risks.

- *Improving Learning/Research Support* – The academic and learning support system required for building the mining and minerals-related human capital needs of industry, government, First Nations/Native Americans, NGOs, and other communities of interest needs strengthening. A collaborative effort is required to oversee this task. Leadership should be assumed by the Society for Mining, Metallurgy and Exploration, Inc. and the Canadian Institute for Mining and Metallurgy working in concert with the North American Working Group on Academic Support for the Mining Industry, the Prospectors and Developers Association of Canada, the Northwest Miners Association, the Mining Association of Canada, and the National Mining Association.

- *Facilitating and Tracking Progress* – A mechanism for facilitating and reporting on progress achieved on the recommendations of MMSD North America should be established.

South America

MMSD South America's activities concentrated on Bolivia, Brazil, Chile, Ecuador, and Peru. The regional report for South America is the result of a process of research and participation by many parties. It is coordinated by CIPMA in Chile and the Mining Policy Research Initiative of the International Development Research Centre in Uruguay. The research component aimed to capture a contemporary image of the mining sector's progress in contributing to sustainable development, based upon extensive review of existing publications. The participatory process sought to identify the existing perspectives on key issues and to produce relevant agendas that suggest where new public and corporate policy directions are needed and where increased research and engagement capacity is required to bridge gaps.

Mining in South America is an activity with pre-

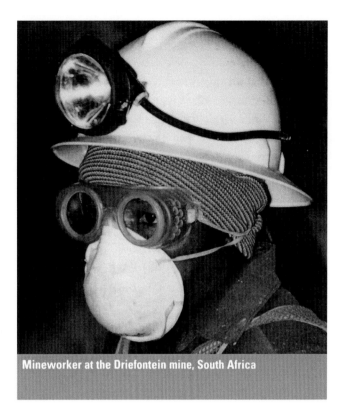

Mineworker at the Driefontein mine, South Africa

Columbian origins that has always developed across multiple ecosystems and in the midst of marked social, cultural, economic, and technological contrasts. Many organizations specializing in the subject have recorded how, despite quantitative progress in basic health, education, and housing services, there persist worrying indices of poverty, a poor quality of life, and income distribution inequities for many people.

The countries in the region have made progress in strengthening their democracies, expressed by new constitutional frameworks with a growing diversity of channels for participation by the general public. This is developing within a dynamic context of role redefinition for the many parties involved and the search for institutional consolidation.

The region enjoyed significant mining investment in the 1990s and the sector now contributes over 20% of world metal production (and in some cases up to 80%) while consumption of these materials is a mere 8%. In the words of the regional Advisory Group, 'mining is both essential and strategic for the development of our countries'. Therefore, the issue is how and where to do it. Mining may contribute to sustainable development if it is conducted within a context of economic growth, social equity, respect for cultural diversity, and responsible environmental management and with transparent mechanisms for participation in the decision-making process.

With this in mind and acknowledging the positive contributions of the sector, a series of key issues of concern were identified. In the five focus countries, the basic proposal involved the need to improve the visions of sustainable development so that they might act as a strategic guide for long-term natural resource management; the perfecting of national, local, and regional development tools and plans; and coordination with the mining sector's development plans.

At the start of the project, MMSD identified 17 key issues in mining and sustainable development in the region as guides for the study:

- public management tools and capacities;
- opportunities, mechanisms, and capacities for the general public to participate in decisions regarding mining;
- access to, and use and generation of, pertinent information about mining;
- distribution of mining taxes and duties at local, regional, and national levels;
- assessments of current taxes and duties;
- social and environmental performance of mining;
- quantity and quality of mining employment;
- small-scale and artisanal mining;
- mining in natural protected areas and high biodiversity zones;
- mining in indigenous territory;
- local development (social, economic, cultural, environmental);
- resource rights and management (land, water, biodiversity, minerals, and so on);
- scientific and technological development;
- planning and management of social and environmental impacts of mine closures;
- environmental and social inheritance from mining activity in the past (environmental and social passives);
- market access; and
- incidence of international agreements, treaties, and standards.

These factors were defined by the work team, taking into account dilemmas identified by the global MMSD Project, and with the collaboration of experts and members of the Advisory Group. Following this, priorities were discussed, detailed, and defined through the MMSD process, so that they would serve to shed light on what is currently understood in the region by 'mining from a sustainable development perspective'. The project uncovered different approaches to the development of mining, while emphasizing that there are complementary visions about mining development projects.

The priority issues identified in the region are:
- more direct and equitable contribution by mining to local development;
- improved capacities and more efficient tools for public management of non-renewable natural resources, by means of greater use of informed and participative processes of land use planning; and
- sustained improvements in the social and environmental performance of mining.

In addition, in light of the social importance of artisanal and small-scale mining and its potential to contribute to local development and overcome poverty, the project identified the need for national developments in this sector's categorization and management.

Discussion of these issues focused on the need to improve decision-making processes with better information (availability and access) and participation; the need for more research and training became clear as part of capacity-building. Key issues for indigenous peoples (such as recognition and the exercise of collective rights regarding resource use) were also identified through the participative process in the region. Relevant issues for labour were identified as occupational health, employment stability, differences between company employees and contract workers, and compliance with international laws.

A call was made to the respective governments to consolidate an agile, effective, democratic, and transparent institutional and political framework that protects the rights of the most vulnerable groups, while ensuring a healthy and stable investment climate in order to attract companies with the highest standards of social and environmental performance.

The mining companies have been called to play a more committed and caring role with local development, building citizenship and strengthening governance, without undermining the role of the state.

Last, civil society in general – including mining workers – should take up its rights to citizen participation, in accordance with individual capacities and knowledge, and thus recognize responsibility in building society's future with governments and the private sector.

This implies that all parties must progress decisively towards greater levels of sustainability, within the limits of their capacities. Notwithstanding whether the states manage to govern well and build on citizenship in the national arenas, fair and equitable international relationships are needed in order to make an effective transition towards sustainable development viable.

Australia

The Australian regional report – *Facing the Future* – prepared by the Australian Minerals, Energy and Environment Foundation has evolved through comprehensive research and consultation with numerous stakeholders.

For an industrial economy, Australia has a relatively high level of dependence on the minerals sector. *Facing the Future* does not argue that the sustainable development of Australian society necessarily depends on the viability of the minerals sector. Minerals development will play an important role in the continuing health of the Australian economy. But it seems likely that the sector is entering an important transitional phase. Mining may take a less prominent role as the industry moves further down the value chain – exploring the economic benefits of the reuse, recycling, and reprocessing of metals. Such a strategy might offer more efficient management of minerals resources.

Facing the Future recognizes the important progress the minerals industry has made over recent years, and the commitment shown by individuals at all levels to improving the industry's social and environmental performance. The Australian minerals sector plays a critical role in national and local economies and in the development of regional Australia. The sector has brought forward important technical innovations in environmental management. It has also begun to work constructively with regional, remote, and indigenous communities. Broader stakeholder recognition of the leadership shown by the industry in these areas is not only fair – it will also do much to reinforce the industry's commitment through difficult economic times.

Voluntary initiatives in community relations and

environmental management – notably the Australian Mineral Industry Code for Environmental Management – have helped sustain the industry's licence to operate. But *Facing the Future* suggests that if voluntary codes of practice are to reduce the need for government regulation, they must remain responsive to changing social conditions and stakeholder expectation. They need to be able to demonstrate that they address real problems, that compliance levels are appropriate and enforced, and that they contribute to significantly improved performance. Given the social contract implicit in voluntary codes of conduct, it is appropriate that codes include recognition of the rights of communities and other stakeholders and incorporate opportunities for independent review and verification.

MMSD Australia research addressed issues of critical concern to Australian stakeholders and areas where Australia had particular experience to share with other minerals-producing regions. It also helped to frame the project's substantial stakeholder engagement programme.

Facing the Future identifies seven critical issues, defined in a series of regional multistakeholder workshops conducted during February 2002:
* the sustainability of the Australian minerals sector and its capacity to support the social, economic, and environmental processes that underpin sustainable development;
* the need to improve governance of the sector, including clearer definition of roles and responsibilities, increased transparency, inclusiveness, and accountability, and new mechanisms to deliver sustainability;
* the need to improve resource valuation and management of minerals resources and ecological values, of the human, intellectual, and community resources that drive development, and of the social and cultural heritage values that enrich the quality of life and define humanity's relationship to each other and to the natural environment;
* the need to improve stakeholder engagement, recognizing the technical and political complexities inherent in more open and transparent engagement processes;
* fairer distribution of costs and benefits to ensure lasting equitable social benefit from the exploitation of mineral resources;
* the promotion of inter-generational benefits by improving understanding of sectoral impacts on the health, economic well-being, and cultural and social

relations of communities, by developing social baseline data for all operations, and by establishing effective monitoring systems to measure long-term benefits to local communities; and

• the promotion of the rights and well-being of indigenous communities by ensuring that operations receive the free and prior informed consent of local indigenous communities, that traditional owners are able to assess and respond to mining proposals, and that there is an equitable distribution of benefits between companies, communities, and government.

Facing the Future proposes specific actions to enhance the minerals sector's contribution to Australia's sustainable development. The most important of these are:

• The dialogue and cooperation established by the project should continue. Future stakeholder engagement processes should ensure the broadest stakeholder participation in defining governance structures, processes, and objectives.

• The sector should recognize the rights of stakeholders to participate in decisions that affect their lives and interests. It should define the precise nature of stakeholder rights and work collaboratively to establish the most effective means of presenting those rights and ensuring their implementation.

• The sector should consider – in an open and participatory manner – the need to establish independent mechanisms for stakeholder complaints and complaints resolution, and should report on the nature and outcomes of stakeholder complaints.

• Companies should make clearly articulated statements of business principles and sustainable development policy commitments. They should develop the systems necessary to ensure those commitments are reflected in strategic and operational decision-making; in the allocation of capital, staffing, and other resources; and in process monitoring, evaluation, and reporting.

• Companies should introduce independent third-party verification of their social and environmental performance and reporting standards.

• The sector should explore the economic case for increasing the emphasis on minerals processing and other value-adding activities.

• The environmental, social, and other costs of resource extraction and processing should be reflected in the price of minerals products. This will

require dialogue and the engagement of all key stakeholders.

• Some areas are off-limits to exploration and mining activity. These should be identified through stakeholder consultation, informed by rigorous risk assessment processes, and communicated in a manner that is accessible and appropriate to stakeholder needs.

• The sector should improve understanding of mining operations' impacts on community health, economic well-being, and cultural and social relations. It should establish social baseline data and effective monitoring systems – based on sound social science methodology and community participation – to measure long-term effects on local communities.

• The sector should respect indigenous communities' right of prior and informed consent to minerals development on their lands. This will require provision of comprehensive information on proposals, access to independent advice and expertise, and appropriate time frames in which to respond to proposals.

Western Europe

As a result of early meetings with stakeholders, a decision was made to focus specifically on the questions surrounding metals in use through a desk study incorporating commentary and interviews with key actors. This activity was limited in extent and not meant to replicate the more extensive processes of engagement undertaken elsewhere.

The following key questions were addressed in the report:

• Who are the key stakeholders when it comes to European Union (EU) environmental policy-making? What is their function, how do they work, and what power do they have?

• What are the main principles of EU environmental policy-making and how does this affect the non-ferrous metals industry? What do different stakeholders think about it?

• How do the EU Waste Management Strategy and the Revision of the Chemicals Policy affect the non-ferrous metals industry's licence to market? What drives these policies? What are the different stakeholder perspectives?

• What stakeholder processes/dialogues have been set in place (at EU or European national level) around

REGIONAL PERSPECTIVES **CHAPTER 15**

mining and metals related to sustainable development in Europe? What are they about? How do they function? Who is taking part?

Western Europe, together with the US, is the largest user of metals. Europe uses around 25% of the global total of major non-ferrous metals while it produces only 2–3% of the global metal ore production. Further, the European mining and mineral sector plays an important role in the development of the economic activities of the European Union. Around 190,000 people are directly employed in the European minerals and metals mining industry, which generates a turnover in excess of 5 billion euros.

The sector for construction minerals is by far the biggest employer, with direct employment of about 140,000 people. Many others are employed indirectly in associated industries such as equipment manufacture, exploration, processing, and manufacturing industries. In the European non-ferrous metals industry, for example, thousands of associated companies of different sizes employ more than 1 million people. European consumption trends indicate that Europe has a significant role to play in determining the patterns of metal use needed to make the transition to sustainable development.

The regional study focuses on the perspectives of key stakeholder groups with regard to six initiatives that have implications for practice and consumer trends in Europe with respect to the use of metals. These are the EU Strategy for Sustainable Development, the Sixth Environmental Action Plan, the precautionary principle, risk assessment strategies, the EU waste management and minimization strategy, and the revision of the EU Chemicals Policy, all of which have implications for the mining, minerals, and metals sector. This summary addresses the issues raised by the European Union Sustainable Development Strategy and the use of the precautionary principle.

In 2001, the European Commission proposed an EU Sustainable Development Strategy, later endorsed by the European Council, which was based on the need to integrate sustainable development into planning within the EU. From an industry perspective, the Sustainable Development Strategy raises several questions. One of the biggest concerns is to make sure that it does not limit industry's space to innovate; technological innovation must be placed at the heart

of environmental strategy and not be impeded by over-regulation. Fabrizio d'Adda, Chairman of UNICEF's Environment Committee and CEO of the Italian company Enichem, states that 'autonomous initiatives by companies are the main source of cost-effective progress in many environmental areas' as opposed to the 'command and control' regulation of the European Commission.

Environmental organizations are also critical of the Sustainable Development Strategy and criticize the failure to tackle the international footprint of the EU's agriculture, fisheries, and trade activities. It is maintained that the strategy risks creating an 'ecological Fortress Europe'. Tony Long of the Brussels office of the World Wide Fund for Nature notes that the EU has for long been 'strong on words and weak on action'. The lack of clear targets and a timetable supports his observation. The European Environment Bureau, an NGO, regrets that the European Council did not adopt the phasing out of environmentally perverse subsidies, environmental tax reform, greening of public procurement, and strict environmental liability.

Another key debating point is the operationalization of the precautionary principle. The non-ferrous metals industry believes that the EU has given the impression that its use implies a search for zero risk. The principle should only be used after the completion of a risk assessment (that is, of exposure to risk) and when there is scientific uncertainty and reasonable grounds for concern as to the potentially dangerous effects of a substance.

Equally, there is a sense that the definition of an 'acceptable level of risk for society' has become politicized. Restrictions on the marketing and use of certain substances (subject to precaution) will hence be driven by a political agenda rather than scientific evaluation. Measures based on the principle should be proportionate and be preceded by a cost-benefit analysis that takes into account the impact of substitution of materials.

The environmental movement is aware that a 'zero-risk' environment is impossible to achieve, but wants to stimulate the prevention of harm. It is therefore in favour of an approach that includes:
• early action on the basis of reasonable suspicion of harm;
• the reversal of the burden of proof, because the

MMSD THE MINING, MINERALS AND SUSTAINABLE DEVELOPMENT PROJECT traditional approach, which lies with legislators, may cause considerable delays before action is taken;

- the substitution principle: if safer alternatives are or may be available, they should be considered; and
- transparency and democratic decision-making to decide about the acceptability of technologies and activities and the ways to control them.

Some consider that environmental issues will increasingly come to the fore in the EU's policy agenda – this will affect the sector. It is widely recognized that the production and the use of target metals must be environmentally acceptable. A key debate is centred on precaution as a tool to manage hazard and risks from certain substances. This is an important debate for the non-ferrous metals sector since certain uses of some metals have the potential to present risks to public health and the environment. Examples of this are lead in gasoline and cadmium in batteries, if not properly recycled.

The report makes several key recommendations:

- Development of a proactive stance (as opposed to a reactive one) towards legislation. The non-ferrous metals industry needs to share responsibility with authorities and civil society groups.
- Maintenance of an ongoing stakeholder dialogue, through which knowledge and information is shared. Different interest groups need to recognize their mutual dependency. The European Aluminium Association and Friends of the Earth Italy, for instance, cooperated on a study on the environmental performance of aluminium in road vehicles in the EU member states, plus Norway and Switzerland.
- Initiation of more meaningful dialogue at a national level between national associations, NGOs, governments of member states, and others. The United Kingdom Stakeholder Forum on Chemicals, for example, was set up by the UK Department of the Environment, Transport and the Regions in 2000 to promote a better understanding between different stakeholders (government, business, environment, and consumer groups) of people's concerns about chemicals in the environment.
- Increase in exchange of data and information between producers and downstream users.
- Development of more effective public policy and greater transparency to influence the growth and evolution of patterns of production and consumption.

- Development of better systems for determining the transboundary impact of metals use within the community on other states and environments outside the EU.

National Baseline Studies

Baseline studies were also commissioned at the national level in some countries. These projects were generally restricted to desk studies, but with the incorporation of perspectives gained from a limited consultation with key stakeholders. The national studies do not attempt to replicate the full stakeholder engagement process undertaken at the regional level.

In general, the national studies were developed according to specific terms of reference and tailored to address key issues in the respective countries. Baseline studies were commissioned to increase understanding of:

- the main areas of contention and conflict associated with the sector, including legacy issues;
- the structural and political constraints to progress in key areas;
- key drivers of change in particular areas;
- good practice in particular areas of activity; and
- new initiatives that are being proposed and ones that are currently under way.

India

The study on India was prepared by the Tata Energy Research Institute in Goa.

India produces as many as 84 minerals – 4 fuel, 11 metallic, 49 non-metallic industrial, and 20 minor minerals. The aggregate production of minerals for 1999–2000 was about 550 million tonnes, from approximately 3100 reporting mines, producing among other things coal, lignite, limestone, iron ore, bauxite, copper, lead, and zinc.

More than 80% of the mineral production comes from open cast mines. Mining leases numbering 9244 are spread over 21 states and about 13,000 mineral deposits occupying about 700,000 hectares, which is 0.21% of the total land mass of the country. The aggregate value of minerals production in 1999–2000 was more than Rs.450 billion (approximately US$10 billion).

The contribution of mining and quarrying to gross domestic product has declined marginally – from 2.47% in 1993–94 to 2.26% in 2000–01. The 1991 census data indicates that out of the total work force of 286 million main workers, the mining sector employed about 800,000 workers. Employment of women in the mining and quarrying division was 68,600, which is about 10% of the total employment in the organized mining and quarrying sector, although this is believed to be in decline.

The National Mineral Policy of 1993 has been revised in the form of the Mines and Minerals Act (Regulation and Development, 1994 and 1999) and Mineral Conservation Rules (1988). These revisions allow foreign equity in projects up to a level of 50%. They also sanction private-sector exploitation of the 13 minerals previously reserved for public-sector mining companies (iron ore, manganese ore, sulphur, chromite, gold, diamond, copper, lead, zinc, molybdenum, tungsten, nickel, and platinum group of minerals), and include the requirement for effective mine planning, including environmental management provisions that have to be approved by the Indian Bureau of Mines. Other amendments include provisions for the review of mining plans after five years, including foresight planning for a further five years, the payment of compensation to landowners, the requirement for rehabilitation of mining lands, and restrictions on the use of forestland.

Key issues revolve around land and the lack of a clear rehabilitation and resettlement policy by central government. Equally, the relationship between mining companies and communities has been characterized by a lack of consultation with local communities, which means that their needs and concerns are only marginally satisfied and that they are rarely involved in decision-making. The result has been a relationship in which confrontations, tensions, and conflict have been predominant.

Campaigns against unjust mining, by people's organizations and social action groups, have been prominent and have pressed for people's rights over natural resources. Land acquisition is an issue around which many social action groups have agitated for change, forcing companies and government to address that issue along with resettlement and rehabilitation. Policy reform, while potentially far-reaching, is still evolving. Other issues include displacement, human

rights violations, environmental degradation, and health hazards.

The negative public perception of the mining industry will not change overnight. The mining industry must re-establish the connection between its products and the people who use them through a comprehensive public outreach effort accompanied by a need to re-examine each mining operation and to improve or maintain community relations programmes and sustainable environmental management systems. In addition, the sector must come to grips with the economic, environmental, and ethical consequences of closure of mines. There are several priority areas.

Developing tri-sector partnerships in mining areas – There is a need for multidimensional research that integrates activities ranging from the technical to the social, including training and capacity building for partnerships among companies, government, and communities.

Mine closure – Presently there is no specific legislation in India requiring environmental protection during the closure of a mine. Viable economic alternatives post-closure may include transforming mined land to areas for crop production. Timing new mining projects in the region to follow on consecutively would help local economies. Adequate planning is a key to, among other things, reducing tensions and conflicts with local communities.

Small-scale mining – In India, there are more than 10,000 small-scale mines, many of which are not illegal. In particular, there is a need to better understand occupational health and safety issues related

Woman using metal cooking pots, India

to small-scale mining, issues related to women and child labour, the improvement of the legislative framework, and improvement of the linkages between large and small-scale mining.

Policy reforms – In spite of an elaborate mining legislation and policy framework in the country, there exist a number of gaps. There is a need to make the minerals investment process more user-friendly and the licensing system less bureaucratic, to increase private-sector participation, to clarify the compensation system, and to overhaul the tax and royalty systems. There is also a need for policies and practices that encourage openness and transparency from all stakeholders.

Indonesia

The baseline study on Indonesia was prepared by Dr R Wiriosudarmo of Yayasan Ecomine Nusa Lestari (Ecomine) in Jakarta.

According to the Indonesian constitution, both land and minerals are under the control of the state. According to Agrarian Law No. 5 of 1960, state control over land covers the power of the government to regulate the use and maintenance of land as well as the legal relationship between humans, land, water, and air space.

Rapid economic development in the last two decades has increased competition for land use. Mining projects, which have a long gestation period, could not compete in the race for land. Land use conflicts between mining and other industries, as well as between mining and communities, have increased. Mining no longer enjoys any priority in this respect.

Further, Indonesia is a country of diverse cultures, and the traditional laws governing land ownership are not well codified. As a general rule, it is safe to assume that most communities, particularly outside Java, are strongly influenced by varieties of cultural law (*hukum adat*). Each area may have completely different traditional rules and tolerance for different types of land use.

Land problems associated with mining have been escalating in complexity for the last three years. To some extent, this problem has affected mining investment and has led to the postponement of exploration activities and the closing of mining

operations. It has also become the prime source of conflict, triggering anti-mining sentiment. Unless an acceptable resolution is found, it is predicted that the land problem will escalate. Specific problems include:

- repressive intervention from the local authority,
- absence of sustainability criteria in assessing the value of compensation, and
- the loss of cultural values associated with the loss of land.

The complexity of cultural land ownership would not be a barrier to investment if industry were willing and prepared to deal with it. One of the problems with cultural land ownership concerns boundaries, which while uncertain in a formal legal sense are definitive among the tribal communities. Legal boundary demarcation in turn confuses issues of compensation. In general, the mining industry may have no objection to the payment of land compensation. The problem arises when the status of land ownership is uncertain. Ideally, codification of cultural land ownership throughout the country would assist investors.

Post-mining land use in Indonesia is not well regulated. Mining Law No. 11 of 1967 and other subordinate mining regulations only stipulate the responsibility of the mining industry to compensate and conduct land rehabilitation after mine closure. The move towards regional autonomy is expected to foster the implementation of spatial planning at the regional level to address such issues.

A general lack of government interest in the social aspects of mining is evident throughout the structure of the Department of Energy and Mineral Resources (DEMR, formerly the Department of Mines and Energy). There is no single agency or even a desk in the DEMR that deals with the social aspects of mining. Further, the government has not established a policy framework for the accommodation of social considerations associated with mining. Social issues are commonly approached through the narrow window afforded by the environmental impact assessment regime. The relationship between the mining industry and the community has never been part of the development framework. This lack of attention to community perspectives has created the perception that the community is a liability to the sector rather than an asset that can be nurtured for mutual benefit.

Mining is also associated with an adversarial approach

to recruiting local and particularly unskilled labourers, most of whom are poorly qualified. For certain job specifications, pre-employment training would be a practical option to increase the capacity of local labour to fill such positions; a policy rarely practised by mining projects, particularly those with short timelines.

The absence of a government social policy framework and the voluntary nature of community development have succeeded in separating development implementation from the integrated planning of mining projects. Most mining companies do not even think of community development as a strategic issue. There have been many complaints from mining companies that they have spent heavily on development, but the present framework narrows the chances of a successful outcome.

Lack of transparency in the mining industry is another issue. While the mining companies perceive transparency as a controlled flow of official information from the company to the public, people perceive it as the right to know. This is a question of good will versus good governance. The first is voluntary, while the latter should be obligatory.

Despite laws to the contrary, environmental impact assessment reports and data obtained from environmental monitoring and environmental audits, for example, are not always available to the public. Further, the government is often reluctant to release information concerning environmental issues. This situation is exacerbated by the inability of the government to collect information concerning environmental baseline conditions. In the event of environmental conflict, the government relies greatly on information provided by the mining industry.

Past development in Indonesia has created imbalances between the wealthy and the poor. These imbalances are not acceptable to any standard of human values. The current multidimensional crisis in Indonesia is an expression of these imbalances. One group enjoys excessive benefits from the development of natural resources, while the other struggles for existence without the means to produce even a bare subsistence livelihood. Within this context, the mining industry is perceived as one that creates social injustice.

Several key points emerge from the Indonesia national report:

- Development practised in the past supported increases in economic output that depended on unsustainable depletion of natural resources and the life-support capabilities of the ecosystem.
- The development practised in the past systematically excluded large segments of society, which has resulted in alienation and social conflict. Inclusiveness means that everyone who chooses to be a productive, contributing community member has a right to the opportunity to do so and to be recognized and respected for these contributions.
- The discussion of land use for mining should include use during exploration and production periods and post-mining, as well as the right of the landowner to reject mining.
- The role of the community in mining is controversial. Work is needed to build the capacity of communities and to explore procedures for involving communities in decision-making.
- The devastating impact of illegal mining has negated the positive values of small-scale mining. The challenge is to establish a concept of community-based small-scale mining.
- On the question of regional autonomy, two main issues surfaced. What is the role of local government? And what adjustments does the sector have to make to work within a sustainable regionalized structure?

Throughout the Indonesia baseline study, several areas have been identified in which the perspective of the various parties concerned are not in accord:

Land access for mining – In preparation for the reform of land policy, industry should initiate with others a discussion of land use for mining, which should include land use during exploration, the status of land during production, rehabilitation of land after mining, and the right of the landowner to reject mining. Access to traditional land for mining is another issue that needs research and in-depth discussion in a series of extensive stakeholder engagements.

The role and position of the community in mining – The role of the community in mining is controversial and in need of in-depth research to understand the capacity of the community for involvement in decision-making and to explore procedures for community involvement and the prospect of establishing a legislative framework to enable this.

Small-scale mining – The challenge is to establish a better understanding of community-based small-scale mining. Research and stakeholder discussion should cover issues that may relate to the linkages between SSM and large-scale operations, environmental management, socio-economic and socio-cultural development, technical assistance and funding possibilities, marketing prospects and assistance, and institutions.

The role of local government in mining – Regional autonomy is being implemented in Indonesia. Two main issues subject to discussion and research are the role of local government in mining and the meaning of regional autonomy for mining in terms of sustainable development of mineral resources.

Philippines

The study on the Philippines was done by M V Cabalda, M A Banaag, P N T Tidalgo, and R B Garces, other independent consultants, and a Steering Committee in Manila.

The Philippines is well endowed with metallic and non-metallic mineral resources. In the past two decades, the growth of the industry has been seriously impeded by lack of foreign investment due to political instability, a 60:40 limitation on foreign ownership; soft metal prices; excessive taxation; high operating, production, labour, and energy costs; civil unrest; and a series of natural disasters.

The approval of the long-awaited new Mining Act in 1995 gave hope to the industry's impending resurgence and was met with enthusiasm by both local and foreign mining investors. Not long after, however, the Act became the target of NGOs and the central focus of opposition, primarily because it allowed wholly owned foreign mining companies to operate mines within the country and was regarded as giving them tacit permission to plunder the national patrimony at the expense of the environment and the Filipino people.

Meanwhile, the local mining industry has been hard pressed to meet current regulations as well as societal expectations, despite applying a lot of effort to these demands. Given the industry's precarious situation, however, progress towards this end has been slow.

The government, on the other hand, is faced with accusations that it is in collusion with the industry and is not doing enough to punish errant mining companies. Yet government is at the same time being accused by the industry of being an 'anti-mining NGO', because of what is seen as a highly prescriptive approach to regulation as well as the lengthy and tedious period needed to permit a mine and to complete a mining contract.

One thing is certain, a culture of change – a paradigm shift – must be integrated into the way in which mineral resources development is undertaken in the country, one that considers the concerns of the government, industry, and other stakeholders.

In terms of regulation, the Philippine Environmental Impact Statement system was formally established under Presidential Decree No. 1586. Under the system, mining (and quarrying) projects are classified as 'environmentally critical projects', hence they require an Environmental Compliance Certificate prior to development.

The Contingent Liability and Rehabilitation Fund is the primary financial mechanism for mine rehabilitation. Multipartite monitoring is mandated through the Mine Rehabilitation Fund (MRF) and damage compensation through the Mine Wastes and Tailings Reserve Fund. The MRF is established and maintained by each operating mine as a deposit to ensure the availability of funds for the satisfactory compliance with these statutes and commitments.

The Philippine Mining Act of 1995 in one of its governing principles clearly states 'the grant[ing] of mining rights shall harmonize existing activities, policies and programs of the government that directly/indirectly promote self-reliance, development and resource management'.

Current regulations mandate mining contractors to rehabilitate land disturbed by mining activities to a physically and chemically stable and self-sustaining ecosystem, based on a final land use more productive or approximating to the original land use as agreed with communities and local governments; to establish safety and health management systems and ensure continual improvement of safety and health performance based on a risk management approach;

to contribute to the establishment of sustainable/ alternative livelihood opportunities and skills for the host and neighbouring communities during and after the operation of the mine; and to share equitably the economic benefits derived from mining with major stakeholders – national and local government and communities. The overriding objective is to guarantee that future environmental conditions are not compromised, that social stability is maintained, and that no financial liability is absorbed either by the government or the community.

The Mining Act notes that 'activities, policies, and programs that promote community-based, community-oriented, and process development shall be encouraged, consistent with the principles of people's empowerment and grassroots development.'

The challenges that need to be faced in the Philippine Mining Sector include:
• addressing the low level of government support;
• a lack of local government unit acceptance – the industry needs strong national government leadership to work with local government units in assisting investors to meet requirements;
• industry conservatism – the industry needs to showcase new 'world best practice' mines, and the government must strategically support remaining development proposals that demonstrate examples of best practice;
• a lack of clarification or codification and clear land title for all stakeholder groups, which impedes access to 'ground';
• the fiscal regime for foreign mining companies – an acceptable agreement on the fiscal regime is needed that allows for an equitable sharing of revenues between the government and the investing company;
• the Supreme Court challenge to the Mining Act – investors will not make high-risk investments in mining while there is uncertainty over the unresolved Supreme Court case on the constitutionality of the Mining Act filed in 1997; and
• the Indigenous Peoples' Rights Act – uncertainty will continue until this matter is resolved and it is determined who owns the mineral resources of the Philippines.

Other key issues include:
• environmental degradation – contamination of water

and crops, water depletion, and siltation of water bodies, and so on;
• land disputes – conflict between mining claims, tenurial rights and other claims (with indigenous people, for example), and the comprehensive Agrarian Reform Law;
• land conversion or use; and
• the presence of large-scale mining companies that results in the displacement of panning and small-mining activities within neighbouring areas, leading to competition for scarce resources.

Papua New Guinea

The Papua New Guinea (PNG) study was prepared by Dr Glenn Banks, independent consultant – Australian Defence Force Academy at the University of New South Wales.

The current mining industry in PNG ranks as one of the largest in the Asia-Pacific region. There are five operating mines, and a vibrant small-scale sector involving up to 50,000 small-scale miners.

PNG has seen several dramatic changes that undermine, or make largely irrelevant, existing policies, including:
• greater emphasis on the involvement of local communities in the mineral development process before any mining plan is submitted;
• a marked shift in the distribution of revenue flows from mining operations from central government to local communities and institutions; and
• the de facto surrender of state sovereignty over mineral resources with the payment of the full value of royalties from the sector to local communities and provincial institutions.

Some of these changes have led to an exodus of large companies from the country.

The small-scale mining sector is increasingly being recognized as a significant contributor to gold production and, more important, local livelihoods across at least ten provinces in Papua New Guinea. Small-scale mining has considerable economic impact estimated at K100 million in gold and silver per year, with high-end estimates placing production closer to K150 million, or over 1% of gross national product.

Local communities, while always involved in or affected by mining in PNG, came to prominence as stakeholders in the minerals sector in the late 1980s. This period was marked both by the beginnings of the 'minerals boom' and the closure of the BCL mine. The two events meant that local communities became engaged in negotiations and discussions to a far larger extent than they had previously. The Mining Act 1992 enshrined this participation in legislation, and subsequent developments have seen communities become major economic beneficiaries of large-scale mines.

Any brief discussion of mining and community issues is sure not to reflect adequately the variety and complexity of the issues at different mining operations. Mining has wrought massive social and economic changes for local communities in Papua New Guinea. Three areas where new initiatives of note are proposed or currently under way are the development of a national-level mine closure policy and guidelines, a sustainability policy for the minerals sector, and some of the initiatives occurring in terms of the relationships between mining corporations and local communities and governments.

The development of a sustainability policy for PNG will focus on:
- definition and measurement of the economic sustainability of the industry and the implications of this for communities;
- definition of the interface between the social and environmental impacts;
- effective arrangements for benefits distribution;
- development of systems or institutions to ensure the development initiated by a mine project can be sustained after mining ceases;
- identification and establishment of sustainable income replacement economic activities for communities post-mine;
- measures required to sustain essential services provided by the mining company beyond mine life; and
- the creation and management of long-term funds to provide resources for the continuation of sustainable development activities.

The PNG mining industry has experienced a boom in the past decade, and despite the problems described, it has continued to operate – in some places very successfully for most stakeholders. Given this experience, there are a number of key

areas where in particular the structure and management of relationships between stakeholders in PNG could provide positive models applicable more widely.

Four of these are:

- *The Development Forum* – premised on the view that all key stakeholders should be involved in discussions concerning a potential mine from the time that the developer submits a proposal for development.
- *Communication and relationships* – developed using a number of different means of communicating with local stakeholders. These various channels seek to provide information to other stakeholders, to receive information about the community, or both.
- *Local-level initiatives* – focusing on facilitating and nurturing the capacity of local-level government and institutions so they are able to deliver, on a sustainable basis, community-level development. This is an important shift in emphasis from previous corporate efforts that had sought to provide local-level infrastructure and governance directly.
- *Sustainability and Mine Closure Policy* – The Department of Mining and the Office of Environment and Conservation drew up a draft policy and set of guidelines for mine closure in late 2000. This comprehensive document seeks to ensure that mine closure is an integral part of mine development and operational planning. There is provision for mine closure bonds and trusts, and detailed guidelines for both physical (environmental) and social aspects of mine closure. Following discussions with industry, NGOs, and government departments, and the receipt of a World Bank loan for mining sector institutional strengthening, the social aspects of mine closure were incorporated into the development of the sustainability policy.

While there has been a raft of studies and reports on various aspects of the industry, particularly in the last decade, the understanding of a number of critical aspects is still relatively thin:

- *Economic impact of the industry at the national level* – The recent mining and hydrocarbon fiscal review drew largely on Internal Revenue Commission figures, and did not, for example, calculate the contribution of the personal income taxes of mining company employees, nor import duties paid by the companies.

- *Revenue flows and utilization at the local level* –
An assessment of how these revenues can better
contribute to sustainable development requires a
more complete knowledge of the variations that
exist within the sector.
- *Processes of change in communities.* – While there have
been a number of detailed and high-quality studies
on processes of community change in Papua New
Guinea, the vast majority of these have been limited
in terms of the time period over which the research
has been carried out.
- *Communication* – Linked to the above issue, there is a
need for more detailed work on the form and
effectiveness of current mechanisms for
communication between mining companies, local-
level government, and affected communities.
- *Long-term impacts on flora, fauna, and water quality* –
There is still a need to draw together and summarize
more effectively the environmental information
gathered from the various mining projects over
the years.
- *Policy* – There is a need for a more coherent policy
focus within Papua New Guinea in terms of the
minerals sector.
- *Practice* – Three areas where efforts by corporations
and governments can be targeted to improve
practice are communication, links between local
authorities, and the mining operations and social
monitoring.

There are also three areas of significance where
capacity needs to be strengthened to enhance the
ability of the minerals sector to contribute to
sustainable development: government regulators,
community affairs sections, and provincial and local-
level governments.

Kyrgyzstan

The Community and Business Forum was responsible
for the baseline study on the mining industry and
sustainable development in Kyrgyzstan.

Kyrgyzstan is fortunate to have a geologic database
containing technical information that can be
favourably compared with and sometimes exceeds
those of many other countries. Yet the organization of
this database is not compatible with modern
computerized information systems.

Since the demise of the Soviet Union, the industry has

been beset with problems, including:
- the deterioration of equipment, the absence of a
high-quality repair base, and a lack of funds for
maintenance of equipment at operational capacity or
for reconstruction and modernization;
- an inability to comply with state health and
environmental standards;
- the insolvency of domestic consumers and
unregulated increases in prices for equipment and
services;
- an antiquated legislative system, especially with
regard to taxation (in particular, an extremely high
rate of royalty of up to 30% for gold; 12% for
lanthanide, mercury, and antimony; and a custom
duty of 70% for rare-earth elements), which hinders
the existence and development of the industry; and
- ineffective mechanisms for the production, sale, and
purchasing of materials – functions that are loaded onto
enterprises that have little experience in this field.

The industry has also gone through profound crisis
and transformation, including:
- drastic increases in the cost of fuel for energy,
- increased burden of social infrastructure costs after
the collapse of the former Soviet Union,
- the loss of markets for and production of antimony
and uranium to Russia and Kazakhstan,
- the need to export all production, and
- the need to import most raw materials.

At present, the cost of labour in Kyrgyzstan is low in
comparison to world standards due to an oversupply
of labour. So as the Kyrgyz economy opens to the
international market, the wage component will be
treated with increased concern and will inevitably lead
to reductions in labour. One of the key problems for
the industry is the emigration of highly skilled and
experienced staff to Russia and other republics.
Regardless of production decreases, the importance
of the industry for the economy of the republic is
still great.

The industry has also gone through a major
restructuring in a struggle to reduce production costs,
which has led to job losses of 50–70%. In some
instances, minimal subsidies have been granted to the
worst affected communities. Counter to this, the
government has also been taking measures to try and
improve the contribution of the mining and minerals
sector to the development of local communities. The
Government of Kyrgyzstan has developed a long-term

plan for the development of new mining enterprises in all regions of the republic in an attempt to create jobs and increase foreign exchange.

At present, potential investors, when making marketing, legal, financial, and project decisions, generally resort to the services of international experts who are well known but unfamiliar with local conditions. It is necessary to build up a native infrastructure and expertise base that can contribute to decision-making and that factors in market conditions, local circumstances, and leading-edge thinking, while still reflecting local specificity and national concerns.

With regard to the regulatory environment in Kyrgyszstan:

- Deposits are state-owned.
- The developer is obliged to pay a royalty for the right to exploit the deposits and a one-time 'bonus'.
- There is mandatory reclamation and rehabilitation of land and natural heritage sites after mining.
- The law favours investment and mining business development.
- Foreign investors are encouraged and capital repatriation is allowed.
- The transfer of licences to third parties is permitted with the authorization of an appropriate governmental body.

In the present environment, small enterprise development can play an important role in strengthening the Kyrgyz economy. Small deposits can be developed by using comparatively inexpensive portable equipment, and this sector does not require the same degree of extensive infrastructure, which allows a reduction in the volume of inputs and the degree of financial commitment, as well as a potential reduction in the degree of environmental and social impact. Further, the rehabilitation of small areas involves less environmental performance cost. Reduced costs also allow the entry of local developers into the sector. The development of small deposits can create the new jobs that are important in the absence of other economic activity and helps to support local development through contributions to revenues, providing that local administrative systems facilitate the use of such revenues to achieve development-focused objectives.

Other challenges include the legacy of uranium mine

tailings left after the demise of the former Soviet Union, which used Kyrgyzstan as a major source of supply until the late 1970s. Present estimates determine that 18 closed mines have been responsible for 520 million cubic metres of waste stored in 63 dumps, and 56 million cubic metres of beneficiation and metallurgical processing wastes stored in 44 tailings and slag carriages. Few funds are available for rehabilitation, although a draft law on 'tailings and dumps' is pending.

The Ministry of Environment and Emergency is not well enough organized, lacks appropriately prepared personnel and equipment, and is unsure of its roles and responsibilities. Further, existing legislation in the field of environmental protection is based on the practices extant in the former Soviet Union and does not consider the specific environmental problems caused by these hazards.

Citizens and public unions are able to take part in decision-making related to the siting of tailings disposal facilities. People living on land near tailings dumps are entitled to receive compensation for damage caused by radiation and other forms of pollution that exceed specified concentrations. Since the break-up of the former Soviet Union, such payments have not been maintained.

In terms of a way forward for Kyrgyzstan, a provisional list of challenges has been grouped according to stakeholders. First, there is a need for national level reporting on decision-making and policy development that is transparent and accessible to the public through the media and other sources. There is also a need to develop clear rules around the use of information as well as procedures that outline the responsibilities of all stakeholders. Better knowledge and policy is required around whose interests are affected by a particular project. While the country has signed the Aarhus convention, there is no such legislation at present. There needs to be investment in increased skills education for government employees involved with the sector. Policy needs to be developed for the integration of impact assessment on a wider scale for projects. Equally, policy frameworks need to be more favourable to investment for the development of local communities, observance of environmental requirements, and community health.

There are several areas in which international organizations could assist through consultation and financing: sociological studies (awareness, attitude, participation, and so on); publication of independent research, analysis, and assessment results; organization and support of public hearings on mining sector issues; assistance in the provision of modern technologies, especially in health care and environment protection areas; knowledge transfer in the area of assessment of the nature and scale of environmental and social impacts; public participation; involvement of national experts in decision-making processes; and improved legislation and law enforcement practices.

Mining companies can facilitate the move to a more open sector that contributes more fully to sustainable development through the publication of concise accessible reports on their activities, facilitating with government public hearings on anticipated projects, and providing briefings and press releases as appropriate and in discussion with stakeholders. Companies can also provide support for some of the activities of local NGOs in acting as facilitators on certain issues. Companies should cooperate in the establishment of policies that recognize the rights of local communities, particularly with regard to compensation issues, and should conduct surveys to assess community response to any project proposal. Policies should also be established for the conduct of social and environmental impact assessment.

Local communities might have a greater interest in the presence of mining companies on their territories if they were informed, regarded as partners, and afforded different forms of participation (including revenue distribution, development of appropriate business opportunities and the nomination of representatives for inclusion in the decision-making process).

The main value of interaction with the NGO sector lies in the establishment of partnerships. The main obstacle to this is that the non-governmental sector has a weak infrastructure at present and is uncoordinated. NGOs can assist with, among other things, independent studies, analysis, and assessments and the collection and distribution to the public and other interested parties of impartial information about mining. NGOs can also help with the public monitoring of environmental requirements by mining companies and with ensuring the participation of independent qualified experts, the monitoring of human rights observance as outlined in national legislation and international agreements, and assistance

with training and educational seminars to increase awareness of project implications.

Increased capacity is required in the education system to train the specialists required in each of the areas outlined above, and for the provision of courses at all levels to increase public awareness of the issues.

Republic of Khakassia

The baseline study on Khakassia in the former Soviet Union was prepared by Strana Zapovednaya of the Protected Land National Fund.

The Republic's mineral resources are represented by deposits of coal, iron, gold, molybdenum, polymetallic ores (lead and zinc), marble, barites, bentonites, limestone, rock phosphorites, asbestos, uranium, gypsum, jadeite, nephrite, and mineral waters. There are good prospects for developing deposits of manganese, wolfram, antimony, cobalt, oil, gas and gas condensate.

More than 100 enterprises are engaged in recovering commercial minerals in the Republic, including two iron ore mines, four gold mines, six open cast mines and two pits for recovering hard coal, the Sorsk molybdenum combine, two combines mining for marble and granite, more than 30 artels and small enterprises mining gold, and 36 enterprises extracting widely distributed commercial minerals.

The 20 main mining enterprises in the Republic contribute almost 20% of the tax revenue to its budget and provide permanent employment for 8% of the population. Virtually all of Russia's molybdenum is mined in the Republic, and recovery of coal, gold, and iron ore constitutes respectively 3%, 1.5%, and 4% of the amount for Russia as a whole. There are no enterprises in state ownership, and shareholdings are being turned over to the private sector.

The success of the mining, minerals, and metals sector in the republic is currently constrained by:
• a lack of significant investment,
• the progressively ageing industrial base of the sector,
• the low level of added value in the mining enterprises' products,
• a weak legislative and regulatory base, and
• difficulties in promoting export production from Khakassia.

According to V Tsyganok, First Deputy President of the Government of the Republic of Khakassia, the state is faced with the need to reinforce state control in the whole field of the use of natural resources and protection of the natural environment, setting out a system of precise and transparent relationships of authority with the business community that exploits natural resources, and laying the basis of a balanced regional policy on a range of issues.

The private sector is currently undergoing a process of reform. IPG Sibal's approach, for example, has been to move towards preventing harmful environmental and social impacts through:

- the introduction into the production process of world-class methods and technologies that are environmentally safe and save resources;
- the certification of production output in accordance with international standards;
- increased control of solid wastes, of emissions into the atmosphere, and of effluent and reduction in the levels of harmful emissions and sewage as well as increased recycling of solid wastes;
- constant monitoring of the ecological situation in the regions where IPG Sibal enterprises are located;
- active liaison with the environmental protection movement and ecological awareness training among employees at the Group's plants;
- computer classes connected to the internet in institutions of general education in a number of Russia's regions; and
- funding for construction of the Holy Trinity Church in the city of Abakan as well as other sponsorships.

Yet privatization and the sale of previously state-owned property to companies outside the republic has destabilized production and often means that concern by the owners for the social conditions of their employees in such enterprises is minimal.

The baseline study was still undergoing final editing when this report went to press, but the interim agenda for change noted the following:

- There are few resources for the improvement of the an official tax register of ownership, boundaries, and value of real property.
- Some of the regulations with regard to mining and in particular with respect to nature protection and natural resources legislation are incompatible and require revision.

- Expert assessment of existing projects and proposals is constrained by lack of funding and expertise.
- Federal regulations 'on expert ecological assessment' are not fully adhered to by the territorial authorities for monitoring and supervision.
- Projects in special land use areas are often not submitted for assessment and there is inadequate liaison between state and federal bodies.
- Site information relating to environmental protection and conditions for the use of natural resources are not reported in full.
- Public discussion of expert state ecological assessment for projects is inadequate.

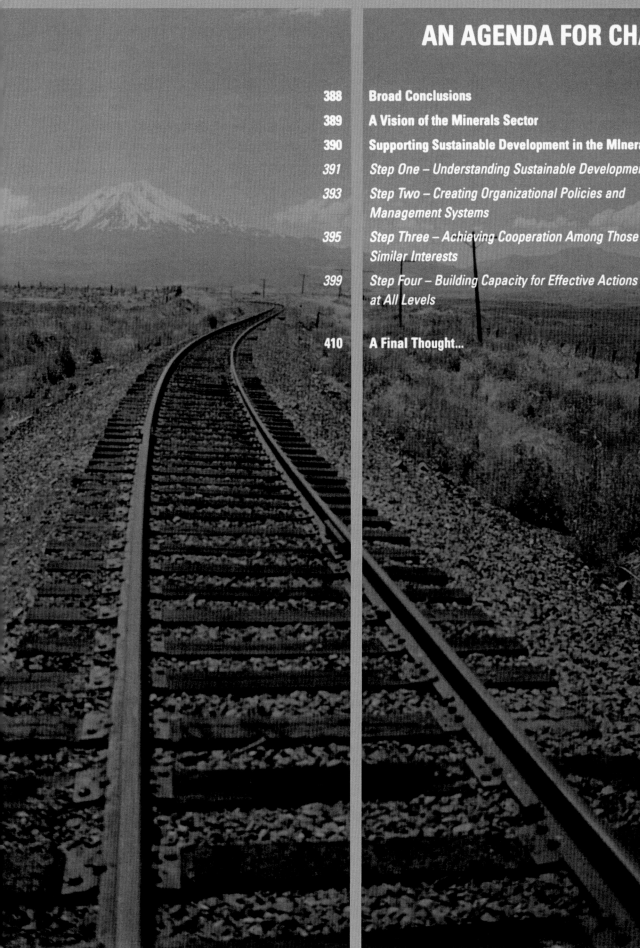

CHAPTER 16

AN AGENDA FOR CHANGE

The many people and organizations – in business, government, civil society, and elsewhere – who together constitute the minerals sector have differing roles, perspectives, and values. But there is more convergence than might be expected. There is a broad acceptance that the various costs and benefits do not fall equally on all. There is a strong desire for improved performance, a better quality of life, and constructive engagement that produces results. There are experienced and committed people throughout the sector, in government, labour unions, civil society organizations, companies, and elsewhere, with useful ideas and considerable energy. Yet there is frustration about how hard it is to make change, to put ideas and energy into practice, or to produce concrete results.

The MMSD Project found from the beginning that sustainable development could provide a useful framework to guide the minerals sector. It also believed that by setting out the challenges – from all perspectives, in a fair and balanced way – new ways forward would emerge. It has not been an easy process, given the low levels of trust in the sector on the one hand and the complexity of the issues on the other.

This final chapter contains the broad conclusions that emerged from the MMSD process and an Agenda for Change. (See Box 16–1 for a description of the Project that formed the basis for this agenda.) The agenda sets out various actions for improving the mineral sector's contribution to sustainable development. In all the discussion the project has provoked, few quarrelled with the basic definition of sustainable development contained in the 1987 report of the World Commission on Environment and Development. The Agenda for Change assumes a broad set of goals that flow from that definition:
• material and other needs for a better quality of life have to be fulfilled for people of this generation
• as equitably as possible
• while respecting ecosystem limits and
• building the basis on which future generations can meet their own needs.

Box 16–1. The MMSD Project at a Glance

MMSD has tried to do three things: provide a means for surfacing ideas and information; offer some opportunity to test those ideas with diverse, knowledgeable audiences; and provide a 'snapshot' of where this evolution of ideas stands and what conclusions can be drawn.

The project has surfaced ideas through working and engaging with organizations and individuals from different regions of the world. This has included:
• a review of existing knowledge;
• assimilation of suggestions submitted to MMSD by many organizations and individuals;
• research conducted by staff of the International Institute for Environment and Development;
• four regional processes that have, in turn, drawn on contributions from many researchers to produce regional reports; and
• the commissioning of 12 country baseline studies and more than 100 expert studies on a range of topics.

It has tested those ideas as widely as possible through:
• posting important documents on the MMSD website and asking for comment;
• the distribution of Bulletins detailing MMSD progress and soliciting response sent to the MMSD database of over 5000 people;
• informal conversations with individuals and organizations working in the field;
• responses received when these emerging ideas were presented at meetings and conferences throughout the world;
• regional consultations in four key mineral-producing and -consuming regions around the globe;
• national processes of consultation in several countries;
• peer review and comment on critical pieces of background research;
• 23 global workshops on topics ranging from biological diversity and corruption to managing mineral wealth and indigenous concerns about mineral development, attended by 600–700 diverse stakeholders and interested parties;
• close work with a 25-member Assurance Group consisting of people from a broad spectrum of backgrounds and perspectives;
• wide publication of a draft report on 4 March 2002, with an invitation to submit comments and criticisms, which resulted in more than 100 sets of written comments as well as numerous less formal suggestions and an intense effort to evaluate, respond to, and where appropriate adopt the comments into this final report; and
• four regional forums to discuss the draft report.

MMSD has not been able to reach every group that is concerned about these issues or to engage all the relevant actors from all interest groups. It has not completed the analytical task, nor has it attempted to state a consensus where none exists.

From this MMSD derived a framework based on a set of guiding principles, as described in Chapter 1. (See Table 16–1.)

This framework requires that most decisions be based on multiple rather than single criteria. Choices, or trade-offs, are needed where a decision cannot satisfy all criteria simultaneously. But there is a need to maintain some limits with respect to parameters for trade-offs. This agenda assumes that there are some values subscribed to by all, such as basic human rights or honest justice systems, that cannot be cast aside. The idea of 'critical natural capital' should join this list once it has been more fully debated and is more widely understood.

Decision-makers have to operate within certain constraints. Different stakeholders emphasize different priorities: poverty alleviation and equity for those concerned with development; the 'triple bottom line' for industry; the integrity of ecosystems and their continued viability for environmentalists. To reach consensus through negotiation – especially for individuals such as the CEO of a company or the director of a non-governmental organization (NGO) – is a demanding task. This is complicated by the fact that not all groups have the same level of economic power or influence. Time is another constraint: time is needed to build trust, to even out power differentials, to learn to understand different perspectives and identify commonalities.

The right incentives need to be in place to encourage different actors to pursue their own objectives in ways that contribute to the wider goals of sustainable development. What is appropriate for each to do will be based on responsibilities and capacities. For each, it is important that actions:
- be consistent with organizational objectives as well as the objectives of sustainable development;
- build on strengths; and
- be measurable, so there must be some way to distinguish success from failure.

The next section outlines some overall conclusions from Part III, followed by a vision of the future for the mining and minerals sector in a sustainable world that provides some guidance on the actions needed to move this agenda forward.

Table 16–1. Sustainable Development Principles

Economic Sphere
- Maximize human well-being.
- Ensure efficient use of all resources, natural and otherwise, by maximizing rents.
- Seek to identify and internalize environmental and social costs.
- Maintain and enhance the conditions for viable enterprise.

Social Sphere
- Ensure a fair distribution of the costs and benefits of development for all those alive today.
- Respect and reinforce the fundamental rights of human beings, including civil and political liberties, cultural autonomy, social and economic freedoms, and personal security.
- Seek to sustain improvements over time; ensure that depletion of natural resources will not deprive future generations through replacement with other forms of capital.

Environmental Sphere
- Promote responsible stewardship of natural resources and the environment, including reparations for past damages.
- Minimize waste and environmental damage along the whole of the supply chain.
- Exercise prudence where impacts are unknown or uncertain.
- Operate within ecological limits and protect critical natural capital.

Governance Sphere
- Support representative democracy, including participatory decision-making.
- Encourage free enterprise within a system of clear and fair rules and incentives.
- Avoid excessive concentration of power through appropriate checks and balances.
- Ensure transparency through providing all stakeholders with access to relevant and accurate information.
- Ensure accountability for decisions and actions, which are based on comprehensive and reliable analysis.
- Encourage cooperation in order to build trust and shared goals and values.
- Ensure that decisions are made at the appropriate level, adhering to the principle of subsidiarity where possible.

Broad Conclusions

Breaking New Ground contains only a fraction of the analysis generated by the MMSD process, much of which is provided on the accompanying CD. Given the heterogeneous nature of this sector, few generalizations can or should be made. With that disclaimer in mind, here are some general conclusions of the MMSD Project:

Need – Society's need for mineral commodities is clear, as they provide the substrate for numerous products upon which modern society depends. Even in the case of non-recyclable mineral commodities such as coal, it will take years to phase out use, given current dependencies. It is not currently possible to meet the world's legitimate basic needs without more of at least some kinds of mineral commodities in circulation.

Structure of the Sector – Though there is a great deal of interdependence among companies along the value chain, the lack of vertical integration in some of the minerals industry can be an obstacle to effective product stewardship. Improving this situation will require much more collaboration in the industry than has occurred in the past. If the industry is to move towards providing mineral 'services' as opposed to material supply, restructuring and alliances will need to be established.

Stakeholders – The sector includes stakeholders from the local to the global – with a wide variety of interests. There is a difference between those with a direct and often involuntary interest and those who are concerned indirectly because they choose to be. The term 'stakeholder' therefore requires further clarification. Talking of multistakeholder processes without some clarity around the different kinds of 'stakes' is too simplistic.

Subsidiarity – Local issues should be solved locally, as local endowments and priorities differ from place to place. Local actors will be directly involved when their interests are threatened. While international action and solidarity remain crucial, decentralizing decision-making to the point as close to the impact as possible should be the norm. Local actors often resent interventions from national or international quarters 'on their behalf', particularly if this involves the assumption of a mandate.

Best Practice – Similarly, the concept of 'best practice' requires local solutions. A frequent response to questions about what constitutes 'best practice' is that 'it all depends'. Best practice should be defined by decentralized and iterative processes, not by a fixed set of parameters that can be read out of a manual.

Incentives – Win-win solutions are not always possible; voluntary approaches alone are insufficient where there is a compelling social priority but little or no business case to justify the additional expenditures needed to meet it. There are then two options: collective action on a voluntary basis that is enforced internally by a group, or governmental intervention or regulation to achieve the same result. Unless the law is clear and enforced, some enterprises will resist change. In addition, if civil society groups put pressure only on a large few companies and fail to recognize progress, the rest will ride free. From the MMSD finance dialogue, it is clear that market-base incentives on sustainable development criteria are difficult though probably not impossible to design. At present, the discussion is couched in terms of the management of risk, increasing shareholder value, and the occasional marketing advantage. Devising a system of customer-driven certification is also problematic due to the heterogeneity of the industry.

Capacities – There is a genuine and critical need to build the capacity of all the actors. Though MMSD has not surveyed in detail respective capacities, the overall conclusion must be that sustainable development for the sector calls for a new and different mix of skills. The current mix, whether looking at companies, NGOs, or governments, will need to improve for the sector to contribute to sustainable development.

Managing Mineral Wealth – The full potential contribution of minerals to national economies is mostly far from realized. In all too many instances, incentives for foreign investment reduce the wealth available to the host nation. The ability of mineral-rich countries to add value to their wealth by way of beneficiation and processing is often denied by lack of capacity, tariff, and other trade barriers. In some cases, subsidies make the position worse for others. The mismanagement of wealth through inefficiency and corruption does not help. Those who have mineral wealth now should be determined to use it to produce diverse and stable economies for tomorrow – and they need help to do so.

Legacies – The negative social and environmental legacy of the sector is a major obstacle to building trust and moving forward. Abandoned sites and communities, persistent waste and pollution issues, aggrieved peoples: the list is long. Historically, consumers – mostly in the industrial world – have not paid the full costs of using mineral commodities; the failure to internalize many of these costs has only been recognized recently. The obstacles to progress in dealing with legacies include establishing priorities on the worst sites, identifying who will pay, and deciding on the source of the funding.

Collective Efforts – Corporate performance in the minerals sector, measured against any indicator, is variable. Some good companies are improving , but the bad are inexcusable, and the past record is even worse. Action by companies, individually and collectively, is clearly required. In an open trading and competitive world, a 'rush to the bottom' caused by 'free riders' is a real danger. In many areas, small companies are crucial to the standards of large ones. If, for example, projects near closure are simply sold by multinationals to private, less visible entities, other routes are opened to avoid obligations. Collective action must include companies of all sizes in order to produce positive results.

Use of Existing Institutions – Existing organizations should be encouraged to continue facilitating collective action. Institutions such as national and international chambers of mining and regional governmental organizations currently offer the best opportunity for collective action to move forward. Mutual recognition of their respective roles and collaboration is needed. All need to engage more openly with other constituencies.

Dilemmas remain on a range of issues, including how to:
- raise the capacity of all to act to the best of standards,
- define the boundaries of responsibility among different actors when governance is weak,
- balance the role of regulation with that of voluntary initiatives,
- apply the precautionary principle so as to have a proportional response,
- remove subsidies and trade barriers that favour the better-off,
- achieve better balances between risks and opportunities,

- act when there is a democratic and governance deficit,
- stop the free riders yet maintain competition in an open trading world, and
- ensure that the price of a product reflects its total costs.

A Vision of the Minerals Sector

The MMSD process sought to create a picture of what the minerals sector would look like if it were to maximize its contribution to sustainable development. (See Table 16–2.) In this vision of the future, the minerals industry is integrated throughout the value chain and providing mineral services rather than primary products. To raise the performance of all, a leading group of companies – both large and small – provides a model and supports the efforts of others.

Legal and regulatory frameworks will be complemented by voluntary initiatives, such as mine-site or company-wide verification. These measures will be developed through transparent and inclusive processes, defining concrete performance standards at the global, national, and local levels. Governments will have sufficient capability and willingness to impose sanctions on those who will not meet these standards. There will be fair and accepted mechanisms to facilitate access to information, public participation in decision-making processes, and access to justice to resolve disputes.

All actors will have sufficient capacity to meet higher standards, to define and enforce constructive interventions, and to monitor performance and facilitate sustainable development objectives. Costs will be much better internalized, and there will be a concerted effort to address the legacies of abandoned mines.

There will be clear incentives for all actors. Companies that perform well will retain their social licence to operate – including lower operating costs, favourable borrowing terms, and lower insurance rates. Governments will benefit from harmonious social, economic, and political relations. Labour will enjoy better working conditions and better health. NGOs will play a positive role in meeting society's needs. Consumers will be assured that their use of mineral products is supporting sustainable livelihoods. And communities overall will have better standards of living and greater involvement in decision-making processes.

Table 16–2. Towards a Sustainable Future for the Mining and Minerals Sector

The Worst of the Past	A Vision of the Future
Mineral revenues that are spent outside the public view for the benefit of a few	Mineral wealth spent transparently to support social and economic goals
Long-running disputes with landowners about compensation	Disputes resolved efficiently and fairly
Tariff and non-tariff barriers that deter developing countries from establishing downstream industries	A level playing field where free trade works more equitably
Minerals development as a threat to protected areas and biological diversity	Mineral development in appropriate places and as a source of revenue to ensure the protection of areas critical to biodiversity
Companies that set their own rules in protected enclaves	A shared system of laws and practices that applies to everyone
Government decisions taken privately and unaccountably, based on poor information	Decisions taken publicly, after consultation with affected parties, based on clear criteria
Mining and recycling industries seeing each other as competitors	An integrated, complementary approach to management of materials in use
Consumers who have no idea of the source of the minerals they use	Consumers who know the source of the products they use and increasingly act on that knowledge
Minerals development as a threat to indigenous peoples' cultures and societies	A minerals industry that works in partnership with indigenous peoples and communities
Frequent disputes and armed conflicts	Fair, equitable, and accepted ways of preventing and resolving disputes
Minerals operations endangering worker and public health and causing deaths	A minerals industry that promotes improvements in public health
A legacy of ghost towns, poverty, and pollution	Integrated planning for sustained post-closure environmental, social, and economic benefits
Infrequent exchanges among a few stakeholders	Ongoing and inclusive dialogue among all stakeholder groups

Supporting Sustainable Development in the Minerals Sector

One of the principal difficulties in adopting the agenda of sustainable development is the multiplicity of the individual issues, problems, and proposed solutions. This Agenda for Change proposes a relatively small number of overarching ideas that can be used to organize those many individual concerns and priorities into manageable tasks. In each chapter in Part III, risks and opportunities are outlined and current problems identified, with some specific steps suggested that may lead to progress in problem solving.

This chapter does not attempt to capture and summarize all those proposals and suggestions; its function is quite different. The goal here is to recommend some broader steps that can be taken to integrate many of the suggestions in Part III. These can be grouped into four major categories of actions to support sustainable development in the minerals sector:

- Increase understanding of sustainable development.
- Create organizational-level policies and management systems for implementing the principles of sustainable development.

• Collaborate with others with common interests to take joint steps towards sustainable development.
• Increase the ability to work towards sustainable development at local, national, and global levels.

The proposals are directed principally to those with a high level of interest and involvement in the sector. Many of the proposals are more applicable to some actors than to others.

Step One – Understanding Sustainable Development
Realizing the potential of sustainable development requires a commitment to education and research, including a focus on the development of practical tools for making decisions and taking actions.

Education
There is a need to increase the understanding of sustainable development among employees of minerals companies, relevant government agencies, labour and civil society organizations, and others with important roles in the sector.

• Institutions such as mining schools that have a role in educating future mining and minerals professionals – who may work in the future in companies, governments, or elsewhere in the sector – should incorporate sustainable development in their curricula.
• Donors to these institutions should support, encourage, and insist on these broadened curricula.
• Industry associations, labour unions, and NGOs should work with educational institutions on their curricula. They could also assist in developing short courses or distance learning modules for current professionals.
• Educational institutions with more general mandates should strive to incorporate broader understanding of the role of minerals in society, as well as the sector's contribution to sustainable development.

Research on Priority Issues
While the MMSD Project has compiled a considerable amount of information, it has also highlighted areas where more research is needed. Research will face increasing demands to ensure relevance to the concerns of stakeholders in the sector, and there is a need to find mechanisms to ensure this broadening of focus occurs. In the minerals sector, research has also

been used in the past to gain political capital, or to ensure that research reaches conclusions that are not damaging to particular interests. This leads to dismissal and rejection on one or another side of even good research results.

• Any organization funding significant research in this area should have clearly stated policies ensuring the rigour of the research it is supporting, including publication of data, citation to publicly available sources, and peer review.
• There is an important role for panels with representatives selected by a variety of stakeholders to establish research priorities for organizations supporting research related to sustainable development in the minerals sector, especially in reflecting the needs of developing countries.
• Many research priorities are identified throughout Part III. Specific areas needing attention include the development of a business case relating to the use and recycling of metals and minerals, and the positive and negative impacts of minerals development on community health.
• More funding could be committed to research that aims to integrate existing disparate sets of knowledge or expertise within a sustainable development framework.
• International mechanisms exist to coordinate and fund research of public interest on topics such as public health and climate change. While there are already some international alliances for research in the minerals sector, it is hoped that either research networks with specialist university departments, national research institutions, or a UN agency would convene meetings of interested parties to discuss research of public interest.

Development of Practical Tools
There is great emphasis on the development of tools for taking concrete steps towards the goals and principles of sustainable development, especially in the business world. This is necessary and should be encouraged; but there is also a danger that the market may be flooded with duplicative and poorly thought out tools that will ultimately discredit the idea.

• An industry body, such as the International Council on Mining & Metals (ICMM) or the Prospectors and Developers Association of Canada (PDAC), could commission respected institutions – perhaps involving a partnership of leading business schools –

to survey industry needs and develop criteria to distinguish appropriate types of decision-making tools. These tasks should be undertaken with the appropriate participation of affected stakeholders.
- Many specifics tools should be developed or refined. These include, for example, indicators on human rights, conflict, or social conditions.
- Donor governments, regional and international organizations, or a group of like-minded governments could support surveys on the kind of decision-making tools needed to enhance decision-making in governments.

Improving Professional Practice and Knowledge
The knowledge and practice of the various professions needed by organizations may not encourage practices consistent with sustainable development, or may even serve as obstacles to progress. In companies, for example, current accounting standards may not provide clear answers for integrated planning for mine closure, purchasing standards may not be appropriate to the emerging concepts of supply chain assurance or community development, and methods for evaluating mineral prospects may not take into account the best current understanding of sustainable development.

Specialists of different disciplines and technical fields at all stages of the minerals cycle – from geology to accounting – will need to evaluate how to apply the principles of sustainable development to their current activities. This task may be aided by collaboration with others in the same fields, through, for example, the work of professional associations.

- At the international level, appropriate industry bodies from all stages of the minerals chain, such as ICMM or PDAC, in partnership with international associations of professionals and specialists, could convene meetings to examine priority issues facing different disciplines working to apply the principles of sustainable development. Associations of exploration geologists, accountants, engineers, human resource directors, purchasing managers, marketing professionals, lawyers, and others would be among the high priorities for such meetings.
- At the national level, national mining associations or organizations of processing, fabricating or recycling companies could convene similar events with national associations of professionals.
- Labour unions, working with other actors, could convene events designed to understand workers' concerns about sustainable development, to

Key Actions for Understanding Sustainable Development	
Actions	**Responsibilities**
Education and Research	
• Incorporate sustainable development into curricula for mineral professionals	• Educational institutions supported by donors, industry associations, labour unions, and NGOs
• Policies for transparency and rigour for research	• Donors, research institutions
• Establish research priorities	• Multistakeholder panel
• Undertake research	• Research institutes and other organizations that undertake research
• Fund integrative research	• Donors
Development of Practical Tools	
• Quality assurance for decision tools	• Industry bodies such as ICMM or PDAC, business schools, and research institutions
• Development of specific tools	• All actors
• Survey of government decision-making tools	• Donors, governments, regional, and international organizations
Improving Professional Practice and Knowledge	
• Meetings at the international level	• Industry bodies such as ICMM and PDAC, international professional associations
• Meetings at the national level	• National industry associations, national professional associations
• Meetings focused on the role and concerns of labour	• Labour unions

strengthen their roles in dealing with a variety of issues, and to identify areas in which the training of workers should be improved. These can build on existing work in areas of health and safety, retrenchment, and broader community issues.

Step Two – Creating Organizational Policies and Management Systems

Most organizations do not have sustainable development policies and should consider developing them. This is important for all actors, including large consumers of mineral products, lenders, and institutional investors. Such a policy can be used to create internal change and to integrate sustainable development into mainstream thinking in ways that add value to the organization.

As a first step in developing such a policy, an organization should review its overall objectives and functions from a sustainable development perspective. This could include understanding how the organization can contribute to sustainable development; identifying the potential costs and benefits of doing so; and maximizing the benefits for the organization as a whole by integrating individual activities into a coherent, organization-wide management system. Institutions, government agencies, businesses, and other groups that already have sustainable development policies should review the extent to which these have penetrated the organization and its decision-making processes, and should consider more effective ways of integrating them into practices and deriving organizational value from them.

Sustainable development policies are a starting point for action, but integrated management systems are required to ensure their effective implementation. These will involve the integrated use of specific tools and may be based on models such as those that have driven improvements in worker health and safety or environmental impacts. All actors need to review existing organizational management systems to assess whether the right mechanisms are in place and to determine whether they have sufficient capacity to undertake necessary changes. In particular, organizations need to ensure that mechanisms are in place to evaluate progress in implementation and to report findings to management and key stakeholders in a credible manner.

The remainder of this section considers the development of policy and management systems by individual actors. Actions that involve cooperative efforts with others are dealt with later in the chapter.

Companies

A company-level sustainable development policy can incorporate other relevant company policies such as those on environmental issues, worker health and safety, employee integrity, community relations, human rights, reporting, and so on. This should enable the integration of these policies within a coherent, more efficient and effective, and less costly management system. The whole company should be engaged, as this partial list of the departments that might be included indicates:

- Human resources – recruiting and retaining good-quality staff, evaluation and compensation.
- Legal departments – permitting, contracts, managing liabilities, better due diligence, making clear that no corruption will be tolerated, adequate provisions for enforcement.
- Purchasing – supply chain assurance, community development.
- Accounting – treatment of risks, costs, and liabilities; accurate and informative reporting to senior management, boards of directors, and external audiences.
- Boards of directors and senior management – identification of sources of risk and potential business opportunities.
- Exploration and property acquisition – better due diligence in identifying liabilities, more effective assessment of the pros and cons on acquisitions and divestitures.
- Health, safety, and environment – further progress in integrating programmes into employee consciousness; improved relations with regulators.
- Site management – long-term planning; improved relations with local communities.
- Marketing – moving beyond selling commodities to more complex relationships with customers that are harder for competitors to match.
- Corporate strategy – better planning and assessment of future business opportunities.
- Communications and external relations – improving communications and delivery of information to external stakeholders, whether they be shareholders, surrounding communities, or NGOs.

Companies can develop management systems for key issues to help implement sustainable development policies, or even where such policies have not been established. An example is establishing a management system to review end-of-life plans at existing operations, to take necessary action to strengthen them, and to continue to monitor them throughout the project life.

The company review should focus on whether existing plans fully address the end-of-life environmental, social, and economic conditions of affected communities; care and opportunities for displaced workers; and the implications for government at all levels. Key questions are whether the different actors share an understanding of their respective roles and responsibilities, and whether these are clearly spelled out. Appropriate measures should be in place to ensure that benefits achieved during the project life can be sustained to the maximum extent and that negative impacts at closure are eliminated or minimized. This process can be useful in surfacing potential future liabilities and allowing them to be managed.

The company should extend this review to involve key stakeholders and should facilitate discussion among the principal actors in the community and local government. The aim is to develop a shared vision of the environmental, economic, and social life of the community post-closure; to elaborate specific objectives; and to allocate the roles, responsibilities, and obligations for achieving those goals. Plans should build on and supplement any existing government planning processes and requirements.

Labour Organizations

Labour organizations can develop policies for sustainable development as a way of bringing members together in a shared understanding of priorities and objectives for themselves and for the organization as a whole. The policy can identify priority areas in which the organization seeks to collaborate with other actors to promote sustainable development. In addition to its traditional responsibilities towards workers, this could include involvement in broader community concerns such as health and local development.

Government

Government policy on sustainable development in the minerals sector can be a useful tool to integrate, coordinate, and harmonize the missions of different departments in pursuit of common objectives. It can provide guidance to all departments in orienting their policies and enable an increased level of cooperation and integration of efforts. The departments involved in developing and adopting the policy should at a minimum include those dealing with minerals exploration and development, the environment, trade and industry, labour, and economic development.

A country with significant mineral endowments should consider undertaking a comprehensive review of the impact of its legal and policy framework for the minerals sector. This should focus on looking at how the mineral endowment is managed for sustainable development, identifying deficiencies, and finding ways to remedy them. It should consider different parts of the minerals sector, from exploration to the manufacture of mineral-related products, and should consider all sizes of operations. Of equal importance is ensuring that the government departments involved have adequate resources and the tools they need to do their work effectively.

Any review would be most beneficial if it takes the form of an open discussion involving key actors in industry, labour, and civil society. The World Bank Group is already active in a number of countries promoting national mining policy dialogues, development frameworks, and country strategies; it may well be a source of advice or assistance for those countries that desire its support. At the same time, the Bank can use the conclusions of its ongoing Extractive Industries Review to examine how its activities in the minerals sector can best contribute to sustainable development and improve performance.

Non-Governmental Organizations

NGOs could develop policies to clarify the link between organizational purposes and broader sustainable development goals, to provide guidance to employees, to serve as guidance in making decisions, and to make the organization's position clear to other actors.

NGOs can also enhance their effectiveness and reduce risks by developing clear and public policies of investigation and assurance that they apply to data they use. Although accuracy of information is important to all actors, this is particularly so for campaigning NGOs, since their effectiveness is closely tied to their reputation for accuracy and since they are increasingly

Key Actions for Creating Organizational Policies and Management Systems	
Actions	**Responsibilities**
Organizational-Level Policy	
• Policy review and development	• Companies, labour organizations, government, NGOs, international organizations
• Coordination among government agencies to implement sustainable development policies	• Government ministries
• NGO policies to deliver developmental services for companies	• NGOs
• World Bank Extractive Industries Review	• Eminent Person and World Bank
Management Systems	
• End-of Life planning	• Companies, with stakeholder input
• Identifying gaps in government capacity	• Government, with assistance from international organizations
• Systems for assuring quality of information	• NGOs

asked to campaign on issues arising in parts of the world far from their home base. NGOs that have adopted explicit policies and management systems to ensure thorough investigation of information, as is the case with some human rights organizations, have clearly enhanced their effectiveness and credibility.

Step Three – Achieving Cooperation Among Those With Similar Interests

Groups of actors with common roles, responsibilities, and interests can benefit from collaboration in a number of ways. For example, they can form associations or networks to share understanding and lessons of good practice, to enable more effective communication with other groups to pool resources, and to minimize transaction costs. Groups of actors, whether at the national or international level, focus more effectively on the concerns of a broad association of organizations than on the opinions of single organizations or communities. Collaboration may occur from the local to international level and may take a number of different forms – everything from informal information-sharing networks to formal associations requiring membership and adherence to certain norms.

Existing Associations
• *Review and Formulation of Sustainable Development Policies*
Associations and networks should review existing policies with a view to developing sustainable

development policies. In some cases these already exist. The Sustainable Development Charter of ICMM is one example; several national industry associations have also either developed or are developing such policies. Networks such as the World Mines Ministries Forum, regional associations such as the Mines Ministries of the Americas (CAMMA) and ministries in Asia Pacific Economic Cooperation (APEC), and NGO initiatives such as the Global Mining Campaign should also consider adopting sustainable development policies.

• *Sharing Information and Capacity Building Among Members*
International bodies of ministers, including those of mines, finance, and the environment, can be instrumental in sharing experience and ideas for improving the contribution of the minerals sector to sustainable development. National, regional, and international industry associations, such as Eurométaux and the International Zinc Association, have also done valuable work in sharing ideas and approaches among member companies. They provide a platform for companies to share experiences and facilitate capacity building among members. The same is true of national associations of artisanal and small-scale miners (ASM). Labour unions have among the best developed networks for these purposes. Other associations or networks such as the Global Mining Campaign or ICMM are newer but have considerable potential in information sharing and capacity building. Associations and networks should examine ways they can strengthen and expand these roles.

Forming Associations or Networks

Where appropriate, stakeholder groups in the minerals sector should be encouraged to form associations to advance their interests and improve their contribution. The impetus must come from within the groups themselves, but others can help create opportunities for engagement. More powerful groups of actors should provide financial and other support to groups that are shy of resources to organize themselves into associations. To be represented effectively, groups must select leaders in a way regarded as legitimate and ensure that the mandate of leadership is periodically renewed.

• *Stronger Networks for Artisanal and Small-Scale Miners*
Associations of artisanal and small-scale miners exist in some countries but not others. Even where they do exist, their ability to participate in global policy processes is limited. A key goal is to develop the ability of small-scale and artisanal miners to speak for themselves, through their own organizations, in policy and other processes that affect their interests. The Communities and Small-Scale Mining initiative is critical in providing a forum to facilitate communication and coordination between miners, communities, donors, governments, industry, and other stakeholders and in actively promoting the sharing of knowledge, lessons learned, good practices, and policies. Continued and increased support of this initiative is needed in order for it to have a real impact.

• *Stronger Networks for Communities*
Communities affected by mining could benefit from the development of stronger networks for sharing experience and as a means of bringing their views to attention at the national and global level. Conferences of local governments and other community organizations, supported by donors and organized on an inclusive basis, might be a first step towards building these stronger networks. They could take place at the national, regional, and global levels. One challenge in assuring the effectiveness and value of this approach is ensuring a balance and representation of all community views. In addition, local governments in areas with minerals development should be encouraged to network with each other to share experiences, so that their concerns can be reflected internationally.

• *International Indigenous Peoples Organization*
In two workshops held by MMSD on indigenous people and mining, it was suggested that an international indigenous peoples organization be established to share experience and strategically advise, direct, and monitor industry performance in the arena of indigenous relations. With the help of governments and the international community, this organization could oversee development and implementation of a set of core principles on relationships with indigenous people. Leadership from existing indigenous organizations will be necessary if this new group is to succeed. Its value would in part depend on inclusiveness and the ability to attract a wide range of indigenous organizations with disparate views. It should also build on the networks established through the efforts of other groups.

Protocols and Statements of Principle

Within associations of actors, standards can be improved collectively through the development of and agreement on norms and principles. As described in Chapter 14, these range from non-binding statements to requirements for specified practices as a condition of membership, and sometimes include codes or protocols that verify performance through third-party audits.

• *A Global Declaration and Establishment of a Protocol*
The mining industry should consider adopting a Declaration on Sustainable Development and establishing a Protocol to support its commitment. These tools are intended to complement, not replace, other priorities and initiatives identified at other points in this chapter. The proposal is designed to simplify the current multiple codes of conduct and sources of guidance by providing a way to bring these together over time into one management system. It would start by building on the recently adopted Sustainable Development Charter of ICMM.

The Declaration is a means to address two potentially competing objectives. First, there is a strong interest among many in industry, made evident in the MMSD process, for some kind of rigorous process to define a better level of performance through means recognized by and acceptable to key external stakeholders, and to verify that performance. Second, there is a strong desire to act promptly, to maintain momentum, and to show seriousness of purpose. Some variety of a certification system, a Protocol, or a stewardship council might meet the first objective but will take time to create, and more immediate action is important.

Phase I – ICMM and other appropriate organizations could develop the Declaration. (See Box 16–2 for suggested basic elements and Box 14–4 for principles contained in existing initiatives, identified as strong candidates for inclusion.) While it would inform and consult key stakeholders in the process, the Declaration would be a unilateral action by industry. Companies would be encouraged to adopt and sign on to it. The Declaration might be most effective if it:

- pledges to review the ICMM charter in light of the conclusions of the MMSD report;
- includes a commitment to developing specific, measurable criteria as a set of protocols, to be brought together in a Protocol to the ICMM Charter, dealing with specific areas of concern such as those identified in this report, along with a system of verification of performance; and
- suggests how that system of protocols could be extended more broadly to others in all parts of the industry.

Phase II – This phase would establish a fully articulated Protocol, dealing with key areas of concern for sustainable development and industry performance. This would be done through a process encouraged and catalysed by ICMM, but managed in a way acceptable

---

Box 16–2. Basic Elements of the Declaration on Mining, Minerals, and Sustainable Development

Companies could agree to:

- Participate in review of their association charters and policies in light of the conclusions of this report.
- Work with other companies, within a defined time, to establish a Protocol dealing with key issues of sustainable development and corporate performance, in a process acceptable to key external stakeholders.
- Work with other companies to develop an accepted system of verification to accompany the Protocol.
- Devise a set of immediate commitments embodied in the Declaration; one approach would be adoption of the basic principles outlined in a manageable number of existing agreements and guidelines.
- Develop internal management procedures to familiarize employees with the meaning of these commitments, their importance as company policy, and their alignment with business success.
- Develop reporting procedures that address the principles in the Declaration.
- Conduct, over a defined period, an independent audit by a reputable outside organization of the state of company compliance with the requirements of the Declaration.

---

to principal constituencies and including them in appropriate roles to which they agree. The goal of Phase II would be to create the basis for an accepted Protocol for individual minerals facilities or projects. Elements for individual sets of issues could be adopted as they were agreed; there is no reason to wait for agreement on every issue before adopting measures that are not in dispute. The Protocol should be accompanied by a clear system of rigorous third-party verification. There should be a comprehensive investigation of whether this should lead to a certification system at the project level.

Representatives of key stakeholder groups should be involved in development of the Protocol and the verification process. Commercial lenders could support the Declaration and Protocol as a means to the better management of risk. Insurers would benefit from risk reduction. Where the risk is better managed, they can make a broader range of insurance products available, or offer existing products to higher limits. Equity investors may want to evaluate the extent to which company participation in the proposed Declaration and Protocol is likely to be relevant to investor risks and share value. As the Protocol becomes company-wide, it will be increasingly relevant to investors, particularly those who publish 'sustainability listings' for share issues, and ethical or sustainable development funds. The World Bank Group could also use the Protocol as a tool for considering its lending conditions for mineral projects.

Phase III – This phase is envisioned to be an expanded Protocol for company-wide application. Participation by external stakeholders in management of the process would be deepened at this stage. It may lead to a system of company-wide certification or verification. Phase III could ultimately, if the parties deem it appropriate, approach the question of product certification for certain mineral commodities.

While ICMM must have the key role in reviewing its own Charter, and should take leadership in developing the language of the Declaration and the subsequent adoption of the Protocol, it should be absolutely clear that companies choosing not to join ICMM should be able to participate in this system. It should be open to all levels of the industry, and therefore should be a subject of early discussion with national associations and such bodies as PDAC or Eurométaux. Any or all of these bodies could eventually decide that adhering to the Protocol is a requirement of membership. But the Protocol should not require membership in ICMM.

The Declaration could call for an immediate set of commitments that could be adopted by individual companies, together with a commitment to a longer-term process of multistakeholder engagement to develop the more comprehensive and specific guidelines for responsible management in the minerals industry. It should also provide for a company commitment to adopt and comply with national or regional industry codes of conduct where they exist. For example, companies operating in Australia should initially comply with the Australian Minerals Industry Code for Environmental Management, and those in Canada should adhere to the Mining Association of Canada's environmental policy and sustainable development principles as they are developed.

• *National and Regional Industry Codes of Conduct*
Many issues can be dealt with more effectively at the national or regional level, such as within the region defined by the Southern African Development Community (SADC). A number of national industry

associations have adopted sustainable development policies. There may be benefits in developing these further into codes of conduct, on the model of the environmental codes already in place in some associations.

• *Regional Statements of Principle by Governments*
Regional government organizations such as SADC, APEC, or CAMMA may want to consider adopting sustainable development policies for the minerals sector that can help governments seek greater convergence and harmonization.

• *Statements of Principles by Nongovernmental Organizations*
A collective statement of principles by NGOs that focuses on mineral-related issues might strengthen their influence and increase the contribution they are able to make in the sector.

Developing the Capacity to Prevent and Respond to Emergencies
Preventing accidents is a high priority. When they occur, their impacts are greatly magnified if the capacity to deal with them promptly and effectively is lacking. Moreover, uncertainty, lack of knowledge, and

Key Actions for Achieving Cooperation Among Stakeholders

Actions	Responsibilities
Existing Associations and Networks • Policy review and development • Sharing information and capacity building among members	• All associations and networks including intergovernmental bodies such as ICMM and PDAC, other regional and international industry associations, international bodies of ministers, labour unions
Forming Associations and Networks • National and international networks for small-scale and artisanal miners • National and international networks of local governments and community organizations • International indigenous peoples organization	• Artisanal and small-scale mining organizations, donors • Community representatives, local governments, donors • Indigenous organizations, governments, donors
Protocols and Statements of Principle • A global industry Declaration and Sustainable Development Protocol • National and regional industry codes • Regional governmental statements of principle • NGO statements of principles	• ICMM and other international industry bodies • National industry associations • Governments, regional bodies such as SADC and CAMMA • Global Mining Campaign or other associations of NGOs
Preventing and Responding to Emergencies • Emergency Response Facility	• Industry associations, with governments, NGOs, experts, insurance companies

inaccurate information may cause as much public concern as the accident itself.

An international Emergency Response Facility, supported principally by industry and with appropriate involvement of other stakeholders, could play an important role. It could mobilize world-class experts to supplement government capacity to assess, respond, and control accidents and emergencies or to reduce the chance of them happening. This approach could assure the public that the best possible advice is available to responsible officials. This function would not have ongoing staff beyond a coordinator but would rely on experts from consulting firms, universities, governments, companies, NGOs, or other institutions on an 'as needed' basis. Minimizing the impact of one incident could achieve considerable direct and indirect savings.

The insurance industry is keen to prevent accidents and emergencies. Most insurance companies would like to see more frequent and effective inspections of key facilities such as tailings dams. The transaction costs to insurers of conducting these inspections themselves are high. The proposed emergency response capability could be of significant interest to insurers. They could participate in the design of the facility and in defining its tasks to ensure maximum business benefits. They could consider whether these benefits are sufficient to merit financial support from the insurance industry, just as this industry has supported other collective risk-reduction organizations in the past.

Step Four – Building Capacity for Effective Actions at All Levels
Community Level
Where a local community is affected by minerals development, a shared vision of the development path for the community is required, including agreement on how the costs and benefits of minerals activity are apportioned and how decisions taken. A key issue is who the 'community' is and how it makes decisions.

• *Community Engagement*
For most mining operations, engagement with local communities must begin at the exploration stage. There is no universal formula appropriate to every community or situation. Exploration companies through their associations are in some cases, such as PDAC's 3Es initiative, developing programmes or

guidelines designed to promote fairer and more equitable dealings with communities at this early stage.

Companies should develop plans for continuous engagement during the operational life – from exploration through to closure. This plan should be discussed with the community to ensure that the mechanisms it proposes are considered appropriate. Companies must ensure that those in charge have the right skills and proper authority and that there is continuity of involvement. They must also be willing to invest time in the community.

• *Integrated Impact Assessment*
Currently, the almost universal tool used at the early stage of any large mining or minerals processing project and many smaller ones is environmental impact assessment. This is supplemented on an ad hoc basis by social impact assessments and a variety of other kinds of appraisals, often in a poorly integrated framework. Environmental and social assessment tools should be combined to enable a transition to integrated impact assessment.

An integrated impact assessment should include all significant social, economic, and environmental issues. It should be universal for new projects and include an early phase of consultation with the community to identify local concerns, and to design the assessment to ensure those concerns are addressed. It should include a community-level resource inventory and examine the whole spectrum of sustainable development issues in the project's area of influence, in addition to those required by legislation. Such an assessment should become an inclusive, dynamic, ongoing process of integrating knowledge on potential impacts into decision-making and management practices. It should be endorsed by the local community and government, and entail independent monitoring of impacts. It could become the basis for developing effective communication with a community that will lead to development of a Community Sustainable Development Plan (CSDP). The Seven Questions framework developed by MMSD NORTH AMERICA provides a useful example of an integrated assessment framework that goes beyond 'impacts'.

• *Community Sustainable Development Plans*
Establishing a Community Sustainable Development Plan is a step that needs to be evaluated on a case-by-case basis. In some areas, the existing government

framework and local or regional planning processes will suffice. Elsewhere, leadership from companies, labour organizations, or community organizations will be needed. The objective is not to replace but to supplement government while attempting to build or improve local capacity in the process.

The CSDP should be based on the community's concept of how the mine can best contribute to achieving its social, environmental, and economic goals. It should be grounded in the willingness and ability of the company and appropriate levels of government to contribute to and support those goals. It should be designed through a process of consultation that begins during the permitting phase (for new projects) and that is supported by the studies prepared in the integrated impact assessment process.

The plan should provide the fundamental framework for relationships among the company, the community, and the government (and any other parties) through the project life and into post-closure. It should identify the specific actions needed and the respective roles and responsibilities to achieve the agreed-upon vision. It could also create some obligations, on all sides, for taking those steps. Independent mechanisms for monitoring and evaluation, including clear and agreed indicators of performance, need to be included. The plan will need to evolve and be amended over the life of the project to reflect changing priorities and capacities.

While a company may facilitate and promote the process, the leadership role belongs to local government to the extent it has the capacity and willingness. Otherwise an NGO or development organization could step into this role. The process could also become, for example, part of the forum for discussion between local and national government over revenue sharing and responsibility for services.

Some companies are moving in this direction; it would be helpful if these arrangements were formalized. A system for learning by all from the growing experience in this or other sectors would also be valuable.

The World Bank could evaluate the usefulness of requiring or encouraging contractual Community Sustainable Development Plans, where they will be useful, in projects funded by the International Finance Corporation (IFC) or insured by the Multilateral

Investment Guarantee Agency (MIGA). These could clarify the roles and responsibilities of the community, the company, and the host government for sustainable development, extending through closure into the post-closure phase. Commercial banks could review whether adopting a parallel requirement would be a way to reduce their exposure to the results of proceeding without such plans.

• *Integrated Planning for Closure*
Since many mineral projects depend on specific deposits that have a finite life span, there is a need to focus on where the community wants to be when the project closes. This requires defining desired end-of-life environmental, social, and economic conditions; identifying the resources required to achieve them; and clearly allocating the roles and responsibilities of each of the actors. There needs to be a focus on sustaining benefits in areas such as housing, community health, and education. Plans could be developed through consultation with the community as part of the CSDP. Improving performance in closure planning will be helped by actions at the national and even global levels, as discussed later in this agenda.

• *Labour and Management Cooperation*
Employees have important bridging roles between the smelter, factory, or mine and the community in or around it. Employees could be central in the community-level processes: reviewing end-of-life plans and assisting in the design of CSDPs. This could be in the context of a labour-management agreement. If there is no leadership from the company in initiating the processes, labour could consider taking on that role. International labour organizations can also play a role in informing their national and local affiliates about the opportunities these processes could present, and how they might most effectively participate in them.

• *Dispute Resolution Mechanisms*
When problems, disputes, and controversies arise, government should usually be turned to first. But where there is restricted access to justice, especially at the community level, or when existing mechanisms are inadequate or not trusted, it may be necessary to design dispute resolution mechanisms at the community level. The question of how to resolve disputes should be discussed and agreed at the earliest stage of negotiations; they should be part of the consultation process or the CSDP. It may be impossible

Key Actions at the Community Level	
Actions	**Responsibilities**
• Community engagement	• Companies, communities, local institutions
• Integrated impact assessment	• Companies, communities, local government, consultants
• Community Sustainable Development Plans (CSDP)	• Companies, labour unions, local government, communities, civil society organizations
• Integrated planning for closure	• Companies, labour unions, local government, communities, civil society organizations
• Labour-management agreement for sustainable development	• Labour organizations, companies
• Disputes and conflict resolution mechanisms	• Companies, communities, labour unions, local government, civil society organizations
• Cooperation between large companies and artisanal and small-scale miners	• Companies, artisanal and small-scale miners

to design effective mechanisms that are self-contained at the community level. There may not be a 'neutral' organization in the community acceptable to everyone in a dispute resolution role.

• *Large Companies and Artisanal and Small-Scale Mining*
Large companies could engage directly with small-scale miners and their communities, helping them to work in a more sustainable fashion and where necessary to find alternative economic activities.

National Level
National governments have many roles to play in the minerals sector. They are the facilitators of investment, regulators, and also the providers of public goods and services. Effective policy, coordination, and action at the national level will help to maximize the benefits of minerals activities and minimize the negative impacts. Different government agencies that deal with the minerals sector need to coordinate their activities to ensure coherence and consistency, from exploration to fabrication. In addition, as suggested earlier in the chapter, governments with mineral activities may consider comprehensive reviews of their legal and policy frameworks for the minerals sector to ensure that they are consistent with the vision of sustainable development.

• *Access to Information*
National legislation is needed to give interested parties the legal right to access information. Effective public participation cannot take place without it, nor can the building of trust and cooperation among actors. All levels of governments should have legal provisions and regulatory provisions for citizens to access information

in government possession for which there is not a valid and publicly stated reason for non-disclosure. Mechanisms to support this may include contact points for regular exchange of information with civil society. Governments and civil society organizations should also establish clear and agreed procedures for requesting, receiving, and disseminating information, including the opportunity for the public to identify the information they need for effective and responsible participation in the decision-making process.

• *Public Participation*
In its most developed form, public participation involves civil society in decision-making around strategy, policy, and practice and in setting the agenda for discussion of these. There is a growing trend at the national level in some countries towards contractual and quasi-contractual arrangements to satisfy public participation and public benefit interests. National governments should continue the process of regulatory reform to facilitate public participation and access to information. They should introduce the systems needed to ensure consistency with emerging international norms in this field. Access to information and public participation cannot be established and maintained unless there is a right to access to the legal means to enforce them.

• *Clarifying Land Regimes*
In some places, land rights issues, including compensation and dealing fairly with informal occupation and use, cannot now be resolved without substantial conflict with communities. Resolving conflict over land must start at the national level with clear rules for access to and use of land. These must be

accepted as fair by those most likely to be affected by development proposals involving land negotiations. The best long-run solution is for governments to establish laws and policies in these areas that offer better opportunities for avoiding and resolving conflicts.

No system of laws can accommodate all situations that are likely to arise in land negotiations. In some places, these issues require extensive private negotiations among companies and local occupants of land or those requiring compensation. Governments could consider revising existing laws to include elements such as extensive consultation with local communities; clearly defined rights for those with established occupancy and use of land or communal land holdings, even where they hold no legal title; compensation for loss of rights; and effective access to systems of justice. Governments should also ensure that when bilateral negotiations do take place around land issues, the rules are understood and followed by all actors.

• *Traditional Indigenous Territories*
Indigenous land claims deserve special consideration in this process. Failure to resolve land claims creates significant tensions and often causes affected communities to be suspicious of any activity that requires use of or access to indigenous territories. Governments and companies could make considerable progress by maintaining respect for the principle of prior informed consent freely given. For companies, this would mean behaving as if consent is required to gain access to indigenous lands even when this is not the case in law; this is a prelude to free and fair negotiation on land access issues. For governments, it does not mean that they would subordinate all sovereign national interests to local concerns, but rather that indigenous communities should be recognized as having clear rights within the territories they occupy. The extent of indigenous territories needs to be clearly defined for the security of traditional peoples, and open dialogue needs to be maintained on this issues. Other actors such as the NGO community can assist with these processes.

• *Frameworks to Maximize and Sustain the Benefits of Minerals Development*
Governments should consider developing long-term strategic plans for the creation and management of mineral wealth that include appropriate methods of capturing the rent from minerals and distributing the

revenues; the creation of human, physical, and other forms of capital; and planning for the effects of mine closure at both the local and the national/macro level. In addition, governments could develop measures, such as commodity loans and fiscal restraint, to prevent undue stress on public financing resulting from minerals price volatility.

A proportion of the benefits, such as revenue received in royalties or taxes, needs to be distributed through local administrative structures to enable them to take advantage of some important development opportunities for communities. It is clearly inappropriate, however, to have a universal formula for the distribution of wealth within countries, as the choice should be determined by governments according to domestic priorities and political systems. What is clear is that the problem must be resolved in acceptable and fair fashions, or it may lead to conflict inimical to all interests that undermines any potential for sustainable development.

International organizations such as the World Bank, the UN Development Programme, and the UN Conference on Trade and Development (UNCTAD) should continue to promote study and discussion of wealth distribution issues in their dialogues with governments, with a view to improving the spread of resources at lower levels of government and in communities, or to build essential human and physical capital for economic development.

• *Frameworks for Artisanal and Small-Scale Mining*
Governments need to develop an appropriate, consistent, and transparent policy and regulatory framework that focuses on both the facilitation and management of artisanal and small-scale mining. For the framework to be effective, governments should ensure that sufficient financial and regulatory incentives exist for small-scale miners to formalize their activities, as described earlier. It is also important that any framework recognizes the linkages between large-scale mining and ASM and that there is coherence in policy, regulation, and legislation for the whole spectrum of mining activities. ASM activities also should be incorporated in relevant regional and local development programmes. These policies should also provide the means for dealing with priority problems, such as hazardous working conditions or the use of mercury.

• *Frameworks for Community Development*
Building on existing elements, governments should consider establishing a coordinated legal and institutional framework to incorporate integrated impact assessments, Community Sustainable Development Plans, and integrated closure planning and to assign responsibilities among agencies – in consultation with relevant stakeholder groups.

Legal requirements for developing closure plans for mines tend to be heavily oriented towards environmental concerns. Governments should ensure that mine-closure planning also includes consideration of economic activities in affected communities, opportunities for displaced workers, social infrastructure, and other appropriate issues. In addition, governments could legally require that mine closure planning clarify the roles, responsibilities, and obligations of the different actors.

There is a need to establish and clarify quality standards for impact assessments for mining projects. Government agencies charged with managing impact assessment processes should develop standards for baseline data and analysis, and for special issues such as acid drainage assessment, closure planning, and water quality. National-level industry associations need to make such standards explicit to their membership and pursue mechanisms to inculcate them thoroughly into project development practices.

• *Legislating for Mining-Induced Displacement and Resettlement*
Experiences with resettlement have often been unfavourable. At present, the mining industry, financiers, and governments often externalize displacement costs onto the weakest party – the displaced. It may also be the case that compensation cannot adequately restore and improve the income and livelihood standards of people subjected to involuntary resettlement. Governments must put in place regulations that ensure free and willing negotiation on any resettlement proposal, including freedom from harassment or coercion at the local level and full participation in the decision-making process. Mechanisms for monitoring and fair arbitration procedures are a natural accompaniment to such regulation.

It is too early to expect harmonization and the emergence of a detailed industry-wide approach on this issue. One option in the future might be to

institute involuntary displacement and resettlement insurance to protect the involuntarily displaced – but this too is politically premature at present. In the interim, a displacement and resettlement contingency clause could be proposed as an on-the-ground solution, which is an agreement that all likely risks of these outcomes be assessed, goals set, costs estimated, organizational arrangements proposed, and financing secured before a mining project goes forward.

• *Anti-Corruption Initiatives*
Corruption siphons off the potential benefits of mineral activities, posing a serious threat to sustainable development. Concerted effort is needed to combat corruption – governments should adopt national legislation to put the anti-corruption convention of the Organisation for Economic Co-operation and Development into effect. There are also many examples of national coalitions among companies, national chambers of commerce, and civil society organizations against corruption. Companies could work with organizations such as Transparency International at the national level to establish industry-wide guidance.

Governments and companies should adopt more widely the practice of open publication of basic information about how much wealth is generated from projects, the amounts of revenue received by government departments, and how that money has been spent. Industry organizations should consider taking the initiative, possibly in partnership with an international organization such as the World Bank, to establish an international and public register of all payments by mining companies to governments at all levels.

• *Audits, Guidelines, and Standards for Environment Management*
Governments and funding agencies should require regular independent audits of all tailings storage facilities and find ways to act on the results. Equally, governments should set up clear guidelines for evaluating different disposal methods for mining waste on a case-by-case basis, with a clear value in the short term of the need to avoid riverine disposal.

Government agencies charged with managing impact assessment processes should develop standards for baseline data and analysis and for special issues such as acid drainage assessment, closure planning, and water quality. A high priority in many countries should be communicating the results of an assessment of the

Key Actions at the National Level	
Actions	**Responsibilities**
Review and Development of Legal and Policy Frameworks	
• Access to information	• Governments and relevant stakeholders
• Public participation	
• Land rights regimes and compensation systems	
• Traditional indigenous territories	
• Maximizing the benefits of mineral development	
• Artisanal and small-scale mining	
• Community development	
• Mining-induced displacement and resettlement	
Other Actions	
• An international register of payments to combat corruption	• Companies, industry associations, NGOs, governments, international organizations
• Audits, guidelines, and standards for environmental management	• Government, affected communities, companies
• Capacity building	• Governments, international organizations such as the World Bank, the UN, NGOs, donors
• Labour-company agreements	• National unions, companies
• National multistakeholder processes	• All relevant actors

potential for acid drainage more effectively to interested parties, and integrating this concern into decision-making from the permitting stage through closure.

• *Capacity Building*
Although the World Bank and the United Nations have been supporting capacity building in this sector, it would be helpful to develop a clearer picture of the kind of capacities needed and those that are already in place at the national level. These international organizations could work with member governments and others to develop an understanding of the levels of capacities required and specific guidelines or benchmarks.

• *Labour-Company Agreements*
Workers and organized labour could be major advocates for many aspects of sustainable development such as community development and health, and they have a special responsibility to implement good practices in safety and training. Governments could promote agreements between labour and industry at the national level to promote sustainable development for the minerals sector.

• *National Multistakeholder Processes*
Governments, in consultation with stakeholders, could

be effective convenors of multistakeholder processes at the national level for policy discussions and change.

Global Level
Many mineral companies, markets for mineral products, and capital markets that finance projects operate at the global level. Moreover, in a broad sense, the challenges faced by the sector are global concerns, including the need for economic development, poverty alleviation, and an end to human rights abuses. This and other factors mean that some action is needed at the regional and global level.

The rationales for global initiatives include:

• *Growing international pressure to observe higher standards* – The spread of economic globalization has created more connections between economies than ever before. Where commodities are traded in global markets, consumers and investors are increasingly concerned about environmental and social performance at the source.
• *Free trade and fairer markets* – The world trading system is seen to be failing to deal with aspects of market access. Tariff and non-tariff barriers impede minerals beneficiation, which may inhibit economic development of mineral-dependent economies. This can only be addressed in ongoing trade negotiations.

- *Skills and technology transfer* – One important way to address the disparities in wealth, capacity, and resources is to facilitate access to new technologies, innovation, and skills training between nations.
- *Need for a level playing field* – Better internalization of environmental and social costs will provide more rent for national governments and other resource owners, more income for local communities, better environmental performance, greater incentives for materials efficiency, and greater margins for producers. If these measures are required in some places but not in others, production may simply shift to regions where costs are not internalized. This may place a cap on what can be achieved in countries that want better performance.
- *Legacy issues* – The failure to internalize costs in the past means that consumers in wealthier countries have been subsidized, paying lower prices for the minerals they have used. Assistance to the poorest countries to address legacy issues may be a step in the right direction to redress this.

To move towards collective action, initiatives from everyone in the sector are required. Current programmes and priorities show limited coherence and agreement. Stronger international action by government is an important goal and greater understanding among other actors is the first step to achieving it. In the meantime, there can be other serious initiatives; but they will largely be voluntary and non-binding.

Any proposal for global action for sustainable development faces serious hurdles. First, international organizations tend to be dominated by those with the most resources, capacity, and access to institutions of power, and therefore tend to reflect the values of those in industrial economies. Efforts must be made to redress power imbalances to ensure that the values of people and institutions in developing economies are given equal weight. Second, very few global or international institutions have authority to establish binding rules and requirements or to impose sanctions for non-compliance. And few of the limited number with such powers (such as the World Trade Organization) have the mandate for or interest in addressing the challenges of sustainable development in the minerals sector. Third, while government initiatives can create effective international organizations with mandatory powers, governments are not pressured to move in this direction. And finally, there is resistance to

creating any new international institutions unless funding sources can be identified.

The remainder of this section suggests initiatives that can be taken at the global level by different groups of actors working together on general and specific challenges. Some are already under way in some form and need to be supported. Others have yet to be initiated. It should be noted that calling for action at the international level does not preclude these initiatives being undertaken at other levels. The Forum and disputes resolution mechanism, for example, could also be developed (or may already be in place) at the national or regional level.

- *A Complaints and Dispute Resolution Mechanism*
All parties in the sector should have a serious interest in establishing fair, reasonable ways to resolve grievances and disputes. A dispute resolution mechanism should bring parties together, in a neutral forum, to work out a mutually acceptable facilitated settlement. The elements of the mechanism are envisioned as similar to the methods and procedures of an ombudsman, such as the IFC's Advisor/Ombudsman (CAO)or the Mining Ombudsman Project operated by Community Aid Abroad in Australia. Clearly, where possible, complaints would be better handled by an independent organization operating at a regional or national level.

- The process would be available only in cases of foreign direct investment; it would not apply where the parties were all domestic.
- Where the IFC or MIGA are involved in projects, the process would not supersede the work of the CAO.
- The overall rules for the complaints and dispute resolution mechanism would be set at the global level and managed in a transparent fashion. The mechanism would be guided by principles designed to avoid conflicts of interest.
- A prerequisite to invoking the mechanism would be an effort to solve the problem at the local level.
- The dispute resolution professionals who operate the system would not act as judge or jury to decide who was right, but would mediate to try to achieve a solution acceptable to all.
- The focus would be on problem solving and addressing complaints in a way satisfactory to all parties.
- Anyone with a grievance that fell within the established subject matter could request assistance from the service.

The overall programme could be overseen by a balanced multistakeholder Board. The Board would periodically issue public reports of its activities and the overall process. It would establish rules for the conduct of the process, and amend them as necessary based on stakeholder feedback and experience.

- Complainants would have the option of having their complaints handled privately and in confidence. There would be clear rules of evidence and procedure.
- Parties would agree to cooperate with the process of dispute resolution, provide appropriate information as reasonably requested, and show a commitment to making the process work.

Commercial lenders could support this proposal by requiring a demonstration that an effective dispute resolution mechanism is available as a condition of loans.

- *A Product Stewardship Initiative*
Industry needs to collaborate with regulatory authorities, downstream users, and other groups to develop sound, science-based means of ensuring safe use, re-use, and eventual disposal of its products. A Product Stewardship Initiative could promote greater exchange of information and integration of views with the industry's principal customers and intermediary processors, recyclers, and others. This initiative could build on the work already undertaken by the Non-Ferrous Metals Consultative Forum on Sustainable Development, which has indicated that further development of the stewardship concept needs to be done by selecting some real issues in real settings and working with companies and stakeholders on a pilot basis.

As part of this process, national governments need to continue to identify incentives and disincentives for recycling and innovative design in metals use and to develop policies on them. They need to develop national strategies for recycling and extending product life, with measurable targets, to include collection networks, infrastructure, and investment in recycling technologies.

A Product Stewardship Initiative would lead to improved understanding of:

- energy, water, land use, recycling, and re-use issues;
- life-cycle analysis as a management tool for sustainable development;
- appropriate recycling technology transfers to developing countries; and
- possible product certification schemes.

- *A Sustainable Development Support Facility*
There is wide agreement that the complex and demanding tasks of proper management of the minerals sector may tax available expertise and the capacity of government and other essential actors, particularly where they do not have a great deal of prior experience with the sector's operations. A Sustainable Development Support Facility could be developed to serve as a central clearinghouse for information on who is doing what in the sector and suggest ways to coordinate and target efforts of donors and others. It could serve:

- as an independent source of capacity building or advice to government on issues such as emergency planning or implementation of local emergency preparedness plans;
- as a supplement to government departments charged with technical tasks such as safety inspection of tailings dams;
- to help develop the technical standards necessary for effective impact assessment in the minerals sector;
- to assess potential for acid rock drainage and strategies for dealing with it; and
- to assist local governments, companies, or others in the development of Community Sustainable Development Plans and to strengthen the capacity needed for effective planning for closure.

The Facility could be supported by one or more donor agencies, with a pledge to support it long enough to give it a chance to prove its worth, and could be administered by the World Bank Group as a trust fund. An important and useful role in its management could also be played by the World Conservation Union–IUCN.

Applications for assistance could be made by any government, NGO, UN body, trade union, or other appropriate organization that was committed to cooperative approaches to sustainable development concerns in the minerals sector. General policies would be established and applications reviewed by a balanced panel with representation of various stakeholder interests at the global level, or by several such panels operating at the regional level.

• *Reporting Guidelines*
A harmonized system of reporting guidelines is needed
to ensure that key aspects of company practice are
publicly reported to a standard that informs internal
and external stakeholders about the sustainable
development performance of corporations and major
projects. This requires reporting and performance
indicators that allow for innovation and for differences
at the level of specifics. The system will only be
effective if there is trust, transparency, and
accountability in terms of those doing the reporting –
in the systems devised, the mechanisms used to
generate the information, and the process for reporting
the data in a usable form to the target audience.

A multilateral organization such as the World Bank
could convene an experts group to draft a broad set of
principles and operational guidelines for reporting.
Organizations such as the World Bank and the UN
Environment Programme (UNEP) as well as minerals
associations and minerals corporations should participate
in developing the guidelines. Appropriate and meaningful
NGO and community involvement is also key.

In defining guidelines, the sector should work with
organizations such as the Global Reporting Initiative
and the International Organization for Standardization
to achieve comparability between sectors and to ensure
the transfer of existing knowledge.

Research into the identification and development of
key indicators for public reporting needs to continue.
Organizations such as the Minerals and Energy
Research Network (MERN) that have taken a lead in
this field should continue to develop indicators and to
explore how they relate to each other and how they fit
into management systems. The eventual aim is to
construct a set of 'must have' generic yet sector-specific
indicators at the project and corporate level, supported
by a secondary set of indicators that could be
applicable at particular sites.

The UN, the World Bank, and governments have a
role to play in creating a feedback loop. Equally,
industry organizations such as ICMM and others have
a role to play in ensuring that their members
understand and adopt the standards specified in the
principles, guidelines, and public reporting criteria.

• *Protected Areas and Mining Initiative*
Increased collaboration is required at the international

level among key actors including IUCN and other
conservation organizations, governments, and NGOs to
resolve issues related to protected areas management.
The MMSD process highlighted the following possible
actions, among others:

• Establish a multistakeholder forum that aims to
achieve consensus on 'no-go' zones for mining, on a
case-by-case basis, with a priority for World Heritage
Sites.
• Develop a package of published 'better-practice'
guidance on mining and protected areas, developed
through collaborative research and capacity building
partnerships, to be showcased at the next World
Parks Congress in 2003 and the next conference of
the Parties to the Convention on Biological
Diversity in 2004.
• Establish clear criteria that can be used to decide if
mining is possible near protected areas, which should
then be applied to its control and to the assessment
of inherited mines in protected areas (especially
those existing before the area was protected).
• Work towards improving the transparency of
decision-making around the assignment of protected
areas categories, developing more detailed technical
guidance regarding the application of the categories
system.
• Undertake 'high resolution' mapping through key
institutions that will identify the scale and extent of
threats to and opportunities for protected areas
posed by mining and other sectoral activities.

• *Mineral Legacies Initiative*
During the MMSD process, an overwhelming majority
of participants agreed on the importance of
remediating abandoned mine sites where there is a
clear threat to public health and safety or ongoing
impact on important water resources. Improving
conditions at abandoned sites can yield immense social
and environmental benefits for a relatively small
investment.

The focus at least initially should be on true 'orphan'
sites, where no former owner or operator can be
identified and all would agree that the problem is a
public responsibility. Priority should be given to sites
where remedial action will offer a clear payoff in
improved public health and safety, more usable water
supplies, or other demonstrable benefits, such as
protection of biodiversity. Another priority is projects
in low-income countries with significant abandoned

mine legacy problems and those with particularly pressing social legacies of mining communities.

Governments with many abandoned mines but few resources could be given grants to determine priorities for the cases most urgently needing attention and to develop project proposals that could then be funded. High priority should be given to sites where the rehabilitation of the environmental legacy will generate needed employment and skill-building and be a source of livelihoods.

Most observers agree to the need to such action, but not on its financing or administration. Yet there are good if not perfect models for the administration – the Global Environment Facility is one; a trust fund established by donors and administered by the World Bank or regional development banks would be another. The World Bank has financed work at abandoned mines or other mineral facilities in the past. At a minimum it could coordinate its future support for such activities with a trust or other entity managing this work. The Bank might well find other ways to support the effort.

Mining companies could raise the profile of this issue by ensuring that it is discussed and debated at the Global Mining Initiative meeting in Toronto in May 2002. One possibility would be for a group of companies to take the initiative by pledging an initial contribution to the trust fund on the condition that it be matched by government and other donors in some specified percentage.

At the World Summit on Sustainable Development in August–September 2002, world leaders could use the opportunity of meeting in one of the world's most important mining centres – and one that shares with others a legacy of problems from that activity – to call for a full-scale feasibility study for a Mineral Legacies Initiative. Establishing this fund would require a number of nations to commit together to a programme to make it viable for at least several years. Protection of public goods such as water supply and public health and safety would have to be the primary goals, but the programme could also be useful in building skills and generating employment.

• *Financial Surety*
Governments recognize that some industries (such as

power plants, chemical facilities, and mines) have the potential to leave behind large social costs. To make sure they do not inherit these costs, some insist that companies provide a bond or financial guarantee to ensure that they will comply with closure plans. The company guarantees in this way that the specific obligations for mine closure will be carried out; it also ensures internalization of costs and promotes economic efficiency. Without such surety, the legacy of abandoned sites and their attendant problems are certain to grow.

Developing countries have often not adopted financial surety for a number of reasons. Many have just finished revising their laws and regulations to create incentives for investment; guarantees and new requirements may be seen as a disincentive. Small and medium-sized companies with limited capacity to comply with bonding or financial surety obligations may collectively be a significant source of jobs. Finally, developing an effective plan requires flexibility, which implies discretionary authority. Discretionary authority implies delays and may lead to corruption. Despite these obstacles, some way must be found to capture the benefits of financial surety. Progress on this issue is important. The World Bank recognizes this as a priority concern.

The best way forward seems to be for the World Bank and the world's mines ministers together to convene a dialogue, starting with a high-level conference, to find ways of reconciling the clear benefits to be achieved by appropriate guarantee systems, national policies for minerals investment, and the growing desire of many commercial and non-commercial lenders to ensure that the projects they finance do not wind up adding to the world's inventory of sites abandoned without proper precaution.

• *A Global Labour-Management Agreement*
There could be a global-level agreement between labour federations representing workers in the minerals sector, such as the International Federation of Chemical, Energy, Mine and General Workers' Unions (ICEM), and international organizations representing companies for broad cooperation in support of sustainable development. Organized labour could take the lead to suggest elements of the agreement. These may include traditional areas of interest such as the training, health, and safety of workers, but could also

include broader community concerns. The agreement could be linked to counterpart agreements at the national and local levels.

• *Forum on Mining, Minerals, and Sustainable Development*
To drive the sustainable development debate forward, it is important to establish effective and ongoing dialogues. Much of the dialogue to date has been partial. Many actors in the sector have felt the need to move towards an ongoing results-oriented dialogue that adds value. During the course of MMSD, many serious issues were raised. While few people deny the validity of these issues, they may phrase them differently, or see different solutions ahead, or distrust others' intentions in raising them. It is impossible to deal with all the issues facing the sector at once. Effective leadership could focus the agenda on a manageable number of issues and attempt to achieve convergence on a ranking of priorities without agreeing on solutions. Discussion of this kind requires a neutral space or spaces where ideas can be aired openly without excessive concern. The MMSD regional processes that have begun this task would hope to continue in differing forms, at either the national or the regional levels.

This argues for a process or processes that can stay in effective communication with all principal stakeholders and that is not controlled by any of them individually but 'belongs' to all of them as a group. In the forest products industry, a similar need led to the creation

of a Forest Stewardship Council. In the dam building sector, it led to the World Commission on Dams. The Responsible Care initiative in the chemicals industry has a multistakeholder stewardship council. In the minerals sector, this model has been pursued, with variations, for things such as the recent cyanide code, the White Horse Mining Initiative, and the MMSD Project itself. Processes of this type can create results that could not be created in any other way. Whatever anyone's view of the cyanide code, for instance, it is clearly a better and stronger product for having come through such a process.

With these models in mind, a Forum on Mining, Minerals, and Sustainable Development could be established. This would not have to be a permanent bureaucracy. It could, for example, resemble the Toronto Conference in May 2002, but in a more advanced version at some determined intervals in the future. The Forum could perhaps achieve these goals:

• Establishing priorities, not just for industry or for government, but for a wide range of actors in the sector, so that each could focus on a manageable number of tasks in the near term.
• Setting guidelines for processes directed at individual issues, to give all concerned a greater confidence in their legitimacy and reduce the transaction costs in setting them up.
• Endorsing processes if they met those guidelines, adding to their legitimacy and increasing peoples'

Key Actions at the Global Level	
Actions	**Responsibilities**
• Complaints and dispute resolution mechanism	• Companies, representatives of affected stakeholder groups, commercial lenders
• Product Stewardship Initiative	• Non-Ferrous Metals Consultative Forum on Sustainable Development, industry associations, NGOs, governments, labour
• Sustainable Development Support Facility	• Governments, international organizations, NGOs such as IUCN, stakeholders
• Reporting guidelines	• ICMM–industry associations, NGOs and stakeholders, Global Reporting Initiative, companies, international organizations
• Protected areas and mining	• Conservation NGOs such as IUCN, governments, companies, associations such as ICMM, communities
• Dialogue on Mineral Legacies	• Mining industry, world leaders
• Dialogue on financial surety	• World Bank, mine ministers
• Global labour-management agreement	• International labour unions such as ICEM and international industry associations such as ICMM
• Forum on Mining, Minerals, and Sustainable Development	• All actors

confidence in participating in them.
* Endorsing the results of those processes, giving them broader acceptance and ensuring that their principles are more quickly incorporated into company policy, industry protocols, best practice guidelines, lending policies of banks, and laws and regulations.

Setting up such an endeavour requires a significant amount of time, energy, and money. The World Commission on Dams, for example, spent an entire year establishing the rules under which the Commission would operate and selecting its members before it began its work programme. But if it can be achieved once, it should not be allowed to die, which would involve repeating the investment the next time high-level dialogue were needed. Investment is made not only by the management of the process and its sponsors but by everyone – all stakeholders have to invest in examining the process, setting the rules under which it will go forward, and developing confidence that it will not work to their disadvantage.

The MMSD Project has identified a number of issues ripe for progress in a Forum – management of tailings and other large-volume wastes, action against corruption, integrated planning for closure, community health and mining, and biodiversity and protected areas, to name just a few. But progress on any of them will require engagement of a variety of stakeholders. Effective engagement that produces results will require attention to process, which requires investment.
There is no effective alternative. A way to proceed, and one that could yield better long-term results, would be to make the investment once, instead of every time an issue came up.

Whatever the reaction to this suggestion, it is clear that it is easier to seek solutions with some kind of a structure. If the mineral sector returns to dialogues among some but not all key actors, happening more or less by accident, and fading as fast as they began, the sector will be going backwards. The goal for sustainable development in the mining and minerals sector should instead be increasingly inclusive and intentional dialogues that are deliberately planned and that engage ever-broader circles, leading to ongoing engagement for the long term.

There is an informal proposal for such a forum from the UN family. Others suggest that the Forum could develop out of existing mechanisms such as the

International Study Group's Non-Ferrous Metals Consultative Forum on Sustainable Development.

Whatever the future of the Forum proposal, at a minimum there should be a recognition that establishing communication and discussion among interested parties on a national, regional, or global basis requires a committed effort and a significant investment of time and money. Processes are expensive at least in part because of the investment needed to establish these links. Finding a home in an institution capable of maintaining the databases that projects – including MMSD – have established and of circulating periodic bulletins, perhaps containing a registry of current research activities, is an important investment in the future of dialogue. MERN, the UNCTAD/UNEP Mineral Resources Forum, or a new Union for Minerals and Sustainable Development are all possible homes for such a body.

A Final Thought...

The MMSD Project did not try to resolve the many economic, environmental, social, and governance issues facing the mining and minerals sector – no single effort could. But the project did try to turn a spotlight on the range of challenges raised by society's need for and production of minerals. Judging by the input and reactions during the two years of the Project, that goal was achieved. The many people who made contributions to the process – through papers, workshop participation, comments on successive drafts, emails with news from all corners of the world – confirmed that the minerals sector involves much more than digging ore out of the ground.

Although *Breaking New Ground* is the final report of the MMSD Project, it is not, of course, the final word on this complex subject. But we hope that for the minerals sector it is a helpful step along a road towards sustainable development that includes all those affected: policymakers, business leaders, public interest campaigners, people working in mines, local communities, and – very important – consumers. All these people must join the discussion and take action if the world is to find a better way to meet society's needs.

APPENDICES

Appendix 1: The MMSD Project

Appendix 2: MMSD Consultation Activities

APPENDIX 1: THE MMSD PROJECT

The Sponsors Group

The Sponsors Group was convened by the World Business Council for Sustainable Development to represent the organizations supporting and financing the project. Its members included 25 of the world's largest mining companies as well as a variety of governments, international institutions, non-governmental organizations, universities, and foundations. The Sponsors Group did not have any influence over the project's conclusions but contributed information and contacts. Members of the group also actively participated in MMSD workshops and meetings. The Sponsors Group adhered to a charter (available on the CD-ROM) and signed a joint statement on the MMSD project and this report (see page viii). Yolanda Kakabadse (President of IUCN – The World Conservation Union) and Sir Robert Wilson (Chairman of Rio Tinto plc) acted as co-chairs of the group.

Sponsors were:

Alcan Inc
Alcoa Inc
Anglo American plc
Anglovaal Mining Ltd
BHP Billiton
Caterpillar Inc
Codelco Chile – Corporación Nacional del Cobre
Colorado School of Mines
Comisión Chilena del Cobre
Conservation International
CRU International Ltd
*Department for International Development, Government of the United
    Kingdom*
Environment Australia, Government of Australia
Freeport-McMoRan Copper and Gold Inc
Gold Fields Ltd
HATCH Associates Ltd
*International Federation of Chemical, Energy, Mine and General Workers'
    Unions (ICEM)*
IUCN – The World Conservation Union
KPMG
Lonmin plc
Mackay School of Mines, University of Nevada, Reno
M.I.M. Holdings Ltd
Mitsubishi Materials Corporation / Mitusbishi Corporation
Mitsui Mining and Smelting Co., Ltd
Natural Resources Canada, Government of Canada
Newmont Mining Corporation
Nippon Mining & Metals Co., Ltd
Noranda Inc
Norsk Hydro ASA
Pasminco Ltd
Phelps Dodge Corporation
Placer Dome Inc
PricewaterhouseCoopers
Rio Tinto plc
Sibirsky Aluminium Group (Sibal)
Somincor
Sumitomo Metal Mining
Teck Cominco Ltd
United Nations Environment Programme
WMC Resources Ltd
The World Bank Group

Support from the Rockefeller Foundation is gratefully acknowledged. We also thank the Global Reporting Initiative for its collaboration with MMSD.

The assistance of Robert Court and Peter Eggleston of Rio Tinto plc, who acted as special liaisons with the Sponsors Group, was greatly appreciated.

This list excludes additional regional sponsorship.

APPENDIX 1: Continued

The Assurance Group

The Assurance Group was an independent international panel of 25 individuals from key stakeholder groups representing diverse areas of expertise in the mining and minerals sector. The members offered advice and guidance to the Work Group and met seven times to discuss progress. Initial members were appointed by the Project Coordinator in consultation with the Project Director. Subsequent members were selected and approved by the Assurance Group through its Nominations Committee, which assessed under-represented stakeholder clusters, held independent consultations to identify candidates, and selected individuals. The Assurance Group adhered to a charter (available on the CD-ROM) and signed a joint statement on the MMSD project and its outputs (see page vii).

Assurance Group members were:

Duma Nkosi (Chair), Executive Mayor of Ekurhuleni Metro, South Africa (May 2000)★

Glenn Miller (Vice-Chair), Director, Graduate Program in Environmental Sciences and Health at the University of Nevada, United States (May 2000)

Jacqueline Aloisi de Larderel, Director of the Division of Technology, Industry and Economics of UNEP, France (January 2001)

Richard Baldes, independent biological consultant on tribal lands in the United States (September 2001)

Patricia Caswell, Executive Director, Global Sustainability at RMIT University, Australia (May 2000)

Anna Cederstav, Staff Scientist at the International Program of Earthjustice Legal Defense Fund, United States (January 2001)

Mick Dodson, Chair of the Australian Institute of Aboriginal and Torres Strait Islander Studies, Australia (September 2001)

Cholpon Dyikanova, National Manager of the Community Business Forum, Kyrgyzstan (January 2001)

Colin Filer, Head of the Social and Environmental Studies Division, Papua New Guinea National Research Institute and part-time Fellow in the Department of Anthropology and the Resource Management in Asia-Pacific Project at the Research School of Pacific and Asian Studies in the Australian National University (January 2001)

Douglas Fraser, private consultant providing guidance and advice in the strategic application of sustainable business practices. Former Vice President of Sustainable Development of Placer Dome Inc., Canada (May 2000)

Reg Green, Head of Health, Safety and Environmental Affairs at the International Federation of Chemical, Energy, Mine and General Workers' Unions, Belgium (September 2001)

Gerard Holden, Managing Director and Global Head of Mining and Metals, Barclays Capital, United Kingdom (January 2001)

Namakau Kaingu, Chair of the Southern African Development Community's Women in Mining Trust, Zambia (January 2001)

Antonio La Viña, Director of the Biological Resources Program of the World Resources Institute, United States. Former Undersecretary for Legal and Legislative Affairs of the Department of Environment and Natural Resources of the Philippines (May 2000)

Kathryn McPhail, Program Manager in the World Bank, United States (January 2001)

Daniel Meilán, independent consultant and former Sub-secretary of Mining of Argentina (May 2000)

Maria Ligia Noronha, Fellow of the Policy Analysis Division of the Tata Energy Research Institute, India (May 2000)

Manuel Pulgar-Vidal, Executive Director of the Peruvian Society for Environmental Law, Peru (May 2000)

Leon Rajaobelina, Executive Director of the Conservation International's Madagascar Programme, Madagascar (May 2000)

Charles Secrett, Executive Director of Friends of the Earth, United Kingdom (May 2000)

John Stewart, consultant associated with the Chamber of Mines of South Africa (January 2001)

Osvaldo Sunkel, Professor of Economics and Director of the Centre for Public Policy Analysis, University of Chile (May 2000)

Helmut Weidner, Senior Researcher at the Social Science Research Centre in Berlin, Germany (May 2000)

Doug Yearley, Chairman Emeritus of Phelps Dodge Corporation, United States (May 2000)

Senzeni Zokwana, President of the National Union of Mineworkers of South Africa (January 2001)

Jay Hair was Chair of the Assurance Group until September 2001.

Roger Augustine and Damien Roland were members of the Assurance Group until September 2001.

★Joining dates are shown in brackets.

APPENDIX 1: Continued

The Work Group

The Work Group was responsible for executing MMSD at the global level and for coordinating regional activities under the leadership of a Project Director. The group's main duties were undertaking research, commissioning and supervising research projects, convening workshops, communicating with stakeholders, writing the report, and disseminating information about the project. The Work Group, a multidisciplinary team from 10 countries, was headquartered at the IIED in London and adhered to a charter (available on the CD-ROM).

Work Group members were:

Richard Sandbrook, Project Coordinator

Luke Danielson, Project Director
Caroline Digby, Research Manager
Bernice Lee, Assistant Project Coordinator
Frank McShane, Coordinator of Stakeholder Engagement
Elisabeth Wood, Assistant Project Manager

Linda Starke, Report Editor

Sarah Henson, Project Administrator
Lucy Brain-Gabbott, Project PA
Tonia Savage, Project PA

Gabriela Flores Zavala, Communications and External Relations Executive
Guy Collis, Information Assistant
Ben Sandbrook, Report Coordinator
Andrea Steel, Project Assistant

Research Fellows:
Juan Carlos Altamirano
Stijn De Lameilleure
Gabriel Eweje
Anne-Marie Fleury
Benoit Gervais
Bruce Howard
Silvia Kyeyune
Patricio Leyton
Juan Velasquez

Other Researchers:
Wai Lee Kui
Hannah Reid
Amy Twigge

Other Contributors to the Report:
Robin Adams, Steve Bass, Josh Bishop, Nigel Cross, George Greene, Maryanne Grieg-Gran, Mark Halle, Izabella Koziell, Charlie Pye-Smith, Meredith Sassoon, Omar Sattaur, Peter Stalker, Jeanne Tan, and Halina Ward

Also thanks to Priyanka Anand, Beatrice Blumenthal, Alissa Chapman, Lilian Chatterjee, Kimberly Clarke, Bob Dick, Pedro-Andres Garzon, Vanessa Gordon, Rob Lake, Frances MacDermott, Catherine McCloskey, Lutske Newton, Clare Palmer, Katharine Pincham, Anthony Polak, Frances Reynolds, Ben Richardson, Nick Robins, Jacqueline Saunders, Glenn Sigurdson, Jonathan Sinclair-Wilson, Fernando Wittig, and the staff at Asset Graphics

APPENDIX 1: Continued

Regional Partners

MMSD Australia
The Australian Minerals and Energy Environment Foundation (AMEEF)

Postal address:
C/O Swinburne University
PG Building
144 High Street
Prahran, Victoria 3181
Australia
Tel: +61 0 3 9214 6804
Fax: +61 0 3 9214 6805
E-mail: ameef@ameef.org.au
http://www.ameef.com.au/mmsd

Regional team: Bren Sheehy (coordinator), Chris Burnup, and Victoria Cole

MMSD North America
The International Institute for Sustainable Development (IISD) in Winnipeg, Canada

Postal address:
161 Portage Avenue East
6th Floor
Winnipeg
Manitoba
R3B 0Y4
Canada
Tel: +1 204 958 7700
Fax: +1 204 958 7710
E-mail: info@iisd.ca
http://www.iisd.org/mmsd

Regional team: Anthony Hodge (coordinator), Michael McPhie, and Dirk van Zyl

MMSD South America

Regional Coordinators:
The Mining Policy Research Initiative (MPRI) of the International Development Research Center (IDRC) in Montevideo, Uruguay

Postal address:
Av. Brasil 2655
CP 11300
Montevideo
Uruguay
Tel: +598 2 709 0042
Fax: +598 2 708 6776
E-mail: mpri@idrc.org.uy
http://www.mmsd-la.org

The Centro de Investigación y Planificación del Medio Ambiente (CIPMA) in Santiago, Chile

Postal address:
Bucarest 046-D
Providencia
Casilla 16362
Santiago 9
Chile
Tel: +56 2 334 1091/2
Fax: +56 2 334 1095
E-mail: info@cipma.cl

Regional team: Hernán Blanco and Cristina Echavarría (coordinators), Patricia González, Carolina Quintana and Enrique Gallicchio (MPRI), Gustavo Lagos (Pontificia Universidad Católica de Chile), Valeria Torres, Beatriz Bustos, and Claudia Gana (CIPMA)

National Coordinators:

Bolivia
Servicios Ambientales S.A. in La Paz

Postal address:
Edificio Fortaleza 302
Av. Arce 2799
Zona de San Jorge
P.O. Box 1387
La Paz
Bolivia
Tel: +591 2 243 4512 / 243 5014
Fax: +591 2 243 5014
E-mail: jceu_eco@ceibo.entelnet.bo

Fundación MEDMIN in La Paz

Postal address:
Rosendo Gutierrez
Esq. Sanchez Lima N° 482
La Paz
Bolivia

Tel: +591 2 235 9409
Fax: +591 8 211 2337
E-mail: medmin@mail.megalink.com

National team: Juan Carlos Enríquez and Mario Luna

APPENDIX 1: Continued

Brazil
Centro de Tecnologia Mineral – CETEM in Rio de Janeiro

Postal address:
Av. Ipê, 900, Cidade Universitaria
Ilha do Fundão
21941-590
Rio de Janeiro, RJ
Brazil
Tel: +55 21 386 57302
Fax: +55 21 2260 9154 - 260 2837
E-mail: webmaster@cetem.gov.br

National team: María Laura Barreto (coordinator), Bruce Jonson, Francisco Fernández, Gloria Janaina de Castro Sirotheau, María Helena Rocha Lima, and Samir Nahass

Chile
The Centro de Investigación y Planificación del Medio Ambiente – CIPMA in Santiago (See above for details)

National team: Hernán Blanco, Gustavo Lagos (Pontificia Universidad Católica de Chile), Valeria Torres, Beatriz Bustos, and Claudia Gana

Ecuador
Fundación Ambiente y Sociedad in Quito

Postal address:
Alemania N30-92 y Av. Eloy Alfaro
Quito
Ecuador
Tel: +593 2 223 7064 / 290 4815
Fax: +593 2 290 4815
E-mail: ambientesociedad@porta.net

Fundación Futuro Latinoamericano in Quito

Postal address:
Casilla Postal 17-17-558
Quito
Ecuador
Tel and fax: +593 2 292 9635 - 292 0636
E-mail: ffla@fulano.org

National team: Fabián Sandoval (coordinator), Jorge Albán, Miguel Carvajal, Carlos Chamorro, and Diego Pazmiño

Peru
Grupo de Análisis para el Desarrollo (GRADE) in Lima

Postal address:
Av. Del Ejército 1870
Lima 27
Peru
Tel. +51 1 264 1780
Fax: +51 1 264 1882
E-mail: postmaster@grade.org.pe

National team: Manuel Glave and Juana Kuramoto

MMSD Southern Africa
The University of the Witwatersrand in Johannesburg, South Africa

Postal address:
School of Mining Engineering
Private Bag 3
WITS 2050
South Africa
Tel: +27 11 717 7422
Fax: +27 11 339 8295
E-mail: Hoadley@egoli.min.wits.ac.za
http://www.mining.wits.ac.za/mmsd

The Council for Scientific and Industrial Research (CSIR) in Stellenbosch, South Africa

Postal address:
Environmentek Integration Unit (EIU)
P.O. Box 320
Jan Cilliers Street
Stellenbosch
7599
South Africa
Tel: +27 21 888 2400
Fax: +27 21 888 2693
E-mail: aweaver@csir.co.za
http://csir.co.za

Regional team: Alex Weaver, Daniel Limpitlaw, and Marie Hoadley

APPENDIX 2: MMSD CONSULTATION ACTIVITIES

MMSD Global Workshops

MMSD convened a series of workshops on specific themes. These served to gather stakeholders from mining companies and labour, non-governmental organizations, research institutions, academia, community groups, and international organizations from throughout the world. They provided valuable opportunities for sharing perspectives and played a pivotal role in informing the project report. More than 750 participants attended MMSD workshops organized at the global level:

- *Strategic Planning Workshop*, 4–6 May 2001, London, United Kingdom
- *Preparing for Implementation*, 24–25 July 2000, Geneva, Switzerland
- *The Role of Financial Institutions in Sustainable Development: The Case of Mining*, 10–12 January 2001, Washington DC, United States, jointly organized by MMSD, World Bank, and UNEP
- *Small-scale Mining in South America*, 24 January 2001, Santiago, Chile
- *Planning Meeting for Research on Access to Information in the Mining and Minerals Sector*, 14 March 2001, Toronto, Canada
- *Finance, Mining, and Sustainability*, 8–9 April 2001, Washington DC, United States, jointly organized by MMSD, World Bank, and UNEP
- *Long-run Minerals Availability*, 22–23 April 2001, Washington DC, United States
- *The Role of Public Participation*, 25–27 May 2001, Woodstock VT, United States
- *Mining and Biodiversity I*, 11–12 June 2001, London, United Kingdom
- *Armed Conflict and Natural Resources*, 11 July 2001, London, United Kingdom, co-hosted with the International Institute for Strategic Studies
- *Large Volume Waste*, 15–17 July 2001, Vancouver BC, Canada
- *Voluntary Initiatives for the Mineral Sector*, 18 July 2001, Santa Fe NM, United States
- *Life Cycle Analysis*, 9–10 August 2001, New York, United States
- *Managing Mineral Wealth*, 15–17 August 2001, London, United Kingdom
- *Meeting of the MMSD/GRI Multistakeholder Advisory Panel on Public Reporting in the Mining and Minerals Sector*, 23–24 August 2001, Boston, MA, United States
- *Human Rights Issues in the Mining and Minerals Sector*, 6 September 2001, Transparency International, Berlin, Germany
- *Corruption Issues in the Mining and Minerals Sector*, 7 September 2001, Transparency International, Berlin, Germany
- *Worker and Community Health in the Mining Sector*, 10 September 2001, London, United Kingdom, co-hosted by MMSD and the Environmental Epidemiology Unit of the London School of Hygiene & Tropical Medicine's Department of Public Health and Policy
- *Indigenous Peoples and Relationships with the Mining Sector*, 27–28 September 2001, Quito, Ecuador
- *Corporate Social Responsibility – From Words to Action*, 15–16 October 2001, London, United Kingdom, jointly organized by the Royal Institute of International Affairs
- *Mining and Biodiversity II*, 25–26 October 2001, London, United Kingdom
- *Artisanal and Small-scale Mining*, 19–20 November 2001, London, United Kingdom

- *Second Meeting of the MMSD/GRI Multistakeholder Advisory Panel on Public Reporting in the Mining and Minerals Sector*, 27 November 2001, Vancouver, BC, Canada
- *Dialogue on Access to Information in the Mining Sector*, 28–30 November 2001, Vancouver, BC, Canada
- *Financing, Mining, and Sustainability – Exploring Sound Investment Decision Processes*, 14–15 January 2002, Paris, France, jointly organized by MMSD, World Bank, and UNEP
- *Indigenous Peoples and the Mining Sector*, 4–6 February 2002, Melbourne, Australia

Principles of Engagement

The following Principles of Engagement governed the way MMSD approached engaging stakeholders in its activities:

Those involved in an MMSD activity do so with the assurance that the Project is committed to providing the opportunity for participants to interact, with these expectations:

- MMSD provides an opportunity for people both to inform each other within the context of a project which seeks to describe the global mineral cycle, and also to offer advice and guidance to the Project.

- We hope to identify and understand the diversity of perspectives, values and interests that can help build the foundation for positive change. Views have to be freely expressed and the risks of such expression reduced. This is a forum in which individuals or groups can investigate ideas.

- There is a need for a place where views can be exchanged frankly and openly. MMSD has no authority to impose solutions on anyone.

- The Project should strive to identify where it can best help to guide the flow of discussion. The objective should be to help develop areas of common ground, understand where differences exist, and the underlying reasons for them.

- Wherever possible, we should widen the networks of connections and identify ways of addressing challenges, within and beyond the life of the Project.

- Participating in, or contributing to workshops or other events, commenting on documents produced, suggesting participants for meetings, and other interactions with the Project are not and will not be portrayed as an endorsement of MMSD. It is important that the basis for participation be widely understood.

- Notes or minutes prepared by MMSD will report important comments and points of view but will not attribute them to specific participants unless this is requested by the person making the statement. Exchange of ideas is freer when unknown consequences can be minimised.

- The notes from workshops should be reviewed by a representative group of attendees, agreed at the meeting, prior to finalisation. Notes will typically be of a summary nature and will include a list of participants. There should be an opportunity to discuss the contents of the notes and ensure that everyone is comfortable with them prior to their wider circulation.

- There should be an opportunity to discuss these Principles of Engagement at the outset of any activity to ensure that participants are comfortable with it and that it is appropriate for the purpose. It is in no way a constraint on the participants to develop further or additional understandings as are appropriate in the circumstances.

APPENDIX 2: Continued

MMSD Draft Report Comment Process

The commenting process for the MMSD Draft Report took place between 4 March and 17 April 2002. In total, MMSD received comments from 102 individuals and organizations, with over 510 pages of text. All but five sets of comments were submitted in English. The five non-English submissions were in Spanish. All comments received are included in the CD-ROM.

Profession of comment providers:

Academics	17
Consultants (corporate and independent)	20
Governments	14
Industry Associations	13
International Organisations	4
Labour	1
Mining companies	8
NGOs	19
Private Sector (other industries, banks, etc)	6

Origins of comment providers (in terms of organizational affiliation):

Asia	6
Australia	11
Europe	37
North America	35
South America	7
Southern Africa	6

Together with MMSD regional partners in Australia, North America, South America and southern Africa, four regional forums were held in March and April 2002 to obtain comments from regional stakeholders. Over 250 stakeholders took part in these forums.

Region Forums	Number of Participants
Australia	150
North America	19
South America	58
Southern Africa	29

Acronyms and Abbreviations

AAG	Academic Advisory Group
AAID	Accelerated Area Integrated Development (Philippines)
AD	acid drainage
AFR	average fatalities ratio
AI	Amnesty International
AMEEF	Australian Minerals and Energy Environment Foundation
ANCSA	Alaska National Interest Land Conservation Act
APEC	Asia Pacific Economic Cooperation
APELL	Awareness and Preparedness for Emergencies at a Local Level
ASM	artisanal and small-scale mining
BPD	Business Partners for Development
CAMA	Canadian Aboriginal Minerals Association
CAMMA	Annual Conference of Mines Ministers of the Americas
CAO	Compliance Advisor / Ombudsman
CASM	Communities and Small-scale Mining
CBD	United Nations Convention on Biodiversity
CBO	community-based organization
CDA	Cooperative Development Authority (Philippines)
CIPMA	Centro de Investigación y Planificación del Medio Ambiente (Chile)
CEPMLP	Centre for Energy, Petroleum and Mineral Law and Policy, University of Dundee (UK)
CERES	Coalition for Environmentally Responsible Economies
CETEM	Centro de Tecnologia Mineral (Brazil)
CIZ	Community Interest Zone (Canada)
Conama	National Environmental Commission (Chile)
Corema	Regional Environmental Commission (Chile)
CPI	Corruption Perceptions Index
CSDP	Community Sustainable Development Plan
CTE	Centro Técnico Escondida (Chile)
DEMR	Department of Energy and Mineral Resources (Indonesia)
DFID	Department for International Development (UK)
DRC	Democratic Republic of Congo
DRI	direct reduced iron
E3	Environmental Excellence in Exploration (Canada)
EAP	electric arc furnace
ECA	export credit agencies
ECJ	European Court of Justice
ECDG	Export Credits Guarantee Department (UK)
EDC	Export Development Canada
EFIC	Export Finance and Insurance Corporation (Australia)
EIA	environmental impact assessment
EMS	environmental management system
EMU	European Monetary Union
EU	European Union
FDI	foreign direct investment
FSC	Forest Stewardship Council
GDP	gross domestic product
GMI	Global Mining Initiative
GRADE	Grupo de Análisis para el Desarrollo (Peru)
GRI	Global Reporting Initiative
HBI	Hot Briquetted Iron
HP	Hewlett-Packard
HPAL	high-pressure acid leaching
HWG	Huascaran Working Group (Peru)
IBA	International Bar Association
IBRD	International Bank for Reconstruction and Development (US)
ICC	indigenous cultural communities
ICEM	International Federation of Chemical, Energy, Mine and General Workers Unions (Belgium)
ICME	International Council on Metals and the Environment (Canada)
ICMM	International Council on Mining and Metals (UK)
IDA	International Development Association (US)
IFC	International Finance Corporation (US)
IIA	integrated impact assessment

IIED	International Institute for Environment and Development (UK)
IISD	International Institute for Sustainable Development (Canada)
ILO	International Labour Organization (Switzerland)
IMF	International Monetary Fund (US)
INAP	International Network for Acid Prevention (Canada)
IP	indigenous peoples
IPC	Integrated Pollution Control Licence (Ireland)
IPEC	International Programme on the Elimination of Child Labour
IPRA	Indigenous Peoples Rights Act (Philippines)
ISO	International Organization for Standardization
ITDG	Intermediate Technology Development Group (Zimbabwe)
IUCN	International Union for Conservation of Nature and Natural Resources
KG	kilograms
LCA	life-cycle assessment
LME	London Metal Exchange (UK)
MEND	Mine Environment Neutral Drainage program (Canada)
MERN	Mining and Energy Research Network (UK)
MIDR	mining-induced displacement and resettlement
MIGA	Multilateral Investment Guarantee Agency (US)
MRF	Mineral Resources Forum (Switzerland)
MRF	Mine Rehabilitation Fund (Philippines)
MMSD	Mining, Minerals and Sustainable Development (UK)
MPRI	Mining Policy Research Initiative (Uruguay)
NANA	North West Alaska Native Association (US)
NGO	non-governmental organization
NFM	non-ferrous metal
NPI	National Pollutant Inventory (Australia)
NUM	National Union of Mineworkers (South Africa)
OECD	Organisation for Economic Co-operation and Development
OHCHR	United Nations Office of the High Commissioner for Human Rights
OHS	occupational health and safety
OPIC	Overseas Private Investment Corporation (US)
PDAC	Prospectors and Developers Association of Canada
PGM	Platinum Group Metal
PNG	Papua New Guinea
PRTR	Pollutant Release and Transfer Register
QMM SA	QIT Madagascar Minerals SA
RMI	Rocky Mountain Institute (US)
SADC	Southern African Development Community
SBI	Sustainable Budget Index (Botswana)
SDA	sustainable development assessment
SEIA	social and environmental impact assessment
SETAC	Society for Environmental Toxicology and Chemistry
SHM	strategic health management
SIA	social impact assessment
SRI	socially responsible investment
TI	Transparency International
TRAC	Transfer Risk and Accelerate Closure Programme
TRAINS	United Nations Conference on Trade and Development, Trade Analysis and Information System
TRI	Toxics Release Inventory (USA)
UNCTAD	United Nations Conference on Trade and Development
UNDP	United Nations Development Programme
UNEP	United Nations Environment Programme
UNHCR	United Nations High Commission for Refugees
WBCSD	World Business Council for Sustainable Development
WBG	World Bank Group
WCD	World Commission on Dams
WEF	World Economic Forum
WGIP	Working Group on Indigenous Peoples
WHO	World Health Organization
WMMF	World Mines Ministers Forum
WRI	World Resources Institute
WTO	World Trade Organization

Bibliography

Adams, W W, and Kolhos, M E (1941) 'Metal and non-metal mine accidents in the United States during the calendar year 1939 (excluding coal mines)'. *Bureau of Mines Bulletin* 440. US Department of the Interior, Washington, D.C.

Adams, W W, and Wrenn, V E (1941) 'Quarry accidents in the United States during the calendar year 1939'. *Bureau of Mines Bulletin* 438. US Department of the Interior, Washington, D.C.

AllAfrica.com (2001) *Small Scale Gemstone Miners Cry for Help.* http://allafrica.com/stories/200107300021.html

AMEEF (2001 in prep.) *Managing the Impacts of the Australian Minerals Industry on Biodiversity.* Australian Centre for Mining and Environmental Research. Paper prepared for MMSD.

Amnesty International (1993) *Brazil: Amnesty International Calls For Protection of Indigenous Communities Following Massacre of Yanomami Indians.* Amnesty International, 20 August 1993.

Amnesty International (1997) *Amnesty International 1997 Annual Report.* Amnesty International, London.

Amnesty International (2001) *Human Rights Guidelines for Companies.* The Business Group, Amnesty International, UK.

Anderson, M, Fraser, D, and Zandvliet, D (2001) *Corporate Options: Constructive Engagement in Conflict Zones: Case Study of the Porgera Joint Venture (PJV) Gold Mining Operation, PNG.* Collaborative for Development Action.

Anglo American (2001) *Safety, Health and Environment Report 2000.* Anglo American, London.

AngloGold (1998) *Small & Medium Enterprise Development Initiative.* AngloGold, London.

Angola Peace Monitor (2001) Special Report VIII (2). 22 October.

Annan, K (1999) *A Compact for the New Century.* Speech at the World Economic Forum, Davos, Switzerland, 31 January.

Annan, K (2000) *Report to the Millennium Assembly.* United Nations, New York.

Appleton, J D et al. (1999) 'Mercury contamination associated with artisanal gold mining on the island of Mindanao: the Philippines'. *Science of the Total Environment* 228: 95–109.

Applied Geology Associates (1989) *Environmental, Socio-Economic and Public Health Review of Bougainville Copper Mine Panguna.* AGA Limited, New Zealand.

Archibald, L and Crnkovich, M (1999) *If Gender Mattered: A Case Study of Inuit Women, Land Claims and the Voisey Bay Nickel Project.* Status of Women Canada, Ottawa.

Ashton, P J, Love, D, Mahachi, H, and Dirks, P (2001) *An Overview of the Impact of Mining and Mineral Processing Operations on Water Resources and Water Quality in the Zambezi, Limpopo and Olifants Catchments in Southern Africa.* CSIR-Environmentek, Pretoria, South Africa, and Geology Department, University of Zimbabwe, Harare, Zimbabwe. Paper prepared for MMSD Southern Africa.

Asian Development Bank (1998) *Handbook on Resettlement: A Guide to Good Practice.* Asian Development Bank. Manila, Philippines.

Asogwa, S E (1988) 'The health benefits of mechanization at the Nigerian Coal Corporation'. *Accid. Anal. Prev.* 20(2) 103–108.

Aspinall, C (2001) *Final Report on Research of Small Scale Mining in Indonesia.* Paper prepared for MMSD.

Aste, J (2001) Presentation at the MMSD Managing Mineral Wealth Workshop, London, 15–17 August.

Australian Asia-Pacific Mining Network (1998) *Principles for the Conduct of Company Operations within the Minerals Industry, New South Wales.* Minerals Policy Institute, Australia.

Auty, R M, and Mikesell, R F (1998) *Sustainable Development in the Mineral Economies.* Clarendon Press, Oxford.

Ayres, R U, Ayres, L W, and Rade, I (2001) *The Life Cycle of Copper, its Co-products and Bi-products.* Paper prepared for MMSD.

Azcue, J M (ed) (1999) *Environmental Impacts of Mining Activities.* Springer, Germany.

Baldwin, R E (1966) *Economic Development and Export Growth: A Study of Northern Rhodesia, 1920–1960.* University of California Press, Berkeley.

Ballard, C (2001) *Human Rights and the Mining Sector in Indonesia.* Paper prepared for MMSD.

Bangulot, I J (2001) Affidavit of Retraction. Subscribed and sworn, September 26, Pasig City, Philippines, to Public Notary L M Lawas-Yutok.

Banks, G (1994) *Porgera Social Monitoring Program: Economic Modelling Project: Second Report.* PJV/ENV–20/93, February.

Banks, G (2001) *Baseline Study for Papua New Guinea.* Paper prepared for MMSD.

Banks, G, and Ballard, C (1997) *The Ok Tedi Settlement: Issues, Outcomes and Implications.* National Centre for Development Studies and Australia National University, Canberra.

Barberis, D (1998) *Negotiating Mining Agreements: Past, Present and Future Trends.* Kluwer Law International, London.

Barnett, H J, and Morse, C (1963) *Scarcity and Growth.* Johns Hopkins for Resources for the Future, Baltimore.

Barreto, L M (2001) *Projeto MMSD Relatório do Brasil.* Paper prepared for MMSD South America.

Barron, B B (1957) *Out of the Depths: The Story of John R. Lawson, a Labor leader.* Colorado Historical Commission and Denver Trades and Labor Assembly, Denver.

Bass, S (2001) *Change Towards Sustainability in Resource Use: Lessons for MMSD from the Forest Sector.* Paper prepared for MMSD.

Bass, S, and Hearne, R (1997) *Private Sector Forestry: A Review of Instruments for Ensuring Sustainability.* International Institute for Environment and Development, London.

Bass, S, Font, X, and Danielson, L (2001) 'Standards and certification: a leap forward or a step back for sustainable development?' *The Future Is Now.* Volume 2. International Institute for Environment and Development, London.

Bass, S, Thornber, K, Markopoulos, M, Roberts, S, and Grieg-Gran, M (2001) *Certification's Impact on Forests, Stakeholders and Supply Chains.* Instruments for Sustainable Private Sector Forestry Series. International Institute for Environment and Development, London.

Bastida, E (2001a) 'A review of the concept of security of mineral tenure: issues and challenges'. *Journal of Energy and Natural Resources Law* 19(1) pp. 31–43.

Bastida, E (2001b) *Integrating Sustainability into Legal Frameworks for Mining in some Selected Latin American Countries.* Paper prepared for MMSD.

Baumol, W, and Oates, W (1988) *The Theory of Environmental Policy* (2nd edition). Cambridge University Press, Cambridge.

BBC News (2001) 'Blood diamonds'. BBC News Internet Edition, 19 October. Available at http://news.bbc.co.uk/hi/english/audiovideo/programmes/correspondent/newsid_1604000/1604165.stm

Beattie, A (2000) 'Wolfensohn spends time with bank's critics'. *The Financial Times*, 23 September. London.

Beder, S (1997) *Global Spin: The Corporate Assault on Environmentalism.* Green Books, Totnes, UK.

Bell, L C (2001) 'Establishment of native ecosystems after mining – Australian experience across diverse biogeographical zones'. *Ecological Engineering* 17: 179–186.

BGR Hannover (1995) Mineralische Rohstoffe: Bausteine für die Wirtschaft. BGR, Hannover.

BHP Billiton (2001) *Health, Safety, Environment and Community Policy.* BHP Billiton, Melbourne.

Blair, T (2001) 'Foreword'. In *Resource Productivity: Making More with Less.* UK Government Policy and Innovation Unit.

Bonnell, S (2000) 'Social change in the Porgera Valley'. In Filer, C (ed) *Dilemmas of Development: The Social and Economic Impact of the Porgera Gold Mine 1989–1994*. Asia Pacific Press, The Australian National University and The National Research Institute Boroko, Australia.

Borax (2001) *Borax and Sustainable Development: 2000 Progress Report*. Published by Borax.

Botts, S (2001) *Antamina 'La Mina Peruana del Futuro'*. Presentation at the Sullivan Round Table, Kimberley, Canada, November.

Bourassa, M J, and Vaughan, W S (1999) *The Impact of Politics, Economics and Local Legislation on Exploration and Mining in PacRim Countries*. Presented at the PacRim /99 Congress, Bali, Indonesia, 13 October.

Brazilian Bureau of Mines (2001) *Anuário Mineral Brasileiro e Sumário Mineral Brasileiro*. Brazilian Bureau of Mines.

Brehaut, H (2001) *The Community Health Dimension of Sustainable Development in Developing Countries*. Global Sustainability Services Inc. Paper prepared for MMSD.

Brewer, K (2001) *Creating and Capturing Mineral Wealth: Government Perspectives*. Presentation at MMSD Managing Mineral Wealth Workshop, London, August 15–17.

British Petroleum (1986) *BP Statistical Review of World Energy*. British Petroleum, London.

British Petroleum (2001) *BP Statistical Review of World Energy*. British Petroleum, London.

Brooks, R R, Chambers M F, Nicks, L J, and Robinson, B H (1998) 'Phytomining'. *Trends in Plant Sciences* 3: 359–362.

Brown, L, and Flavin, C (1999) *State of the World 1999*. Worldwatch Institute, Washington D.C.

Brown, L , Flavin, C, French, H, Abramovitz, J, Dunn, S, Gardner, G, Mattoon, A, Platt McGinn, A, O'Meara, M, Renner, M, Bright, C, Postel, S, Halweil, B, and Starke, L (2000) *State of the World 2000*. Earthscan, London.

Brundtland, G H (1994) *Oslo Symposium on Sustainable Consumption*. January.

Buitelaar, R M (ed) (2001) *Aglomeraciones Mineras y Desarrollo local en América Latina*. Alfaomega, Bogotá.

Business Week (2000) 'Business week global 1000'. Business Week Online website, 10 July. http://www.businessweek.com/1999/99_28/g1000.htm

Cabalda, M V, Banaag M A, Tidalgo, P N and Garces, R B (2002) *Sustainable Development in the Philippine Minerals Industry*. Paper prepared for MMSD.

Cale, S (1997) 'Pregnant problems: keeping it under wraps'. *Mining Environmental Management*, December.

Cameco (2001) *Building Communities – The Community Vitality Monitoring Partnership Process (CVMPP)*. Cameco website, http://www.cameco.com/social_responsibility/communities/community_dialogue.php#cvmpp

Camus, J P (2002) 'Management of mineral resources'. *Mining Engineering*, January.

Canadian Institute of Mining, Metallurgy and Petroleum (1998) 'International reserve initiative'. *CIM Bulletin* 91 (1017): 44–45, February.

Carley, M, and Christie, I (2000) *Managing Sustainable Development*. Earthscan, London.

CASM (2001) 'Charter'. Collaborative Group on Artisanal and Small-Scale Mining website, http://wbln1018.worldbank.org/IFCEXT/casmsite.nsf/weblinks/charter?opendocument

Castilla, J C (1983) 'Environmental impact in sandy beaches of copper mine tailings at Chañaral, Chile'. *Marine Pollution Bulletin*, 14(12) December.

Castillo, R F (1998) 'El Cobre tailings dam failure, Chile'. In *Proceedings of the Workshop on Risk Management and Contingency Planning in the Management of Mine Tailings*. International Council on Metals and the Environment and Division of Technology, Industry and Economics. United Nations Environment Programme (November 1998).

Cawood, F (2001) *Aligning Mineral Wealth with Sustainable Development: The Southern African Perspective*. Paper prepared for MMSD Southern Africa.

CEE Bankwatch Network (2000) *Cyanide to Dresdner Bank*. CEE Bankwatch Network website at http://www.bankwatch.org

Centro de Estudios y Proyectos SRL and Netherlands Embassy (1999) *Cochambamba, Potosí, Chuquisaca: Genero y Medio Ambiente*. Muelas del Diablo Editores, La Paz.

Cernea, M M (2000) 'Risks, safeguards and reconstruction: a model for population displacement and resettlement'. In Cernea, M M, and McDowell, C (eds) *Risks and Reconstruction: Experiences of Resettlers and Refugees*. World Bank, Washington D.C.

CFMEU (2001) *Mining and Energy Division*. Construction, Forestry, Mining and Energy Union website, http://www.cfmeu.asn.au/mining-energy

Chakravorty, S L (2001) *Country Paper on Artisanal and Small-Scale Mining – India*. Paper prepared for MMSD.

Chamber of Mines of South Africa (2001) *SA Mining Industry Statistical Tables 2000*. Mining Statistics Library, Chamber of Mines of South Africa.

Chilean Copper Commission (2001) *Estadisticas del Cobre y otros Minerales: 1991–2000*. COCHILCO, Santiago de Chile.

Chinese Statistical Information Network (2000) *Chinese Statistical Yearbook '99*. Available at http://www.stats.gov.cn/yearbook/ml/1999_e.htm

Choshi, S (2001) *Mining and Society: Local Development*. African Institute of Corporate Affairs. Paper prepared for MMSD Southern Africa.

Cleveland, C J (1991) 'Natural resources scarcity and economic growth revisited: economic and biophysical perspectives'. In Constanza, R (1991) *Ecological Economies: The Science and Management of Sustainability*. Columbia University Press, New York.

Coelho, J M (2001) *The Mining of Aggregates in the Metropolitan Region of São Paulo*. Paper prepared for MMSD.

Constanza, R (1991) *Ecological Economies: The Science and Management of Sustainability*. Columbia University Press, New York.

Collier, P (2000) *The Economic Causes of Civil Conflict and their Implications for Policy*. The World Bank, Washington D.C.

Commission of the European Communities (2000) *Proposal for a Directive of the European Parliament and of the Council on Waste Electrical and Electronic Equipment*. COM(2000) 347 Final. 13 June.

Commission of the European Communities (2001a) *Green Paper on Integrated Product Policy*. COM(2001) 68 Final. 7 February.

Commission of the European Communities (2001b) *White Paper. Strategy for a Future Chemicals Policy*. COM(2001) 88 Final. 27 February. Brussels.

Commission of the European Communities (2001c) *Working Paper for a Directive of the European Parliament and of the Commission on the Impact on the Environment of Electrical and Electronic Equipment*. Version 1. February.

Commission on Human Rights, United Nations (2001) *Economic and Social Council Situations of Human Rights in Myanmar*. Agenda item 9, fifty-fifth session, E/CN.4/2001.L20, April 12.

Compania Minera Antamina (2001) *Estudio de Impacto Ambiental-Impacto Socieconomico*. Proyecto Antamina, Compania Minera Antamina website, http://www.mem.gob.pe/wmem/antamina/proyectoantamina.htm

Compliance Advisor Ombudsman (2000) *Investigation into the Mercury Spill of June 2, 2000 in the Vicinity of San Juan, Choropampa and Magdalena, Peru*. Report of the Independent Commission to the Office of Compliance Advisor/Ombudsman of the International Finance Corporation and the Multilateral Investment Guarantee Agency. July.

Conservation International (2000) *Lightening the Lode: A Guide to Responsible Large-scale Mining*. Conservation International and WWF International, Washington D.C.

Considine, T J (1991) 'Economic and technological determinants of the material intensity of use'. *Land Economics* 67: 99–115.

Convention on Biological Diversity (1992) Convention on Biological Diversity. 5 June.

Cooke, J (1999) 'Ecosystems of disturbed ground'. In Walker, L R (ed) *Ecosystems of the World*. Elsevier, Oxford.

Cornes, R, and Sandler, T (1996) *The Theory of Externalities, Public Goods and Club Goods*. Cambridge University Press, Cambridge.

Cosbey, A (2001) *Mining, Minerals and Sustainable Development: The Links to Trade and Investment Rules*. Paper prepared for MMSD.

Coumans, C (1999a) 'Placer Dome dumps waste, shares, and responsibility on Marinduque Island, Philippines'. *Mining Watch Canada Bulletin*, April.

Coumans, C (1999b) 'The sore that keeps festering'. *The Financial Post*, 8 April, Ontario.

Crain, A M (2001) *Indigenous Land Regularisation in Latin America*. Resource Center, NativeWeb. Available at http://www.nativeweb.org/ papers

Crocombe, R, and Meleisea, M (1994). *Land Issues in the Pacific*. MacMillan Brown Centre for Pacific Studies, University of Canterbury, Institute of Pacific Studies and the University of the South Pacific, Australia.

Crowson, P (2002) *Sustainability and the Economics of Mining – What Future?* Presentation at MMSD/UNEP/WB Mining Finance Workshop, Paris, January.

CRU International (2001a) *Precious Metals Market Outlook*. CRU International, London.

CRU International (2001b) *Development of the Minerals Cycle and the Need for Minerals*. CRU International, London.

CSIRO Minerals (2001) *People, Power, Participation: A Study of Mining – Community Relationships*. Paper prepared for MMSD.

Dalal-Clayton, B, and Bass, S (2001) *Taking a Systematic and Strategic Approach to Sustainability*. IIED, London.

Dalisay, J (ed) (1999) *Mining Revisited*. Environmental Science for Social Change, Quezon City, the Philippines.

Dalupan, C (2001) *Mining and Sustainable Development: Insights from International Law*. Unpublished paper, 2001.

Daniel, P (1992) 'Economic policy in mineral-exporting countries: what have we learned?' In Tilton, J E (ed) *Mineral Wealth and Economic Development*. Resources for the Future, Washington D.C.

Danielson, L, and Nixon, M (2000) 'Current regulatory approaches to mine closure in the United States'. In Warhurst, A, and Noronha, L (eds) *Environmental Policy in Mining. Corporate Strategy and Planning for Closure*. Lewis Publishers, Boca Raton, FL.

Davidson, J (1998) *Building Partnerships with Artisanal Miners on Las Cristinas: The Minera Las Cristinas Experience in Southern Venezuela*. Pan-American Workshop on the Safe Use of Minerals and Metals, Lima, Peru, 1–3 July (updated from *Mining Environmental Management*, March 1998).

Denoon, D. (2000) *Getting Under the Skin: The Bougainville Copper Agreement and the Creation of the Panguna Mine*. Melbourne: Melbourne University Press.

Derickson, A (1989) 'Part of the yellow dog: U.S. coal miners' opposition to the company doctor system, 1936–1946'. *International Journal of Health Services* 19(4): 709–720.

Derickson, A (1991) 'The United Mine Workers of America and the recognition of occupational respiratory diseases, 1902–1968'. *American Journal of Public Health* 81(6): 782–90.

De Soto, H (2000) *The Mystery of Capital: Why Capitalism Triumphs in the West and Fails Everywhere Else*. Bantam Press, London.

Development Bank of Japan (2001) *Introduction of a Home Appliance Recycling System: Effects and Prospects: Progress Towards Utilisation of Recycling Infrastructure*. DBJ Research Report No. 18, Japanese Ministry of Economy, Trade and Industry.

Diavik-Diamonds Mines Inc. (2000) *The Distribution of the Project Resource Income*. News Room, Diavik-Diamonds Mines Inc. website, http://www.diavik.ca/html/visitor_center.html

Dobb, E (1996) 'Pennies from hell: in Montana, the bill for America's copper comes due'. *Harper's Magazine*, October.

Dodd, T (2000) 'Rio Tinto miners face sex claims in Borneo'. *Australian Financial Review*, 30 June.

Dollar, D, and Pritchett, L (1998) *Assessing Aid: What Works, What Doesn't and Why*. Oxford University Press, Oxford.

Downing, T E (2002) *Avoiding New Poverty: Mining-Induced Displacement and Resettlement*. Paper prepared for MMSD.

Downing, T E, Moles, J, McIntosh, I, and Garcia-Downing, C (2002) *Indigenous Peoples and Mining: Strategies and Tactics for Encounters*. Paper prepared for MMSD.

Drechsler, B (2001) *Small Scale Mining and Sustainable Development in the SADC Region*. Paper prepared for MMSD Southern Africa.

Dudley, N, and Stolton, S (2001) *To Dig or Not to Dig? Criteria to Determine the Suitability of Mineral Exploration, Extraction and Transport from Social and Ecological Perspectives*. A draft discussion paper for WWF.

Dunn, W (2001) Presentation at MMSD Managing Mineral Wealth workshop, London, 15–17 August.

Ebinghaus, R, Tripathi, R M, Wallschlager, D, Wallschlager, L, and Steven, E (1999) 'Natural and anthropogenic mercury sources and their impact on the air-surface exchange of mercury on regional and global scales'. In Ebinghaus, R, Turner, R R, Lacerda, D, Vasiliev, O, and Salomons, W (eds) (1999) *Mercury Contaminated Sites – Characterisation, Risk Assessment and Remediation*. Springer Verlag, Heidelberg.

Ebinghaus, R, Turner, R R, Lacerda, D, Vasiliev, O, and Salomons, W (eds) (1999) *Mercury Contaminated Sites – Characterisation, Risk Assessment and Remediation*. Springer Verlag, Heidelberg.

Echavarría, C, and Correa, H D (2000) *Environmental/Social Performance Indicators for Minerals Development: Nuclear Issues for Indigenous Peoples*. Mining Energy Research Network Working paper, Warwick.

Eggert, R G (1990) 'The passenger car industry: faithful to steel'. In Tilton, J E (ed) (1990) *World Metal Demand. Trends and Prospects*. Resources for the Future.

Eggert, R (2001) *Mining and Economic Sustainability: National Economies and Local Communities*. Paper prepared for MMSD.

Elias, R, and Taylor I (2001) *HIV/AIDS, the Mining and Minerals Sector and Sustainable Development in Southern Africa*. Paper prepared for MMSD.

Elkington, J (1998) *Cannibals with Forks: the Triple Bottom Line of 21st Century Business*. New Society Publishers, Canada.

Ellis, D V, Poling, G W, and Baer, R L (1995) 'Submarine tailings disposal (STD) for mines: an introduction'. *Marine Georesources and Geotechnology* 13: 3–18.

Ellis, D V, and Robertson, J D (1999) 'Underwater placement of mine tailings: case examples and principles'. Chapter 9, pp. 123–141. In Azcue, J M (ed) *Environmental Impacts of Mining Activities*. Springer, Berlin.

Emberson-Bain, A (1994) *Labour and Gold in Fiji*. Cambridge University Press, Cambridge.

Emsley, I (2001) *Technological Development and Skills Requirements in Modern Mining.* Paper presented at MMSD Managing Mineral Wealth Workshop, London, 15–17 August.

ENDS Magazine (2001) 'Danish can ban gets a legal pasting'. 14 September. Environmental Data Services, London.

Enriquez, J C (2001) *Minería y Minerales de Bolivia en la Transición hacia el Desarrollo Sustentable.* Paper prepared for MMSD South America.

Environment Australia (2002) Environment Australia-National Pollutant Inventory website, http://www.npi.gov.au/

Environment Canada (2002) Environment Canada-National Pollutant Release Inventory website, http://www.ec.gc.ca/ pdb/npri/

Erickson, R L (1973) *Crustal Abundance of Elements, and Minerals Reserves and Resources.* United States Minerals Resources, Geological Survey Professional Paper 820.

ERM (2000) *ERM Survey of UK Pension Funds.* ERM, London.

Eurométaux (2001) *Comments on the White Paper on a Future Chemicals Policy.* May 2001. Eurométaux.

FAO/World Health Organization (1999) *Codex Alimentarius Commission Guidelines for Production, Processing, Labelling and Marketing of Organically Produced Foods.* GL32–1999, Rev 1, 2001. FAO, Rome.

Filer, C (1990) 'The Bougainville rebellion, the mining industry and the process of social disintegration in Papua New Guinea'. In May, R J, and Spriggs, M (eds) (1990) *The Bougainville Crisis.* Crawford House Press, Australia.

Fisher, J. (1993) *The Road from Rio.* Praeger publishers, New York.

Fitzgerald, B (1999) 'BHP in two minds about pulling plug on Ok Tedi'. The Age Internet Edition. Melbourne, 12 August, http://www.theage.com.au/daily/990812/bus/bus11.html

Five Winds International (2001) *Eco-efficiency and Materials.* International Council on Metals and the Environment, Ottawa.

Fraser, D (2001) Presentation at MMSD Workshop on Armed Conflict and Natural Resources: The Case of the Minerals Sector. London, 11 July.

Foreit, K G, Haustein D, Winterhalter, M, and LaMata, E (1991) 'Costs and benefits of implementing child survival services at a private mining company in Peru'. *American Journal of Public Health* 81(8): 1055–1057.

Forest Peoples Programme, Philippine Indigenous Peoples Links and the World Rainforest Movement (2000) *Undermining the Forests. The need to Control Transnational Mining Companies: A Canadian Case Study.* FPP, PIP Links and WRM, UK.

Fox, H R, and Moore, H M (2000) *Land Reclamation and Regeneration. Proceedings of the British Land Reclamation Society and National Land Reclamation Panel Conference.* Camborne School of Mines, Cornwall, September.

Fukuyama, F (1996) *Trust: The Social Virtues and the Creation of Prosperity.* Free Press Paperbacks-Simon & Schuster, New York.

Fulop, S, and Kiss, C (2001) *Information Availability: A Key to Building Trust in the Minerals Sector, Review of Systems for Making Information Available.* Paper prepared for MMSD.

Fundación MEDMIN (in press) *Impactos Económicos y Ambientales de la Liberalización del Comercio: Una Aplicación al Sector Minero.* MEDMIN, La Paz.

Gamble, D (1978) 'The Berger Inquiry: an impact assessment process'. *Science* 199(3): 946–952.

Gardner, G, and Sampat, P (1998) *Mind over Matter: Recasting the Role of Materials in Our Lives.* Worldwatch Paper 144. Worldwatch Institute, Washington D.C.

Gereffi, G, Jumphrey, J, Kaplinsky, R, and Sturgeon, T J (2001) 'Introduction: globalisation, value chains and development'. In Gereffi, G and Kaplinsky, R (eds) 'The value of value chains: spreading the gains of globalisation'. *Institute of Development Studies Bulletin* 32: 1–8.

German, T, and Rande, J (1998) *The Reality of Aid 1998/1999: an Independent Review of Poverty Reduction and Development Assistance, 1998/1999.* Earthscan, London.

Gertsch, R E, and Maryniak, G E (1991) 'Space mining: boondoggle or the next gold rush'. *Mining Engineering* 43(8): 1029–1041.

Gibson, R (2000) 'Favouring the Higher Test: Contributions to sustainability as the central criterion for reviews and decisions under the Canadian Environmental Assessment Act'. *Journal of Environmental Law and Practice*, 10 (1): 39–54.

Gibson, G (2001a) *Building Partnerships. Key Elements of Capacity Building.* Paper prepared for MMSD.

Gibson, G (2001b) *Community Information Needs: Access to Information Through the Mining Life Cycle.* Paper prepared for MMSD.

Gingerich, J C, Mathews, L W, and Peshko, M J (2002) *The Development of New Exploration Technologies at Noranda: Seeing more with Hyperspectral and Deeper with 3-D Seismic.* Canadian Institute of Mining Metallurgy and Petroleum Issue (Geology) vol. 95 no. 1058, February.

Glave, M A, and Kuramoto, J (2001) *Proyecto Minerales, Mineria y Desarrollo Sustentable – MMSD – Informe final del Proyecto – Peru.* Paper prepared for MMSD South America.

Global Reporting Initiative (1999) *GRI Overview.* Global Reporting Initiative website, http://globalreporting.org/AboutGRI/Overview.htm

Global Reporting Initiative (2000) *Sustainability Reporting Guidelines on Economic, Environmental and Social Performance.* June. London.

Global Response (2001) *Stop Irresponsible Mining in Kenya.* Guest book, Swahili Coast website, http://www.mwambao.com/dongo.htm

Global Witness (2000) *Conflict Diamonds: Possibilities for the Identification, Certification and Control of Diamonds.* Global Witness, London.

Gold Fields Mineral Services Ltd (2001) *Gold Survey 2001.* Gold Fields Mineral Services Ltd.

Gordon, R B, Koopmans, J J, Nordhaus, W B, and Skinner, B J (1987) *Towards a New Iron Age.* Harvard University Press, Cambridge MA.

Government of Australia (1993) *The Native Title Act. An Act about Native Title in Relation to Land or Waters, and for Related Purposes.* Commonwealth Consolidated Acts, Canberra.

Government of Chile (1997) *Reglamento del Sistema de Evaluación de Impacto Ambiental.* Legislacion, Comision Chilena del Cobre website, http://www.cochilco.cl/home/esp/frameset-legislacion.htm

Government of Fiji (1999) *Compensation Policy for Fiji's Mining Sector.* Mineral Resource Department, Suva.

Government of India (2001) *Annual Report 2000–01 of the Ministry of Labour.* Government of India.

Government of South Africa, Department of Minerals and Energy (2001) *South Africa's Mineral Industry Yearbook for 1999/2000.* Government of South Africa, Department of Minerals and Energy.

Government of the Province of Manitoba (2000) *Land Access Sustainable Development: Land Access Action Plant.* Mineral Resource Division-Mines branch (Regulation), 23 and 26 October. Province of Manitoba website, http://www.gov.mb.ca/itm/mrd/index.html

Government of United States of America – Department of State (2001) *Voluntary Principles on Security and Human Rights. Fact Sheet.* US Department of State website, http://www.state.gov/g/drl/rls/index.cfm?docid=2931

Granville, A (2001) *Baseline Survey of the Mining and Minerals Sector.* Paper prepared for MMSD Southern Africa.

Grassle, J F (1991) 'Deep-sea benthic biodiversity'. *Bio-science* 41(7): 464–468.

Greene, G, Moffett, J, Meyer, S, and Middelkoop, M J (2001) *Voluntary Initiatives and Application to the Mining and Metals Sector.* Stratos Inc. Ottawa, Canada. Paper prepared for MMSD.

Greene, G (2001) *Planning For Outcomes: A Framework For the Consideration of Options.* Paper prepared for MMSD.

Greenhouse, S (2002) 'Alabama coal giant is sued over 3 killings in Columbia'. *New York Times,* 22 March.

Grieg-Gran, M (2002) *Financial Incentives for Improved Sustainability Performance: The Business Case and the Sustainability Dividend.* Paper prepared for MMSD.

Gueye, D (2001) *National Study in Artisanal and Small-Scale Mining: Case of Burkina Faso.* Paper prepared for MMSD.

Gunson, A J, and Yue Jian (2001) *Artisanal Mining in The People's Republic of China.* Paper prepared for MMSD.

Hall, D C, and Hall, J V (1984) 'Concepts and measures of natural resource scarcity and a summary of recent trends'. *Journal of Environmental Economics and Management* 11(4): 363–379.

Hall, K G (2001) 'Tapping an angry vein: Peruvian farmers battle Canadian mining giant over future of their lands'. *The Seattle Times,* 13 July.

Hamilton, K, and Lutz, E (1996) *Green National Accounts: Policy Issues and Empirical Evidence.* Environmental Economic Series 39, The World Bank, Washington.

Hancock, P M (2001) *Baseline Assessment Australia.* Paper prepared for MMSD.

Handelsman, S D (2001) *Report on Human Rights and the Mineral Industry.* Paper prepared for MMSD.

Hannesson, R (2001a) *Investing for Sustainability: The Management of Mineral Wealth.* Klewer Academic Publishers, Boston.

Hannesson, R (2001b) Presentation at MMSD Managing Mineral Wealth Workshop, London, 15–17 August.

Harden, B (2001) 'A black mud from Africa helps power the new economy'. *New York Times Magazine,* 12 August.

Hart, S and Ahuja, G (1996) 'Does it pay to be green? An empirical examination of the relationship between emission reduction and firm performance'. *Business Strategy and the Environment* 5: 30–37.

Hawken, P, Lovins, A, and Lovins, L H (1999) *Natural Capitalism. Creating the Next Industrial Revolution.* Little, Brown and Company, New York.

Heathcote, I (undated) *Balancing Economic Development Against Indigenous Values: Nickel Mining in Coastal Labrador.* Regional updates. Available at http://cwx.prenhall.com/bookbind/pubbooks/nebel2/medialib/update3.html

Heiler, K, Pickersgill, R, and Briggs, C (2000) *Working Time Arrangements in the Australian Mining Industry: Trends and Implications with Particular Reference to Occupational Health and Safety.* Sectoral Activities Programme Working Paper no. 162, ILO, Geneva.

Hemmati, M (2002) *Multi-Stakeholder Processes for Governance and Sustainability – Beyond Deadlock and Conflict.* Earthscan, London.

Henstock, M (1996) *The Recycling of Non-Ferrous Metals.* ICME, Ottawa.

Hentschel, T (1998) 'Implementing environmental protection projects in small-scale mining'. In *The Proceedings of the Workshop on the Sustainable Development of Non-Renewable Resources Towards the 21st Century.* UNRFNRE, New York.

Hentschel, T, Hruschka, F, and Priester, M (2001) *Global Report on Artisanal and Small Scale Mining.* Paper prepared for MMSD.

Hilson, G (2001a) *A Contextual Review of the Ghanaian Small-Scale Mining Industry.* Paper prepared for MMSD.

Hilson, G (2001b) 'Putting theory into practice: how has the gold mining industry interpreted the concept of sustainable development?' *Mineral Resources Engineering* 10: 397–413.

Hirschman, A O (1958) *The Strategy of Economic Development.* Yale University Press, New Haven.

Hoffmann, U, and Wilson, B (2000) 'Requirements for, and benefits of, environmentally sound and economically viable management of battery recycling in the Philippines in the wake of Basel Convention trade restrictions'. *Journal of Power Sources* 88: 115–123.

Holden, A and O'Faircheallaigh, C (1995) *The Economic and Social Impact of Silica Mining in Hope Vale.* Aboriginal Politics and public Sector Management Monograph No 1 Griffith University. Centre for Australian Public Sector Management, Brisbane.

Horswill, D, Riley, D, and Parker, D (1999) *Zinc and Sustainable Development: The Case of the Red Dog Mine.* Cominco Ltd. See http://www.iza.com/zwo_org/Environment/040107.htm

Horswill, D (2001) Presentation at the Sullivan Mine Round Table, Kimberley, Canada.

Houghton, J T, Ding, Y, Griggs, D J, Noguer, M, van der Linden, P J, and Xiaosu, D (eds) (2001) *Climate Change 2001: The Scientific Basis.* Contribution of Working Group I to the Third Assessment Report of the Intergovernmental Panel on Climate Change (IPCC). Cambridge University Press, UK.

Howard, M (1988) *The Impact of the International Mining Industry on Native Peoples.* Transnational Corporations Research Project, University of Sydney.

Howie, P (2001) 'Real prices for selected mineral commodities, 1870–1997'. Colorado School of Mines. Appendix in: Tilton, J E (2002 in print) *On Borrowed Time? Assessing the Threat of Mineral Depletion.* Resources for the Future, Washington D.C.

HSBC (2001) *Senior Gold Book.* HSBC, January.

Humphreys, D (2001a) 'Sustainable development: can the mining industry afford it?' *Resources Policy* 27: 1–7.

Humphreys, D (2001b) *The Role of China in the World Mining Industry.* Paper presented in the China Mining 2001 Conference, Xi'an, Shaanxi Province, 20–22 September.

Hutchinson (2001) 'Barrick's African tribulations'. *National Post (Canada).* 29 December.

IAEA (1993) *Uranium Extraction Technology.* IAEA Technical Reports Series No. 359. International Atomic Energy Agency, Vienna.

ICBP (1992) *Putting Biodiversity on the Map: Priority Areas for Global Conservation.* International Council for Bird Preservation, Cambridge.

ICF (2000) *Greenhouse Gas Emissions from the Aluminium Industry.* Report by ICF Consulting (Washington D.C.) submitted to IEA Greenhouse Gas Research and Development Programme (Cheltenham, UK). January.

ICFTU (2001) *Annual Survey of Violations of Trade Union Rights.* International Confederation of Free Trade Unions, Brussels.

ICMM (2001) 'Our charter'. International Council on Mining and Metals website, http://www.icme.com/html/charter_intro.php

ICOLD (2001) *Tailings Dams: Risk of Dangerous Occurrences, Lessons Learnt from Practical Experiences.* United Nations Environment Programme. International Commission on Large Dams and Division of Technology, Industry and Economics, Bulletin 121.

IENIM (1996) *A Mining Strategy for Latin America and the Caribbean.* World Bank Technical Paper no. 345, The World Bank, Washington D.C.

IIED (1994) *Whose Eden? A Review of Community Based Approaches to Wildlife Management.* IIED, London.

IIED (1996) *Towards a Sustainable Paper Cycle.* IIED, London.

IIED (1999) *Mining, Minerals and Sustainable Development, The Results of a Scoping Project for the World Business Council for Sustainable Development,* 26 October. IIED, London.

ILO (1991) *Safety and Health in Opencast Mines.* ILO, Geneva.

ILO (1995) *Safety and Health Convention.* ILO, Geneva.

ILO (1999a) *C182 Worst Forms of Child Labour Convention.* International Programme on the Elimination of Child Labour, International Labour Organization. ILO, Geneva.

ILO (1999b) *Social and Labour Issues in Small-scale Mines.* Report for discussion at the Tripartite Meeting on Social and Labour Issues in Small-scale Mines, Geneva, 17–22 May. ILO, Geneva.

ILO (2001a) *Code of Practice on HIV/AIDS and the World of Work.* ILO, Geneva.

ILO (2001b) *Labour Statistics Database* (LABORSTA). ILO, Geneva.

ILO (2001c) *Mining (Coal, other Mining).* Sectorial Activities. ILO, Geneva.

ILO (2001d) *Peru: Project Benefits Children in Gold Mining Industry.* International Programme on the Elimination of Child Labour, International Labour Organization. ILO, Geneva.

Innu Nation (1995) 'Guidelines for a respectful relationship between the Innu Nation at Nitassinan Mineral Exploration and Development at Emish (Voisey's Bay): an introduction to the issues'. In *Proceedings of the Canadian Aboriginal Minerals Association Conference: Exploring Common Ground: Aboriginal Communities and Base Metals Mining.* Sudbury, Ontario.

International Council on Metals and the Environment (1996) *Report of the International Workshop on Risk Assessment of Metals and their Inorganic Compounds.* Angers, France, November 13–15, 1996. ICME, Ottawa (Canada).

International Council on Metals and the Environment (1999) 'The Red Dog Mine story'. In ICME, *Mining and Indigenous People: Case Studies.* pp. 31–40, Ottawa.

International Development Research Centre (2001) *Large Mines and the Community.* IDRC.

International Programme on Chemical Safety (1990) *Beryllium. Environmental Health Criteria 106.* World Health Organisation, Geneva.

International Programme on Chemical Safety (1992) *Cadmium. Environmental Health Criteria 134.* World Health Organisation, Geneva.

International Union for the Conservation of Nature, UNESCO World Heritage Centre and International Council on Metals and the Environment (2000) *Proceeding of a Technical Workshop on World Heritage and Mining.* Gland, Switzerland.

International University of Kyrgystan (1999) *Barskoon: Yesterday, Today, Tomorrow.* International University of Kyrgystan (EMK).

InterPress Service (1994) *UNDP Helps Revive Indigenous Trade.* InterPress Service. Worldwide distribution via the APC networks. 28 November. Available at http://nativenet.uthscsa.edu/archive/nl/9412/0105.html

IUCN (1994) *Protected Area Management Categories.* IUCN, Gland.

IUCN (1998) *1997 United Nations List of Protected Areas.* Prepared by UNEP-WCMC and WCPA. IUCN, Gland.

IUCN (2002) *Environmental Sustainability Guidelines on Mining and Petroleum Extraction Activities in Arid and Semi-Arid Zones.* Draft copy. IUCN, Gland.

IUCN and WWF (1999) 'Metals from the forests: mining and forest degradation'. Special edition of *Arbovitae.* WWF International and IUCN, Gland.

IUCN, UNESCO World Heritage Centre and ICME (2001) *Proceedings of the Technical Workshop on World Heritage and Mining.* 21–23 September 2000, Gland Switzerland.

IUCN-WCPA and WCMC (1994) *Guidelines for Protected Area Management Categories.* IUCN, Gland.

Jackson, T (1996) *Material Concerns, Pollution, Profit and Quality of Life.* Routledge, London.

Jeffrey, W G (2001) *A World of Metals: Finding, Making and Using Metals.* 2nd edition, International Council on Metals and the Environment, Ottawa.

Jenkin, L E T (2000) 'Regeneration of abandoned metalliferous mine sites by enhanced recolonisation of natural ecosystems – the role of amendments'. In Fox, H R, and Moore, H M (2000) *Land Reclamation and Regeneration. Proceedings of the British Land Reclamation Society and National Land Reclamation Panel Conference.* Camborne School of Mines, Cornwall, September.

Jennings, N S (2001) *Improving Safety and Health in Mines: A Long and Winding Road?* Paper prepared for MMSD.

Johnson, M H, Bell, J, and Bennett, J (1980) 'Natural resource scarcity: empirical evidence and public policy'. *Journal of Environmental Economics and Management* 7(4): 256–271.

Johnstone, N (1998) 'The implications of the Basel Convention for developing countries: the case of trade in non-ferrous metal-bearing waste'. *Resources, Conservation and Recycling* 23: 1–28.

Johnstone, N (2001) *Resource Efficiency and the Environment.* OECD Environment Directorate, Paris.

Jolly, J L W (2000) *The US Copper-Base Scrap Industry and its By-Products.* Technical Report, Copper Development Assoc. Inc.

Jones, D S G (2000) 'Deep sea tailings placement (DSTP)'. *Australian Journal of Mining.* December, pp. 38–42.

Jones, S, and Jones, M (2001) *Overview of Deep Sea Tailing Placement.* January 2001 update. NSR Environmental Consultants Pty Ltd, Victoria, Australia for BHP Minerals.

Joyce, S, and MacFarlane, M (2001) *Social Impact Assessment in the Mining Industry: Current Situation and Future Directions.* Paper prepared for MMSD.

Kangwa, J (2001) *Privatisation and Social Management.* Paper prepared for MMSD Southern Africa.

Karen National Union (1998) Newsletter, 27 August.

Keynes, J M (1936) *The General Theory of Employment, Interest and Money.* Macmillan, UK.

Keita, S (2001) Presentation at MMSD Artisanal and Small-Scale Miners Workshop, London, 19–20 November.

Kenny, T (2000) *Zambia: Deregulation and the Denial of Human Rights.* Submission to UN Committee on Economic and Social Rights, RAID, Oxford.

Khanna, T (ed) (2000) *Mine Closure and Sustainable Development.* Results of the Workshop organized by the World Bank Group Mining Department and the Metal Mining Agency of Japan, Mining Journal Book, London.

King, A, and Lenox, M (2000) 'Industry self regulation without sanctions: the chemical industry's responsible care program'. *Academy of Management Journal* 43(4): 698–716.

King, D (1997) *The Big Polluter and the Constructing of Ok Tedi: Eco-Imperialism and Underdevelopment along the Ok Tedi and Fly Rivers of Papua New Guinea.* Presented at the European Society of Oceanists Conference, Copenhagen, 4 January.

King, M (2000) Presentation by King, M (Richards Bay Minerals) on Greater St Lucia Wetlands Park, South Africa at the Technical Workshop on World Heritage and Mining, Gland, Switzerland, 21–23 September.

Kirsch, S (2002) *Mining, Indigenous Peoples and Human Rights: A Case Study of the Ok Tedi Mine, Papua New Guinea.* Draft of case study prepared for a workshop on 'Indigenous Peoples, Private Sector Natural Resource, Energy and Mining Companies and Human Rights', Geneva, January. Organized by UN High Commissioner for Human Rights in collaboration with UN Conference on Trade and Development and International Labour Organisation, Geneva.

Koziell, I (2001) *Diversity not Adversity: Sustaining Livelihoods with Biodiversity.* IIED, London.

Labat-Anderson Inc (1997) Final Social Audit Report, 15 July, Labat-Anderson Inc, USA.

Labonne, B (1997) *Small-Scale Mining and Energy: Contribution to Poverty Reduction and Perspectives for Technical Cooperation in Africa.* Presented to the Second Conference of African Ministers Responsible for the Development and Utilization of Mineral and Energy Resources, Durban, 17–22 November.

Labonne, B, and Gilman, J (1999) *Towards Building Sustainable Livelihoods in the Artisanal Mining Communities.* Presented at the Tripartite Meeting on Social and Labor Issues in Small-scale Mines, ILO, Geneva, 17–21 May.

Lacerda, L D, and Salomons, W (1998) *Mercury from Gold and Silver Mining. A Chemical Time Bomb?* Springer, New York.

Lagos, G E (1994) *Instrumentos Regulatorios y Económicos para la Gestión Ambiental de los Recursos Mineros: el caso de la Pequeña y Mediana Minería.* Libro publicado por el Centro de Economía de los Recursos Naturales, Facultad de Economía, Universidad de Chile y por el Ministerio de Bienes Nacionales, Santiago de Chile.

Lagos, G E, Blanco, H, Torres, V, and Bustos, B (2001) *Minería y Minerales de Chile en la Transición Hacia el Desarrollo Sustentable.* Paper prepared for MMSD.

Lagos, G, and Velasco, P (1999) 'Environmental policies and practice in Chilean mines'. In *Mining and the Environment: Case Studies from the Americas.* International Development Research Centre (IDRC), Canada.

Lahiri-Dutt, K (1998) 'From gin girls to scavengers: women in Raniganj Collieries'. University of Burdwan, India; Census of India 1991. Cited in *Labour File, A Monthly Journal of Labour and Economic Affairs* 6(6 and 7) June/July 2000.

Lahiri-Dutt, K (2000) 'Gender dimension of mining: women workers in Indian coalmines' *Mining Environment Management* 8(5), London.

Lamont, J (2001) 'Economy must prove there is life after diamonds: diversification, a survey on Botswana'. *The Financial Times,* 26 September, London.

Landell-Mills, N, Bishop, J, and Porras, I (forthcoming) *Silver Bullets or Fools Gold? Markets for Environmental Services and the Poor.* IIED, London.

Lange, G-M (2000) *The Contribution of Minerals to Sustainable Economic Development in Botswana.* Draft report for the Botswana Natural Resource Accounting Programme.

Lash, J (ed) (2001) 'Forward'. *Sustainable Measures: Evaluation and Reporting on Social and Environmental Performance.* Greenleaf Publishing Limited, UK.

Lee, T and Yao, C L (1970) 'Abundance of chemical elements in the Earth's crust and its major tectonic units'. *International Geological Review* 12(7): 778–786.

Leigh, J D, and Briggs, J H (1992) *Rare or Threatened Australian Plants.* Australian National Parks and Wildlife Service, Canberra.

Leopold, A (1949) *A Sand County Almanac: And Sketches Here and There.* Oxford University Press. Reprinted 1977.

Levy, A, and Scott-Clark, C (2001) 'Between hell and the stone of Heaven'. *The Observer,* 11 November, London.

Littlepage, I L, Ellis, D V, and Mcinerney, I (1984) 'Marine disposal of mine tailings'. *Marine Pollution Bulletin,* 15(7).

Lloyd, M V, Barnett, G, Doherty, M D, Jeffree, R A, John, J, Majer, J D, Osborne, J M, and Nichols, O G (in prep) *Managing the Impacts of the Australian Mineral Industry on Biodiversity.* Paper prepared for MMSD Australia.

Loayza, F C (2001) *Access to Information: A key to Building Trust in the Minerals Sector: The Government Role.* Paper prepared for MMSD.

Loayza, F, Franco, I, Quezada, F, and Alvarado, M (2001) 'Bolivia: turning gold into human capital'. Part 1, Chapter 2 in International Development Research Centre. *Large Mines and the Community.*

Lodenius, M, and Malm, O (1998) 'Mercury in the Amazon'. *Reviews of Environmental Contamination and Toxicology* 157: 25–52.

Lovins, A B, Feiler, T E, and Rábago, K R (2002) *Energy and Sustainable Development in the Mining and Minerals Industries.* Paper prepared for MMSD.

Luzenac (2000) *Balancing the Needs.* Luzenac Social and Environmental Report 2000.

Lyon, J S, Hilliard, T J, and Bethell, T N (1993) *Burden of Gilt.* Mineral Policy Center, Washington, D.C.

McDivitt, J (2001) *Survey of Mining Educational Institutions and the Current State of their Programs.* Paper prepared for MMSD.

McDivitt, J (2002) *Status of Education of Mining Industry Professionals.* Paper prepared for MMSD.

MacDonald, A (2000) 'Risky Business: the Movement of Vancouver-based Mining Firms to Latin America'. M A thesis, Department of Geography, Simon Fraser University, Vancouver.

MacDonald, A (2002) *Industry in Transition: A Profile of the North American Mining Sector.* Paper prepared for MMSD.

McDonald, R J (2000) *The Economic Performance of an 'Old' Industry: Mineral Extraction and Processing.* Prepared for Australasian Institute of Mining and Metallurgy's Annual Conference, Sydney.

McMahon, G (ed) (1997) *Mining and the Community. Results of the Quito Conference.* Output of the Conference on Mining and the Community held in Quito, Ecuador, 6–8 May. World Bank Energy, Mining and Telecommunications Department.

McMahon, G, Evia, J L, Pasco-Font, A, and Sanchaz, J (1999) *An Environmental Study of Artisanal, Small, and Medium Mining in Bolivia, Chile, and Peru.* World Bank Technical Paper no. 429, The World Bank, Washington D.C.

MacMillan, M (2000). *Smoke Wars: Anaconda Copper, Montana Air Pollution, and the Courts, 1890–1920.* Montana Historical Society Press, Montana.

McNamee, K (1999) 'Undermining the wilderness: the Canadian mining industry is abandoning its support for a national network of protected areas'. *Alternatives Journal* 25(4): 24–31.

McPhail, K (2001) *The Revenue Dimension of Mining, Oil and Gas Projects.* World Bank, Washington D.C.

McShane, F (2002) *Mining Tradition or Breaking New Ground: Stakeholder Relationships in the Fijian Mining Sector.* Unpublished Draft PhD Thesis. McGill University, Montreal.

Mamadou, B (ed) (1995) *A Summary of the Proceedings of the International Roundtable on Artisanal Mining Organized by the World Bank.* Regularizing Informal Mining, World Bank.

Manu, K S (2001) Presentation at MMSD Managing Mineral Wealth Workshop, London, 15–17 August.

Marshall, A R, and Rau, M T (1999) *Lower Ok Tedi and Middle Fly – Estimate of Current Vegetation Dieback and Classification of Flood Plain Vegetation.* Report prepared for Ok Tedi Mining Limited's Mine Waste Management Project.

Marshall, I E (2001) *A Survey of Corruption Issues in the Mining and Minerals Sector.* Paper prepared for MMSD.

Martin, T E, Davies, M P, Rice, S Higgs, T, and Lighthall, P C (2001) *Stewardship of Tailings Facilities for Sustainable Development.* Paper prepared for MMSD.

Martinez Cobo, J (1987) *Study of the Problem of Discrimination Against Indigenous Populations.* United Nations Special Rapporteur.

Mate, K (1998) 'Boom in Ghana's golden enclave: major new investments boost output, but environmental concerns are growing'. *Africa Recovery* 11(3): 11.

Matthews, E (principal author) (2000) *The Weight of Nations: Material Outflows from Industrial Economies.* World Resources Institute, Washington D.C.

May, R M (1998) 'How many species are there on earth?' *Science,* 247: 1441–49.

Meadows, D H, Meadows, D L, Randers, J, and Behrens, W (1972) *The Limits to Growth.* Pan, London.

Meadows, D H, Meadows, D L, and Randers, J (1992) *Beyond the Limits*. Chelsea Green Publishing, Post Mills, VT.

Meeran, R (2002) 'Cape pays the price as justice prevails'. *The Times*, 15 January.

MEM (1998) 'Mining in the Emerald Isle' *Mining Environmental Management* 6 (5), London, September.

Miller, C G (1998) *Use of Financial Surety for Environmental Purposes*. ICME.

Mineral and Energy Policy Centre (2001) *A Case Study of Community Involvement in Developing the Minerals Policy in South Africa*. Paper prepared for MMSD.

Mineral Policy Center (1997) *Golden Dreams, Poisoned Streams: How Reckless Mining Pollutes America's Waters and How We Can Stop It*. Minerals Policy Center, Washington D.C.

Minerals Council of Australia (1999) *Safety Culture Survey Report of the Australian Minerals Industry*. July, Minerals Council of Australia, Canberra.

Minerals Council of Australia (2001) *Safety & Health Performance 1999–2000 Report of the Australian Minerals Industry*. Minerals Council of Australia, Canberra.

Minesite (2001) *New Gold Marketing Initiative Edges into World Gold Council Territory*. 22 October 2001. http://www.minesite.com

Mining Association of Canada (1998) *A Guide to the Management of Tailings Facilities*. Mining Association of Canada.

Mining Association of Canada (2001) *Facts and Figures 2000*. Available at http://mining.ca/english/publications/index.html

Mining Industry Associations of Southern Africa (2001) *Introduction of the Adapted Minataur Process for Gold Recovery to Small-Scale Miners*. Submitted to the SADC Mining Sector Technical Committee.

Mining Magazine (2000) 'New technology at Cortez'. *Mining Magazine* 8 (2), February.

Mining Policy Institute (2001) *Chairperson Quits over River Pollution at Placer Dome's Porgera Mine in Papua New Guinea*. Press release.

MiningWatch Canada (2001) *Stakeholder Report*. Report to Mines Ministers from MiningWatch Canada, 12 September.

Mining Web (2000) *The World's Biggest Mining Companies*. The MiningWeb website, http://www.theminingweb.com/

MINTEK (2001) *The Minataur Process: An Alternative Gold-Refining Technology*. Extractive Metallurgy Division, MINTEK, South Africa.

Mitchell, D, Varangis, P, and Akiyama, T (1996) *Managing Commodity Booms and Busts*. The World Bank, Washington D.C.

Mitchell, P (2000) 'Prediction, prevention, control, and treatment of acid rock drainage'. In Warhurst, A and Noronha, L (eds) *Environmental Policy in Mining. Corporate Strategy and Planning for Closure*. Lewis Publishers, Boca Raton, FL.

Mittermeier, R A, Myers, N, Robles Gil, P and Mittermeier, C G (1999) *Hotspots: Earth's Biological Richest and most Endangered Terrestrial Ecoregions*. CEMEX, Mexico City.

Mittermeier, R A, Myers, N, Thomsen, J B, da Fonseca, G A B and Olivieri, S (1998) 'Biodiversity hotspots and major tropical wilderness areas: approaches to setting conservation priorities'. *Conservation Biology* 12(3): 516–520.

Mkapa, B W (2001) *Turning Idle Mineral Wealth Into a Potent Weapon Against Poverty*. Address to the Chamber of Mines of South Africa, 15 November.

MMSD (2001a) *How can the Minerals Sector Support the Development of Mineral Economies and Contribute to Building Sustainable Communities*. Report of the MMSD Managing Mineral Wealth Workshop, London, 15–17 August.

MMSD (2001b) *Meeting Report on Corruption Issues in the Mining and Minerals Sector*. Co-hosted by MMSD and Transparency International. Berlin, September.

MMSD (2001c) *Workshop Report on Armed Conflict and Natural Resources: The Case of the Minerals Sector*. Co-organized by MMSD and the International Institute for Strategic Studies, London, 11 July.

MMSD (2001d) *Workshop Report on Life Cycle Assessment: The Application of Life Cycle Assessment to Mining, Minerals and Metals*. New York, 9–10 August.

MMSD (2001e) *Workshop Report on Voluntary Initiatives for the Mineral Sector*. Workshop at Santa Fe, NM, July.

MMSD (2001f) *Worker and Community Health and Safety Informal Experts Meeting*. Report of the MMSD Worker and Community Health in the Mining Sector in the Context of Sustainable Development Workshop, London, 10 September.

MMSD (2001g) *Meeting Report. Finance, Mining and Sustainability Conference*. Organized jointly by MMSD, World Bank Group and UN Environmental Programme, Washington DC, 8–9 April.

MMSD (2001h) *Workshop Report on Access to Information and the Mining, Minerals and Metals Sector*. Vancouver, 29–30 November.

MMSD (2002) *Meeting Report. Finance, Mining and Sustainability: Exploring Sound Investment Decision Processes*. Organized jointly by MMSD, World Bank Group and UN Environmental Programme, Paris, 14–15 January.

MMSD Southern Africa (2001) *Mining, Minerals and Sustainable Development in Southern Africa*.

Mokopanele, T (2001) 'Mines shut eyes to dump hazard'. *Business Day, 1st Edition*. 30 August. Available at: http://www.saep.org/forDB/forDBAug01/MININGminesshuteyesBD300801.htm

Moody, R (2000) *Gravediggers: A Report on Mining in Burma*. Canada Asia Pacific Resource Network, Canada.

Moody, R (2001) *Into the Unknown Regions. The hazards of STD (Submarine Tailings Disposal)*. SSC and International Books, April, commissioned by Minewatch Asia-Pacific ISBN 90 5727 040 4.

Moore, D J, and Tilton, J E (1996) 'Economic growth and the demand for construction materials'. *Resources Policy* 22: 197–205.

Morales Bonilla, C, and Mauss, E A (1998) 'A community-initiated study of blood lead levels of Nicaraguan children living near a battery factory'. *American Journal of Public Health* 88(12): 1843–1845.

Moran, R E (1999) *Misuse of Water Quality Prediction in Mining Impact Studies*. Paper presented at the Geological Society of America's Workshop on Predictions in the Earth Sciences: Use and Misuse in Policy Making. Colorado, January.

Moran, R E (2001) *An Alternative look at a Proposed Mine in Tambogrande, Peru*. Prepared for Oxfam America. Minerals Policy Centre and Environmental Mining Council of British Columbia, Washington D.C.

MSHA (1999) *Quarterly Employment and Coal Production: Accidents/Injuries/Illnesses Reported to MSHA under 30 CFR Part 50, 1986–1997*. US Department of Labor, Mine Safety and Health Administration, Office of Injury and Employment Information, Denver.

Mudder, T, and Harvey, K (1998) 'Closure concepts'. *Mining and Environmental Management*. November.

Mugova, A (2001) *The Shamva Mining Project*. Presentation at MMSD Artisanal and Small-Scale Miners Workshop, London, 19–20 November.

Mulcahy, R (1999) 'Replacing the company doctor: Pruden Valley, Tennessee, and the development of the miners' clinics'. *Tennessee Medicine* 92(3): 91–5.

Müller, G P (1997) *Jade: The Stone of Heaven*. Documentary film, TomTom Film Productions.

Musvoto, A N (2001) *Gender and Mining: Community*. Paper prepared for MMSD Southern Africa.

Myers, N, Mittermeier, R A, Mittermeier, C G, da Fonseca, G A B, and Kent, J (2000). 'Biodiversity hotspots for conservation priorities'. *Nature* (London), 403: 853–858.

Naito, K, Remy, F, and Williams, J (forthcoming) *A Comparative Review of Legal and Fiscal Frameworks for Exploration and Mining: Best Practices*. The World Bank, Washington D.C.

Nappi, C (1990) 'Food and beverage container industries, change and diversity'. In Tilton, J (ed) *World Metal Demand. Resource for the Future*, Washington, D.C.

National Mining Association (2001) 'Employment data-mining statistics'. Available at http://www.nma.org/

National Research Council (1996) *Understanding Risk: Informing Decisions in a Democratic Society*. National Academy Press, Washington D.C.

National Research Council (1999) *Our Common Journey. A Transition Toward Sustainability*. National Academy Press, Washington D.C.

National Research Council (forthcoming) *Evolutionary and Revolutionary Technologies for Mining*. National Academy Press, Washington D.C.

Ndubula, B (2001) National Union of Mine Workers, Presentation made at MMSD Workshop on Worker and Community Health and Safety.

Noranda (2000) *Sustainable Development Report*. Noranda, Toronto.

Noronha, L (2001) *Costs and Returns of Sustainability?* Tata Energy Research Institute. Paper prepared for MMSD/UNEP/WB Mining Finance Workshop, Washington D.C. 9 April.

Norwatch (1999) Norwatch Newsletter, No. 11, May.

Nostromo Research (2001) *The case against QMM/Rio Tinto in Madagascar*. Report commissioned by Friends of the Earth (England, Wales and Northern Ireland) for presentation to the Malagasy government, London. Available at Mines and Communities website http://www.minesandcommunities.org/Company/foemadagascar1.htm

Nriagu, J O (1996) 'A history of global metal pollution'. *Science* 272: 223–224. 12 April.

Nriagu, J O, and Pacyna, J M (1988) 'Quantitative assessment of worldwide contamination of air, water and soils by trace metals'. *Nature* (London) 333: 134–139.

NSR Consultants (2001) *Overview of Deep Sea Tailing Placement for BHP Minerals*. NSR Consultants.

OECD (1996) *Recommendation of the Council on Implementing Pollutant Release and Transfer Registers, C(96)41/Final*. OECD, Paris.

OECD (1997) *Convention on Combating Bribery of Foreign Public Officials in International Business Transactions*. OECD, Paris.

OECD (2001a) *Extended Producer Responsibility. A Guidance Manual for Governments*. OECD, Paris.

OECD (2001b) *OECD Guidelines for Multinational Enterprises*. Global Instruments for Corporate Responsibility. OECD Annual Report 2001.

OECD (2001c) 'Resource use efficiency'. Chapter 23 in *OECD Environmental Outlook*. No. 69. OECD, Paris.

OECD (2001d) *The Firm, The Environment, and Public Policy*. OECD, Paris.

O'Faircheallaigh, C (1984) *Mining and Development: Foreign-Financed Mines in Australia, Ireland, Papua New Guinea and Zambia*. London: Croom Helm.

O'Faircheallaigh, C (1995) *Mineral Development Agreements Negotiated by Aboriginal Communities in the 1990s*. Centre for Aboriginal Economic Policy Research, Australian National University, No. 85/1995.

O'Faircheallaigh, C (1996) *Resource Development and Inequality in Indigenous Societies*. Aboriginal Politics and Public Sector Management Research Paper No. 2.

Office of the High Commissioner for Human Rights (1991) *Convention (No. 169) concerning Indigenous and Tribal Peoples in Independent Countries*. Adopted on 27 June 1989 by the General Conference of the International Labour. Organisation at its seventy-sixth session. Entry into force 5 September 1991.

OIT/IPEC and AECI (2000) *Programa de Erradicación del Trabajo Infantil en el Caserío Minero Artesanal Santa Filomena II Fase*. OIT/IPEC, Lima.

O'Neill, I (2001) *Landowners Blockade BHP's Rat Run from Ok Tedi*. Mineral Policy Institute website, 26 November, http://www.mpi.org.au/rr/page.php?page=23

Onorato, W T, Fox, P, and Strongman, J E (1997) *Assistance for Minerals Sector Development and Reform in Member Countries*. The World Bank, Washington D.C.

Orellana, M (2001) *Washington Agreement on Gold*. Paper prepared for MMSD.

Organization of American States (1996) Inter-American Convention Against Corruption. OAS website, http://www.oas.org/EN/PINFO/CONVEN/corrupt.htm

Organization of American States (2000) *The Inter-American Strategy for Public Participation in Sustainable Development*. The Organization of American States' Permanent Executive Committee of the Inter-American Council for Integral Development (CEPCIDI). Draft text available at http://www.oas.org/usde/news/news7.htm

Organization of American States, Inter-American Commission on Human Rights (1997) *Report on the Events at Amayapampa, Llallagua, and Capasirca: Northern Part of the Department of Potosi, Bolivia, December 1996*. Organization of American States, Inter-American Commission on Human Rights, Washington DC.

Ostensson, O (1997) 'Mining and the environment: the economic agenda'. *Industry and Environment* 20(4): 20–31.

Ostensson, O (2001) Presentation at MMSD Managing Mineral Wealth Workshop, London, 15–17 August.

Otto, J (1992) *A Global Survey of Mineral Company Investment Preferences. Mineral Investment Conditions in Selected Countries of the Asia-Pacific Region*. United Nations ST/ESCAP/1197.

Otto, J, Beraun, M, and Cordes, J (2000) *Global Mining Taxation Comparative Study*. Institute for Global Resources Policy and Management, Colorado School of Mines, Golden, Colorado.

Otto, J M (2002) *Creating a Positive Investment Climate*. World Mine Ministries Forum, Toronto 13–15 March.

Oxfam America (2001) *The Extractive Sectors and the Poor*. Oxfam report, October.

Oxfam Community Aid Abroad (2001) *Mining Ombudsman Report 2000–2001*. OCAA, Fitzroy, Australia.

Packard, V (1960) *The Waste Makers*. Penguin, London.

Pacyna, J M, and Pacyna, E G (2001) 'An assessment of global and regional emissions of trace metals to the atmosphere from anthropogenic sources worldwide'. *Canadian Journal of Environmental Reviews* 9: 1–30.

Palmer, A (2001) *Voluntary Initiatives and the World Trade Organization*. Paper prepared for MMSD.

Parr, C (2002) *Operational Needs and Realities in the Search for and Development of a Mine*. Paper prepared for MMSD.

Pasco-Font, A (2001) Presentation at MMSD Managing Mineral Wealth Workshop, London, 15–17 August.

Pearce, D W (1993) *Economic Values and the Natural World*. MIT Press, Cambridge, MA.

Pearce, D, Turner, K R, and O'Riordan, T (1994) *Measuring Sustainable Development*. Earthscan, London.

Phelps, R. W. (2000) 'Moving a mountain a day – Grasberg grows six-fold'. *Engineering & Mining Journal*, 1 Jun. pp. 22–28.

Phelps Dodge (1999) *Phelps Dodge Annual Report 1998*. Phelps Dodge, USA.

Philippine International Forum (1999) *Mining Mining: Lessons from the Philippines*. PIF, Quezon City, The Philippines.

Pintz, W S (1984) *Ok Tedi: Evolution of a Third World Mining Project*. Mining Journal Books, London.

Placer Dome (2001) *Sustainability Policy*. Placer Dome, Vancouver.

Placer Dome Asia Pacific (1998) *Porgera Mine Sustainability Report*. PDAP, Milton.

Placer Dome Asia Pacific (1999) *Porgera Mine Sustainability Report*. PDAP, Milton.

Plumlee, G S, Morton, R A, Boyle, T P, Medlin, J H, and Centeno, J A (2000) *Placer Dome Dumps Waste, Shares, and Responsibility on Marinduque Island, Philippines*. Mining Watch Canada Bulletin.

Porter, G, Carter, A, Bakarr, M, and Cormos, C (2001) *Review of an Ileminite Project in South East Madagascar*. Unpublished report. Conservation International, Washington D.C.

Porter, M E, and van der Linde, C (1995) 'Green and competitive'. *Harvard Business Review* 3: 120–134.

Porter, R N (2000) Presentation by Porter, R N (Site manager) on Greater St Lucia Wetlands Park, South Africa at the Technical Workshop on World Heritage and Mining, Gland, Switzerland, 21–23 September.

Portney, P R, and Stavins, R N (eds) (2000) *Public Policies for Environmental Protection* (2nd edition). Resources for the Future, Washington, D.C.

Potter, N, and Christy, Jr F T (1962) *Trends in Natural Resource Commodities: Statistics of Prices, Output, Consumption, Foreign Trade, and Employment in the US, 1870–1957*. Johns Hopkins for Resources for the Future, Baltimore.

Powell, D, and Leiss, W (1997) *Mad Cows and Mothers Milk*. McGill-Queen's University Press, Montreal.

Powell, I (1999) 'Rautenbach's Congo war role behind fraud squad raid'. *The Daily Mail and Guardian. Johannesburg Internet Edition*. 26 November. http://www.mg.co.za/mg/news/99nov2/26nov-rautenbach.html

PricewaterhouseCoopers (2001) *Mining and Sustainability: Survey of the Mining Industry*. PricewaterhouseCoopers/MMSD, London.

Priester, M, and Hruschka, F (1996) *New Approaches to Improve the Environmental Management of Small-Scale Mining*. Natural Resources and Development.

Pring, R (2001) *The Law of Public Participation in Mining and Resources Development*. Paper prepared for MMSD.

Quinkertz, R, Rombach, G, and Liebeg, D (2001) 'A scenario to optimise the energy demand of aluminium production depending on the recycling quota'. *Resources, Conservation and Recycling* 33: 217–234.

QMM S.A. (2001) *Ilmenite Project: Social and Environmental Impact Assessment and Environmental Management Plan*. QMM S.A.

Radetzki, M, and Tilton, J (1990) 'Conceptual and methodological issues'. In Tilton, J E (ed) *World Metal Demand: Trends and Prospects*. Resources for the Future, Washington D.C.

Rae, M, and Rouse, A (2001) *Mining Certification Evaluation Project*. World Wildlife Fund Australia, Melbourne.

Ramos, B (2000) Case Study: Doñana National Park. Presentation at the IUCN/ICME/UNESCO World Heritage and Mining Workshop, Gland, Switzerland.

Ramos, H (2001) Presentation at MMSD Managing Mineral Wealth Workshop, London, 15–17 August.

Ranchod, S (2001) *Women in the Workplace*. Paper prepared for MMSD Southern Africa.

Redmond, I (2001) *Coltan Boom, Gorilla Bust: The Impact of Coltan Mining on Gorillas and Other Wildlife in Eastern DR Congo*. A report for the Diane Fossey Gorilla Fund Europe and the Born Free Foundation, May.

Reese, S T, Wrenn, V E, and Reid, E J (1955) 'Injury experience in coal mining, 1952: analysis of mine safety factors, related employment, and production data'. *Bureau of Mines Bulletin* 559. US Department of the Interior, Washington D.C.

Regan, J (2001) *BHP Billiton nears Ok Tedi mine exit*. Planet Ark Environmental News Website, 13 December, http://www.planetark.org/dailynewsstory.cfm?newsid=13700&newsdate=13-Dec-2001.

Regueiro, M, Martins, L, and Arvidsson, S (2000) *Minerals in Europe: the Risks of Outsourcing*. EuroGeoSurveys Opinion 9, 27 March.

Reimann, M A, O'Kane, P T, and Cruz, E D (1999) *Nickel Laterites, An Increasingly Economic Resource*. Geostar Metals Inc. Available at http://www.geostarmetals.com/nickel.html

Richards, D G (2001) 'Risk review and corporate assurance in tailings management in Rio Tinto'. In Workshop on Mine Waste Management Brussels – 5 July 2000 *Les Techniques de l'Industrie Minerale* No. 9, March, pp. 95–97.

Ricks, G (1994) 'Closure considerations in environmental impact statements'. *Minerals Industry International* No. 1022.

Rio Tinto (2000) *Social and Environmental Review*. Published by Rio Tinto.

Rio Tinto (2001) *Yandicoogina Land Use Agreement*. Paper prepared for MMSD.

Roberts, S (2000) *Supply Chains as a Lever for Sustainability? Progress, Prospects and Pitfalls*. Available at http://www.iied.org/pdf/Supply_Chains.pdf

Robins, N (1995) *Citizen Action to Lighten Britain's Ecological Footprints*. A report from the International Institute for Environment and Development to the UK Government Department of the Environment, February.

Robins, N, and Roberts, S (1996) *Rethinking Paper Consumption*. Discussion paper, IIED, London.

Robinson, A (2001) 'Placer Dome cleanup threatened: Philippines rejects firm's plan to dump mine waste in ocean'. *Globe and Mail*, 6 November p.B12. Toronto.

Rosenfeld Sweeting, A, and Clark, A P (2000) *Lightening the Lode: A Guide to Responsible Large-Scale Mining*. Conservation International, Washington D.C.

Ross, M (2001) *The Extractive Sector and the Poor*. Oxfam America, Washington D.C.

Rössler, M (2000) 'World Heritage Convention: goals, objectives, criteria, issues and challenges with respect to world heritage and mining'. In International Union for the Conservation of Nature, UNESCO World Heritage Centre and International Council on Metals and the Environment, *Proceeding of a Technical Workshop on World Heritage and Mining*. Gland, Switzerland.

Roulet, M M, Lucotte, N, Farella, G, Serique, H, Coelho, C J, Sousa Passos, E, de Jesus da Silva, P, Scavone de Andrade, D, Mergler and Amorim, M (1999) 'Effects of recent human colonization on the presence of mercury in Amazonian ecosystems'. *Water, Air and Soil Pollution* 112: 297–313.

Sachs, J D, and Warner, A M (1995) *Natural Resource Abundance and Economic Growth*. Working paper 5398, National Bureau of Economic Research, Cambridge, MA.

Samel, R (2001) 'Materials in cars: options for change'. *Materials Technology* 16: 4–7.

Sassoon, M (1998) 'Los Frailes aftermath'. *Mining Environmental Management* 6(4): 8–12.

Sassoon, M (2000) 'Effective environmental impact assessment'. In Warhurst, A, and Noronha, L (eds) (2000) *Environmental Policy in Mining. Corporate Strategy and Planning for Closure*. Lewis Publishers. Boca Raton, FL.

Scheyvens, R, and Lagisa, L (1998) 'Women, disempowerment and resistance: an analysis of logging and mining activities in the Pacific'. *Singapore Journal of Tropical Geography* 19(1). National University of Singapore, Blackwell Publishers.

Schmidt-Bleek, F (aided by Waginger H, and Moos, H) (1999) Ökodesign – vom Produkt zur Dienstleistungserfüllungsmaschine. Wirtschaftskammer Österreich, WIFI Broschüre No 303, Wien.

Schloss, M (2000) Combating Corruption for Development. Transparency International, Berlin.

Schumacher, K, and Sathaye, J (1999) India's Aluminium Industry: Productivity, Energy Efficiency and Carbon Emissions. Ernst Orlando Lawrence Berkeley National Laboratory, Berkeley, California. Report No. LBNL 41845.

Schumacher, O L (ed) (1999) Mining Cost Service. Western Mine Engineering Inc., Washington State, US.

Scott-Russel, H (1993) 'A survival strategy towards mining in the year 2000'. Journal of the South African Institute of Mining and Metallurgy 93: 237–251.

Secretariat of the Convention on Biological Diversity (2001) Handbook of the Convention on Biological Diversity. Earthscan, London.

Secrett, C (1995) Defining Sustainable Development for the Transport Sector. Paper produced for the UK Round Table on Sustainable Development. Friends of the Earth, London.

Seers, D (1959) An Approach to the Short Period Analysis of Primary Producing Economies. Oxford Economic Papers, UK.

Seidman, A, Seidman, R, and Wälde, T (eds) (1999) Making Development Work: Legislative Reform for Institutional Transformation and Good Governance. Kluwer Law International, London.

Seidman, R, and Seidman, A (1994) State and Law in the Development Process: Problem Solving, Law and Institutional Change in the Third World. Macmillan, London.

Sen, A (1999) Development as Freedom. Alfred A. Knopf, New York.

Senior, C (1998) 'The Yandigicoogina process: a model for negotiating land use agreements'. In Moore, P (ed) Land, Rights, Laws: Issues of Native Title. Native Title Research Unit, Australian Institute of Aboriginal and Torres Strait Islander Studies, Canberra.

Shihata, I F (1994) The World Bank Inspection Panel. Oxford University Press, New York.

Silva-Forsberg, M C, Forsberg, B R, and Zeidemann, V K (1999) 'Mercury contamination in humans linked to river chemistry in the Amazon Basin'. Ambio 28: 519–521.

Skinner, B J (1976) 'A second iron age ahead?' American Scientist 64: 158–169.

Slade, M E (1982) 'Trends in natural-resource commodity process: an analysis of the time domain'. Journal of Environmental Economics and Management 9: 122–137.

Sol, V M, Peters, S W M, and Aiking, H (1999) Toxic Waste Storage Sites in EU Countries, a Preliminary Risk Inventory. Report commissioned by WWF from the Institute for Environmental Studies.

South Africa National Union of Mineworkers Gender Policy (1998) Women, Work and the Union: Towards a Gender Perspective. Discussion paper for NUM Policy Workshop, 16–18 October.

South African Minerals Bureau (2000) South Africa's Mineral Industry 1999/2000.

South African Women in Mining Association (2000) Summary of Women in Mining Trust Chairperson's Speech. South African Department of Minerals and Energy, Johannesburg.

Southern African Development Community (1997) Heads of Government Declaration on Gender.

Southern African Development Community (2001) Review of the Performance of the Mining Industry in the SADC Region. SADC, Rep. SADMIN/TC/1/2001/3. 10 June.

State of Wisconsin (1997) Wisconsin Act 171. 1997 Senate Bill 3.

Stephens, C, and Ahern, M (2001) Worker and Community Health Impacts Related to Mining Operations Internationally: A Rapid Review of the Literature. Paper prepared for MMSD.

Stewart, J (2000) Emerging and Future Technologies for Mining in South Africa. Presented at MINExpo International, Las Vegas, 9–12 October.

Stokes, M, and Derham J (2000) The Regulation and Construction of a New Zinc Mine. Workshop on Mine Waste Management, Brussels, July.

Storey, K, and Shrimpton, M (1995) Lessons Long Distance Labour Community in the Canadian Mining Industry. Working Paper No.43, Centre for Resource Studies, Queen's University.

Stratos Inc. (2002) Stepping Forward (excerpts) Corporate Sustainability Reporting in Canada. Draft paper.

Subramanian, V R (1997) 'Impact of Basel Convention on secondary-lead industry in economies in transition'. Journal of Power Sources 67: 237–242.

Sunley, E, and Baunsgaard, T (2001) The Tax Treatment of the Mining Sector: An IMF Perspective. Background paper for The World Bank workshop on Taxation of the Mining Sector, 4–5 April.

Susapu, B, and Crispin, G (2001) Country Study Report on Small Scale Mining in Papua New Guinea. Paper prepared for MMSD.

SustainAbility (2001) Buried Treasure: Uncovering the Business Case for Corporate Sustainability. SustainAbility, London.

Swanson, T, and Johnston, S (1999) Global Environmental Problems and International Environmental Agreements: The Economics of International Institution Building. Edward Elgar, UK.

Tauli-Corpuz, V (1996) The Marcopper Toxic Mine Disaster – Philippines' Biggest Industrial Accident. Third World Network website, http://www.twnside.org.sg/title/toxic-ch.htm

Tata Energy Research Institute (2001) Overview of Mining and Mineral Industry in India. Tata Energy Research Institute, New Delhi. Paper prepared for MMSD.

Third World Network-Africa (2001) NGOs Express Concern about Mining Activities in Africa. Press release.

Thomson, I, and Joyce, S (1997) 'Exploration and the challenge of community relations'. In McMahon, G (ed) (1997) Mining and the Community. Results of the Quito Conference. Output of the Conference on Mining and the Community held in Quito, Ecuador, 6–8 May. World Bank Energy, Mining and Telecommunications Department.

Thomson, I, and MacDonald, A (2001) Access to Information: A Key to Building Trust in the Minerals Sector. Corporate Communication Standards, Practice and Issues. Paper prepared for MMSD.

Thornton, I (1995) Metals in the Global Environment: Facts and Misconceptions. International Council on Metals in the Environment, Ottawa, Canada.

Tilton, J E (ed.) (1990) World Metal Demand. Trends and Prospects. Resources for the Future, Washington, D.C.

Tilton, J E (ed.) (1992) Mineral Wealth and Economic Development. Resources for the Future, Washington, D.C.

Tilton, J E (1999) 'The future of recycling'. Resources Policy 25: 197–204.

Tilton, J E (2002 in print) On Borrowed Time? Assessing the Threat of Mineral Depletion. Resources for the Future, Washington, D.C.

Tonamiut Inuit Annait Ad Hoc Committee on Aboriginal Women and Mining in Labrador (1997) 52% of the Population Deserves a Closer Look: A Proposal for Guidelines Regarding the Environmental and Socio-Economic Impacts on Women from the Mining Development at Voisey Bay. Available at http://www.innu.ca/womenguidelines.html

Tomic, F (2001) Presentation at the MMSD Managing Mineral Wealth Workshop, London, 15–17 August.

Toulmin, C, and Quan, J (2000) Evolving Land Rights Policy and Tenure in Africa. Department for International Development (DFID) and IIED, London.

UNCTAD (2001) *Handbook of World Mineral Trade Statistics 1994–1999.* UNCTAD New York and Geneva.

UNDP (1997) *Governance for Sustainable Human Development.* UNDP, New York.

UNDP (1998) *Human Development Report.* Oxford University Press, New York.

UNDP (1999a) *Artisanal Mining and Sustainable Livelihoods.* United Nations Development Program Sustainable Livelihoods.

UNDP (1999b) *Human Development Report: Globalization with a Human Face.* Oxford University Press, New York.

UNDP (2000) *Human Development Report: Human Rights and Human Development.* Oxford University Press, New York.

UNDP (2001) *Human Development Report: Making new Technologies Work for Human Development.* Oxford University Press, New York.

UNDP/UNEP/World Bank/WRI (2000) *World Resources 2000–2001. People and Ecosystems: The Fraying Web of Life.* Prepared by the United Nations Development Programme (UNDP), the United Nations Environment Programme (UNEP), the World Bank, and the World Resources Institute. World Resources Institute, Washington D.C.

UNEP/WWF/IUCNNR (1980) *World Conservation Strategy.* International Union for Conservation of Nature and Natural Resources, Gland.

UNEP (1988) *APELL Awareness and Preparedness for Emergencies at Local Level.* UNEP.

UNEP (1996) *Environmental and Safety Incidents Concerning Tailings Dams at Mines.* United Nations Environment Programme, Industry and Environment, with Mining Journal Research Services.

UNEP (1999) *Emerging Environmental Issues for Mining in the PECC Region.* UNEP, Paris.

UNEP (2000) 'Dissection of an accident: lessons learned and follow-up actions from Baia Mare'. In *Mining and Sustainable Development II, Challenges and Perspectives* (2000) Division of Technology, Industry and Economics, United Nations Environment Programme.

UNEP-Infoterra Network (2000) *The Dublin Declaration.* World Resources Institute – Governance and Institutions.

UNEP / Standard Bank (2002) *The Role of Financial Institutions in Sustainable Mineral Development.* UNEP/Standard Bank, Paris.

UNEP-UNDESA (1994) *Environmental Guidelines for Mining Operations.* UNEP-Mineral Resource Forum.

UNESCO (2000) 'Potosi silver tears'. *UNESCO Courier Internet edition.* March 2000. UNESCO website, http://www.unesco.org/courier/2000_3/uk/dici/txt1.htm

United Nations (1948) *The Universal Declaration on Human Rights.* Adopted and proclaimed by United Nations General Assembly Resolution 217 A (III) of 10 December.

United Nations (1989) *International Standard Industrial Classification of all Economic Activities.* Third Revision (ISIC, Revision 3, 1989).

United Nations (1992) *United Nations Conference on Environment and Development.* Agenda 21.

United Nations (1995) *UN Fourth World Conference on Women in Beijing.* China; 4–15 September.

United Nations (2000) *World Investment Report,* July.

United Nations (2002) *Berlin II Guidelines for Mining and Sustainable Development.* Available at http://www.mineralresourcesforum.org/Berlin/index.htm

United Nations Commission on Human Rights (2001) *Economic and Social Council Situations of Human Rights in Myanmar.* Agenda item 9, fifty-fifth session, E/CN.4/2001.L20, 12, April.

United Nations Economic and Social Council (1996) *Developments in Small-Scale Mining-Report of the Secretary General.* UN Documentation Centre.

United Nations Environment and Human Settlement Division (1998) *Convention on Access to Information, Public Participation in Decision-Making and Access to Justice in Environmental Matters.* Aarhus, Denmark, 25 June.

Unit for the Promotion of Democracy-Organization of American States (1997) *Natural Resources, Foreign Concessions and Land Rights: A Report on the Village of Nieuw Koffiekamp.* OAS, Washington, D.C.

UNRISD (2000) *Visible Hands: Taking Responsibility for Social Development.* United Nations Research Institute for Social Development, Geneva.

US Bureau of Mines (1977) *Commodity Data Summaries 1977.* US Bureau of Mines, Washington, D.C.

US Department of Energy (1999) *Energy Matters.* Newsletter, May.

US Department of Energy (2000) *Mining Industry Roadmap for Cross Cutting Technologies.* US Department of Energy Office of Industrial Technologies.

US Department of Energy, Office of Industrial Technologies (2001) *Automotive Aluminium Scrap Sorting.* Available at: http://www.oit.doe.gov/factsheets/aluminum/pdfs/autoalscrapsorting.pdf

US EPA (1983) *Development Document for Effluent Limitations Guidelines and Standards for the Nonferrous Metals Point Source Category.* Vol 3, part 1. Washington, D.C.

US EPA (1998) *Macroeconomic Importance of Recycling and Remanufacturing.* US Environmental Protection Agency Office of Solid Waste. October 28.

US Geological Survey (2000a) *Mineral Commodities Summaries 2000.* Available at http://minerals.usgs.gov/minerals/pubs/mcs/.

US Geological Survey (2000b) *Minerals Yearbook: Volume I Metals and Minerals.* Available at http://minerals.usgs.gov/minerals/pubs/commodity/myb/.

US Geological Survey (2001) *Obsolete Computers, 'Gold Mine' or High-Tech Trash? Resource Recovery from Recycling.* United States Geological Survey Fact Sheet FS-060-01. July.

van der Veen (2000) *The World Bank Experience. Lessons from 10 years of Mining Sector Reform: The Road Traveled.* Presentation made at the Mining Taxation Workshop, Washington, D.C. April 4–5.

van der Veen, P (2001) Presentation at the Sullivan Roundtable in Kimberly, British Columbia, Canada, November.

van Zyl, D, Sassoon, M, Digby, C, Fleury, A-M, and Kyeyune, S (2002) *Mining for the Future.* Paper prepared for MMSD.

Vargas, G G G, Andrade, M R, Razo, L M D, Aburto, B V, Aguilar, E V, and Cebrian M E (2001) 'Lead exposure in children living in a smelter community in region Lagunera, Mexico'. *Journal of Toxicology and Environmental Health* 62(6): 417–429.

Vaughan, S (1995) *The Greening of Financial Markets.* UNEP, Geneva.

Vaughan, W S, and Bourassa, M J (2000) *The Impact of Politics, Economics and Local Legislation on Exploration and Mining in Pacrim Countries.* Paper presented at the PacRim/99 Congress, Bali, Indonesia, 13 October.

Veiga, M, and Hinton, J (2002) 'Abandoned artisanal gold mines in the Brazilian Amazon: a legacy of mercury pollution'. *Natural Resources Forum,* forthcoming.

Vermuelen, S, and Koziell, I (forthcoming) *Integrating Local and Global Biodiversity Values: A Review of Biodiversity Assessment.* IIED, London.

Vitousek, P M, Mooney, H A, Lubchenco, J, and Melillo, J M (1997) 'Human domination of earth's ecosystems'. *Science* 277: 494–499.

von Weizsäcker, E U, Lovins, A B, and Lovins, L H (1997) *Factor Four – Doubling Wealth, Halving Resource Use.* Earthscan, London.

Wackernagel, M, and Rees, W (1996) *Our Ecological Footprint; Reducing Human Impact on the Earth.* New Society Publishers, Gabriola Island, BC, Canada.

Walker, L R (ed) (1999) *Ecosystems of the World*. Elsevier, Oxford.

Ward, B, and Dubos, R (1972) *Only One Earth: The Care and Maintenance of a Small Planet*. Penguin Books, London.

Ward, H (2001) 'Securing transnational corporate accountability through national courts: implications and policy options'. *Hastings Int'l & Comp. L. Rev. 24(451)*.

Warden-Fernandez, J (2001) *Indigenous Communities and Mineral Development*. Paper prepared for MMSD.

Warhurst, A, and Noronha, L (eds) (2000) *Environmental Policy in Mining: Corporate Strategy and Planning for Closure*. Lewis Publishers, New York.

Warhurst, A (2002) *Sustainability Indicators as part of a Sustainability Performance Management System for Mining*. The Mining Environment Research Network (MERN). Warwick Business School, University of Warwick. Paper prepared for MMSD.

Wayne Dunn and Associates (2001) *Cameco in Northern Saskatchewan*. Wayne Dunn and Associates.

WBCSD (1996) *Eco-efficiency Principles from WBCSD. Eco-efficient Leadership for Improved Economic and Environmental Performance*. World Business Council for Sustainable Development, Geneva.

WBCSD (2001) *The Business Case for Sustainable Development – Making a Difference Toward the Johannesburg Summit 2002 and Beyond*. WBCSD, Switzerland.

WBCSD (2002 in print) *Toward a Sustainable Cement Industry*. Summary report. An independent study commissioned by WBCSD. Battelle, the Business of Innovation.

Weber-Fahr, M, Strongman, Kunanayagam, J, McMahon, R, and Sheldon, G (2001) *Mining and Poverty Reduction*. Draft paper April 2001. World Bank, Washington, D.C.

Wedepohl, K H (1995) 'The composition of the continental crust'. *Geochimica et Cosmochimica Acta* 59: 1217–1232.

Whiteman, G, and Mamen, K (2002) *Meaningful Consultation and Participation in the Mining Sector? A Review of the Consultation and Participation of Indigenous Peoples within the International Mining Sector*. The North-South Institute, Ottawa.

Wilburn, D R, and Goonan, T G (1998) *Aggregates from Natural and Recycled Sources. Economic Assessments for Construction Applications–A Materials Flow Analysis*. US Geological Survey. Available at http://greenwood.cr.usgs.gov/pub/circulars/c1176/c1176.html

Wilderness Society (2000) *Westpac and Jabiluka: The Facts*. Campaigns, Wilderness Society website, http://www.wilderness.org.au/member/tws/projects/Jabiluka/westpac.html

Williams, J (2001) 'Worldwide observations on the Latin American mining law model'. In *Proceedings of the Dundee Annual Mining Seminar*. June.

Williamson, J. (ed) (1990) *Latin American Adjustment: How much has Happened*. Institute for International Economics, Washington, D.C.

Wilson, R (1998) Address to the Centennial Conference of the Canadian Institute of Mining, Metallurgy and Petroleum, Montreal.

Wiriosudarmo, R (2001) *Baseline Study and Gap Analysis on Mining in Indonesia*. Paper prepared for MMSD.

WMC Resources (2000a) *Community – Environment Report. Toward Sustainable Development*. Published by WMC Limited, Australia.

WMC Resources (2000b) *Safety and Health Report. Toward Incident and Injury free*. Published by WMC Limited, Australia.

Womack, J P, and Jones, D T (1996) *Lean Thinking: Banish Waste and Create Wealth in Your Corporation*. Simon and Schuster, New York.

Wood, T (2001) *Battle Over Las Cristinas Takes Another, Ugly Turn*. MiningWeb website, posted 10/12/2001. Available at http://m1.mny.co.za/mgjr.nsf/Current/85256ACE0035918D85256AE3006DCE72?OpenDocument

World Bank (1997) *World Development Report 1997: The State in a Changing World*. Oxford University Press, New York.

World Bank (1999) *Myanmar: An Economic and Social Assessment*. Draft paper.

World Bank (2000a) 'Managing the recent commodity price cycle'. In *Global Economic Prospects and the Developing Countries*. The World Bank, Washington, D.C.

World Bank (2000b) *World Development Report 2000/2001: Attacking Poverty*. Oxford University Press, New York.

World Bank (2001a) *Tanzania: Women in the Mining Sector*. Findings 189, August, Africa Region Findings. World Bank, Washington, D.C.

World Bank (2001b) *World Development Indicators 2001*. World Bank, Washington, D.C.

World Bank (2001c) *World Development Report 2002: Building Institutions for Markets*. Oxford University Press, New York.

World Bank (2001d) *Operational Policy Involuntary Resettlement*. Policy 4.12, approved 10/23/01 Washington, D.C.

World Bank-International Finance Corporation (2001) *HIV/AIDS and Mining*. World Bank Group Mining.

World Bank-International Finance Corporation (2002) *Treasure or Trouble? Mining in Developing Countries*. Draft.

World Commission on Dams (2000) *Dams and Development: A New Framework for Decision-Making. The Final Report of the World Commission on Dams*. Earthscan, London.

World Commission on Environment and Development (1987) *Our Common Future*. Oxford University Press.

World Gold Council (2001) *An Indian Love Affair*. Gold – Global Issues and Debate, Issue 3, 20 March.

World Rainforest Movement (2000) 'ABN Amro Bank clients protest against Freeport's activities in Indonesia'. World Rainforest Movement website at http://www.wrm.org.uy/bulletin/20/Indonesia3.html

World Resource Institute (2001) *The Access Initiative: An Initiative to Promote Access to Information, Participation and Justice in Environmental Decision-Making*. World Resources Institute/ Environmental Law Association/ PARTICIPA, Washington, D.C.

Wotruba, H, Hrushka, F, Preister, M, and Hentschel, T (1998) *Manejo Ambiental en la Pequena Mineria*. COSUDE/MEDMIN, La Paz, Bolivia.

WWF (2000) *Living Planet Report 2000*. WWF – World Wide Fund For Nature, Gland.

WWF (2002) *To Dig or Not to Dig? Criteria for Determining the Suitability or Acceptability of Mineral Exploration, Extraction and Transport from Ecological and Social Perspectives*. World Wide Fund For Nature, Gland.

Young, A (1996) *Choices for the Future of Mining in B.C.* Article edited from a speech given to mining industry representatives on 22 October at a symposium on the future of mining in B.C. Available at http://www.bcen.bc.ca/bcerart/Vol7/choicesf.htm

Young, J E (2000) 'The coming materials efficiency revolution'. In Fishbein, B, Ehrenfeld, J and Young, J E (eds) *Extended Producer Responsibility: A Materials Policy for the 21st Century*. Inform, Inc., New York.

Young, J E (2000b) *Gold: at What Price? The Need for a Public Debate on National Gold Reserves*. Mineral Policy Center, Washington, D.C. Available at http://www.mineralpolicy.org/publications/pdf/0024.Gold-At_What_72dpi.pdf

Zadek, S, Pruzan, P, and Evans, R (1997) *Building Corporate Accountability: Emerging Practices in Social and Ethical Accounting*. Earthscan, London.

Zillman, D, Lucas, A and Pring, G (eds) (2002) *Human Rights in Natural Resources Development: The Law of Public Participation in the Sustainable Development of Mining and Energy Resources*, Oxford University Press, New York.

Index

International Institute for Environment and Development

The International Institute for Environment and Development (IIED) is an independent, non-profit research institute working in the field of sustainable development. IIED aims to provide expertise and leadership in researching and achieving sustainable development at local, national, regional and global levels. In alliance with others we seek to help shape a future that ends global poverty and delivers and sustains efficient and equitable management of the world's natural resources.

Postal address:
3 Endsleigh Street,
London WC1H 0DD
United Kingdom
Tel: +44 20 7388 2117
Fax: +44 020 7388 2826
http://www.iied.org

World Business Council for Sustainable Development

The World Business Council for Sustainable Development (WBCSD) is a coalition of 160 international companies united by a shared commitment to sustainable development via the three pillars of economic growth, ecological balance and social progress. Our members are drawn from more than 30 countries and 20 major industrial sectors. We also benefit from a Global Network of 35 national and regional business councils and partner organizations involving some 1000 business leaders globally.

Our mission
To provide business leadership as a catalyst for change toward sustainable development, and to promote the role of eco-efficiency, innovation and corporate social responsibility.

Our aims
Our objectives and strategic directions, based on this dedication, include:
Business leadership – to be the leading business advocate on issues connected with sustainable development.
Policy development – to participate in policy development in order to create a framework that allows business to contribute effectively to sustainable development.
Best practice – to demonstrate business progress in environmental and resource management and corporate social responsibility and to share leading-edge practices among our members.
Global outreach – to contribute to a sustainable future for developing nations and nations in transition.

Postal address:
4, chemin de Conches
1231 Conches-Geneva
Switzerland
Tel: +41 22 839 3100
Fax: +41 22 839 3131
http://www.wbcsd.org

IIED and WBCSD publications are available from Earthprint:
P.O. Box 119
Stevenage
Hertfordshire SG1 4TP
England
Tel: +44 1438 748 111
Fax: +44 1438 748 844
E-mail: orders@earthprint.com
http://www.earthprint.com